PRAISE FOR OTHER AMERICA'S TEST KITCHEN TITLES

"The sum total of exhaustive experimentation . . . anyone interested in gluten-free cookery simply shouldn't be without it."
NIGELLA LAWSON ON *THE HOW CAN IT BE GLUTEN FREE COOKBOOK*

"Even ultra-experienced gluten-free cooks and bakers will learn something from this thoroughly researched, thoughtfully presented volume."
PUBLISHERS WEEKLY ON *THE HOW CAN IT BE GLUTEN FREE COOKBOOK*

"The 21st-century *Fannie Farmer Cookbook* or *The Joy of Cooking*. If you had to have one cookbook and that's all you could have, this one would do it."
CBS SAN FRANCISCO ON *THE NEW FAMILY COOKBOOK*

"This book upgrades slow cooking for discriminating, 21st-century palates—that is indeed revolutionary."
THE DALLAS MORNING NEWS ON *SLOW COOKER REVOLUTION*

"One bag, 3 meals? Get the biggest bang for your buck."
FOX NEWS ON *THE MAKE-AHEAD COOK*

"The go-to gift book for newlyweds, small families or empty nesters."
ORLANDO SENTINEL ON *THE COMPLETE COOKING FOR TWO COOKBOOK*

"Some 2,500 photos walk readers through 600 painstakingly tested recipes, leaving little room for error."
ASSOCIATED PRESS ON *THE AMERICA'S TEST KITCHEN COOKING SCHOOL COOKBOOK*

"Ideal as a reference for the bookshelf . . . will be turned to time and again for definitive instruction on just about any food-related matter."
PUBLISHERS WEEKLY ON *THE SCIENCE OF GOOD COOKING*

"A one-volume kitchen seminar, addressing in one smart chapter after another the sometimes surprising whys behind a cook's best practices. . . . You get the myth, the theory, the science and the proof, all rigorously interrogated as only America's Test Kitchen can do."
NPR ON *THE SCIENCE OF GOOD COOKING*

"Carnivores with an obsession for perfection will likely have found their new bible in this comprehensive collection."
PUBLISHERS WEEKLY (STARRED REVIEW) ON *THE COOK'S ILLUSTRATED MEAT BOOK*

"This encyclopedia of meat cookery would feel completely overwhelming if it weren't so meticulously organized and artfully designed. This is Cook's Illustrated at its finest."
THE KITCHN ON *THE COOK'S ILLUSTRATED MEAT BOOK*

"This book is a comprehensive, no-nonsense guide . . . a well-thought-out, clearly explained primer for every aspect of home baking."
THE WALL STREET JOURNAL ON *THE COOK'S ILLUSTRATED BAKING BOOK*

"Buy this gem for the foodie in your family, and spend the extra money to get yourself a copy too."
THE MISSOURIAN ON *THE BEST OF AMERICA'S TEST KITCHEN 2015*

"The perfect kitchen home companion . . . The practical side of things is very much on display . . . cook-friendly and kitchen-oriented, illuminating the process of preparing food instead of mystifying it."
THE WALL STREET JOURNAL ON *THE COOK'S ILLUSTRATED COOKBOOK*

"If this were the only cookbook you owned, you would cook well, be everyone's favorite host, have a well-run kitchen, and eat happily every day."
THECITYCOOK.COM ON *THE AMERICA'S TEST KITCHEN MENU COOKBOOK*

"This comprehensive collection of 800-plus family and global favorites helps put healthy eating in an everyday context, from meatloaf to Indian curry with chicken."
COOKING LIGHT ON *THE AMERICA'S TEST KITCHEN HEALTHY FAMILY COOKBOOK*

"There are pasta books . . . and then there's this pasta book. Flip your carbohydrate dreams upside down and strain them through this sieve of revolutionary, creative, and also traditional recipes."
SAN FRANCISCO BOOK REVIEW ON *PASTA REVOLUTION*

"These dishes taste as luxurious as their full-fat siblings. Even desserts are terrific."
PUBLISHERS WEEKLY ON *THE BEST LIGHT RECIPE*

"Further proof that practice makes perfect, if not transcendent. . . . If an intermediate cook follows the directions exactly, the results will be better than takeout or Mom's."
THE NEW YORK TIMES ON *THE NEW BEST RECIPE*

"The entire book is stuffed with recipes that will blow your dinner-table audience away like leaves from a sidewalk in November."
SAN FRANCISCO BOOK REVIEW ON *THE COMPLETE COOK'S COUNTRY TV SHOW COOKBOOK*

"Rely on this doorstopper for explicit and comprehensive takes on recipes from basic to sophisticated."
TOLEDO BLADE ON *THE COMPLETE AMERICA'S TEST KITCHEN TV SHOW COOKBOOK*

THE COMPLETE
VEGETARIAN
COOKBOOK

A FRESH GUIDE TO EATING WELL
WITH 700 FOOLPROOF RECIPES

BY THE EDITORS AT
AMERICA'S TEST KITCHEN

Contents

Welcome to America's Test Kitchen

This book has been tested, written, and edited by the folks at America's Test Kitchen, a very real 2,500-square-foot kitchen located just outside of Boston. It is the home of *Cook's Illustrated* magazine and *Cook's Country* magazine and is the Monday-through-Friday destination for more than four dozen test cooks, editors, food scientists, tasters, and cookware specialists. Our mission is to test recipes over and over again until we understand how and why they work and until we arrive at the "best" version.

We start the process of testing a recipe with a complete lack of preconceptions, which means that we accept no claim, no theory, no technique, and no recipe at face value. We simply assemble as many variations as possible, test a half-dozen of the most promising, and taste the results blind. We then construct our own hybrid recipe and continue to test it, varying ingredients, techniques, and cooking times until we reach a consensus. The result, we hope, is the best version of a particular recipe, but we realize that only you can be the final judge of our success (or failure). As we like to say in the test kitchen, "We make the mistakes, so you don't have to."

All of this would not be possible without a belief that good cooking, much like good music, is indeed based on a foundation of objective technique. Some people like spicy foods and others don't, but there is a right way to sauté, there is a best way to cook a pot roast, and there are measurable scientific principles involved in producing perfectly beaten, stable egg whites. This is our ultimate goal: to investigate the fundamental principles of cooking so that you become a better cook. It is as simple as that.

If you're curious to see what goes on behind the scenes at America's Test Kitchen, check out our daily blog, The Feed, at AmericasTestKitchenFeed.com, which features kitchen snapshots, exclusive recipes, video tips, and much more. You can watch us work (in our actual test kitchen) by tuning in to *America's Test Kitchen* (AmericasTestKitchen.com) or *Cook's Country from America's Test Kitchen* (CooksCountryTV.com) on public television. Tune in to *America's Test Kitchen Radio* (ATKradio.com) on public radio to listen to insights, tips, and techniques that illuminate the truth about real home cooking. Want to hone your cooking skills or finally learn how to bake—from an America's Test Kitchen test cook? Enroll in a cooking class at our online cooking school at OnlineCookingSchool.com. And find information about subscribing to *Cook's Illustrated* magazine at CooksIllustrated.com or *Cook's Country* magazine at CooksCountry.com. Both magazines are published every other month. However you choose to visit us, we welcome you into our kitchen, where you can stand by our side as we test our way to the best recipes in America.

f FACEBOOK.COM/AMERICASTESTKITCHEN

y TWITTER.COM/TESTKITCHEN

▶ YOUTUBE.COM/AMERICASTESTKITCHEN

◉ INSTAGRAM.COM/TESTKITCHEN

ⓟ PINTEREST.COM/TESTKITCHEN

t AMERICASTESTKITCHEN.TUMBLR.COM

8+ GOOGLE.COM/+AMERICASTESTKITCHEN

Preface

My first brush with vegetarianism began in March 1970. I hitchhiked up from Santa Fe to visit a college friend in Colorado but made it only as far as the Hog Farm, a commune founded by Wavy Gravy in Taos. Here were the children of the '60s trying to make the transition from suburbia to rural life. After almost freezing to death in a bunkhouse that was poorly heated (nobody knew how to bank a fire), I spent the next day cleaning the filthy kitchen and cooking brown rice and vegetables. This began my almost year-long introduction to vegetarian cookery.

Many years later, I had taken over *East West Journal*, a small macrobiotic magazine (I soon transformed it into *Natural Health Magazine*). Lunches were gobs of glutinous brown rice and overcooked rutabaga and carrots. Most of the staff secretly migrated to the ice cream parlor next door mid-afternoon for something satisfying to eat. Others resorted to bowls of chocolate mousse made with soft tofu and carob. So much for early vegetarian fare!

If one looks back at the first edition of *Moosewood*, one would find a less than inspiring selection of dishes, most of which had heavy additions of cheese and cream. Most folks back then still viewed vegetables as side dishes, and turning them into main courses was an exercise in compromise and substitution. Just taking out the meat and replacing it with something else clearly was not the answer.

So, why does the world need yet another vegetarian cookbook? For starters, vegetables, grains, and legumes are very different from animal protein. For the most part, trying to make a beef stew without beef is a futile enterprise. Resorting to incredibly complicated recipes is also not necessary—good vegetarian cooking should be and can be simple. Forget about fat and cheese being the go-to solution; there are plenty of ways to add flavor without dairy. We found a long list of items that boost flavor, including soy sauce, tomato paste, dried mushrooms, and nuts, and we finished dishes with citrus juice, vinegar, and/or fresh herbs.

Perhaps the biggest reason for this book is the need to rethink the underlying approach. Plenty of other cuisines, and not just from around the Mediterranean, have embraced vegetables for their own distinctive flavors and uses. In addition to Morocco, Turkey, and the Middle East, we found inspiration in South America, Korea, and Mexico. Plus the modern supermarket offers choices—unfamiliar to most home cooks—that enhance vegetarian cooking, such as tempeh, red and black rice, millet, oat berries, and substitutes for items such as fish sauce.

Yes, we found that some meat dishes do translate well into vegetarian alternatives. A burger can be made from a wide variety of grains, legumes, and vegetables. Some of our other meatless classics include Shepherd's Pie, Vegetable Moussaka, Butternut Squash Chili, and Mushroom Bolognese. We came up with lots of other new ideas as well: Parsnip Hummus was a hit in the test kitchen as were Spiced Crispy Chickpeas and even the odd-sounding Turkish Nut Sauce. And some of my personal favorites are Millet Cakes with Spinach and Carrots, Super Greens Soup with Lemon-Tarragon Cream, Chilled Marinated Tofu, and White Lentil Soup with Coconut Milk and Mustard Greens.

You get more than vegetarian recipes in this collection: 500 of the recipes are gluten-free, 250 are vegan, and 300 qualify as "fast," meaning they take 45 minutes or less start to finish.

After my stint as a vegetarian cook, I didn't look back for more than 30 years since those initial results did not stir the soul. Today, I still eat meat but in smaller quantities, and often as a flavoring in vegetable-based recipes. (Okay, I still love a good steak and pork in any form.) But now I know how to think about vegetables and grains in a whole new way. This can be four-star cooking, and it also can be simple.

So, the world does need another vegetarian cookbook since the folks at our test kitchen have labored long and hard to rethink the repertoire, to start out with a fresh take on how to cook everything but meat, poultry, and fish. These are new days, an exciting time to be a home cook and to work in a test kitchen.

In fact, this is not really a "vegetarian" cookbook per se—it's just a well-considered cookbook for the 21st century. We ought to treat vegetables better, as ingredients worthy of main course attention. Someday we will no longer refer to this style of cooking as vegetarian, as if taking vegetables and grains seriously is something surprising.

It's simply good cooking.

Cordially,

CHRISTOPHER KIMBALL
Founder and Editor,
Cook's Illustrated and *Cook's Country*
Host, *America's Test Kitchen* and
Cook's Country from America's Test Kitchen

Vegetarian Basics

Photos: Stuffed Acorn Squash with Barley; Roasted Butternut Squash Salad with Za'atar and Parsley

Introduction

As we tackled this, our first collection of vegetarian recipes, we thought hard about who would use this book and how they would cook from it. For vegetarians, this comprehensive cookbook offers a fresh, modern take on everyday cooking that will keep them busy and well fed for years to come. For cooks who want to incorporate more vegetables and hearty grains into their daily cooking repertoire and omit meat, at least on occasion, this book teaches new techniques for building flavor and new methods for assembling meals. And we think all cooks will find plenty of appealing recipes here—we've included more than 700 recipes for everything from snacks and sandwiches to egg dishes and salads. The selection is eclectic and wide ranging, with comfort food classics (like Shepherd's Pie and Hearty Vegetable Lasagna) as well as less well known peasant dishes from around the globe (like Lentils, Rice, and Crispy Onions and Potato Vindaloo).

Because putting a satisfying vegetarian dinner on the table is the reason we think most people need this book, we've made these recipes the centerpiece: The Hearty Vegetable Mains chapter offers more than 50 recipes from casseroles and gratins to vegetable cakes and fritters to stuffed vegetables, stir-fries, and curries. Other chapters, including Salads Big and Small, Rice and Grains, and Beans and Soy, contain many recipes that can stand alone as a meal or can serve as the anchor for a meal when paired with a simple side. We've given serving suggestions where we think they will be helpful, and we encourage you to pair recipes across the book to make interesting vegetarian meals.

Vegetarian cooking can be labor-intensive, so we made an effort to simplify recipes wherever possible. Throughout the book you will find icons for recipes that can be made in 45 minutes from start to finish (including vegetable prep, which is generally quite considerable for vegetarian recipes); we hope this helps you navigate your way through this collection and pick out the recipes that work best for busy weeknights. There are also icons for vegan and gluten-free dishes on the pages and in the index. And we've often added notes to recipes indicating when a simple ingredient swap will make it gluten-free, like using tamari instead of soy sauce, or when a single ingredient can be changed or omitted to make a dish vegan.

Because we hoped to make this book a complete guide to vegetarian cooking, we didn't want to leave out simple recipes like basic tomato sauces, eggs every way, our favorite ways to cook rice, pestos, vinaigrettes, and more. Good home cooks rely on these cornerstone recipes again and again: A perfect fried egg turns a simple vegetable dish into hearty meal, while a dollop of pesto adds complexity to countless soups and stews. You'll find these basic recipes grouped together throughout the book on featured recipe collection pages.

Whether you are new to vegetarian cooking or an old hand at it, a good resource can be helpful in encouraging you to try new ingredients, and perhaps more importantly to cook with them in new and surprising ways. We use quinoa to make Spanish-inspired vegetarian meatballs, change up a classic Caesar salad with flavor-packed raw kale, and roast chickpeas with warm spices for an easy, addictive snack. This book is packed with sidebars that will help you shop for and prep ingredients like the array of hearty greens on the market today, different types of tofu and tempeh, the world of beans and grains, and more. Spices and flavor builders are key, too, from za'atar, sumac, and dried mushrooms to vegetarian fish sauce (we found a surprising vegetarian alternative, but we also tell you how to make your own).

Over the years in the test kitchen, we have learned a few things about how to make vegetarian recipes that have universal appeal. To get you started, this first section of the book offers tips on our favorite ingredients for building flavor, the equipment you really need for vegetarian cooking, and everything you need to know about buying, storing, and prepping vegetables.

Flavor-Building Ingredients for the Vegetarian Cook

Vegetarian cooking should never mean dishes that are bland or boring; there are myriad options for giving dishes rich, savory flavor without the meat. Here are the ingredients we turn to again and again to lend bold flavor to vegetarian recipes.

OIL

Oil is essential for most methods of cooking, whether sautéing, pan frying, baking, or broiling, and because many vegetarian recipes are naturally lean, they often need a bit more oil to lend richness. The two we reach for most often are vegetable oil and extra-virgin olive oil. Vegetable oils can be made from any number of "vegetable" sources, but usually they consist of soybean oil. These oils have high smoke points and almost no flavor; we use them for shallow frying, sautéing, and stir-frying, and in dressings with strong flavors. Vegetable oils are also fine for deep frying, but canola oil (a vegetable oil made from rapeseed) can give food an off-flavor when heated for a long time. We reach for flavorful extra-virgin olive oil to dress vegetables, to drizzle over soups and grilled or roasted foods, and in most vinaigrettes. Extra-virgin olive oil's strong flavors dissipate when exposed to high heat, so we generally use it only in dishes that are cooked relatively quickly.

VINEGAR

Vinegar isn't just for making vinaigrettes; we also use it to perk up sauces, stews, soups, and rice and bean dishes. Much like lemon or lime juice, a drizzle of acidic vinegar before serving can brighten and balance a dish. Different types lend distinct flavors to dishes, and we reach for several varieties in the book to lend nuanced flavor to recipes. Because their more complex flavors can have a big impact on simple vegetarian dishes, we recommend you buy a good red wine vinegar, balsamic vinegar, and sherry vinegar. See page 265 for more information.

VEGETABLE BROTH

A good vegetable broth is an essential ingredient in the vegetarian kitchen. It provides a flavorful backbone to a wide range of dishes, from soups and stews to risottos and pasta. But it's important to be a savvy shopper—we've found that many commercial vegetable broths are terrible, with overly sweet, tinny flavors or distinct vegetable flavors that overwhelm dishes. We recommend **Orrington Farms Vegan Chicken Flavored Broth Base & Seasoning** and **Swanson Certified Organic Vegetable Broth** (see page 76 for more information), or you can make your own broth or broth concentrate with our recipes on pages 76–77.

SOY SAUCE

Soy sauce is an essential ingredient in vegetarian cooking; this salty liquid is made from fermented soybeans and wheat, barley, or rice, and it is rich in glutamates, taste bud stimulators that give food the meaty, savory flavor known as umami. Although it is traditionally an Asian ingredient, we use it in all types of dishes to add great savory flavor. If you cannot eat gluten, be sure to look for gluten-free soy sauce or tamari.

BRAGG AMINO ACIDS

Bragg Liquid Aminos is made from 16 amino acids derived from soybeans (amino acids are the structural units that make up proteins). It made a great vegetarian stand-in for fish sauce. It gave our Asian recipes the same meaty, savory, fermented flavor of traditional fish sauce. You can also make your own vegetarian fish sauce with our recipe on page 60.

CHEESES

Whether crystalline or creamy, sharp or mild, blue or orange, cheese is a great way to add flavor, richness, and protein to vegetarian dishes. We use ricotta, goat cheese, and feta to lend richness and creaminess to dishes ranging from casseroles to salads. We rely on mild cheddar, Monterey Jack, and mozzarella for their smooth flavor and great melting qualities. And we reach for sharp cheddar, Parmesan, Pecorino Romano, or blue cheese when we want to add bold flavor to a dish. Wrap cheese in parchment paper and then in aluminum foil before refrigerating; the paper allows the cheese to breathe, while the foil keeps out off-flavors and prevents the cheese from drying out.

YOGURT

Add bacteria to whole, low-fat, or nonfat milk and you get yogurt. We add whole-milk yogurt to sauces, soups, and dressings to give them richness and a thick, creamy texture. We especially love Greek yogurt, which is thicker, drier, and tangier than ordinary yogurt. It is made by allowing the watery whey to drain from the yogurt, giving it a smooth, thick texture. Simply stir a few spices or herbs into yogurt to make a creamy spread for sandwiches, a dip for crudités, or a cool accompaniment to dollop on vegetable fritters, soups, or curries. We don't recommend cooking with nonfat yogurt.

NUTS AND SEEDS

Nuts and seeds are essential for vegetarian cooking because they are rich in healthy fats and protein. They are also great for adding flavor and crunch; we use them frequently to lend richness and texture to recipes. We also grind nuts in the food processor to give dishes like our Ultimate Vegetarian Chili (page 105) great flavor and body throughout. Because nuts and seeds are high in oil, they will become rancid quickly, so we recommend that you store them in the freezer. Frozen nuts and seeds will keep for months, and there's no need to defrost them before toasting or chopping.

DRIED MUSHROOMS

Mushrooms are particularly high in savory umami flavor, which is the reason they are often used as a stand-in for meat. Dried mushrooms offer that same flavor in a concentrated package, giving recipes a major dose of meatiness. We often use dried porcini or shiitakes to build deep flavor in longer-cooking dishes. When buying dried mushrooms, always inspect them closely. Avoid those with small holes, which indicate the mushroom may have been subjected to pinworms. The mushrooms should also be free of dust and grit.

TOMATO PASTE

Tomato paste is tomato puree that has been cooked to remove almost all moisture. It is our secret ingredient in many recipes where we want lots of savory flavor. Because it's so concentrated, it's naturally full of glutamates, which provide the meaty flavor known as umami. When tomato paste is added to dishes, we've found that it brings out subtle depths and savory notes.

SPICE BLENDS

Blends of spices are a great way to give a dish complex flavor in one fell swoop. They also make it easy to make interesting ethnic dishes with authentic flavor. Garam masala is one of our favorites; it is a potent Indian spice blend that usually includes cinnamon, cloves, coriander, cumin, cardamom, and dried chiles. Curry powder, a blend of various herbs, spices, and seeds, is essential for making curries with authentic flavor. For dishes with Middle Eastern flavors, we reach for *za'atar*, a pungent combination of toasted sesame seeds, thyme, marjoram, and sumac. *Ras el hanout* is a complex Moroccan blend that features warm spices like ginger, anise, cinnamon, nutmeg, cloves, and cardamom. We also often reach for chili powder to add a bold, multilayered heat to spicy dishes.

CITRUS JUICE

We frequently add lemon or lime juice (depending on the flavor profile of the dish) toward the end of cooking or just before serving to balance dishes with some bright acidity. When purchasing lemons or limes at the supermarket, choose large ones that give to gentle pressure; hard ones have thicker skin and yield less juice. To get the most juice out of a lemon or lime, we recommend rolling it vigorously on a hard surface before slicing it open. This will bruise, break up, and soften the rind's tissues while it tears the membrane of the juice vesicles (tear-shaped juice sacs), thereby filling the inside of the fruit with juice even before it is squeezed. For juicing, we prefer either a wooden reamer with a sharp tip that can easily pierce the flesh, or a manual citrus juicer. And always juice lemons and limes at the last minute, as their flavor mellows quickly.

FRESH HERBS

We often use a sprinkling of minced herbs to give dishes a fresh finish, or whole herb leaves to brighten salads or sandwiches. Parsley, cilantro, and basil are the herbs we use most often and are good to have on hand (or, even better, to grow in small pots in your kitchen). Fresh herbs are highly perishable; to get the most life out of your herbs, gently rinse and dry them (a salad spinner works well), wrap them in a damp paper towel, and place them in a partially open zipper-lock bag in the crisper drawer. Delicate basil is the exception; don't wash it before you need to use it (the added moisture will shorten its shelf life), but do wrap it in paper towels to shield it from the cold in your refrigerator.

SALT AND PEPPER

Seasoning dishes with salt and pepper is always important, but it's especially crucial in vegetarian dishes that rely on just a few simple flavors. We use salt to bring out the flavors of vegetables and to brine beans, and we salt the cooking water for pasta, rice, and grains to season them as they cook. We recommend you stock both table salt and kosher salt. Table salt can be used in any application; it dissolves quickly and easily and is best for baking and using in a brine. The large crystals of kosher salt are good for seasoning foods before cooking and for salting vegetables to pull out excess moisture. As for pepper, fresh is always best. Its flavor dissipates quickly once it's ground, so we recommend buying whole peppercorns and grinding them as needed.

Essential Equipment for Vegetarian Cooking

Vegetarian cooking naturally requires a good amount of vegetable prep, and while prepping vegetables generally doesn't necessitate an arsenal of specialty tools, getting good-quality basics will save you a lot of time and frustration. When it's time to cook, skillets, baking sheets (and wire racks), and a Dutch oven will cover most bases.

CHEF'S KNIFE

When it comes to vegetable prep, a good chef's knife is absolutely essential. This one knife will handle 90 percent of your kitchen cutting work, from chopping onions and splitting butternut squash to mincing fresh herbs. Look for a chef's knife that is 8 inches long with a pointed tip, a comfortable grip, and a curved edge, which helps when rhythmically rocking the blade to chop a pile of carrots or dice an onion. A good chef's knife will be substantial but lightweight—it should have enough heft to get the job done but not be so heavy that it's tiring to use. And the handle should resist slipping, even when your hand is wet or greasy. Look for one made from high-carbon stainless steel, a hard metal that, once sharpened, tends to stay that way. Our favorite is the **Victorinox Swiss Army 8-Inch Fibrox Chef's Knife**, $39.95. See page 9 for details on caring for and using your knives.

PARING KNIFE

For detail work like peeling a hot potato, coring tomatoes, or julienning small vegetables, we turn to a paring knife. Its smaller, more maneuverable, and slightly curved blade makes precision tasks faster and easier. We also use its pointed tip to test the tenderness of the vegetables being cooked. Although paring knives come in a range of shapes, we prefer those that resemble a mini chef's knife, with a slightly curved blade and pointed tip. Blades of 3 to 3½ inches are the most versatile. The handle should be comfortable and the blade should be somewhat flexible for easy maneuvering into tight spots and for handling curves when peeling and paring. Our favorite is the **Wüsthof Classic with PEtec 3½-Inch Paring Knife**, $39.95.

CUTTING BOARDS

When you're prepping a pile of vegetables, a good cutting board is absolutely essential. You'll want one with a large cutting area (think about the vegetable prep for ratatouille, a gratin, or a curry or stir-fry): We recommend buying a board with a work space that measures at least 20 by 15 inches. The board should be sturdy but not too hard. We prefer wood and bamboo boards to plastic, glass, and acrylic because their softer surfaces offer just enough give and "grip" for the knife to stick lightly with each stroke. Knives can slip on plastic boards, while glass and acrylic boards are so hard they dull knives more quickly than the others do. However, wooden and bamboo boards must be washed by hand and require occasional maintenance, while a plastic board can be cleaned in the dishwasher. The **Proteak Edge Grain Teak Cutting Board**, $84.99, is our favorite.

VEGETABLE PEELERS

A dull, subpar peeler makes a mountain of tiresome work out of a simple task. A good peeler should be fast and smooth—no clogging up with peels, jamming on bumps, or making you go over and over the same spot. It should make thin peels, not waste a lot of good food. It should have a comfortable, no-slip handle, and it should stay sharp. In the test kitchen, we keep two peelers: a classic model that handles the usual tasks, and one with a serrated blade to remove peels from delicate foods like peaches and tomatoes. Ceramic blades will dull very quickly and become discolored, so stick with metal blades. Luckily, you don't have to pay a lot to get a great peeler—our winner, the **Kuhn Rikon Original Swiss Peeler**, costs just $4.

MANDOLINE

Even if you have the knife skills of a professional chef, slicing a pile of potatoes (or any other vegetable) razor-thin with the help of only a chef's knife is a trying task. The mandoline is a device that makes the job easy and precise (which is important for getting even slices of vegetables that will cook through at the same rate). This countertop tool resembles a horizontal grater, and slicing requires nothing more than running a piece of food against the blade. Look for a mandoline with a hand guard to shield your fingers, gripper tongs to grasp food, and clear measurement markings for precision cuts. We like the **Swissmar Börner Original V-Slicer Plus Mandoline**, $29.99.

FOOD PROCESSOR

A food processor is great for chopping messy things such as canned tomatoes, grinding delicate foods like fresh bread into fine crumbs, and shredding cheese without straining an arm muscle, plus it can chop or grind nuts, mix dough, make pesto, and puree squash. When shopping for a food processor, resist the temptation to buy a cheap model; less-expensive food processors can't perform even the most basic tasks very well. The better, pricier models have more powerful motors, run more quietly, and don't slow down under a heavy load of bread dough. The blades should be sharp and sturdy, or they will mangle the food rather than cut through it. A large feed tube is also key. It should be large enough to fit potatoes, hunks of cheese, and other larger pieces of food. But the tube shouldn't be too big or food will fall out of position for the blade. Our favorite model is the **Cuisinart Custom 14-Cup Food Processor**, $199.

SALAD SPINNER

It's essential to dry greens for salads carefully or the dressing won't coat the leaves, resulting in a soggy salad with the dressing puddling at the bottom of the bowl. We also use a salad spinner to wash and dry herbs and to spin away the excess liquid from salted vegetables. After extensive testing, we've found that a pump mechanism is best. Compared with a crank or a pull-cord mechanism, a top-mounted pump requires very little effort to use. A nonskid bottom is nice to prevent slipping and sliding in the sink. And choose a model with a solid, leakproof bowl so you can wash greens right in the spinner. We recommend the **OXO Good Grips Salad Spinner**, $29.99.

COARSE GRATER

A sharp grater with large holes is indispensable for many tasks, from uniformly grating blocks of cheddar cheese to shredding potatoes or carrots. Razor-sharp teeth are a must to allow you to grate quickly and efficiently. The grater should have a generous, inflexible grating plane with extra-large holes for efficiency. A solid, rigid frame with a larger surface area enables continuous grating, rather than short bursts. We also look for a comfortable handle and rubber feet to ensure the grater will stay put when held at any angle. Our favorite is the **Rösle Coarse Grater**, $35.95; its flat design makes it easy to store, and its big, sharp holes and large surface area make shredding and grating a breeze.

RASP-STYLE GRATER

A finely textured rasp-style grater (so-called because it's modeled after the woodworker's file-like tool) is perfect for finely grating hard Parmesan or Pecorino Romano, zesting citrus fruits, grating fresh ginger, or making a garlic paste. It should have sharp teeth so that it will require little effort or pressure when grating, and a comfortable handle. We like the **Microplane Classic Zester Grater**, $12.95.

GARLIC PRESS

You can always mince garlic by hand, but we've found that a garlic press does a better job, producing a fuller, less-acrid flavor that is more evenly distributed throughout a dish. It keeps the garlic off your fingers, too. However, many garlic presses are poorly made. The handle and hopper should be sturdy and durable, and the hopper should be large enough to hold two cloves of garlic. A long handle is more comfortable and requires less effort. **The Kuhn Rikon Stainless Steel Epicurean Garlic Press**, $39.95, is our winner.

FINE-MESH STRAINER

A fine-mesh strainer is essential for rinsing rice, grains, or canned beans; draining tomatoes; and straining stocks and pureed soups. Look for a deep bowl, and make sure to pick a sturdy model that won't bend or twist over time. An ergonomic handle is best; an uncomfortable handle makes slow jobs (like straining pudding) a chore. Our favorite is the **CIA Masters Collection 6¾-Inch Fine Mesh Strainer**, $27.49.

COLANDER

A good colander is essential for draining pasta and for salting and draining vegetables. Look for a large capacity so you can cook a lot of veggies or pasta and not worry about the food spilling into the sink. The colander should have some kind of base to keep food out of the range of the sink floor (and unsanitary backwash). Lots of small, mesh-like perforations are better than large, widely spaced holes because water drains faster and food won't slip through. Avoid collapsible colanders; their annoying tendency to tip over and dump pasta all over the sink cancels out their flat storage appeal. We like the **RSVP International Endurance Precision Pierced 5-Quart Colander**, $25.99.

SKILLETS

You will reach for a 12-inch skillet more often than any other pan when using this book—this multiuse pan is key for everything from stir-fries to braised vegetables to stovetop pasta dishes. The flared, shallow sides encourage rapid evaporation, so foods brown rather than steam. A good-quality skillet is essential for getting good, even browning, which translates to more flavor. A traditional (not nonstick) skillet is best when you want to develop lots of fond (the flavorful browned bits that lend savoriness to pan sauces). We use nonstick skillets to cook or sauté delicate items that tend to stick or break apart, like vegetable cakes, stir-fries, and egg dishes. Plus, cleanup is a snap. Look for a 12-inch pan with at least a 9-inch cooking surface and a comfortable, ovensafe handle. For traditional skillets, stainless-steel, fully clad pans are best; we like the **All-Clad 12-Inch Stainless Fry Pan**, $154.95. For nonstick pans, we like the **T-Fal Professional Non-Stick 12½-Inch Fry Pan**, $34.99.

BAKING SHEETS AND WIRE RACKS

We use rimmed aluminum baking sheets for everything from roasting, broiling, and oven frying to keeping food warm in the oven or spreading food out to speed up cooling. We also often fit a baking sheet with a cooling rack so that air can circulate all around the food for even crisping or faster cooling. We prefer baking sheets that are 18 by 13 inches with a 1-inch rim all around—parchment paper and standard cooling racks won't fit if you buy a pan with smaller dimensions. Look for a heavy-duty pan; a pan that isn't thick enough can buckle and transfer heat too intensely, burning the food. A light-colored surface will heat and brown evenly, making for perfectly cooked vegetables. Be sure to buy at least two baking sheets; they have so many different uses that having more than one available is a good plan. Our favorite baking sheet is the **Wear-Ever 13-Gauge Half Size Heavy Duty Sheet Pan by Vollrath**, $14.99, and our favorite cooling rack is the **CIA BakeWare 12 x 17-Inch Cooling Rack**, $15.95.

DUTCH OVEN

A Dutch oven is ideal for frying, braising, steaming, and boiling as well as for simmering soups, stews, and pasta sauces. Built for both oven and stovetop use, a Dutch oven is generally wider and shallower than a conventional stockpot—it's easier to reach into and provides a wider surface area for browning. Its heft translates into plenty of heat retention—perfect for keeping frying oil hot or maintaining a low, steady simmer. A large Dutch oven—at least 6 quarts—is essential for making big batches of chili or for wilting down large bunches of hearty greens. Our favorite pots measure more than 9 inches across—any less and you'll be stuck browning in batches. The handles should be sturdy and wide enough to grab with thick oven mitts, and the lid should be tight-fitting and heavy to keep steam from escaping. We have two winning Dutch ovens: the **Le Creuset 7¼-Quart Round French Oven**, $304.95, and the **All-Clad Stainless 8-Quart Stockpot**, $279.95.

PEPPER MILL

Vegetarian cooking often relies on just a few simple flavors or ingredients, so ensuring that dishes are well seasoned is especially critical. The preground pepper sold in the spice aisle is insipid when compared with freshly ground, so it's essential to own a good pepper mill and grind your own pepper. A pepper mill should offer a wide range of grinds, from very coarse to very fine. A large hopper means less refilling, while a weak grinder makes grinding fresh pepper a chore. We like the **Cole & Mason Derwent Gourmet Precision Pepper Mill**, $40.

Knife School

Vegetarian cooking often requires a good amount of prep work, so having good, sharp knives and knowing how to use them can really save you time. Here are the key points to remember.

GOOD TECHNIQUE = LESS RISK

If you use proper techniques, you are less likely to injure yourself with the knife. It is crucial to keep knives sharp so that they cut through food without slipping. It is also important to grip the knife and know how to position your noncutting hand.

GOOD TECHNIQUE = FASTER RESULTS

If you use proper techniques, you will be able to prepare food faster. This one is pretty simple. Would you rather take two minutes or five minutes to chop an onion? It may not seem like a big difference, but in a recipe with a lot of vegetable prep, all those extra minutes can really add up.

GOOD TECHNIQUE = BETTER RESULTS

If you use proper techniques, you will produce food that is evenly cut and therefore will cook at an even rate. Cooks with poor knife skills end up with unevenly diced carrots or minced garlic with large hunks. Poorly cut food will not cook properly. For instance, those large hunks of garlic will burn and impart a harsh flavor to your food.

The Three Knives You Really Need

Buying an all-in-one set of knives may seem convenient, but most sets are loaded with superfluous pieces. So instead of wasting your money (and your counter space) on these products, just invest in a few good knives. We consider just three knives to be essential: a chef's knife, a paring knife, and a serrated knife (or bread knife).

CHEF'S KNIFE

PARING KNIFE

SERRATED KNIFE

Caring for Your Knives

A sharp knife is a fast knife, and a dull knife is an accident waiting to happen. Dull knives are dangerous because a dull blade requires more force to do the job and so has a higher chance of slipping and missing the mark. Even the best knives will dull over time with regular use.

IS IT SHARP?

To determine if your knife needs sharpening, put it to the paper test. Hold a folded, but not creased, sheet of newspaper by one end. Lay the blade against the top edge at an angle and slice outward. If the knife fails to slice cleanly, try steeling it (see right). If it still fails, it needs sharpening.

WHEN TO USE A SHARPENING STEEL

A sharpening steel doesn't really sharpen a knife; it hones the edge of a slightly dulled blade. Sweeping the blade along the steel realigns the edge. Throughout this motion, make sure to maintain a 20-degree angle between the blade and the steel. Four or five strokes on each side of the blade should realign the edge.

WHEN TO USE A KNIFE SHARPENER

If your knife is quite dull, you'll need to reshape its edge. This requires removing a fair amount of metal. To restore a very dull knife, you have three choices: You can send it out; you can use a whetstone (tricky for anyone but a professional); or—the most convenient option—you can use an electric or manual sharpener.

Cleaning and Caring for Your Cutting Boards

Depending on the type of board, you will need to clean and care for it differently. Here are some basic tips.

SCRUB YOUR BOARD

Routine cleaning is essential; scrub your board thoroughly in hot, soapy water (or put it through the dishwasher if it's dishwasher-safe) to kill harmful bacteria, then rinse it well and dry it completely. For stubborn odors, scrub the cutting board with a paste of 1 tablespoon of baking soda and 1 teaspoon of water, then wash with hot, soapy water.

SOAK IT IN BLEACH AND WATER

To remove stubborn stains from plastic boards, mix a solution of 1 tablespoon of bleach per quart of water in the sink and immerse the board, dirty side up. When the board rises to the surface, drape a dish towel or two over its surface and sprinkle the towel with about ¼ cup bleach solution. Let it sit overnight, then wash it with hot, soapy water.

APPLY OIL

If using a wood or bamboo board, maintain it by applying a food-grade mineral oil every few weeks when the board is new, and a few times a year thereafter. The oil soaks into the fibers, creating a barrier to excess moisture. (Don't use olive or vegetable oil, which can become rancid.) Avoid leaving wood or bamboo boards in water, or they will eventually split.

Setting Up Your Cutting Station

In our test kitchen, "setting up your board" means setting up your cooking station before you begin to prep and cook. Setting up your board at home is just as important, so that you're organized and efficient.

ANCHOR YOUR BOARD

A cutting board that slides all over the counter not only is annoying, it is unsafe. If your cutting board doesn't have non-slip grips on the bottom, place either a square of wet paper towel or a small piece of shelf liner between the counter and the cutting board to hold it in place.

ORGANIZE YOUR PREP

Organizing your prepped ingredients into little bowls isn't just for TV chefs—it's a great idea for home cooks too. This setup makes it easy to grab an ingredient and add it to a hot pan at just the right moment.

KEEP IT TIDY

Don't push vegetable trimmings to one side of the cutting board. This reduces the usable work area on your board, and those trimmings always have a way of getting back under your knife. Designate a small bowl or a plastic grocery bag for trimmings.

Holding a Knife

Much as how someone holds a baseball bat, how you hold a knife makes a difference in terms of control and force. And don't forget about the other hand—the one that holds the food securely in place while you cut. How you hold the food steady makes a difference in terms of fingertip safety.

CONTROL GRIP

For more control, choke up on the handle and actually grip the blade of the knife between your thumb and forefinger.

FORCE GRIP

Holding the knife on the handle allows you to use more force and is helpful when cutting through hard foods.

PROTECT YOUR FINGERTIPS

Use the "bear claw" grip to hold food in place and minimize danger. Tuck your fingertips in, away from the knife, and rest your knuckles against the blade. During the upward motion of slicing, reposition your guiding hand for the next cut.

Basic Cutting Motions

Depending on the food being prepared, you will use different parts of the knife blade and different motions. Here are four basic motions used.

**SMALL ITEMS:
KEEP TIP DOWN**

To cut small items, such as celery, push the blade forward and down, using the blade's curve to guide the middle of the knife through smooth strokes. The tip of the blade should touch the board at all times when cutting small food.

**LARGE ITEMS:
LIFT BLADE UP**

To cut large items, such as eggplant, lift the entire blade off the board to help make smooth strokes.

**MINCING:
USE BOTH HANDS**

To mince herbs and garlic, grip the handle with one hand and rest the fingers of the other hand lightly on the knife tip. This grip facilitates the up-and-down rocking motion needed for mincing. To make sure the food is evenly minced, pivot the knife as you work through the pile of food.

**TOUGH ITEMS:
USE THE HEEL**

To cut tough foods like winter squash, use the heel of the knife. Use one hand to grip the handle and place the flat palm of your other hand on top of the blade. Cut straight down, pushing the blade gently. Be careful and make sure your hand and the knife are dry to prevent slippage.

Vegetables from A to Z

Over the years, we've developed some preferences in the test kitchen when it comes to sizes and varieties of vegetables you should buy. We've summarized this advice in the entries that follow. We also describe any unusual techniques that we've developed to prolong freshness, along with general cooking information for vegetables that can often cause confusion. Also see salad greens on pages 252–253.

ARTICHOKES
- Buy small or medium artichokes; larger ones can be tough and fibrous. Look for artichokes that are compact, unblemished, and bright green. Avoid those with shriveled brown stems or leaves. If you tug at a leaf, it should snap off cleanly.
- It is important to submerge artichokes in acidulated water (water with a small amount of vinegar, or lemon or lime juice) as soon as they are cut to prevent browning.
- It is best to steam medium artichokes and serve with a lemony vinaigrette. Small or baby artichokes are best roasted.
- Artichokes will keep for up to five days if sprinkled lightly with water and stored in a zipper-lock bag.

ASPARAGUS
- Medium-thick asparagus (about ⅝ inch) work best in most recipes, since larger spears must be peeled and pencil-thin specimens overcook easily.
- White asparagus has no color because it is grown without light. It costs more than traditional asparagus, and its delicate flavor doesn't survive long-distance shipping. Buy white asparagus only if very fresh.
- To perk up slightly limp asparagus, trim ends and stand spears up in a glass or jar filled with 1 inch of water; refrigerate overnight. We also store asparagus this way, covered with plastic wrap.

AVOCADOS
- Buy small, rough-skinned Hass variety rather than larger, smooth-skinned Fuerte; Hass are creamier and less watery.
- Don't use an avocado until it is ripe; it should yield slightly to a gentle squeeze. If in doubt, try to remove the small stem; it should flick off easily and reveal green underneath.
- Halved and pitted avocados can be stored cut side down on a plate drizzled with olive oil.
- Underripe avocados will ripen in about two days on the counter, but they will do so unevenly; it's better to ripen them in the refrigerator, though this will take about four days. Ripe avocados stored in the refrigerator can last up to five days.

BEETS
- Healthy leaves are an easy-to-recognize sign of freshness when buying beets with stems and leaves attached. If buying roots only, make sure they are firm and the skin is smooth.
- Beets are best steamed or roasted (wrapped in foil). Do not peel the skin or slice off the tops prior to cooking to minimize bleeding.
- It's easiest to peel whole beets after cooking. To minimize mess, simply use a paper towel to wipe the skin off.
- To remove beet stains from a cutting board, scrub the board with salt.
- Beets with greens attached can be stored in the refrigerator in a loosely sealed plastic bag for several days. If you remove the greens, beets will keep for one week.

BELL PEPPERS
- Choose sweeter red, yellow, and orange bell peppers over green peppers, which taste bitter. Look for brightly colored peppers that are glossy and firm to the touch. If you are stuffing peppers, choose those with a well-rounded shape and even bottoms.
- Roasted bell peppers have many applications and are easy to make (see page 81). Bell peppers are also great in salads and stir-fries.
- You can store peppers in a loosely sealed plastic bag in the refrigerator for up to one week.

BOK CHOY
- Buy bok choy with leaves that are bright green and crisp; wilted leaves are a sign of age. Stalks should be bright white and not be covered with any brown spots.
- Bok choy is best stir-fried or braised; tough stalks need a head start and should go into the pan before the leaves.
- Store bok choy in the refrigerator in a loosely sealed plastic bag for up to three days. Don't wash bok choy until you are ready to cook it.

BROCCOLI

- Buy whole broccoli, not just the crowns or florets, as the stalks are quite flavorful. Avoid broccoli with stalks that have dry cracks or that bend easily, or with florets that are yellow or brown. The cut ends of the stalks should look fresh, not dry and brown.
- Broccoli is best steamed, stir-fried, pan-roasted, or roasted. Note that for all methods other than steaming, the tougher stems must be cooked before the florets.
- To revive limp broccoli, trim the stalk, stand it in 1 inch of water, and refrigerate it overnight.
- Store broccoli unrinsed in an open plastic bag in the crisper drawer. It will keep for about one week.

BROCCOLINI

- Buy broccolini that is bright green with firm stems.
- Broccolini will keep for several days unrinsed in an open plastic bag in the crisper drawer.
- It is best to steam-cook broccolini in a small amount of water and add seasonings after all the water has evaporated.

BROCCOLI RABE

- Buy broccoli rabe with fresh leaves and an abundance of small green florets.
- Store broccoli rabe unrinsed in an open plastic bag in the crisper drawer, where it will keep for several days.
- It is best to blanch and then sauté broccoli rabe; blanching tames its bitterness.

BRUSSELS SPROUTS

- For the best flavor, buy Brussels sprouts with small, tight heads, no more than 1½ inches in diameter, although larger sprouts can often be trimmed of loose leaves along the stem and still be quite good. Look for sprouts that are bright green and have no black spots or yellowing.
- The best way to cook Brussels sprouts is to braise or roast them. Braising produces tender, nutty-flavored, and bright-green sprouts. Roasting produces Brussels sprouts that are well caramelized on the outside and tender on the inside. Larger sprouts cook best when cut in half.
- Store Brussels sprouts in a vented container in the refrigerator for up to five days. Don't wash them until you are ready to cook them. If you have bought them on the stem, remove the stem for storage.

CABBAGES

- When buying red or green cabbage, look for smaller, looser heads covered with thin outer leaves.
- Red and green cabbage are best braised or salted and used to make coleslaw. Napa cabbage is perfect for stir-frying and salads.
- Store cabbage loosely wrapped in plastic in the refrigerator for about four days. Remove the tough outer leaves before using.

CARROTS

- Buy fresh carrots with greens attached for the best flavor. If buying bagged carrots, check that they are evenly sized and firm (they shouldn't bend). Don't buy extra-large carrots, which are often woody and bitter.
- The most flavorful ways to cook carrots are roasting and braising.
- To prevent shriveling, store carrots in the crisper drawer in a partially open zipper-lock bag or in their original plastic bag. Before storing green-topped carrots, remove and discard the greens or the carrots will become limp. Both bagged and fresh carrots will keep for several weeks.

CAULIFLOWER

- Buy heads of cauliflower with tight, firm florets without any discoloration.
- When cooking cauliflower, the key is not to cook it in a lot of liquid since it is a very porous vegetable. It is best to steam or roast cauliflower.
- Cauliflower wrapped in plastic can be stored in the refrigerator for several days.

CELERY

- Buy loose celery heads, not bagged celery heads (with clipped leaves) or bagged celery hearts. Loose celery heads tend to be fuller and fresher. Look for glossy green stalks without brown edges or yellowing leaves.
- Revive limp celery stalks by cutting off about 1 inch from both ends and submerging the stalks in a bowl of ice water for 30 minutes.
- The best way to store celery is to wrap it in foil and store it in the refrigerator. It will keep for several weeks.

CELERY ROOT

- Buy celery root that feels heavy for its size and has a hard and firm exterior.
- Store celery root in the refrigerator wrapped tightly in plastic wrap for up to two weeks. If you buy celery root with stalks and leaves attached, remove these before storing.

CORN

- Corn loses it sweetness soon after it is harvested, so buy the freshest corn you can find. Look for plump ears with green husks and golden silk extending from the tops (the more silk the better since it is an indicator of the number of kernels). Peel back the husk to check for brown spots and to make sure the kernels are firm.
- If you must store corn, wrap it, husk and all, in a wet paper bag and then in a plastic bag and place it in the refrigerator for up to 24 hours.

CUCUMBERS

- Buy regular American cucumbers that are dark green, firm, and without shriveled ends. Seedless English cucumbers have a weak cellular structure that turns them mushy when cut and salted (which we do for salads), and they have less flavor.
- We use cucumbers primarily to make cucumber salads or relishes. Cucumbers must be salted and weighted to ensure a crunchy, not soggy, salad.
- Cucumbers can be stored in the crisper drawer as is; the waxed coating most wholesalers apply will keep cucumbers fresh for at least one week. Unwaxed cucumbers can be stored in a loosely sealed plastic bag for up to one week.

EGGPLANTS

- Buy globe eggplants unless a recipe specifies a specific type of eggplant. Look for eggplant that is firm, deep purple, glossy, and without blemishes. A ripe eggplant will feel heavy in your hand. Larger eggplants tend to be more bitter and have more seeds.
- We cook globe eggplants in many ways, including roasting, baking, sautéing, stewing, and stir-frying. In most applications, the eggplant must be salted first to draw out excess water.
- Store eggplants at room temperature away from direct sunlight.

ENDIVES

- Choose endives with crisp, unblemished outer leaves. The leaves should be compact and tightly closed, and the stem should be firm and white.
- Endive is great braised, roasted, or grilled. We also like it thinly sliced in salads.
- Store endive in a partially open zipper-lock bag; it will stay fresh for several days.

FENNEL

- Buy fennel bulbs that are creamy white and firm with little or no discoloration. Stems should be crisp and the feathery fronds bright green.
- Fennel bulbs are great sautéed, grilled, or roasted, all of which concentrate its anise flavor. Braising is another good cooking method. Use the fronds as a garnish.
- Store fennel in the refrigerator in a zipper-lock bag for up to three days.

GARLIC

- Buy heads of garlic with firm, tightly bound cloves. Do not buy garlic with green sprouts emerging from the cloves (the sprouts taste bitter). For more information on garlic, see page 286.
- Store garlic at room temperature in an open basket that allows for air circulation. Do not remove the papery outer skin until you are ready to use the cloves.

GREEN BEANS

- Buy green beans that are brightly colored and fresh-looking. Thinner beans are generally sweeter and more tender.
- The best ways to cook green beans are boiling, braising, and roasting.
- Store green beans in the refrigerator in a loosely sealed plastic bag.

HEARTY (WINTER) GREENS

- Buy kale, Swiss chard, or collard greens with leaves that are dark green and crisp with no signs of wilting or yellowing. We recommend cleaning these greens in a sink full of water, where there is ample room to swish the leaves.
- These assertive greens are best blanched and then sautéed or braised. They also work well in soups and stews.
- You can store greens in the refrigerator in an open plastic bag for several days. Blot up any excess moisture on leaves before storing. Do not clean the greens until you are ready to cook them.

LEEKS

- Buy leeks that have not been trimmed (some markets remove the tops when leeks start to wilt) and that appear to have most of their green leaves intact. Look for leeks that are firm with crisp, dark green leaves.
- Leeks are best braised or steamed.
- Store leeks in the crisper drawer wrapped tightly in plastic; they will stay fresh for up to one week.

MUSHROOMS

- There are many varieties of fresh mushrooms available at the supermarket now: the humble white button mushroom, as well as cremini, shiitake, oyster, and portobello mushrooms, for starters. We find cremini mushrooms to be firmer and more flavorful than white button mushrooms; the two are interchangeable in any recipe.
- Buy mushrooms loose if possible so that you can inspect their quality. When buying button or cremini mushrooms, look for mushrooms with whole, intact caps; avoid those with discoloration or dry, shriveled patches. Pick mushrooms with large caps and minimal stems.
- When you are ready to cook mushrooms, they can be rinsed under cold running water. If you are planning to serve them raw, do not rinse them but rather brush them clean with a pastry brush or soft cloth.
- You can store loose mushrooms in the crisper drawer in a partially open zipper-lock bag for several days. Store packaged mushrooms in their original containers, as these are designed to "breathe," maximizing the life of the mushrooms. After removing the amount of the mushrooms called for in a recipe, simply rewrap the box with plastic wrap.

ONIONS

- Choose onions with dry, papery skins. They should be rock-hard, with no soft spots or powdery mold on the skin. Avoid onions with green sprouts. Everyday yellow onions have the richest flavor, but milder, sweeter red onions are great grilled or minced raw for a salad or salsa. For more on various types of onions and their uses, see page 304.
- Store onions in a cool, well-ventilated spot away from light. Do not store onions in the refrigerator, where their odors can permeate other foods.

PARSNIPS

- Look for parsnips that are on the smaller side (about 4 ounces) because they are sweeter. Large parsnips (8 ounces and larger) have a core that must be cut out. Look for hard parsnips without any soft spots.
- Parsnips can be prepared and cooked in the same way as carrots and are particularly well-suited to braising and roasting.
- You can store parsnips in the refrigerator in a partially open zipper-lock bag for at least one week.

PEAS

- When buying snow peas or sugar snap peas, look for those that are crisp and bright green without obvious blemishes or dry spots. If buying shelling peas, look for pods that are filled out. (Note that shelling peas are hard to find and require a lot of work, so we use frozen peas in many applications. They are frozen right after being shucked and are often sweeter and fresher-tasting than shelling peas.)
- Snow peas are best stir-fried. Sugar snap peas should be blanched and then sautéed or stir-fried. Shelling peas are best boiled and buttered or braised, or used in soups and stews.
- Store peas in the refrigerator in a partially open zipper-lock bag. Fresh shelling peas are very perishable and should be used right away. Snow and sugar snap peas will keep for several days.

POTATOES

- Since potatoes have varying textures (determined by starch level), you can't just reach for any potato and expect great results. Potatoes fall into three main categories (baking, boiling, or all-purpose) depending on texture. For more details on how to match types of potatoes and cooking methods, see page 308.
- Buy potatoes that show no signs of sprouting. Potatoes with a greenish tinge beneath the skin have had too much exposure to light and should also be avoided.
- Try to buy loose potatoes since bagged potatoes can hasten deterioration and sprouting. Store potatoes in a paper bag in a cool, dry place and away from onions, which give off gases that hasten sprouting. New potatoes should be used within one month, but other potato varieties will hold for several months.

RADISHES

- Try to buy radishes with their greens attached; if the greens are healthy and crisp, it is a good sign that the radishes are fresh. If the radishes are sold without their greens, make sure they are firm and the skin is smooth and not cracked. Avoid very large radishes, which can be woody.
- Radishes can be braised, roasted, or eaten raw in salads.
- You can store radishes in a partially open zipper-lock bag for up to one week. If you buy radishes with greens attached, remove the greens before storing them.

RUTABAGAS

- Most rutabagas are quite large (1 to 2 pounds) and usually waxed to prolong their shelf life. Buy small, unwaxed rutabagas if you can. Avoid those that have cracks or look shriveled.
- Rutabagas are best when mashed or roasted.
- Store rutabagas in the crisper drawer; they will stay fresh for several weeks.

SPINACH

- Flat-leaf spinach is available in bunches, baby spinach is sold either loose or in bags, and curly-leaf spinach is bagged. Look for spinach that is a deep green in color (never yellow), with smooth leaves and crisp stems.
- Curly-leaf and baby spinach (if bought bagged) should be stored in their original packaging, which is designed to keep the spinach fresh. Flat-leaf spinach should be stored in a dry, open zipper-lock bag.

SWEET POTATOES

- Choose firm sweet potatoes with skins that are taut, not wrinkled.
- Many varieties are available, and they can range quite a bit in color, texture, and flavor. Beauregard (usually sold as a conventional sweet potato) and Jewel are sweet and moist and have the familiar sweet-potato flavor. Red Garnet is more savory and has a looser texture. Nontraditional varieties that are lighter in color, like the Japanese White, White Sweet, Batata, and purple potatoes, tend to be starchier and drier.
- Store sweet potatoes in a dark, well-ventilated spot (do not store them in a plastic bag); they will keep for about one week.

TOMATOES

- Choose locally grown tomatoes if at all possible, as this is the best way to ensure a flavorful tomato. Heirloom tomatoes are some of the best local tomatoes you can find. Choose tomatoes that smell fruity and feel heavy.
- If supermarket tomatoes are your only option, look for tomatoes sold on the vine. They are better than regular supermarket tomatoes, which are picked when still green and blasted with ethylene gas to develop texture and color.
- Never refrigerate tomatoes; the cold damages enzymes that produce flavor compounds, and it ruins their texture. Even cut tomatoes should be kept at room temperature (wrap them tightly in plastic wrap).
- If the vine is still attached, leave it on and store the tomatoes stem end up. Store stemmed tomatoes stem side down at room temperature. This prevents moisture from escaping and bacteria from entering, and thus prolongs shelf life.
- To quickly ripen hard, unripened tomatoes, store them in a paper bag with a banana or an apple, both of which emit ethylene gas, which hastens ripening.

WINTER SQUASH

- Whether acorn, butternut, delicata, or another variety, squash should feel hard; soft spots are an indication that the squash has been mishandled. Squash should also feel heavy for its size, a sign that the flesh is moist and soft.
- Most supermarkets sell butternut squash that has been completely or partially prepped. Whole squash you peel yourself has the best flavor and texture, but if you are looking to save a few minutes of prep, we have found the peeled and halved squash is fine. We don't like the butternut squash sold in chunks; while it's a timesaver, the flavor is wan and the texture stringy.
- You can store winter squash in a cool, well-ventilated spot for several weeks.

ZUCCHINI AND YELLOW SUMMER SQUASH

- Choose zucchini and yellow summer squash that are firm and without soft spots. Smaller squash are more flavorful and less watery than larger specimens; they also have fewer seeds. Look for zucchini and summer squash no heavier than 8 ounces, and preferably just 6 ounces.
- Unless grilling or shredding squash, salting is often necessary to eliminate excess water.
- You can store the squash in the refrigerator in a partially open zipper-lock bag for several days.

Prep School

Whether you are simply steaming a vegetable or using it as one component of a more involved recipe, usually some basic vegetable prep is required. True, you might cook a vegetable any number of ways—for example, a potato could be fried, mashed, or roasted—but generally there are some standard prep steps required first. After years of peeling, seeding, and chopping vegetables in the test kitchen, we've found the following methods are the easiest and most efficient ways to prepare a number of vegetables for myriad uses. Also see How to Wash and Dry Salad Greens (page 251).

ARTICHOKES: Preparing

1. Grasp artichoke by stem and hold horizontal to counter. Use kitchen shears to trim pin-sharp thorns from tips of leaves, skipping top two rows.

2. Rest artichoke on cutting board. Holding stem in one hand, cut off top two rows of leaf tips with chef's knife.

3. Cut stem flush with base of bulb. To prevent browning, drop trimmed artichoke into bowl of water mixed with juice of 1 lemon until ready to steam.

ASPARAGUS: Trimming

1. Remove one stalk of asparagus from bunch and bend it at thicker end until it snaps.

2. With broken asparagus as guide, trim tough ends from remaining asparagus bunch, using chef's knife.

AVOCADOS: Cutting Up

1. After slicing avocado in half around pit with chef's knife, lodge edge of knife blade into pit and twist to remove.

2. Use dish towel to hold avocado steady. Make ½-inch crosshatch incisions in flesh of each avocado half with knife, cutting down to, but not through, skin.

3. Insert soupspoon between skin and flesh and gently scoop out avocado cubes.

BEETS: Peeling Cooked

To avoid stained dish towels or messy hands, cradle cooked beets in paper towel and gently rub off skin.

BELL PEPPERS: Cutting Up

1. Slice off top and bottom of pepper and remove seeds and stem.

2. Slice down through side of pepper.

3. Lay pepper flat, trim away remaining ribs and seeds, then cut into pieces or strips as desired.

BOK CHOY: Preparing

1. Trim bottom 1 inch from head of bok choy. Wash and pat leaves and stalks dry. Cut leafy green portion away from either side of white stalk.

2. Cut each white stalk in half lengthwise, then crosswise into thin strips.

3. Stack leafy greens and slice crosswise into thin strips. Keep sliced stalks and leaves separate.

BROCCOLI: Cutting Up

1. Place head of broccoli upside down on cutting board and use chef's knife to trim off florets very close to heads. Cut florets into 1-inch pieces.

2. After cutting away tough outer peel of stalk, square off stalk, then slice stalk into ¼-inch thick pieces.

BROCCOLI RABE: Trimming

Trim off and discard thick stalk ends (usually bottom 2 inches of each stalk).

BROCCOLINI: Trimming

For any stems ½ inch or thicker, use paring knife to trim bottom 2 inches from stems.

BRUSSELS SPROUTS: Preparing

Peel off any loose or discolored leaves and use paring knife to slice off bottom of stem end, leaving leaves attached.

CABBAGE: Shredding

1. Cut cabbage into quarters, then trim and discard hard core.

2. Separate cabbage into small stacks of leaves that flatten when pressed.

3. Use chef's knife to cut each stack of leaves into thin shreds (you can also use slicing disk of food processor to do this).

CARROTS: Cutting on Bias and into Matchsticks

1. Slice carrot on bias into 2-inch-long oval-shaped pieces.

2. For matchsticks, lay ovals flat on cutting board, then slice into 2-inch-long matchsticks, about ¼ inch thick.

CAULIFLOWER: Cutting Up

1. Pull off any leaves, then cut out core of cauliflower using paring knife.

2. Separate florets from inner stem using tip of paring knife.

3. Cut larger florets into smaller pieces by slicing through stem.

CELERY: Chopping Quickly

Using chef's knife, trim leaves from top of celery bunch. Then chop across bunch until you have desired amount.

CELERY ROOT: Peeling

1. Using chef's knife, cut ½ inch from both root end and opposite end.

2. To peel, cut from top to bottom, rotating celery root while removing wide strips of skin.

CORN: Cutting Kernels off the Cob

After removing husk and silk, stand ear upright in large bowl and use paring knife to slice kernels off of cob.

CORN: Preparing for the Grill

1. Remove all but innermost layer of husk from each ear of corn.

2. Use scissors to snip off tassel.

CUCUMBERS: Seeding

Halve peeled cucumber lengthwise. Run small spoon inside each cucumber half to scoop out seeds and surrounding liquid.

ENDIVES: Preparing for Braising

1. Trim off discolored end of endive (cut thinnest slice possible so leaves remain intact).

2. Cut endive in half lengthwise through core end.

FENNEL: Preparing

1. Cut off stems and feathery fronds. Trim thin slice from base and remove any tough or blemished outer layers from bulb.

2A. For braising or grilling, slice bulb vertically through base into ½-inch-thick slices, making sure to leave core intact.

2B. For sautéing, roasting, or salads, cut bulb in half through base, then use paring knife to remove pyramid-shaped core. Slice each half into thin strips, cutting from base to stem end.

GARLIC: Mincing

1. Trim off root end of garlic clove, then crush clove gently between side of chef's knife and cutting board to loosen papery skin (it will fall away from garlic).

2. Using two-handed chopping motion, run knife over garlic repeatedly to mince it.

GARLIC: Mincing to a Paste

Sprinkle minced garlic with salt, then scrape blade of knife back and forth over garlic until it forms sticky paste.

GREEN BEANS: Trimming

Line beans up on cutting board and trim ends with one slice.

GREENS: Washing

Fill salad spinner bowl with cool water, add cut greens, and gently swish them around. Let grit settle to bottom of bowl, then lift greens out and drain water. Repeat until greens no longer release any dirt.

HEARTY (WINTER) GREENS: Preparing Swiss Chard, Kale, or Collard Greens

1. Cut away leafy portion from stalk or stem using chef's knife.

2. Stack several leaves and either slice crosswise or chop into pieces according to recipe.

3. If using chard stems in recipe, cut into pieces as directed after separating from leafy portion. (Discard collard and kale stems.)

LEEKS: Preparing

1. Trim and discard root and dark green leaves.

2. Cut trimmed leek in half lengthwise, then slice crosswise into ½-inch-thick pieces.

3. Rinse cut leeks thoroughly to remove dirt and sand using salad spinner or bowl of water.

MUSHROOMS: Preparing

1. Rinse mushrooms under cold water just before cooking. Don't wash mushrooms that will be eaten raw; brush dirt away with soft pastry brush or cloth.

2. Tender stems on white button and cremini mushrooms should be trimmed, then prepped and cooked alongside caps. Tough, woody stems on shiitakes and portobellos should be removed.

MUSHROOMS: Removing Gills

When cooking portobello mushrooms in soups and stews, use soupspoon to scrape gills off underside of mushroom cap.

ONIONS: Chopping

1. Halve onion through root end, then peel onion and trim top. Make several horizontal cuts from one end of onion to other but don't cut through root end.

2. Make several vertical cuts. Be sure to cut up to but not through root end.

3. Rotate onion so root end is in back; slice onion thinly across previous cuts. As you slice, onion will fall apart into chopped pieces.

PEAS: Trimming Snow and Snap Peas

Use paring knife and thumb to snip off tip of pod and pull along flat side to remove string at same time.

POTATOES: Cutting into Evenly Sized Pieces

1. Using chef's knife, cut 1 thin sliver from one side of potato. Set potato on cut side, and slice potato crosswise into even planks.

2. Stack several planks and cut crosswise, then rotate 90 degrees and cut crosswise again to create evenly sized pieces as directed in recipe.

SHALLOTS: Mincing

1. Make closely spaced horizontal cuts through peeled shallot, leaving root end intact.

2. Next, make several vertical cuts through shallot.

3. Finally, thinly slice shallot crosswise, creating fine mince.

TOMATOES: Coring and Dicing

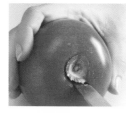

1. Remove core of tomato using paring knife.

2. Slice tomato crosswise.

3. Stack several slices of tomato, then slice both crosswise and widthwise into pieces as desired.

TOMATOES: Peeling

1. Score X at each tomato's base using paring knife. Using slotted spoon, lower tomatoes, a few at a time, into large pot of boiling water and boil for 30 to 60 seconds, just until skin at X begins to loosen.

2. Using slotted spoon, quickly transfer tomatoes to prepared ice bath and let cool for 1 minute.

3. Starting at X, use paring knife to remove loosened peel in strips.

TOMATOES: Seeding

Halve tomato through equator, then use your finger to pull out seeds and surrounding gel.

WINTER SQUASH: Seeding Safely

1. Set squash on damp dish towel. Position cleaver on skin of squash. Strike back of cleaver with mallet to drive cleaver deep into squash. Continue to hit cleaver until it cuts completely through squash.

2. Using soupspoon, scoop out and discard seeds.

WINTER SQUASH: Cutting Up Butternut Squash

1. After peeling squash, use chef's knife to trim off top and bottom and then cut squash in half where narrow neck and wide curved bottom meet.

2. Cut neck of squash into evenly sized planks according to recipe.

3. Cut planks into evenly sized pieces according to recipe.

4. Cut base in half lengthwise and scoop out and discard seeds and fibers. Slice each base half into evenly sized lengths according to recipe.

5. Cut lengths into evenly sized pieces according to recipe.

ZUCCHINI: Seeding

Halve zucchini lengthwise. Run small spoon inside each zucchini half to scoop out seeds.

CHAPTER 1

Hearty Vegetable Mains

GRATINS, CASSEROLES, AND MORE

■ FAST (Less than 45 minutes start to finish)   ■ VEGAN   ■ GLUTEN-FREE
Photos: Stuffed Eggplant with Bulgur; Potato-Tomato Gratin

Summer Vegetable Gratin

SERVES 4

✔ **WHY THIS RECIPE WORKS:** We loved the idea of a rich, bread crumb–topped gratin showcasing our favorite summer vegetables: zucchini, summer squash, and ripe tomatoes. But every version we tried ended up a watery, soggy mess thanks to the liquid the vegetables released. To fix this problem, we salted the vegetables and let them drain before assembling the casserole. We baked the dish uncovered so that the remaining excess moisture would evaporate in the oven. Layering the tomatoes on top exposed them to more heat so that they ended up roasted and caramelized. To flavor the vegetables, we tossed them with an aromatic garlic-thyme oil then drizzled more oil over the top. Fresh bread crumbs tossed with Parmesan and shallots made an elegant topping. The success of this recipe depends on high-quality vegetables. Buy zucchini and summer squash of roughly the same diameter. We like the combination, but you can also use just zucchini or summer squash.

1	pound zucchini, sliced ¼ inch thick
1	pound yellow summer squash, sliced ¼ inch thick
	Salt and pepper
1½	pounds ripe tomatoes, cored and sliced ¼ inch thick
6	tablespoons extra-virgin olive oil
2	onions, halved and sliced thin
2	garlic cloves, minced
1	tablespoon minced fresh thyme
1	slice hearty white sandwich bread, torn into quarters
2	ounces Parmesan cheese, grated (1 cup)
2	shallots, minced
¼	cup chopped fresh basil

1. Toss zucchini and summer squash with 1 teaspoon salt and let drain in colander until vegetables release at least 3 tablespoons liquid, about 45 minutes. Pat zucchini and summer squash dry firmly with paper towels, removing as much liquid as possible.

2. Spread tomatoes out over paper towel–lined baking sheet, sprinkle with ½ teaspoon salt, and let stand for 30 minutes. Thoroughly pat tomatoes dry with more paper towels.

3. Heat 1 tablespoon oil in 12-inch nonstick skillet over medium heat until shimmering. Add onions and ½ teaspoon salt and cook, stirring occasionally, until softened and dark golden brown, 20 to 25 minutes; set aside.

4. Combine 3 tablespoons oil, garlic, thyme, and ½ teaspoon pepper in bowl; set aside. Process bread in food processor until finely ground, about 10 seconds, then combine with 1 tablespoon oil, Parmesan, and shallots in separate bowl; set aside.

5. Adjust oven rack to upper-middle position and heat oven to 400 degrees. Grease 3-quart gratin dish (or 13 by 9-inch baking dish) with remaining 1 tablespoon oil. Toss zucchini and summer squash with half of garlic-oil mixture and arrange in greased baking dish. Sprinkle evenly with caramelized onions, then top with tomato slices, overlapping them slightly. Spoon remaining garlic-oil mixture evenly over tomatoes. Bake until vegetables are tender and tomatoes are starting to brown on edges, 40 to 45 minutes.

6. Remove baking dish from oven and increase heat to 450 degrees. Sprinkle bread-crumb mixture evenly over top and continue to bake gratin until bubbling and cheese is lightly browned, 5 to 10 minutes. Let cool for 10 minutes, then sprinkle with basil and serve.

Assembling a Summer Vegetable Gratin

1. Arrange zucchini and yellow squash in greased baking dish.

2. Sprinkle caramelized onions evenly over top.

3. Lay tomato slices over onions, overlapping them slightly, and spoon remaining garlic-oil mixture evenly over top.

4. Bake until vegetables are tender and tomatoes are starting to brown on edges, then sprinkle bread-crumb mixture evenly over top. Bake until cheese is lightly browned, 5 to 10 minutes.

Potato-Tomato Gratin

SERVES 4 TO 6 `GF`

✅ **WHY THIS RECIPE WORKS:** We wanted a rustic, hearty potato gratin lightened by layers of sweet, bright tomatoes. To balance the moisture in our gratin (and avoid ending up with a watery mess), we chose plum tomatoes, which released less juice than other varieties, and russet potatoes, because their higher starch content meant they soaked up more of the tomato juices. Baking the gratin uncovered allowed any remaining excess water to evaporate, giving us a moist but not waterlogged gratin. To boost the gratin's flavor, we layered in caramelized onions and added garlic, thyme, and chopped kalamata olives. A bubbling, browned topping of nutty Gruyère cheese finished the dish. Thinly sliced potatoes are key to an evenly cooked gratin—use a mandoline, a V-slicer, or the slicing disk on a food processor (tomatoes are better sliced by hand).

> 2 **tablespoons extra-virgin olive oil**
> 2 **onions, halved and sliced thin**
>   **Salt and pepper**
> 2 **garlic cloves, minced**
> ¼ **cup water**
> ½ **cup pitted kalamata olives, chopped**
> 3 **pounds plum tomatoes, cored and sliced ¼ inch thick**
> 2 **pounds russet potatoes, peeled and sliced ⅛ inch thick**
> 2 **teaspoons minced fresh thyme**
> 8 **ounces Gruyère cheese, shredded (2 cups)**

1. Adjust oven rack to upper-middle position and heat oven to 400 degrees. Grease 3-quart gratin dish (or 13 by 9-inch baking dish). Heat oil in 12-inch skillet over medium heat until shimmering. Add onions, ½ teaspoon salt, and ¼ teaspoon pepper and cook, stirring frequently, until onions are soft and golden brown, 15 to 20 minutes.

2. Stir in garlic and cook until fragrant, about 30 seconds. Add water and cook until nearly evaporated, scraping up any browned bits, about 2 minutes. Off heat, stir in olives.

Slicing Onions Thin

Halve onion through root end, then peel. Place onion flat side down, then slice it from pole to pole into ¼-inch-thick slices.

3. Shingle half of tomatoes in even layer in prepared dish. Shingle half of potatoes over tomatoes and sprinkle with 1 teaspoon thyme, ½ teaspoon salt, and ¼ teaspoon pepper. Top evenly with onion mixture, then repeat layering with remaining potatoes, tomatoes, and 1 teaspoon thyme, ½ teaspoon salt, and ¼ teaspoon pepper.

4. Bake, uncovered, for 1 hour. Sprinkle with Gruyère and continue to bake until cheese is browned and bubbly and potatoes are completely tender, 25 to 30 minutes. Let cool for 30 minutes before serving.

Root Vegetable Gratin

SERVES 4 TO 6

✅ **WHY THIS RECIPE WORKS:** This hearty gratin, a cousin to classic scalloped potatoes, swaps out some of the potatoes for carrots and parsnips. Bathed in a rich béchamel sauce, this satisfying dish is topped with nutty Gruyère cheese. To make sure the different vegetables cooked at the same rate, we cut each one to the same thinness and baked them together in a casserole tightly wrapped in aluminum foil at a moderate temperature for an hour and a half. Then we removed the foil, sprinkled Gruyère over the top, and baked it uncovered for another 20 minutes, allowing the cheese to brown. We used a shallow 2-quart gratin dish, which allowed for the most surface area (and browned crust), but a 13 by 9-inch baking dish also worked. Prep and assemble all of the other ingredients before slicing the potatoes and parsnips, or they will begin to brown (do not store them in water; this will make the gratin bland and watery). Thinly sliced potatoes, carrots, and parsnips are key to an evenly cooked gratin—use a mandoline, a V-slicer, or the slicing disk on a food processor. Parmesan cheese can be substituted for the Gruyère, if desired.

> 1 **pound russet potatoes, peeled and sliced ⅛ inch thick**
> 1 **pound carrots, peeled and sliced ⅛ inch thick**
> 1 **pound parsnips, peeled and sliced ⅛ inch thick**
> 2 **tablespoons unsalted butter**
> 2 **shallots, minced**
> 1½ **teaspoons salt**
> 3 **garlic cloves, minced**
> 2 **teaspoons minced fresh thyme**
> ¼ **teaspoon pepper**
> ⅛ **teaspoon ground nutmeg**
> ⅛ **teaspoon cayenne pepper**
> 1 **tablespoon all-purpose flour**
> 1½ **cups heavy cream**
> 3 **ounces Gruyère cheese, shredded (¾ cup)**

1. Adjust oven rack to middle position and heat oven to 350 degrees. Grease 2-quart gratin dish. Place potatoes, carrots, and parsnips in large bowl.

2. Melt butter in small saucepan over medium heat. Stir in shallots and salt and cook until shallots are softened, about 2 minutes. Stir in garlic, thyme, pepper, nutmeg, and cayenne and cook until fragrant, about 30 seconds. Stir in flour and cook until incorporated, about 1 minute. Whisk in cream, bring to simmer, and cook until thickened, about 2 minutes.

3. Pour sauce over vegetables and toss to coat. Transfer mixture to prepared dish and gently pack into even layer, removing any air pockets. Cover dish with aluminum foil and bake until vegetables are almost tender (paring knife can be slipped in and out of potatoes with some resistance), about 1½ hours.

4. Remove foil and sprinkle with Gruyère. Continue to bake, uncovered, until lightly browned on top and fork inserted into center meets little resistance, 20 to 30 minutes. Let cool for 10 minutes before serving.

Sweet Potato and Swiss Chard Gratin

SERVES 4 TO 6 **GF**

✔ **WHY THIS RECIPE WORKS:** To move sweet potatoes squarely to the center of the dinner plate, we created a decidedly savory and elegant sweet potato gratin. Sweet potatoes got their name for a reason, so to mitigate some of their sweetness we turned to earthy, bitter Swiss chard, which we sautéed with shallot, garlic, thyme, and butter. We shingled half the sliced potatoes along the bottom of the gratin dish, topped them with the chard, then layered on the remaining potatoes. Pouring a combination of water, wine, and cream over the vegetables encouraged the potatoes to cook evenly and imparted a welcome richness. Covering the gratin dish for the first half of baking gave the potatoes enough time to cook through, then we uncovered the dish to ensure the excess liquid could evaporate and the cheesy topping could brown. Thinly sliced potatoes are key to an evenly cooked gratin—use a mandoline, a V-slicer, or the slicing disk on a food processor.

We balance hearty, bitter Swiss chard with sweet potatoes and nutty, savory Parmesan cheese in this elegant gratin.

- 2 tablespoons unsalted butter
- 2 shallots, minced
  Salt and pepper
- 2 pounds Swiss chard, stemmed and cut into ½-inch-wide strips
- 3 garlic cloves, minced
- 2 teaspoons minced fresh thyme
- ⅔ cup heavy cream
- ⅔ cup water
- ⅔ cup dry white wine
- 3 pounds sweet potatoes, peeled and sliced ⅛ inch thick
- 2 ounces Parmesan cheese, grated (1 cup)

1. Adjust oven rack to middle position and heat oven to 350 degrees. Melt butter in Dutch oven over medium-high heat. Add shallots and 1 teaspoon salt and cook until shallots are softened, about 2 minutes. Stir in chard and cook until wilted, about 2 minutes. Stir in garlic, thyme, and ¾ teaspoon pepper and cook until fragrant, about 30 seconds; transfer to bowl.

2. Add cream, water, wine, and 1 teaspoon salt to now-empty pot and bring to simmer over medium-high heat. Remove pot from heat and cover to keep warm.

3. Shingle half of potatoes evenly into 3-quart gratin dish (or 13 by 9-inch baking dish). Spread wilted chard mixture evenly over potatoes, then shingle remaining potatoes over top. Pour cream mixture evenly over top.

4. Cover dish with aluminum foil and bake for 45 minutes. Uncover, sprinkle with Parmesan, and continue to bake until gratin is golden brown and nearly all liquid has evaporated, about 45 minutes. Let cool for 10 minutes before serving.

Vegetable Pot Pie

SERVES 4 TO 6

✔ **WHY THIS RECIPE WORKS:** We wanted a vegetable pot pie that featured a rich, flavorful gravy, a flaky, tender crust, and a hearty combination of vegetables. When choosing the vegetables, we thought about flavor but also about the cooking method. Delicate vegetables like asparagus or leeks turned an unappealing army green in the gravy, and they overcooked by the time the sauce was thickened and the crust was browned. Instead we chose a combination of longer-cooking vegetables: mushrooms, sweet potato, turnip, and Swiss chard. So that each vegetable came out tender, we sautéed the mushrooms, sweet potato, and turnip before stirring in the chard. This also helped us to create a flavorful gravy—all those vegetables left behind a good amount of fond in the pot. When we whisked in the broth, the fond was incorporated into the sauce, lending it deep, complex flavor. You can use our homemade All-Butter Single-Crust Pie Dough (page 398) or store-bought pie dough in this recipe. If using store-bought dough, you will still need to roll the dough into a 10-inch circle. Cremini mushrooms are also known as baby bella mushrooms.

- 1 single-crust pie dough
- 4 tablespoons unsalted butter
- 1 onion, chopped fine
- 8 ounces cremini mushrooms, trimmed and quartered if large or halved if small
  Salt and pepper
- 1 sweet potato (12 ounces), peeled and cut into ½-inch pieces
- 8 ounces turnips, peeled and cut into ½-inch pieces
- 3 garlic cloves, minced
- ½ teaspoon grated lemon zest plus 1 tablespoon juice
- 8 ounces Swiss chard, stemmed and cut into 1-inch pieces
- 2 tablespoons all-purpose flour
- 2 cups vegetable broth
- 1 ounce Parmesan cheese, grated (½ cup)
- 2 tablespoons minced fresh parsley
- 1 large egg
- 1 teaspoon water

1. Roll dough between 2 large sheets parchment paper into 10-inch circle. Remove parchment on top of dough. Fold over outer ½-inch edge of dough, then crimp into tidy fluted edge using fingers. Using paring knife, cut four 2-inch, oval-shaped vents in center. Slide parchment paper with crust onto baking sheet and refrigerate until needed.

2. Meanwhile, adjust oven rack to middle position and heat oven to 400 degrees. Melt 2 tablespoons butter in Dutch oven

Preparing Pot Pie Crust

1. Roll dough to 10-inch circle between sheets parchment paper. Remove top piece of parchment. Fold over outer ½-inch rim of dough.

2. Using fingers, crimp folded edge of dough to make attractive fluted rim.

3. Using paring knife, cut four 2-inch, oval-shaped vents in center of dough.

over medium heat. Stir in onion, mushrooms, and ½ teaspoon salt and cook until mushrooms have released their liquid, about 5 minutes.

3. Stir in sweet potato and turnips. Reduce heat to medium-low, cover, and cook, stirring occasionally, until potato and turnips begin to soften around edges, 7 to 9 minutes. Stir in garlic and lemon zest and cook until fragrant, about 30 seconds. Stir in chard and cook until wilted, about 2 minutes; transfer to bowl.

4. Melt remaining 2 tablespoons butter in now-empty pot over medium-high heat. Stir in flour and cook for 1 minute. Gradually whisk in broth, scraping up any browned bits and smoothing out any lumps. Bring to simmer and cook until sauce thickens slightly, about 1 minute. Off heat, whisk in Parmesan, parsley, lemon juice, and ½ teaspoon salt. Stir in cooked vegetables, along with any accumulated juices, and season with salt and pepper to taste.

5. Transfer filling to 9½-inch deep-dish pie plate set on aluminum foil–lined rimmed baking sheet. Place chilled crust on top. Lightly beat egg, water, and pinch salt together in bowl, then brush over crust. Bake until crust is golden brown and filling is bubbling, about 30 minutes. Let cool for 10 minutes before serving.

These crowd-pleasing enchiladas boast spicy roasted poblano peppers and hearty black beans in a bright tomatillo sauce.

Roasted Poblano and Black Bean Enchiladas

SERVES 4 TO 6 `GF`

✔ **WHY THIS RECIPE WORKS:** For truly great vegetarian enchiladas, we wanted a bright, rich green enchilada sauce featuring the sweet-tart flavor of tomatillos. We tried using fresh tomatillos but found that their quality depended largely on the season. Even after roasting, the mealy texture and watery flavor of out-of-season tomatillos was underwhelming. Instead we turned to canned tomatillos, which promised consistent flavor and texture throughout the year without any of the prep work, making our sauce as easy as turning on a food processor. We rounded out the sauce with onion, garlic, cilantro, and lime juice. A splash of heavy cream lent richness without making the sauce greasy. For the filling, we started with spicy, fruity, roasted poblano chiles. Then we smashed canned black beans to create a quick refried bean base and stirred in a little of the tomatillo sauce, Monterey Jack cheese, and some classic seasonings, which we bloomed on the stovetop with basic aromatics.

4 poblano chiles
2 (13-ounce) cans tomatillos, drained
2 onions, chopped fine
1 cup fresh cilantro leaves
⅓ cup vegetable broth
¼ cup heavy cream
¼ cup vegetable oil
5 garlic cloves, peeled (3 whole, 2 minced)
1 tablespoon lime juice
1 teaspoon sugar
Salt and pepper
1 (15-ounce) can black beans, rinsed
1 teaspoon chili powder
½ teaspoon ground coriander
½ teaspoon ground cumin
8 ounces Monterey Jack cheese, shredded (2 cups)
12 (6-inch) corn tortillas

1. Adjust oven rack 6 inches from broiler element and heat broiler. Place poblanos on aluminum foil–lined rimmed baking sheet and broil, turning as needed, until skins are charred, 15 to 20 minutes. Transfer poblanos to large bowl, cover with plastic wrap, and let steam for 5 minutes. Remove skins, stems, and seeds, then chop poblanos into ½-inch pieces. Reduce oven temperature to 400 degrees and adjust oven rack to middle position.

2. Process tomatillos, half of onion, ½ cup cilantro, broth, cream, 1 tablespoon oil, 3 whole garlic cloves, lime juice, sugar, and 1 teaspoon salt in food processor until sauce is smooth, about 2 minutes, scraping down sides of bowl as needed. Season with salt and pepper to taste.

3. Mash half of beans in large bowl with potato masher or fork until mostly smooth. Heat 1 tablespoon oil in 12-inch skillet over medium heat until shimmering. Add remaining onion and cook until softened and lightly browned, 5 to 7 minutes. Stir in remaining 2 cloves minced garlic, chili powder, coriander, and cumin and cook until fragrant, about 30 seconds. Stir in chopped poblanos, mashed beans, and remaining whole beans and cook until warmed through, about 2 minutes.

4. Transfer bean mixture to large bowl and stir in 1 cup Monterey Jack, ½ cup pureed tomatillo sauce, and remaining ½ cup cilantro. Season with salt and pepper to taste. Spread ½ cup pureed tomatillo sauce over bottom of 13 by 9-inch baking dish. Brush both sides of tortillas with remaining 2 tablespoons oil. Stack tortillas, wrap in damp dish towel, and place on plate; microwave until warm and pliable, about 1 minute.

5. Working with 1 warm tortilla at a time, spread ¼ cup bean-cheese filling across center of tortilla. Roll tortilla tightly around filling and place, seam side down, in baking dish; arrange enchiladas in 2 columns across width of dish.

Pour remaining sauce over top to cover completely and sprinkle remaining 1 cup Monterey Jack down center of enchiladas. Cover dish tightly with greased aluminum foil. Bake until enchiladas are heated through, about 25 minutes. Let cool for 5 minutes before serving.

VARIATION

Roasted Poblano, Black Bean, and Zucchini Enchiladas GF

Roast 2 red bell peppers alongside poblanos in step 1; stem, seed, and chop as directed and add to filling with poblanos. Add 1 seeded and finely chopped zucchini to skillet with onion in step 3.

Making Poblano and Black Bean Enchiladas

1. BROIL POBLANOS: Broil poblanos until skins are charred. Transfer to bowl, cover, and let steam for 5 minutes. Remove skins, stems, and seeds, then chop poblanos into ½-inch pieces.

2. MAKE SAUCE AND FILLING: Process sauce ingredients until smooth; set aside. Sauté onion, garlic, and spices, then stir in broiled poblanos and black beans. Stir in cheese.

3. ASSEMBLE ENCHILADAS: Spread ½ cup sauce over bottom of baking dish. Roll each tortilla around ¼ cup filling and place in dish. Pour remaining sauce over top and sprinkle with cheese.

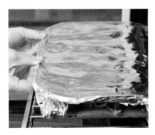

4. COVER AND BAKE: Cover dish tightly with greased aluminum foil and bake until enchiladas are heated through, about 25 minutes.

A smoky, spicy sauce made with ancho chiles, cumin, garlic, and oregano is the star of these cheesy Tex-Mex enchiladas.

Tex-Mex Cheese Enchiladas

SERVES 4 TO 6

✓ **WHY THIS RECIPE WORKS:** Tex-Mex enchiladas have no meat or tomatoey sauce. Instead, a smoky chile gravy provides the bulk of the flavor. Dried ancho chiles, along with cumin, garlic, and oregano, were the perfect backbone for our roux-based sauce, and a splash of vinegar brightened it up. Instead of using the processed cheese typical of the dish, we opted for a mixture of cheddar for flavor and Monterey Jack for smooth meltability. Finally, while traditional recipes call for frying the corn tortillas one at a time, we found a shortcut that reduced the time (and excess grease): brushing the tortillas with oil and microwaving them for a minute. Dried chiles vary in size and weight, so it's best to seed and tear them before measuring; you need about ½ cup of prepped chiles. You'll lose some flavor, but you can substitute 2 tablespoons of ancho chile powder and 1 tablespoon of ground cumin for the whole ancho chiles and cumin seeds; reduce the toasting time to 1 minute.

Dried Ancho Chiles

The sauce in the Tex-Mex Cheese Enchiladas, often called "gravy," gets its hallmark flavor and red color from toasted and ground ancho chiles. When fresh, these broad, blackish-green chiles are called poblanos. Because anchos are naturally smoky and fruity, their complex flavor and mild heat make them an excellent option for grinding into powder for use in spice rubs and chili. Look for dried chiles that are pliable and brightly colored. For more information on fresh and dried chiles, see pages 102 and 107.

2 dried ancho chiles, stemmed, seeded, and torn into ½-inch pieces (½ cup)
1 tablespoon cumin seeds
1 tablespoon garlic powder
2 teaspoons dried oregano
5 tablespoons vegetable oil
3 tablespoons all-purpose flour
  Salt and pepper
2 cups vegetable broth
2 teaspoons distilled white vinegar
8 ounces Monterey Jack cheese, shredded (2 cups)
6 ounces sharp cheddar cheese, shredded (1½ cups)
12 (6-inch) corn tortillas
1 onion, chopped fine

1. Toast chiles and cumin in 12-inch skillet over medium-low heat, stirring often, until fragrant, about 2 minutes. Transfer to spice grinder and let cool for 5 minutes. Add garlic powder and oregano and grind to fine powder.

2. Heat 3 tablespoons oil in now-empty skillet over medium-high heat until shimmering. Stir in ground chile mixture, flour, ½ teaspoon salt, and ½ teaspoon pepper and cook until fragrant and slightly deepened in color, about 1 minute. Slowly whisk in broth and bring to simmer. Reduce heat to medium-low and cook, whisking often, until sauce has thickened and measures 1½ cups, about 5 minutes. Whisk in vinegar and season with salt and pepper to taste. Remove from heat and cover to keep warm.

3. Adjust oven rack to middle position and heat oven to 450 degrees. Spread ½ cup sauce over bottom of 13 by 9-inch baking dish. Combine cheeses in bowl; set ½ cup cheese mixture aside for topping. Brush both sides of tortillas with remaining 2 tablespoons oil. Stack tortillas, wrap in damp dish towel, and place on plate; microwave until warm and pliable, about 1 minute.

4. Working with 1 warm tortilla at a time, spread ¼ cup cheese mixture across center of tortilla and sprinkle with 1 tablespoon onion. Roll tortilla tightly around filling and place, seam side down, in baking dish; arrange enchiladas in 2 columns across width of dish.

5. Pour remaining sauce over top to cover completely and sprinkle with reserved cheese. Cover dish tightly with greased aluminum foil. Bake until sauce is bubbling and cheese is melted, about 15 minutes. Sprinkle with remaining onion and serve.

Vegetarian Tamale Pie

SERVES 6 TO 8 `GF`

✔ **WHY THIS RECIPE WORKS:** Loaded with beans, vegetables, and cheese and topped with a cornmeal crust, this vegetarian take on tamale pie is a rich, hearty casserole. To pack our pie with deep, bold flavor, we focused our efforts on the sauce. We used the traditional Mexican technique of roasting the main ingredients (canned diced tomatoes, onion, and garlic) until darkly browned, then simply blended them with chipotle chile, chili powder, and lime juice to make a complexly flavored sauce. We combined the sauce with two types of canned beans, corn, zucchini, and fresh cilantro in a baking dish and topped it with a layer of cheese, then a quick cornmeal batter. When our casserole emerged from the oven, the crust was browned, the filling was bubbling, the beans absorbed the sauce's flavor, and the vegetables retained their firm texture. For a spicier version of the pie, add an additional chipotle chile to the sauce and substitute Pepper Jack cheese for the Monterey Jack.

2 (28-ounce) cans diced tomatoes, drained with 2 cups juice reserved
1 onion, chopped coarse
4 garlic cloves, chopped coarse
1 tablespoon vegetable oil
  Salt and pepper
1 tablespoon minced canned chipotle chile in adobo sauce
1 tablespoon chili powder
4 teaspoons lime juice
2 (15-ounce) cans black beans, rinsed
1 (15-ounce) can pinto beans, rinsed

1½ cups fresh or frozen corn
1 zucchini, cut into ½-inch cubes
¼ cup minced fresh cilantro
1 teaspoon dried oregano
8 ounces Monterey Jack cheese, shredded (2 cups)
4 cups water
1½ cups coarse cornmeal

1. Adjust oven rack to middle position and heat oven to 475 degrees. Toss tomatoes, onion, garlic, oil, and ½ teaspoon salt together in bowl, then spread out onto aluminum foil–lined rimmed baking sheet. Roast vegetables, stirring occasionally, until they begin to brown darkly at edges, 35 to 40 minutes.

2. Remove vegetables from oven and reduce oven temperature to 375 degrees. Transfer roasted vegetables and any accumulated juices to blender. Add chipotle, chili powder, lime juice, and reserved tomato juice. Puree until mixture is slightly chunky, 8 to 10 seconds. Season sauce with salt and pepper to taste. Combine sauce, black beans, pinto beans, corn, zucchini, cilantro, and oregano in 13 by 9-inch baking dish and top evenly with cheese.

3. Bring water to boil in large heavy-bottomed saucepan over high heat. Add ¾ teaspoon salt, then slowly pour in cornmeal, whisking vigorously to prevent lumps from forming. Reduce heat to medium-high and cook, whisking constantly, until cornmeal begins to soften and mixture thickens, about 3 minutes. Off heat, season with salt and pepper to taste. Spread warm cornmeal mixture evenly over casserole with rubber spatula, pushing it to edges of baking dish.

4. Cover dish with foil and bake for 30 minutes. Remove foil and continue to bake until crust is beginning to brown and filling is bubbling, 30 to 35 minutes. Let cool for 10 minutes before serving.

Rustic Polenta Casserole with Mushrooms and Swiss Chard

SERVES 6 TO 8 `GF`

✔ **WHY THIS RECIPE WORKS:** For a hearty vegetarian polenta casserole, we turned to meaty-tasting mushrooms, which we sautéed until all their liquid evaporated and they were well browned. Garlic and thyme added depth of flavor, and simmering the tomatoes with the mushrooms ensured we didn't lose any of the flavorful fond developed while cooking the mushrooms. To bulk up this dish and add a bright vegetal flavor, we used Swiss chard, which we cooked briefly in the skillet to take away its raw bite. Since the chard continues to cook in the oven, we found that it was important to reduce all the liquid from our sauce first, so the extra moisture from the chard didn't turn the sauce watery. Sprinkled with flavorful fontina cheese to finish, this combination of creamy polenta, meaty mushrooms, tomatoes, and Swiss chard made a satisfying main course. For information on buying polenta, see page 195.

3 cups water
1 cup whole milk
   Salt and pepper
1 cup coarse-ground polenta
2 ounces Parmesan cheese, grated (1 cup)
3 tablespoons unsalted butter
3 tablespoons extra-virgin olive oil
1 onion, chopped fine
1½ pounds white mushrooms, trimmed and sliced thin
3 garlic cloves, minced
1 tablespoon minced fresh thyme or 1 teaspoon dried
1 (28-ounce) can diced tomatoes
8 ounces Swiss chard, stemmed and cut into 1-inch pieces
4 ounces fontina cheese, shredded (1 cup)

1. Adjust oven rack to middle position and heat oven to 400 degrees. Bring water and milk to boil in large saucepan over medium-high heat. Stir in 1 teaspoon salt. Slowly pour polenta into liquid in steady stream while stirring back and forth with wooden spoon. Reduce to gentle simmer, cover, and cook, stirring often, until mixture has uniformly smooth, thick consistency, 15 to 20 minutes. Off heat, stir in Parmesan and butter, and season with salt and pepper to taste. Pour polenta into 13 by 9-inch baking dish and smooth into even layer.

2. Meanwhile, heat oil in 12-inch skillet over medium heat until shimmering. Add onion and ½ teaspoon salt and cook until onion is softened, about 5 minutes. Add mushrooms and cook until they have released their liquid and are well browned, about 25 minutes.

3. Stir in garlic and thyme and cook until fragrant, about 30 seconds. Stir in tomatoes and their juice, bring to simmer, and cook, stirring occasionally, until sauce has thickened, about 10 minutes. Stir in chard, 1 handful at a time, and cook until wilted, 2 to 4 minutes. Season with salt and pepper to taste.

4. Spread mushroom mixture evenly over polenta, then sprinkle with fontina. Bake casserole until warmed through and cheese is melted, 10 to 15 minutes. Let cool for 5 minutes before serving.

Vegetable Moussaka

SERVES 6 TO 8

✔ **WHY THIS RECIPE WORKS:** Traditional recipes for this Greek dish combine ground lamb with cinnamon, nutmeg, and tomatoes then top that with eggplant and a thick béchamel sauce. For our vegetarian interpretation, we used bulgur and potatoes to create a hearty foundation. Blooming the cinnamon with sautéed onion and garlic built great flavor, and simmering the potatoes before baking ensured they would come out tender. Bulgur requires just a soak to tenderize, so we simply stirred it into the potato-tomato mixture and let it sit off the heat until it had absorbed all the excess liquid (and flavor). As for our layer of eggplant, we simply stuck it in the oven to roast while we created our potato-bulgur base. Finally, we made a thick, rich béchamel to spread over the top, then we baked the dish until it was hot and bubbling. When buying eggplant, look for those that are glossy, feel firm, and are heavy for their size. You can swap fine-grind bulgur for the medium-grind in this recipe. For information on different types of bulgur, see page 184. Do not substitute low-fat or skim milk in the sauce.

4	pounds eggplant, peeled and cut into ¾-inch pieces
¼	cup extra-virgin olive oil
	Salt and pepper
1	onion, chopped fine
4	garlic cloves, minced
1	tablespoon minced fresh oregano or 1 teaspoon dried
1	teaspoon ground cinnamon
½	cup dry white wine
1	pound russet potatoes, peeled and cut into ½-inch pieces
2	cups vegetable broth
1	(28-ounce) can crushed tomatoes
1	cup medium-grind bulgur, rinsed
3	tablespoons unsalted butter
¼	cup all-purpose flour
2	cups whole milk
2	ounces Parmesan cheese, grated (1 cup)
	Pinch ground nutmeg
2	tablespoons chopped fresh basil

1. Adjust oven racks to upper-middle and lower-middle positions and heat oven to 450 degrees. Line 2 rimmed baking sheets with aluminum foil and spray with vegetable oil spray. Toss eggplant with 3 tablespoons oil, 1 teaspoon salt, and ¼ teaspoon pepper and spread evenly over prepared sheets. Bake until eggplant is light golden brown and tender, 40 to 50 minutes, switching and rotating sheets halfway through roasting. Set eggplant aside to cool. Reduce oven temperature to 400 degrees and adjust oven rack to middle position.

2. Meanwhile, heat remaining 1 tablespoon oil in Dutch oven over medium heat until shimmering. Add onion and ½ teaspoon salt and cook until onion is softened, about 5 minutes. Stir in garlic, oregano, and cinnamon and cook until fragrant, about 30 seconds. Stir in wine, scraping up any browned bits, until nearly all liquid is evaporated, about 2 minutes. Stir in potatoes and broth and bring to simmer. Cover, reduce heat to low, and cook until potatoes are nearly tender, about 15 minutes.

3. Stir in tomatoes and their juice and cook, uncovered, until flavors meld, about 5 minutes. Off heat, stir in bulgur and let sit until grains are tender and most of liquid is absorbed, about 15 minutes. Transfer to 13 by 9-inch baking dish and top evenly with roasted eggplant to form compact layer.

4. Melt butter in now-empty pot over medium heat. Stir in flour and cook for 1 minute. Gradually whisk in milk, bring to simmer, and cook, whisking often, until sauce thickens and no longer tastes of flour, about 5 minutes. Off heat, whisk in Parmesan and nutmeg and season with salt and pepper to taste. Pour sauce over eggplant and smooth into even layer.

5. Cover with foil and bake until bubbling around edges, about 15 minutes. Uncover and continue to bake until top is light golden brown around edges, about 15 minutes. Let cool for 10 minutes. Sprinkle with basil and serve.

Butternut Squash and Spinach Bread Pudding

SERVES 6 TO 8

✔ **WHY THIS RECIPE WORKS:** To make a rich and creamy savory bread pudding that was decidedly an entrée, we added roasted butternut squash, earthy spinach, and Parmesan cheese. After trying several types of bread, we settled on a French baguette for its strong crumb and neutral flavor. Instead of cubing our bread, we had better results tearing the baguette into rustic, ragged pieces. Toasting the torn pieces to a deep golden brown enriched their flavor and gave the bread a crispness that helped prevent the finished dish from turning soggy. For the custard, we found that a mixture of 3 cups cream to 2 cups milk was rich but not too heavy for dinner. To prevent curdling in the oven, we replaced the traditional whole eggs with just egg yolks, which stabilized the custard. We prefer the flavor and texture of a high-quality French baguette here, but a conventional supermarket baguette will also work.

1½	pounds butternut squash, peeled, seeded, and cut into ¾-inch pieces (4 cups)
1	tablespoon extra-virgin olive oil
	Salt and pepper

1　(18- to 20-inch) French baguette, torn or cut into
　　1-inch pieces (10 cups)
3　cups heavy cream
2　cups whole milk
8　large egg yolks
2　ounces Parmesan cheese, grated (1 cup)
2　teaspoons minced fresh thyme
2　garlic cloves, minced
10　ounces frozen spinach, thawed, squeezed dry,
　　and chopped

1. Adjust oven racks to upper-middle and lower-middle positions and heat oven to 450 degrees. Toss squash with oil, ½ teaspoon salt, and ¼ teaspoon pepper in bowl, then spread out onto aluminum foil–lined rimmed baking sheet. Arrange bread in single layer on second rimmed baking sheet.

2. Place squash on lower-middle rack and bread on upper-middle rack. Bake bread until crisp and browned, about 12 minutes, stirring halfway through baking. Remove bread from oven and stir squash; continue to cook squash until tender, 10 to 15 minutes.

3. Whisk cream, milk, yolks, ½ cup Parmesan, thyme, garlic, 1 teaspoon salt, and ¾ teaspoon pepper together in large bowl. Stir in toasted bread and let sit, stirring occasionally, until bread softens and is beginning to absorb custard, 30 to 45 minutes. When bread is softened, stir in roasted squash and spinach.

4. Spray 13 by 9-inch baking dish with vegetable oil spray. Adjust oven rack to middle position and heat oven to 350 degrees. Pour half of bread mixture into prepared dish and sprinkle with ¼ cup Parmesan. Top with remaining bread mixture and remaining ¼ cup Parmesan. Bake until custard is just set, about 1 hour, rotating dish halfway through baking. Let cool for 10 minutes before serving.

For an *involtini* that showcases the eggplant, we baked the eggplant separately before rolling it around the flavorful filling.

could use less filling without sacrificing flavor. Lastly, we threw together a simple but bright tomato sauce in a skillet, added the eggplant bundles to it, and finished the dish under the broiler so we could skip dirtying a casserole dish. Select shorter, wider eggplants for this recipe. We like whole-milk ricotta in this recipe, but part-skim may be used. Do not use fat-free ricotta.

Eggplant Involtini
SERVES 4 TO 6

WHY THIS RECIPE WORKS: Eggplant *involtini* is like a lighter and more summery version of eggplant Parmesan, with the flavorful eggplant planks rolled around a creamy ricotta filling. Traditional recipes require a two-step process of salting the eggplant and then frying it, but we decided to skip the breading and instead incorporate the bread crumbs right into the filling. This method allowed the eggplant's flavor and meaty texture to take center stage in the dish, and it let us sidestep the salting and draining step; without a coating to turn soggy, we could simply bake the eggplant until its excess moisture evaporated. Adding some Pecorino Romano to the ricotta meant we

2　large eggplants (1½ pounds each), peeled and
　　sliced lengthwise into ½-inch-thick planks (about
　　12 planks), end pieces trimmed to lie flat
6　tablespoons vegetable oil
　　Kosher salt and pepper
2　garlic cloves, minced
¼　teaspoon dried oregano
　　Pinch red pepper flakes
1　(28-ounce) can whole peeled tomatoes, drained,
　　juice reserved, and tomatoes chopped coarse
1　slice hearty white sandwich bread, torn into 1-inch pieces
8　ounces (1 cup) whole-milk ricotta cheese
1½　ounces Pecorino Romano cheese, grated (¾ cup)
¼　cup plus 1 tablespoon chopped fresh basil
1　tablespoon lemon juice

1. Adjust 1 oven rack to lower-middle position and second rack 8 inches from broiler element. Heat oven to 375 degrees. Line 2 rimmed baking sheets with parchment paper and spray generously with vegetable oil spray. Brush 1 side of eggplant slices with 2½ tablespoons oil, then season with ½ teaspoon salt and ¼ teaspoon pepper. Flip slices over and repeat on second side with another 2½ tablespoons oil, ½ teaspoon salt, and ¼ teaspoon pepper. Arrange eggplant slices in single layer on prepared baking sheets. Bake until tender and lightly browned, 30 to 35 minutes, switching and rotating sheets halfway through baking. Let eggplant cool for 5 minutes, then flip each slice over using thin spatula.

2. Meanwhile, heat remaining 1 tablespoon oil in 12-inch broiler-safe skillet over medium-low heat until just shimmering. Add garlic, ½ teaspoon salt, oregano, and pepper flakes and cook, stirring occasionally, until fragrant, about 30 seconds. Stir in tomatoes and their juice, increase heat to high, and bring to simmer. Reduce heat to medium-low and simmer until thickened, about 15 minutes. Cover to keep warm.

3. Pulse bread in food processor until finely ground, 10 to 15 pulses. Combine bread crumbs, ricotta, ½ cup Pecorino, ¼ cup basil, lemon juice, and ½ teaspoon salt in bowl.

4. With widest short side of eggplant facing you, spoon about 3 tablespoons ricotta mixture over bottom third of each eggplant slice (use slightly more filling for larger slices and slightly less for smaller slices). Gently roll up each eggplant slice and place seam side down in tomato sauce in skillet.

5. Heat broiler. Bring sauce to simmer over medium heat and cook for 5 minutes. Transfer skillet to oven and broil until eggplant is well browned and cheese is heated through, 5 to 10 minutes. Remove from broiler. Sprinkle with remaining ¼ cup Pecorino and let stand 5 minutes. Sprinkle with remaining 1 tablespoon basil and serve.

Eggplant Parmesan
SERVES 6 TO 8

✔ **WHY THIS RECIPE WORKS:** Frying the eggplant for this classic Italian dish not only is time-consuming but also can make the dish heavy and dull. In the hope of eliminating most of the grease as well as some of the prep time, we opted to cook the breaded eggplant in the oven. Baking the eggplant on preheated and oiled baking sheets resulted in crisp, golden-brown slices. To keep its excess moisture from turning the eggplant soggy, we salted and drained the slices before baking. A traditional bound breading of flour, egg, and fresh bread crumbs worked best for giving the eggplant a crisp, browned coating. While the eggplant was in the oven, we made a quick tomato sauce using garlic, red pepper flakes, basil, and canned diced tomatoes. Then we layered the sauce, eggplant slices, and mozzarella in a baking dish and baked it until hot and bubbling. Leaving the top layer of eggplant mostly unsauced ensured it would crisp up nicely in the oven. We like to use kosher salt when salting the eggplant because the coarse grains don't dissolve as readily as table salt, so any excess can be easily wiped away.

EGGPLANT

- **2 pounds eggplant, sliced into ¼-inch-thick rounds**
  Kosher salt and pepper
- **8 slices hearty white sandwich bread, torn into quarters**
- **2 ounces Parmesan cheese, grated (1 cup)**
- **1 cup all-purpose flour**
- **4 large eggs**
- **6 tablespoons vegetable oil**

Making Eggplant Involtini

1. SLICE EGGPLANT: Lay each peeled eggplant on its side and slice it lengthwise into ½-inch-thick planks (you should have about 12 planks).

2. BAKE SLICES: Brush both sides of eggplant with oil, season with salt and pepper, and bake until tender and lightly browned, 30 to 35 minutes.

3. STUFF AND ROLL: With widest end facing you, place portion of ricotta mixture on bottom third of slice. Roll into cylinder, then place seam side down in skillet.

4. SIMMER AND BROIL: Simmer sauce for 5 minutes. Transfer skillet to oven and broil until eggplant is well browned and cheese is heated through, 5 to 10 minutes.

SAUCE

- 3 (14.5-ounce) cans diced tomatoes
- 2 tablespoons extra-virgin olive oil
- 4 garlic cloves, minced
- ¼ teaspoon red pepper flakes
- ¼ cup chopped fresh basil
  Kosher salt and pepper

- 8 ounces mozzarella, shredded (2 cups)
- 1 ounce Parmesan cheese, grated (½ cup)
- 10 fresh basil leaves, roughly torn

1. FOR THE EGGPLANT: Toss eggplant with 1½ teaspoons salt and let drain in colander until eggplant releases about 2 tablespoons liquid, 30 to 45 minutes. Wipe excess salt from eggplant, then spread out over baking sheet lined with paper towels and thoroughly pat dry with more paper towels to remove as much liquid as possible.

2. Meanwhile, adjust oven racks to upper-middle and lower-middle positions, place rimmed baking sheet on each rack, and heat oven to 425 degrees. Pulse bread in food processor to fine, even crumbs, about 15 pulses (you should have about 4 cups). Transfer crumbs to shallow dish and stir in Parmesan and ½ teaspoon pepper. Wipe out food processor bowl.

3. Combine flour and 1 teaspoon pepper in large zipper-lock bag and shake to combine. Beat eggs in second shallow dish. Working with 8 to 10 eggplant slices at a time, add eggplant to bag with flour mixture and shake to coat. Shake off excess flour, dip eggplant in eggs, then coat with bread-crumb mixture; transfer to wire rack set in separate rimmed baking sheet.

4. Remove preheated baking sheets from oven. Add 3 table-spoons oil to each sheet, tilting to coat pan evenly. Place breaded eggplant on baking sheets in single layer and bake until well browned and crisp, about 30 minutes, switching and rotating baking sheets after 10 minutes, and flipping eggplant slices after 20 minutes.

5. FOR THE SAUCE: Process 2 cans diced tomatoes and their juice in now-empty food processor until almost smooth, about 5 seconds. Heat oil, garlic, and pepper flakes in large saucepan over medium-high heat, stirring occasionally, until fragrant and garlic is light golden, about 3 minutes. Stir in processed tomatoes and remaining can diced tomatoes and their juice, and bring to boil. Reduce heat to simmer and cook until slightly thickened and reduced to 4 cups, about 15 minutes. Off heat, stir in basil and season with salt and pepper to taste.

6. Spread 1 cup tomato sauce over bottom of 13 by 9-inch baking dish. Layer half of eggplant slices into dish, overlapping

Getting to Know Eggplant

Though it's commonly thought of as a vegetable, eggplant is actually a fruit. Eggplants are available year-round. When shopping, look for eggplants that are firm, with smooth skin and no soft or brown spots. They should feel heavy for their size. Eggplants are very perishable and will get bitter if they overripen, so aim to use them within a day or two. They can be stored in a cool, dry place short-term, but for more than one or two days, refrigeration is best.

There are many varieties of eggplant, ranging anywhere from 2 to 12 inches long, from round to oblong, and from dark purple to white. Here are a few of the most common varieties:

GLOBE

The most common variety in the United States, globe eggplant has a mild flavor and a tender texture that works well in most cooked applications. It can be sautéed, broiled, grilled, and stir-fried. Because of its high water content, it's often best to salt and drain it before cooking.

ITALIAN

Also called baby eggplant, Italian eggplant looks like a smaller version of a globe eggplant. It has moderately moist flesh and a distinct spicy flavor and can be sautéed, broiled, grilled, and stir-fried.

CHINESE

Chinese eggplant has firm, somewhat dry flesh with an intense, slightly sweet taste. It is best for sautéing, stewing, or stir-frying.

THAI

With crisp, applelike flesh and a bright, grassy flavor with a hint of spiciness, Thai eggplant can be eaten raw. It's also good sautéed or stir-fried.

SALTING EGGPLANT

We often recommend salting eggplant before cooking. Salting eggplant not only draws out excess moisture, it also draws out flavor molecules that are tightly bound to proteins that make them inaccessible to our tastebuds. The salt draws flavor compounds out of the cell walls while forcing the proteins to separate from these molecules, resulting in eggplant with more intense flavor—that won't water down your dish.

All About Spices

Just one or two spices can elevate an everyday dish to the next level. But spices can go rancid or stale, and often home cooks reach for old bottles of spices with little flavor. Here are a few tips to help you get the most from your spice rack.

BUYING SPICES

Grinding releases the compounds that give a spice its flavor and aroma, so it's best to buy spices whole and grind them before using; the longer a spice sits, the more its flavor fades. That said, there's no denying the convenience of preground spices. Try to buy preground spices in small quantities, from places (like spice shops) likely to have high turnover.

STORING SPICES PROPERLY

Don't store spices and herbs on the counter close to the stove; heat, light, and moisture shorten their shelf life. Keep them in a cool, dark, dry place in well-sealed containers. To check whole spices for freshness, grind or finely grate a small amount and take a whiff. If the spice releases a lively aroma, it's still good to go. It's helpful to label each spice with the date opened; whole spices are generally good for two years and ground spices for one year.

SPICE RACK ESSENTIALS

From arrowroot to mountain pepper to sumac to *za'atar*, there are hundreds of spices out there to choose from, but in the test kitchen there are only a few we believe are a must in every pantry. We have found we go through chili powder, cinnamon, cayenne, paprika, and peppercorns fairly quickly; all others we recommend buying on a need-to-use basis.

BLOOMING SPICES BUILDS FLAVOR

In the test kitchen, we often like to bloom spices, a technique that removes any raw flavor or dustiness from spices and intensifies their flavor. To bloom spices, cook them briefly on the stovetop or in the microwave in a little oil or butter. As they dissolve, their essential oils are released from a solid state into solution form, where they mix and interact, producing a more complex flavor. Be careful to avoid burning them.

GETTING A GOOD GRIND

Freshly ground spices have superior aroma and vibrancy, and because whole spices have a longer shelf life than preground, grinding your own will help you get more out of the spices you buy. We recommend buying a designated blade-type coffee grinder for grinding spices.

slices to fit. Top evenly with 1 cup sauce and sprinkle with 1 cup mozzarella. Layer remaining eggplant into dish, then dot with 1 cup sauce, leaving majority of eggplant exposed so it will remain crisp. Sprinkle with Parmesan and remaining 1 cup mozzarella. Bake until sauce is bubbling and cheese is browned, 13 to 15 minutes. Let cool for 10 minutes, then sprinkle with basil and serve with remaining sauce.

Baked Squash Kibbeh

SERVES 4 TO 6

✔ **WHY THIS RECIPE WORKS:** Middle-Eastern kibbeh is a finely ground combination of beef or lamb, bulgur, and onions either formed into balls and deep-fried or pressed into a pan and baked. For a vegetarian version of this flavorful dish, we loved the idea of pairing butternut squash with the warm spices. We combined the squash with hearty bulgur, spices, and aromatics. To streamline our recipe, we microwaved the prepped squash; in just 15 minutes, it was tender enough to be pureed. We preferred baking our kibbeh over the mess of deep-frying, but we swapped the traditional 12-inch baking pan for a 9-inch springform pan, which made slicing and serving the baked kibbeh easier—plus the thicker slices baked up more moist and tender. Because bulgur soaks up a fair amount of liquid as it cooks, when we stirred raw bulgur into the squash, the kibbeh initially turned out dry and crumbly. Soaking the bulgur in water for 10 minutes solved this problem. A garnish of feta and toasted pine nuts added some creaminess and crunch. You can use medium-grind bulgur here, but the texture of the kibbeh will be more coarse and moist. For information on different types of bulgur, see page 184. Serve with any of the sauces on page 43.

- 2 **pounds butternut squash, peeled, seeded, and cut into ½-inch pieces (6 cups)**
- 3 **tablespoons extra-virgin olive oil**
- 1 **onion, chopped fine**
- 2 **garlic cloves, minced**
- 1 **teaspoon ground coriander**
- ¼ **teaspoon five-spice powder**
- 1½ **cups fine-grind bulgur, rinsed**
- ½ **cup all-purpose flour**
- ¼ **cup minced fresh cilantro**
- 2 **tablespoons minced fresh mint**
- 1 **teaspoon salt**
- ½ **teaspoon pepper**
- 4 **ounces feta cheese, crumbled (1 cup)**
- 2 **tablespoons pine nuts, toasted and chopped**

This flavorful baked dish features pureed butternut squash and bulgur flavored with aromatics, spices, and cilantro.

1. Adjust oven rack to middle position and heat oven to 400 degrees. Spray 9-inch springform pan with vegetable oil spray. Microwave squash in covered bowl, stirring occasionally, until tender, 15 to 20 minutes. Process cooked squash in food processor until smooth, about 1 minute; let cool.

2. Heat 1 tablespoon oil in 12-inch nonstick skillet over medium heat until shimmering. Add onion and cook until softened, about 5 minutes. Stir in garlic, coriander, and five-spice and cook until fragrant, about 30 seconds. Stir in pureed squash and cook until slightly thickened, 2 to 4 minutes. Transfer squash mixture to large bowl and let cool.

3. Meanwhile, place bulgur in separate bowl and add water to cover by 1 inch. Let sit until tender, about 10 minutes. Drain bulgur through fine-mesh strainer, then wrap in clean dish towel and wring tightly to squeeze out as much liquid as possible.

4. Stir bulgur, flour, cilantro, mint, salt, and pepper into squash mixture until well combined. Transfer to prepared pan and press into even layer with wet hands. Using paring knife, score surface into 8 even wedges, cutting halfway down through mixture. Brush top with remaining 2 tablespoons oil and bake until golden brown and set, about 45 minutes.

5. Sprinkle with feta and pine nuts and continue to bake until cheese is softened and warmed through, about 10 minutes. Let kibbeh cool in pan for 10 minutes. Run thin knife around inside of springform pan ring to loosen, then remove ring. Slice kibbeh into wedges along scored lines and serve.

VARIATION
Baked Pumpkin Kibbeh
This kibbeh will have a milder flavor than the squash version.

Substitute 1 (15-ounce) can unsweetened pumpkin puree for squash; skip microwaving and processing squash in step 1.

Spinach Strudel
SERVES 4

✔ **WHY THIS RECIPE WORKS:** Sweet strudels might be better known, but savory strudels have a long and delicious history. Our starting point for this recipe was a filling of spinach with ricotta and feta cheeses. We added golden raisins and pine nuts for their contrasting textures. Next we turned to simplifying the strudel assembly. We found that we could simply stack the greased phyllo sheets, mound the filling on one side, then roll up the strudel into a log. We left a 2-inch border and kept the sides open to guard against leaking filling. A few vents to allow steam to escape kept the top crisp during baking and cooling. Carefully squeezing the spinach dry before making the filling prevented excess moisture from watering down the filling and causing leaks. Phyllo dough is also available in larger 18 by 14-inch sheets; if using, cut them in half to make 14 by 9-inch sheets. Be sure to use phyllo that is fully thawed or it will crack and flake apart when handled. Don't thaw the phyllo in the microwave; let it sit in the refrigerator overnight or on the counter for 4 to 5 hours.

10 ounces frozen spinach, thawed, squeezed dry, and chopped coarse
6 ounces (¾ cup) whole-milk ricotta cheese
3 ounces feta cheese, crumbled (¾ cup)
6 scallions, sliced thin
½ cup golden raisins
2 tablespoons pine nuts, toasted
2 tablespoons lemon juice
1 tablespoon minced fresh oregano
2 garlic cloves, minced
½ teaspoon ground nutmeg
   Salt and pepper
10 (14 by 9-inch) phyllo sheets, thawed
   Olive oil spray

1. Adjust oven rack to middle position and heat oven to 400 degrees. Line rimmed baking sheet with parchment paper. Mix spinach, ricotta, feta, scallions, raisins, pine nuts, lemon juice, oregano, garlic, and nutmeg together in bowl and season with salt and pepper to taste.

2. On clean counter, layer phyllo sheets on top of one another, coating each sheet thoroughly with olive oil spray. Mound spinach mixture into narrow log along bottom edge of phyllo, leaving 2-inch border at bottom and ½-inch border on sides. Fold bottom edge of dough over filling, then continue to roll dough around filling into tight log, leaving ends open.

3. Gently transfer strudel, seam side down, to prepared baking sheet. Lightly spray with olive oil and cut four 1½-inch vents diagonally across top of strudel.

Making Strudel

1. STACK PHYLLO SHEETS: On clean counter, layer phyllo sheets on top of one another, coating each sheet thoroughly with olive oil spray.

2. COMPACT FILLING INTO MOUND: Mound spinach mixture into narrow log along bottom edge of phyllo, leaving 2-inch border at bottom and ½-inch border on sides.

3. ROLL DOUGH AROUND FILLING: Fold bottom edge of dough over filling, then continue to roll dough around filling into tight log, leaving ends open.

4. CUT VENTS: Gently transfer strudel, seam side down, to prepared baking sheet. Lightly spray with olive oil and cut four 1½-inch vents diagonally across top of strudel.

4. Bake strudel until golden, about 20 minutes, rotating baking sheet halfway through baking. Let cool on baking sheet for 5 minutes, then slice and serve.

VARIATION

Spinach Strudel with Olives and Goat Cheese

Substitute ½ cup pitted and chopped kalamata olives for raisins, and crumbled goat cheese for feta.

Easy Vegetable and Bean Tostadas

SERVES 4 TO 6 `FAST` `GF`

✔ WHY THIS RECIPE WORKS: These easy tostadas boast big flavor and appealing textures, combining refried beans, sautéed onions and peppers, a crunchy coleslaw topping spiced with jalapeños, and a drizzle of a cool *crema*. We used convenient bagged coleslaw mix and tossed it with the brine from jarred jalapeños to make an easy slaw. Canned refried beans saved time, needing only to be warmed in the oven while we sautéed the onions and peppers. We then topped the tostadas with the cooked vegetables, slaw, and some tangy *queso fresco*. We imitated traditional Mexican crema by brightening sour cream with some fresh lime juice and drizzled it over the top along with a sprinkle of whole cilantro leaves. Both store-bought and homemade tostadas will work well here; our favorite store-brought brand is Mission Tostadas Estilo Casero. Serve with Sweet and Spicy Pickled Onions, page 43, if desired.

- 1 (14-ounce) bag green coleslaw mix
- 1 tablespoon finely chopped jarred jalapeños, plus ¼ cup brine
  Salt and pepper
- ½ cup sour cream
- 3 tablespoons lime juice (2 limes)
- 1 (15-ounce) can vegetarian refried pinto beans
- 12 (6-inch) corn tostadas
- 2 tablespoons vegetable oil
- 2 onions, halved and sliced thin
- 3 green bell peppers, stemmed, seeded, and cut into 2-inch-long strips
- 3 garlic cloves, minced
- 4 ounces queso fresco or feta cheese, crumbled (1 cup)
- ¼ cup fresh cilantro leaves

To brighten our vegetable tostadas, we make an instant pickled topping by tossing coleslaw mix with jalapeño brine.

1. Toss coleslaw mix with 3 tablespoons jalapeño brine in bowl and season with salt and pepper to taste. In separate bowl, whisk sour cream and 2 tablespoons lime juice together.

2. Adjust oven racks to upper-middle and lower-middle positions and heat oven to 450 degrees. Combine refried beans, jalapeños, and remaining 1 tablespoon jalapeño brine in bowl and season with salt and pepper to taste. Spread bean mixture evenly over tostadas and arrange on 2 rimmed baking sheets. Bake tostadas until beans are warm, 5 to 10 minutes.

3. Meanwhile, heat oil in 12-inch skillet over medium-high heat until just smoking. Add onions and peppers and cook until softened and lightly browned, 5 to 7 minutes. Stir in garlic and cook until fragrant, about 30 seconds. Off heat, stir in remaining 1 tablespoon lime juice and season with salt and pepper to taste.

4. Top warm tostadas with cooked vegetables, slaw, and queso fresco. Drizzle with sour cream–lime juice mixture, sprinkle with cilantro leaves, and serve.

Easy Tomato and Corn Tostadas `FAST` `GF`
Substitute vegetarian refried black beans for refried pinto beans. Substitute 2 ears corn, kernels cut from cobs, for peppers; cook with onions as directed. Before adding garlic to skillet, stir in 1 pound halved cherry tomatoes and let soften and warm through, about 3 minutes.

Making Tostadas

1. Using fork, poke center of each tortilla 3 or 4 times (to prevent puffing and allow for even cooking).

2. Add 1 tortilla at a time to hot oil. Place metal potato masher on top to keep tortilla flat and submerged in oil. Fry until crisp and lightly browned, 45 to 60 seconds (no flipping is necessary). Sprinkle with salt.

Zucchini Fritters
SERVES 3 TO 4 `FAST`

✔ **WHY THIS RECIPE WORKS:** These crispy zucchini fritters, packed with feta cheese and dill and served with a cucumber-yogurt sauce, make an appealing and easy entrée. The key to success was to prevent the zucchini, which has a high moisture content, from turning the fritters soggy. Salting the shredded zucchini, letting it drain, and then squeezing it out in a clean dish towel solved this issue. To allow the delicate flavor of the zucchini to shine through, we avoided heavy batters and bound the zucchini with just a few eggs and a little flour. A combination of feta, scallions, dill, and garlic nicely balanced the zucchini flavor without overwhelming it. Use a coarse grater or the shredding disk of a food processor to shred the zucchini. Make sure to squeeze the zucchini until it is completely dry, or the fritters will fall apart in the skillet. Do not let the zucchini sit on its own for too long after it has been squeezed dry, or it will turn brown. In addition to the sauce, you can also serve with lemon wedges.

1 pound zucchini, shredded

Salt and pepper

8 ounces feta cheese, crumbled (2 cups)

2 scallions, minced

2 large eggs, lightly beaten

2 tablespoons minced fresh dill

1 garlic clove, minced

¼ cup all-purpose flour

6 tablespoons extra-virgin olive oil

1 recipe Cucumber-Yogurt Sauce (page 43)

1. Adjust oven rack to middle position and heat oven to 200 degrees. Toss shredded zucchini with 1 teaspoon salt and let drain in fine-mesh strainer for 10 minutes.

2. Wrap zucchini in clean dish towel, squeeze out excess liquid, and transfer to large bowl. Stir in feta, scallions, eggs, dill, garlic, and ¼ teaspoon pepper. Sprinkle flour over mixture and stir to incorporate.

3. Heat 3 tablespoons oil in 12-inch nonstick skillet over medium heat until shimmering. Drop 2-tablespoon-size portion of batter into skillet and use back of spoon to press batter into 2-inch-wide fritter (you should fit about 6 fritters in pan at a time). Fry until golden brown on both sides, 4 to 6 minutes.

4. Transfer fritters to paper towel–lined baking sheet and keep warm in oven. Wipe out skillet with paper towels and repeat with remaining 3 tablespoons oil and remaining batter. Serve fritters warm or at room temperature with cucumber sauce.

Squeezing Zucchini Dry

To prevent soggy, fragile zucchini fritters, it's important to remove excess moisture.

1. Shred zucchini on large holes of box grater.

2. Squeeze shredded zucchini in clean dish towel or several layers of paper towels until dry.

Cauliflower Cakes

SERVES 4

✓ **WHY THIS RECIPE WORKS:** These hearty cauliflower cakes feature complex flavors, a creamy interior, and a crunchy browned exterior. Since cauliflower is a frequent addition to curries, we turned to warm spices like turmeric, coriander, and ground ginger for our flavor base. To ensure that the flavor of the cauliflower stood up to all those additions, and to drive off excess moisture that would otherwise make our cakes fall apart, we cut the cauliflower into florets and roasted them until they were well browned and tender. Next we needed a binder to hold the shaped cakes together. Egg and flour are standard additions, but we also added some goat cheese to provide extra binding, creaminess, and tangy flavor. Although these cakes held together, they were very soft and tricky to flip in the pan. Refrigerating the cakes for 30 minutes before cooking them proved to be the best solution. Chilled, these cakes transferred from baking sheet to skillet without a problem and were much sturdier when it came time to flip them. In addition to the lemon wedges, serve with any of the sauces on page 43.

1 head cauliflower (2 pounds), cored and cut into 1-inch florets

¼ cup vegetable oil

1 teaspoon ground turmeric

1 teaspoon ground coriander

½ teaspoon ground ginger

Salt and pepper

4 ounces goat cheese, softened

2 scallions, sliced thin

1 large egg, lightly beaten

2 garlic cloves, minced

1 teaspoon grated lemon zest, plus lemon wedges for serving

¼ cup all-purpose flour

1. Adjust oven rack to middle position and heat oven to 450 degrees. Toss cauliflower, 1 tablespoon oil, turmeric, coriander, ginger, 1 teaspoon salt, and ¼ teaspoon pepper together in bowl. Transfer to aluminum foil–lined rimmed baking sheet and roast until cauliflower is well browned and tender, about 25 minutes. Let cool, then transfer to large bowl.

2. Line clean rimmed baking sheet with parchment paper. Mash cauliflower coarsely with potato masher. Stir in goat cheese, scallions, egg, garlic, and lemon zest until well combined. Sprinkle flour over mixture and stir to incorporate. Using wet hands, divide mixture into 4 equal portions, pack

EASY ACCOMPANIMENTS FOR VEGETARIAN BURGERS, FRITTERS, AND MORE

These easy, versatile sauces and toppings are perfect for adding a little extra flavor, texture, or contrast to dishes. They're perfect as toppings for vegetable cakes and fritters, rice bowls, or curries, as spreads for sandwiches, as dips for crudités, chips, or crackers, or as a cool accompaniment to dollop on soups.

Cucumber-Yogurt Sauce

MAKES ABOUT 2½ CUPS `FAST` `GF`

Cilantro, mint, parsley, or tarragon can be substituted for the dill if desired.

- 1 cup plain Greek yogurt
- 2 tablespoons extra-virgin olive oil
- 2 tablespoons minced fresh dill
- 1 garlic clove, minced
- 1 cucumber, peeled, halved lengthwise, seeded, and shredded
  Salt and pepper

Whisk yogurt, oil, dill, and garlic together in medium bowl. Stir in cucumber and season with salt and pepper to taste. Serve. (Sauce can be refrigerated for up to 1 day.)

Yogurt-Herb Sauce

MAKES 1 CUP `FAST` `GF`

- 1 cup whole milk or low-fat plain yogurt
- 1 garlic clove, minced
- 2 tablespoons minced fresh cilantro
- 2 tablespoons minced fresh mint
  Salt and pepper

Combine yogurt, garlic, cilantro, and mint in small bowl; season to taste with salt and pepper. Let stand at least 30 minutes to blend flavors. (Sauce can be refrigerated for up to 2 days).

Sriracha Mayo

MAKES ABOUT ¾ CUP `FAST` `GF`

- ½ cup mayonnaise
- 1 scallion, chopped fine
- 2 tablespoons Sriracha
- 1 tablespoon lime juice

Combine all ingredients in bowl. (Mayo can be refrigerated for up to 2 days.)

Garlic Aïoli

MAKES 1¼ CUPS `FAST` `GF`

Using a combination of vegetable oil and extra-virgin olive oil is crucial to the flavor of the aïoli.

- 2 large egg yolks
- 2 teaspoons Dijon mustard
- 2 teaspoons lemon juice
- 1 garlic clove, minced
- ¾ cup vegetable oil
- 1 tablespoon water
- ½ teaspoon salt
- ¼ teaspoon pepper
- ¼ cup extra-virgin olive oil

Process yolks, mustard, lemon juice, and garlic in food processor until combined, about 10 seconds. With processor running, slowly drizzle in vegetable oil, about 1 minute. Transfer mixture to medium bowl and whisk in water, salt, and pepper. Whisking constantly, slowly drizzle in olive oil. (Aïoli can be refrigerated for up to 4 days.)

Cilantro-Mint Chutney

MAKES ABOUT 1 CUP `FAST` `GF`

Any type of yogurt will work in this recipe.

- 2 cups packed fresh cilantro leaves
- 1 cup packed fresh mint leaves
- ⅓ cup plain yogurt
- ¼ cup minced onion
- 1 tablespoon lime juice
- 1½ teaspoons sugar
- ½ teaspoon ground cumin
- ¼ teaspoon salt

Process all ingredients in food processor until smooth, about 20 seconds, stopping to scrape down bowl as needed. Serve. (Chutney can be refrigerated for up to 1 day.)

Easy Cherry Tomato Salsa

MAKES ABOUT 1 CUP
`FAST` `VEGAN` `GF`

- 6 ounces cherry tomatoes, quartered
- 1 tablespoon extra-virgin olive oil
- 1 tablespoon minced fresh cilantro
- 1½ teaspoons lime juice
  Salt and pepper

Combine all ingredients in bowl and season with salt and pepper to taste. (Salsa can be refrigerated for up to 1 day.)

Sweet and Spicy Pickled Onions

MAKES ABOUT 2 CUPS
`FAST` `VEGAN` `GF`

- 1 red onion, sliced thin (1½ cups)
- 1 cup red wine vinegar
- ⅓ cup sugar
- 2 jalapeño chiles, stemmed, seeded, and cut into thin rings
- ¼ teaspoon salt

Place onion in medium heat-resistant bowl. Bring vinegar, sugar, jalapeños, and salt to simmer in small saucepan over medium-high heat, stirring occasionally, until sugar dissolves. Pour vinegar mixture over onion, cover loosely, and let cool to room temperature, about 30 minutes. Once cool, drain and discard liquid. (Onions can be refrigerated for up to 1 week.)

gently into ¾-inch-thick cakes, and place on prepared sheet. Refrigerate cakes until chilled and firm, about 30 minutes.

3. Heat remaining 3 tablespoons oil in 12-inch nonstick skillet over medium heat until shimmering. Gently lay cakes in skillet and cook until deep golden brown and crisp on both sides, 10 to 14 minutes, flipping gently halfway through cooking. Drain cakes briefly on paper towels. Serve with lemon wedges.

Millet Cakes with Spinach and Carrots

SERVES 4 GF

✔ **WHY THIS RECIPE WORKS:** Technically a seed rather than a grain, millet makes a perfect base for pan-fried cakes because as it cooks the seed bursts, releasing starch and becoming sticky. It has a mellow, cornlike flavor and is easily adaptable to many types of cuisines, though it is a staple in Asia and its nutty flavor lends itself particularly well to bold flavor profiles. We liked the combination of millet and curry, and adding bright spinach and carrot along with shallot and garlic created a highly flavorful but nicely balanced mixture. Though millet holds together well on its own, we found that the addition of an egg and plain yogurt was helpful to keep the cakes together during cooking. Chilling the formed cakes for 30 minutes further ensured that they were sturdy and easy to handle. Baking was an appealing hands-off cooking method, but we found that the heat of the oven dried them out and didn't add much flavor, so we decided to pan-fry them to create a flavorful crust on the exterior while maintaining a moist interior. Serve with any of the sauces on page 43.

Millet seeds burst as they cook, releasing sticky starches that become a natural binder for our pan-fried cakes.

1	**cup millet, rinsed**
2	**cups water**
	Salt and pepper
3	**tablespoons vegetable oil**
1	**shallot, minced**
6	**ounces (6 cups) baby spinach, chopped**
2	**carrots, peeled and shredded**
2	**garlic cloves, minced**
2	**teaspoons curry powder**
¼	**cup plain yogurt**
1	**large egg, lightly beaten**
2	**tablespoons minced fresh cilantro**

1. Line rimmed baking sheet with parchment paper. Combine millet, water, and ½ teaspoon salt in medium saucepan and bring to simmer over medium heat. Reduce heat to low, cover, and simmer until grains are tender and liquid is absorbed, 15 to 20 minutes. Off heat, let millet sit, covered, for 10 minutes; transfer to large bowl.

2. Heat 1 tablespoon oil in 12-inch nonstick skillet over medium heat until shimmering. Add shallot and cook until softened, about 3 minutes. Stir in spinach and carrots and cook until spinach is wilted, about 2 minutes. Stir in garlic, curry powder, ½ teaspoon salt, and ¼ teaspoon pepper and cook until fragrant, about 30 seconds. Transfer to bowl with millet and wipe out now-empty skillet with paper towels.

3. Stir yogurt, egg, and cilantro into millet mixture until well combined. Divide mixture into 8 equal portions, pack firmly into 3½-inch-wide cakes, and place on prepared sheet. Refrigerate cakes until chilled and firm, about 30 minutes.

4. Adjust oven rack to middle position and heat oven to 200 degrees. Set wire rack in rimmed baking sheet. Heat 1 tablespoon oil in now-empty skillet over medium heat until shimmering. Gently lay 4 cakes in skillet and cook until deep golden brown and crisp on both sides, 10 to 14 minutes, turning gently halfway through cooking. Transfer cakes to prepared sheet and keep warm in oven. Repeat with remaining cakes and oil. Serve.

Crispy Potato Latkes

MAKES 10 LATKES, SERVING 3 TO 4 `GF`

✓ **WHY THIS RECIPE WORKS:** To achieve latkes that were light and not greasy, with buttery, soft interiors surrounded by a shatteringly crisp outer shell, we needed to do two things: First, we removed as much water as possible from the potato shreds by wringing them out in a dish towel. Then we briefly microwaved them. This caused the starches in the potatoes to form a gel that held on to the potatoes' moisture so it didn't leach out during cooking. With the water taken care of, the latkes crisped up quickly and absorbed minimal oil. We prefer shredding the potatoes on a coarse grater, but you can also use the large shredding disk of a food processor; cut the potatoes into 2-inch lengths first. Serve with a green salad or sautéed hearty greens and top with applesauce and sour cream.

2 **pounds russet potatoes, unpeeled and shredded**
½ **cup grated onion**
　 Salt and pepper
2 **large eggs, lightly beaten**
2 **teaspoons minced fresh parsley**
　 Vegetable oil

1. Adjust oven rack to middle position, place rimmed baking sheet on rack, and heat oven to 200 degrees. Toss potatoes, onion, and 1 teaspoon salt together in bowl. Working in 2 batches, wrap potato mixture in clean dish towel and wring tightly to squeeze out as much liquid as possible into measuring cup, reserving drained liquid. Let liquid sit until starch settles to bottom, 5 to 10 minutes.

2. Microwave dried potato mixture in covered bowl until just warmed through but not hot, 1 to 2 minutes, stirring mixture with fork every 30 seconds. Spread potato mixture evenly over second rimmed baking sheet and let cool for 10 minutes.

3. Pour off water from reserved potato liquid, leaving potato starch in measuring cup. Whisk in eggs until smooth. Return cooled potato mixture to bowl. Add parsley, ¼ teaspoon pepper, and potato starch mixture and toss to combine.

4. Set wire rack in clean rimmed baking sheet and line with triple layer of paper towels. Heat ¼-inch depth of oil in 12-inch skillet over medium-high heat until shimmering. Place ¼-cup mound of potato mixture in oil and press with nonstick spatula into ⅓-inch-thick disk. Repeat until 5 latkes are in pan.

5. Cook, adjusting heat so oil bubbles around latke edges, until golden brown on both sides, about 6 minutes. Let latkes drain briefly on paper towels, then transfer to baking sheet in oven. Repeat with remaining potato mixture, adding oil as needed to maintain ¼-inch depth between batches. Season with salt and pepper to taste and serve.

Celery Root and Potato Roesti with Lemon-Parsley Crème Fraîche

SERVES 2 TO 3 `GF`

✓ **WHY THIS RECIPE WORKS:** Hugely popular in Switzerland, roesti is a large golden-brown pancake of simply seasoned grated potatoes fried in butter. We set out to master this recipe with a crunchy, crisp exterior encasing a tender, creamy interior. Wanting to produce cakes with plenty of hearty potatoes but with a decidedly fresh flavor, we swapped out some of the potatoes for celery root, which gave our roesti a brighter flavor without masking the delicate flavor of the potatoes. Producing a golden-brown crust was easy, but the inside of the roesti came out gluey and half-cooked. To solve these problems we eliminated excess moisture by salting our vegetables, then wringing them dry in a dish towel. To ensure our potato cake held together, we tossed the potatoes and celery root with a small amount of cornstarch. Creating a rich but bright sauce to accompany our roesti was as simple as combining tangy crème fraîche with parsley and lemon zest and juice. We were pleased to find that a beet variation worked just as well as our master recipe: We simply tweaked the seasoning and our sauce to match the flavor profile of the sweeter, earthy-tasting beet roesti.

¼ **cup crème fraîche**
3 **tablespoons minced fresh parsley**
2½ **teaspoons grated lemon zest plus ½ teaspoon juice**
　 Salt and pepper
1 **pound russet potatoes, peeled and shredded**
1 **celery root (14 ounces), peeled and shredded**
2 **teaspoons cornstarch**
4 **tablespoons unsalted butter**

1. Combine crème fraîche, 1 tablespoon parsley, ½ teaspoon lemon zest, lemon juice, and ⅛ teaspoon salt in bowl, cover, and refrigerate until needed. Meanwhile, toss potatoes and celery root with ¾ teaspoon salt, then let drain in colander for 30 minutes.

2. Working in 3 batches, wrap potato mixture in clean dish towel and wring tightly to squeeze out as much liquid as possible; transfer to large bowl. Add remaining 2 tablespoons parsley, remaining 2 teaspoons lemon zest, cornstarch, and ¼ teaspoon pepper, and toss to combine.

3. Melt 2 tablespoons butter in 10-inch nonstick skillet over medium-low heat. Add potato mixture and spread into even layer. Cover and cook for 5 minutes. Uncover and, using greased spatula, gently press potato mixture to form compact, round cake. Cook, pressing on cake occasionally, until bottom is deep golden brown, about 10 minutes.

4. Run spatula around edge of pan and shake pan to loosen roesti; slide onto large plate. Melt remaining 2 tablespoons butter in now-empty skillet. Invert roesti onto second plate, then slide it, browned side up, back into skillet. Cook, pressing on cake occasionally, until bottom is well browned, about 15 minutes. Transfer roesti to wire rack and let cool for 5 minutes. Cut into wedges and serve with crème fraîche sauce.

VARIATION

Beet and Potato Roesti with Orange-Chive Crème Fraîche `GF`

Substitute chives for parsley, orange zest and juice for lemon zest and juice, and 1 pound peeled and grated beets for celery root.

Flipping Potato Roesti

1. After browning first side, run spatula around edge of pan and shake pan gently to loosen roesti. Slide roesti onto large plate.

2. Place second plate face down over roesti. Invert roesti onto second plate so it is browned side up.

3. Slide roesti back into pan, browned side up. Tuck edges into pan with spatula.

Stuffed Eggplant with Bulgur
SERVES 4

✔ **WHY THIS RECIPE WORKS:** Italian eggplants are the perfect size for stuffing, and they take on a rich, creamy texture when baked. Roasting the eggplants prior to stuffing was key to preventing them from turning watery and tasteless. The slight caramelizing effect of roasting them on a preheated baking sheet added depth of flavor, too. We then let the eggplants drain briefly on paper towels (which got rid of excess liquid) before adding the stuffing. Hearty, nutty bulgur, which requires only soaking before it's ready to eat, made a perfect filling base. Pecorino Romano cheese added richness while tomatoes lent bright flavor and a bit of moisture. You can use fine-grind bulgur in this recipe, but do not use coarse-grind or cracked-wheat bulgur or skip the step of rinsing the bulgur before cooking. For information on different types of bulgur, see page 184. The time it takes for the bulgur to become tender and fluffy in step 3 will depend on the age and type of bulgur used.

- 4 **(10-ounce) Italian eggplants, halved lengthwise**
- 2 **tablespoons extra-virgin olive oil**
   Salt and pepper
- ½ **cup medium-grind bulgur, rinsed**
- ¼ **cup water**
- 1 **onion, chopped fine**
- 3 **garlic cloves, minced**
- 2 **teaspoons minced fresh oregano or ½ teaspoon dried**
- ¼ **teaspoon ground cinnamon**
   Pinch cayenne pepper
- 1 **pound plum tomatoes, cored, seeded, and chopped**
- 2 **ounces Pecorino Romano cheese, grated (1 cup)**
- 2 **tablespoons pine nuts, toasted**
- 2 **teaspoons red wine vinegar**
- 2 **tablespoons minced fresh parsley**

1. Adjust oven racks to upper-middle and lowest positions, place parchment paper–lined rimmed baking sheet on lowest rack, and heat oven to 400 degrees.

2. Score flesh of each eggplant half in 1-inch diamond pattern, about 1 inch deep. Brush scored sides of eggplant with 1 tablespoon oil and season with salt and pepper. Lay eggplant, cut side down, on hot baking sheet and roast until flesh is tender, 40 to 50 minutes. Transfer eggplant, cut side down, to paper towel–lined baking sheet and let drain. Do not wash rimmed baking sheet.

3. Meanwhile, toss bulgur with water in bowl and let sit until grains are tender and fluffy, 20 to 40 minutes.

4. Heat remaining 1 tablespoon oil in 12-inch skillet over medium heat until shimmering. Add onion and cook until softened, 5 minutes. Stir in garlic, oregano, cinnamon, cayenne, and ½ teaspoon salt and cook until fragrant, about 30 seconds. Stir in soaked bulgur, tomatoes, ¾ cup Pecorino, pine nuts, and vinegar and let warm through, about 1 minute. Season with salt and pepper to taste.

5. Return eggplant, cut side up, to rimmed baking sheet. Using 2 forks, gently push eggplant flesh to sides to make room for filling. Mound bulgur mixture into eggplant halves and pack lightly with back of spoon. Sprinkle with remaining ¼ cup Pecorino. Bake on upper-middle rack until cheese is melted, 5 to 10 minutes. Sprinkle with parsley and serve.

Scoring Eggplant

Using tip of chef's knife (or paring knife), score each eggplant half in 1-inch diamond pattern, about 1 inch deep.

Roasting the empty mushroom caps to release their moisture before stuffing them keeps them from getting weighed down.

Stuffed Portobello Mushrooms with Spinach and Gorgonzola

SERVES 4

✔ **WHY THIS RECIPE WORKS:** With their naturally concave shape and wide surface area, portobello mushroom caps are perfect for roasting and stuffing. Yet getting these thick, meaty mushrooms to cook through while weighed down by filling can take a long time. To speed up the process, we roasted the empty caps in a superhot 500-degree oven first. Roasting them gill side down allowed any moisture released during cooking to drain away, plus it protected the delicate underside of the mushrooms from burning. While the mushrooms roasted, we made an easy stuffing with baby spinach, flavorful Gorgonzola cheese, and toasted walnuts that we topped with panko bread crumbs. A quick run under the broiler heated everything through and crisped up the crown of bread crumbs. You can substitute cream sherry with a squeeze of lemon juice for the dry sherry here, but do not substitute cooking sherry. Feta or goat cheese can be substituted for the Gorgonzola if desired.

5 tablespoons extra-virgin olive oil
10 large portobello mushroom caps, 8 whole, 2 chopped fine
    Salt and pepper
12 ounces (12 cups) baby spinach

2 tablespoons water
1 onion, chopped fine
4 garlic cloves, minced
½ cup dry sherry
4 ounces Gorgonzola cheese, crumbled (1 cup)
1 cup walnuts, toasted and chopped
¾ cup panko bread crumbs

1. Adjust oven rack to upper-middle position and heat oven to 500 degrees. Brush rimmed baking sheet with 1 tablespoon oil. Lay 8 mushroom caps, gill side down, on baking sheet and brush tops with 2 tablespoons oil. Roast until tender, 10 to 12 minutes. Remove baking sheet from oven, flip mushrooms gill side up, and season with salt and pepper.

2. Meanwhile, microwave spinach, water, and ¼ teaspoon salt in covered bowl until spinach is wilted, about 2 minutes. Drain spinach in colander, let cool slightly, then place in clean dish towel and squeeze out excess liquid. Transfer spinach to cutting board and chop coarse.

3. Cook onion and remaining 2 tablespoons oil in 12-inch skillet over medium-high heat until softened, about 3 minutes. Stir in chopped mushrooms and cook until they begin

With their substantial, meaty texture and great flavor, mushrooms are a staple of the vegetarian diet. We love the complex meatiness they add to soups, sauces, stir-fries, and stuffings, and we also enjoy them simply sautéed, stuffed, marinated, or grilled on their own. Here's everything you need to know about buying, storing, and preparing mushrooms.

Buying Mushrooms

There are many varieties of fresh mushrooms available at the supermarket now: the humble white button mushroom, as well as cremini, shiitake, oyster, and portobello mushrooms, for starters. We find cremini mushrooms to be firmer and more flavorful than less-expensive white button mushrooms, but the two are interchangeable in any recipe. If possible, always buy mushrooms loose so that you can inspect their quality. When buying button or cremini mushrooms, look for mushrooms with whole, intact caps; avoid those with discoloration or dry, shriveled patches. Pick mushrooms with large caps and minimal stems.

Storing Mushrooms

Because of their high moisture content, mushrooms are very perishable; most mushrooms can be kept fresh for only a few days. To extend their shelf life as long as possible, store loose mushrooms in the crisper drawer in a partially open zipper-lock bag. Store packaged mushrooms in their original containers, as these are designed to "breathe," maximizing the life of the mushrooms. Once the package has been opened, simply rewrap it with plastic wrap.

Cleaning Mushrooms

When it comes to cleaning, you can ignore the advice against washing mushrooms, which exaggerates their ability to absorb water. As long as they are washed before they are cut, we found that 6 ounces of mushrooms gain only about a quarter-ounce of water. However, rinsing can cause discoloration, so don't wash mushrooms that will be eaten raw; simply brush dirt away with a soft pastry brush or cloth. If you are cooking the mushrooms, rinse away dirt and grit with cold water just before using, then spin dry in a salad spinner.

Preparing Mushrooms

For mushrooms with tender stems, such as white button and cremini, trim the stems, then prep and cook the stems alongside the caps.

For mushrooms with tough, woody stems, such as shiitakes and portobellos, the stems should be removed.

Buying and Preparing Dried Porcini

We often turn to dried porcini to add potent savory flavor to dishes. Because the mushrooms are dried, their flavor is concentrated and they are conveniently shelf-stable. When buying dried porcini, always inspect the mushrooms. Avoid those with small holes, which indicate the mushrooms may have been subjected to pinworms. Look for large, smooth porcini free of holes, dust, and grit. Because porcini mushrooms are foraged, not farmed, they vary in cleanliness. Always remove any grit before using; we like to swish them in a bowl of water to loosen dirt, then rinse them.

Buying and Preparing Portobellos

Portobellos are the giants of the mushroom family, ranging from 4 to 6 inches in diameter. They are the mature form of cremini mushrooms, and, as a result of the extra growing time, they have a particularly intense, meaty flavor and a steaklike texture. They are ideal for being sautéed, stir-fried, roasted, grilled, or stuffed. Look for mushrooms with fully intact caps and dry gills. Wet, damaged gills are a sign of spoilage. The stems are woody and are often discarded, so buy mushrooms with stems only if you plan to use them (such as in soup, stock, or stuffing). To clean portobellos, simply wipe them with a damp towel. When cooking portobellos in soups or stews, you may want to remove the gills on the underside of the cap so that your dish won't taste or look muddy.

to release their liquid, about 4 minutes. Stir in garlic and cook until fragrant, about 30 seconds. Stir in sherry and cook until evaporated, about 2 minutes. Stir in chopped spinach, Gorgonzola, and walnuts and cook until heated through, about 1 minute. Season with salt and pepper to taste.

4. Spoon filling into roasted mushroom caps, press filling flat with back of spoon, then sprinkle with panko. Bake until panko is golden and filling is hot, 5 to 10 minutes. Serve.

Stuffed Acorn Squash with Barley

SERVES 4

✓ **WHY THIS RECIPE WORKS:** For a simple but elegant stuffed squash recipe, we started with halved acorn squash. To ensure that we achieved both tender squash and a perfectly cooked filling, we roasted the squash on its own until tender and made an easy filling in the meantime. First we simmered hearty pearl barley under tender. While the barley cooked, we sautéed chopped fennel and onion, then folded this mixture into the barley along with pine nuts, Parmesan, and herbs. We topped the squash with a sprinkle of additional cheese and baked it for just a few minutes to warm it through. A drizzle of sweet, bright balsamic vinegar was the perfect balancing touch. Be sure to look for similar-size squash (1½ pounds each) to ensure even cooking. Make sure to use pearl barley, not hulled barley, in this recipe—hulled barley takes much longer to cook. For more information on barley, see page 184.

- 3 tablespoons extra-virgin olive oil
- 2 acorn squashes (1½ pounds each), halved pole to pole and seeded
  Salt and pepper
- ¾ cup pearl barley, rinsed and drained
- 1 onion, chopped fine
- 1 fennel bulb, stalks discarded, bulb halved, cored, and chopped fine
- 6 garlic cloves, minced
- 1 teaspoon minced fresh thyme or ¼ teaspoon dried
- 1 teaspoon ground coriander
- 2 ounces Parmesan cheese, grated (1 cup)
- 2 tablespoons minced fresh parsley
- 2 tablespoons pine nuts, toasted
- 1 tablespoon unsalted butter
- 4 teaspoons balsamic vinegar

1. Adjust oven racks to upper-middle and lower-middle positions and heat oven to 400 degrees. Line rimmed baking sheet

Guidelines for Using Dried Herbs

Dried herbs are often more convenient than fresh because they don't spoil and need no more prep than a twist of a lid. But they can add a dusty quality to dishes, especially when added at the end. Here are the tricks we've found for using them successfully.

WHEN DRIED HERBS SHINE AND HOW TO SUBSTITUTE
Only some dried herbs give good results, mainly in recipes with longer cooking times (20 minutes or more) and a good amount of moisture. Dishes like chili and pasta sauce are actually often better when made with dried oregano than with fresh. Dried rosemary, sage, marjoram, and thyme also fare reasonably well in certain applications; the flavor compounds in these herbs are relatively stable at high temperatures, so they maintain their flavor through the drying process. To replace fresh herbs with dried, use one-third the amount, and add them early in the cooking process so they have time to soften.

WHEN FRESH IS BEST
Those herbs that we consider delicate (like basil, chives, and parsley) lose most of their flavor when dried, so we prefer fresh forms of these herbs. Two herbs, tarragon and dill, fall into a middle category: They do add flavor in their dried form, but it is more muted than that provided by hardier dried herbs, so we generally prefer fresh when possible.

SMART STORAGE
Like spices, dried herbs should be stored in a cool, dark, dry place and not near the stove, where heat, light, and moisture will shorten their shelf life. However, even when properly stored, dried herbs lose their potency 6 to 12 months after opening, so it's important to replace them frequently. You can test dried herbs for freshness by rubbing them between your fingers—if they don't release a bright fragrance, it's time to buy a new jar.

with aluminum foil and grease with 1 tablespoon oil. Brush cut sides of squash with 1 tablespoon oil, season with salt and pepper, and lay cut side down on prepared baking sheet. Roast on lower-middle rack until tender (paring knife can be slipped into flesh with no resistance), 45 to 55 minutes. Remove squash from oven and increase oven temperature to 450 degrees.

2. Meanwhile, bring 3 quarts water to boil in large saucepan. Stir in barley and ¼ teaspoon salt. Return to boil, then reduce to simmer and cook until barley is tender, 20 to 25 minutes; drain.

3. Wipe now-empty saucepan dry, add remaining 1 tablespoon oil, and heat over medium heat until shimmering. Add onion and fennel and cook until softened, about 10 minutes. Stir in garlic, thyme, and coriander and cook until fragrant, about 30 seconds. Off heat, stir in cooked barley, ¾ cup Parmesan, parsley, pine nuts, and butter. Season with salt and pepper to taste.

4. Flip roasted squash over and scoop out flesh, leaving ⅛-inch thickness of flesh in each shell. Gently fold squash flesh into barley mixture. Spoon mixture into squash shells, mounding it slightly, and sprinkle with remaining ¼ cup Parmesan. Bake on upper-middle rack until cheese is lightly browned, 5 to 10 minutes. Drizzle with balsamic vinegar and serve.

Stuffed Tomatoes with Couscous and Zucchini

SERVES 4

✔ **WHY THIS RECIPE WORKS:** To turn stuffed tomatoes into a great entrée, we needed to find a solution to the problem that plagues most recipes: drab, soggy fillings. Our first step was to core and seed the tomatoes, salt their interiors, and let them drain, drawing out their excess liquid. After 30 minutes, the tomatoes had given up most of their liquid, ensuring that we could pack them with filling without them becoming soggy. For the stuffing, we chose nutty-tasting whole-wheat couscous instead of bread crumbs and paired it with sautéed zucchini and fennel. We built the filling in one saucepan, adding broth toward the end, then let the couscous finish cooking off the heat. Goat cheese and Parmesan added richness and kept the filling cohesive. We stuffed our tomatoes and sprinkled them with Parmesan before baking them until the cheese was browned and the tomatoes were tender. Look for tomatoes of equal size with flat, sturdy bottoms that can sit upright on their own.

8   large tomatoes (8 ounces each)
     Salt and pepper
3   tablespoons extra-virgin olive oil
1   fennel bulb, stalks discarded, bulb halved, cored,
     and chopped fine
2   shallots, minced
1   zucchini (8 ounces), cut into ¼-inch pieces
4   garlic cloves, minced
⅔   cup whole-wheat couscous
¾   cup vegetable broth
2   ounces Parmesan cheese, grated (1 cup)

Salting and draining the tomatoes before stuffing keeps their juice from making the couscous and vegetable filling soggy.

2   ounces goat cheese, crumbled (½ cup)
¼   cup chopped fresh basil

1. Slice top ⅛ inch off each tomato and carefully remove core and seeds. Sprinkle inside of each tomato with ⅛ teaspoon salt. Place upside down on several layers of paper towels and let drain for 30 minutes.

2. Meanwhile, adjust oven rack to upper-middle position and heat oven to 375 degrees. Heat 2 tablespoons oil in large saucepan over medium heat until shimmering. Add fennel and shallots and cook until softened and lightly browned, 10 to 12 minutes.

3. Stir in zucchini and cook until tender, about 5 minutes. Stir in garlic and cook until fragrant, about 30 seconds. Stir in couscous and cook until lightly toasted, 1 to 2 minutes. Stir in broth and bring to brief simmer. Remove pan from heat, cover, and let sit for 5 minutes. Using fork, gently fluff couscous and stir in ½ cup Parmesan, goat cheese, and basil. Season with salt and pepper to taste.

4. Pat inside of each tomato dry with paper towels. Arrange tomatoes, cut side up, in 13 by 9-inch baking dish lined with aluminum foil. Brush cut edges of tomatoes with remaining

1 tablespoon oil. Mound couscous filling into tomatoes and pack lightly with back of spoon. Sprinkle with remaining ½ cup Parmesan. Bake until cheese is lightly browned and tomatoes are tender, about 15 minutes. Serve.

Preparing Tomatoes for Stuffing

1. Using sharp knife, slice top ⅛ inch off each tomato.

2. Using fingers (or paring knife), remove and discard core and any seeds inside tomato.

3. Sprinkle inside of each tomato with ⅛ teaspoon salt, place upside down on paper towels, and let drain for 30 minutes.

For a satisfying Tex-Mex supper, we fill subtly spicy poblano peppers with a melty, cheesy bean and corn stuffing.

Cheesy Stuffed Poblanos

SERVES 4 TO 6 **GF**

✔ **WHY THIS RECIPE WORKS:** Inspired by the Mexican dish chiles rellenos, we set out to make a recipe for cheesy stuffed poblano peppers. Chiles rellenos are traditionally poblano peppers that are stuffed with cheese and then battered and fried. We felt the bright, vegetal flavor of the pepper was lost during frying (not to mention we didn't want to contend with the mess that frying created), and most of the cheese fillings we came across were bland and oozed out of the pepper during cooking. To fix these problems, we first decided to roast the stuffed peppers to deepen their flavor and tenderize the peppers. Stuffing raw poblanos without tearing them was tricky, but after a quick trip to the microwave, they were more pliable. To improve our filling's flavor and to anchor the cheese in the peppers during

roasting, we added a couple of cans of pinto beans (half of which we mashed), corn, garlic, onion, and spices to a combination of Monterey Jack and cheddar cheeses. A quick fresh tomato salsa nicely balanced the rich, cheesy peppers.

2 (15-ounce) cans pinto beans, rinsed
1 cup water
1 tablespoon vegetable oil
1 onion, chopped fine
4 garlic cloves, minced
1 tablespoon ground cumin
1 tablespoon minced fresh oregano or 1 teaspoon dried
1 teaspoon chili powder
1 teaspoon grated lime zest plus 1 tablespoon juice
Salt and pepper
⅛ teaspoon cayenne pepper
2 cups frozen corn
4 ounces Monterey Jack cheese, shredded (1 cup)
4 ounces sharp cheddar cheese, shredded (1 cup)
¼ cup minced fresh cilantro
8 poblano chiles
1 recipe Easy Cherry Tomato Salsa (page 43)

1. Adjust oven racks to upper-middle and lower-middle positions and heat oven to 425 degrees. Line 2 rimmed baking sheets with aluminum foil and set wire rack in each. Using potato masher, mash half of beans and water together in bowl until mostly smooth.

2. Heat oil in 12-inch nonstick skillet over medium heat until shimmering. Add onion and cook until softened, about 5 minutes. Stir in garlic, cumin, oregano, chili powder, lime zest, ½ teaspoon salt, and cayenne and cook until fragrant, about 30 seconds. Stir in mashed bean mixture and cook, stirring constantly, until nearly all liquid has evaporated, 3 to 5 minutes. Stir in remaining beans and corn and cook until warmed through, about 2 minutes. Off heat, stir in Monterey Jack, cheddar, cilantro, and lime juice. Season with salt and pepper to taste.

3. Leaving stem intact, cut slit lengthwise down 1 side of each poblano. Microwave poblanos in covered bowl until just pliable, about 2½ minutes. Gently pry open poblanos, remove seeds, and stuff evenly with bean-cheese mixture. Lay poblanos, stuffed side up, on prepared sheets. Bake until tender, switching and rotating sheets halfway through baking, 30 to 40 minutes. Serve with salsa.

Stuffing Poblano Chiles

1. Leaving stem intact, cut slit lengthwise down 1 side of poblanos.

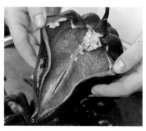

2. Microwave poblanos in covered bowl until just pliable, about 2½ minutes.

3. Gently pry open poblanos, remove seeds, and stuff evenly with bean-cheese mixture.

Twice-Baked Potatoes with Broccoli, Cheddar, and Scallions
SERVES 4 `GF`

✔ **WHY THIS RECIPE WORKS:** Twice-baked potatoes are simple enough to make, but the process can be time-consuming and too often results in rubbery skins filled with pasty, bland fillings. We wanted to perfect the process to achieve twice-baked potatoes with slightly crisp skins and a rich, creamy filling. We oiled the potatoes before baking for a crisp skin, then we let the baked potatoes cool slightly before slicing them open and removing the flesh. We found that we could prevent the hollowed-out shells from turning soggy by crisping them in the oven while making the filling. And for the filling, we found it best to combine the potatoes with dairy ingredients—tangy sour cream and half-and-half were ideal—plus a small amount of butter, and sharp cheddar cheese for its bold flavor. For a perfect finish, we placed the filled potatoes under the broiler for a browned, crisp topping.

4 (8- to 9-ounce) russet potatoes, unpeeled
  Vegetable oil
4 tablespoons unsalted butter
1 pound broccoli florets, cut into ½- to 1-inch pieces
  Salt and pepper
2 tablespoons water
1 teaspoon lemon juice
6 ounces sharp cheddar cheese, shredded (1½ cups)
3 scallions, sliced thin
½ cup sour cream
¼ cup half-and-half
¼ teaspoon dry mustard

1. Adjust 1 oven rack to middle position and second rack 8 inches from broiler element. Heat oven to 400 degrees. Rub potatoes with vegetable oil, place on aluminum foil–lined baking sheet, and roast until skewer can be inserted into potatoes with little resistance, 60 to 70 minutes. Let potatoes cool for 10 minutes.

2. Meanwhile, melt 2 tablespoons butter in 12-inch skillet over medium-high heat. Add broccoli and ½ teaspoon salt and cook, stirring occasionally, until lightly browned, about 2 minutes. Add water, cover, and cook until broccoli is crisp-tender, about 1 minute. Uncover and let water evaporate, about 1 minute. Transfer broccoli to bowl and drizzle with lemon juice.

3. Halve each potato lengthwise. Using soupspoon, scoop flesh from each half into bowl, leaving about ⅜-inch thickness of flesh. Place shells, cut sides up, on baking sheet and return to oven until dry and slightly crisp, about 10 minutes.

4. Meanwhile, add remaining 2 tablespoons butter to potato flesh in bowl and mash with fork until potatoes are smooth and butter is melted. Stir in 1 cup cheddar, scallions, sour cream, half-and-half, mustard, and ¾ teaspoon salt. Season with pepper to taste, then gently fold in broccoli.

5. Remove shells from oven and heat broiler. Mound filling into shells and sprinkle with remaining ½ cup cheddar. Broil until spotty brown, 6 to 10 minutes. Let cool for 5 minutes before serving.

Preparing Potatoes for Stuffing

1. Halve baked potatoes lengthwise through narrower side so that potatoes will lie flat on wider side when stuffed.

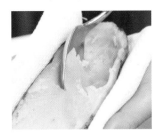

2. Using soupspoon, scoop flesh from each potato half, leaving about ⅜-inch thickness of flesh to support potato skin.

To get perfect stir-fired asparagus, we cook the spears over high heat until browned, then steam them through in the sauce.

Stir-Fried Asparagus with Shiitake Mushrooms

SERVES 4   FAST VEGAN GF

✓ **WHY THIS RECIPE WORKS:** To achieve stir-fried asparagus with a flavorful browned exterior and a crisp-tender texture, we had to start with a hot pan and stir the asparagus only occasionally. This allowed the asparagus to char and caramelize before it overcooked. To ensure that the asparagus cooked evenly we diluted the sauce with water, creating a small amount of steam that cooked the spears through before evaporating and leaving behind a flavorful, clingy glaze. To keep our recipe simple, we used just five bold ingredients in our stir-fry sauce. To complement the fresh-flavored asparagus, we added in some thinly sliced shiitake mushrooms. Look for spears that are no thicker than ½ inch. In order for this recipe to be gluten-free, you must use gluten-free soy sauce or tamari. Serve with rice.

SAUCE
- 2 tablespoons water
- 1 tablespoon soy sauce
- 1 tablespoon dry sherry
- 2 teaspoons packed brown sugar
- 2 teaspoons grated fresh ginger
- 1 teaspoon toasted sesame oil

VEGETABLES
- 1 tablespoon vegetable oil
- 1 pound asparagus, trimmed and cut on bias into 2-inch lengths
- 4 ounces shiitake mushrooms, stemmed and sliced thin
- 2 scallions, green parts only, sliced thin on bias

1. FOR THE SAUCE: Whisk all ingredients together in bowl.

2. FOR THE VEGETABLES: Heat oil in 12-inch nonstick skillet over high heat until smoking. Add asparagus and mushrooms and cook, stirring occasionally, until asparagus is spotty brown, 3 to 4 minutes. Add sauce and cook, stirring once or twice, until pan is almost dry and asparagus is crisp-tender, 1 to 2 minutes. Transfer to serving platter, sprinkle with scallions, and serve.

With a wide variety of vegetables and lots of bold flavor, many Asian dishes are naturally vegetarian or easy to make vegetarian. To make great stir-fries, curries, or other Asian dishes, you'll need some Asian ingredients, but nowadays most supermarkets have an Asian foods section full of options. The following list includes common Asian ingredients that you'll find in many of our recipes.

Asian Chile Sauces

Used both in cooking and as a condiment, these sauces come in a variety of styles. Sriracha contains garlic and is made from chiles ground into a smooth paste. Asian chili-garlic sauce is similar to Sriracha, but the chiles are coarsely ground. Sambal oelek is made purely from ground chiles without the addition of garlic or other spices, thus adding heat but not additional flavor. Once opened, these sauces will keep for several months in the refrigerator.

Chinese Rice Wine

This rich-flavored liquid made from fermented glutinous rice or millet is used for both drinking and cooking. It ranges in color from clear to amber and tastes slightly sweet and aromatic. Chinese rice wine is also called yellow wine, Shao Hsing, or Shaoxing. If you can't find Chinese rice wine, dry sherry is a decent substitute.

Coconut Milk

Widely available in cans, coconut milk adds rich flavor and body to soups, curries, and stir-fries. Coconut milk comes in both regular and light versions. Regular coconut milk is creamier than the light, but it also contains more fat. Do not confuse coconut milk with cream of coconut, which contains added sugar and is much sweeter.

Fish Sauce

Fish sauce is a salty, amber-colored liquid made from fermented fish. It is used as both an ingredient and a condiment in certain Asian cuisines, most commonly in Southeast Asia. In very small amounts, it adds a well-rounded, salty flavor to sauces, soups, and marinades. You can make your own vegetarian fish sauce or substitute an equal amount of Bragg Liquid Aminos. For more information, see page 60.

Five-Spice Powder

Often called Chinese five-spice powder, this aromatic blend of spices typically contains cinnamon, clove, fennel seed, star anise, and Sichuan peppercorn (white pepper or ginger are common substitutes). Available in the spice aisle of the supermarket, five-spice powder is great in sauces and in spice rubs for grilled foods.

Hoisin Sauce

Hoisin sauce is a thick, reddish-brown mixture of soybeans, sugar, vinegar, garlic, chiles, and spices, the most predominant of which is five-spice powder. It is used in many classic Chinese dishes and as a table condiment, much like ketchup. The ideal hoisin sauce balances sweet, salty, pungent, and spicy elements so that no one flavor dominates.

Mirin

This Japanese rice wine has a subtle salty-sweet flavor prized in Asian marinades and glazes. The most traditional method for creating mirin uses glutinous rice, malted rice, and distilled alcohol. Many supermarket brands in this country, however, combine sake or another type of alcohol with salt, corn syrup, other sweeteners, and sometimes caramel coloring and flavoring. We use mirin to brighten the flavor of stir-fries, teriyaki, and other Asian dishes. If you cannot find mirin, substitute 1 tablespoon dry white wine and ½ teaspoon sugar for every 1 tablespoon of mirin.

Miso

Made from a fermented mixture of soybeans and rice, barley, or rye, miso is incredibly versatile, suitable for use in soups, braises, dressings, and sauces as well as for topping grilled foods. Although countless variations of salty, deep-flavored miso are available, three common types are white *shiro* (actually light golden in color), red *aka*, and brownish-black *hatcho*. Shiro miso is mild and sweet; hatcho miso is strong, complex, and prunelike. Aka miso nicely balances salty and sweet elements and is the best all-purpose miso. If you are gluten-free, be aware that some brands include wheat, barley, or rye, and check the label carefully.

Oyster Sauce

This thick, salty brown sauce is a rich, concentrated mixture of oysters, soy sauce, brine, and seasonings. Very salty and fishy-tasting, oyster sauce is too strong to be used as a condiment. Rather, it is used to enhance the flavor of many dishes and stir-fries and is the base for many Asian dipping sauces. You can find vegetarian oyster sauces, made from mushrooms, in stores and online. This sauce will keep indefinitely when refrigerated.

Rice Vinegar

Rice vinegar is made from glutinous rice that is broken down into sugars, blended with yeast to ferment into alcohol, and aerated to form vinegar. It has a sweet-tart flavor that is used to accentuate many Asian dishes. It comes in an unseasoned version and a seasoned version with added sake, sugar, and salt.

Sesame Oil

Raw sesame oil, which is very mild and light in color, is used mostly for cooking, while toasted sesame oil, which has a deep amber color, is primarily used for seasoning because of its intense, nutty flavor. For the biggest hit of sesame flavor, we prefer to use toasted sesame oil. Just a few drops will give stir-fries, noodle dishes, and salad dressings a deep, rich flavor. Purchase sesame oil in tinted glass and refrigerate it to extend its shelf life.

Soy Sauce

Soy sauce is a dark, salty, fermented liquid made from soybeans and roasted grain. It is used throughout Asia to enhance flavor and contribute complexity to food. Soy sauce is rich in the amino acid glutamate, which contributes potent savory, meaty flavor to dishes. Pasteurized soy sauce can be stored at room temperature, but unpasteurized soy sauce should be refrigerated.

Thai Green Curry Paste

Store-bought green curry paste is made from fresh green Thai chiles, lemon grass, galangal (Thai ginger), garlic, and other spices. It quickly adds rich herbal flavor, complexity, and a bit of heat and is most often used in curries. It is usually sold in small jars with the other Thai ingredients at the supermarket.

Thai Red Curry Paste

Store-bought Thai red curry paste combines a number of hard-to-find, authentic Thai aromatics—including galangal (Thai ginger), bird's eye chiles, lemon grass, and kaffir lime leaves—in one easy-to-find ingredient. It is usually sold in small jars with the other Thai ingredients at the supermarket.

Wasabi

Hot and pungent, wasabi is commonly used as a condiment for sushi and sashimi but is also useful as an ingredient in other Japanese dishes. Fresh wasabi root (also known as Japanese horseradish) is hard to find and expensive (about $8 per ounce). More widely available is wasabi that is sold in paste or powder form (the powder is mixed with water to form a paste). Because fresh wasabi root is so expensive, most pastes and all powders contain no wasabi at all, but instead comprise a mixture of garden-variety horseradish and mustard, along with cornstarch and food coloring. We advise seeking out wasabi paste made from real wasabi root for its complex flavor.

Tips for Stir-Fry Success

The beauty of stir-frying is that you can do it quickly with just about anything in your fridge—but it's not a free-for-all. Here are some of our best tips and tricks for making great stir-fries.

PREP EVERYTHING AHEAD

Stir-fries come together and cook quickly, so it's helpful to measure out and prep all of your ingredients beforehand. This way, you have exactly what you need on hand and won't risk overcooking the vegetables or burning the sauce while you're mincing some garlic or grating ginger.

CHOOSE THE RIGHT VEGETABLES

Choose relatively sturdy vegetables that can withstand high heat but that cook quickly. Some of our favorites include onions, bell peppers, broccoli, eggplant, and snow peas. Remember that they'll cook best if the pieces are uniform in size and that a crisp-tender or al dente texture is desirable.

SWAP YOUR WOK FOR A SKILLET

It may seem like a traditional wok is the best pan for stir-frying, but the conical bottom of a wok is designed for a pit-style stove, where the flames lick and engulf the pan. On a flat, Western-style burner, the broad surface of a skillet makes more contact than a round-bottomed wok, making it a better choice for browning. We also prefer to use nonstick skillets for stir-frying. Be sure to use the skillet size called for in the recipe; if the skillet is too small, the ingredients will steam rather than sear; if it's too big, the sauce can overreduce.

DON'T CROWD THE PAN

Adding all the ingredients at once will cause the vegetables to steam rather than sear. Be sure to add the food to the pan in an even layer and leave space between the vegetables so that they brown well.

ADD AROMATICS LATER

Waiting to add aromatics like ginger and garlic until the protein and vegetables have been cooked prevents them from scorching over the high heat. Once the vegetables are tender, we clear the center of the skillet and mash the aromatics into the skillet until fragrant, which takes only about 30 seconds.

DON'T STIR TOO MUCH

Nomenclature aside, it's best not to stir your stir-fry too much. Western-style burners have a relatively low heat output, so stirring frequently during cooking inhibits proper browning.

Stir-Fried Eggplant with Garlic-Basil Sauce

SERVES 4 FAST VEGAN GF

✔ **WHY THIS RECIPE WORKS:** We wanted to achieve a great Thai-style eggplant stir-fry without having to take the extra effort to salt or pretreat the eggplant before cooking (after all, stir-fries are supposed to come together quickly, not involve a lot of additional work). We started by cooking the eggplant for a full 10 minutes. In that time we were able to drive off the excess moisture and brown the eggplant, all in one 12-inch skillet. To complement the earthy eggplant, we also added a sweet red bell pepper to the skillet. We tested adding additional vegetables, but anything more felt superfluous and hid the great flavor and texture of the sautéed eggplant. For the Thai-style sauce, we used a combination of water and fish sauce substitute flavored with brown sugar, lime, and red pepper flakes. Stirring in a generous amount of basil and scallions to finish perfected our quick eggplant stir-fry. Do not peel the eggplant; leaving the skin on helps it hold together during cooking. Serve with rice.

SAUCE
- ½ cup water
- ¼ cup fish sauce substitute (see page 60)
- 2 tablespoons packed brown sugar
- 2 teaspoons grated lime zest plus 1 tablespoon juice
- 2 teaspoons cornstarch
- ⅛ teaspoon red pepper flakes

VEGETABLES
- 2 tablespoons plus 1 teaspoon vegetable oil
- 6 garlic cloves, minced
- 1 tablespoon grated fresh ginger
- 1 pound eggplant, cut into ¾-inch pieces
- 1 red bell pepper, stemmed, seeded, and cut into ¼-inch pieces
- ½ cup fresh basil leaves, torn into rough ½-inch pieces
- 2 scallions, sliced thin

1. FOR THE SAUCE: Whisk all ingredients together in bowl.

2. FOR THE VEGETABLES: Combine 1 teaspoon oil, garlic, and ginger in bowl. Heat remaining 2 tablespoons oil in 12-inch nonstick skillet over high heat until shimmering. Add eggplant and bell pepper and cook, stirring often, until well browned and tender, 8 to 10 minutes.

3. Clear center of skillet, add garlic mixture, and cook, mashing mixture into skillet, until fragrant, about 30 seconds. Stir garlic mixture into vegetables. Whisk sauce to recombine, then add to skillet. Cook, stirring constantly, until sauce is thickened, about 30 seconds. Off heat, stir in basil and scallions and serve.

Stir-Fried Portobellos, Carrots, and Snow Peas with Soy-Maple Sauce

SERVES 4 VEGAN GF

✓ **WHY THIS RECIPE WORKS:** When designing a recipe for a satisfying mushroom stir-fry, we chose hefty, meaty portobellos for the mushrooms, then settled on complementary vegetables to round out the meal. The trick was infusing this stir-fry with flavor and ensuring each vegetable was properly cooked. Cooking the mushrooms in two batches guaranteed even cooking and kept them from steaming in their own juices. In addition to the sauce, we found that adding a simple soy-maple glaze really boosted the mushrooms' flavor. As for the other vegetables, we chose snow peas and carrots, stir-frying them until crisp-tender in the same skillet that we used for the mushrooms. We heated garlic and ginger until just fragrant, then stirred in the sauce until everything was glossy and coated. In order for this recipe to be gluten-free, you must use gluten-free soy sauce or tamari. Serve with rice.

GLAZE

- 3 tablespoons maple syrup
- 2 tablespoons mirin
- 1 tablespoon soy sauce

SAUCE

- ½ cup vegetable broth
- 2 tablespoons soy sauce
- 1½ tablespoons mirin
- 2 teaspoons rice vinegar
- 2 teaspoons cornstarch
- 2 teaspoons toasted sesame oil

VEGETABLES

- 2 garlic cloves, minced
- 2 teaspoons grated fresh ginger
- ¼ teaspoon red pepper flakes
- 3 tablespoons vegetable oil
- 2 pounds portobello mushroom caps, gills removed, cut into 2-inch wedges
- 8 ounces snow peas, strings removed and sliced ¼-inch-thick on bias
- 2 carrots, peeled and cut into 2-inch-long matchsticks

1. FOR THE GLAZE: Whisk all ingredients together in bowl.

2. FOR THE SAUCE: Whisk all ingredients together in bowl.

3. FOR THE VEGETABLES: Combine garlic, ginger, pepper flakes, and 1 teaspoon oil in small bowl. Heat 1 tablespoon oil in 12-inch nonstick skillet over high heat until shimmering. Add half of mushrooms and cook, without stirring, until browned on one side, 2 to 3 minutes. Flip mushrooms over, reduce heat to medium, and cook until second side is browned and mushrooms are tender, about 5 minutes; transfer to bowl. Repeat with 1 tablespoon oil and remaining mushrooms.

4. Return all mushrooms to pan, add glaze, and cook over medium-high heat, stirring frequently, until glaze is thickened and mushrooms are coated, 1 to 2 minutes. Transfer mushrooms to bowl.

5. Wipe now-empty skillet clean with paper towels, add remaining 2 teaspoons oil, and place over high heat until shimmering. Add snow peas and carrots and cook, stirring occasionally, until vegetables are crisp-tender, about 5 minutes. Clear center of skillet, add garlic mixture, and cook, mashing mixture into skillet, until fragrant, about 30 seconds. Stir garlic mixture into vegetables.

6. Return mushrooms to skillet. Whisk sauce to recombine, then add to skillet. Cook, stirring constantly, until sauce is thickened, 1 to 2 minutes. Transfer to platter and serve.

Stir-Fried Bok Choy with Noodle Cake

SERVES 6 FAST

✓ **WHY THIS RECIPE WORKS:** For a change of pace, we wanted to serve this simple vegetable stir-fry atop a crispy pan-fried noodle cake. To make the noodle cake, we boiled fresh Chinese noodles, drained them, and then packed them into a nonstick skillet to get a crisp and crunchy exterior with a tender and chewy center. We found that the best way to flip the cake without breaking was to slide it onto a plate, invert it onto a second plate, then slide it back in the pan. We kept the vegetables for our stir-fry simple: Bok choy and red bell pepper are a classic combination. A mixture of broth, soy sauce, sherry, and vegetarian oyster sauce gave us the thick, full-flavored sauce we were after. We added in some classic Chinese aromatics, ginger and garlic, to give the sauce deep flavor. Fresh Chinese noodles are often kept in the produce section of the grocery store. If they aren't available, you can substitute fresh Italian spaghetti.

SAUCE

- ¼ cup vegetable broth
- 2 tablespoons soy sauce
- 1 tablespoon dry sherry
- 1 tablespoon vegetarian oyster sauce
- 1 teaspoon sugar
- 1 teaspoon cornstarch
- ⅛ teaspoon red pepper flakes

NOODLE CAKE AND VEGETABLES

- 9 ounces fresh Chinese noodles
  Salt
- 2 scallions, sliced thin
- 5 tablespoons plus 1 teaspoon vegetable oil
- 1 tablespoon grated fresh ginger
- 1 garlic clove, minced
- 1 small head bok choy (1 pound), stalks and greens separated, stalks sliced ¼ inch thick on bias and greens cut into ½-inch strips
- 1 red bell pepper, stemmed, seeded, and cut into ¼-inch strips

1. FOR THE SAUCE: Whisk all ingredients together in bowl.

2. FOR THE NOODLE CAKE AND VEGETABLES: Bring 4 quarts water to boil in Dutch oven. Add noodles and 1 tablespoon salt and cook, stirring often, until tender, 2 to 3 minutes (do not overcook). Drain thoroughly. Add scallions and ½ teaspoon salt to noodles and toss to combine.

3. Adjust oven rack to middle position and heat oven to 200 degrees. Set wire rack in rimmed baking sheet. Heat 2 tablespoons oil in 12-inch nonstick skillet over medium heat until shimmering. Spread noodles evenly into skillet and press into cake with spatula. Cook until crisp and golden brown on first side, 5 to 8 minutes.

4. Slide noodle cake onto large plate. Add 2 tablespoons oil to skillet and swirl to coat. Invert noodle cake onto second plate and slide it, browned side up, into skillet. Cook until golden brown on second side, 5 to 8 minutes. Slide noodle cake onto prepared rack and keep warm in oven.

Pan-Frying a Noodle Cake

1. Heat 2 tablespoons oil in 12-inch nonstick skillet over medium heat until shimmering. Spread noodles evenly into skillet and press into cake with spatula. Cook until crisp and golden brown on first side, 5 to 8 minutes.

2. Slide noodle cake onto large plate. Add 2 tablespoons oil to skillet and swirl to coat. Invert noodle cake onto second plate and slide it, browned side up, into skillet. Cook until golden brown on second side, 5 to 8 minutes.

5. Combine 1 teaspoon oil, ginger, and garlic in bowl. Add remaining 1 tablespoon oil to now-empty skillet and return to high heat until just smoking. Add bok choy stalks and red bell pepper and cook until lightly browned, 2 to 3 minutes.

6. Clear center of skillet, add ginger mixture, and cook, mashing mixture into skillet, until fragrant, about 30 seconds. Stir ginger mixture into vegetables. Stir in bok choy greens and cook until beginning to wilt, about 30 seconds. Whisk sauce to recombine, then add to skillet. Cook, stirring constantly, until sauce is thickened, about 30 seconds. Serve with noodle cake.

Stir-Fried Tofu and Bok Choy
SERVES 4 VEGAN GF

✓ **WHY THIS RECIPE WORKS:** Tofu stir-fries make a quick and satisfying vegetarian meal, but many recipes result in lackluster tofu and limp vegetables in a gummy sauce. We found several key techniques to achieve creamy tofu with a browned crust and crisp-tender vegetables, all lightly coated in a flavorful sauce. Removing as much of the tofu's moisture as possible by letting it drain on paper towels helped it brown in its relatively short cooking time. Coating the pieces in cornstarch further helped in creating a crispy crust while keeping the interior creamy, and also made a craggy surface that held on to the sauce nicely. We stir-fried the tofu in a skillet over high heat, then we cooked the vegetables until just crisp-tender. We cleared a spaced in the skillet and sautéed the aromatics, added back the tofu with quick-cooking bok choy greens, and poured in a garlic-ginger sauce lightly thickened with cornstarch so that it clung to the tofu and vegetables without being gloppy. In order for this recipe to be gluten-free, you must use gluten-free soy sauce or tamari. Serve with rice.

SAUCE
- ½ cup vegetable broth
- ¼ cup soy sauce
- 2 tablespoons Chinese rice wine or dry sherry
- 1 tablespoon sugar
- 2 teaspoons cornstarch
- 1 teaspoon toasted sesame oil

STIR-FRY
- 14 ounces extra-firm tofu, cut into 1-inch cubes
- ⅓ cup cornstarch
- 3 scallions, minced
- 3 garlic cloves, minced
- 1 tablespoon grated fresh ginger

3 tablespoons vegetable oil

1 small head bok choy (1 pound), stalks and greens separated, stalks sliced thin and greens cut into 1-inch pieces

2 carrots, peeled and cut into 2-inch-long matchsticks

1. FOR THE SAUCE: Whisk all ingredients together in bowl.

2. FOR THE STIR-FRY: Spread tofu out over paper towel–lined baking sheet and let drain for 20 minutes. Gently pat tofu dry with paper towels, then toss with cornstarch in bowl. Transfer coated tofu to strainer and shake gently over bowl to remove excess cornstarch.

3. Combine scallions, garlic, ginger, and 1 teaspoon oil in bowl; set aside. Heat 2 tablespoons oil in 12-inch nonstick skillet over high heat until just smoking. Add tofu and cook until crisp and well browned on all sides, 10 to 15 minutes; transfer to bowl.

4. Add remaining 2 teaspoons oil to now-empty skillet and return to high heat until shimmering. Add bok choy stalks and carrots and cook until vegetables are crisp-tender, about 4 minutes. Clear center of skillet, add garlic mixture, and cook, mashing mixture into skillet, until fragrant, about 30 seconds. Stir garlic mixture into vegetables.

5. Return tofu to skillet. Stir in bok choy greens. Whisk sauce to recombine, then add to skillet. Cook, stirring constantly, until sauce is thickened, 1 to 2 minutes. Serve.

For great curried cauliflower, we steam it until tender, sauté it until well browned, then simmer it in the flavorful curry sauce.

Thai Red Curry with Cauliflower
SERVES 4 | FAST | VEGAN | GF

✔ **WHY THIS RECIPE WORKS:** Thai cooking is all about balance, so when we set out to make a red curry with cauliflower, we knew that developing the deep, nutty flavor of the cauliflower was important. Typically we turn to the oven to achieve this, but for a curry dish that could otherwise be on the table in about 15 minutes, this felt like an unnecessary step. Instead, we confined ourselves to the skillet. Achieving tender, golden-brown cauliflower without scorching turned out to be a two-step process that took just about 10 minutes. First, we cooked the cauliflower along with water in a covered skillet for about 5 minutes, steaming it until it was just tender, then we uncovered the skillet to finish the cooking. This final uncovered cooking time drove off any remaining water left in the skillet, tenderized the cauliflower further, and allowed it to develop deep golden browning without any charring. A few minutes in the skillet at the very end of cooking was all the red curry sauce needed to bloom its flavors and thicken enough to coat the cauliflower nicely. Serve with rice.

1 (13.5-ounce) can coconut milk

3 tablespoons fish sauce substitute (see page 60)

1 teaspoon grated lime zest plus 1 tablespoon juice

1 tablespoon packed light brown sugar

2 teaspoons Thai red curry paste

⅛ teaspoon red pepper flakes

2 tablespoons plus 1 teaspoon vegetable oil

2 garlic cloves, minced

1 teaspoon grated fresh ginger

1 large head cauliflower (3 pounds), cored and cut into ¾-inch florets

¼ cup water

¼ teaspoon salt

¼ cup fresh basil leaves, torn into rough ½-inch pieces

1. Whisk coconut milk, fish sauce, lime zest and juice, sugar, curry paste, and pepper flakes together in bowl. In separate bowl, combine 1 teaspoon oil, garlic, and ginger.

2. Heat remaining 2 tablespoons oil in 12-inch nonstick skillet over high heat until shimmering. Add cauliflower, water, and salt, cover, and cook until cauliflower is just tender and translucent, about 5 minutes. Uncover and continue to cook,

Vegetarian Substitutes for Fish Sauce

Traditional fish sauce is a salty, amber-colored liquid made from fermented fish. It's rich in glutamates, taste bud stimulators that give food the meaty, savory flavor known as umami. Many recipes in Asian cuisines rely on fish sauce to provide a distinctive rich, salty, fermented flavor.

In search of a convenient vegetarian alternative, we found a variety of brands that offered a "vegetarian fish sauce." These sauces varied drastically in consistency (some were thick, some were thin), ingredients (some were fruit-flavored, others were mushroom based), and flavor (some were simply funky, some almost cheese-flavored). Overall, the products were inconsistent, and none of them were similar enough to traditional fish sauce to make a reliable substitute.

Luckily, with a little more research, we discovered **Bragg Liquid Aminos**. Made from 16 amino acids derived from soybeans (amino acids are the structural units that make up proteins), it is advertised as a healthy alternative to soy sauce. Tasters found it to be surprisingly similar to fish sauce, offering a great saltiness, with a bit of fermented flavor.

We also wanted to develop an option for a homemade substitute for fish sauce. We started with a base of water and soy sauce, which is rich in meaty-tasting glutamates, then we looked for ingredients that would amplify its savory flavor. Dried shiitake mushrooms turned out to be the solution—they are rich in flavor-amplifying compounds called nucleotides. When used together, nucleotides and glutamates can boost savory, umami-like flavors exponentially. Simmering both the dried mushrooms and soy sauce in a salty broth provided just the right meaty punch; this recipe worked perfectly as a 1:1 substitute for fish sauce.

VEGETARIAN FISH SAUCE SUBSTITUTE

MAKES ABOUT 1¼ CUPS FAST VEGAN GF

In order for this recipe to be gluten-free, you must use gluten-free soy sauce or tamari.

- 3 **cups water**
- 3 **tablespoons salt**
- 2 **tablespoons soy sauce**
- ¼ **ounce dried sliced shiitake mushrooms**

Simmer all ingredients in large saucepan over medium heat until mixture is reduced by half, about 20 to 30 minutes. Strain liquid and let cool completely. (Fish sauce can be refrigerated for up to 2 months.)

stirring occasionally, until liquid is evaporated and cauliflower is tender and well browned, 8 to 10 minutes.

3. Clear center of skillet, add garlic mixture, and cook, mashing mixture into skillet, until fragrant, about 30 seconds. Stir garlic mixture into cauliflower and reduce heat to medium-high. Whisk coconut milk mixture to recombine, add to skillet, and simmer until slightly thickened, about 4 minutes. Off heat, stir in basil and serve.

VARIATION

Thai Red Curry with Bell Peppers and Tofu VEGAN GF

Omit cauliflower, water, and salt. Toss 14 ounces extra-firm tofu, pressed dry with paper towels and cut into ¾-inch cubes, with ⅓ cup cornstarch; transfer to strainer and shake gently to remove excess cornstarch. Add coated tofu to heated oil in step 2 and cook until crisp and browned on all sides, 10 to 15 minutes; transfer to clean bowl. Add 2 red bell peppers, cut into 2-inch-long matchsticks, to oil left in skillet and cook until crisp-tender, about 2 minutes, before adding garlic mixture. Return tofu to skillet with sauce.

Thai Vegetable Green Curry with Jasmine Rice Cakes

SERVES 4 FAST

✔ **WHY THIS RECIPE WORKS:** Herbaceous and aromatic, green curry is a bright-tasting alternative to the red variety. Making your own requires a laundry list of ingredients, not to mention a fair amount of time, so we looked to the grocery store for a convenient ready-made version. We used just a few tablespoons of green curry paste as the base for our sauce and added a whole can of coconut milk (along with fish sauce substitute and a little brown sugar) for richness and depth. To soak up all the extra sauce, we made jasmine rice cakes to go along with our vegetable curry. Pulsing some of the cooked rice in a food processor helped to create a sticky base so the cakes wouldn't crumble apart when served. We loved the combination of bamboo shoots and green beans for the vegetables, but the real key was finishing the dish with chopped radishes and fresh cilantro to bring some color and fresh flavor to our dish. You can either use store-bought precooked jasmine rice or use our recipe for Stovetop White Rice (page 158). Basmati or long-grain white rice can be substituted for the jasmine rice; however, the cakes will be slightly less flavorful.

4 cups cooked jasmine rice
1 large egg, lightly beaten
2 tablespoons all-purpose flour
   Salt and pepper
3 tablespoons vegetable oil
1 (13.5-ounce) can coconut milk
3 tablespoons Thai green curry paste
2 tablespoons fish sauce substitute (see page 60)
1 tablespoon packed brown sugar
12 ounces green beans, trimmed and cut into
   2-inch lengths
1 (8-ounce) can bamboo shoots, rinsed
1 tablespoon lime juice
2 radishes, trimmed and chopped fine
2 tablespoons minced fresh cilantro

1. Adjust oven rack to middle position and heat oven to 200 degrees. Microwave rice in covered bowl until hot, about 90 seconds. Pulse half of rice in food processor until coarsely ground, about 10 pulses. Return processed rice to bowl with unprocessed rice, let cool, then stir in egg, flour, ¾ teaspoon salt, and ½ teaspoon pepper. Using wet hands, pack rice mixture into eight 3-inch-wide cakes and place on baking sheet.

2. Set wire rack in rimmed baking sheet. Heat 1 tablespoon oil in 12-inch nonstick skillet over medium-high heat until shimmering. Gently lay cakes in skillet and cook until golden brown and crisp on both sides, about 6 minutes, turning gently halfway through cooking. Transfer cakes to prepared rack and keep warm in oven.

3. Whisk coconut milk, curry paste, fish sauce, and sugar together in bowl. Wipe out now-empty skillet with paper towels, add remaining 2 tablespoons oil, and heat over medium-high heat until shimmering. Add green beans and cook, stirring occasionally, until tender, about 5 minutes.

4. Stir in coconut milk mixture and bamboo and simmer until sauce is slightly thickened, about 4 minutes. Off heat, stir in lime juice and season with salt and pepper to taste. Sprinkle with radishes and cilantro and serve with rice cakes.

Trimming Green Beans

Line beans up on cutting board, with stem ends pointing in same direction, and trim off stems using chef's knife.

Braised Winter Greens and Squash with Coconut Curry
SERVES 4 `VEGAN` `GF`

✔ **WHY THIS RECIPE WORKS:** For a one-pot approach to turning hearty kale and sweet butternut squash tender without spending hours at the stovetop, we turned to a technique typically reserved for large cuts of meat: braising. Building flavor with aromatics like onion and garlic first was a given, but to balance the flavor of bitter-tasting kale, we turned to curry and coconut milk. A mere teaspoon of curry powder was all we needed for its flavor to carry through. It was important to bloom the curry powder in oil to bring out and deepen its flavor before adding the braising liquid. A combination of creamy coconut milk and vegetable broth proved the right combination for our braising liquid, and reserving a half-cup of the coconut milk to stir in at the end of cooking was important to reinforce the creamy sauce. To brighten the flavor of our hearty winter dish, we finished with a squeeze of lime juice and a sprinkle of crunchy roasted pepitas. Serve with rice.

3 tablespoons extra-virgin olive oil
1 onion, chopped fine
2 pounds butternut squash, peeled, seeded, and cut into ½-inch pieces (6 cups)
5 garlic cloves, minced
2 teaspoons grated fresh ginger
1 teaspoon curry powder
2 pounds kale, stemmed and chopped
1 cup vegetable broth
1 (13.5-ounce) can coconut milk
   Salt and pepper
1 tablespoon lime juice
⅓ cup roasted pepitas

1. Heat 2 tablespoons oil in Dutch oven over medium heat until shimmering. Add onion and cook, stirring frequently, until softened, about 5 minutes. Add squash and cook, stirring occasionally, until just beginning to brown, about 5 minutes; transfer to bowl.

2. Add garlic, ginger, and curry powder to oil left in pot and cook over medium-high heat until fragrant, about 30 seconds. Add half of greens and stir until beginning to wilt, about 1 minute. Stir in remaining greens, broth, all but ½ cup coconut milk, and ½ teaspoon salt. Cover pot, reduce heat to medium-low, and cook, stirring occasionally, until kale is wilted, about 15 minutes.

3. Stir in squash and any accumulated juices, cover, and continue to cook until kale and squash are tender, 10 to 20 minutes.

4. Uncover, increase heat to medium-high, and cook, stirring occasionally, until most of liquid has evaporated and sauce has thickened, 2 to 5 minutes. Off heat, stir in remaining ½ cup coconut milk, lime juice, and remaining 1 tablespoon oil. Season with salt and pepper to taste, sprinkle with pepitas, and serve.

Indian-Style Vegetable Curry with Potatoes and Cauliflower

SERVES 4 TO 6 `VEGAN` `GF`

✓ **WHY THIS RECIPE WORKS:** We wanted a recipe for the ultimate vegetable curry, with a wide variety of perfectly cooked vegetables and a deeply flavorful (but weeknight-friendly) red curry sauce. We started with the sauce. Toasting store-bought curry powder in a skillet turned it into a flavor powerhouse, and garam masala added even more spice flavor. To build the rest of our flavor base, we started with a generous amount of sautéed onion, garlic, ginger, and fresh chile, as well as tomato paste for sweetness. For the vegetables, we chose hearty potatoes, cauliflower, and peas plus convenient canned chickpeas. We found that sautéing the spices and main ingredients together enhanced and melded the flavors. Finally, we rounded out our sauce with a combination of water, pureed canned tomatoes, and a splash of coconut milk. For more heat, include the chile seeds and ribs when mincing. We prefer the richer flavor of regular coconut milk here; however, light coconut milk can be substituted. Serve over rice with Indian-Style Onion Relish (page 63) or Cilantro-Mint Chutney (page 43).

1 (14.5-ounce) can diced tomatoes
3 tablespoons vegetable oil
4 teaspoons curry powder
1½ teaspoons garam masala
2 onions, chopped fine
12 ounces red potatoes, unpeeled, cut into ½-inch chunks
  Salt and pepper
3 garlic cloves, minced
1 serrano chile, stemmed, seeded, and minced
1 tablespoon grated fresh ginger
1 tablespoon tomato paste
½ head cauliflower (1 pound), cored and cut into 1-inch florets

This hearty vegetable curry features cauliflower, potatoes, chickpeas, tomatoes, and peas in a deeply flavorful sauce.

1½ cups water
1 (15-ounce) can chickpeas, rinsed
1½ cups frozen peas
½ cup coconut milk
¼ cup minced fresh cilantro

1. Pulse diced tomatoes with their juice in food processor until nearly smooth, with some ¼-inch pieces visible, about 3 pulses.

2. Heat oil in Dutch oven over medium-high heat until shimmering. Add curry powder and garam masala and cook until fragrant, about 10 seconds. Stir in onions, potatoes, and ¼ teaspoon salt and cook, stirring occasionally, until onions are browned and potatoes are golden brown at edges, about 10 minutes.

3. Reduce heat to medium. Stir in garlic, chile, ginger, and tomato paste and cook until fragrant, about 30 seconds. Add cauliflower florets and cook, stirring constantly, until florets are coated with spices, about 2 minutes.

4. Gradually stir in water, scraping up any browned bits. Stir in chickpeas and processed tomatoes and bring to simmer.

A combination of red and sweet potatoes, warm spices, and mustard seeds gives our vindaloo deep, complex flavor.

Cover, reduce to gentle simmer, and cook until vegetables are tender, 20 to 25 minutes.

5. Uncover, stir in peas and coconut milk, and continue to cook until peas are heated through, 1 to 2 minutes. Off heat, stir in cilantro, season with salt and pepper to taste, and serve.

VARIATION

Indian-Style Vegetable Curry with Sweet Potatoes and Eggplant `VEGAN` `GF`

Omit peas and substitute 12 ounces sweet potato (about 1 medium), peeled and cut into 1-inch chunks, for red potatoes. Substitute 8 ounces green beans, trimmed and cut into 1-inch lengths, and 1 medium eggplant (about 1 pound), cut into ½-inch pieces, for cauliflower.

Potato Vindaloo

SERVES 6 `VEGAN` `GF`

WHY THIS RECIPE WORKS: Vindaloo is a complex, spicy dish that blends Portuguese and Indian cuisines into a potent braise featuring warm spices, chiles, wine vinegar, tomatoes, onions, garlic, and mustard seeds. We set out to translate its comfort food appeal into a hearty vegetarian version. Centering our dish around potatoes seemed right, as it required low and slow cooking to develop complex flavors, and a combination of red and sweet potatoes elevated our stew's flavor even further. However, after 45 minutes of simmering, the potatoes still weren't fully cooked. A second look at our ingredients showed us why: The acidic environment created by the tomatoes and vinegar was preventing our potatoes from becoming tender. To test our theory, we whipped up another batch, this time leaving out the tomatoes and vinegar until the end, cooking them just enough to mellow their flavors. Sure enough, after just 15 minutes, our potatoes were perfectly tender. To give our vindaloo exceptionally deep flavor, we used a mix of Indian spices plus bay leaves and mustard seed, and simmered them with the potatoes, which soaked up the flavors as they cooked. Serve over rice with a dollop of yogurt.

  2 **tablespoons vegetable oil**
  2 **onions, chopped fine**
  1 **pound red potatoes, unpeeled and cut into ½-inch pieces**
  1 **pound sweet potatoes, peeled and cut into ½-inch pieces**
     Salt and pepper
 10 **garlic cloves, minced**
  4 **teaspoons paprika**
  1 **teaspoon ground cumin**
  ¾ **teaspoon ground cardamom**
  ½ **teaspoon cayenne pepper**
  ¼ **teaspoon ground cloves**
 2½ **cups water**
  2 **bay leaves**

1 tablespoon mustard seeds
1 (28-ounce) can diced tomatoes
2½ tablespoons red wine vinegar
¼ cup minced fresh cilantro

1. Heat oil in Dutch oven over medium heat until shimmering. Add onions, red potatoes, sweet potatoes, and ½ teaspoon salt and cook, stirring occasionally, until onions are softened and potatoes begin to soften at edges, 10 to 12 minutes.

2. Stir in garlic, paprika, cumin, cardamom, cayenne, and cloves and cook until fragrant and vegetables are well coated, about 2 minutes. Gradually stir in water, scraping up any browned bits. Stir in bay leaves, mustard seeds, and 1 teaspoon salt and bring to simmer. Cover, reduce heat to medium-low, and cook until potatoes are tender, 15 to 20 minutes.

3. Stir in tomatoes and their juice and vinegar and continue to simmer, uncovered, until flavors are blended and sauce has thickened slightly, about 15 minutes. Discard bay leaves, stir in cilantro, and season with salt and pepper to taste. Serve.

Sautéed Spinach with Chickpeas and Garlicky Yogurt

SERVES 2 TO 3 FAST GF

✔ **WHY THIS RECIPE WORKS:** For a spinach-based dish that was more satisfying than a side, we turned to convenient and tender baby spinach and added hearty chickpeas and an aromatic yogurt sauce. The trickiest part of cooking spinach is getting it tender but not mushy, so we knew we'd need a strategy for ridding the spinach of excess liquid. Parcooking it in the microwave and then draining it turned out to be the best solution. We pressed the microwaved spinach in a colander to eliminate more water, coarsely chopped it, and pressed it again. Then all we had to do was quickly sauté it. As for seasonings, we started by toasting a good amount of sliced garlic in oil, then added coriander and turmeric to the skillet to bloom. Canned chickpeas bulked up this dish without adding any more work, and thinly sliced sun-dried tomatoes contributed another layer of bright flavor. For the final touch to this dish, we put together a quick garlicky yogurt sauce with a dash of fresh mint for brightness. Serve with hearty, crusty bread.

1 cup plain yogurt
2 tablespoons chopped fresh mint
6 garlic cloves, peeled (4 sliced thin, 2 minced)
 Salt and pepper
18 ounces (18 cups) baby spinach
6 tablespoons water

2 tablespoons plus 2 teaspoons extra-virgin olive oil
½ teaspoon ground coriander
½ teaspoon ground turmeric
1 (15-ounce) can chickpeas, rinsed
½ cup oil-packed sun-dried tomatoes, sliced thin

1. Combine yogurt, mint, 2 cloves minced garlic, and ¼ teaspoon salt together in bowl, cover, and refrigerate until needed.

2. Microwave spinach and ¼ cup water in covered bowl until spinach is wilted and has reduced in volume by half, 3 to 4 minutes. Remove bowl from microwave and keep covered for 1 minute. Carefully transfer spinach to colander and, using back of rubber spatula, gently press spinach to release excess liquid. Transfer spinach to cutting board and chop coarsely. Return spinach to colander and press again.

3. Cook 2 tablespoons oil and sliced garlic in 10-inch skillet over medium-high heat, stirring constantly, until garlic is light golden brown and beginning to sizzle, 3 to 6 minutes. Stir in coriander and turmeric and cook until fragrant, about 30 seconds. Stir in chickpeas, tomatoes, and remaining 2 tablespoons water. Reduce heat to medium and cook, stirring occasionally, until water evaporates and tomatoes are softened, 1 to 2 minutes.

4. Stir in spinach and ¼ teaspoon salt and cook until uniformly wilted and glossy green, about 2 minutes. Transfer spinach to platter, drizzle with remaining 2 teaspoons oil, and season with salt and pepper to taste. Serve with yogurt sauce.

Indian-Style Spinach with Fresh Cheese (Saag Paneer)

SERVES 4 TO 6 GF

✔ **WHY THIS RECIPE WORKS:** *Saag paneer*, soft cubes of creamy cheese in a spicy pureed spinach sauce, is an Indian restaurant classic. We found that re-creating this dish at home wasn't as difficult as we expected. We made our own cheese by heating whole milk and buttermilk, squeezing the curds of excess moisture, then weighting the cheese down until it was firm enough to slice. For the spinach sauce, instead of cooking the spinach in batches on the stovetop, we simply wilted it all in the microwave. Adding mustard greens lent additional complexity that worked well with the warm spices. Canned diced tomatoes brightened the dish, and buttery cashews—both pureed and chopped—gave our Indian classic a subtle nutty richness. To ensure that the cheese is firm, wring it tightly in step 2 and use two plates that nestle together snugly. Use commercially produced cultured buttermilk in this recipe. Serve with basmati rice.

This traditional Indian dish combines soft cubes of fresh, homemade cheese with a complex, aromatic spinach sauce.

CHEESE

- 3 quarts whole milk
- 3 cups buttermilk
- 1 tablespoon salt

SPINACH SAUCE

- 1 (10-ounce) bag curly-leaf spinach, rinsed
- ¾ pound mustard greens, stemmed and rinsed
- 3 tablespoons unsalted butter
- 1 teaspoon cumin seeds
- 1 teaspoon ground coriander
- 1 teaspoon paprika
- ½ teaspoon ground cardamom
- ¼ teaspoon ground cinnamon
- 1 onion, chopped fine
  Salt and pepper
- 3 garlic cloves, minced
- 1 tablespoon grated fresh ginger
- 1 jalapeño chile, stemmed, seeded, and minced
- 1 (14.5-ounce) can diced tomatoes, drained and chopped coarse
- ½ cup roasted cashews, chopped coarse

Making Paneer

1. BOIL MILK: Line colander with triple layer of cheesecloth and set in sink. Bring milk to boil, then whisk in buttermilk and salt.

2. DRAIN CURDS: Carefully pour milk mixture into colander and let curds drain in sink for 15 minutes.

3. SQUEEZE OUT LIQUID: Twist edges of cheesecloth together, firmly squeezing out as much liquid as possible from cheese curds.

4. WEIGHT CHEESE: Place taut, twisted cheese pouch between 2 large plates and weigh down top plate with heavy Dutch oven. Set aside at room temperature until cheese is firm and set, about 45 minutes.

- 1 cup water
- 1 cup buttermilk
- 3 tablespoons minced fresh cilantro

1. FOR THE CHEESE: Line colander with triple layer of cheesecloth and set in sink. Bring milk to boil in Dutch oven over medium-high heat. Whisk in buttermilk and salt, turn off heat, and let stand for 1 minute. Pour milk mixture through cheesecloth and let curds drain for 15 minutes.

2. Pull edges of cheesecloth together to form pouch. Twist edges of cheesecloth together, firmly squeezing out as much liquid as possible from cheese curds. Place taut, twisted cheese pouch between 2 large plates and weigh down top plate with heavy Dutch oven. Set aside at room temperature until cheese is firm and set, about 45 minutes, then remove cheesecloth.

(Cheese can be wrapped in plastic wrap and refrigerated for up to 3 days.) Cut cheese into ½-inch pieces.

3. FOR THE SPINACH SAUCE: Microwave spinach in covered bowl until wilted, about 3 minutes. Let cool slightly, then chop enough spinach to measure ⅓ cup. Transfer remaining spinach to blender. Microwave mustard greens in covered bowl until wilted, about 4 minutes. Let cool slightly, then chop enough mustard greens to measure ⅓ cup; combine with chopped spinach. Transfer remaining mustard greens to blender with remaining spinach.

4. Meanwhile, melt butter in 12-inch skillet over medium-high heat. Add cumin seeds, coriander, paprika, cardamom, and cinnamon and cook until fragrant, about 30 seconds. Add onion and ¾ teaspoon salt and cook, stirring frequently, until softened, about 3 minutes. Stir in garlic, ginger, and jalapeño and cook, stirring frequently, until lightly browned and just beginning to stick to pan, 2 to 3 minutes. Stir in tomatoes and cook mixture until pan is dry and tomatoes are beginning to brown, 3 to 4 minutes. Remove skillet from heat.

5. Transfer half of onion mixture, ¼ cup cashews, and water to blender with greens and process until smooth, about 1 minute. Stir puree, chopped greens, and buttermilk into skillet with remaining onion mixture and bring to simmer over medium-high heat. Reduce heat to low, cover, and cook until flavors have blended, 5 minutes. Season with salt and pepper to taste. Gently fold in cheese cubes and cook until just heated through, 1 to 2 minutes. Transfer to serving dish, sprinkle with remaining ¼ cup cashews and cilantro, and serve.

Vegetable Bibimbap

SERVES 4 `GF`

WHY THIS RECIPE WORKS: A staple in Korean cuisine, bibimbap features short-grain rice topped with sautéed vegetables, beef, and a fried egg. We swapped the beef for shiitake mushrooms flavored with soy sauce, garlic, and toasted sesame oil. Then we made a quick pickle of bibimbap toppings: Grated carrot, bean sprouts, and cucumber steeped in rice vinegar lent bright flavor and crunch. The final step was topping each bowl with a fried egg. Traditionally, the yolk is left runny so it can be broken and stirred throughout the rice and vegetables to provide richness to this otherwise lean dish. Grate the carrots on a coarse grater. You can use either seasoned or unseasoned rice vinegar in this recipe. You can substitute sushi rice for the short-grain rice; if using medium- or long-grain rice, increase the amount of water to 3 cups and simmer until the grains are tender, 18 to 20 minutes, in step 2.

Our vegetarian version of bibimbap features shiitakes, spinach, and pickled vegetables topped with a buttery, runny fried egg.

In order for this recipe to be gluten-free, you must use gluten-free soy sauce or tamari.

PICKLED VEGETABLES
- 4 ounces (2 cups) bean sprouts
- 1 carrot, peeled and shredded
- 1 cucumber, peeled, halved lengthwise, seeded, and sliced ¼ inch thick
- 1 cup rice vinegar

RICE
- 2 cups short-grain white rice
- 2 cups water
- 2 teaspoons rice vinegar
- 1 teaspoon salt

VEGETABLES AND EGGS
- 2 tablespoons vegetable oil
- 12 ounces shiitake mushrooms, stemmed and sliced ½ inch thick
- 3 garlic cloves, minced

10 ounces (10 cups) baby spinach

2 tablespoons soy sauce

2 tablespoons toasted sesame oil

1 tablespoon rice vinegar

   Salt and pepper

4 large eggs

1. FOR THE PICKLED VEGETABLES: Combine all ingredients in bowl, pressing to submerge vegetables in vinegar. Cover and refrigerate for at least 30 minutes or up to 24 hours. Before serving, strain vegetables, discarding liquid.

2. FOR THE RICE: Bring rice, water, vinegar, and salt to boil in medium saucepan over high heat. Cover, reduce heat to low, and cook until liquid has been absorbed, 7 to 9 minutes. Remove rice from heat and let sit, covered, until tender, about 15 minutes.

3. FOR THE VEGETABLES AND EGGS: Heat 1 tablespoon vegetable oil in 12-inch nonstick skillet over medium-high heat until just smoking. Add mushrooms and cook, stirring occasionally, until they release their liquid, 5 to 7 minutes. Stir in garlic and cook until fragrant, about 30 seconds. Stir in spinach, 1 handful at a time, and cook until wilted, about 3 minutes. Off heat, stir in soy sauce, toasted sesame oil, and vinegar, and season with salt and pepper to taste. Transfer to platter and tent loosely with aluminum foil.

4. Crack eggs into 2 small bowls (2 eggs per bowl) and season with salt and pepper. Wipe out now-empty skillet with paper towels, add remaining 1 tablespoon oil, and heat over medium heat until shimmering. Working quickly, pour 1 bowl of eggs in 1 side of pan and second bowl of eggs in other side. Cover and cook until whites are set but yolks are still runny, 2 to 3 minutes.

5. To serve, portion rice into bowls, top with vegetables and fried egg, and serve with pickled vegetables.

Roasted Root Vegetables with Lemon-Caper Sauce
SERVES 4   VEGAN   GF

✔ **WHY THIS RECIPE WORKS:** For the ultimate roasted vegetable recipe, we chose a combination of Brussels sprouts, red potatoes, and carrots. To ensure the vegetables would roast evenly, we cut them into equal-size pieces. Arranging the Brussels sprouts in the center of the baking sheet, with the hardier potatoes and carrots around the perimeter, kept the more delicate sprouts from charring in the hot 450-degree oven. Before roasting, we tossed the vegetables with olive oil,

thyme, rosemary, and a little sugar (to promote browning). Whole garlic cloves and halved shallots softened and mellowed in the oven, lending great flavor to the finished dish. Once all of the vegetables were perfectly tender and caramelized, we tossed them with a bright dressing of parsley, capers, and lemon juice. Use Brussels sprouts no bigger than golf balls for this recipe.

1 pound Brussels sprouts, trimmed and halved

1 pound red potatoes, unpeeled and cut into 1-inch pieces

8 shallots, peeled and halved

4 carrots, peeled and cut into 2-inch pieces, thick ends halved lengthwise

6 garlic cloves, peeled

3 tablespoons extra-virgin olive oil

2 teaspoons minced fresh thyme

1 teaspoon minced fresh rosemary

1 teaspoon sugar

   Salt and pepper

2 tablespoons minced fresh parsley

1½ tablespoons capers, rinsed and roughly chopped

1 tablespoon lemon juice, plus lemon wedges for serving

1. Adjust oven rack to middle position and heat oven to 450 degrees. Toss Brussels sprouts, potatoes, shallots, carrots, garlic, 1 tablespoon oil, thyme, rosemary, sugar, ¾ teaspoon salt, and ¼ teaspoon pepper together in bowl.

2. Spread vegetables into single layer on rimmed baking sheet, arranging Brussels sprouts cut side down in center of pan. Roast until vegetables are tender and golden brown, 30 to 35 minutes, rotating pan halfway through cooking.

3. Whisk parsley, capers, lemon juice, and remaining 2 tablespoons oil together in large bowl. Add roasted vegetables, toss to combine, and season with salt and pepper to taste. Serve with lemon wedges.

VARIATION

Roasted Radicchio, Fennel, and Parsnips with Lemon-Basil Sauce   VEGAN   GF
Substitute the following for Brussels sprouts and carrots: 2 fennel bulbs, halved, cored, and sliced into ½-inch wedges; ½ pound parsnips, peeled and cut into 2-inch pieces; and 1 head radicchio, cored and cut into 2-inch wedges. Arrange radicchio in center of baking sheet before roasting. Omit capers and parsley and add 2 tablespoons chopped fresh basil and 2 tablespoons minced fresh chives to oil mixture in step 3.

We top sweet roasted butternut squash with pecans and goat cheese, then drizzle it with cayenne-spiked maple syrup.

Roasted Butternut Squash with Goat Cheese, Pecans, and Maple

SERVES 4 TO 6 `GF`

🗸 **WHY THIS RECIPE WORKS:** Inspired by famed chef Yotam Ottolenghi's technique of roasting thin half-moons of squash, we sought to create a savory recipe for roasted butternut squash that was simple and presentation-worthy. We chose to peel the squash to remove not only the tough outer skin but also the rugged fibrous layer of white flesh just beneath, ensuring supremely tender squash. To encourage the squash slices to caramelize, we used a hot 425-degree oven, placed the squash on the lowest oven rack, and increased the baking time to evaporate the water. We also swapped in melted butter for olive oil, giving us even more flavorful browning. Finally, we selected a mix of toppings that added crunch, creaminess, and a little sweetness: pecans, goat cheese, and maple syrup spiked with cayenne. This dish can be served warm or at room temperature. For the best texture, be sure to peel the squash thoroughly, removing all of the fibrous flesh just below the squash's skin.

Cutting Up Squash for Roasting

1. Using sharp vegetable peeler or chef's knife, remove skin and fibrous threads just below skin from squash.

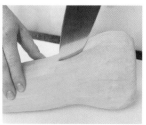

2. Carefully drive tip of chef's knife into center of peeled squash. Place folded dish towel on top of squash, over tip of knife.

3. Drive rest of knife down through end of squash. Turn squash around and repeat from opposite side to cut squash in half.

4. Scrape out seeds using spoon, then place squash flat side down on cutting board and slice crosswise into ½-inch-thick pieces.

2½–3 pounds butternut squash
    3 tablespoons unsalted butter, melted
    ½ teaspoon salt
    ½ teaspoon pepper
    2 tablespoons maple syrup
       Pinch cayenne pepper
  1½ ounces goat cheese, crumbled (⅓ cup)
    ⅓ cup pecans, toasted and chopped coarse
    2 teaspoons fresh thyme leaves

1. Adjust oven rack to lowest position and heat oven to 425 degrees. Using sharp vegetable peeler or chef's knife, remove skin and fibrous threads just below skin from squash (squash should be completely orange, with no white flesh). Halve squash lengthwise and scrape out seeds. Place squash, cut side down, on cutting board and slice crosswise into ½-inch-thick pieces.

2. Toss squash with melted butter, salt, and pepper and arrange on rimmed baking sheet in single layer. Roast squash until side touching sheet toward back of oven is well browned, 25 to 30 minutes. Rotate sheet and continue to bake until side touching sheet toward back of oven is well browned, 6 to 10 minutes.

3. Remove squash from oven and use metal spatula to flip each piece. Continue to roast until squash is very tender and side touching sheet is browned, 10 to 15 minutes.

4. Transfer squash to platter. Combine maple syrup and cayenne in bowl, then drizzle over squash. Sprinkle squash with goat cheese, pecans, and thyme and serve.

VARIATION

Roasted Butternut Squash with Tahini and Feta GF

Omit maple syrup and cayenne. Whisk 1 tablespoon tahini, 1 tablespoon extra-virgin olive oil, 1½ teaspoons lemon juice, 1 teaspoon honey, and pinch salt together in bowl; drizzle over cooked squash. Substitute ¼ cup finely crumbled feta cheese for goat cheese, ¼ cup toasted and finely chopped pistachios for pecans, and 2 tablespoons chopped fresh mint for thyme.

Mediterranean Braised Green Beans with Potatoes and Basil

SERVES 4 TO 6 VEGAN GF

✓ **WHY THIS RECIPE WORKS:** Unlike crisp-tender green beans that have been steamed or sautéed, braised green beans boast a uniquely soft, velvety texture without being mushy. Unfortunately, achieving this usually takes as much as 2 hours of simmering. To get ultratender braised green beans in half the time, we first simmered them with a pinch of baking soda to dissolve the pectin in their cell walls. Once the beans were partially softened, we stirred in acidic diced tomatoes to add sweet flavor and neutralize the baking soda so the beans wouldn't soften too much. The beans turned meltingly tender after less than an hour of simmering in a low oven. To infuse the beans with bright Mediterranean flavors, we added sautéed garlic and onion plus some bright lemon juice, basil, and a drizzle of olive oil. Finally, to ensure the beans were hearty enough for dinner, we added in chunks of potatoes; 1-inch pieces turned tender in the same amount of time as the beans. Serve with a dollop of plain yogurt and rice or crusty bread.

5 tablespoons extra-virgin olive oil
1 onion, chopped fine
4 garlic cloves, minced
2 teaspoons dried oregano
1½ cups water
1½ pounds green beans, trimmed and cut into 2- to 3-inch lengths
1 pound Yukon Gold potatoes, peeled and cut into 1-inch pieces
½ teaspoon baking soda
1 (14.5-ounce) can diced tomatoes, drained with juice reserved, chopped coarse
1 tablespoon tomato paste
2 teaspoons salt
¼ teaspoon pepper
3 tablespoons chopped fresh basil
Lemon juice

1. Adjust oven rack to lower-middle position and heat oven to 275 degrees. Heat 3 tablespoons oil in Dutch oven over medium heat until shimmering. Add onion and cook until softened, 5 to 7 minutes. Stir in garlic and oregano and cook until fragrant, about 30 seconds. Stir in water, green beans, potatoes, and baking soda and bring to simmer. Reduce heat to medium-low and cook, stirring occasionally, for 10 minutes.

2. Stir in tomatoes and their juice, tomato paste, salt, and pepper. Cover pot, transfer to oven, and cook until sauce is slightly thickened and green beans can be cut easily with side of fork, 40 to 50 minutes.

3. Stir in basil and season with lemon juice to taste. Transfer to bowl, drizzle with remaining 2 tablespoons oil, and serve.

Braised Fennel with Radicchio and Parmesan

SERVES 4 GF

✓ **WHY THIS RECIPE WORKS:** Although it's most often used only as an aromatic, fennel deserves a chance in the limelight. To turn this flavorful vegetable into a main course, we cut the fennel into thick slabs and braised them with wine and aromatics. To achieve deeper flavor, we opted to leave the fennel in the skillet even after the braising liquid had evaporated. Seven minutes per side was all it took to achieve a deep golden, caramelized crust on the fennel and develop some serious flavor-boosting fond in the pan. To take advantage of these browned bits, and to balance the sweetness of the fennel, we stirred in a whole head of radicchio, cooking it briefly with water, honey, and butter to tame its harsh edge and create a

Cooking with Wine

Over the years, the test kitchen has developed hundreds of recipes with wine. Here's what we've found works best.

RED WINE

When cooking with red wine, it's best to stick with blends like Côtes du Rhône or generically labeled "table" wines that use a combination of grapes to yield a balanced, fruity finish. If you prefer single-grape varietals, choose medium-bodied wines, such as Pinot Noir or Merlot. Avoid oaky wines like Cabernet Sauvignon, which turn bitter when cooked.

WHITE WINE

The best white wines for cooking are medium-bodied unoaked varieties that aren't terribly sweet. We prefer clean, crisp, dry Sauvignon Blancs to sweet Rieslings or heavily oaked Chardonnays, which can dominate subtle flavors. We have found that only Sauvignon Blanc consistently boils down to a "clean" yet sufficiently acidic flavor that meshes nicely with a variety of ingredients in savory recipes.

VERMOUTH

Dry vermouth makes a good substitute for white wine in many sauces and other savory recipes, and because it has a shelf life of several months, it's easy to keep a bottle on hand. Vermouth adds herbaceous notes to any dish and is a bit more alcoholic than white wine. Replace white wine with an equal amount of vermouth.

COOKING WINE

We've learned that when it comes to wine, it's best not to cook with anything you would not drink. This includes "cooking wines" sold in many supermarkets. They taste horrible and include a lot of sodium, so if the wine is cooked down it can make your recipe unappetizingly salty. That said, there's no need to spend a fortune on wine destined for sauces or stews. We've tested good $10 bottles versus better-tasting $30 wines and found that any differences in the glass disappear in a cooked application.

NONALCOHOLIC SUBSTITUTIONS FOR WINES

An equal amount of broth can work as a replacement in dishes that call for a small amount of wine. The dish won't taste exactly the same, but the recipe will work. For every ½ cup broth used, you should also stir in ½ teaspoon red or white wine vinegar or lemon juice before serving to mimic some of the acidity otherwise provided by the wine.

richly flavored pan sauce. All this dish needed was a sprinkle of Parmesan cheese and toasted pine nuts for added richness and crunch, and some of the minced fennel fronds for brightness. Serve over polenta.

- 4　tablespoons unsalted butter
- 3　fennel bulbs, 2 tablespoons fronds minced, stalks discarded, bulbs cut vertically into ½-inch-thick slabs
- ½　teaspoon grated lemon zest plus 2 teaspoons juice
　　Salt and pepper
- ½　cup dry white wine
- 1　head radicchio (10 ounces), halved, cored, and sliced thin
- ¼　cup water
- 2　teaspoons honey
- 2　tablespoons pine nuts, toasted and chopped
　　Shaved Parmesan cheese

1. Melt 3 tablespoons butter in 12-inch skillet over medium heat. Add fennel slabs, lemon zest, ½ teaspoon salt, and ¼ teaspoon pepper, then pour wine over fennel. Cover, reduce heat to medium-low, and cook for 15 minutes. (Skillet will be crowded at first, but fennel will fit into single layer as it cooks.)

2. Flip fennel pieces and continue to cook, covered, until fennel is tender and well browned, about 7 minutes. Flip fennel pieces and continue to cook, covered, until well browned on second side, about 7 minutes. Transfer fennel to platter and tent loosely with aluminum foil.

3. Add radicchio, water, and honey to any liquid left in skillet and cook over low heat, scraping up any browned bits, until wilted, 3 to 5 minutes. Stir in lemon juice and remaining 1 tablespoon butter and let sauce thicken slightly, about 1 minute. Season with salt and pepper to taste. Pour radicchio and sauce over fennel and sprinkle with pine nuts, minced fennel fronds, and shaved Parmesan. Serve.

Slicing Fennel for Braising

1. Cut off tops and feathery fronds, trim very thin slice from bottom of base, and remove any tough or blemished outer layers.

2. Place trimmed fennel bulb upright on base and cut vertically into ½-inch-thick slabs.

This classic Tunisian dish combines simple grilled vegetables with a potent dressing of warm spices and fresh herbs.

Tunisian-Style Grilled Vegetables (Mechouia)

SERVES 4 TO 6 VEGAN GF

✓ **WHY THIS RECIPE WORKS:** For our take on this robustly flavored Tunisian dish of grilled vegetables, we started by prepping the vegetables for the grill. To get good charring, we wanted to expose as much surface area to the heat as possible, so we halved the eggplant, zucchini, and plum tomatoes lengthwise and stemmed and flattened the bell peppers. We also scored the eggplant and zucchini before putting them over the coals so they would release their excess moisture as they cooked. We used a potent combination of coriander, caraway, cumin, paprika, and cayenne to replace the traditional Tunisian spice blend *tabil* and infuse our vegetables with exotic flavor. The heat of the grill worked to bloom the flavor of the spices so they didn't taste raw or harsh, and more of the spices plus garlic, lemon, and a trio of herbs provided a bright, fresh-tasting dressing. Equal amounts of ground coriander and cumin can be substituted for the whole spices. Serve with grilled pita bread or with hard-cooked eggs and olives.

DRESSING

- 2 teaspoons coriander seeds
- 1½ teaspoons caraway seeds
- 1 teaspoon cumin seeds
- 5 tablespoons extra-virgin olive oil
- ½ teaspoon sweet paprika
- ⅛ teaspoon cayenne pepper
- 3 garlic cloves, minced
- ¼ cup chopped fresh parsley
- ¼ cup chopped fresh cilantro
- 2 tablespoons chopped fresh mint
- 1 teaspoon grated lemon zest plus 2 tablespoons juice
  Salt

VEGETABLES

- 2 bell peppers (1 red and 1 green), top and bottom trimmed, stemmed and seeded, and peppers flattened
- 1 small eggplant, halved lengthwise and scored on cut side
- 1 zucchini (8 to 10 ounces), halved lengthwise and scored on cut side
- 4 plum tomatoes, cored and halved lengthwise
  Salt and pepper
- 2 shallots, unpeeled

1. FOR THE DRESSING: Grind coriander seeds, caraway seeds, and cumin seeds in spice grinder until finely ground. Whisk ground spices, oil, paprika, and cayenne together in bowl. Reserve 3 tablespoons oil mixture for brushing vegetables before grilling. Heat remaining oil mixture and garlic in 8-inch skillet over low heat, stirring occasionally, until fragrant and small bubbles appear, 8 to 10 minutes. Transfer to large bowl, let cool for 10 minutes, then whisk in parsley, cilantro, mint, and lemon zest and juice and season with salt to taste.

2. FOR THE VEGETABLES: Brush interior of bell peppers and cut sides of eggplant, zucchini, and tomatoes with reserved oil mixture and season with salt.

3A. FOR A CHARCOAL GRILL: Open bottom vent completely. Light large chimney starter three-quarters filled with charcoal briquettes (4½ quarts). When top coals are partially covered with ash, pour evenly over grill. Set cooking grate in place, cover, and open lid vent completely. Heat grill until hot, about 5 minutes.

3B. FOR A GAS GRILL: Turn all burners to high, cover, and heat grill until hot, about 15 minutes. Turn all burners to medium-high.

4. Clean and oil cooking grate. Place bell peppers, eggplant, zucchini, tomatoes, and shallots, cut sides down, on grill. Cook (covered if using gas), turning as needed, until tender and slightly charred, 8 to 16 minutes. Transfer eggplant, zucchini, tomatoes, and shallots to baking sheet as they finish cooking;

place bell peppers in bowl, cover with plastic wrap, and let steam to loosen skins.

5. Let vegetables cool slightly. Peel bell peppers, eggplant, tomatoes, and shallots. Chop all vegetables into ½-inch pieces, then toss gently with dressing in bowl. Season with salt and pepper to taste. Serve warm or at room temperature.

Prepping Grilled Tunisian-Style Vegetables

1. To flatten bell pepper, trim off top and bottom, then remove stem and seeds. Cut through 1 side of pepper, then press flat and trim away any remaining ribs.

2. Using tip of chef's knife (or paring knife), score cut sides of halved zucchini and eggplant in ½-inch diamond pattern, cutting down to but not through skin.

Grilled Eggplant and Bell Peppers with Mint-Cumin Dressing

SERVES 4 TO 6 `GF`

✓ **WHY THIS RECIPE WORKS:** Our perfect grilled vegetable recipe would have to produce charred-on-the-outside, tender-on-the-inside veggies with great smoky flavor and a lively dressing. To double up our recipe's flavor, we wanted a combination of two vegetables. Mindful of complementary cooking times, we paired eggplant with sweet red bell peppers. We built a moderate, medium-heat fire and cooked the vegetables for about 20 minutes, until they were perfectly tender and full of smoky flavor. To boost the taste further, we whisked up a quick mint-cumin dressing to accompany the vegetables after they came off the grill. Drizzled with dressing while still warm, the vegetables had enough flavor to be the star attraction of a meal. Once we had perfected our recipe, we made an easy variation with zucchini, red onion, and a lemon-basil dressing. After about 5 minutes, faint grill marks should begin to appear on the undersides of the vegetables; if necessary, adjust their position on the grill or adjust the heat level. The vegetables can be served hot, warm, or at room temperature.

1 pound eggplant, sliced into ½-inch-thick rounds
2 red bell peppers, stemmed, seeded, and cut into 2-inch planks
5 tablespoons extra-virgin olive oil
   Salt and pepper
2 tablespoons plain yogurt
1 tablespoon chopped fresh mint
1 tablespoon lemon juice
1 small garlic clove, minced
½ teaspoon ground coriander
½ teaspoon ground cumin

1. Brush eggplant and bell peppers with ¼ cup oil, sprinkle with 1 teaspoon salt, and season with pepper. Whisk remaining 1 tablespoon oil, yogurt, mint, lemon juice, garlic, coriander, cumin, and ¼ teaspoon salt together in bowl.

2A. FOR A CHARCOAL GRILL: Open bottom vent completely. Light large chimney starter half filled with charcoal briquettes (3 quarts). When top coals are partially covered with ash, pour evenly over grill. Set cooking grate in place, cover, and open lid vent completely. Heat grill until hot, about 5 minutes.

2B. FOR A GAS GRILL: Turn all burners to high, cover, and heat grill until hot, about 15 minutes. Turn all burners to medium.

3. Clean and oil cooking grate. Place vegetables, cut sides down, on grill. Cook (covered if using gas), turning as needed, until tender and caramelized, 16 to 18 minutes; transfer to platter as they finish cooking. Whisk dressing to recombine, drizzle over vegetables, and serve.

VARIATION

Grilled Zucchini and Red Onion with Lemon-Basil Dressing

SERVES 4 TO 6 `VEGAN` `GF`

After about 5 minutes, faint grill marks should begin to appear on the undersides of the vegetables; if necessary, adjust their position on the grill or adjust the heat level. The vegetables can be served hot, warm, or at room temperature. You will need two 12-inch metal skewers for this recipe.

1 large red onion, peeled and sliced into ½-inch-thick rings
1 pound zucchini, sliced lengthwise into ¾-inch-thick planks
6 tablespoons extra-virgin olive oil
   Salt and pepper
1 teaspoon grated lemon zest plus 1 tablespoon juice
1 small garlic clove, minced
¼ teaspoon Dijon mustard
1 tablespoon chopped fresh basil

1. Thread onion rounds, from side to side, onto 2 metal skewers. Brush onion and zucchini with ¼ cup oil, sprinkle with 1 teaspoon salt, and season with pepper. Whisk remaining 2 tablespoons oil, lemon zest and juice, garlic, mustard, and ¼ teaspoon salt together in bowl.

2A. FOR A CHARCOAL GRILL: Open bottom vent completely. Light large chimney starter half filled with charcoal briquettes (3 quarts). When top coals are partially covered with ash, pour evenly over grill. Set cooking grate in place, cover, and open lid vent completely. Heat grill until hot, about 5 minutes.

2B. FOR A GAS GRILL: Turn all burners to high, cover, and heat grill until hot, about 15 minutes. Turn all burners to medium.

3. Clean and oil cooking grate. Place vegetables, cut sides down, on grill. Cook (covered if using gas), turning as needed, until tender and caramelized, 18 to 22 minutes; transfer to platter as they finish cooking. Remove skewers from onion and discard any charred outer rings. Whisk dressing to recombine, and drizzle over vegetables. Sprinkle with basil and serve.

Grilled Vegetable Kebabs with Grilled Lemon Dressing

SERVES 4 VEGAN GF

✔ **WHY THIS RECIPE WORKS:** Vegetables are often added as an afterthought or as a filler on grilled meat kebabs, leading to mushy or charred vegetables. However, vegetables on their own can be a great option for grilled kebabs, because they cook quickly and, when done right, offer a crisp, charred exterior and a juicy, tender interior. Tossing grilled vegetables with a bold dressing can do wonders to brighten up an otherwise boring dinner, but for our take on vegetable kebabs, we took the idea one step further. We tossed the vegetables with half of our dressing base before skewering and grilling them, giving them great flavor from the start. We also grilled lemon quarters to tone down their bright acidity and give the juice a deeper, more complex flavor when added to the dressing. Bell peppers and zucchini are classic grilling vegetables for good reason: Bell peppers sweeten over the flame, while zucchini hold their shape and meaty texture. Portobello mushroom caps were the perfect addition to the kebabs; as they released their moisture over the flame, they picked up great char flavor and developed a deep, meaty taste. You will need eight 12-inch metal skewers for this recipe.

¼ cup extra-virgin olive oil
1 teaspoon Dijon mustard
1 teaspoon minced fresh rosemary
1 garlic clove, minced
  Salt and pepper
6 portobello mushroom caps (5 inches in diameter), quartered
2 zucchini, halved lengthwise and sliced ¾ inch thick
2 red bell peppers, stemmed, seeded, and cut into 1½-inch pieces
2 lemons, quartered

1. Whisk oil, mustard, rosemary, garlic, ½ teaspoon salt, and ¼ teaspoon pepper together in large bowl. Measure half of mixture into separate bowl and set aside for serving. Toss mushrooms, zucchini, and bell peppers with remaining oil mixture, then thread in alternating order onto eight 12-inch metal skewers.

2A. FOR A CHARCOAL GRILL: Open bottom vent completely. Light large chimney starter half filled with charcoal briquettes (3 quarts). When top coals are partially covered with ash, pour evenly over grill. Set cooking grate in place, cover, and open lid vent completely. Heat grill until hot, about 5 minutes.

2B. FOR A GAS GRILL: Turn all burners to high, cover, and heat grill until hot, about 15 minutes. Turn all burners to medium.

3. Clean and oil cooking grate. Place kebabs and lemons on grill. Cook (covered if using gas), turning as needed, until vegetables are tender and well browned and lemons are juicy and slightly charred, 16 to 18 minutes. Transfer kebabs and lemons to platter, removing skewers.

4. Juice 2 lemon quarters and whisk into reserved oil mixture. Drizzle vegetables with dressing and serve.

Cleaning and Oiling a Cooking Grate

1. To prevent food from sticking and picking up off-flavors, use grill brush to scrape cooking grate clean.

2. Using tongs, dip wad of paper towels in vegetable oil and wipe cooking grate several times.

CHAPTER 2

Soups, Stews, and Chilis

■ FAST (Less than 45 minutes start to finish)　■ VEGAN　■ GLUTEN-FREE
Photos: Black Bean Chili; Wild Rice and Mushroom Soup

Buying the Best Vegetable Broth

Vegetable broth is an essential ingredient in the vegetarian kitchen, providing a flavorful backbone to everything from soups and stews to risottos and pasta. Good vegetable broth should underscore the flavor of fresh vegetables, adding depth to a recipe without overwhelming the dish's flavor. To find a commercial vegetable broth that could stand in for homemade, we tested 25 nationally available broths sold as liquids, pastes, powders, concentrates, or cubes. We also included versions called "vegetarian chicken." Since they have vegetable ingredients and contain no meat, we decided these were technically vegetable broth. We avoided broths with more than 750 mg of sodium per cup; concentrated in risotto or sauce, they can be unbearably salty.

Once we had our contenders, we tasted each in vegetable soup and in risotto. The broths offered a spectrum of flavors, colors, and textures—and most were terrible: too sweet, salty, or sour, or just fake. Some broths stamped out the fresh taste of our recipes with an umami bomb of packaged-soup flavor. Several suffered from a lack of balance, whether they were too sweet, or too sour, or relied too heavily on a single vegetable flavor. Only a few succeeded, enhancing but not overwhelming the recipes. Their flavor was mild and balanced, with enough saltiness to heighten other flavors without going overboard. Colors also influenced our rankings. Dark red, brown, or gray broths made fresh risotto and soup look gloomy; our tasters liked light, pale yellow broths best.

Ultimately, we could recommend only three vegetable broths. Each comes in a different form. Our highest-ranked broth, **Orrington Farms Vegan Chicken Flavored Broth Base & Seasoning**, is a 6-ounce jar of powder that makes up to 28 cups of broth. Well-balanced, nicely savory, and fairly salty, this powdered broth was almost as good as our own homemade vegetable broth base. Swanson Certified Organic Vegetable Broth is our runner-up. While this ready-to-use liquid broth is more expensive, its 32-ounce carton is quick and convenient. In third place was Better Than Bouillon Vegetable Base, Reduced Sodium, a concentrated paste that makes 38 cups of broth from an 8-ounce jar. If you want to limit your sodium intake, we recommend Edward & Sons Low-Sodium Not-Chick'n Natural Bouillon Cubes, with 130 mg of sodium per cup. Any of these satisfies our basic need for a mild, neutral vegetable broth, but homemade is still our first choice.

Vegetable Broth Base

MAKES ABOUT 1¾ CUPS BASE, OR ABOUT 1¾ GALLONS BROTH   `FAST` `VEGAN` `GF`

WHY THIS RECIPE WORKS: The vegetable broth bases found on supermarket shelves promise a convenient and economical alternative to liquid broth, but they usually deliver harsh, overwhelming flavors. Our goal was to develop a homemade broth base that would deliver on both flavor and convenience. To make a vegetable concentrate that would pack bold flavor, we started with a classic *mirepoix* of onion, carrots, and celery. However, the celery gave the broth a bitter flavor, and the onion was too pungent. We swapped in celery root and leeks, which lent similar but milder flavors. Some parsley added a fresh, herbal note. To amp up the savory flavor and give the broth more depth and complexity, we added dried onion, tomato paste, and soy sauce. A hefty dose of salt ensured the broth was well seasoned and kept the base from freezing solid, so we could store it in the freezer for months and easily remove a tablespoon at a time without having to thaw the container. For the best balance of flavors, measure the prepped vegetables by weight. Kosher salt aids in grinding the vegetables. In order for this recipe to be gluten-free, you must use gluten-free soy sauce or tamari.

> 2   leeks, white and light green parts only, chopped and washed thoroughly (2½ cups, 5 ounces)
> 2   carrots, peeled and cut into ½-inch pieces (⅔ cup, 3 ounces)
> ½   small celery root, peeled and cut into ½-inch pieces (¾ cup, 3 ounces)
> ½   cup (½ ounce) fresh parsley leaves and thin stems
> 3   tablespoons dried minced onion
> 2   tablespoons kosher salt
> 1½   tablespoons tomato paste
> 3   tablespoons soy sauce

1. Process leeks, carrots, celery root, parsley, dried minced onion, and salt in food processor, pausing to scrape down sides of bowl frequently, until paste is as fine as possible, 3 to 4 minutes. Add tomato paste and process for 1 minute, scraping down sides of bowl every 20 seconds. Add soy sauce and continue to process for 1 minute. Transfer mixture to airtight container and tap firmly on counter to remove air bubbles. Press small piece of parchment paper flush against surface of mixture and cover tightly. Freeze for up to 6 months.

2. TO MAKE 1 CUP BROTH: Stir 1 tablespoon fresh or frozen broth base into 1 cup boiling water. If particle-free broth is desired, let broth steep for 5 minutes, then strain through fine-mesh strainer.

Traditional Vegetable Stock

MAKES 8 CUPS `VEGAN` `GF`

WHY THIS RECIPE WORKS: Store-bought vegetable broths are often unappealingly sweet or loaded with sodium. We wanted a nicely balanced, robust vegetable stock that would lend flavor to soups and stews without being overwhelming. Caramelizing plenty of onions, scallions, and garlic, plus carrots and celery in modest amounts, until we had some flavorful fond on the bottom of the pot gave our stock depth and a sweetness that wasn't one-dimensional. We found that cauliflower, although nontraditional, added a nutty complexity that tasters loved, while a single plum tomato provided the acidity and brightness that balanced the sweetness of our stock. Bay leaves and some thyme contributed the right herbal notes. We simmered the stock gently for 90 minutes to develop plenty of rich flavor. The fond is important for the flavor and color of the stock, so be sure to let it form on the bottom of the pot in step 1. To prevent the stock from looking cloudy, be sure to simmer it gently (don't boil), and don't press on the solids when straining. You will need at least a 7-quart Dutch oven for this recipe.

- 3   **onions, chopped**
- 2   **celery ribs, chopped**
- 2   **carrots, peeled and chopped**
- 8   **scallions, chopped**
- 15 **garlic cloves, peeled and smashed**
- 1   **teaspoon vegetable oil**
- 1   **teaspoon salt**
- 12 **cups water**
- 1   **head cauliflower (2 pounds), cored and cut into 1-inch florets**
- 1   **plum tomato, cored and chopped**
- 8   **sprigs fresh thyme**
- 3   **bay leaves**
- 1   **teaspoon black peppercorns**

1. Combine onions, celery, carrots, scallions, garlic, oil, and salt in large Dutch oven or stockpot. Cover and cook over medium-low heat, stirring often, until golden brown fond has formed on bottom of pot, 20 to 30 minutes.

2. Stir in water, cauliflower, tomato, thyme sprigs, bay leaves, and peppercorns, scraping up any browned bits, and bring to simmer. Partially cover pot, reduce heat to gentle simmer, and cook until stock tastes rich and flavorful, about 1½ hours.

3. Strain stock gently through fine-mesh strainer (do not press on solids). (Stock can be refrigerated for up to 4 days or frozen for up to 1 month.)

Making Vegetable Stock

1. SWEAT VEGETABLES: Cook vegetables, garlic, oil, and salt, covered, in large Dutch oven over medium-low heat until golden-brown fond has formed on bottom of pot, 20 to 30 minutes.

2. ADD WATER: Stir in water, cauliflower, tomato, thyme sprigs, bay leaves, and peppercorns and bring to simmer.

3. SIMMER UNTIL FLAVORFUL: Partially cover pot, reduce heat to gentle simmer, and cook until stock tastes rich and flavorful, about 1½ hours.

4. STRAIN STOCK: Strain stock gently through fine-mesh strainer without pressing on solids.

Creamless Creamy Tomato Soup

SERVES 6 TO 8 `FAST` `VEGAN`

WHY THIS RECIPE WORKS: We wanted a tomato soup recipe that would have velvety smoothness and a bright tomato taste—without flavor-dulling cream. We started with canned tomatoes for their convenience and year-round availability. A little brown sugar balanced the tomatoes' acidity, and a surprise ingredient—slices of white bread torn into pieces and blended into the soup—helped give our tomato soup luxurious body without added cream. Make sure to purchase canned whole tomatoes in juice, not in puree. If half of the soup fills your blender by more than two-thirds, process the soup in three batches. For an even smoother soup, pass the pureed mixture through a fine-mesh strainer after blending it. Serve with Classic Croutons (page 85).

¼ cup extra-virgin olive oil, plus extra for serving
1 onion, chopped fine
3 garlic cloves, minced
1 bay leaf
  Pinch red pepper flakes (optional)
2 (28-ounce) cans whole peeled tomatoes
3 slices hearty white sandwich bread, crusts removed, torn into 1-inch pieces
1 tablespoon packed brown sugar
2 cups vegetable broth
2 tablespoons brandy (optional)
  Salt and pepper
¼ cup minced fresh chives

1. Heat 2 tablespoons oil in Dutch oven over medium-high heat until shimmering. Add onion, garlic, bay leaf, and pepper flakes, if using. Cook, stirring often, until onion is translucent, 3 to 5 minutes. Stir in tomatoes and their juice. Using potato masher, mash until no pieces bigger than 2 inches remain. Stir in bread and sugar and bring soup to boil. Reduce heat to medium and cook, stirring occasionally, until bread is completely saturated and starts to break down, about 5 minutes. Discard bay leaf.

2. Transfer half of soup to blender. Add 1 tablespoon oil and puree until soup is smooth and creamy, 2 to 3 minutes. Transfer to large bowl and repeat with remaining soup and remaining 1 tablespoon oil. Return pureed soup to clean pot.

3. Stir in broth and brandy, if using. Return soup to boil and season with salt and pepper to taste. Serve, sprinkling individual bowls with chives and drizzling with oil.

Carrot-Ginger Soup
SERVES 6 VEGAN GF

❤ **WHY THIS RECIPE WORKS:** Sometimes the simplest recipes get overcomplicated as more and more versions appear. Case in point: carrot-ginger soup, whose flavors often get elbowed out with the addition of other vegetables, fruits, or dairy. For a fresh, clean-tasting soup, we decided to go back to the basics. With a combination of cooked carrots and carrot juice, we were able to get well-rounded, fresh carrot flavor. Using a mixture of grated fresh ginger and crystallized ginger gave us bright, refreshing ginger flavor with a moderate kick of heat. Finally, for a silky-smooth texture, we added a touch

Spicy ginger (both fresh and crystallized) punches up the sweet carrot in this creamy pureed soup.

of baking soda to help break down the carrots and ginger, producing a perfectly creamy soup. We finished with some simple garnishes of sour cream and chopped chives to provide texture and tang. In addition to these accompaniments, serve the soup with Classic Croutons (page 85). To make this recipe vegan, omit the sour cream.

2 tablespoons unsalted butter or vegetable oil
2 onions, chopped fine
¼ cup minced crystallized ginger
1 tablespoon grated fresh ginger
2 garlic cloves, peeled and smashed
  Salt and pepper
1 teaspoon sugar
2 pounds carrots, peeled and sliced ¼ inch thick
4 cups water
1½ cups carrot juice
2 sprigs fresh thyme
½ teaspoon baking soda
1 tablespoon cider vinegar
  Chopped chives
  Sour cream

1. Melt butter in large saucepan over medium heat. Stir in onions, crystallized ginger, fresh ginger, garlic, 2 teaspoons salt, and sugar. Cook, stirring often, until onions are softened but not browned, 5 to 7 minutes.

2. Stir in carrots, water, ¾ cup carrot juice, thyme sprigs, and baking soda. Increase heat to high and bring to simmer. Reduce heat to medium-low, cover, and simmer gently until carrots are very tender, 20 to 25 minutes.

3. Discard thyme sprigs. Working in batches, process soup in blender until smooth, 1 to 2 minutes. Return pureed soup to clean pot and stir in vinegar and remaining ¾ cup carrot juice.

4. Return soup to brief simmer over medium heat. Season with salt and pepper to taste. Serve, garnishing individual bowls with chives and sour cream.

Creamy Cauliflower Soup

SERVES 4 TO 6 GF

WHY THIS RECIPE WORKS: We wanted a cauliflower soup with a creamy texture but without adding any cream, which tends to dull the cauliflower's delicate flavor. Instead, we relied on the cauliflower's low insoluble fiber content to produce a velvety-smooth puree. To ensure that the cauliflower flavor remained at the forefront, we cooked the cauliflower in water instead of broth, skipped the spice rack entirely, and bolstered the soup with sautéed onion and leek. We added the cauliflower to the simmering water in two stages so that we got the grassy flavor of just-cooked cauliflower and the sweeter, nuttier flavor of longer-cooked cauliflower. Finally, we browned florets in butter and used both as a flavorful garnish. White wine vinegar may be substituted for the sherry vinegar. Be sure to thoroughly trim the cauliflower's core of green leaves and leaf stems, which can be fibrous and can contribute to a grainy texture in the soup.

- 1 head cauliflower (2 pounds)
- 8 tablespoons unsalted butter, cut into 8 pieces
- 1 leek, white and light green parts only, halved lengthwise, sliced thin, and washed thoroughly
- 1 small onion, halved and sliced thin
  Salt and pepper
- 4½–5 cups water
- ½ teaspoon sherry vinegar
- 3 tablespoons minced fresh chives

1. Pull off outer leaves of cauliflower and trim stem. Using paring knife, cut around core to remove; thinly slice core and reserve. Cut heaping 1 cup of ½-inch florets from head of

Browned butter and a few sautéed cauliflower florets make an elegant garnish for our cauliflower soup.

cauliflower; set aside. Cut remaining cauliflower crosswise into ½-inch-thick slices.

2. Melt 3 tablespoons butter in large saucepan over medium-low heat. Add leek, onion, and 1½ teaspoons salt. Cook, stirring often, until leek and onion are softened but not browned, about 7 minutes.

3. Add 4½ cups water, sliced core, and half of sliced cauliflower. Increase heat to medium-high and bring to simmer. Reduce heat to medium-low and simmer gently for 15 minutes. Add remaining sliced cauliflower and simmer until cauliflower is tender and crumbles easily, 15 to 20 minutes.

4. Meanwhile, melt remaining 5 tablespoons butter in 8-inch skillet over medium heat. Add reserved florets and cook, stirring often, until florets are golden brown and butter is browned and has nutty aroma, 6 to 8 minutes. Remove skillet from heat and use slotted spoon to transfer florets to small bowl. Toss florets with vinegar and season with salt to taste. Pour browned butter in skillet into separate bowl and reserve for garnishing.

5. Process soup in blender until smooth, about 45 seconds. Return pureed soup to clean pot, bring to brief simmer over medium heat, and adjust consistency with remaining water as needed (soup should have thick, velvety texture but should be thin enough to settle with flat surface after being stirred). Season with salt to taste. Serve, garnishing individual bowls with browned florets, drizzle of browned butter, chives, and pepper.

VARIATION
Curried Cauliflower Soup GF

Before adding water to saucepan, stir 1½ tablespoons grated fresh ginger and 1 tablespoon curry powder into vegetables and cook until fragrant, about 30 seconds. Substitute ½ teaspoon lime juice for sherry vinegar, and 2 scallions, sliced thin on bias, for chives. Stir ½ cup canned coconut milk and 1 tablespoon lime juice into pureed soup before serving.

Roasted Red Pepper Soup with Paprika and Cilantro Cream
SERVES 8

✔ **WHY THIS RECIPE WORKS:** Roasting red peppers turns their raw, sweet crunch into something smoky and rich. We wanted to concentrate that flavor in a silky pureed soup. We started by broiling the peppers until they were charred and puffed. Next, we built an aromatic base for our soup with garlic, red onion, cumin, and smoked paprika. Sautéing some tomato paste and flour gave the soup intense umami flavor and a velvety thickness. Finally, we whisked in broth, added the roasted peppers, and simmered them until they were tender before whirring the soup smooth in the blender. For a garnish, we make a bright cilantro-lime cream to top our soup. The flavor of this soup depends on homemade roasted red peppers; do not substitute jarred red peppers. Keep your eye on the peppers as they broil in step 2; the broiling time may vary depending on the intensity of your broiler. Sweet paprika can be substituted for the smoked paprika if necessary.

CILANTRO CREAM
- ¾ cup sour cream
- ¼ cup whole milk
- 1 tablespoon minced fresh cilantro
- ½ teaspoon grated lime zest plus 1 tablespoon juice
  Salt and pepper

SOUP
- 8 red bell peppers, cored and flattened
- 1 tablespoon extra-virgin olive oil
- 2 garlic cloves, minced
- 1 red onion, chopped

To give our roasted red pepper soup warm, complex flavors, we add smoked paprika, cumin, and a splash of sherry.

- ½ teaspoon ground cumin
- ½ teaspoon smoked paprika
- 2 tablespoons tomato paste
- 1 tablespoon all-purpose flour
- 4 cups vegetable broth, plus extra as needed
- 1 bay leaf
- ½ cup half-and-half
- 2 tablespoons dry sherry
- 2 tablespoons minced fresh cilantro
  Salt and pepper

1. FOR THE CILANTRO CREAM: Whisk all ingredients together in bowl and season with salt and pepper to taste. Cover and refrigerate until needed.

2. FOR THE SOUP: Adjust oven rack 3 inches from broiler element and heat broiler. Spread half of peppers, skin side up, onto aluminum foil–lined baking sheet. Broil until skin is charred and puffed but flesh is still firm, 8 to 10 minutes, rotating sheet halfway through broiling. Transfer broiled peppers to bowl, cover with plastic wrap or foil, and let steam until skins peel off easily, 10 to 15 minutes. Repeat with remaining peppers. Peel broiled peppers, discarding skins, and chop coarse.

Roasting Red Peppers

1. Cut off top and bottom of pepper, then remove core and stem. Slice down through side of pepper, then lay flat on cutting board and trim away any remaining ribs.

2. Place flattened peppers, pepper tops, and pepper bottoms on aluminum foil–lined baking sheet. (You can fit up to 4 peppers on sheet.)

3. Broil peppers until skin is charred and puffed but flesh is still firm, 8 to 10 minutes, rotating sheet halfway through broiling.

4. Transfer broiled peppers to bowl, cover with plastic wrap, and let steam until skins peel off easily, 10 to 15 minutes.

3. Cook oil and garlic together in Dutch oven over low heat, stirring constantly, until garlic is foamy, sticky, and straw-colored, 8 to 10 minutes. Stir in onion, increase heat to medium, and cook until softened, 5 to 7 minutes.

4. Stir in cumin and paprika and cook until fragrant, about 30 seconds. Stir in tomato paste and flour and cook for 1 minute. Gradually whisk in vegetable broth, smoothing out any lumps. Stir in bay leaf and chopped roasted peppers, bring to simmer, and cook until peppers are very tender, 5 to 7 minutes.

5. Discard bay leaf. Working in batches, puree soup in blender until smooth, 1 to 2 minutes. Return soup to clean pot and stir in half-and-half, sherry, and additional broth as needed to adjust consistency. Heat soup gently over low heat until hot (do not boil). Stir in cilantro and season with salt and pepper to taste. Serve, drizzling individual portions with cilantro cream.

NOTES FROM THE TEST KITCHEN

Pureeing Soup

The texture of a pureed soup should be as smooth and as creamy as possible. With this in mind, we tried pureeing several soups with a food processor, a handheld immersion blender, and a regular countertop blender. It pays to use the right appliance to produce a silky-smooth soup. And because pureeing hot soup can be dangerous, follow our safety tips.

BLENDER IS BEST
A standard blender turns out the smoothest pureed soups. The blade on the blender does an excellent job with soups because it pulls ingredients down from the top of the container. No stray bits go untouched by the blade. And as long as plenty of headroom is left at the top of the blender, there is no leakage.

IMMERSION BLENDER LEAVES BITS BEHIND
The immersion blender has appeal because it can be brought to the pot, eliminating the need to ladle hot ingredients from one vessel to another. However, we found that this kind of blender can leave unblended bits of food behind.

PROCESS WITH CAUTION
The food processor does a decent job of pureeing, but some small bits of vegetables can get trapped under the blade and remain unchopped. Even more troubling is the tendency of a food processor to leak hot liquid. Fill the bowl more than halfway and you are likely to see liquid running down the side of the food processor base.

WAIT BEFORE BLENDING, AND BLEND IN BATCHES
When blending hot soup, follow a couple of precautions. Wait 5 minutes for moderate cooling, and fill the blender only two-thirds full; otherwise, the soup can explode out the top.

KEEP LID SECURE
Don't expect the lid on a blender to stay in place. Hold it securely with a folded dish towel to keep it in place and to protect your hand from hot steam. And pulse several times before blending continuously.

Creamy Butternut Squash Soup

SERVES 4 TO 6 `GF`

✓ **WHY THIS RECIPE WORKS:** Butternut squash soup should be a simple soup—little more than squash, cooking liquid, and a few aromatic ingredients—that comes together easily yet is creamy and deeply flavorful. But many squash soups fail to live up to their potential, often ending up too sweet or with too little squash flavor. We got the most flavor out of our squash by sautéing a shallot in butter with the reserved squash seeds and fibers, simmering the mixture in water, and then using the flavorful liquid to steam the unpeeled squash. This method gave us doubly flavorful, tender squash with the added bonus of avoiding the difficult task of peeling raw squash. To complete our soup, we scooped out the cooked squash from its skin, then pureed it with some of the strained steaming liquid for a perfectly smooth texture. Some heavy cream added richness, and a little brown sugar and nutmeg balanced the squash's earthy flavor. Serve with Cinnamon-Sugar Croutons (page 85).

- 4 tablespoons unsalted butter, cut into ½-inch pieces
- 1 large shallot, chopped
- 3 pounds butternut squash, quartered and seeded, with fibers and seeds reserved
- 6 cups water
  Salt and pepper
- ½ cup heavy cream
- 1 teaspoon packed dark brown sugar
  Pinch ground nutmeg

1. Melt 2 tablespoons butter in Dutch oven over medium heat. Add shallot and cook until softened, 2 to 3 minutes. Stir in squash seeds and fibers and cook until butter turns orange, about 4 minutes.

2. Stir in water and 1 teaspoon salt and bring to boil. Reduce heat to simmer, place squash cut side down in steamer basket, and lower basket into pot. Cover and steam squash until completely tender, 30 to 40 minutes.

3. Using tongs, transfer cooked squash to rimmed baking sheet. Let squash cool slightly, then scrape cooked squash from skin using soupspoon; discard skin.

4. Strain cooking liquid through fine-mesh strainer into large liquid measuring cup. Working in batches, puree cooked squash with 3 cups strained cooking liquid in blender until smooth, 1 to 2 minutes. Return pureed soup to clean pot and stir in cream, sugar, nutmeg, and remaining 2 tablespoons butter. Return to brief simmer, adding additional strained cooking liquid as needed to adjust consistency. Season with salt and pepper to taste, and serve.

VARIATIONS

Creamy Butternut Squash Soup with Fennel `GF`
Reduce amount of squash to 2 pounds and add 1 teaspoon fennel seeds to pot with squash seeds and fibers. Add 1 large fennel bulb, stalks discarded, bulb halved, cored, and cut into 1-inch-thick strips, to steamer basket with squash.

Curried Butternut Squash and Apple Soup `GF`
A tart apple, such as a Granny Smith, adds a nice contrast to the sweet squash, but any type of apple may be used.

Reduce amount of squash to 2½ pounds. Add 1 large apple, peeled, cored, and quartered, to steamer basket with squash. Substitute 2 teaspoons curry powder for nutmeg.

Southwestern Butternut Squash Soup `GF`
Substitute 1 tablespoon honey for brown sugar and ½ teaspoon ground cumin for nutmeg. Stir 2 tablespoons minced fresh cilantro and 2 teaspoons minced canned chipotle chile in adobo sauce into soup before serving.

Harvest Pumpkin Soup

SERVES 4 TO 6 `FAST` `GF`

✓ **WHY THIS RECIPE WORKS:** The perfect dish for cold fall evenings, pumpkin soup is warm, velvety, and, when you use canned pumpkin, surprisingly easy. The trick is getting rich, balanced pumpkin flavor out of a can. We started by creating a deeply flavorful base for our soup by softening onion and then adding cumin, coriander, and nutmeg, which gave us a warm-spiced flavor that paired well with pumpkin. Maple syrup was the ideal sweetener, adding depth and enhancing the nutty flavor of the soup without overwhelming it with sweetness. A combination of vegetable broth and water gave the soup a subtle savory backbone, and just ½ cup of half-and-half gave us the creamy texture we were looking for. Simmering the pumpkin in the flavorful liquid for 15 minutes allowed the flavors to meld and cooked off the tinny flavor of the canned pumpkin, then we pureed the soup to a silky consistency. Be sure to buy pure canned pumpkin, not pumpkin pie filling, which has sugar and spices added. Crumbled blue cheese and toasted, chopped walnuts make nice garnishes to this soup.

- 2 tablespoons unsalted butter
- 1 onion, minced
- 2 garlic cloves, minced
- ½ teaspoon ground cumin
- ½ teaspoon ground coriander
- ¼ teaspoon ground nutmeg

3 cups vegetable broth, plus extra as needed

2 cups water

1 (15-ounce) can unsweetened pumpkin puree

¼ cup maple syrup

½ cup half-and-half

   Salt and pepper

1. Melt butter in Dutch oven over medium heat. Add onion and cook until softened, about 5 minutes. Stir in garlic, cumin, coriander, and nutmeg and cook until fragrant, about 30 seconds.

2. Stir in broth, water, pumpkin, and maple syrup, scraping up any browned bits, and bring to boil. Reduce to simmer and cook until flavors have melded, about 15 minutes.

3. Working in batches, process soup in blender until smooth, 1 to 2 minutes. Return pureed soup to clean pot and stir in half-and-half and additional broth as needed to adjust consistency. Heat soup gently over low heat until hot (do not boil). Season with salt and pepper to taste and serve.

Super Greens Soup with Lemon-Tarragon Cream

SERVES 4 TO 6   **GF**

✔ WHY THIS RECIPE WORKS: We wanted a deceptively delicious, silky-smooth soup that delivered a big dose of healthy greens. It would be packed with all the essential nutrients of hearty greens and would boast a deep, complex flavor brightened with a garnish of lemon and herb cream. First, we built a flavorful foundation of sweet caramelized onions and earthy sautéed mushrooms. We added broth, water, and lots of leafy greens (we liked a mix of chard, kale, arugula, and parsley), and simmered the greens until tender before blending them until smooth. We were happy with the soup's depth of flavor, but it was watery and too thin. Many recipes we found used potatoes as a thickener, but they lent an overwhelmingly earthy flavor. Instead, we tried using Arborio rice. The rice's high starch content thickened the soup to a velvety, lush consistency without clouding its bright, vegetal flavors. For a vibrant finish, we whisked together heavy cream, sour cream, lemon zest, lemon juice, and tarragon and drizzled it over the top.

¼ cup heavy cream

3 tablespoons sour cream

2 tablespoons plus ½ teaspoon extra-virgin olive oil

¼ teaspoon finely grated lemon zest plus ½ teaspoon juice

½ teaspoon minced fresh tarragon

   Salt and pepper

We use a surprising ingredient—Arborio rice—to thicken our Super Greens Soup without dulling its clean, vegetal flavors.

1 onion, halved through root end and sliced thin

¾ teaspoon light brown sugar

3 ounces white mushrooms, trimmed and sliced thin

2 garlic cloves, minced

   Pinch cayenne pepper

3 cups water

3 cups vegetable broth

⅓ cup Arborio rice

12 ounces Swiss chard, stemmed and chopped coarse

9 ounces kale, stemmed and chopped coarse

¼ cup fresh parsley leaves

2 ounces (2 cups) baby arugula

1. Combine cream, sour cream, ½ teaspoon oil, lemon zest and juice, tarragon, and ¼ teaspoon salt in bowl. Cover and refrigerate until ready to serve.

2. Heat remaining 2 tablespoons oil in Dutch oven over medium-high heat. Stir in onion, sugar, and 1 teaspoon salt and cook, stirring occasionally, until onion releases some moisture, about 5 minutes. Reduce heat to low and cook, stirring often and scraping up any browned bits, until onion is deeply browned and slightly sticky, about 30 minutes. (If onion

Successful Soup Making

Making a great pot of soup, stew, or chili requires attention to detail, the right ingredients, well-made equipment, and a good recipe.

SAUTÉ AROMATICS

The first step in making many soups is sautéing aromatics such as onion and garlic. Sautéing softens their texture so that there is no unwelcome crunch in the soup, and it tames harsh flavors and develops complex flavors in the process.

START WITH GOOD BROTH

Homemade vegetable broth offers the best flavor, but store-bought broth is a convenient option. However, it's important to be a savvy shopper—many commercial vegetable broths have overly sweet, tinny flavors and are loaded with too much salt. To learn more and for our recommended brands, see Buying the Best Vegetable Broth on page 76.

CUT VEGETABLES TO THE RIGHT SIZE

Haphazardly cut vegetables will cook unevenly—larger pieces will be underdone and crunchy, while smaller ones will be soft and mushy. Cutting vegetables evenly to the size specified in the recipe ensures that they will be perfectly cooked.

STAGGER THE ADDITION OF VEGETABLES

When a soup contains a variety of vegetables, they are often added in stages to account for their varied cooking times. Hardy vegetables like potatoes and winter squash need much more cooking than delicate asparagus or spinach.

SIMMER, DON'T BOIL

The fine line between simmering and boiling can make a big difference in your soups. A simmer is a restrained version of a boil; fewer bubbles break the surface. Simmering heats food through more gently and more evenly; boiling can cause vegetables such as potatoes to break apart.

SEASON JUST BEFORE SERVING

In general, we add salt, pepper, and other seasonings—such as delicate herbs and lemon juice—after cooking, just before serving. The saltiness of the stock and of ingredients like canned tomatoes and beans can vary greatly, so it's best to taste and adjust the seasonings at the end. For our simple vegetable soups, particularly pureed soups, we also like to include flavorful garnishes like cilantro cream, harissa, seeds or chopped nuts for crunch, or a dollop of bright pesto.

is sizzling or scorching, reduce heat. If onion is not browning after 15 to 20 minutes, increase heat.)

3. Stir in mushrooms and cook until they have released their moisture, about 5 minutes. Stir in garlic and cayenne and cook until fragrant, about 30 seconds. Stir in water, broth, and rice, scraping up any browned bits, and bring to boil. Reduce heat to low, cover, and simmer for 15 minutes.

4. Stir in chard, kale, and parsley, 1 handful at a time, until wilted and submerged in liquid. Return to simmer, cover, and cook until greens are tender, about 10 minutes.

5. Off heat, stir in arugula until wilted. Working in batches, process soup in blender until smooth, about 1 minute. Return pureed soup to clean pot and season with salt and pepper to taste. Drizzle individual portions with lemon-tarragon cream, and serve.

White Gazpacho

SERVES 6 TO 8 ｜ VEGAN

✔ **WHY THIS RECIPE WORKS:** Spanish white gazpacho is a silky chilled soup with intense flavor. At its best, it is a study in contrasts: Some bites offer a nutty crunch, while others are sharply fruity and floral. But the versions we tried were watery and bland, or even grainy. We found that the order in which we added ingredients to the blender made all the difference. First, we ground almonds, then we added bread (which had been soaked briefly in water), garlic, sherry vinegar, salt, and cayenne pepper. Then we drizzled in olive oil and water. To get just a hint of almond flavor without overwhelming the soup, we mixed a tablespoon of the pureed soup with almond extract, then stirred a teaspoon of the mixture back into the soup. Sliced green grapes and toasted almonds added fruitiness and crunch. An extra drizzle of olive oil made for a rich finish and a beautiful presentation. This rich soup is best when served in small portions (about 6 ounces). Use a good-quality extra-virgin olive oil; our favorite is Columela Extra Virgin Olive Oil.

- 6   slices hearty white sandwich bread, crusts removed
- 4   cups water
- 2½   cups (8¾ ounces) plus ⅓ cup sliced blanched almonds
- 1   garlic clove, peeled
- 3   tablespoons sherry vinegar
-   Salt and pepper
-   Pinch cayenne pepper
- ½   cup extra-virgin olive oil, plus extra for drizzling
- ⅛   teaspoon almond extract
- 2   teaspoons vegetable oil
- 6   ounces seedless green grapes, sliced thin (1 cup)

1. Combine bread and water in bowl and let soak for 5 minutes. Process 2½ cups almonds in blender until finely ground, about 30 seconds, scraping down sides of blender jar as needed. Using your hands, remove bread from water, squeeze it lightly, and transfer to blender with almonds. Measure out 3 cups soaking water and set aside; transfer remaining soaking water to blender. Add garlic, vinegar, ½ teaspoons salt, and cayenne to blender and process until mixture has consistency of cake batter, 30 to 45 seconds. With blender running, add olive oil in thin, steady stream, about 30 seconds. Add reserved soaking water and process for 1 minute.

2. Season with salt and pepper to taste. Strain soup through fine-mesh strainer set in bowl, pressing on solids to extract liquid. Discard solids.

3. Measure 1 tablespoon soup into separate bowl and stir in almond extract. Return 1 teaspoon extract-soup mixture to soup; discard remaining mixture. Chill soup for at least 3 hours or up to 24 hours.

4. Heat vegetable oil in 8-inch skillet over medium-high heat until oil begins to shimmer. Add remaining ⅓ cup almonds and cook, stirring constantly, until golden brown, 3 to 4 minutes. Immediately transfer to bowl and stir in ¼ teaspoon salt.

5. Ladle soup into shallow bowls. Mound grapes in center of each bowl, sprinkle with cooled almonds, and drizzle with extra olive oil. Serve immediately.

Classic Gazpacho

SERVES 8 TO 10 VEGAN   GF

✓ **WHY THIS RECIPE WORKS:** A good gazpacho should showcase the brightness of fresh vegetables, yet many recipes turn out bland, thin soups. We wanted to develop a foolproof recipe with distinct vegetables in a bright tomato broth. We started by chopping the vegetables by hand, which ensured they retained their color and firm texture. Letting them sit briefly in a sherry vinegar marinade guaranteed well-seasoned vegetables, while a combination of tomato juice and ice cubes (which helped chill the soup) provided the right amount of liquid. Chilling our soup for a minimum of 4 hours was critical to allow the flavors to develop and meld. Use a Vidalia, Maui, or Walla Walla onion here. This recipe makes a large quantity because the leftovers are so good, but it can be halved if you prefer. Traditionally, diners garnish their gazpacho with more of the same diced vegetables that are in the soup, so cut some extra vegetables when you prepare those called for in the recipe. Serve with Garlic Croutons, chopped pitted black olives, chopped hard-cooked eggs, and finely diced avocados. For a finishing touch, serve in chilled bowls.

CLASSIC CROUTONS FAST VEGAN

Either fresh or stale bread can be used in this recipe, although stale bread is easier to cut and crisps more quickly in the oven.

> 6 slices hearty white sandwich bread, crusts removed, cut into ½-inch cubes (3 cups)
> 3 tablespoons unsalted butter, melted, or extra-virgin olive oil
> Salt and pepper

Adjust oven rack to middle position and heat oven to 350 degrees. Toss bread with melted butter, season with salt and pepper, and spread onto rimmed baking sheet. Bake until golden brown and crisp, 20 to 25 minutes, stirring halfway through baking. Let cool and serve. (Croutons can be stored at room temperature for up to 3 days.)

VARIATIONS

GARLIC CROUTONS FAST VEGAN

Whisk 1 minced garlic clove into melted butter before tossing with bread.

CINNAMON-SUGAR CROUTONS FAST VEGAN

These croutons pair best with sweet soups like Creamy Butternut Squash Soup.

Toss buttered bread with 6 teaspoons sugar and 1½ teaspoons ground cinnamon before baking.

1½ pounds tomatoes, cored and cut into ¼-inch dice
2 red bell peppers, stemmed, seeded, and cut into ¼-inch dice
2 small cucumbers, 1 cucumber peeled, both sliced lengthwise, seeded, and cut into ¼-inch dice
½ small sweet onion or 2 large shallots, minced
⅓ cup sherry vinegar
2 garlic cloves, minced
Salt and pepper
5 cups tomato juice
8 ice cubes
1 teaspoon hot sauce (optional)
Extra-virgin olive oil

1. Combine tomatoes, bell peppers, cucumbers, onion, vinegar, garlic, and 2 teaspoons salt in large (at least 4-quart) bowl and season with pepper to taste. Let stand until vegetables just begin to release their juices, about 5 minutes. Stir in tomato

juice, ice cubes, and hot sauce, if using. Cover and refrigerate to blend flavors, at least 4 hours or up to 2 days.

2. Discard any unmelted ice cubes and season with salt and pepper to taste. Serve cold, drizzling individual portions with oil.

VARIATION

Spicy Gazpacho with Chipotle Chile and Lime `VEGAN` `GF`

We recommend garnishing bowls of this spicy soup with finely diced avocado. If desired, reduce the amount of chipotles to make the soup less spicy.

Omit hot sauce. Add 2 tablespoons minced fresh cilantro, 1 tablespoon minced canned chipotle chile in adobo sauce, and 2 teaspoons grated lime zest plus 6 tablespoons juice (3 limes) with tomato juice and ice cubes.

Provençal Vegetable Soup

SERVES 6 `GF`

✓ **WHY THIS RECIPE WORKS:** Provençal vegetable soup is a classic French summer soup with a delicate broth that is intensified by a dollop of *pistou*, the French equivalent of Italy's pesto. We wanted a simple version that focused on fresh seasonal vegetables. Leeks, green beans, and zucchini all made the cut; we like their summery flavors, different shapes, and varying shades of green. We added canned white beans (which were far more convenient than dried in this quick-cooking soup) and orecchiette pasta (for its easy-to-spoon shape). To simplify the traditional pistou, we just whirred basil, Parmesan, olive oil, and garlic together in our food processor. If you cannot find haricots verts (thin green beans), substitute regular green beans and cook them for an extra minute or two. You can substitute small shells or ditalini for the orecchiette (the cooking times might vary slightly). In order for this recipe to be gluten-free, you must use gluten-free pasta. Serve with Garlic Toasts (page 97) or crusty bread, if desired.

PISTOU

½ cup fresh basil leaves

1 ounce Parmesan cheese, grated (½ cup)

⅓ cup extra-virgin olive oil

1 garlic clove, minced

SOUP

1 tablespoon extra-virgin olive oil

1 leek, white and light green parts only, halved lengthwise, sliced ½ inch thick, and washed thoroughly

A quick basil *pistou* is the perfect accent for this bright, fresh vegetable soup.

1 celery rib, cut into ½-inch pieces

1 carrot, peeled and sliced ¼ inch thick

Salt and pepper

2 garlic cloves, minced

3 cups vegetable broth

3 cups water

½ cup orecchiette

8 ounces haricots verts, trimmed and cut into ½-inch lengths

1 (15-ounce) can cannellini or navy beans, rinsed

1 small zucchini, halved lengthwise, seeded, and cut into ¼-inch pieces

1 large tomato, cored, seeded, and chopped medium

1. FOR THE PISTOU: Process all ingredients together in food processor until smooth, scraping down bowl as needed, about 15 seconds. (Pistou can be refrigerated for up to 4 hours.)

2. FOR THE SOUP: Heat oil in Dutch oven over medium heat until shimmering. Add leek, celery, carrot, and ½ teaspoon salt and cook until vegetables are softened, 8 to 10 minutes. Stir in garlic and cook until fragrant, about 30 seconds. Stir in broth and water and bring to simmer.

3. Stir in pasta and simmer until slightly softened, about 5 minutes. Stir in haricots verts and simmer until bright green but still crunchy, about 3 minutes. Stir in cannellini beans, zucchini, and tomato and simmer until pasta and vegetables are tender, about 3 minutes. Season with salt and pepper to taste. Serve, topping individual portions with generous tablespoon pistou.

Seeding Zucchini

Halve zucchini lengthwise, then gently scrape out seeds using soupspoon.

Root Vegetable Soup

SERVES 6 TO 8 **VEGAN GF**

✔ **WHY THIS RECIPE WORKS:** We wanted to feature a variety of hearty root vegetables in a satisfying winter soup. We started with a combination of leeks, russet potatoes, celery root, and carrots. Canned diced tomatoes gave the soup a subtle sweetness. Sweating the leeks until they were tender so they would melt into the broth gave the soup a flavorful, aromatic backbone. We cut the potatoes, celery root, and carrots to the same size to ensure they cooked at the same rate. Once the potatoes were tender, we mashed some of them into the soup to give the broth more body and thickness. At the end of cooking, we stirred in escarole and convenient frozen lima beans until the greens were wilted and the beans were heated through. A sprinkling of fresh parsley brightened our winter vegetable soup. Serve with crusty bread.

- 1 tablespoon extra-virgin olive oil
- 1 pound leeks, white and light green parts only, halved lengthwise, sliced ¼ inch thick, and washed thoroughly
  Salt and pepper
- 3 garlic cloves, minced
- 6 cups vegetable broth
- 1 (14.5-ounce) can diced tomatoes, drained and chopped coarse
- 12 ounces russet potatoes, peeled and cut into ½-inch pieces
- 12 ounces celery root, peeled and cut into ½-inch pieces
- 12 ounces carrots, peeled and cut into ½-inch pieces

Storing and Reheating Soups, Stews, and Chilis

Soups, stews, and chilis make a generous number of servings, making it convenient to stock your freezer with last night's leftovers so you can reheat them whenever you like. First you'll need to cool the pot. As tempting as it might seem, don't transfer the hot contents straight to the refrigerator. This can increase the fridge's internal temperature to unsafe levels, which is dangerous for all the other food stored in the fridge. We find that letting the pot cool on the countertop for an hour helps the temperature drop to about 75 degrees, at which point you can transfer it safely to the fridge. If you don't have an hour to cool the whole pot to room temperature, you can divide the contents of the pot into a number of storage containers to allow the heat to dissipate more quickly, or you can cool it rapidly by using a frozen bottle of water to stir the contents of the pot.

To reheat soups, stews, and chilis, we prefer to simmer them gently on the stovetop in a sturdy, heavy-bottomed pot, but a spin in the microwave works too. Just be sure to cover the dish to prevent a mess. And note that while most soups, stews, and chilis store just fine, those that contain dairy or pasta do not—the dairy curdles as it freezes, and the pasta turns bloated and mushy. Instead, make and freeze the dish without including the dairy or pasta component. After you have thawed the soup, stew, or chili, and it has been heated through, you can stir in the uncooked pasta and simmer until just tender, or stir in the dairy and continue to heat gently until hot (do not boil).

- 1 small head escarole (12 ounces), trimmed and cut into 1-inch pieces
- 1 cup frozen baby lima beans, thawed (optional)
- 2 tablespoons minced fresh parsley

1. Heat oil in Dutch oven over medium-low heat until shimmering. Stir in leeks and ½ teaspoon salt, cover, and cook, stirring occasionally, until leeks are softened, 8 to 10 minutes.

2. Stir in garlic and cook until fragrant, about 30 seconds. Stir in broth, tomatoes, potatoes, celery root, and carrots and bring to boil. Cover, reduce heat to gentle simmer, and cook until vegetables are tender, about 25 minutes.

3. Using back of wooden spoon, mash some of potatoes against side of pot to thicken soup. Stir in escarole and lima beans, if using, and cook until escarole is wilted and beans are heated through, about 5 minutes. Off heat, stir in parsley and season with salt and pepper to taste. Serve.

Rustic Leek and Potato Soup

SERVES 6 TO 8

✔ **WHY THIS RECIPE WORKS:** We prefer a hearty version of leek and potato soup with big bites of tender potatoes, but all too often the soup ends up more like a chowder, with potatoes that are flaking and falling apart. We found that low-starch red potatoes were the best option for a flavorful country-style soup because they held their shape and didn't become waterlogged during cooking. Removing the pot from the heat toward the end allowed the potatoes to finish cooking in the hot broth without becoming overcooked or mushy. To infuse our soup with the delicate flavor of the leeks, we used a hefty 5 pounds of leeks and sautéed them in butter to deepen their flavor. We cooked the leeks until they were tender but not falling apart so that there would still be bites of leeks in our rustic soup. Garlic, thyme, and a couple of bay leaves were all we needed to round out the flavors of this simple soup. Leeks can vary in size. If yours have large white and light green sections, use fewer leeks.

6	tablespoons unsalted butter
4–5	pounds leeks, white and light green parts only, halved lengthwise, sliced 1 inch thick, and washed thoroughly (11 cups)
	Salt and pepper
4	garlic cloves, minced
1	teaspoon minced fresh thyme
1	tablespoon all-purpose flour
3	cups vegetable broth
2¼	cups water
2	bay leaves
1¾	pounds red potatoes, peeled and cut into ¾-inch chunks

1. Melt butter in Dutch oven over medium heat. Stir in leeks and 1 teaspoon salt, cover, and cook, stirring occasionally, until leeks are tender but not mushy, 15 to 20 minutes (do not brown). Stir in garlic and thyme and cook until fragrant, about 30 seconds. Stir in flour and cook for 2 minutes.

2. Increase heat to high and gradually stir in broth and water. Stir in bay leaves and potatoes, cover, and bring to boil. Reduce heat to medium-low and simmer until potatoes are almost tender, 5 to 7 minutes.

3. Remove pot from heat and let stand, covered, until potatoes are tender and flavors meld, 10 to 15 minutes. Discard bay leaves and season with salt and pepper to taste. Serve.

Preparing Leeks

1. Trim and discard root and dark green leaves.

2. Cut trimmed leek in half lengthwise, then slice into pieces sized according to recipe.

3. Rinse cut leeks thoroughly using salad spinner or bowl of water to remove dirt and sand.

Hearty Cabbage Soup

SERVES 6 TO 8 GF

✔ **WHY THIS RECIPE WORKS:** More often than not, cabbage soup is just a bowl of wilted, sad cabbage and watery, bland broth. We set out to make a soup full of crisp-tender cabbage and chunks of potato floating in a rich, flavorful broth. As a starting point, we needed to choose the most appropriate variety of cabbage for a hearty soup. Tasters preferred the more assertive flavor of green cabbage over napa or savoy cabbages. For the potatoes, low-starch red potatoes beat out other varieties because they held their shape after a period of simmering. Many cabbage soup recipes also call for a pork product—most often smoky bacon. We swapped out the bacon for hot smoked paprika. This gave the soup more backbone and a hint of smokiness. We also added caraway seed for its delicate anise flavor, which brought out the sweetness of the cabbage, and we finished the soup with fresh dill. A dollop of sour cream added a rich, tangy counterpoint to the sweetness of the soup. You can substitute smoked paprika and a pinch of cayenne for the hot smoked paprika.

3 tablespoons unsalted butter

1 onion, chopped fine

Salt and pepper

4 garlic cloves, minced

1 teaspoon caraway seeds

1 teaspoon minced fresh thyme or ¼ teaspoon dried

½ teaspoon hot smoked paprika

¼ cup dry white wine

6 cups vegetable broth

1 small head green cabbage (1¼ pounds), cored and cut into ¾-inch pieces

12 ounces red potatoes, unpeeled and cut into ¾-inch pieces

3 carrots, peeled and cut into ½-inch pieces

1 bay leaf

1 tablespoon minced fresh dill

1 cup sour cream

1. Melt butter in Dutch oven over medium heat. Stir in onion and 1 teaspoon salt and cook until softened, 5 to 7 minutes. Stir in garlic, caraway, thyme, and paprika and cook until fragrant, about 30 seconds.

2. Stir in wine, scraping up any browned bits, and simmer until nearly evaporated, about 1 minute. Stir in broth, cabbage, potatoes, carrots, and bay leaf and bring to boil. Cover, reduce to gentle simmer, and cook until vegetables are tender, about 30 minutes.

3. Discard bay leaf. Season with salt and pepper to taste and sprinkle with dill. Top individual portions with sour cream, and serve.

Vegetable Shabu-Shabu with Sesame Sauce

SERVES 6 TO 8   FAST   GF

 WHY THIS RECIPE WORKS: Shabu-shabu is a Japanese hot-pot dish in which beef, vegetables, and tofu are simmered in broth, then served with chewy udon noodles and dipping sauces. We wanted to develop a version without the meat (or the hot pot). The traditional dashi broth is made from glutamate-rich kombu seaweed and bonito (tuna) flakes. We needed to find a way to replicate the bonito's fishy flavor. After a good deal of trial and error, we found that adding a second variety of seaweed (wakame), plenty of fish sauce substitute, rice wine, and sugar replicated the depth of the bonito. Shabu-shabu typically includes carrots, napa cabbage or bok choy, enoki or shiitake mushrooms, tofu, and chrysanthemum leaves. Luckily, the hard-to-find chrysanthemum leaves were not missed when omitted. We preferred bok choy to cabbage and the fuller flavor of shiitake

This traditional Japanese soup features chewy udon noodles, silky tofu, and tender vegetables in a simple, savory broth.

mushrooms to enoki. A dollop of a sesame sauce made with mayonnaise, miso, garlic, and lemon juice was the perfect garnish. We prefer the flavor of red miso here, but white miso can be substituted; do not substitute "light" miso because its flavor is too mild. See page 55 for information about buying miso.

SESAME SAUCE

¼ cup sesame seeds, toasted

1 garlic clove, minced

2 tablespoons mayonnaise

1 tablespoon red miso

2 teaspoons lemon juice

2 teaspoons sugar

½ teaspoon water

SOUP

8 ounces dried udon noodles

Salt

9 cups water

½ ounce kombu seaweed, rinsed

½ ounce wakame seaweed, rinsed

½ cup mirin

¼ cup fish sauce substitute (see page 60)

1½ teaspoons sugar

3 heads baby bok choy (4 ounces each), sliced ⅛ inch thick

3 carrots, peeled and sliced ⅛ inch thick

14 ounces soft tofu, cut into ½-inch cubes

8 ounces shiitake mushrooms, stemmed and sliced thin

1. FOR THE SESAME SAUCE: Stir all ingredients together in bowl until smooth.

2. FOR THE SOUP: Bring 2 quarts water to boil in large pot. Add udon noodles and ½ tablespoon salt and cook, stirring often, until tender; drain and set aside.

3. Meanwhile, bring water, kombu, and wakame to brief boil in large pot over medium heat. Remove from heat and discard seaweed.

4. Stir in mirin, fish sauce, and sugar and bring to simmer over medium heat. Stir in bok choy and carrots and simmer until crisp-tender, 2 to 4 minutes. Stir in tofu, mushrooms, and cooked noodles and let heat through, about 1 minute. Drizzle individual portions with sesame sauce and serve.

Winter Squash Chowder

SERVES 6 TO 8

✔ **WHY THIS RECIPE WORKS:** We wanted to pair the sweet, subtle flavor of winter squash with warm, nutty spices in a satisfying chowder. Our biggest challenge would be accentuating the mild flavor of the squash without overpowering it. We started with some thyme and a single bay leaf. Warm, spicy nutmeg and slightly bitter sage provided just the right savory notes we were looking for. We also found that a small amount of dark brown sugar added rich, caramel notes that enhanced the squash's natural sweetness. Next we needed to address the chowder's consistency. The squash's starches didn't thicken the soup enough alone, so we stirred in some flour and cream to impart richness and a velvety texture. To balance the sweet richness of the squash, we also added some healthy, hearty kale. A sprinkling of nutty, salty Parmesan made for the perfect garnish. At last, our chowder was a wonderful balance of hearty and rich, sweet and savory. We prefer smaller squash over larger squash because it has a more concentrated flavor and a finer texture. Delicata or carnival squash can be substituted for the butternut squash.

2 tablespoons unsalted butter

1 onion, chopped fine

Salt and pepper

3 garlic cloves, minced

1 teaspoon minced fresh thyme or ¼ teaspoon dried

Pinch freshly grated nutmeg, plus extra to taste

⅓ cup all-purpose flour

7 cups vegetable broth

3 pounds butternut squash, peeled, seeded, and cut into ½-inch pieces (9 cups)

1 bay leaf

8 ounces kale, stemmed and cut into ½-inch pieces

½ cup heavy cream

1 tablespoon minced fresh sage

1 teaspoon packed dark brown sugar

Grated Parmesan cheese

1. Melt butter in Dutch oven over medium heat. Stir in onion and 1½ teaspoons salt and cook until softened, 5 to 7 minutes. Stir in garlic, thyme, and nutmeg and cook until fragrant, about 30 seconds. Stir in flour and cook for 2 minutes.

2. Gradually whisk in broth, scraping up any browned bits and smoothing out any lumps. Stir in squash and bay leaf and bring to boil. Cover, reduce to gentle simmer, and cook until squash begins to soften, 10 to 15 minutes.

3. Stir in kale, cover, and continue to simmer until squash and kale are tender, about 10 minutes.

4. Off heat, discard bay leaf and stir in cream, sage, and sugar. Season with salt, pepper, and nutmeg to taste. Sprinkle individual portions with Parmesan, and serve.

Celeriac, Fennel, and Apple Chowder

SERVES 6

✔ **WHY THIS RECIPE WORKS:** Celeriac (known more commonly as celery root) is a staple in supermarkets, but most cooks walk right by it. That's a shame because this knobby tuber boasts refreshing herbal flavors with notes of anise, mint, mild radish, and celery. Its creamy (rather than starchy) texture makes it the perfect choice for a hearty vegetable chowder. To further enhance its anise flavor, we sautéed a chopped fennel bulb along with big pieces of onion. For a sweet, fruity counterpoint, we added some grated apple. Chunks of tender red potatoes bulked up the chowder. For a bright citrus note, we simmered a strip of orange zest in the broth. To get the perfect amount of body, we pureed 2 cups of the chowder with a modest amount of cream and then stirred the puree back into the pot. Finally, we stirred in minced fresh fennel fronds to brighten the dish.

This sweet-and-savory chowder combines hearty potato with delicately anise-flavored celery root and shredded apple.

2 tablespoons unsalted butter
1 onion, cut into ½-inch pieces
1 fennel bulb, 1 tablespoon fronds minced, stalks discarded, bulb halved, cored, and cut into ½-inch pieces
  Salt and pepper
6 garlic cloves, minced
2 teaspoons minced fresh thyme or ¾ teaspoon dried
2 tablespoons all-purpose flour
½ cup dry white wine
4 cups vegetable broth
1½ cups water
1 celery root (14 ounces), peeled and cut into ½-inch pieces
12 ounces red potatoes, unpeeled, cut into ½-inch pieces
1 Golden Delicious apple, peeled and shredded
1 bay leaf
1 (3-inch) strip orange zest
¼ cup heavy cream

1. Melt butter in Dutch oven over medium heat. Add onion, fennel pieces, and 1½ teaspoons salt and cook until vegetables are softened, 5 to 7 minutes. Stir in garlic and thyme and cook until fragrant, about 30 seconds. Stir in flour and cook

for 1 minute. Stir in wine, scraping up any browned bits, and cook until nearly evaporated, about 1 minute.

2. Stir in broth, water, celery root, potatoes, apple, bay leaf, and orange zest and bring to boil. Reduce heat to low, partially cover, and simmer gently until stew is thickened and vegetables are tender, 35 to 40 minutes.

3. Off heat, discard bay leaf and orange zest. Puree 2 cups chowder and cream in blender until smooth, about 1 minute, then return to pot. Stir in fennel fronds, season with salt and pepper to taste, and serve.

Peeling Celery Root

Because of its thick skin, you can't use a vegetable peeler to peel celery root. Use this method instead.

1. Trim slice from top and bottom of celery root, then stand root on flat bottom.

2. Starting from top, carefully cut away tough outer skin in strips.

Wild Rice and Mushroom Soup
SERVES 6 TO 8 `GF`

✓ **WHY THIS RECIPE WORKS:** The combination of nutty, chewy wild rice and mushrooms should produce a soup that's substantial—but not heavy—and full of earthy depth. To make good on that promise, we kept the focus on the main ingredients by choosing supporting players that amplified the nutty, earthy, umami-rich flavor profile we were after: tomato paste, soy sauce, dry sherry, and plenty of garlic. For the mushrooms, we chose fresh cremini mushrooms and added dried shiitakes for a dose of potent mushroom flavor. Grinding the shiitakes ensured their flavor permeated the broth. Simmering the wild rice with baking soda decreased its cooking time and brought out more robust flavor. Then we used the rice simmering liquid as our broth, infusing the entire soup with wild rice flavor. Cornstarch helped thicken the broth, and some cream gave our soup a velvety texture. We finished the soup with chives and lemon zest for brightness. White mushrooms can be substituted for the cremini mushrooms. We used a spice grinder to process the dried shiitake mushrooms, but a blender also works. In order for this recipe to be gluten-free, you must use gluten-free soy sauce or tamari.

4¼ cups water
1 sprig fresh thyme
1 bay leaf
5 garlic cloves, peeled (1 whole, 4 minced)
 Salt and pepper
¼ teaspoon baking soda
1 cup wild rice
4 tablespoons unsalted butter
1 pound cremini mushrooms, trimmed and sliced ¼ inch thick
1 onion, chopped fine
1 teaspoon tomato paste
⅔ cup dry sherry
¼ ounce dried shiitake mushrooms, finely ground using spice grinder
4 cups vegetable broth
1 tablespoon soy sauce
¼ cup cornstarch
½ cup heavy cream
¼ cup minced fresh chives
¼ teaspoon finely grated lemon zest

1. Adjust oven rack to middle position and heat oven to 375 degrees. Bring 4 cups water, thyme sprig, bay leaf, whole garlic clove, ¾ teaspoon salt, and baking soda to boil in medium saucepan over high heat. Add rice and return to boil. Cover saucepan, transfer to oven, and bake until rice is tender, 35 to 50 minutes. Drain rice through fine-mesh strainer set in 4-cup liquid measuring cup, discarding thyme sprig, bay leaf, and garlic. Add enough water to reserved cooking liquid to measure 3 cups.

2. Melt butter in Dutch oven over high heat. Add cremini, onion, minced garlic, tomato paste, ¾ teaspoon salt, and 1 teaspoon pepper. Cook, stirring occasionally, until vegetables are browned and dark fond develops on bottom of pot, about 15 minutes.

3. Stir in sherry, scraping up any browned bits, and cook until nearly evaporated, about 2 minutes. Stir in ground shiitakes, reserved rice cooking liquid, broth, and soy sauce and bring to boil. Reduce heat to low, cover, and simmer until onion and mushrooms are tender, about 20 minutes.

4. Whisk cornstarch and remaining ¼ cup water together in bowl. Stir cornstarch slurry into soup and simmer until thickened, about 2 minutes. Off heat, stir in cooked rice, cream, chives, and lemon zest. Cover and let stand for 20 minutes. Season with salt and pepper to taste, and serve.

Farmhouse Vegetable and Barley Soup

SERVES 6 TO 8 **VEGAN**

✔ **WHY THIS RECIPE WORKS:** We wanted a simple, satisfying soup with lots of vegetables accented by nutty, chewy grains of barley. We started by simmering leeks, carrots, and celery in a combination of wine and soy sauce until we had a potent aromatic backbone for our soup. Then we added in the barley along with vegetable broth (cut with water so its sweetness wouldn't be overwhelming), dried porcini mushrooms, and herbs. As the barley softened, the mushrooms and herbs infused the broth with flavor. Next, we added the remaining vegetables: chunks of Yukon Gold potatoes, turnip, and some cabbage. Once all the vegetables were tender, we stirred in some frozen peas, lemon juice, and parsley for a pop of bright flavor. We prefer an acidic, unoaked white wine such as Sauvignon Blanc for this recipe. Garnish this soup with crumbled cheddar cheese or Classic Croutons (page 85).

8 sprigs fresh parsley plus 3 tablespoons chopped
4 sprigs fresh thyme
1 bay leaf
2 tablespoons unsalted butter or vegetable oil
1½ pounds leeks, white and light green parts only, halved lengthwise, sliced ½ inch thick, and washed thoroughly
2 carrots, peeled and cut into ½-inch pieces
2 celery ribs, cut into ¼-inch pieces
⅓ cup dry white wine
2 teaspoons soy sauce
 Salt and pepper
6 cups water
4 cups vegetable broth
½ cup pearl barley
1 garlic clove, peeled and smashed
⅛ ounce dried porcini mushrooms, finely ground using spice grinder
1½ pounds Yukon Gold potatoes, peeled and cut into ½-inch pieces
8 ounces turnip, peeled and cut into ¾-inch pieces
1½ cups chopped green cabbage
1 cup frozen peas
1 teaspoon lemon juice

1. Using kitchen twine, tie together parsley sprigs, thyme sprigs, and bay leaf. Melt butter in Dutch oven over medium heat. Add leeks, carrots, celery, wine, soy sauce, and 2 teaspoons salt. Cook, stirring occasionally, until liquid has evaporated and celery is softened, about 10 minutes.

2. Stir in water, broth, barley, garlic, mushroom powder, and herb bundle. Increase heat to high and bring to boil. Reduce heat to medium-low, partially cover, and simmer gently for 25 minutes.

3. Stir in potatoes, turnip, and cabbage and simmer until barley, potatoes, turnip, and cabbage are tender, 18 to 20 minutes. Off heat, discard herb bundle. Stir in peas, lemon juice, and chopped parsley. Season with salt and pepper to taste and serve.

Beet and Wheat Berry Soup with Dill Cream

SERVES 6

✓ **WHY THIS RECIPE WORKS:** Traditional hot borscht is a heavy affair, with starchy vegetables and a beef or pork broth base. We wanted a lighter, fresh vegetarian version that kept the focus on the beets. To complement the earthy shredded beets, we swapped the waxy, starchy potatoes for fiber-loaded wheat berries. Toasting the wheat berries gave them a rich, nutty flavor and a pleasant chewy consistency in the soup. To build a flavorful backbone, we sautéed onion, garlic, thyme, and tomato paste before stirring in the broth. Red wine vinegar, red cabbage, and a dash of cayenne helped to round out the flavor of the beets as well. A dollop of dill cream added tang to this satisfying and vitamin-packed soup. You can use the shredding disk of the food processor to grate the beets and carrot and to shred the cabbage. Do not use presteamed or quick-cooking wheat berries here, as they have a much shorter cooking time; be prepared to read the package carefully to determine what kind of wheat berries you are using.

SOUP

- ⅔ cup wheat berries, rinsed
- 3 tablespoons vegetable oil
- 2 onions, chopped fine
- 4 garlic cloves, minced
- 1 teaspoon minced fresh thyme or ½ teaspoon dried
- 2 tablespoons tomato paste
- ¼ teaspoon cayenne pepper
- 8 cups vegetable broth
- 3 cups water
- 1½ cups shredded red cabbage
- 1 pound beets, trimmed, peeled, and shredded
- 1 small carrot, peeled and shredded
- 1 bay leaf
- Salt and pepper
- 1 tablespoon red wine vinegar

Chewy, nutty toasted wheat berries and a tangy dill cream give a fresh spin to our borscht-inspired beet soup.

DILL CREAM

- ½ cup sour cream
- ¼ cup minced fresh dill
- ½ teaspoon salt

1. FOR THE SOUP: Toast wheat berries in Dutch oven over medium heat, stirring often, until fragrant and beginning to darken, about 5 minutes; transfer to bowl.

2. Heat oil in now-empty pot over medium heat until shimmering. Stir in onions and cook until softened, about 5 minutes. Stir in garlic and thyme and cook until fragrant,

Avoiding Beet Stains

To prevent beet juice from staining your cutting board, spray surface lightly with vegetable oil spray before prepping beets.

about 30 seconds. Stir in tomato paste and cayenne and cook until darkened slightly, about 2 minutes.

3. Stir in broth and water, scraping up any browned bits. Stir in toasted wheat berries, cabbage, beets, carrot, bay leaf, and ¾ teaspoon pepper, and bring to boil. Reduce heat to low and simmer until wheat berries are tender but still chewy and vegetables are tender, 45 minutes to 1¼ hours.

4. FOR THE DILL CREAM: Meanwhile, combine all ingredients in bowl.

5. Off heat, discard bay leaf, and stir in vinegar and 1 teaspoon salt. Season with additional salt and pepper to taste. Top individual portions with dill cream and serve.

Classic Tuscan White Bean Soup

SERVES 8 VEGAN GF

✓ **WHY THIS RECIPE WORKS:** One of our favorite bean soups is Tuscan white bean soup, which boasts creamy, tender beans and hearty vegetables in a light, velvety broth. Determined to avoid tough, exploded beans in our soup, we soaked the beans overnight in salted water, which softened the skins. Then we experimented with cooking times and temperatures, discovering that bringing the soup to a simmer, then gently cooking it in a 250-degree oven, produced perfectly tender beans that stayed intact. We added the tomatoes toward the end of cooking, because their acid kept the beans from softening properly when added at the outset. To round out our soup, we chose other traditional Tuscan ingredients and flavors—hearty greens, lots of garlic, and a sprig of rosemary. To keep its herbal flavor from overwhelming the soup, we steeped the rosemary in the broth for just 15 minutes. For more information on the science behind salt-soaking beans, and how to speed up the process if you're tight on time, see page 204. Serve with Garlic Toasts (page 97).

Salt and pepper
1 pound (2½ cups) dried cannellini beans, picked over and rinsed
1 tablespoon extra-virgin olive oil, plus extra for serving
1 large onion, chopped
2 carrots, peeled and cut into ½-inch pieces
2 celery ribs, cut into ½-inch pieces
8 garlic cloves, peeled and crushed
½ ounce dried porcini mushrooms, rinsed and minced
5 cups water
3 cups vegetable broth
2 bay leaves
1 pound kale or collard greens, stemmed and chopped into 1-inch pieces
1 (14.5-ounce) can diced tomatoes, drained
1 sprig fresh rosemary

1. Dissolve 3 tablespoons salt in 4 quarts cold water in large container. Add beans and soak at room temperature for at least 8 hours or up to 24 hours. Drain and rinse well.

2. Adjust oven rack to lower-middle position and heat oven to 250 degrees. Heat oil in Dutch oven over medium heat until shimmering. Add onion, carrots, and celery and cook until vegetables are softened and lightly browned, 10 to 15 minutes.

Making Classic Tuscan White Bean Soup

1. BRINE BEANS: Dissolve 3 tablespoons salt in cold water in large container. Add beans and soak at room temperature for at least 8 hours.

2. BROWN AROMATICS: Heat oil and cook onion, carrots, and celery until softened and lightly browned. Then stir in garlic and mushrooms before adding water, broth, bay leaves, and soaked beans; bring to simmer.

3. TRANSFER TO OVEN: Cover pot, transfer to oven, and cook until beans are almost tender, 45 minutes to 1 hour. Stir in chopped kale and drained tomatoes and return pot to oven. Cook until beans and greens are fully tender.

4. STEEP ROSEMARY: Remove pot from oven and submerge sprig of fresh rosemary in stew. Cover and let stand 15 minutes.

3. Stir in garlic and mushrooms and cook until fragrant, about 1 minute. Stir in water, broth, soaked beans, and bay leaves. Increase heat to high and bring to simmer. Cover pot, transfer to oven, and cook until beans are almost tender (very center of beans will still be firm), 45 minutes to 1 hour.

4. Stir in kale and tomatoes and continue to cook in oven, covered, until beans and greens are fully tender, 30 to 40 minutes.

5. Remove pot from oven. Submerge rosemary sprig in stew, cover, and let stand 15 minutes. Discard bay leaves and rosemary sprig. Season soup with salt and pepper to taste. If desired, use back of spoon to press some beans against side of pot to thicken soup. Drizzle extra olive oil over individual bowls and serve.

VARIATION

Quicker Tuscan White Bean Soup VEGAN GF

Skip step 1, reduce amount of water to 2 cups and substitute 4 (15-ounce) cans cannellini beans, rinsed, for soaked cannellini beans. Add water, broth, beans, bay leaves, kale, and tomatoes to pot at same time and simmer gently on stovetop until vegetables and greens are fully tender, 20 to 25 minutes; add rosemary sprig off heat as directed.

Black Bean Soup

SERVES 6 VEGAN GF

✔ **WHY THIS RECIPE WORKS:** A great black bean soup has carefully balanced sweet, spicy, and smoky flavors and a luscious consistency. But too often it ends up watery, thin, and bland, or overspiced and bitter. We wanted to create a foolproof black bean soup with great flavor and a dark, thick broth. Because the beans are the star of this dish, we used dried beans, which released flavor into the broth as they cooked. Usually we soak dried beans overnight to soften their skins and promote even cooking, but because we didn't mind getting some blown-out beans, we were able to skip this step. To give the beans great savory flavor, we added dried porcini mushrooms and bay leaves to the simmering liquid. Aromatic onions, celery, and carrot, plus cumin and red pepper flakes, rounded out the flavors. Dried beans tend to cook unevenly, so be sure to taste several beans to determine their doneness in step 1. For efficiency, you can prepare the soup ingredients while the beans simmer, and the garnishes while the soup simmers. Garnishes are essential for this soup, as they add not only flavor, but texture and color as well. Serve with lime wedges, minced fresh cilantro, finely diced red onion, diced avocado, and sour cream.

BEANS

- 1 pound (2½ cups) dried black beans, picked over and rinsed
- 5 cups water, plus extra as needed
- 1 ounce dried porcini mushrooms, rinsed and minced
- 2 bay leaves
- 1 teaspoon salt
- ⅛ teaspoon baking soda

SOUP

- 3 tablespoons extra-virgin olive oil
- 2 large onions, chopped fine
- 3 celery ribs, chopped fine
- 1 large carrot, peeled and chopped fine
- 6 garlic cloves, minced
- 1½ tablespoons ground cumin
- ½ teaspoon red pepper flakes
- 6 cups vegetable broth
- 2 tablespoons cornstarch
- 2 tablespoons water
- 2 tablespoons lime juice
- Salt and pepper

1. FOR THE BEANS: Combine beans, water, mushrooms, bay leaves, salt, and baking soda in large saucepan. Bring to boil, skimming any impurities that rise to surface. Cover, reduce heat to low, and simmer gently until beans are tender, 1¼ to 1½ hours. (If after 1½ hours beans are not tender, add 1 cup more water and continue to simmer until beans are tender.) Discard bay leaves; do not drain beans.

2. FOR THE SOUP: Heat oil in Dutch oven over medium heat until shimmering. Add onions, celery, and carrot and cook until vegetables are softened and lightly browned, 12 to 15 minutes.

3. Stir in garlic, cumin, and pepper flakes and cook until fragrant, about 1 minute. Stir in broth and cooked beans with their cooking liquid and bring to boil. Reduce heat to medium-low and cook, uncovered and stirring occasionally, until flavors have blended, about 30 minutes.

4. Puree 1½ cups beans and 2 cups liquid in blender until smooth, about 1 minute, then return to pot. Whisk cornstarch and water together in bowl, then gradually stir half of cornstarch mixture into simmering soup. Continue to simmer soup, stirring occasionally, until slightly thickened, 3 to 5 minutes. (If at this point soup is thinner than desired, repeat with remaining cornstarch mixture.) Off heat, stir in lime juice and season with salt and pepper to taste. Serve.

Hearty 15-Bean and Vegetable Soup

SERVES 8 TO 10 VEGAN GF

👍 **WHY THIS RECIPE WORKS:** Bean soup mixes promise a shortcut to a flavorful bean soup, but the results are invariably disappointing. Different beans cook at different rates, leaving some blown-out and disintegrating while others remain hard. We wanted to doctor up a mix with fresh flavors and a smarter technique. To get the various beans to cook evenly, we started by brining them to soften their skins, preventing blowouts. Then we brought the soup to a simmer before transferring it to the oven to cook gently in the low, constant heat. To build flavor, we sautéed plenty of aromatics and added thyme, bay leaves, and savory dried porcini. Swiss chard, white mushrooms, and fresh tomato balanced the hearty beans. You can find 15-bean soup mix alongside the other bagged dried beans in the supermarket; any 1-pound bag of multiple varieties of beans will work in this recipe. For more information on the science behind salt-soaking beans, and how to speed up the process if you're tight on time, see page 204. The different varieties of beans cook at different rates, so be sure to taste several beans to ensure they are all tender before serving.

Salt and pepper
1 pound 15-bean soup mix, flavoring pack discarded, beans picked over and rinsed
2 tablespoons extra-virgin olive oil
1 small onion, chopped medium
1 carrot, peeled and chopped fine
1 pound Swiss chard, stems chopped medium, leaves sliced ½ inch thick
½ ounce dried porcini mushrooms, rinsed and minced
12 ounces white mushrooms, trimmed and quartered
6 garlic cloves, minced
2 teaspoons minced fresh thyme or ½ teaspoon dried
8 cups vegetable broth
2 bay leaves
1 large tomato, cored and chopped medium

1. Dissolve 3 tablespoons salt in 4 quarts cold water in large container. Add beans and soak at room temperature for at least 8 hours or up to 24 hours. Drain and rinse well.

2. Adjust oven rack to lower-middle position and heat oven to 250 degrees. Heat oil in Dutch oven over medium heat until shimmering. Stir in onion, carrot, chard stems, and porcini mushrooms and cook until vegetables are softened, 7 to 10 minutes.

3. Stir in white mushrooms, cover, and cook until mushrooms have released their liquid, about 5 minutes.

Uncover and continue to cook until mushrooms are dry and browned, 5 to 10 minutes.

4. Stir in garlic and thyme and cook until fragrant, about 30 seconds. Stir in broth, soaked beans, and bay leaves and bring to boil. Cover pot, transfer to oven, and cook until beans are almost tender, 1 to 1¼ hours.

5. Stir in chard leaves and tomato and continue to cook in oven, covered, until beans and vegetables are fully tender, 30 to 40 minutes. Remove pot from oven and discard bay leaves. Season with salt and pepper to taste and serve.

Sicilian Chickpea and Escarole Soup

SERVES 6 TO 8 GF

👍 **WHY THIS RECIPE WORKS:** In Sicily, chickpeas are the favored legume to use in soup. We found dozens of soup recipes starring chickpeas but were most interested in versions in which the mild bean shared the stage with escarole. We knew that dried beans were the way to go for our traditional soup because we could infuse the chickpeas with lots of flavor as they cooked. For aromatics, we started with the classic flavors of the region: onion, garlic, oregano, and red pepper flakes. We also added fennel, which grows wild throughout much of the Mediterranean; its mild anise bite complemented the nutty chickpeas. A strip of orange zest added a subtle citrusy note, while a Parmesan rind added a nutty richness and complexity that bolstered the chickpeas' flavor. When stirred in for the last 5 minutes of cooking, the escarole leaves wilted until velvety and the stems retained a slight crunch. For more information on the science behind salt-soaking beans, and how to speed up the process if you're tight on time, see page 204. Parmesan rind can be replaced with a 2-inch chunk of the cheese. Serve with Garlic Toasts (page 97).

Salt and pepper
1 pound (2¾ cups) dried chickpeas, picked over and rinsed
2 tablespoons extra-virgin olive oil, plus extra for serving
2 fennel bulbs, stalks discarded, bulbs halved, cored, and chopped fine
1 small onion, chopped medium
5 garlic cloves, minced
2 teaspoons minced fresh oregano or ½ teaspoon dried
¼ teaspoon red pepper flakes
7 cups water
5 cups vegetable broth
1 (5-inch) piece Parmesan cheese rind plus 2 ounces cheese, grated (1 cup)

The elegant soup of creamy chickpeas, mildly bitter escarole, fennel, and fresh tomato is finished with a drizzle of olive oil.

2 bay leaves
1 (3-inch) strip orange zest
1 head escarole (1 pound), trimmed and cut into 1-inch pieces
1 large tomato, cored and chopped medium

1. Dissolve 3 tablespoons salt in 4 quarts cold water in large container. Add chickpeas and soak at room temperature for at least 8 hours or up to 24 hours. Drain and rinse well.

2. Heat oil in Dutch oven over medium heat until shimmering. Add fennel, onion, and 1 teaspoon salt and cook until vegetables are softened, 7 to 10 minutes. Stir in garlic, oregano, and pepper flakes and cook until fragrant, about 30 seconds.

3. Stir in water, broth, drained chickpeas, Parmesan rind, bay leaves, and orange zest and bring to boil. Reduce to gentle simmer and cook until chickpeas are tender, 1¼ to 1¾ hours.

4. Stir in escarole and tomato and cook until escarole is wilted, 5 to 10 minutes.

5. Off heat, remove bay leaves and Parmesan rind (scraping off any cheese that has melted and adding it back to pot). Season with salt and pepper to taste. Sprinkle individual portions with grated Parmesan, drizzle with extra oil, and serve.

GARLIC TOASTS

MAKES 8 SLICES `FAST` `VEGAN`

Be sure to use a high-quality crusty bread, such as a baguette; do not use sliced sandwich bread.

8 (1-inch-thick) slices rustic bread
1 large garlic clove, peeled
3 tablespoons extra-virgin olive oil
Salt and pepper

Adjust oven rack 6 inches from broiler element and heat broiler. Spread bread out evenly over rimmed baking sheet and broil, flipping as needed, until well toasted on both sides, about 4 minutes. Briefly rub 1 side of each toast with garlic, drizzle with oil, and season with salt and pepper to taste. Serve.

Moroccan-Style Chickpea Soup

SERVES 4 TO 6 `FAST` `VEGAN` `GF`

✓ **WHY THIS RECIPE WORKS:** This satisfyingly hearty and easy-to-make chickpea soup is infused with the rich, complex flavors of Moroccan cuisine. To make this soup easy enough for a weeknight, we used convenient canned chickpeas. Sautéing onion with a little sugar sped up their cooking, then we added a substantial amount of garlic to the pot with paprika, saffron, ginger, and cumin for a potent aromatic flavor base. The saffron lent the soup a distinct aroma and rich color, while the cumin and ginger added a pungent kick that would fool anyone into thinking this soup was cooked for hours. Once the spices were fragrant, we added in the chickpeas along with potatoes, canned diced tomatoes, and chopped zucchini. After just 20 minutes of simmering, the vegetables were tender and the rich flavors of the soup had melded. Mashing some of the potatoes into the soup helped to give it a rich consistency. You can substitute regular paprika and a pinch of cayenne for the hot paprika. Serve with plenty of hot sauce.

3 tablespoons unsalted butter or extra-virgin olive oil
1 onion, chopped fine
1 teaspoon sugar
Salt and pepper
4 garlic cloves, minced
½ teaspoon hot paprika
¼ teaspoon saffron threads, crumbled

¼ teaspoon ground ginger
¼ teaspoon ground cumin
2 (15-ounce) cans chickpeas, rinsed
1 pound red potatoes, unpeeled and cut into ½-inch pieces
1 (14.5-ounce) can diced tomatoes
1 zucchini, cut into ½-inch pieces
3½ cups vegetable broth
¼ cup minced fresh parsley and/or mint
  Lemon wedges

1. Melt butter in Dutch oven over medium-high heat. Add onion, sugar, and ½ teaspoon salt and cook until onion is softened, about 5 minutes. Stir in garlic, paprika, saffron, ginger, and cumin and cook until fragrant, about 30 seconds. Stir in chickpeas, potatoes, tomatoes and their juice, zucchini, and broth. Simmer, stirring occasionally, until potatoes are tender, 20 to 30 minutes.

2. Using wooden spoon, mash some of potatoes against side of pot to thicken soup. Off heat, stir in parsley and season with salt and pepper to taste. Serve with lemon wedges.

Curried Lentil Soup

SERVES 4 TO 6   VEGAN   GF

✔ **WHY THIS RECIPE WORKS:** When done right, lentils should have a delicate, firm-tender bite and deep, earthy flavor. We wanted to take advantage of their appeal in a simple but flavorful curried lentil soup. We starting by sautéing plenty of aromatics, then we added the lentils and cooked them until the vegetables were softened and the lentils had darkened, which helped them hold their shape and boosted their flavor. We deglazed the pan with white wine before adding the liquid and simmering the lentils until tender. Pureeing part of the soup ensured the broth had a luscious consistency. *Lentilles du Puy*, also called French green lentils, are our first choice for this recipe, but brown, black, or regular green lentils will work (note that cooking times will vary depending on the type used). Be sure to sort through the lentils carefully to remove small stones and pebbles, and rinse them before cooking.

2 tablespoons extra-virgin olive oil
1 large onion, chopped fine
2 carrots, peeled and chopped
3 garlic cloves, minced
1 teaspoon curry powder
1 (14.5-ounce) can diced tomatoes, drained
1 bay leaf

1 teaspoon minced fresh thyme
1 cup lentils, picked over and rinsed
  Salt and pepper
½ cup dry white wine
4½ cups vegetable broth
1½ cups water
3 tablespoons minced fresh parsley

1. Heat oil in Dutch oven over medium-high heat until shimmering. Stir in onion and carrots and cook until vegetables begin to soften, about 2 minutes. Stir in garlic and curry and cook until fragrant, about 30 seconds. Stir in tomatoes, bay leaf, and thyme and cook until fragrant, about 30 seconds. Stir in lentils and ¼ teaspoon salt. Cover, reduce heat to medium-low, and cook until vegetables are softened and lentils have darkened, 8 to 10 minutes.

2. Uncover, increase heat to high, add wine, scraping up any browned bits, and bring to simmer. Stir in broth and water and bring to boil. Partially cover pot, reduce heat to low, and simmer until lentils are tender but still hold their shape, 30 to 35 minutes.

3. Discard bay leaf. Puree 3 cups soup in blender until smooth, then return to pot. Warm soup over medium-low heat until hot, about 5 minutes. Stir in parsley and serve.

VARIATION
Curried Lentil Soup with Spinach   VEGAN   GF
Substitute 5 cups baby spinach for parsley; cook spinach in soup, stirring often, until wilted, about 3 minutes.

White Lentil Soup with Coconut Milk and Mustard Greens
SERVES 4   VEGAN   GF

✔ **WHY THIS RECIPE WORKS:** White lentils might be rare in your local market, but throughout India they are used in a variety of stews or are ground into flour for dumplings and thin crêpes. White lentils are skinned and split black lentils; they have a unique flavor similar to mung beans, and they cook to a particularly viscous, starchy texture that makes for a great soup. Our inspiration for this soup came from the spicy, largely vegetarian cuisine of southern India, which uses a lot of garlic, chiles, ginger, and coconut milk. Mustard greens provided the perfect foil to the creamy soup base. We preferred the softer texture and milder flavor of the greens when we wilted them briefly in the microwave before stirring them into the finished soup. For a bright, fresh garnish, we made a chutney-inspired blend of diced fresh tomatoes, lime juice,

White lentils have a particularly delicate bean flavor and cook down to a thick, creamy texture perfect for a satisfying soup.

1. Toast cumin in 8-inch skillet over medium heat until fragrant, about 1 minute; transfer to bowl.

2. Heat oil in Dutch oven over medium heat until shimmering. Add onion and ½ teaspoon salt and cook until onion is softened and lightly browned, 5 to 7 minutes. Stir in half of jalapeño, ginger, and garlic and cook until fragrant and beginning to brown, about 3 minutes. Stir in lentils, broth, bay leaf, turmeric, and 1 teaspoon toasted cumin and bring to simmer. Reduce heat to low, partially cover, and simmer until lentils are tender, 40 to 50 minutes.

3. Meanwhile, microwave mustard greens in bowl until wilted and tender, 3 to 4 minutes; transfer to colander and let drain. In separate bowl, toss tomatoes, lime juice, remaining 1 teaspoon toasted cumin, remaining jalapeño, and ¼ teaspoon salt.

4. Discard bay leaf from soup. Puree ¾ cup soup and coconut milk in blender until smooth, about 30 seconds, then return to pot. Stir in mustard greens and bring to brief simmer. Season with salt and pepper to taste. Top individual portions with tomato mixture, and serve.

and toasted whole cumin seeds. Be sure to rinse the white lentils well—they can come coated in a thin layer of oil. White lentils can be found in well-stocked supermarkets, specialty Indian markets, and online. If you can't find white lentils, substitute *lentilles du Puy*; reduce the lentil cooking time to 25 minutes and note that the soup will be more brothy.

- 2 teaspoons cumin seeds
- 3 tablespoons vegetable oil
- 1 onion, chopped fine
  Salt and pepper
- 2 jalapeño chiles, stemmed, seeded, and minced
- 2 tablespoons grated fresh ginger
- 4 garlic cloves, minced
- 1 cup white lentils, picked over and rinsed
- 5½ cups vegetable broth
- 1 bay leaf
- ½ teaspoon turmeric
- 14 ounces mustard greens, stemmed and chopped
- 3 plum tomatoes, cored and chopped fine
- 1 tablespoons lime juice
- ¾ cup canned coconut milk

Italian Vegetable Stew (Ciambotta)

SERVES 6 TO 8   VEGAN   GF

✔ **WHY THIS RECIPE WORKS:** Italy's *ciambotta* is a ratatouille-like stew, chock-full of veggies, that makes for a hearty one-bowl meal. We wanted to avoid the sorry fate of most recipes—mushy vegetables floating in a weak, one-note broth. To keep the zucchini and peppers from watering down the stew, we used a skillet to cook off their excess water before adding them to the pot. To thicken the broth, we embraced the eggplant's natural tendency to fall apart and simmered it until it completely broke down into the tomato-enriched sauce (microwaving it first helped to rid it of its excess moisture). To deepen the flavor of the stew, we browned the eggplant along with the onion and potato, then sautéed some tomato paste to develop lots of flavorful fond before adding the liquid to the pot. Finally, we found that a quick basil and oregano pesto—whirred together in the food processor and stirred into the zucchini and peppers before we added them to the pot—gave the soup a bold, bright herbal flavor. Serve with crusty bread.

PESTO
- ⅓ cup chopped fresh basil
- ⅓ cup fresh oregano leaves
- 6 garlic cloves, minced
- 2 tablespoons extra-virgin olive oil
- ¼ teaspoon red pepper flakes

STEW

12 ounces eggplant, peeled and cut into
½-inch pieces
Salt
¼ cup extra-virgin olive oil
1 large onion, chopped
1 pound russet potatoes, peeled and cut into
½-inch pieces
2 tablespoons tomato paste
2¼ cups water
1 (28-ounce) can whole peeled tomatoes,
drained with juice reserved and chopped coarse
2 zucchini, halved lengthwise, seeded,
and cut into ½-inch pieces
2 red or yellow bell peppers, stemmed,
seeded, and cut into ½-inch pieces
1 cup shredded fresh basil

1. FOR THE PESTO: Process all ingredients in food processor until finely ground, about 1 minute, scraping down sides of bowl as needed.

2. FOR THE STEW: Toss eggplant with 1½ teaspoons salt in bowl. Line surface of large plate with double layer of coffee filters and lightly spray with vegetable oil spray. Spread eggplant evenly over coffee filters and microwave until eggplant is dry to touch and slightly shriveled, 8 to 12 minutes, tossing halfway through cooking.

3. Heat 2 tablespoons oil in Dutch oven over high heat until shimmering. Add eggplant, onion, and potatoes, and cook, stirring frequently, until eggplant browns, about 2 minutes.

4. Push vegetables to sides of pot. Add 1 tablespoon oil and tomato paste to clearing and cook, stirring often, until brown fond develops on bottom of pot, about 2 minutes. Stir in 2 cups water and tomatoes and their juice, scraping up any browned bits. Bring to boil. Reduce heat to medium, cover, and gently simmer until eggplant is completely broken down and potatoes are tender, 20 to 25 minutes.

5. Meanwhile, heat remaining 1 tablespoon oil in 12-inch skillet over high heat until just smoking. Add zucchini, bell peppers, and ½ teaspoon salt and cook, stirring occasionally, until vegetables are browned and tender, 10 to 12 minutes. Push vegetables to sides of skillet. Add pesto to clearing and cook until fragrant, about 1 minute. Stir pesto into vegetables and transfer to bowl. Off heat, add remaining ¼ cup water to skillet and scrape up any browned bits.

6. Remove Dutch oven from heat and stir in vegetable mixture and water from skillet. Cover and let stew stand for 20 minutes to let flavors blend. Stir in basil, season with salt to taste, and serve.

Mushroom and Farro Stew

SERVES 4 VEGAN

 WHY THIS RECIPE WORKS: A mushroom ragout is a rich, intensely flavorful stew made with a variety of exotic wild mushrooms. We wanted a recipe for a simple mushroom ragout with great savory flavor. Meaty, substantial portobellos plus a mix of assorted mushrooms (usually some combination of white button, cremini, and oyster mushrooms) gave the dish balanced mushroom flavor. A small amount of dried porcini added even more complexity. To make our ragout hearty, we wanted to include a grain. Delicate quinoa disappeared next to the big bites of mushrooms, and wheat berries took too long to cook, but farro was a hit: Its nutty flavor and chewy texture complemented the mushrooms nicely. Tomatoes and a splash of dry Madeira wine cut through the richness. For the best flavor, we prefer to use a combination of white, shiitake, and oyster mushrooms; however, you can choose just one or two varieties if you like. The woody stems of shiitakes are unpleasant to eat so be sure to remove them. Drizzle individual portions with good balsamic vinegar before serving, if desired. For information on farro, see page 185.

1½ cups farro
3½ cups vegetable broth
Salt and pepper
1 pound portobello mushroom caps,
halved and sliced ½ inch wide
18 ounces assorted mushrooms, trimmed and
halved if small or quartered if large
2 tablespoons extra-virgin olive oil
1 onion, chopped fine
½ ounce dried porcini mushrooms, rinsed and minced
3 garlic cloves, minced
1 teaspoon minced fresh thyme or ¼ teaspoon dried
¼ cup dry Madeira
1 (14.5-ounce) can diced tomatoes, drained and chopped
2 tablespoons minced fresh parsley

1. Simmer farro and broth in large saucepan over medium heat until farro is tender and creamy, 20 to 25 minutes. Season with salt and pepper to taste; cover and keep warm.

2. Meanwhile, microwave portobello and assorted mushrooms in covered bowl until tender, 6 to 8 minutes. Drain, reserving mushroom juices.

3. Heat oil in Dutch oven over medium-high heat until shimmering. Add onion and porcini and cook until softened and lightly browned, 5 to 7 minutes. Stir in drained mushrooms and cook, stirring often, until mushrooms are dry and lightly browned, about 5 minutes.

4. Stir in garlic and thyme and cook until fragrant, about 30 seconds. Stir in Madeira and reserved mushroom juices, scraping up any browned bits. Stir in tomatoes and simmer gently until sauce is slightly thickened, about 8 minutes. Off heat, stir in parsley and season with salt and pepper to taste. Portion farro into 4 individual serving bowls and top with mushroom mixture. Serve.

Quinoa and Vegetable Stew

SERVES 6 TO 8 GF

✔ **WHY THIS RECIPE WORKS:** Quinoa stews are common in many South American regions. But authentic recipes call for obscure ingredients, such as annatto powder or Peruvian varieties of potatoes and corn. We set out to make a traditional quinoa stew with an easy-to-navigate ingredient list. We found that paprika has a similar flavor profile to annatto powder; we rounded it out with cumin and coriander. Red bell pepper, tomatoes, red potatoes, sweet corn, and frozen peas were a nice mix of vegetables. We added the quinoa after the potatoes had softened and cooked it until it released starch to help give body to the stew. Finally, we added the traditional garnishes: *queso fresco*, avocado, and cilantro. We like the convenience of prewashed quinoa. If you buy unwashed quinoa (or if you are unsure whether it's washed), be sure to rinse it before cooking to remove its bitter protective coating (called saponin). This stew tends to thicken as it sits; add additional warm vegetable broth as needed before serving to loosen. Do not omit the garnishes; they are important to the flavor of the stew.

- 2 **tablespoons vegetable oil**
- 1 **onion, chopped**
- 1 **red bell pepper, stemmed, seeded, and cut into ½-inch pieces**
- 5 **garlic cloves, minced**
- 1 **tablespoon paprika**
- 2 **teaspoons ground coriander**
- 1½ **teaspoons ground cumin**
- 6 **cups vegetable broth**
- 1 **pound red potatoes, unpeeled, cut into ½-inch pieces**
- 1 **cup prewashed white quinoa**
- 1 **cup fresh or frozen corn**
- 2 **tomatoes, cored and chopped coarse**
- 1 **cup frozen peas**
  Salt and pepper
- 8 **ounces queso fresco or feta cheese, crumbled (2 cups)**
- 1 **avocado, halved, pitted, and diced**
- ½ **cup minced fresh cilantro**

With nutty, chewy quinoa and a mix of fresh vegetables, this South American stew is as nourishing as it is delicious.

1. Heat oil in Dutch oven over medium heat until shimmering. Add onion and bell pepper and cook until softened, 5 to 7 minutes. Stir in garlic, paprika, coriander, and cumin and cook until fragrant, about 30 seconds. Stir in broth and potatoes and bring to boil over high heat. Reduce heat to medium-low and simmer gently for 10 minutes.

2. Stir in quinoa and simmer for 8 minutes. Stir in corn and simmer until potatoes and quinoa are just tender, 5 to 7 minutes. Stir in tomatoes and peas and let heat through, about 2 minutes.

3. Off heat, season with salt and pepper to taste. Sprinkle portions with queso fresco, avocado, and cilantro before serving.

VARIATION

Quinoa and Vegetable Stew with Eggs GF

Serving this stew with a cooked egg on top is a common practice in Peru.

Crack 6 large eggs evenly over top of stew after removing from heat and seasoning with salt and pepper in step 3; cover and let eggs poach off heat until whites have set but yolks are still soft, about 4 minutes. To serve, carefully scoop cooked egg and stew from pot with large spoon.

All About Fresh Chile Peppers

Chiles get their heat from a group of chemical compounds called capsaicinoids, the best known being capsaicin. If you like a lot of heat, you can use the entire chile when cooking. If you prefer a milder dish, remove the ribs and seeds. Here are the chiles we reach for most in the test kitchen.

JALAPEÑO

Perhaps the best-known chile, jalapeños are moderately hot and have a bright, grassy flavor similar to a green bell pepper. They can be dark green or scarlet red.

POBLANO

These chiles are very dark green in color. When ripe, they turn a reddish-brown. They have a fruity, subtly spicy flavor. Thanks to their large size, they are also ideal for stuffing. Poblanos can be found in Latin markets and many supermarkets.

ANAHEIM

With their acidic, lemony flavor, mild spiciness, and crisp texture, these popular chiles can be eaten raw, roasted, or fried; they are also frequently stuffed or used in salsa. Anaheim chiles are medium green in color and have a long, tapered shape.

SERRANO

Similar in appearance to jalapeños but with a slightly more slender shape and brazen heat, these chiles have a fresh, clean, fruity flavor. They are good both raw in salsa and cooked in chilis and curries.

HABANERO

These small, lantern-shaped chiles pack intense heat. They have a floral, fruity flavor that makes them a great addition to marinades, salsas, and cooked dishes. They range from light green to orange to red in color.

THAI

These tiny multicolored chiles look ornamental, but they mean business. They have a flavor similar to that of black peppercorns and a bold, lingering heat. They are best when used sparingly in cooked dishes.

We re-create this traditional Caribbean spicy squash stew by swapping in Swiss chard for the local callaloo leaves.

Caribbean-Style Swiss Chard and Butternut Squash Stew

SERVES 4 **VEGAN** **GF**

✔ **WHY THIS RECIPE WORKS:** Inspired by an earthy, spicy Caribbean stew that pairs the local callaloo leaves with squash in a rich, coconut-infused broth, we set out to re-create a vegetarian version (since it traditionally includes pork). We found that Swiss chard was a good alternative to replicate the earthy, slightly citrusy notes of the callaloo leaves. A combination of fresh chile and cayenne pepper gave the soup a robust heat that balanced the sweetness of the butternut squash. A handful of recipes called for a few dashes of angostura bitters, an aromatic alcohol infused with herbs and citrus. While not a must, the bitters gave the stew a uniquely authentic flavor. We pureed a small portion of the stew to give it a thick consistency and bright green color, while leaving most of the greens and squash in large bites. You can substitute delicata or carnival squash for the butternut squash if you prefer. To make this dish spicier, mince the ribs and seeds from the chile and add them in.

2 tablespoons vegetable oil

2 onions, chopped fine

4 scallions, minced

    Salt

4 garlic cloves, minced

1 habanero or Scotch bonnet chile, stemmed, seeded, and minced

1 teaspoon minced fresh thyme or ¼ teaspoon dried

    Pinch cayenne pepper

3½ cups vegetable broth

2 pounds butternut squash, peeled, seeded, and cut into ½-inch pieces (6 cups)

1 pound Swiss chard, stemmed and cut into 1-inch pieces

1 cup canned coconut milk

    Angostura bitters (optional)

1. Heat oil in Dutch oven over medium heat until shimmering. Stir in onions, scallions, and ½ teaspoon salt and cook until vegetables are softened, 5 to 7 minutes. Stir in garlic, habanero, thyme, and cayenne and cook until fragrant, about 30 seconds.

2. Stir in broth and squash, scraping up any browned bits, and bring to boil. Reduce to gentle simmer and cook for 15 minutes. Stir in chard and continue to simmer until squash and chard are tender, 10 to 15 minutes. Stir in coconut milk and bring to brief simmer.

3. Process 2 cups stew in blender until smooth, about 45 seconds; return to pot. Season with salt and bitters, if using, to taste, and serve.

Prepping Chiles Safely

Wear gloves when working with very hot peppers like habaneros to avoid direct contact with oils that supply heat. Wash your hands, knife, and cutting board well after prepping chiles.

North African Vegetable and Bean Stew

SERVES 6 TO 8 **VEGAN**

✅ **WHY THIS RECIPE WORKS:** North African stews combine heady, potent spices with hearty, filling vegetables, pasta, and beans. We used a combination of chickpeas and butter beans to give our stew a balance of bite, earthiness, and creaminess. For the vegetables, we chose Swiss chard and chunks of carrot. While handmade pasta is standard in North African cooking, it's a bit more work than we had in mind. We opted for dried pasta and chose to use tiny ditalini after tasters found the traditional thin, short noodles difficult to scoop up with a spoon. However, we stuck with tradition when it came to the harissa, a ubiquitous North African ingredient. It's essentially a spicy paste of ground chiles, cumin, coriander, garlic, and olive oil. Spooned over individual bowls of stew, our homemade paste added great spice, heat, and depth of flavor. In fact, tasters like the harissa addition so much that we chose to stir ¼ cup of it directly into the stew with some minced parsley. You can substitute 1 (10-ounce) bag frozen baby lima beans for the butter beans. You can substitute store-bought harissa if you wish, but be aware that spiciness can vary greatly by brand.

1 tablespoon extra-virgin olive oil

1 onion, minced

8 ounces Swiss chard, stems chopped fine, leaves cut into ½-inch pieces

4 garlic cloves, minced

1 teaspoon ground cumin

½ teaspoon paprika

½ teaspoon ground coriander

¼ teaspoon ground cinnamon

2 tablespoons tomato paste

2 tablespoons all-purpose flour

7 cups vegetable broth

2 carrots, peeled and cut into ½-inch pieces

1 (15-ounce) can chickpeas, rinsed

1 (15-ounce) can butter beans, rinsed

½ cup ditalini

⅓ cup minced fresh parsley

1 recipe harissa (page 104)

    Salt and pepper

1. Heat oil in Dutch oven over medium heat until shimmering. Add onion and chard stems and cook until softened, 5 to 7 minutes. Stir in garlic, cumin, paprika, coriander, and

HARISSA

MAKES 6 TABLESPOONS FAST VEGAN GF

Harissa is a traditional Tunisian condiment that is great for flavoring sauces and dressings, or dolloping on hummus, couscous, eggs, and sandwiches.

        5 tablespoons extra-virgin olive oil
    1½ tablespoons paprika
        4 garlic cloves, minced
        2 teaspoons ground coriander
     ¾ teaspoon ground cumin
     ¼ teaspoon cayenne pepper
     ⅛ teaspoon salt

Combine all ingredients in bowl and microwave until bubbling and fragrant, 15 to 30 seconds. Let cool.

cinnamon and cook until fragrant, about 30 seconds. Stir in tomato paste and flour and cook for 1 minute.

2. Stir in broth and carrots and bring to boil. Reduce to gentle simmer and cook for 10 minutes. Stir in chard leaves, chickpeas, butter beans, and pasta and continue to simmer until vegetables and pasta are tender, 10 to 15 minutes.

3. Off heat, stir in parsley and ¼ cup harissa. Season with salt and pepper to taste. Serve, passing remaining harissa separately.

Artichoke, Pepper, and Chickpea Tagine

SERVES 4 TO 6

✔ **WHY THIS RECIPE WORKS:** We wanted a filling tagine packed with big bites of artichokes and peppers and tender chickpeas, flavored with pungent garlic, lots of warm spices, briny olives, and tangy lemon. Using only quick-cooking vegetables kept this tagine from being an all-day affair. First we thawed and drained frozen artichokes, then we sautéed them to drive off any remaining moisture. Next we lightly browned bell peppers and onions. Canned chickpeas needed only to be simmered in the flavorful broth. For the aromatic lemon flavor that distinguishes authentic tagines, we used lots of lemon zest. Finally, we enriched the broth by stirring in Greek yogurt just before serving. To thaw the frozen artichokes quickly, microwave them on high, covered, for 3 to 5 minutes. Frozen artichokes are generally quartered; if yours are not, cut the artichoke hearts into quarters before using. While we prefer

the richer, fuller flavor of whole Greek yogurt, regular plain whole-milk yogurt can be substituted, but the sauce will be slightly thinner. A rasp-style grater makes quick work of turning the garlic into a paste. Serve with Couscous (page 186).

     ¼ cup extra-virgin olive oil, plus extra for serving
        2 (9-ounce) boxes frozen artichokes, thawed and patted dry
        2 yellow or red bell peppers, stemmed, seeded, and cut into matchsticks
        1 onion, halved and sliced ¼ inch thick
        4 (2-inch) strips lemon zest plus 1 teaspoon grated zest (2 lemons)
        8 garlic cloves (6 minced, 2 minced to paste)
        1 tablespoon paprika
     ½ teaspoon ground cumin
     ¼ teaspoon ground ginger
     ¼ teaspoon ground coriander
     ¼ teaspoon ground cinnamon
     ⅛ teaspoon cayenne pepper
        2 tablespoons all-purpose flour
        3 cups vegetable broth
        2 (15-ounce) cans chickpeas, rinsed
     ½ cup pitted kalamata olives, halved
     ½ cup golden raisins
        2 tablespoons honey
     ½ cup plain whole Greek yogurt
     ½ cup minced fresh cilantro
        Salt and pepper

1. Heat 1 tablespoon oil in Dutch oven over medium heat until shimmering. Add artichokes and cook until golden brown, 5 to 7 minutes; transfer to bowl.

2. Add 1 tablespoon oil to now-empty pot and heat over medium heat until shimmering. Stir in bell peppers, onion, and lemon zest strips and cook until vegetables are softened and lightly browned, 5 to 7 minutes. Stir in minced garlic, paprika, cumin, ginger, coriander, cinnamon, and cayenne and cook until fragrant, about 30 seconds. Stir in flour and cook for 1 minute.

3. Gradually whisk in broth, scraping up any browned bits and smoothing out any lumps. Stir in browned artichokes, chickpeas, olives, raisins, and honey and bring to simmer. Cover, reduce to gentle simmer, and cook until vegetables are tender, about 15 minutes.

4. Off heat, remove lemon zest strips. Stir ¼ cup of hot liquid into yogurt to temper, then stir yogurt mixture into pot. Stir in remaining 2 tablespoons oil, garlic paste, cilantro, and grated lemon zest. Season with salt and pepper to taste. Serve, drizzling individual portions lightly with additional olive oil.

Easy Weeknight Chili

SERVES 6   VEGAN   GF

✓ **WHY THIS RECIPE WORKS:** For this vegetarian chili, we were after the hearty texture and bold flavors of a classic meat and bean chili, but we wanted it to be easy enough for a weeknight dinner. For texture, we turned to veggie protein crumbles, which make a great stand-in for ground beef, and they're prep-free; we simply stirred them into the chili with the beans and vegetables. To develop rich, complex flavors without hours of simmering, we bloomed garlic, chili powder, cumin, coriander, and chipotle chile in hot oil before adding the liquids. We used canned tomato sauce for the bulk of the liquid; this gave the chili a thick, velvety texture, complemented by sweet chunks of tomatoes and tender, juicy squash. To make this recipe vegan and/or gluten-free, you must use vegan and/or gluten-free veggie protein crumbles. If using frozen veggie protein crumbles, do not thaw before adding to chili. Veggie protein crumbles can be a bit salty, so season your recipe with a light hand. Serve with minced fresh cilantro, sour cream, and lime wedges.

> 2   tablespoons vegetable oil
> 2   onions, chopped fine
> 1   red bell pepper, stemmed, seeded, and cut into ½-inch pieces
>   Salt and pepper
> 4   garlic cloves, minced
> 1   tablespoon chili powder
> 1½ teaspoons ground cumin
> 1   teaspoon ground coriander
> 1   teaspoon minced canned chipotle chile in adobo sauce
> 2   (15-ounce) cans red kidney beans, rinsed
> 1   (28-ounce) can whole peeled tomatoes, drained with juice reserved, chopped coarse
> 1   (15-ounce) can tomato sauce
> 12 ounces veggie protein crumbles, broken into small pieces
> 1   cup vegetable broth
> 1   zucchini, cut into ½-inch pieces
> 1   yellow summer squash, cut into ½-inch pieces

1. Heat oil in Dutch oven over medium-high heat until shimmering. Add onions, bell pepper, and 1 teaspoon salt and cook until vegetables are softened and lightly browned, 6 to 8 minutes. Stir in garlic, chili powder, cumin, coriander, chipotle, and ½ teaspoon pepper and cook until fragrant, about 30 seconds.

2. Stir in kidney beans, tomatoes and their juice, tomato sauce, veggie protein crumbles, broth, zucchini, and yellow squash and bring to boil. Reduce heat to low and simmer until squash is tender and chili is slightly thickened, 35 to 40 minutes. Season with salt and pepper to taste and serve.

Hearty mushrooms, bulgur, and walnuts plus potent dried chiles make our vegetarian chili ultra-satisfying.

Ultimate Vegetarian Chili

SERVES 6 TO 8   VEGAN

✓ **WHY THIS RECIPE WORKS:** We wanted to develop a vegetarian version of classic chili so flavorful, savory, and satisfying that even meat lovers would enjoy it on its own merits. We'd need to find replacements for the different ways that meat adds depth and flavor to chili. Along with two kinds of beans, bulgur bulked up the chili, giving it a substantial texture. A combination of umami-rich ingredients—soy sauce, dried shiitake mushrooms, and tomatoes—added deep, savory flavor. Walnuts are also high in flavor-boosting glutamates; when we ground some and stirred them in, they contributed even more savoriness plus richness and body. Sautéing the spices in oil helped to bloom their flavors. Finally, for the most important ingredient—the chiles—we chose a combination of dried ancho and New Mexican chiles, toasted them in the oven until fragrant, then ground them and added them in. To substitute chili powder for the dried chiles, grind the shiitakes and oregano and add them to the pot with ¼ cup of chili powder in step 4. We recommend a mix of at least two types of beans, one creamy (such as cannellini or navy) and one earthy (such as pinto, black, or red kidney). For more information on the science behind salt-soaking beans, and how to speed up the process if you're tight on time, see page 204. For a spicier chili, use both jalapeños. Serve the chili with lime wedges, sour cream, diced avocado, chopped red onion, and/or shredded Monterey Jack or cheddar cheese, if desired.

Salt
1 pound (2½ cups) assorted dried beans, picked over and rinsed
2 dried ancho chiles
2 dried New Mexican chiles
½ ounce dried shiitake mushrooms, chopped coarse
4 teaspoons dried oregano
½ cup walnuts, toasted
1 (28-ounce) can diced tomatoes, drained with juice reserved
3 tablespoons tomato paste
1-2 jalapeño chiles, stemmed and coarsely chopped
6 garlic cloves, minced
3 tablespoons soy sauce
¼ cup vegetable oil
2 pounds onions, chopped fine
1 tablespoon ground cumin
7 cups water
⅔ cup medium-grind bulgur
¼ cup minced fresh cilantro

1. Dissolve 3 tablespoons salt in 4 quarts cold water in large container. Add beans and soak at room temperature for at least 8 hours or up to 24 hours. Drain and rinse well.

2. Adjust oven rack to middle position and heat oven to 300 degrees. Arrange anchos and New Mexican chiles on rimmed baking sheet and toast until fragrant and puffed, about 8 minutes. Transfer to plate, let cool for 5 minutes, them remove stems and seeds. Working in batches, grind toasted chiles, mushrooms, and oregano in spice grinder (or with mortar and pestle) until finely ground.

3. Process walnuts in food processor until finely ground, about 30 seconds; transfer to bowl. Process drained tomatoes, tomato paste, jalapeño(s), garlic, and soy sauce in food processor until tomatoes are finely chopped, about 45 seconds.

4. Heat oil in Dutch oven over medium-high heat until shimmering. Add onions and 1¼ teaspoons salt and cook, stirring occasionally, until onions begin to brown, 8 to 10 minutes. Reduce heat to medium, add ground chile mixture and cumin, and cook, stirring constantly, until fragrant, about 1 minute. Stir in rinsed beans and water and bring to boil. Cover pot, transfer to oven, and cook for 45 minutes.

5. Stir in bulgur, ground walnuts, tomato mixture, and reserved tomato juice and continue to cook in oven, covered, until beans are fully tender, about 2 hours.

6. Remove pot from oven, stir well, and let stand, uncovered, for 20 minutes. Stir in cilantro before serving.

Making Ultimate Vegetarian Chili

1. TOAST CHILES: Arrange anchos and New Mexican chiles on rimmed baking sheet. Toast in 300-degree oven until fragrant and puffed, about 8 minutes. Working in batches, grind toasted chiles, mushrooms, and oregano in spice grinder until finely ground.

2. PROCESS INGREDIENTS: Process walnuts in food processor until finely ground, about 30 seconds; transfer to bowl. Process drained tomatoes, tomato paste, jalapeño(s), garlic, and soy sauce in food processor until tomatoes are finely chopped, about 45 seconds.

3. BLOOM CHILES AND SPICES: Cook onions and 1¼ teaspoons salt over medium-high heat until beginning to brown, then reduce heat to medium, add ground chile mixture and cumin, and cook, stirring constantly, until fragrant, about 1 minute.

4. SIMMER CHILI: Stir in rinsed beans and water and bring to boil. Cover pot, transfer to oven, and cook for 45 minutes. Stir in bulgur, ground walnuts, tomato mixture, and reserved tomato juice and continue to cook, covered, until beans are fully tender, about 2 hours.

Black Bean Chili

SERVES 6 TO 8 VEGAN GF

✓ **WHY THIS RECIPE WORKS:** We wanted a hearty black bean chili that boasted tender, well-seasoned beans. Dried beans were essential here, but since we didn't mind if some beans burst, we skipped the lengthy step of salt-soaking. White mushrooms gave the chili meaty flavor. Whole cumin seeds and chipotle added depth and smokiness, and, surprisingly, toasted mustard seeds added a pungency and complexity that tasters loved. A sprinkle of minced cilantro brightened the dish. We strongly prefer the texture and flavor of mustard seeds and cumin seeds in this chili, but you can substitute ½ teaspoon dry mustard and/or ½ teaspoon ground cumin, added to the pot with the chili powder in step 3. Serve with lime wedges, sour cream, shredded cheddar or Monterey Jack cheese, chopped tomatoes, and/or minced onion.

1	pound white mushrooms, trimmed and broken into rough pieces
1	tablespoon mustard seeds
2	teaspoons cumin seeds
3	tablespoons vegetable oil
1	onion, chopped fine
9	garlic cloves, minced
1	tablespoon minced canned chipotle chile in adobo sauce
3	tablespoons chili powder
2½	cups vegetable broth
2½	cups water, plus extra as needed
1	pound (2½ cups) dried black beans, picked over and rinsed
1	tablespoon packed light brown sugar
⅛	teaspoon baking soda
2	bay leaves
1	(28-ounce) can crushed tomatoes
2	red bell peppers, stemmed, seeded, and cut into ½-inch pieces
½	cup minced fresh cilantro
	Salt and pepper

1. Adjust oven rack to lower-middle position and heat oven to 325 degrees. Pulse mushrooms in food processor until coarsely chopped and uniform in size, about 10 pulses.

2. Toast mustard seeds and cumin seeds in Dutch oven over medium heat, stirring constantly, until fragrant, about 1 minute. Stir in oil, onion, and processed mushrooms, cover, and cook until vegetables have released their liquid, about 5 minutes. Uncover and continue to cook until vegetables are browned, 5 to 10 minutes.

All About Dried Chiles

Different types of dried chiles have wildly varying flavor— from earthy and fruit-sweet to bright and acidic. While store-bought chili powder is great for many dishes, it is often worth toasting and grinding dried chiles at home.

CHIPOTLE

We use these more than any other dried chile. Smoky, sweet, and moderately spicy, they are jalapeños that are smoked over aromatic wood and dried. They are sold as is or canned in adobo, a tangy tomato-and-herb sauce. We like canned chipotles; they can be added straight to dishes, and leftovers last up to two weeks in the refrigerator or for months when frozen.

ANCHO

These chiles are dried poblanos and are a dark mahogany red. They have a relatively mild flavor with a slightly fruity sweetness. See page 32 for more information.

ÁRBOL

These Mexican chiles are bright red and quite hot, and have a bright, slightly smoky flavor.

NEW MEXICAN

Also called Colorado chiles, these smooth, brick-red chiles are dried Anaheim peppers. They boast a crisp, acidic, earthy flavor reminiscent of roasted peppers and tomatoes.

BIRD

Common in Asian cuisines, these are dried Thai chiles. They are small but pack a lot of heat.

---

3. Stir in garlic and chipotle and cook until fragrant, about 30 seconds. Stir in chili powder and cook, stirring constantly, until fragrant, about 1 minute. Stir in broth, water, beans, sugar, baking soda, and bay leaves and bring to simmer, skimming as needed. Cover, transfer to oven, and cook for 1 hour.

4. Stir in crushed tomatoes and bell peppers and continue to cook in oven, covered, until beans are fully tender, about 1 hour. (If chili begins to stick to bottom of pot or is too thick, add water as needed.)

5. Remove pot from oven and discard bay leaves. Stir in cilantro and season with salt and pepper to taste. Serve.

Roasted Poblano and White Bean Chili

SERVES 4 TO 6 **VEGAN** **GF**

☑ **WHY THIS RECIPE WORKS:** White bean chili is a fresher, lighter cousin of the thick red chili most Americans know and love. Because there are no tomatoes to mask the other flavors, the fresh chiles take center stage. Banana peppers and Italian peppers were dull and uninspiring. Too-hot serranos were also out. A trio of poblanos, Anaheims, and jalapeños provided the complexity and modest heat we were looking for. We broiled the poblanos and Anaheims to develop depth and smokiness. To keep the flavor of the jalapeños bright, we chopped them in the food processor with onions, then sautéed the mixture. To give our chili a sweet quality, we broiled fresh corn, then added it to the chili just before serving. In addition, simmering the cobs with the beans and chiles created sweet undertones that permeated throughout the chili. To thicken the chili, we processed some of the roasted peppers with a portion of the beans and broth. For more spice, do not remove the ribs and seeds from the chiles. If you can't find Anaheim chiles, add 2 additional poblanos and 1 additional jalapeño to the chili. Serve with sour cream, tortilla chips, and lime wedges.

5 poblano chiles, halved lengthwise, stemmed, and seeded
3 Anaheim chiles, halved lengthwise, stemmed, and seeded
3 tablespoons vegetable oil
3 ears corn, kernels cut from cobs and cobs reserved
2 onions, cut into large pieces
2 jalapeño chiles, stemmed, seeded, and chopped
2 (15-ounce) cans cannellini beans, rinsed
4 cups vegetable broth
6 cloves garlic, minced
1 tablespoon tomato paste
1 tablespoon ground cumin
1½ teaspoons ground coriander
   Salt and pepper
1 (15-ounce) can pinto beans, rinsed
4 scallions, green parts only, sliced thin
¼ cup minced fresh cilantro
1 tablespoon lime juice

1. Adjust oven rack 6 inches from broiler element and heat broiler. Toss poblanos and Anaheims with 1 tablespoon oil and arrange, skin side up, on aluminum foil–lined baking sheet. Broil until chiles begin to blacken and soften, about 10 minutes, rotating pan halfway through broiling. Transfer broiled chiles to bowl, cover with plastic wrap, and let steam until skins peel off easily, 10 to 15 minutes. Peel poblanos and Anaheims, then cut into ½-inch pieces, reserving any accumulated juice.

This white bean chili ditches the tomatoes so the delicate, grassy flavors of the fresh chiles can shine through.

2. Meanwhile, toss corn kernels with 1 tablespoon oil, spread evenly over foil-lined baking sheet, and broil, stirring occasionally, until beginning to brown, 5 to 10 minutes; let cool on baking sheet.

3. In food processor, pulse onions and jalapeños together to consistency of chunky salsa, 6 to 8 pulses; transfer to bowl. In now-empty food processor, process 1 cup cannellini beans, 1 cup broth, and ½ cup chopped roasted chiles and any accumulated juice until smooth, about 45 seconds.

4. Heat remaining 1 tablespoon oil in Dutch oven over medium heat until shimmering. Add onion-jalapeño mixture and cook until softened, 5 to 7 minutes. Stir in garlic, tomato paste, cumin, coriander, and ½ teaspoon salt and cook until tomato paste begins to darken, about 2 minutes. Stir in remaining 3 cups broth, scraping up any browned bits. Stir in pureed chile-bean mixture, remaining roasted chiles, remaining cannellini beans, pinto beans, and corn cobs. Bring to simmer, then reduce heat to low and simmer gently until thickened and flavorful, about 40 minutes.

5. Discard corn cobs. Stir in broiled corn kernels and let heat through, about 1 minute. Off heat, stir in scallions, cilantro, and lime juice and season with salt and pepper to taste. Serve.

Butternut Squash Chili with Quinoa

SERVES 6 VEGAN GF

✓ **WHY THIS RECIPE WORKS:** This stick-to-your-ribs African-style butternut squash chili features bold spices, a hefty amount of garlic and ginger, and aromatic coconut milk. It gets its silky body from a combination of blended peanuts and squash, which we roasted with chopped onions until both the squash and the onions started to char around the edges, giving the soup an incredible backbone of flavor. We pureed a portion of the roasted vegetables with the dry-roasted peanuts for a rich, smooth base to our soup. We sautéed sweet bell pepper and spicy jalapeño and briefly bloomed the warm spices before adding in the liquid. A combination of diced tomatoes and coconut milk made a creamy but bright broth, and nutty quinoa added heartiness and a subtle pop of texture. If you buy unwashed quinoa (or if you are unsure whether it's washed), be sure to rinse it before cooking to remove its bitter protective coating (called saponin). For more spice, include the ribs and seeds from the jalapeño. Serve with hot sauce.

Blending peanuts with some of the roasted squash gives this chili silky body and a backbone of intense sweet, nutty flavor.

- 3 **pounds butternut squash, peeled, seeded, and cut into ½-inch pieces (9 cups)**
- 2 **onions, cut into ½-inch pieces**
- 6 **tablespoons vegetable oil**
- **Salt and pepper**
- 5 **cups water, plus extra as needed**
- ¾ **cup dry-roasted salted peanuts, chopped**
- 1 **large red bell pepper, stemmed, seeded, and cut into ½-inch pieces**
- 1 **jalapeño chile, stemmed, seeded, and minced**
- 3 **garlic cloves, minced**
- 2 **tablespoons grated fresh ginger**
- ¾ **teaspoon ground cinnamon**
- ¾ **teaspoon ground coriander**
- ½ **teaspoon cayenne pepper**
- 1 **(14.5-ounce) can diced tomatoes**
- 1 **(13.5-ounce) can coconut milk**
- 1 **cup prewashed white quinoa**
- ¼ **cup minced fresh cilantro or parsley**

1. Adjust oven racks to upper-middle and lower-middle positions and heat oven to 450 degrees. Toss squash, onions, ¼ cup oil, 1 teaspoon salt, and ½ teaspoon pepper together in bowl. Spread vegetables out in even layer over 2 rimmed baking sheets. Roast vegetables, stirring occasionally, until tender, 45 to 50 minutes, rotating and switching sheets halfway through roasting.

2. In food processor, process ½ cup roasted vegetables, 2 cups water, and ¼ cup peanuts until smooth, about 1 minute.

3. Heat remaining 2 tablespoons oil in Dutch oven over medium-high heat until shimmering. Add bell pepper, jalapeño, and 2 teaspoons salt and cook until peppers start to soften, about 5 minutes. Stir in garlic, ginger, cinnamon, coriander, cayenne, and ¾ teaspoon pepper, and cook until fragrant, about 30 seconds.

4. Stir in remaining 3 cups water, tomatoes and their juice, coconut milk, and quinoa and bring to boil. Reduce heat to low and simmer, stirring occasionally, until quinoa is tender, about 15 minutes.

5. Stir in pureed vegetable mixture and remaining roasted vegetables and let heat through, about 3 minutes. Season with salt and pepper to taste. Adjust consistency with additional hot water as needed. Sprinkle individual portions with cilantro and remaining ½ cup peanuts and serve.

CHAPTER 3

Pasta, Noodles, and Dumplings

■ FAST (Less than 45 minutes start to finish)   ■ VEGAN   ■ GLUTEN-FREE
Photos: Fresh Fettuccine with Tomato–Browned Butter Sauce;
Soba Noodles with Roasted Eggplant and Sesame

SIMPLE TOMATO SAUCES

There are infinite variations on the indispensable combination of pasta and tomato sauce. Here are a few of our favorite basic tomato sauces. All of these sauces make 4 cups, enough to sauce 1 pound of pasta. Serve with grated Parmesan cheese.

No-Cook Fresh Tomato Sauce FAST VEGAN GF

The success of this dish depends on using ripe, flavorful tomatoes. This sauce works well with penne, rotini, or campanelle.

- ¼ cup extra-virgin olive oil
- 2 teaspoons lemon juice, plus extra as needed
- 1 shallot, minced
- 1 garlic clove, minced
    Salt and pepper
    Sugar
- 2 pounds very ripe tomatoes, cored and cut into ½-inch pieces
- 3 tablespoons chopped fresh basil

Stir oil, lemon juice, shallot, garlic, 1 teaspoon salt, ¼ teaspoon pepper, and pinch sugar together in large bowl. Stir in tomatoes and let marinate until very soft and flavorful, at least 30 minutes and up to 3 hours. Before serving, stir in basil and season with salt, pepper, sugar, and extra lemon juice to taste. When tossing sauce with cooked pasta, add some pasta cooking water as needed to adjust consistency.

Quick Tomato Sauce
FAST VEGAN GF

This sauce works well with any type of pasta.

- 3 tablespoons extra-virgin olive oil
- 3 garlic cloves, minced
- 1 (28-ounce) can crushed tomatoes
- 1 (14.5-ounce) can diced tomatoes
- 3 tablespoons chopped fresh basil
- ¼ teaspoon sugar
    Salt and pepper

Cook oil and garlic in medium saucepan over medium heat, stirring often, until fragrant but not browned, about 2 min-

utes. Stir in tomatoes and juice. Bring to simmer and cook until slightly thickened, 15 to 20 minutes. Off heat, stir in basil and sugar. Season with salt and pepper to taste. When tossing sauce with cooked pasta, add some pasta cooking water as needed to adjust consistency.

Classic Marinara Sauce
VEGAN GF

This sauce works well with any type of pasta. If you prefer a chunkier sauce, give it just 3 or 4 pulses in the food processor in step 4.

- 2 (28-ounce) cans whole peeled tomatoes
- 3 tablespoons extra-virgin olive oil
- 1 onion, chopped fine
- 2 garlic cloves, minced
- 2 teaspoons minced fresh oregano or ½ teaspoon dried
- ⅓ cup dry red wine
- 3 tablespoons chopped fresh basil
    Salt and pepper
    Sugar

1. Drain tomatoes in fine-mesh strainer set over large bowl. Using hands, open tomatoes and remove and discard seeds and fibrous cores; let tomatoes drain, about 5 minutes. Reserve ¾ cup tomatoes separately. Reserve 2½ cups drained tomato juice; discard extra juice.

2. Heat 2 tablespoons oil in 12-inch skillet over medium heat until shimmering. Add onion and cook until softened and lightly browned, 5 to 7 minutes. Stir in garlic and oregano and cook until fragrant, about 30 seconds. Stir in remaining drained tomatoes and increase heat to medium-high. Cook, stirring often, until liquid has evaporated and tomatoes begin to brown and stick to pan, 10 to 12 minutes.

3. Stir in wine and cook until thick and syrupy, about 1 minute. Stir in reserved tomato juice, scraping up any browned bits. Bring to simmer and cook, stirring occasionally, until sauce is thickened, 8 to 10 minutes.

4. Transfer sauce to food processor, add reserved ¾ cup tomatoes, and pulse until slightly chunky, about 8 pulses. Return sauce to now-empty skillet, stir in basil and remaining 1 tablespoon oil, and season with salt, pepper, and sugar to taste. When tossing sauce with cooked pasta, add some pasta cooking water as needed to adjust consistency.

Tomato Sauce with Vodka and Cream FAST GF

This sauce works well with any type or shape of pasta but is classically served with penne.

- 3 tablespoons extra-virgin olive oil
- 3 garlic cloves, minced
- ½ teaspoon red pepper flakes
- 1 (28-ounce) can crushed tomatoes
- 1 (14.5-ounce) can diced tomatoes
- ⅓ cup vodka
- 1 cup heavy cream
    Salt and pepper

Cook oil, garlic, and pepper flakes in medium saucepan over medium heat, stirring often, until fragrant but not browned, about 2 minutes. Stir in crushed and diced tomatoes and their juice. Bring to simmer and cook for 10 minutes. Stir in vodka and continue to simmer until slightly thickened, 5 to 10 minutes. Stir in cream and simmer until heated through, about 3 minutes. Season with salt and pepper to taste. When tossing sauce with cooked pasta, add some pasta cooking water as needed to adjust consistency.

Penne and Fresh Tomato Sauce with Fennel and Orange

SERVES 4 TO 6 **FAST** **VEGAN** **GF**

✔ **WHY THIS RECIPE WORKS:** To capitalize on the full, lively flavor of great seasonal tomatoes, we found that any type of fresh tomato tasted fine when skinned, seeded, chopped, and simmered in a skillet with garlic and olive oil—as long as it was ripe. To give our fresh tomato sauce an interesting twist, we wanted to balance the tomatoes with some surprising flavors. After testing a variety of ingredients, we chose piney fennel and potent saffron, fruity orange zest, and red pepper flakes for a subtle heat, using them judiciously to keep the sauce in balance. Simmering the sauce just until the tomatoes broke down into a chunky sauce kept the flavor of the tomatoes fresh and bright and made our recipe quick enough for a weeknight. The success of this dish depends on using ripe, flavorful tomatoes. In order for this recipe to be gluten-free, you must use gluten-free pasta.

¼ cup extra-virgin olive oil

1 fennel bulb, stalks discarded, bulb halved, cored, and cut into ¼-inch pieces

2 garlic cloves, minced

2 (3-inch) strips orange zest plus 3 tablespoons juice

½ teaspoon fennel seeds, crushed

⅛ teaspoon red pepper flakes

Pinch saffron, crumbled (optional)

3 pounds tomatoes, cored, peeled, seeded, and cut into ½-inch pieces

1 pound penne

Salt and pepper

3 tablespoons chopped fresh basil

Sugar

1. Heat 2 tablespoons oil in 12-inch skillet over medium-high heat until shimmering. Add fennel pieces and cook until softened and lightly browned, 5 to 7 minutes. Stir in garlic, orange zest, fennel seeds, pepper flakes, and saffron, if using, and cook until fragrant, about 30 seconds. Stir in tomatoes and cook until tomato pieces lose their shape and make chunky sauce, about 10 minutes. Discard orange zest.

2. Meanwhile, bring 4 quarts water to boil in large pot. Add pasta and 1 tablespoon salt and cook, stirring often, until al dente. Reserve ½ cup cooking water, then drain pasta and return it to pot.

3. Stir orange juice, basil, ¼ teaspoon salt, and ⅛ teaspoon pepper into sauce and season with sugar to taste. Add sauce and remaining 2 tablespoons oil to pasta and toss to combine. Add reserved cooking water as needed to adjust consistency. Serve.

Peeling Tomatoes

1. Cut out stem and core of each tomato, then score small X at base.

2. Lower tomatoes into boiling water and simmer until skins loosen, 30 to 60 seconds.

3. Use paring knife to remove strips of loosened skin starting at X on base of each tomato.

VARIATION

Penne and Fresh Tomato Sauce with Mint, Feta, and Spinach

SERVES 4 TO 6 **FAST** **GF**

The success of this dish depends on using ripe, flavorful tomatoes. You can substitute 1 tablespoon chopped fresh oregano for the mint. In order for this recipe to be gluten-free, you must use gluten-free pasta.

3 tablespoons extra-virgin olive oil

2 garlic cloves, minced

3 pounds tomatoes, cored, peeled, seeded, and cut into ½-inch pieces

5 ounces (5 cups) baby spinach

1 pound penne

Salt and pepper

2 tablespoons chopped fresh mint

2 tablespoons lemon juice

Sugar

4 ounces feta cheese, crumbled (1 cup)

1. Cook 2 tablespoons oil and garlic in 12-inch skillet over medium-high heat, stirring often, until garlic is light golden, about 3 minutes. Stir in tomatoes and cook until tomato pieces begin to lose their shape, about 8 minutes. Stir in spinach, 1 handful at a time, and cook until spinach is wilted and tomatoes have made chunky sauce, about 2 minutes.

2. Meanwhile, bring 4 quarts water to boil in large pot. Add pasta and 1 tablespoon salt and cook, stirring often, until al dente. Reserve ½ cup cooking water, then drain pasta and return it to pot.

3. Stir mint, lemon juice, ¼ teaspoon salt, and ⅛ teaspoon pepper into sauce and season with sugar to taste. Add sauce and remaining 1 tablespoon oil to pasta and toss to combine. Add reserved cooking water as needed to adjust consistency. Serve with feta.

Fusilli with Ricotta and Spinach
SERVES 4 TO 6 `FAST` `GF`

✓ **WHY THIS RECIPE WORKS:** Pasta like manicotti and tortellini are often stuffed with a creamy mixture of ricotta and fresh spinach. The combination is irresistible, but making fresh stuffed pasta is a work-intensive project. We decided to turn this dish inside out for a weeknight meal that would make the most of these classic flavors. In order to keep the ricotta texture and flavor distinct (and to prevent the graininess that comes from heating ricotta), we opted to add most of it in dollops over the finished dish rather than fold it into the sauce. To keep the spinach bright and green (and eliminate the tedious task of blanching and squeezing it dry), we cooked it very briefly in the pot along with the pasta. For complexity and balance, we added lots of minced garlic, along with cayenne, nutmeg, lemon juice and zest, and Parmesan cheese, to the sauce. In order for this recipe to be gluten-free, you must use gluten-free pasta.

1 **pound fusilli**
   Salt and pepper
1 **pound (16 cups) baby spinach, chopped coarse**
3 **tablespoons extra-virgin olive oil**
4 **garlic cloves, minced**
¼ **teaspoon ground nutmeg**
⅛ **teaspoon cayenne pepper**
11 **ounces (1⅓ cups) whole-milk ricotta cheese**
¼ **cup heavy cream**
1 **teaspoon grated lemon zest plus 2 teaspoons juice**
1 **ounce Parmesan cheese, grated (½ cup),**
   plus extra for serving

To avoid grainy ricotta, toss the pasta with just a little cheese and cream, then drop large spoonfuls of cheese over the bowl.

1. Bring 4 quarts water to boil in large pot. Add pasta and 1 tablespoon salt and cook, stirring often, until al dente. Stir spinach into pot with pasta and cook for 30 seconds. Reserve 1 cup cooking water, then drain pasta-spinach mixture and return it to pot.

2. Meanwhile, heat 2 tablespoons oil, garlic, nutmeg, and cayenne in small saucepan over medium heat until fragrant, about 1 minute. Off heat, whisk in ⅓ cup ricotta, cream, lemon zest and juice, and ¾ teaspoon salt until smooth. In bowl, whisk remaining 1 cup ricotta, remaining 1 tablespoon oil, ¼ teaspoon pepper, and ⅛ teaspoon salt together until smooth.

3. Add cooked ricotta-cream mixture and Parmesan to pasta and toss to combine. Let pasta rest, tossing frequently, until sauce has thickened slightly and coats pasta, 2 to 4 minutes. Add reserved cooking water as needed to adjust consistency. Transfer pasta to serving platter and dot evenly with seasoned ricotta mixture. Serve with extra Parmesan.

Mushroom Bolognese

SERVES 4 TO 6 `GF`

♥ **WHY THIS RECIPE WORKS:** We wanted to create a vegetarian pasta sauce that mimicked the rich, long-cooked flavor and hearty texture of Bolognese. Traditional Bolognese sauce gets its rich flavor from a combination of several types of meat, so we turned to two types of mushrooms to replicate that complexity: Dried porcini delivered depth of flavor while 2 pounds of fresh cremini gave the sauce a satisfying, substantial texture. To further round out the sauce's savory flavor, we added two umami-rich ingredients: soy sauce and tomato paste. To make prep easy, we used the food processor both to chop the cremini roughly and then to finely chop the onion and carrot. Pulsing whole canned tomatoes in the food processor allowed us to get just the right texture. We also used red wine to lend richness and depth and a little sugar for some balancing sweetness. A dash of heavy cream at the end rounded out the sauce and gave it a decadent silkiness. Cremini mushrooms are also known as baby bella mushrooms. In order for this recipe to be gluten-free, you must use gluten-free pasta and gluten-free soy sauce or tamari.

We make a truly meaty mushroom bolognese with lots of cremini, plus dried porcini, soy sauce, and tomato paste.

2 pounds cremini mushrooms, trimmed and quartered
1 carrot, peeled and chopped
1 small onion, chopped
1 (28-ounce) can whole peeled tomatoes
3 tablespoons unsalted butter
½ ounce dried porcini mushrooms, rinsed and minced
3 garlic cloves, minced
1 teaspoon sugar
2 tablespoons tomato paste
1 cup dry red wine
½ cup vegetable broth
1 tablespoon soy sauce
Salt and pepper
3 tablespoons heavy cream
1 pound fettuccine or linguine
Grated Parmesan cheese

1. Working in batches, pulse cremini mushrooms in food processor until pieces are no larger than ½ inch, 5 to 7 pulses; transfer to large bowl. Pulse carrot and onion in now-empty processor until chopped fine, 5 to 7 pulses; transfer to bowl with mushrooms. Pulse tomatoes and their juice in now-empty processor until chopped fine, 6 to 8 pulses; set aside separately.

2. Melt butter in Dutch oven over medium heat. Add processed vegetables and porcini mushrooms, cover, and cook, stirring occasionally, until they release their liquid, about 5 minutes. Uncover, increase heat to medium-high, and cook until liquid has evaporated and vegetables begin to brown, 12 to 15 minutes.

3. Stir in garlic and sugar and cook until fragrant, about 30 seconds. Stir in tomato paste and cook for 1 minute. Stir in wine and simmer until nearly evaporated, about 5 minutes.

4. Stir in processed tomatoes, vegetable broth, soy sauce, ½ teaspoon salt, and ¼ teaspoon pepper, and bring to simmer. Reduce heat to medium-low and simmer until sauce has thickened but is still moist, 8 to 10 minutes. Off heat, stir in cream.

5. Meanwhile, bring 4 quarts water to boil in large pot. Add pasta and 1 tablespoon salt and cook, stirring often, until al dente. Reserve ½ cup cooking water, then drain pasta and return it to pot. Add sauce and toss to combine. Season with salt and pepper to taste, and adjust consistency with reserved cooking water as needed. Serve with Parmesan.

Vegetarian Spaghetti and Meatballs

SERVES 4 TO 6

✔ **WHY THIS RECIPE WORKS:** Vegetarian meatballs should be tender, moist, and savory, but they're usually either dry and crumbly or soft and mushy, with overwhelming off-flavors. To make a better vegetarian meatball, we first tried to use meaty chopped mushrooms, but tasters found their flavor overwhelming. Veggie protein crumbles, made of texturized soy protein, turned out to be the solution. They gave our meatballs structure, a nice chew, and great savory flavor. Lots of garlic and some onion and rosemary rounded out the flavors. Toasted ground pine nuts added more texture and, along with some grated Parmesan, nutty richness. Because the protein crumbles have less fat and protein than ground meat, we used a combination of a panade of bread and milk and 2 eggs to bind the meatballs. Rather than trying to pan-fry the delicate meatballs, we brushed them with oil and baked them on a sheet tray until they had a nice browned crust. Then we made a simple, fresh-tasting sauce to complement the tender, savory meatballs. Any brand of veggie protein crumbles will work here; we've had good luck using Lightlife Smart Ground Original. If using frozen veggie protein crumbles, do not thaw them before adding them to the food processor.

MEATBALLS

- 2 tablespoons unsalted butter
- ½ onion, chopped fine
- 2 teaspoons chopped fresh rosemary, or ½ teaspoon dried

Salt and pepper
- 4 garlic cloves, minced
- 12 ounces veggie protein crumbles
- 2 large eggs
- 2 slices hearty white sandwich bread, crusts removed, torn into pieces
- ¼ cup milk
- ¼ cup pine nuts, toasted
- 1 ounce Parmesan cheese, grated (½ cup), plus extra for serving

SAUCE AND PASTA

- 2 tablespoons extra-virgin olive oil
- 2 garlic cloves, minced
- 2 (28-ounce) cans whole peeled tomatoes
- ¼ cup chopped fresh basil
  Salt and pepper
- 1 pound spaghetti

1. FOR THE MEATBALLS: Adjust oven rack to upper-middle position and heat oven to 400 degrees. Melt butter in 12-inch nonstick skillet over medium-high heat. Add onion, rosemary, and ¼ teaspoon salt and cook, stirring occasionally, until onions are well browned, soft, and caramelized, 8 to 10 minutes. Stir in garlic and cook until fragrant, about 30 seconds; let mixture cool for 10 minutes.

2. Process cooked onion mixture, veggie protein crumbles, eggs, bread, 2 tablespoons milk, pine nuts, and Parmesan together in food processor until mixture is well combined and has a uniform texture, scraping down bowl as needed, about 20 seconds. If mixture is too dry or does not come

Making Vegetarian Spaghetti and Meatballs

1. BROWN AROMATICS: Cook onion, rosemary, and salt, stirring occasionally, until onions are browned, 8 to 10 minutes. Stir in garlic and cook until fragrant, about 30 seconds.

2. PROCESS MIXTURE: Process onion mixture, veggie protein crumbles, eggs, bread, milk, pine nuts, and Parmesan together, scraping down bowl as needed, until mixture has sticky texture, about 15 seconds.

3. SHAPE AND BAKE MEATBALLS: Shape mixture into 20 meatballs (about 1½ tablespoons each), space evenly on prepared baking sheet, and bake until browned and firm, about 30 minutes.

4. MAKE SAUCE: Cook oil and garlic over medium heat until golden, 1 to 2 minutes. Add tomatoes and mash until coarsely chopped. Bring to boil, then reduce to simmer and cook gently until sauce thickens, about 20 minutes.

together, add 1 tablespoon milk at a time until mixture is desired consistency.

3. Shape mixture into 20 meatballs (about 1½ tablespoons each), and space evenly on lightly oiled baking sheet. Bake meatballs until browned and firm, about 30 minutes.

4. FOR THE SAUCE AND PASTA: Cook oil and garlic in Dutch oven over medium heat until garlic is golden, 1 to 2 minutes. Add tomatoes and mash with a potato masher until coarsely chopped. Bring to boil and simmer gently until sauce thickens, about 20 minutes. Stir in basil; add salt and pepper to taste.

5. Reserve 2 cups sauce separately. Gently add cooked meatballs to Dutch oven and coat thoroughly with remaining sauce.

6. Bring 4 quarts water to boil in large pot. Add pasta and 1 tablespoon salt and cook, stirring often, until al dente. Reserve ½ cup cooking water, then drain pasta, and return it to pot. Add reserved sauce and toss to combine, adding reserved cooking water as needed to adjust consistency. Top individual portions with meatballs and remaining sauce. Serve with extra Parmesan.

Gemelli with Pesto, Potatoes, and Green Beans

SERVES 6 GF

✔ **WHY THIS RECIPE WORKS:** The idea of serving two starches together might seem unusual, but this dish from the Italian region of Liguria is a classic way to serve pesto. The starch from the potatoes lends body to the sauce, and the tender green beans add color and flavor. We started developing our version by testing various types of potatoes and found that red potatoes made the creamiest sauce. Some traditional recipes call for cooking the potatoes, green beans, and pasta simultaneously in the same pot, but that method consistently resulted in one or more elements being overcooked. Cooking them separately made the dish more foolproof. You will need a 10-inch skillet with a tight-fitting lid for this recipe. If gemelli is unavailable, penne or rigatoni make a good substitute. Use red potatoes measuring 3 inches or more in diameter. In order for this recipe to be gluten-free, you must use gluten-free pasta.

¼ **cup pine nuts**
3 **garlic cloves, unpeeled**
2 **cups fresh basil leaves**
1 **ounce Parmesan cheese, grated (½ cup)**
7 **tablespoons extra-virgin olive oil**
   Salt and pepper

This traditional Italian dish combines tender green beans and bright herb pesto with hearty potatoes and pasta.

12 **ounces green beans, trimmed and cut into 1½-inch lengths**
1 **pound large red potatoes, peeled and cut into ½-inch pieces**
1 **pound gemelli**
2 **tablespoons unsalted butter, cut into ½-inch pieces and chilled**
1 **tablespoon lemon juice**

1. Toast pine nuts and garlic in 10-inch skillet over medium heat, stirring often, until pine nuts are golden and garlic darkens slightly, 3 to 5 minutes. Transfer to bowl, let cool slightly, then peel and chop garlic. Process pine nuts, garlic, basil, Parmesan, oil, and ½ teaspoon salt in food processor until smooth, about 1 minute; set aside.

2. Bring ½ cup water and ¼ teaspoon salt to boil in now-empty skillet over medium heat. Add green beans, cover, and cook until tender, 5 to 8 minutes. Drain green beans and transfer to rimmed baking sheet.

3. Meanwhile, bring 3 quarts water to boil in large pot. Add potatoes and 1 tablespoon salt and cook until potatoes are tender but still hold their shape, 9 to 12 minutes. Using slotted spoon, transfer potatoes to sheet with beans.

4. Add pasta to boiling water and cook, stirring often, until al dente. Set colander in large bowl. Drain gemelli, reserving cooking liquid, then return pasta to pot. Add pesto, potatoes and green beans, butter, lemon juice, ¼ cup reserved cooking water, and ½ teaspoon pepper and stir vigorously with rubber spatula until sauce takes on creamy appearance. Season with salt and pepper to taste, and add remaining cooking water as needed to adjust consistency. Serve.

Farfalle and Summer Squash with Tomatoes, Basil, and Pine Nuts

SERVES 4 TO 6   `GF`

✔ **WHY THIS RECIPE WORKS:** For a pasta and squash recipe that would marry the two ingredients in a light, flavorful dish, we kept the skin on the squash to keep the pieces intact, then salted the squash to release excess liquid and concentrate the vegetable's flavor. This step was essential to keep the sauce from ending up watery and bland. It also allowed us to get good browning; it took just 5 minutes in a hot skillet to lightly char each batch. To accompany the squash, we chose halved grape tomatoes, fresh basil, and crunchy pine nuts. We finished the sauce with acidic balsamic vinegar to give it a kick and paired the sauce with farfalle to best trap the flavor-packed ingredients. A combination of zucchini and summer squash makes for a nice mix of colors, but either may be used exclusively if desired. We prefer kosher salt because residual grains are easily wiped away from the squash. If using table salt, be sure to reduce all of the salt amounts in the recipe by half. If farfalle is unavailable, campanelle or fusilli make a good substitute. In order for this recipe to be gluten-free, you must use gluten-free pasta.

  2 **pounds zucchini and/or summer squash, halved lengthwise and sliced ½ inch thick**
    Kosher salt and pepper
  5 **tablespoons extra-virgin olive oil**
  3 **garlic cloves, minced**
  ½ **teaspoon red pepper flakes**
  1 **pound farfalle**
 12 **ounces grape tomatoes, halved**
  ½ **cup chopped fresh basil**
  ¼ **cup pine nuts, toasted**
  2 **tablespoons balsamic vinegar**
    Grated Parmesan cheese

Salting the squash to remove some moisture allows us to get lots of flavorful browning, enriching this bright, summery dish.

1. Toss squash with 1 tablespoon salt in colander and let drain for 30 minutes. Pat squash dry with paper towels and carefully wipe away any residual salt.

2. Heat 1 tablespoon oil in 12-inch nonstick skillet over high heat until just smoking. Add half of squash and cook, stirring occasionally, until golden brown and slightly charred, 5 to 7 minutes, reducing heat if skillet begins to scorch; transfer to large plate. Repeat with 1 tablespoon oil and remaining squash; transfer to plate.

3. Heat 1 tablespoon oil in now-empty skillet over medium heat until shimmering. Add garlic and pepper flakes and cook until fragrant, about 30 seconds. Stir in squash and cook until heated through, about 30 seconds.

4. Meanwhile, bring 4 quarts water to boil in large pot. Add pasta and 2 tablespoons salt and cook, stirring often, until al dente. Reserve ½ cup cooking water, then drain pasta and return it to pot. Add squash mixture, tomatoes, basil, pine nuts, vinegar, and remaining 2 tablespoons oil, and toss to combine. Season with salt and pepper to taste, and add reserved cooking water as needed to adjust consistency. Serve with Parmesan.

Farfalle and Summer Squash with Lemon, Capers, and Goat Cheese

SERVES 4 TO 6 `GF`

A combination of zucchini and summer squash makes for a nice mix of colors, but either may be used exclusively if desired. We prefer kosher salt because residual grains are easily wiped away from the squash. If using table salt, be sure to reduce all of the salt amounts in the recipe by half. If farfalle is unavailable, campanelle or fusilli make a good substitute. In order for this recipe to be gluten-free, you must use gluten-free pasta.

- 2 **pounds zucchini and/or summer squash, halved lengthwise and sliced ½ inch thick**
  Kosher salt and pepper
- 5 **tablespoons extra-virgin olive oil**
- 3 **large shallots, chopped fine**
- ¼ **cup capers, rinsed and chopped**
- 2 **teaspoons grated lemon zest plus 2 tablespoons juice**
- 1 **pound farfalle**
- 12 **ounces grape tomatoes, halved**
- ¼ **cup chopped fresh parsley**
- 4 **ounces goat cheese, crumbled (1 cup)**

1. Toss squash with 1 tablespoon salt in colander and let drain for 30 minutes. Pat squash dry with paper towels and carefully wipe away any residual salt.

2. Heat 1 tablespoon oil in 12-inch nonstick skillet over high heat until just smoking. Add half of squash and cook, stirring occasionally, until golden brown and slightly charred, 5 to 7 minutes, reducing heat if skillet begins to scorch; transfer to large plate. Repeat with 1 tablespoon oil and remaining squash; transfer to plate.

3. Heat 1 tablespoon oil in now-empty skillet over medium heat until shimmering. Add shallots and cook until softened and lightly browned, 2 to 4 minutes. Stir in capers, lemon zest, ½ teaspoon pepper, and squash, and cook until flavors meld, about 30 seconds.

4. Meanwhile, bring 4 quarts water to boil in large pot. Add pasta and 2 tablespoons salt and cook, stirring often, until al dente. Reserve ½ cup cooking water, then drain pasta and return it to pot. Add squash mixture, lemon juice, tomatoes, parsley, and remaining 2 tablespoons oil, and toss to combine. Season with salt and pepper to taste, and add reserved cooking water as needed to adjust consistency. Sprinkle individual portions with goat cheese and serve.

Farfalle and Summer Squash with Tomatoes, Olives, and Feta

SERVES 4 TO 6 `GF`

A combination of zucchini and summer squash makes for a nice mix of colors, but either may be used exclusively if desired. We prefer kosher salt because residual grains are easily wiped away from the squash. If using table salt, be sure to reduce all of the salt amounts in the recipe by half. If farfalle is unavailable, campanelle or fusilli make a good substitute. In order for this recipe to be gluten-free, you must use gluten-free pasta.

- 2 **pounds zucchini and/or summer squash, halved lengthwise and sliced ½ inch thick**
  Kosher salt and pepper
- 5 **tablespoons extra-virgin olive oil**
- 1 **red onion, chopped fine**
- 3 **garlic cloves, minced**
- 1 **teaspoon grated lemon zest plus 1 tablespoon juice**
- 1 **pound farfalle**
- 12 **ounces grape tomatoes, halved**
- ½ **cup pitted kalamata olives, quartered**
- ¼ **cup chopped fresh mint**
- 2 **teaspoons red wine vinegar**
- 4 **ounces feta cheese, crumbled (1 cup)**

1. Toss squash with 1 tablespoon salt in colander and let drain for 30 minutes. Pat squash dry with paper towels and carefully wipe away any residual salt.

2. Heat 1 tablespoon oil in 12-inch nonstick skillet over high heat until just smoking. Add half of squash and cook, stirring occasionally, until golden brown and slightly charred, 5 to 7 minutes, reducing heat if skillet begins to scorch; transfer to large plate. Repeat with 1 tablespoon oil and remaining squash; transfer to plate.

3. Heat 1 tablespoon oil in now-empty skillet over medium heat until shimmering. Add onion and cook until softened and lightly browned, 5 to 7 minutes. Stir in garlic, lemon zest, and ½ teaspoon pepper, and cook until fragrant, about 30 seconds. Stir in squash and cook until heated through, about 30 seconds.

4. Meanwhile, bring 4 quarts water to boil in large pot. Add pasta and 2 tablespoons salt and cook, stirring often, until al dente. Reserve ½ cup cooking water, then drain pasta and return it to pot. Add squash mixture, lemon juice, tomatoes, olives, mint, vinegar, and remaining 2 tablespoons oil, and toss to combine. Season with salt and pepper to taste, and add reserved cooking water as needed to adjust consistency. Sprinkle individual portions with feta and serve.

Pairing Pasta Shapes and Sauces

Pairing a pasta shape with the right sauce might be an art form in Italy, but we think there's only one basic rule to follow: Thick, chunky sauces go with short pastas, and thin, smooth, or light sauces with strand pasta. (Of course, there are a few exceptions—but that's where the art comes in.) Although we specify pasta shapes for every recipe in this book, you should feel free to substitute other pasta shapes as long as you're following this one basic rule. Here are the most common pastas we use, along with what their names really mean, plus some measuring tips.

SHORT PASTAS

Short tubular or molded pasta shapes do an excellent job of trapping and holding on to chunky sauces in dishes such as our Penne and Fresh Tomato Sauce with Fennel and Orange (page 113). Sauces with very large chunks are best with rigatoni or other large tubes. Sauces with small chunks pair better with fusilli or penne.

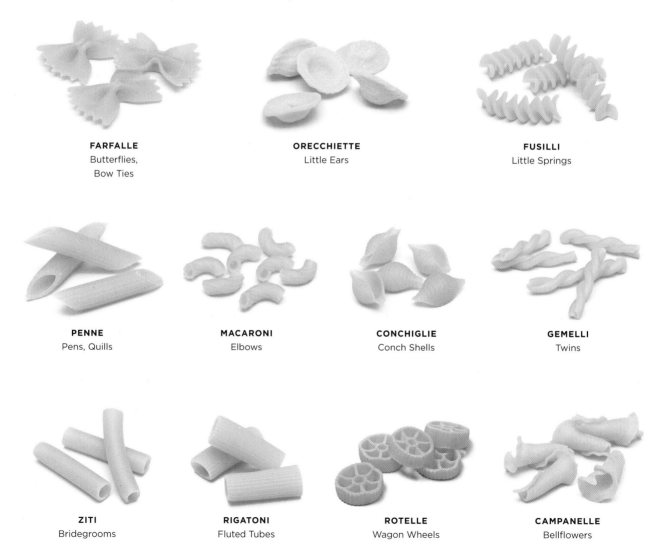

FARFALLE
Butterflies,
Bow Ties

ORECCHIETTE
Little Ears

FUSILLI
Little Springs

PENNE
Pens, Quills

MACARONI
Elbows

CONCHIGLIE
Conch Shells

GEMELLI
Twins

ZITI
Bridegrooms

RIGATONI
Fluted Tubes

ROTELLE
Wagon Wheels

CAMPANELLE
Bellflowers

STRAND PASTAS

Long strands are best with smooth sauces or sauces with very small chunks. In general, wider noodles, such as pappardelle and fettuccine, can support slightly chunkier sauces, like our Mushroom Bolognese (page 115).

VERMICELLI
Little Worms

**SPAGHETTINI
OR THIN SPAGHETTI**
Little Spaghetti

LINGUINE
Little Tongues

FETTUCCINE
Little Ribbons

SPAGHETTI
Little Strings

PAPPARDELLE
Gulp Down

BUCATINI
Little Holes

Measuring Less Than a Pound of Pasta

It's easy enough to measure out a pound of pasta, as most packages are sold in this quantity. But we've included some recipes, most notably "Skillet Pastas," that call for less than 1 pound of pasta. Obviously, you can weigh out partial pounds of pasta using a scale, or you can judge by how full the box is, but we think it's easiest to measure shaped pasta using a dry measuring cup, and strand pasta by determining the diameter.

MEASURING SHORT PASTA

PASTA TYPE*	8 OUNCES	12 OUNCES
Elbow Macaroni and Small Shells	2 cups	3 cups
Orecchiette	2¼ cups	3⅓ cups
Penne, Ziti, and Campanelle	2½ cups	3¾ cups
Rigatoni, Fusilli, Medium Shells, Wagon Wheels, and Wide Egg Noodles	3 cups	4½ cups
Farfalle	3¼ cups	4¾ cups

* These amounts do not apply to whole-wheat pasta.

MEASURING LONG PASTA

When 8 ounces of uncooked strand pasta are bunched together into a tight circle, the diameter measures about 1¼ inches. When 12 ounces of uncooked strand pasta are bunched together, the diameter measures about 1¾ inches.

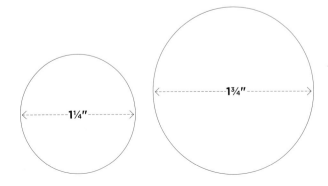

Cooking Pasta 101

Cooking pasta seems simple, but perfect pasta takes some finesse. Here's how we do it in the test kitchen.

USE PLENTY OF WATER

To prevent sticking, you'll need 4 quarts of water to cook up to 1 pound of dried pasta. Pasta leaches starch as it cooks; without plenty of water to dilute it, the starch will coat the noodles and they will stick. Use a pot with at least a 6-quart capacity so that the water won't boil over.

SALT THE WATER

Adding salt to the pasta cooking water is essential; it seasons and adds flavor to the pasta. Add 1 tablespoon of salt per 4 quarts of water. Be sure to add the salt with the pasta, not before, so it will dissolve and not stain the pot.

SKIP THE OIL

It's a myth that adding oil to pasta cooking water prevents the pasta from sticking together as it cooks. Adding oil to cooking water just creates a slick on the surface of the water, doing nothing for the pasta. And when you drain the pasta, the oil prevents the pasta sauce from adhering. To prevent pasta from sticking, simply stir the pasta for a minute or two when you add it to the boiling water, then stir occasionally while it's cooking.

CHECK OFTEN FOR DONENESS

The timing instructions given on the box are almost always too long and will result in mushy, overcooked pasta. Tasting is the best way to check for doneness. We typically prefer pasta cooked al dente, when it still has a little bite left in the center.

RESERVE SOME WATER

Reserve about ½ cup cooking water before draining the pasta—the water is flavorful and can help loosen a thick sauce.

DON'T RINSE

Drain the pasta in a colander, but don't rinse the pasta; it washes away starch and makes the pasta taste watery. Do let a little cooking water cling to the cooked pasta to help the sauce adhere.

KEEP IT HOT

If you're using a large serving bowl for the pasta, place it under the colander while draining the pasta. The hot water heats up the bowl, which keeps the pasta warm longer.

Farfalle with Sautéed Mushrooms and Thyme

SERVES 4 TO 6 FAST GF

✔ **WHY THIS RECIPE WORKS:** For a weeknight pasta and mushroom recipe with a woodsy, full flavor, we used a combination of mushrooms—cremini for their rich, meaty nature and shiitakes for their hearty flavor and chewy texture. Cooking the mushrooms with salt encouraged them to release their juices and enhanced browning. Sautéing the mushrooms in a combination of butter and olive oil gave them a rich, complex flavor and kept the butter from burning. We finished our mushroom pasta recipe with a simple sauce of vegetable broth, heavy cream, and lemon juice rounded out with garlic, shallots, and thyme. To ensure the sauce and pasta finish cooking at the same time, drop the pasta into boiling water just after adding the cremini to the skillet. Cremini mushrooms are also known as baby bella mushrooms. If farfalle is unavailable, campanelle or fusilli make a good substitute. In order for this recipe to be gluten-free, you must use gluten-free pasta.

- 2 **tablespoons unsalted butter**
- 2 **tablespoons extra-virgin olive oil**
- 3 **large shallots, chopped fine**
- 3 **cloves garlic, minced**
- 10 **ounces shiitake mushrooms, stemmed and sliced ¼ inch thick**
- 10 **ounces cremini mushrooms, trimmed and sliced ¼ inch thick**
  - **Salt and pepper**
- 4 **teaspoons minced fresh thyme**
- 1¼ **cups vegetable broth**
- ½ **cup heavy cream**
- 1 **tablespoon lemon juice**
- 1 **pound farfalle**
- 2 **ounces Parmesan cheese, grated (1 cup), plus extra for serving**
- 2 **tablespoons minced fresh parsley**

1. Heat butter and oil in 12-inch skillet over medium heat until butter has melted. Add shallots and cook until softened, about 4 minutes. Stir in garlic and cook until fragrant, about 30 seconds. Add shiitakes, increase heat to medium-high, and cook for 2 minutes. Stir in cremini mushrooms and ½ teaspoon salt and cook, stirring often, until mushrooms are golden brown, about 8 minutes.

2. Stir in thyme and cook until fragrant, about 30 seconds; transfer mixture to bowl. Add broth to now-empty skillet and bring to boil, scraping up any browned bits. Off heat, stir in cream and lemon juice, and season with salt and pepper to taste.

3. Meanwhile, bring 4 quarts water to boil in large pot. Add pasta and 1 tablespoon salt and cook, stirring often, until al dente. Reserve 1 cup cooking water, then drain pasta and return it to pot. Stir in mushroom mixture, broth mixture, Parmesan, and parsley. Cook over medium-low heat, tossing to combine, until pasta absorbs most of liquid, about 2 minutes. Add reserved cooking water as needed to adjust consistency. Serve with extra Parmesan.

VARIATION
Farfalle with Mushrooms, Peas, and Camembert `FAST` `GF`

In order for this recipe to be gluten-free, you must use gluten-free pasta.

Omit thyme. Substitute 6 ounces Camembert, cut into ½-inch cubes (do not remove rind), for Parmesan and minced chives for parsley. Add 1 cup frozen peas to skillet with broth and cook until peas are heated through.

Campanelle with Roasted Cauliflower, Garlic, and Walnuts

SERVES 4 TO 6 `GF`

✔ **WHY THIS RECIPE WORKS:** When done right, high-heat roasting transforms cauliflower from a mild-mannered vegetable to an intensely flavored, sweet, nutty foil for pasta. To achieve a golden exterior, we sliced the cauliflower into wedges to create maximum surface area while leaving the core and florets intact. Tossing the cauliflower with a little sugar jump-started the browning; preheating the baking sheet also helped to develop as much flavor as possible. Cream-based sauces muted the nutty cauliflower flavor, and pestos overwhelmed it, so we focused on a simple lemony dressing with roasted garlic. We rounded out the sauce with fresh parsley and some Parmesan and topped each serving with a handful of walnuts to add a pleasing crunch. If campanelle is unavailable, farfalle or fusilli make a good substitute. In order for this recipe to be gluten-free, you must use gluten-free pasta.

2   garlic heads, top quarter cut off to expose garlic cloves
6   tablespoons plus 1 teaspoon extra-virgin olive oil
1   head cauliflower (2 pounds)
    Salt and pepper
¼   teaspoon sugar
2   tablespoons lemon juice, plus extra as needed
¼   teaspoon red pepper flakes
1   pound campanelle

1   ounce Parmesan cheese, grated (½ cup), plus extra for serving
1   tablespoon chopped fresh parsley
¼   cup walnuts, toasted and chopped coarse

1. Adjust oven rack to middle position, place large rimmed baking sheet on rack, and heat oven to 500 degrees. Place garlic heads, cut side up, in center of 12-inch square of aluminum foil. Drizzle each with ½ teaspoon oil and wrap securely. Place packet on oven rack and roast until garlic is very tender, about 40 minutes.

2. Meanwhile, remove outer leaves from cauliflower and cut stalk flush with bottom. Cut head from pole to pole into 8 equal wedges. Toss cauliflower with 2 tablespoons oil, 1 teaspoon salt, ¼ teaspoon pepper, and sugar in bowl. Remove baking sheet from oven. Carefully lay cauliflower, either cut side down, on hot baking sheet in even layer. Roast cauliflower until well browned and tender, 20 to 25 minutes.

3. Transfer cauliflower to cutting board, let cool slightly, then cut into ½-inch pieces. Transfer garlic packet to cutting board, let cool for 10 minutes, then unwrap garlic. Gently squeeze to remove cloves from skin, transfer to small bowl, and mash smooth with fork. Stir in lemon juice and pepper flakes, then slowly whisk in remaining ¼ cup oil.

4. Bring 4 quarts water to boil in large pot. Add pasta and 1 tablespoon salt and cook, stirring often, until al dente. Reserve 1 cup cooking water, then drain pasta and return it to pot. Add chopped cauliflower, garlic sauce, Parmesan, parsley, and ¼ cup reserved cooking water, and toss to combine. Season with salt, pepper, and extra lemon juice to taste. Add reserved cooking water as needed to adjust consistency. Sprinkle individual portions with walnuts and serve with extra Parmesan.

VARIATIONS
Campanelle with Roasted Broccoli, Garlic, and Almonds

SERVES 4 TO 6 `GF`

If campanelle is unavailable, farfalle or fusilli make a good substitute. In order for this recipe to be gluten-free, you must use gluten-free pasta.

2   garlic heads, top quarter cut off to expose garlic cloves
6   tablespoons plus 1 teaspoon extra-virgin olive oil
1½ pounds broccoli
    Salt and pepper
¼   teaspoon sugar
2   tablespoons lemon juice, plus extra as needed
¼   teaspoon red pepper flakes
1   pound campanelle

1 ounce Manchego cheese, grated (½ cup),
  plus extra for serving
¼ cup chopped fresh basil
¼ cup slivered almonds, toasted

1. Adjust oven rack to middle position, place large rimmed baking sheet on rack, and heat oven to 500 degrees. Place garlic heads, cut side up, in center of 12-inch square of aluminum foil. Drizzle each with ½ teaspoon oil and wrap securely. Place packet on oven rack and roast until garlic is very tender, about 40 minutes.

2. Meanwhile, cut broccoli crowns from large stems. Cut off tough outer layer on stems, then cut into 2- to 3-inch lengths about ½ inch thick. Cut smaller crowns (3 to 4 inches in diameter) into 4 wedges, and cut larger crowns (4 to 5 inches in diameter) into 6 wedges. Toss broccoli with 2 tablespoons oil, 1 teaspoon salt, ¼ teaspoon pepper, and sugar in bowl. Remove baking sheet from oven. Carefully lay broccoli, cut sides down, on hot baking sheet in even layer. Roast broccoli until well browned and tender, 10 to 15 minutes.

3. Transfer broccoli to cutting board, let cool slightly, then cut into ½-inch pieces. Transfer garlic packet to cutting board, let cool for 10 minutes, then unwrap garlic. Gently squeeze to

Preparing Garlic for Roasting

1. Rinse garlic head and remove outer papery skin. Cut top quarter off of garlic head so that tops of cloves are exposed.

2. Place garlic head cut side up in center of 12-inch square of aluminum foil, drizzle with oil, and wrap securely.

3. After roasted garlic head has cooled, remove from foil. Using hand or flat edge of chef's knife, squeeze garlic cloves from skins, starting from root end and working up.

remove cloves from skin, transfer to small bowl, and mash smooth with fork. Stir in lemon juice and pepper flakes, then slowly whisk in remaining ¼ cup oil.

4. Bring 4 quarts water to boil in large pot. Add pasta and 1 tablespoon salt and cook, stirring often, until al dente. Reserve 1 cup cooking water, then drain pasta and return it to pot. Add chopped broccoli, garlic sauce, Manchego, basil, and ¼ cup reserved cooking water, and toss to combine. Season with salt, pepper, and extra lemon juice to taste. Add reserved cooking water as needed to adjust consistency. Sprinkle individual portions with almonds and serve with extra Manchego.

Fusilli with Roasted Portobellos, Garlic, and Pine Nuts

SERVES 4 TO 6 `GF`

In order for this recipe to be gluten-free, you must use gluten-free pasta.

2 garlic heads, top quarter cut off to expose garlic cloves
6 tablespoons plus 1 teaspoon extra-virgin olive oil
8 portobello mushroom caps (3 to 4 inches in diameter), sliced ¾ inch thick
  Salt and pepper
¼ teaspoon sugar
2 tablespoons lemon juice, plus extra as needed
¼ teaspoon red pepper flakes
1 pound fusilli
1 ounce Pecorino Romano cheese, grated (½ cup), plus extra for serving
1 tablespoon chopped fresh rosemary
¼ cup pine nuts, toasted

1. Adjust oven rack to middle position, place large rimmed baking sheet on rack, and heat oven to 500 degrees. Place garlic heads, cut side up, in center of 12-inch square of aluminum foil. Drizzle each with ½ teaspoon oil and wrap securely. Place packet on oven rack and roast until garlic is very tender, about 40 minutes.

2. Meanwhile, toss mushrooms with 2 tablespoons oil, 1 teaspoon salt, ¼ teaspoon pepper, and sugar in bowl. Remove baking sheet from oven. Carefully lay mushrooms, gill side down, on hot baking sheet in even layer. Roast mushrooms until well browned and tender, 20 to 25 minutes, flipping mushrooms halfway through cooking.

3. Transfer mushrooms to cutting board, let cool slightly, then cut into ½-inch pieces. Transfer garlic packet to cutting board, let cool for 10 minutes, then unwrap garlic. Gently squeeze to remove cloves from skin, transfer to small bowl, and mash smooth with fork. Stir in lemon juice and pepper flakes, then slowly whisk in remaining ¼ cup oil.

4. Bring 4 quarts water to boil in large pot. Add pasta and 1 tablespoon salt and cook, stirring often, until al dente. Reserve 1 cup cooking water, then drain pasta and return it to pot. Add chopped mushrooms, garlic sauce, Pecorino, rosemary, and ¼ cup reserved cooking water, and toss to combine. Season with salt, pepper, and extra lemon juice to taste. Add reserved cooking water as needed to adjust consistency. Sprinkle individual portions with pine nuts and serve with extra Pecorino.

Whole-Wheat Fusilli with Kale and White Beans

SERVES 4 TO 6 `FAST` `GF`

✅ **WHY THIS RECIPE WORKS:** Pasta, hearty greens, and beans can make for a sublime experience, but these humble ingredients usually require a lengthy simmer to turn tender and meld into a harmonious dish. To turn this Italian classic into an easy weeknight supper, we swapped out the dried beans for convenient canned cannellini beans and made a potent sauce with garlic, thyme, and red pepper flakes to infuse the dish with flavor in a snap. We chopped the kale into 1-inch pieces then simmered it for just 10 minutes. To give the sauce a thick, luscious consistency, we mashed some of the beans in the pot. To complement our hearty, wintery dish, we chose nutty whole-wheat fusilli. In order for this recipe to be gluten-free, you must use gluten-free pasta.

3	tablespoons extra-virgin olive oil
2	onions, chopped fine
12	garlic cloves, minced
1	teaspoon minced fresh thyme
⅛	teaspoon red pepper flakes
2	(15-ounce) cans cannellini beans, rinsed
2½	cups vegetable broth
1½	pounds kale, stemmed and cut into 1-inch pieces
	Salt and pepper
1	pound whole-wheat fusilli
2	ounces Parmesan cheese, grated (1 cup)

1. Heat 2 tablespoons oil in Dutch oven over medium heat until shimmering. Stir in onions and cook until softened, about 5 minutes. Stir in garlic, thyme, and pepper flakes and cook until fragrant, about 30 seconds. Stir in beans and broth, bring to simmer, and cook until sauce has thickened slightly, about 10 minutes.

2. Stir in kale, cover, and cook, stirring often, until kale is tender, 10 to 12 minutes. Off heat, mash some of beans against

Buying Gluten-Free Pasta

In traditional Italian-style dried pasta, gluten is critically important. This protein matrix provides the structure that keeps noodles intact and pleasantly springy. For people who are avoiding gluten in their diets, finding good wheat-free pasta with the right texture and flavor is a challenge. We sampled eight brands of gluten-free spaghetti made from substitute grains—mainly rice, quinoa, and corn—that lack the specific proteins that form gluten. Each pasta was boiled and tasted with olive oil, then with tomato sauce. The results were unambiguous: Most brands absolutely failed to meet our standards. Most disappointed with textures that managed to be both mushy and gritty, and tasters complained about flavors that ranged from bland to fishy. But there was a lone standout that earned tasters' approval.

Our favorite pasta is made with brown rice, and it contains a relatively high combined total of fiber and protein. It turns out that protein and fiber keep the noodles intact during cooking, forming a barrier around the starch molecules, which prevents them from escaping and leaving the cooked pasta sticky and soft. If the protein network fails, the starch leaches into the cooking water, turning it cloudy—something we observed when cooking the lower-rated brands. In addition, we also learned that proteins in corn are more water-soluble than those in rice, leaving even less protein to surround and control the starch. No surprise, then, that we gave thumbs-down to the texture of corn-based pasta. Our winning brand also uses a low, slow drying method, which helps preserve flavor and ensures that the proteins coagulate and provide structure for the starch. Tasters found that **Jovial Gluten Free Brown Rice Spaghetti** boasted delicate and thin brown rice strands that were springy and clean, with none of the gumminess or off-flavors that plagued other brands.

side of pot with wooden spoon to thicken sauce. Season with salt and pepper to taste.

3. Meanwhile, bring 4 quarts water to boil in large pot. Add pasta and 1 tablespoon salt and cook, stirring often, until al dente. Reserve ½ cup cooking water, then drain pasta and return it to pot.

4. Stir in kale-bean mixture, ½ cup Parmesan, and remaining 1 tablespoon oil and toss to combine. Season with salt and pepper to taste, and add reserved cooking water as needed to adjust consistency. Sprinkle with remaining ½ cup Parmesan and serve.

Whole-Wheat Penne with Butternut Squash and Sage

SERVES 4 TO 6

✔ **WHY THIS RECIPE WORKS:** We wanted a dish that paired hearty whole-wheat pasta with sweet butternut squash. First we sautéed the squash to give it a rich, caramelized flavor. We built a sauce in the same pan, then added the squash back in; after a short braise, we had perfectly cooked, deeply flavorful squash with a silky texture. Lemon juice brightened the sauce, and sage, a natural pairing with butternut squash, lent a balancing herbal note. Mascarpone cheese gave the sauce a velvety texture, and scallions lent a mild onion flavor that complemented the sweet earthiness of the squash. A final sprinkling of sliced almonds added crunch. Fresh sage is crucial to the flavor of this dish; don't substitute dried sage. You can substitute cream cheese for the mascarpone. When simmering the squash in step 3, do not stir too frequently or the squash will begin to fall apart.

2 tablespoons extra-virgin olive oil
2 pounds butternut squash, peeled, seeded, and cut into ½-inch pieces (6 cups)
6 scallions, sliced thin
5 garlic cloves, minced
¼ teaspoon ground nutmeg
1 tablespoon all-purpose flour
2¼ cups vegetable broth
1 cup dry white wine
2 ounces Parmesan cheese, grated (1 cup), plus extra for serving
1½ ounces (3 tablespoons) mascarpone cheese
2 tablespoons minced fresh sage
4 teaspoons lemon juice
Salt and pepper
1 pound whole-wheat penne
¼ cup sliced almonds, toasted

1. Heat 1 tablespoon oil in 12-inch nonstick skillet over medium heat until shimmering. Add squash and cook, stirring occasionally, until spotty brown, 15 to 20 minutes; transfer to bowl.

2. Add remaining 1 tablespoon oil, scallions, garlic, and nutmeg to now-empty skillet and cook over medium heat until scallions are softened, 1 to 2 minutes. Stir in flour and cook for 1 minute. Slowly whisk in broth and wine, scraping up any browned bits.

3. Stir in browned squash and simmer until squash is tender and sauce has thickened slightly, 10 to 15 minutes. Off heat, gently stir in Parmesan, mascarpone, sage, and lemon juice. Season with salt and pepper to taste.

4. Meanwhile, bring 4 quarts water to boil in large pot. Add pasta and 1 tablespoon salt and cook, stirring often, until al dente. Reserve ½ cup cooking water, then drain pasta and return it to pot.

5. Add squash mixture and gently toss to combine. Season with salt and pepper to taste, and add reserved cooking water as needed to adjust consistency. Sprinkle individual portions with almonds, and serve with extra Parmesan.

Whole-Wheat Rotini with Brussels Sprouts

SERVES 4 TO 6 `FAST` `GF`

✔ **WHY THIS RECIPE WORKS:** The combination of earthy Brussels sprouts and nutty whole-wheat pasta makes a uniquely satisfying pasta dish. To ensure the Brussels sprouts were evenly cooked, we sliced them and then sautéed them along with some sliced shallots before simmering them in a combination of vegetable broth and heavy cream. Parmesan imparted a tangy note and gave the sauce some body, while toasted walnuts provided further rich flavor and an appealing crunch. Frozen sweet peas were an easy addition that paired nicely with the Brussels sprouts; we added them at the end to preserve their texture and color. Small, firm Brussels sprouts (about 1 inch in diameter) work best here; see page 260 for information on how to slice Brussels sprouts thinly. In order for this recipe to be gluten-free, you must use gluten-free pasta.

3 tablespoons extra-virgin olive oil
1 pound Brussels sprouts, trimmed and sliced thin
2 shallots, sliced thin
Salt and pepper
1 cup vegetable broth
1 cup heavy cream
¾ cup frozen peas, thawed
1 pound whole-wheat rotini
2 ounces Parmesan cheese, grated (1 cup), plus extra for serving
½ cup walnuts, toasted and chopped

1. Heat oil in 12-inch skillet over medium-high heat until shimmering. Add Brussels sprouts, shallots, ½ teaspoon salt, and ¼ teaspoon pepper and cook until sprouts begin to soften, 3 to 5 minutes. Stir in broth and cream, cover, and simmer until sprouts are tender, about 3 minutes. Off heat, stir in peas, cover, and let sit until heated through, about 2 minutes.

2. Meanwhile, bring 4 quarts water to boil in large pot. Add pasta and 1 tablespoon salt and cook, stirring often, until

A creamy sauce enriched with Parmesan balances earthy Brussels sprouts and hearty whole-wheat pasta in this dish.

al dente. Reserve ½ cup cooking water, then drain pasta and return it to pot.

3. Stir in Brussels sprouts mixture, Parmesan, and walnuts, and toss to combine. Season with salt and pepper to taste, and add reserved cooking water as needed to adjust consistency. Serve with extra Parmesan.

Whole-Wheat Spaghetti with Greens, Beans, and Tomatoes

SERVES 4 TO 6   FAST   GF

✓ **WHY THIS RECIPE WORKS:** For a pasta dish hearty enough to satisfy any hunger, we combined whole-wheat spaghetti with curly-leaf spinach, cannellini beans, and sweet diced tomatoes. Onion, minced garlic, and spicy red pepper flakes created a rich base of flavor. To ensure everything would fit in one pan, we stirred in half of the spinach until just wilted before adding the rest with the broth and tomatoes. We braised the spinach in the broth until it was tender, then added the beans and some briny kalamata olives. The greens, beans, and

Buying Whole-Wheat Pasta

Supermarket shelves now carry a wide range of whole-wheat and multigrain pasta. To find the brand with the best nutty, complex flavor and firm, springy texture, we put 18 brands to the test. We sampled them plain, with olive oil, and with homemade marinara and pesto. Some were puzzlingly similar to white pasta, with none of the hearty, nutty flavor we were looking for, while others were heavy, dense, and rough. So what did our tasting panel find? First, most of the 100 percent whole-wheat and 100 percent whole-grain pastas fell quickly to the bottom of the rankings, garnering descriptions like mushy, doughy, sour, and fishy. But there was one dark horse in the bunch, Italian-made **Bionaturae Organic 100% Whole Wheat Spaghetti** (7 grams protein and 6 grams fiber per serving), made entirely of whole wheat but with an appealing chew and firm texture like the pasta with little or no whole grains. The manufacturer's secret? Custom milling (which ensures good flavor), extrusion through a bronze die (which helps build gluten in the dough), and a slower drying process at low temperatures (which yields sturdier pasta).

sauce had to simmer with the pasta for just a few minutes to create a harmonious flavor. We garnished the dish with crispy garlic chips, a drizzle of olive oil, and Parmesan. In order for this recipe to be gluten-free, you must use gluten-free pasta.

> 3   **tablespoons extra-virgin olive oil, plus extra for drizzling**
> 8   **garlic cloves, peeled, 5 cloves sliced thin lengthwise and 3 cloves minced**
>   **Salt and pepper**
> 1   **onion, chopped fine**
> ½   **teaspoon red pepper flakes**
> 1¼   **pounds curly-leaf spinach, stemmed and cut into 1-inch pieces**
> ¾   **cup vegetable broth**
> 1   **(14.5-ounce) can diced tomatoes, drained**
> 1   **(15-ounce) can cannellini beans, rinsed**
> ¾   **cup pitted kalamata olives, chopped coarse**
> 1   **pound whole-wheat spaghetti**
> 2   **ounces Parmesan cheese, grated (1 cup), plus extra for serving**

1. Cook oil and sliced garlic in 12-inch straight-sided sauté pan over medium heat, stirring often, until garlic turns golden but not brown, about 3 minutes. Transfer garlic to paper towel–lined plate with slotted spoon, and season lightly with salt.

2. Add onion to oil left in pan and cook over medium heat until softened and lightly browned, 5 to 7 minutes. Stir in minced garlic and pepper flakes and cook until fragrant, about 30 seconds. Add half of spinach and cook, tossing occasionally, until starting to wilt, about 2 minutes. Add remaining spinach, broth, tomatoes, and ¾ teaspoon salt, and bring to simmer.

3. Cover (pan will be very full), and cook, tossing occasionally, until spinach is completely wilted, about 10 minutes (mixture will be somewhat soupy). Stir in beans and olives.

4. Meanwhile, bring 4 quarts water to boil in large pot. Add pasta and 1 tablespoon salt and cook, stirring often, until just shy of al dente. Reserve ½ cup cooking water, then drain pasta and return it to pot. Stir in greens mixture and cook over medium heat, tossing to combine, until pasta absorbs most of liquid, about 2 minutes.

5. Off heat, stir in Parmesan. Season with salt and pepper to taste, and add reserved cooking water as needed to adjust consistency. Serve, garnishing individual portions with garlic chips, drizzle of oil, and extra Parmesan.

Skillet Baked Orzo

SERVES 4

✓ **WHY THIS RECIPE WORKS:** For a summery, satisfying dish of creamy orzo and vegetables, we settled on a stovetop-to-oven cooking method to guarantee perfectly cooked vegetables and pasta. First we sautéed our aromatics, then we briefly toasted the orzo to bring out its flavor. We added broth and wine to the skillet and simmered the orzo until it was al dente and had released its starch, creating a luscious, creamy sauce without needing any butter or cream. Stirring in the zucchini, tomatoes, and spinach right before the dish went into the oven kept the vegetables firm and bright-tasting in the finished dish. Salty bites of feta and fresh mint made the perfect finishing touches. Be sure to cook the orzo just until al dente before adding the vegetables and finishing the dish in the oven, or else it will overcook and turn mushy. You will need a 12-inch ovensafe nonstick skillet for this recipe.

- 1 tablespoon extra-virgin olive oil
- 1 onion, chopped fine
- 4 garlic cloves, minced
- 12 ounces (2 cups) orzo
- Salt and pepper
- 3½ cups vegetable broth
- ½ cup white wine

This easy skillet pasta dish combines tender orzo with lots of fresh vegetables and bright Mediterranean flavors.

- 2 zucchini, quartered lengthwise and sliced ½ inch thick
- 8 ounces cherry tomatoes, halved
- 3 ounces (3 cups) baby spinach
- 1 teaspoon grated lemon zest, plus wedges for serving
- 4 ounces feta cheese, crumbled (1 cup)
- 2 tablespoons chopped fresh mint

1. Adjust oven rack to middle position and heat oven to 400 degrees. Heat oil in 12-inch ovensafe nonstick skillet over medium heat until shimmering. Add onion and cook until softened and lightly browned, 5 to 7 minutes. Stir in garlic and cook until fragrant, about 30 seconds. Stir in orzo and 1 teaspoon salt and cook, stirring often, until orzo is coated with oil and lightly browned, about 4 minutes.

2. Stir in broth and wine, bring to simmer, and cook, stirring occasionally, until orzo is al dente, 10 to 12 minutes. Off heat, stir in zucchini, tomatoes, spinach, and lemon zest. Transfer skillet to oven and bake for 10 minutes.

3. Being careful of hot skillet handle, stir orzo thoroughly. Sprinkle feta over top and continue to bake until cheese is lightly browned, about 5 minutes. Sprinkle with mint and serve with lemon wedges.

Baked Ziti with Ricotta and Eggplant

SERVES 4 TO 6

✔ **WHY THIS RECIPE WORKS:** Baked ziti is usually laden with sausage, while vegetarian versions are loaded with cheese. We wanted a substantial vegetarian baked ziti with chunks of roasted, caramelized eggplant that weren't drowning in cheese. To achieve this, we added a hefty 2 pounds of eggplant to our baked ziti, roasting it for 30 minutes before stirring it into the pasta. Cooking the pasta until it was almost al dente ensured that it was tender, but not overcooked, in the finished dish. Sautéed garlic and red pepper flakes provided a savory foundation to our easy sauce, and crushed tomatoes, simmered for just 10 minutes, added rich tomato flavor while keeping the casserole moist. Stirring some of the pasta cooking water into the sauce provided further insurance against a dry baked ziti. For the cheeses, we created a layer of creamy ricotta in the middle of the casserole, then topped the dish with shredded mozzarella and grated Parmesan and baked it until it formed a bubbling, browned crust. Do not use nonfat ricotta or fat-free mozzarella here.

- 2 pounds eggplant, cut into 1-inch pieces
- ¼ cup extra-virgin olive oil
-   Salt and pepper
- 1 pound ziti
- 3 garlic cloves, minced
- ¼ teaspoon red pepper flakes
- 2 (28-ounce) cans crushed tomatoes
- 8 ounces (1 cup) whole-milk ricotta cheese
- 6 ounces mozzarella cheese, shredded (1½ cups)
- 2 ounces Parmesan cheese, grated (1 cup)
- ¼ cup chopped fresh basil

1. Adjust oven rack to middle position and heat oven to 400 degrees. Toss eggplant with 2 tablespoons oil and season with salt and pepper. Spread eggplant over greased rimmed baking sheet and roast, stirring occasionally, until golden brown, about 30 minutes.

2. Meanwhile, bring 4 quarts water to boil in Dutch oven. Add pasta and 1 tablespoon salt and cook, stirring often, until nearly al dente. Reserve ½ cup cooking water, then drain pasta and set aside.

3. Dry now-empty pot, add 1 tablespoon oil, garlic, and pepper flakes, and cook over medium heat until fragrant, about 1 minute. Stir in tomatoes and 1 teaspoon salt and simmer until slightly thickened, about 10 minutes. Off heat, stir in cooked pasta and reserved cooking water, breaking up

All About Canned Tomatoes

Since canned tomatoes are processed at the height of freshness, they deliver more flavor than off-season fresh tomatoes. But with all the options lining supermarket shelves, it's not always clear what you should buy. We tested a variety of canned tomato products to determine the best uses for each and our favorite brands.

WHOLE TOMATOES

Whole tomatoes are peeled tomatoes packed in either their own juice or puree. They are best when fresh tomato flavor is a must. Whole tomatoes are quite soft and break down quickly when cooked. We found that those packed in juice had a livelier, fresher flavor.

DICED TOMATOES

Diced tomatoes are peeled, machine-diced, and packed in either their own juice or puree. Many brands contain calcium chloride, a firming agent that helps the chunks maintain their shape. Diced tomatoes are best for rustic tomato sauces with a chunky texture, and in long-cooked stews and soups in which you want the tomatoes to hold their shape. We favor diced tomatoes packed in juice because they have a fresher flavor than those packed in puree.

CRUSHED TOMATOES

Crushed tomatoes are whole tomatoes ground very finely, then enriched with tomato puree. They work well in smoother sauces, and their thicker consistency makes them ideal when you want to make a sauce quickly. You can also make your own by crushing canned diced tomatoes in a food processor.

TOMATO PUREE

Tomato puree is made from cooked tomatoes that have been strained to remove their seeds and skins. Tomato puree works well in long-simmered, smooth, thick sauces with a deep, hearty flavor.

TOMATO PASTE

Tomato paste is tomato puree that has been cooked to remove almost all moisture. Because it's naturally full of glutamates, tomato paste brings out subtle depths and savory notes. We use it in a variety of recipes, including both long-simmered sauces and quicker-cooking dishes, to lend a deeper, well-rounded tomato flavor and color.

any clumps, and season with salt and pepper to taste. Stir in roasted eggplant.

4. Mix ricotta, remaining 1 tablespoon oil, ¼ teaspoon salt, and ¼ teaspoon pepper together in bowl.

5. Pour half of pasta mixture into 13 by 9-inch baking dish. Top with large spoonfuls of ricotta mixture, then pour remaining pasta over ricotta. Sprinkle with mozzarella and Parmesan. Bake until bubbling around edges and cheese is spotty brown, about 25 minutes. Let cool for 10 to 15 minutes. Sprinkle with basil before serving.

Hearty Vegetable Lasagna

SERVES 8 TO 10

✔ **WHY THIS RECIPE WORKS:** For a hearty vegetable lasagna with bold flavor, we started with a summery mix of zucchini, yellow squash, and eggplant. Salting and microwaving the eggplant and sautéing the vegetables cut down on excess moisture and deepened their flavor. Garlic, baby spinach, and kalamata olives added textural contrast and flavor without much work. We dialed up the usual cheese filling by switching mild-mannered ricotta for a cream sauce made with tangy cottage cheese, heavy cream for richness, and Parmesan and garlic for added flavor. Our quick no-cook tomato sauce added enough moisture to our lasagna that we found that we could skip the usual step of soaking the no-boil noodles before assembling the dish. Part-skim mozzarella can also be used in this recipe, but avoid preshredded cheese, as it does not melt well. We prefer kosher salt because it clings best to the eggplant. If using table salt, reduce all of the salt amounts in the recipe by half.

TOMATO SAUCE

- 1 (28-ounce) can crushed tomatoes
- ¼ cup chopped fresh basil
- 2 tablespoons extra-virgin olive oil
- 2 garlic cloves, minced
- 1 teaspoon kosher salt
- ¼ teaspoon red pepper flakes

CREAM SAUCE

- 8 ounces (1 cup) whole-milk cottage cheese
- 1 cup heavy cream
- 4 ounces Parmesan cheese, grated (2 cups)
- 2 garlic cloves, minced
- 1 teaspoon cornstarch
- ½ teaspoon kosher salt
- ½ teaspoon pepper

LASAGNA

- 1½ pounds eggplant, peeled and cut into ½-inch pieces
  Kosher salt and pepper
- 1 pound zucchini, cut into ½-inch pieces
- 1 pound yellow squash, cut into ½-inch pieces
- 5 tablespoons plus 1 teaspoon extra-virgin olive oil
- 4 garlic cloves, minced
- 1 tablespoon minced fresh thyme
- 12 ounces (12 cups) baby spinach
- 12 no-boil lasagna noodles
- ½ cup pitted kalamata olives, minced
- 12 ounces whole-milk mozzarella cheese, shredded (3 cups)
- 2 tablespoons chopped fresh basil

1. FOR THE TOMATO SAUCE: Whisk all ingredients together in bowl. (Sauce can be refrigerated for up to 1 day.)

2. FOR THE CREAM SAUCE: Whisk all ingredients together in bowl. (Sauce can be refrigerated for up to 1 day.)

3. FOR THE LASAGNA: Adjust oven rack to middle position and heat oven to 375 degrees. Line large plate with double layer of coffee filters and spray with vegetable oil spray. Toss eggplant with 1 teaspoon salt and spread evenly over coffee filters. Microwave eggplant, uncovered, until dry to touch and slightly shriveled, about 10 minutes, tossing halfway through cooking. Let eggplant cool slightly, then toss with zucchini and yellow squash.

4. Combine 1 tablespoon oil, garlic, and thyme in small bowl. Heat 2 tablespoons oil in 12-inch nonstick skillet over medium-high heat until shimmering. Add half of eggplant-squash mixture, ¼ teaspoon salt, and ¼ teaspoon pepper, and cook, stirring occasionally, until vegetables are lightly browned, about 7 minutes. Clear center of skillet, add half of garlic mixture, and cook, mashing with spatula, until fragrant, about 30 seconds. Stir garlic mixture into vegetables and transfer to medium bowl. Repeat with remaining eggplant mixture, 2 tablespoons oil, and remaining garlic mixture; transfer to bowl.

5. Heat remaining 1 teaspoon oil in now-empty skillet over medium-high heat until shimmering. Add spinach and cook, stirring frequently, until wilted, about 3 minutes. Transfer spinach to paper towel–lined plate and drain for 2 minutes. Stir into eggplant mixture. (Cooked vegetables can be refrigerated for up to 1 day.)

6. Grease 13 by 9-inch baking dish. Spread 1 cup tomato sauce evenly over bottom of dish. Arrange 4 noodles on top of sauce (noodles will overlap). Spread half of vegetable mixture over noodles, followed by half of olives. Spoon half of cream sauce over top, and sprinkle with 1 cup mozzarella. Repeat layering with 4 noodles, 1 cup tomato sauce, remaining vegetables, remaining olives, remaining cream sauce, and 1 cup mozzarella. For final layer, arrange remaining 4 noodles on top and cover completely with remaining tomato sauce. Sprinkle with remaining 1 cup mozzarella.

7. Cover dish tightly with aluminum foil that has been sprayed with oil spray, and bake until edges are just bubbling, about 35 minutes, rotating dish halfway through baking. Let lasagna cool for 25 minutes, then sprinkle with basil and serve.

Mushroom Lasagna

SERVES 8 TO 10

✔ **WHY THIS RECIPE WORKS:** American-style mushroom lasagnas often lose the mushrooms in a sea of tomato sauce and mozzarella. Italian-style recipes put the emphasis on the mushrooms, but many call for esoteric or expensive wild mushrooms as well as a lot of preparation time. We wanted to make Italian-style mushroom lasagna approachable, using widely available mushrooms and no-boil noodles. For the primary mushrooms, we found that roasting portobellos concentrated their flavor. The texture of the sauce was a problem (our no-boil noodles sucked up all the moisture), but a very loose béchamel sauce had the right consistency after baking. We attained substantial mushroom flavor when we sautéed chopped white mushrooms and dried porcini until browned, then built the sauce with the mushrooms and the flavorful fond. We rounded out the sauce with garlic, vermouth, and butter plus a little flour for thickening. Parmesan and fontina cheeses added a complementary buttery nuttiness. Finally, we added a gremolata-like topping of minced parsley, basil, lemon zest, and garlic for complexity and freshness. Italian fontina works best in this dish. If it is not available, substitute whole-milk mozzarella.

2	pounds portobello mushroom caps, gills removed, halved and sliced crosswise ¼ inch thick
¼	cup extra-virgin olive oil
	Salt and pepper
4	red onions, chopped
8	ounces white mushrooms, trimmed and halved if small or quartered if large
½	ounce dried porcini mushrooms, rinsed and minced
4	garlic cloves, minced
½	cup dry vermouth
3	tablespoons unsalted butter
3	tablespoons all-purpose flour
1	cup water
3½	cups whole milk

¼	teaspoon ground nutmeg
¼	cup plus 2 tablespoons chopped fresh basil
¼	cup minced fresh parsley
12	no-boil lasagna noodles
8	ounces Italian fontina cheese, shredded (2 cups)
1½	ounces Parmesan cheese, grated (¾ cup)
½	teaspoon grated lemon zest

1. Adjust oven rack to middle position and heat oven to 425 degrees. Toss portobello mushrooms with 2 tablespoons oil, ½ teaspoon salt, and ½ teaspoon pepper and spread onto rimmed baking sheet. Roast until shriveled, about 30 minutes, stirring halfway through roasting; transfer to bowl and let cool.

2. Meanwhile, heat 1 tablespoon oil in 12-inch nonstick skillet over medium heat until shimmering. Add onions, ¼ teaspoon salt, and ¼ teaspoon pepper and cook, stirring occasionally, until onions are softened and lightly browned, 8 to 10 minutes; transfer to bowl with roasted portobellos.

3. Pulse white mushrooms in food processor until coarsely chopped, about 6 pulses. Heat remaining 1 tablespoon oil in now-empty skillet over medium-high heat until shimmering. Add chopped mushrooms and porcini and cook, stirring occasionally, until browned and all moisture has evaporated, 6 to 8 minutes. Stir in 1 tablespoon garlic, 1 teaspoon salt, and 1 teaspoon pepper, reduce heat to medium, and cook, stirring often, until garlic is fragrant, about 30 seconds. Stir in vermouth and cook until liquid has evaporated, 2 to 3 minutes.

4. Stir in butter and cook until melted. Add flour and cook, stirring constantly, for 1 minute. Stir in water, scraping up any browned bits. Stir in milk and nutmeg and simmer until sauce has thickened and measures 4 cups, 10 to 15 minutes. Off heat, stir in ¼ cup basil and 2 tablespoons parsley.

5. Pour 2 inches boiling water into 13 by 9-inch baking dish. Slip noodles into water, 1 at a time, and soak until pliable, about 5 minutes, separating noodles with tip of sharp knife to prevent sticking. Remove noodles from water and place in single layer on clean dish towels; discard water. Dry and grease dish.

6. Combine fontina and Parmesan in bowl. Spread 1 cup mushroom sauce evenly over bottom of prepared dish. Arrange 3 noodles in single layer on top of sauce. Spread ¾ cup sauce evenly over noodles, then sprinkle with 2 cups mushroom-onion mixture and ¾ cup cheese mixture. Repeat layering of noodles, mushroom sauce, mushroom-onion mixture, and cheese mixture 2 more times. Arrange remaining 3 noodles on top, cover completely with remaining sauce, and sprinkle with remaining cheese.

7. Cover dish tightly with aluminum foil that has been sprayed with vegetable oil spray and bake until edges are just bubbling, about 20 minutes, rotating dish halfway through baking. Remove foil, increase oven temperature to 500 degrees, and continue to bake until cheese on top becomes spotty brown, 6 to 8 minutes.

8. Combine remaining 1 teaspoon garlic, remaining 2 tablespoons parsley, remaining 2 tablespoons basil, and lemon zest together and sprinkle over lasagna. Let casserole cool for 15 minutes before serving.

Removing Portobello Gills

Using soupspoon, gently scrape out and discard dark-colored gills from underside of portobello cap.

Spinach Lasagna
SERVES 8 TO 10

✅ **WHY THIS RECIPE WORKS:** For a creamy spinach lasagna with great flavor, we chose hearty curly-leaf spinach and blanched it, then squeezed out all the excess liquid so it wouldn't water down the dish. We flavored the spinach sauce with garlic, shallots, bay leaves, a little nutmeg, and some Parmesan cheese. For the lasagna, we swapped cottage cheese for the usual ricotta; tasters like the extra tang and creaminess it lent to the dish. We also layered in more Parmesan cheese and some creamy, melty fontina. We preferred thinner, easier no-boil noodles to traditional noodles in this dish; soaking them in boiling water for 5 minutes helped to soften them just enough so that they ended up perfectly tender in the finished dish. Our resulting spinach lasagna was a simple success: fresh, green spinach highlighted by a delicate, savory sauce; tender noodles; and mild, creamy cheese. Italian fontina works best in this dish. If it is not available, substitute whole-milk mozzarella. If your lasagna dish is not broiler-safe, brown the lasagna at 500 degrees for about 10 minutes.

SAUCE
- 1¼ pounds curly-leaf spinach, stemmed
-      Salt and pepper
- 5 tablespoons unsalted butter
- 4 large shallots, minced
- 4 garlic cloves, minced
- ¼ cup all-purpose flour
- 3½ cups whole milk
- 2 bay leaves
- ¾ teaspoon ground nutmeg
- 1 ounce Parmesan cheese, grated (½ cup)

LASAGNA
- 8 ounces (1 cup) whole-milk cottage cheese
- 1 large egg
- ¼ teaspoon salt
- 12 no-boil lasagna noodles
- 2 ounces Parmesan cheese, grated (1 cup)
- 8 ounces Italian fontina cheese, shredded (2 cups)

1. FOR THE SAUCE: Bring 4 quarts water to boil in large pot. Fill large bowl with ice water. Add spinach and 1 tablespoon salt to boiling water and cook, stirring continuously, until spinach is just wilted, about 5 seconds. Using slotted spoon, transfer spinach to ice water and soak until completely cool, about 1 minute; drain spinach and transfer to clean dish towel. Wrap towel tightly around spinach to form ball and wring until dry. Chop spinach and set aside.

2. Melt butter in medium saucepan over medium heat. Add shallots and garlic and cook, stirring often, until shallots are softened, about 4 minutes. Stir in flour and cook, stirring constantly, until incorporated, about 1½ minutes. Gradually whisk in milk, smoothing out any lumps. Increase heat to medium-high and bring to boil, whisking often.

3. Stir in bay leaves, nutmeg, ½ teaspoon salt, and ¼ teaspoon pepper. Reduce heat to low and simmer, whisking occasionally, for 10 minutes. Discard bay leaves and whisk in Parmesan until melted. Measure out and reserve ½ cup sauce in bowl; press plastic wrap directly against surface and set aside. Transfer remaining sauce to separate bowl and stir in chopped spinach until well combined and no clumps remain; press plastic directly against surface and set aside.

4. FOR THE LASAGNA: Adjust oven rack to middle position and heat oven to 425 degrees. Process cottage cheese, egg, and salt in food processor until very smooth, about 30 seconds.

5. Pour 2 inches boiling water into 13 by 9-inch broiler-safe baking dish. Slip noodles into water, 1 at a time, and soak until pliable, about 5 minutes, separating noodles with tip of sharp knife to prevent sticking. Remove noodles from water and place in single layer on clean dish towels; discard water. Dry and grease dish.

6. Spread reserved ½ cup sauce evenly over bottom of prepared dish. Arrange 3 noodles in single layer on top of sauce. Spread 1 cup spinach mixture evenly over noodles, sprinkle with Parmesan, and top with 3 more noodles. Spread 1 cup spinach mixture evenly over top, sprinkle with 1 cup fontina, and top with 3 more noodles. Spread 1 cup spinach mixture evenly over top, followed by cottage cheese mixture. Arrange remaining 3 noodles on top, cover completely with remaining spinach mixture, and sprinkle with remaining 1 cup fontina.

7. Cover dish tightly with aluminum foil that has been sprayed with vegetable oil spray and bake until edges are just bubbling, about 20 minutes, rotating dish halfway through baking. Remove dish from oven and remove foil. Adjust oven rack 6 inches from broiler element and heat broiler. Broil lasagna until cheese is spotty brown, 4 to 6 minutes. Let lasagna cool for 15 minutes before serving.

Fideos with Chickpeas and Aïoli

SERVES 4

☑ **WHY THIS RECIPE WORKS:** One of the biggest stars of traditional Spanish cooking is *fideos*. This richly flavored dish toasts thin noodles until nut-brown before cooking them in a garlicky, tomatoey stock loaded with seafood and chorizo. We wanted to streamline the recipe and make it vegetarian but keep the complex flavors of the classic dish. We saved some time by streamlining the *sofrito*, the aromatic base common in Spanish cooking, by finely chopping the onion (so it softened and browned more quickly) and using canned tomatoes instead of fresh. We made the dish vegetarian by subbing out the usual shellfish and chorizo for hearty, creamy chickpeas. A hefty amount of wine and the juice from our canned tomatoes made a stock with good depth of flavor. A topping of garlic aïoli imparts a citrusy component. If you don't make the aïoli, serve the fideos with lemon wedges. In step 4, if your skillet is not broiler-safe, once the pasta is tender, transfer the mixture to a broiler-safe 13 by 9-inch baking dish lightly coated with olive oil. Broil and serve as directed.

8   ounces spaghettini or thin spaghetti,
       broken into 1- to 2-inch lengths
2   tablespoons plus 2 teaspoons extra-virgin olive oil
1   onion, chopped fine
       Salt and pepper
1   (14.5-ounce) can diced tomatoes, drained and
       chopped fine, juice reserved
3   garlic cloves, minced
1½ teaspoons smoked paprika

Nutty toasted noodles and hearty chickpeas are simmered in a smoky tomato sauce and served with a dollop of garlic aïoli.

2¾ cups water
1   (15-ounce) can chickpeas, rinsed
½   cup dry white wine
1   tablespoon chopped fresh parsley
1   recipe Garlic Aïoli (page 43)

1. Toss spaghettini and 2 teaspoons oil in broiler-safe 12-inch skillet until spaghettini is evenly coated. Toast spaghettini over medium-high heat, stirring frequently, until browned and releases nutty aroma (spaghettini should be color of peanut butter), 6 to 10 minutes; transfer to bowl.

2. Wipe out now-empty skillet, add remaining 2 tablespoons oil, and heat over medium-high heat until shimmering. Add onion and ¼ teaspoon salt and cook until onion is softened, about 5 minutes. Stir in tomatoes and cook until mixture is thick, dry, and slightly darkened in color, 4 to 6 minutes.

3. Reduce heat to medium, stir in garlic and smoked paprika, and cook until fragrant, about 30 seconds. Stir in toasted spaghettini until thoroughly combined. Stir in water, chickpeas, wine, reserved tomato juice, ¼ teaspoon salt, and ½ teaspoon pepper. Increase heat to medium-high and bring to simmer. Cook uncovered, stirring occasionally, until liquid is slightly thickened and spaghettini is just tender, 8 to 10 minutes. Meanwhile, adjust oven rack 5 to 6 inches from broiler element and heat broiler.

4. Transfer skillet to oven and broil until surface of spaghettini is dry with crisped, browned spots, 5 to 7 minutes. Let cool for 5 minutes, then sprinkle with parsley and serve with aïoli.

VARIATION
Fideos with Chickpeas and Fennel
Add 1 thinly sliced fennel bulb to skillet with onion and increase cooking time to 10 to 12 minutes. Substitute 1 tablespoon chopped fennel fronds for parsley.

Breaking Pasta for Fideos

 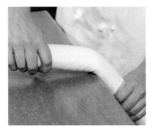

1. Loosely fold 4 ounces of spaghettini in dish towel, keeping pasta flat, not bunched.

2. Press pasta bundle repeatedly against edge of counter to break pasta into 1- to 2-inch lengths. Repeat with remaining 4 ounces spaghettini.

To make our fresh pasta dough easy to roll out, we mix it in the food processor, then knead it by hand for just 2 minutes.

Fresh Egg Pasta
MAKES ABOUT 1 POUND FRESH PASTA

✓ **WHY THIS RECIPE WORKS:** Dried pasta is certainly convenient, but it can't compare to the delicate texture and chew of fresh pasta, plus filled pasta like ravioli require fresh pasta as the starting point. While fresh pasta can be found in many supermarkets and specialty shops—if you're lucky enough to live near one—we wanted a foolproof recipe for fresh pasta that would be easy to knead and roll out. We started with a simple dough, made with just flour and eggs, and found that making it in the food processor kneaded it almost to perfection. Kneading the dough by hand for an additional minute or two made our pasta dough silky and smooth. Running the dough, in pieces, through a manual pasta machine until it was translucent gave us the delicate pasta we

were after. Although the food processor does most of the work, finish kneading this dough by hand. This pasta dough can be used for ravioli or fettuccine.

> 2 cups (10 ounces) all-purpose flour, plus extra as needed
> 3 large eggs, beaten
> Water

1. Pulse flour in food processor to aerate. Add eggs and process until dough forms rough ball, about 30 seconds. (If dough resembles small pebbles, add water, ½ teaspoon at a time; if dough sticks to side of bowl, add flour, 1 tablespoon at a time, and process until dough forms rough ball.)

2. Turn out dough ball and any small bits onto counter and knead by hand until dough is smooth, 1 to 2 minutes. Cover with plastic wrap and set aside to relax for at least 15 minutes or up to 2 hours.

3. Cut dough into 5 even pieces and, using manual pasta machine, roll out dough into sheets. (Leave pasta in sheets for filled and hand-shaped pastas, or cut into long strands to make fettuccine.)

Making Fresh Egg Pasta

1. PROCESS DOUGH: Process flour and eggs, adding water if necessary, until dough forms rough ball, about 30 seconds.

2. KNEAD DOUGH: Turn out dough onto counter and knead until smooth, 1 to 2 minutes.

3. LET REST: Cover dough with plastic wrap and set aside for at least 15 minutes or up to 2 hours.

4. ROLL OUT: Cut dough into 5 even pieces, then use manual pasta machine to roll each piece into thin, satiny sheet (you should be able to see outline of your hand through pasta).

Fresh Fettuccine with Walnut Cream Sauce

SERVES 4

✔ **WHY THIS RECIPE WORKS:** We wanted to come up with some simple but sumptuous sauces that would complement our fresh pasta without masking its delicate flavor and texture. First we made a creamy, nutty walnut sauce. Toasting the walnuts to bring out their flavor, and then processing part of them until finely ground, added great body to our sauce and gave it intense nutty flavor throughout. We balanced the rich nuts and cream with some savory Parmesan, bright white wine, and fresh chives. Next we came up with a simple tomato

sauce enhanced with nutty browned butter. We processed whole canned tomatoes until smooth, then added them to the browned butter with some garlic and a little sugar. We simmered the sauce until its flavors melded and concentrated, then finished it with more butter, some bright sherry vinegar, and basil. In terms of timing, make and cut the pasta first, then make the sauce, then boil the pasta and toss with sauce.

1½ cups (6 ounces) walnuts
¾ cup dry white wine
½ cup heavy cream
1 ounce Parmesan cheese, grated (½ cup)
   Salt and pepper
1 recipe Fresh Egg Pasta (page 134), cut into fettuccine
¼ cup minced fresh chives

1. Toast walnuts in 12-inch skillet over medium heat until golden and fragrant, 2 to 4 minutes. Process 1 cup walnuts in food processor until finely ground, about 10 seconds; transfer to bowl. Pulse remaining ½ cup walnuts in food processor until coarsely chopped, 3 to 5 pulses; combine with finely ground walnuts.

2. Bring wine to simmer in now-empty skillet over medium-high heat and cook until reduced to ¼ cup, about 3 minutes. Whisk in cream, walnuts, Parmesan, ¼ teaspoon salt, and ½ teaspoon pepper. Remove pan from heat and cover to keep warm.

3. Bring 4 quarts water to boil in large Dutch oven. Add 1 tablespoon salt and pasta and cook until pasta is tender but still al dente, 2 to 3 minutes. Reserve 1 cup pasta cooking water and drain pasta.

4. Add pasta and ½ cup pasta cooking water to sauce in skillet and cook over medium heat, tossing constantly, until well coated and hot. Add remaining cooking water as needed to adjust consistency. Stir in chives, season with salt and pepper to taste, and serve.

VARIATION
Fresh Fettuccine with Tomato–Browned Butter Sauce
SERVES 4
In terms of timing, make and cut the pasta first, then make the sauce, then boil the pasta and toss with sauce.

1 (28-ounce) can whole peeled tomatoes
4 tablespoons unsalted butter, cut into 4 pieces
2 garlic cloves, minced
½ teaspoon sugar
   Salt and pepper

2 teaspoons sherry vinegar
1 recipe Fresh Egg Pasta (page 134),
 cut into fettuccine
3 tablespoons chopped fresh basil
 Grated Parmesan cheese

1. Process tomatoes and their juice in food processor until smooth, about 30 seconds. Melt 3 tablespoons butter in 12-inch skillet over medium-high heat, swirling occasionally, until butter is dark brown and releases nutty aroma, about 1½ minutes. Stir in garlic and cook for 10 seconds. Stir in processed tomatoes, sugar, and ½ teaspoon salt, and simmer until sauce is slightly reduced, about 8 minutes.

2. Off heat, whisk in remaining 1 tablespoon butter and vinegar. Season with salt and pepper to taste; cover to keep warm.

Cutting Pasta Dough into Fettuccine

1. Working with one-fifth of dough, flatten dough into disk and run through rollers of pasta machine set to widest position. Bring ends of dough toward middle and press down to seal.

2. Feed open side of pasta through rollers. Fold and roll dough once more. If dough is sticky, lightly dust with flour. Without folding, run pasta through widest setting until dough is smooth.

3. Roll pasta thinner by putting it through machine repeatedly, narrowing setting each time. Roll until dough is thin and satiny and you can see outline of your hand through pasta.

4. Lay pasta on clean dish towel and cover it with damp dish towel. Repeat with other pieces of dough. Affix fettuccine cutting attachment, then run each sheet through pasta machine.

3. Bring 4 quarts water to boil in large Dutch oven. Add 1 tablespoon salt and pasta and cook until pasta is tender but still al dente, 2 to 3 minutes. Reserve ½ cup pasta cooking water, and drain pasta.

4. Add pasta and ¼ cup pasta cooking water to sauce in skillet and cook over medium heat, tossing constantly, until well coated and hot. Add remaining cooking water as needed to adjust consistency. Stir in basil, season with salt and pepper to taste, and serve with Parmesan.

Squash Ravioli with Sage and Hazelnut Browned Butter Sauce

SERVES 6 TO 8, MAKES ABOUT 45 RAVIOLI

✔ **WHY THIS RECIPE WORKS:** We wanted homemade ravioli filled with sweet, earthy butternut squash and bathed in a rich browned butter sauce. We started with the filling, microwaving the squash until tender, then pureeing it with butter, sugar, and nutmeg. We also stirred in some Parmesan cheese to amplify the filling's flavor. After we rolled out the fresh pasta and formed the ravioli, we spread them on a baking sheet and covered them with a damp towel to prevent the pasta from drying out while we made the sauce. We browned a generous amount of butter in a skillet to give it a nutty, caramelized flavor. Chopped hazelnuts, fresh sage, and some lemon juice for brightness rounded out our simple sauce. Do not use frozen squash here; its flavor is very bland and will be disappointing. Sliced or slivered almonds can be substituted for the hazelnuts.

RAVIOLI
1 pound butternut squash, peeled, seeded,
 and cut into 1-inch chunks (3 cups)
4 tablespoons unsalted butter
1 tablespoon packed brown sugar
 Salt and pepper
 Pinch ground nutmeg
2 ounces Parmesan cheese, grated (1 cup)
 All-purpose flour
1 recipe Fresh Egg Pasta (page 134)

SAUCE
8 tablespoons unsalted butter, cut into 4 pieces
¼ cup coarsely chopped hazelnuts
2 tablespoons minced fresh sage
 Salt
2 teaspoons lemon juice
 Shaved Parmesan

Nutty, complex browned butter is the perfect complement to the sweet, earthy butternut squash in our homemade ravioli.

1. FOR THE RAVIOLI: Microwave squash in covered bowl until tender and easily pierced with fork, 10 to 15 minutes. Drain squash well and transfer to food processor. Add butter, sugar, ¼ teaspoon salt, and nutmeg, and process until smooth, 15 to 20 seconds. Transfer to bowl, stir in Parmesan and ⅛ teaspoon pepper, and refrigerate until no longer warm, 15 to 25 minutes.

2. Dust 2 large rimmed baking sheets liberally with flour. Divide pasta dough into 5 even pieces and cover with plastic wrap. Working with 1 piece dough, roll out using pasta machine. Using pizza wheel or sharp knife, cut pasta sheet into long rectangles measuring 4 inches across. Place generous 1-teaspoon dollops of filling over bottom half of dough, spaced about 1¼ inches apart. (If dough edges seem dry, dab with water.) Fold top of pasta over filling and press layers of dough together securely around each filling to seal. Use fluted pastry wheel to cut ravioli apart and trim edges.

3. Transfer finished ravioli to floured baking sheet and cover with damp dish towel. Repeat with remaining pasta and filling. (Towel-covered baking sheets of ravioli can be wrapped with plastic wrap and refrigerated for up to 4 hours. Ravioli can also be frozen for up to 1 month; do not thaw before boiling.)

Forming Ravioli

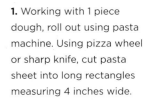

1. Working with 1 piece dough, roll out using pasta machine. Using pizza wheel or sharp knife, cut pasta sheet into long rectangles measuring 4 inches wide.

2. Place generous 1-teaspoon dollops of filling over bottom half of dough, spaced about 1¼ inches apart. (If dough edges seem dry, dab with water.)

3. Fold top of pasta over filling and press layers of dough together securely around each filling to seal.

4. Use fluted pastry wheel to cut ravioli apart and trim edges.

4. FOR THE SAUCE: Before cooking ravioli, cook butter, hazelnuts, sage, and ¼ teaspoon salt in 10-inch skillet over medium-high heat, swirling pan constantly, until butter is melted, has golden brown color, and releases nutty aroma, about 3 minutes. Off heat, stir in lemon juice.

5. Bring 4 quarts water to boil in large pot for ravioli. Add 1 tablespoon salt and half of ravioli. Cook, stirring often and lowering heat if necessary to keep water at gentle boil, until ravioli are tender, about 2 minutes (3 to 4 minutes if frozen). Using slotted spoon or wire spider, transfer cooked ravioli to warm serving platter, spoon some of butter sauce over top, and cover with aluminum foil to keep warm. Return water to boil and repeat with remaining ravioli. Swirl 2 tablespoons of ravioli cooking water into remaining butter sauce, then pour sauce over ravioli. Top with shaved Parmesan and serve immediately.

PESTO SAUCES

Flavorful pestos can be made with lots of different ingredients—from parsley and arugula to sun-dried tomatoes, cherry tomatoes, roasted red peppers, and more. Regardless of the type, a good pesto has two basic requirements: You should use a high-quality extra-virgin olive oil (because its flavor will really shine through), and you should toast the garlic (to help tame its fiery, raw flavor). Note that the flavor and texture of these pestos vary quite a bit, which means that the amount you need to coat your pasta adequately will vary. All the recipes here provide enough pesto to sauce at least 1 pound of pasta.

TO MAKE PESTO: Process all ingredients except oil and cheese in food processor until smooth, scraping down bowl as needed. With processor running, slowly add oil until incorporated. Transfer pesto to bowl, stir in cheese(s), and season with salt and pepper to taste. When tossing pesto with cooked pasta, add some of pasta cooking water as needed (up to ½ cup) to loosen consistency of pesto.

TO MAKE AHEAD: Pesto can be refrigerated for up to 3 days or frozen for up to 3 months. To prevent browning, press plastic wrap flush to surface, or top with thin layer of olive oil.

Classic Basil Pesto

MAKES ¾ CUP **FAST** **GF**

Pounding the basil briefly before processing the pesto helps bring out its flavorful oils. To bruise the basil, place it in a large zipper-lock bag and pound lightly with a rolling pin or meat pounder. The optional parsley helps give the pesto a vibrant green hue. For sharper flavor, substitute Pecorino Romano for the Parmesan.

- 2 cups fresh basil leaves, lightly bruised
- 2 tablespoons fresh parsley leaves (optional)
- ¼ cup pine nuts, toasted
- 3 garlic cloves, toasted and minced
- 7 tablespoons extra-virgin olive oil
- ¼ cup grated Parmesan cheese

Parsley and Toasted Nut Pesto

MAKES 1½ CUPS **FAST** **GF**

Though basil is the go-to herb when making a green pesto, parsley makes a surprisingly delicious substitute. To balance out the grassy, heartier flavor of parsley, we found it necessary to ramp up the nut flavor. Pecans have a

more pronounced flavor than pine nuts. You can substitute walnuts, blanched almonds, skinned hazelnuts, or any combination thereof for the pecans.

- 1 cup pecans, toasted
- ¼ cup fresh parsley leaves
- 3 garlic cloves, toasted and minced
- 7 tablespoons extra-virgin olive oil
- ¼ cup grated Parmesan cheese

Roasted Red Pepper Pesto

MAKES 1½ CUPS **FAST** **GF**

This pesto tastes great when made with homemade roasted red peppers, but jarred roasted red peppers work fine in this recipe. The pesto made with jarred peppers will have a more acidic flavor, so before using them be sure to rinse and dry the jarred peppers well.

- 2 roasted red bell peppers, peeled and chopped (1 cup)
- ¼ cup fresh parsley leaves
- 3 garlic cloves, toasted and minced
- 1 shallot, chopped
- 1 tablespoon fresh thyme leaves
- ½ cup extra-virgin olive oil
- ¼ cup grated Parmesan cheese

Tomato and Almond Pesto

MAKES 1½ CUPS **FAST** **GF**

This is a traditional Sicilian pesto known as *Trapanese*. A single pepperoncini adds a nice, spicy kick; however, you can substitute ½ teaspoon red wine vinegar and ¼ teaspoon red pepper flakes for the pepperoncini if necessary.

- 12 ounces cherry or grape tomatoes
- ½ cup fresh basil leaves
- ¼ cup slivered almonds, toasted
- 1 small pepperoncini (hot pepper in vinegar), stemmed, seeded, and minced
- 1 garlic clove, toasted and minced Pinch red pepper flakes (optional)
- ⅓ cup extra-virgin olive oil
- 1 ounce Parmesan cheese, grated (½ cup)

Sun-Dried Tomato Pesto

MAKES 1½ CUPS `FAST` `GF`

We prefer sun-dried tomatoes packed in oil over those that are packaged dried.

- 1 cup oil-packed sun-dried tomatoes, patted dry and chopped
- ¼ cup walnuts, toasted
- 3 garlic cloves, toasted and minced
- ½ cup extra-virgin olive oil
- 1 ounce Parmesan cheese, grated (½ cup)

Parsley, Arugula, and Ricotta Pesto

MAKES 1½ CUPS `FAST` `GF`

Part-skim ricotta can be substituted here; do not use nonfat ricotta or the pesto will be dry and gummy.

- 1 cup fresh parsley leaves
- 1 cup baby arugula
- ¼ cup pine nuts, toasted
- 3 garlic cloves, toasted and minced
- 7 tablespoons extra-virgin olive oil
- ⅓ cup whole-milk ricotta cheese
- 2 tablespoons grated Parmesan cheese

Kale and Sunflower Seed Pesto

MAKES 1½ CUPS `FAST` `GF`

Kale, with its earthy, slightly bitter flavor, and sunflower seeds, with their strong flavor, are well matched here.

- 2 cups chopped kale leaves
- 1 cup fresh basil leaves
- ½ cup raw sunflower seeds, toasted
- 2 garlic cloves, toasted and minced
- 1 teaspoon red pepper flakes (optional)
- ½ cup extra-virgin olive oil
- 1½ ounces Parmesan cheese, grated (¾ cup)

Green Olive and Orange Pesto

MAKES 1½ CUPS `FAST` `GF`

Using high-quality green olives is crucial to the success of this pesto. Look for fresh green olives (packed in brine) in the supermarket's refrigerated section or at the salad bar.

- 1½ cups fresh parsley leaves
- ½ cup pitted green olives
- ½ cup slivered almonds, toasted
- 2 garlic cloves, toasted and minced
- ½ teaspoon grated orange zest plus 2 tablespoons juice
- ½ cup extra-virgin olive oil
- 1½ ounces Parmesan cheese, grated (¾ cup)

Toasting Garlic

Toast unpeeled cloves in 8-inch skillet over medium heat, shaking pan occasionally, until color of cloves deepens slightly, about 7 minutes. Let toasted garlic cool slightly, then peel and mince.

MAKING THE MOST OF PESTO

Sure, pesto tastes terrific on pasta, but don't sell it short; its robust, concentrated flavor can jazz up just about anything, from sandwiches and omelets to soups and salads. Because a few tablespoons can transform a dish from boring to best in show, it's always nice to have some pesto on hand. Here are some of our favorite ways to use pesto.

- Stir pesto into mashed potatoes for a simple twist on this classic comfort food.
- Dollop pesto onto soups for a heady, herbal aroma.
- Brush pesto on vegetables after roasting, grilling, or steaming for a quick and flavorful glaze.
- Use pesto in place of mayonnaise or mustard on sandwiches.
- Thin pesto with lemon juice to make a quick vinaigrette.

- Drizzle pesto over slices of pizza or calzones.
- Use pesto to flavor fresh cheeses such as mozzarella and ricotta.
- Use a few tablespoons of pesto as an easy marinade for tofu.
- Stir a couple of tablespoons of pesto into equal parts mayonnaise and sour cream for a quick dipping sauce. Serve with veggies or chips.

All About Parmesan

Parmesan is classified as a grana-type cheese: a hard, grainy cheese made from cow's milk. It has a rich, sharp flavor and a melt-in-your-mouth texture. We frequently reach for it to sprinkle on top of pasta dishes or to add a rich, salty flavor to sauces, soups, and stews.

BUYING PARMESAN

We recommend authentic Italian Parmigiano-Reggiano, which has a complex flavor and a smooth, melting texture that none of the others can match. Most of the other Parmesan-type cheeses are too salty and one-dimensional. When shopping, make sure some portion of the words "Parmigiano-Reggiano" is stenciled on the golden rind. To ensure that you're buying a properly aged cheese, examine the condition of the rind. It should be a few shades darker than the straw-colored interior and should penetrate about ½ inch deep (younger or improperly aged cheeses will have a paler, thinner rind). And closely scrutinize the center of the cheese. Those small white spots found on many samples are actually good things—they signify the presence of calcium phosphate crystals, which are formed only after the cheese has been aged for the proper amount of time.

STORING PARMESAN

We found that the best way to preserve Parmesan's flavor and texture is to wrap it in parchment paper, then aluminum foil. However, if you have just a small piece of cheese, tossing it in a zipper-lock bag works almost as well; just be sure to squeeze out as much air as possible before sealing the bag.

PARMESAN VERSUS PECORINO ROMANO

Parmesan and Pecorino Romano have similar textures and flavors, and often you'll see one as an alternative to the other in recipes. We have found that Parmesan and Pecorino Romano generally can be used interchangeably, especially when the amount called for is moderate. However, when Parmesan is called for in larger quantities, stick with the Parmesan, as Pecorino Romano can be fairly pungent.

CAN YOU PREGRATE YOUR OWN PARMESAN?

We've never been tempted by tasteless, powdered Parmesan cheese. But what about grating your own? We found that tasters were hard-pressed to detect any difference between freshly grated Parmesan and cheese that had been grated and stored for up to three weeks. So go ahead and grate your Parmesan ahead; refrigerate in an airtight container.

Mushroom Ravioli with Browned Butter, Sage, and Truffle Sauce

SERVES 6 TO 8, MAKES ABOUT 45 RAVIOLI

✓ **WHY THIS RECIPE WORKS:** For another classic ravioli filling, we swapped out the creamy butternut squash for meaty, hearty mushrooms. For a filling with great mushroom flavor, we chose a combination of white button and porcini mushrooms. To keep the mushrooms from turning the delicate pasta soggy, it was essential to drive off their excess moisture before stuffing the ravioli. We cooked the chopped mushrooms gently over medium-low heat until they released their liquid, then we turned up the heat until the liquid evaporated and the mushrooms browned. We rounded out the filling with shallot, garlic, cream, Parmesan, and some fresh parsley. For the sauce, we kept the browned butter and sage and added some flavorful white truffle oil, which perfectly complemented the earthy mushroom filling. If desired, substitute 2 teaspoons lemon juice for the truffle oil.

RAVIOLI

1½ pounds white mushrooms, trimmed and quartered
2 tablespoons extra-virgin olive oil
2 shallots, minced
5 garlic cloves, minced
1 ounce dried porcini mushrooms, rinsed and minced
   Salt and pepper
¼ cup heavy cream
2 ounces Parmesan cheese, grated (1 cup)
2 tablespoons minced fresh parsley
1 recipe Fresh Egg Pasta (page 134)

SAUCE

8 tablespoons unsalted butter, cut into 4 pieces
2 tablespoons minced fresh sage
   Salt
1 teaspoon white truffle oil
   Shaved Parmesan

1. FOR THE RAVIOLI: Working in 2 batches, pulse white mushrooms in food processor until finely chopped, about 15 pulses; transfer to bowl. Heat oil in 12-inch nonstick skillet over medium heat until shimmering. Add shallots and garlic and cook until fragrant, about 30 seconds. Stir in chopped white mushrooms, porcini mushrooms, and ½ teaspoon salt. Cover, reduce heat to medium-low, and cook, stirring occasionally, until mushrooms are wet and wilted, about 10 minutes.

2. Uncover, increase heat to high, and continue to cook until mushroom liquid has evaporated and mixture is clumpy and starting to brown, about 10 minutes. Stir in cream and cook until mixture is sticky and cohesive but not wet, about 1 minute. Transfer mixture to bowl, stir in Parmesan and parsley, and season with pepper to taste. Refrigerate filling until no longer warm, 15 to 25 minutes.

3. Dust 2 large rimmed baking sheets liberally with flour. Divide pasta dough into 5 even pieces and cover with plastic wrap. Working with 1 piece dough, roll out using pasta machine. Using pizza wheel or sharp knife, cut pasta sheet into long rectangles measuring 4 inches across. Place generous 1-teaspoon dollops of filling over bottom half of dough, spaced about 1¼ inches apart. (If dough edges seem dry, dab with water.) Fold top of pasta over filling and press layers of dough together securely around each filling to seal. Use fluted pastry wheel to cut ravioli apart and trim edges.

4. Transfer finished ravioli to floured baking sheet and cover with damp dish towel. Repeat with remaining pasta and filling. (Towel-covered baking sheets of ravioli can be wrapped with plastic wrap and refrigerated for up to 4 hours. Ravioli can also be frozen for up to 1 month; do not thaw before boiling.)

5. FOR THE SAUCE: Before cooking ravioli, cook butter, sage, and ¼ teaspoon salt in 10-inch skillet over medium-high heat, swirling pan constantly, until butter is melted, has golden brown color, and releases nutty aroma, about 3 minutes. Off heat, stir in truffle oil.

6. Bring 4 quarts water to boil in large pot for ravioli. Add 1 tablespoon salt and half of ravioli. Cook, stirring often and lowering heat if necessary to keep water at gentle boil, until ravioli are tender, about 2 minutes (3 to 4 minutes if frozen). Using slotted spoon or wire spider, transfer cooked ravioli to warm serving platter, spoon some of butter sauce over top, and cover with aluminum foil to keep warm. Return water to boil and repeat with remaining ravioli. Swirl 2 tablespoons of ravioli cooking water into remaining butter sauce, then pour sauce over ravioli. Top with shaved Parmesan and serve immediately.

Browning Butter

Browned butter gives a complex, nutty depth to sauces, but it can go from browned to burnt quickly. Use a skillet with a light-colored interior and keep a close eye on the butter as it begins to brown.

Cook butter in skillet over medium-high heat, swirling pan constantly, until butter has golden brown color and releases nutty aroma, about 3 minutes.

Potato Gnocchi with Browned Butter and Sage Sauce

SERVES 2 TO 3

✔ **WHY THIS RECIPE WORKS:** We wanted a foolproof recipe for impossibly light gnocchi with unmistakable potato flavor. Baking russets (streamlined by parcooking the potatoes in the microwave) produced intensely flavored potatoes—an excellent start to our gnocchi base. To avoid lumps, which can cause gnocchi to break apart during cooking, we turned to a ricer, which gave us a smooth, supple mash. While many recipes offer a range of flour amounts, which ups the chances of overworking the dough (and producing leaden gnocchi), we used an exact amount based on the ratio of potato to flour so that our gnocchi dough was mixed as little as possible. And we found that an egg, while not traditional, tenderized our gnocchi further, delivering delicate, pillowlike dumplings. For the most accurate measurements, weigh the potatoes and flour. After processing, you may have slightly more than the 3 cups (16 ounces) of potatoes required for this recipe. Discard any extra or set aside for another use.

GNOCCHI

- 2 **pounds russet potatoes**
- 1 **large egg, lightly beaten**
- ¾ **cup plus 1 tablespoon (4 ounces) all-purpose flour**
    Salt

SAUCE

- 4 **tablespoons unsalted butter, cut into 4 pieces**
- 1 **small shallot, minced**
- 1 **teaspoon minced fresh sage**
- 1½ **teaspoons lemon juice**
- ¼ **teaspoon salt**

1. FOR THE GNOCCHI: Adjust oven rack to middle position and heat oven to 450 degrees. Poke each potato 8 times with paring knife. Microwave potatoes until slightly softened at ends, about 10 minutes, flipping potatoes halfway through cooking. Transfer potatoes directly to oven rack and bake until skewer glides easily through flesh and potatoes yield to gentle pressure, 18 to 20 minutes.

2. Holding potatoes with dish towel, peel with paring knife. Process potatoes through ricer or food mill onto rimmed baking sheet. Gently spread potatoes into even layer and let cool for 5 minutes.

3. Transfer 3 cups (16 ounces) warm potatoes to bowl. Using fork, gently stir in egg until just combined. Sprinkle flour and 1 teaspoon salt over top and gently combine using fork until no pockets of dry flour remain. Press mixture into rough ball, transfer to lightly floured counter, and gently knead until smooth but slightly sticky, about 1 minute, lightly dusting counter with flour as needed to prevent sticking.

4. Line 2 rimmed baking sheets with parchment paper and dust liberally with flour. Cut dough into 8 pieces. Lightly dust counter with flour. Gently roll piece of dough into ½-inch-thick rope, dusting with flour to prevent sticking. Cut rope into ¾-inch lengths.

5. Holding fork with tines upside down in 1 hand, press each dough piece cut side down against tines with thumb of other hand to create indentation. Roll dough down tines to form ridges on sides. If dough sticks, dust thumb or fork with flour. Transfer formed gnocchi to prepared sheets and repeat with remaining dough.

6. FOR THE SAUCE: Melt butter in 12-inch skillet over medium-high heat, swirling pan occasionally, until butter is browned and releases nutty aroma, about 1½ minutes. Off heat, add shallot and sage, stirring until shallot is fragrant, about 1 minute. Stir in lemon juice and salt and cover to keep warm.

7. Bring 4 quarts water to boil in large pot. Add 1 tablespoon salt. Using parchment paper as sling, add half of gnocchi and cook until firm and just cooked through, about 90 seconds (gnocchi should float to surface after about 1 minute). Remove gnocchi with slotted spoon, transfer to skillet with sauce, and cover to keep warm. Repeat with remaining gnocchi and transfer to skillet. Gently toss gnocchi with sauce to combine and serve.

VARIATION

Potato Gnocchi with Gorgonzola-Cream Sauce

Substitute following for Browned Butter Sauce: Bring ¾ cup heavy cream and ¼ cup dry white wine to simmer in 12-inch skillet over medium-high heat. Gradually whisk in 1 cup crumbled Gorgonzola, and cook until melted and sauce is thickened, 2 to 3 minutes. Off heat, stir in 2 tablespoons minced fresh chives and season with salt and pepper to taste; cover to keep warm.

Creating Gnocchi Ridges

To help gnocchi hold on to sauce, hold fork with tines upside down and press each dough piece (cut side down) against tines to make indentation. Roll gnocchi down tines to create ridges on sides.

We take pasta salad up a notch with an elegant mix of roasted fennel and red onions and sun-dried tomatoes.

Pasta Salad with Arugula and Sun-Dried Tomato Vinaigrette

SERVES 6

✔ **WHY THIS RECIPE WORKS:** We wanted a lighter version of pasta salad, with plenty of vegetables and a flavorful vinaigrette binding everything together. Getting the right balance of acidity was essential; too little and the salad tasted bland, but too much caused the pasta to turn mushy and dulled the vegetables, in both flavor and appearance. Just 2 tablespoons of assertive red wine vinegar was enough to keep the salad tasting bright (for variations with less-acidic lemon juice, ¼ cup was just right). Tossing the pasta with the dressing while the pasta was still hot allowed it to absorb the flavors of the dressing, making the salad more cohesive. For the vegetables, we chose sun-dried tomatoes, briny olives, and peppery arugula. Once we had perfected our pasta salad, we came up with a variation with fennel and red onions, and another with fresh tomatoes and grilled eggplant.

1 **pound fusilli**
  Salt and pepper
2 **tablespoons red wine vinegar**
1 **garlic clove, minced**
½ **cup oil-packed sun-dried tomatoes, drained and chopped, plus 2 tablespoons packing oil**
¼ **cup extra-virgin olive oil**
½ **cup green olives, pitted and sliced**
6 **ounces fresh mozzarella cheese, cut into ½-inch cubes**
4 **ounces (4 cups) baby arugula**

1. Bring 4 quarts water to boil in large pot. Add pasta and 1 tablespoon salt and cook, stirring often, until al dente. Drain pasta and transfer to large bowl.

2. Whisk vinegar, garlic, ¼ teaspoon salt, and ⅛ teaspoon pepper together in small bowl. Whisking constantly, drizzle in tomato oil and olive oil.

3. Stir vinaigrette, tomatoes, and olives into hot pasta and let cool to room temperature, about 30 minutes. (Salad can be refrigerated for up to 1 day; refresh with warm water and additional oil as needed.) Stir in mozzarella and arugula and season with salt and pepper to taste before serving.

VARIATIONS
Pasta Salad with Fennel, Red Onions, and Sun-Dried Tomatoes
SERVES 6 `VEGAN`
If desired, chop 2 tablespoons of the fennel fronds and stir them into the salad before serving.

2 **fennel bulbs, stalks discarded, bulbs halved, cored, and cut into ½-inch wedges**
2 **red onions, halved and sliced ½ inch thick**
2 **tablespoons plus ½ cup extra-virgin olive oil**
  Salt and pepper
1 **pound fusilli**
½ **teaspoon grated lemon zest plus ¼ cup juice (2 lemons)**
1 **garlic clove, minced**
½ **cup oil-packed sun-dried tomatoes, patted dry and sliced thin**
½ **cup chopped fresh basil**

1. Adjust oven rack to middle position and heat oven to 425 degrees. Toss fennel and onions with 2 tablespoons oil, season with salt and pepper, and spread onto rimmed baking sheet. Roast until vegetables are tender and lightly browned, 15 to 20 minutes, stirring halfway through roasting.

2. Meanwhile, bring 4 quarts water to boil in large pot. Add pasta and 1 tablespoon salt and cook, stirring often, until al dente. Drain pasta and transfer to large bowl.

3. Whisk lemon zest and juice, garlic, and ¾ teaspoon salt together in small bowl. Whisking constantly, drizzle in remaining ½ cup oil.

4. Stir dressing, roasted vegetables, and tomatoes into hot pasta and let cool to room temperature, about 30 minutes. (Salad can be refrigerated for up to 1 day; refresh with warm water and additional oil as needed.) Stir in basil and season with salt and pepper to taste before serving.

Pasta Salad with Tomatoes and Grilled Eggplant
SERVES 6 `VEGAN`
The eggplant can also be broiled instead of grilled; spread the eggplant onto a well-greased parchment-lined baking sheet and broil until tender and browned, 5 to 10 minutes, flipping the eggplant halfway through cooking.

1 **pound eggplant, cut into ½-inch-thick rounds**
2 **tablespoons plus ½ cup extra-virgin olive oil**
  Salt and pepper
1 **pound farfalle**
½ **teaspoon grated lemon zest plus ¼ cup juice (2 lemons)**
1 **garlic clove, minced**
½ **teaspoon red pepper flakes**
2 **large tomatoes, cored, seeded, and cut into ½-inch pieces**
½ **cup chopped fresh basil**

1A. FOR A CHARCOAL GRILL: Open bottom vent completely. Light large chimney starter filled with charcoal briquettes (6 quarts). When top coals are partially covered with ash, pour evenly over grill. Set cooking grate in place, cover, and open lid vent completely. Heat grill until hot, about 5 minutes.

1B. FOR A GAS GRILL: Turn all burners to high, cover, and heat grill until hot, about 15 minutes. Leave all burners on high.

2. Lightly brush eggplant with 2 tablespoons oil and season with salt and pepper. Clean and oil cooking grate. Place eggplant on grill and cook (covered if using gas), flipping once, until tender and lightly charred, about 10 minutes. Transfer to cutting board, let cool slightly, then cut into ½-inch pieces.

3. Meanwhile, bring 4 quarts water to boil in large pot. Add pasta and 1 tablespoon salt and cook, stirring often, until al dente. Drain pasta and transfer to large bowl.

4. Whisk lemon zest and juice, garlic, pepper flakes, and ¾ teaspoon salt together in small bowl. Whisking constantly, drizzle in remaining ½ cup oil. Stir dressing, grilled eggplant, and tomatoes into hot pasta and let cool to room temperature, about 30 minutes. (Salad can be refrigerated for up to 1 day; refresh with warm water and additional oil as needed.) Stir in basil and season with salt and pepper to taste before serving.

Orzo Salad with Broccoli and Radicchio

SERVES 4

✓ **WHY THIS RECIPE WORKS:** In this orzo recipe, we set out to make a pilaf that hit all the taste buds: salty, sweet, bitter, and sour. To give the dish a variety of balanced flavors, we included broccoli, bitter radicchio, salty sun-dried tomatoes, pine nuts, and a hefty dose of basil. Cooking the orzo in the same water that we used to quickly blanch the broccoli imparted a delicate vegetal flavor throughout the dish. To round out the salad, we made a sour and sweet dressing with balsamic vinegar and honey. Toasting the pine nuts intensified their nutty flavor and brought further dimension to the orzo. Sharp Parmesan added the perfect salty accent, and chopped fresh basil gave us a fresh finish to lighten this hearty dish. Cooking the pasta until it is completely tender and leaving it slightly wet after rinsing are important for the texture of the finished salad.

¾   **pound broccoli florets, cut into 1-inch pieces**
    Salt and pepper
1⅓ **cups orzo**
1   **head radicchio, cored and chopped fine**
½   **cup sun-dried tomatoes, rinsed, patted dry, and minced, plus 3 tablespoons packing oil**
2   **ounces Parmesan cheese, grated (1 cup)**
½   **cup pine nuts, toasted**
¼   **cup balsamic vinegar**
1   **garlic clove, minced**
1   **teaspoon honey**
3   **tablespoons extra-virgin olive oil**
½   **cup chopped fresh basil**

1. Bring 4 quarts water to boil in large pot. Fill large bowl with ice water. Add broccoli and 1 tablespoon salt to boiling water and cook until crisp-tender, about 2 minutes. Using slotted spoon, transfer broccoli to ice water and let cool, about 2 minutes; drain and pat dry.

2. Return pot of water to boil, add orzo, and cook, stirring often, until tender. Drain orzo, rinse with cold water, and drain again, leaving pasta slightly wet. Toss orzo, broccoli, radicchio, tomatoes, Parmesan, and pine nuts together in large bowl.

3. In small bowl, whisk vinegar, garlic, honey, and 1 teaspoon salt together. Whisking constantly, drizzle in tomato oil and olive oil. Stir vinaigrette into orzo mixture. (Salad can be refrigerated for up to 1 day; refresh with warm water and additional oil as needed.) Stir in basil and season with salt and pepper to taste before serving.

Tortellini Salad with Asparagus and Fresh Basil Dressing

SERVES 8 TO 10

✓ **WHY THIS RECIPE WORKS:** For a super easy pasta salad that would impress any picnic crowd, we paired convenient store-bought cheese tortellini with crisp asparagus and a dressing inspired by the flavors of classic pesto. First, we blanched the asparagus in the same water we later used to cook the tortellini, which instilled the pasta with the asparagus's delicate flavor. Once the tortellini were cooked, we marinated them briefly with bright, juicy cherry tomatoes in a bold dressing of extra-virgin olive oil, basil, lemon juice, shallot, and garlic. To finish the salad, we tossed in some grated Parmesan and toasted pine nuts along with the blanched asparagus just before serving. Cooking the pasta until it is completely tender and leaving it slightly wet after rinsing are important for the texture of the finished salad.

1   **pound asparagus, trimmed and cut into 1-inch pieces**
    Salt and pepper
1   **pound dried cheese tortellini**
12 **ounces cherry tomatoes, halved**
3   **tablespoons lemon juice**
1   **shallot, minced**
1   **garlic clove, minced**
6   **tablespoons extra-virgin olive oil**
½   **cup chopped fresh basil**
1   **ounce Parmesan cheese, grated (½ cup)**
¼   **cup pine nuts, toasted**

1. Bring 4 quarts water to boil in large pot. Fill large bowl with ice water. Add asparagus and 1 tablespoon salt to boiling water and cook until crisp-tender, about 2 minutes. Using slotted spoon, transfer asparagus to ice water and let cool, about 2 minutes; drain and pat dry.

2. Return pot of water to boil. Add tortellini and cook, stirring often, until tender. Drain tortellini, rinse with cold water, and drain again, leaving tortellini slightly wet. Toss tortellini and tomatoes together in large bowl.

3. Whisk lemon juice, shallot, garlic, ½ teaspoon salt, and ½ teaspoon pepper together in small bowl. Whisking constantly, drizzle in oil. Stir dressing into tortellini mixture, cover, and let sit for 15 minutes. (Salad and asparagus can be refrigerated separately for up to 1 day; refresh salad with warm water and additional oil as needed.) Stir in asparagus, basil, Parmesan, and pine nuts and season with salt and pepper to taste before serving.

To replicate the flavor of hard-to-find sesame paste, we blend chunky peanut butter and toasted sesame seeds.

Sesame Noodles with Cucumbers and Radishes

SERVES 4 TO 6 FAST VEGAN GF

✔ **WHY THIS RECIPE WORKS:** Our recipe for easy but authentic-tasting sesame noodles relies on everyday pantry staples to deliver the requisite sweet, nutty, addictive flavor. Chunky peanut butter and toasted sesame seeds, ground together in the blender, made the perfect stand-in for hard-to-find Asian sesame paste. Garlic, ginger, soy sauce, rice vinegar, hot sauce, and brown sugar rounded out the flavors, and thinning the sauce with hot water achieved the best texture to coat the noodles without being gloppy. To avoid the pitfalls of most sesame noodle recipes—gummy noodles and bland, pasty sauce—we rinsed the cooked noodles to rid them of excess starch. Tossing them with sesame oil separately, before adding the sauce, also helped keep the noodles from absorbing too much sauce and becoming pasty. We added in carrot, cucumber, radishes, and scallions to bulk up these noodles and make them hefty enough for a dinner. We like conventional chunky peanut butter here; it tends to be sweeter than natural or old-fashioned versions. If you cannot find fresh Chinese egg noodles, substitute 12 ounces dried spaghetti or linguine. In order for this recipe to be gluten-free, you must use gluten-free spaghetti or linguine, and gluten-free soy sauce or tamari.

SAUCE

- 5 tablespoons soy sauce
- ¼ cup chunky peanut butter
- 3 tablespoons sesame seeds, toasted
- 2 tablespoons rice vinegar
- 2 tablespoons packed light brown sugar
- 1 tablespoon grated fresh ginger
- 2 garlic cloves, minced
- 1 teaspoon hot sauce
- ½ cup hot water

NOODLES AND VEGETABLES

- 1 pound fresh Chinese noodles
- 2 tablespoons toasted sesame oil
- 5 radishes, trimmed, halved, and sliced thin
- 4 scallions, sliced thin on bias
- 1 cucumber, peeled, halved lengthwise, seeded, and sliced thin
- 1 carrot, peeled and grated
- 1 tablespoon chopped fresh cilantro
- 1 tablespoon sesame seeds, toasted

1. FOR THE SAUCE: Process all ingredients except water in blender until smooth, about 30 seconds. With blender running, add hot water, 1 tablespoon at a time, until sauce has consistency of heavy cream (you may not need all of water). (Sauce can be refrigerated for up to 3 days; add warm water as need to loosen consistency before using.)

2. FOR THE NOODLES AND VEGETABLES: Meanwhile, bring 4 quarts water to boil in large pot. Add noodles and cook, stirring often, until tender. Drain noodles, rinse with cold water, and drain again, leaving noodles slightly wet.

3. Transfer noodles to large bowl and toss with oil. Add radishes, scallions, cucumber, carrot, cilantro, and sauce and toss to combine. Sprinkle individual portions with sesame seeds and serve.

Cold Soba Noodle Salad

SERVES 4 FAST VEGAN GF

WHY THIS RECIPE WORKS: Cold soba noodles are traditionally served with a dipping sauce that offers a delicate balance of Japanese flavors. For a fork-friendly take on this simple yet satisfying dish, we decided to turn the dipping sauce into a dressing. Soy sauce, mirin, and wasabi provided a flavorful base. Ginger added some heat, and thin slices of nori (dried seaweed) sprinkled over the top offered subtly briny, grassy notes. Peppery radishes and thinly sliced scallions added freshness and crunch. To prevent the cooked soba noodles from sticking together while we prepped the dressing, we tossed them with vegetable oil. To give this salad more heat, add additional wasabi paste to taste. Nori can be found in the international aisle at the supermarket or at an Asian market or a natural foods market. Do not substitute other types of noodles for the soba noodles here. In order for this recipe to be gluten-free, you must use gluten-free soba noodles and gluten-free soy sauce or tamari.

14 ounces dried soba noodles
   Salt
 1 tablespoon vegetable oil
¼ cup soy sauce
 3 tablespoons mirin
½ teaspoon sugar
½ teaspoon grated fresh ginger
¼ teaspoon wasabi paste or powder
 4 radishes, trimmed and shredded
 2 scallions, sliced thin on bias
 1 (8 by 2½-inch) piece nori, cut into matchsticks with scissors

1. Bring 4 quarts water to boil in large pot. Add noodles and 1 tablespoon salt and cook, stirring often, until tender. Drain noodles, rinse with cold water, and drain again, leaving noodles slightly wet. Transfer to large bowl and toss with oil.

2. Whisk soy sauce, mirin, sugar, ginger, and wasabi together in bowl, then pour over noodles. Add radishes and scallions and toss until well combined. (Salad can be refrigerated for up to 1 day; refresh with warm water and additional oil as needed.) Sprinkle individual portions with nori before serving.

Soba Noodles with Roasted Eggplant and Sesame

SERVES 4 VEGAN GF

WHY THIS RECIPE WORKS: The creamy texture and mild flavor of eggplant is the perfect complement to rich, nutty soba noodles in this recipe. We started with a hearty amount of eggplant. Roasting proved an easy, hands-off way to cook the eggplant; tossing it with soy sauce and vegetable oil beforehand helped to season it and draw out its moisture. For the sauce, we started with more soy sauce for savory richness. Vegetarian oyster sauce, sugar, Asian chili-garlic sauce, and toasted sesame oil provided a nice balance of sweet and spicy flavors, while a little sake contributed clean, acidic notes that bolstered the complexity of the sauce. A sprinkling of fresh cilantro and sesame seeds brightened up our earthy dish. Vermouth can be substituted for the sake if necessary. Do not substitute other types of noodles for the soba noodles here. In order for this recipe to be gluten-free, you must use gluten-free soba noodles and gluten-free soy sauce or tamari.

 3 pounds eggplant, cut into 1-inch pieces
¼ cup vegetable oil
⅓ cup soy sauce
⅓ cup sugar
 3 tablespoons vegetarian oyster sauce
 3 tablespoons toasted sesame oil
 5 teaspoons sake
1½ tablespoons Asian chili-garlic sauce
12 ounces dried soba noodles
¾ cup fresh cilantro leaves
 2 teaspoons sesame seeds, toasted

1. Adjust oven racks to upper-middle and lower-middle positions and heat oven to 450 degrees. Line 2 rimmed baking sheets with aluminum foil and spray with vegetable oil spray. Toss eggplant with vegetable oil and 1 tablespoon soy sauce,

Cutting Up Eggplant

1. Cut eggplant crosswise into 1-inch-thick rounds.

2. Cut rounds into tidy 1-inch cubes.

then spread evenly between prepared baking sheets. Roast until eggplant is well browned and tender, 25 to 30 minutes, stirring and switching sheets halfway through roasting.

2. Combine sugar, oyster sauce, sesame oil, sake, chili-garlic sauce, and remaining soy sauce in small saucepan. Cook over medium heat, whisking often, until sugar has dissolved, about 1 minute; cover and set aside.

3. Meanwhile, bring 4 quarts water to boil in large pot. Add noodles and cook, stirring often, until tender. Reserve ½ cup cooking water, then drain noodles and return them to pot. Add sauce and roasted eggplant and toss to combine. Add reserved cooking water as needed to adjust consistency. Sprinkle individual portions with cilantro and sesame seeds and serve.

Udon Noodles with Mustard Greens and Shiitake-Ginger Sauce

SERVES 4 TO 6   `FAST` `VEGAN`

✔ **WHY THIS RECIPE WORKS:** Noodles and greens are a common pairing in Asia, so we set out to develop a recipe that married the spicy bite of mustard greens with earthy udon noodles. Instead of using store-bought broth, we made our own highly aromatic and flavorful broth. We browned meaty shiitake mushrooms for flavor, then we added water and mirin along with rice vinegar, soy sauce, cloves of garlic, and a chunk of fresh ginger to make a bold, balanced broth. Dried shiitake mushrooms, sesame oil, and chili-garlic sauce rounded out the flavors. After this mixture simmered and reduced, we had a brothy sauce perfect for pairing with our cooked noodles and greens. Because fresh noodles cook so quickly, we made sure to add the greens to the pot before the noodles. Do not substitute other types of noodles for the udon noodles here.

- 1 **tablespoon vegetable oil**
- 8 **ounces shiitake mushrooms, stemmed and sliced thin**
- 2 **cups water**
- ¼ **cup mirin**
- 3 **tablespoons rice vinegar**
- 3 **tablespoons soy sauce**
- 2 **garlic cloves, smashed and peeled**
- 1 **(1-inch) piece ginger, peeled, halved, and smashed**
- ½ **ounce dried shiitake mushrooms, rinsed and minced**
- 1 **teaspoon toasted sesame oil**
- 1 **teaspoon Asian chili-garlic sauce**
- 1 **pound mustard greens, stemmed and chopped into 2-inch pieces**
  Salt and pepper
- 1 **pound fresh udon noodles**

1. Heat vegetable oil in Dutch oven over medium-high heat until shimmering. Add fresh mushrooms and cook, stirring occasionally, until softened and lightly browned, about 5 minutes. Stir in water, mirin, vinegar, soy sauce, garlic, ginger, dried mushrooms, sesame oil, and chili-garlic sauce and bring to simmer. Reduce heat to medium-low, and simmer until liquid has reduced by half, 8 to 10 minutes. Off heat, discard garlic and ginger; cover pot to keep warm, and set aside.

2. Meanwhile, bring 4 quarts water to boil in large pot. Add greens and 1 tablespoon salt and cook until greens are almost tender, 4 to 5 minutes. Add noodles and cook until greens and noodles are both tender, about 2 minutes. Reserve ⅓ cup cooking water, drain noodles and greens, and return them to pot. Add sauce and reserved cooking water, and toss to combine. Cook over medium-low heat, tossing constantly, until sauce clings to noodles, about 1 minute. Season with salt and pepper to taste, and serve.

Vegetarian Pad Thai
SERVES 4 `GF`

✓ **WHY THIS RECIPE WORKS:** With its sweet-sour-salty-spicy sauce, tender rice noodles, and bits of scrambled egg, pad thai is Thailand's most well-known noodle dish. We wanted a great vegetarian version that also featured crispy tofu. To get the noodles right, we soaked rice sticks in hot tap water for 20 minutes before stir-frying for tender but not sticky noodles. To create the balanced salty, sweet, sour, and spicy flavor profile, we combined vegetarian fish sauce, sugar, cayenne, and vinegar. We added tamarind paste for the fresh, bright, fruity taste that is essential to the dish. Chopped peanuts, bean sprouts, thinly sliced scallions, and lime wedges completed our authentic-tasting dish. For an accurate measurement of boiling water, bring a full kettle of water to a boil, then measure out the desired amount. Because this dish comes together very quickly, make sure all your ingredients are prepped before you start cooking. If using a tamarind substitute, use brown sugar instead of granulated sugar in the sauce, and eliminate the lime wedges for serving.

SAUCE
- 3 tablespoons tamarind paste or tamarind substitute
- ¾ cup boiling water
- ¼ cup fish sauce substitute (page 60)
- 3 tablespoons sugar
- 1 tablespoon vegetable oil
- 2 tablespoons rice vinegar
- ¼ teaspoon cayenne pepper

We use tamarind paste, fish sauce substitute, sugar, vinegar, and cayenne to make a pad thai sauce with authentic flavor.

NOODLES, TOFU, AND GARNISH
- 8 ounces (¼-inch-wide) rice noodles
- 14 ounces extra-firm tofu, cut into ¾-inch cubes
- 2 tablespoons cornstarch
- ¼ cup vegetable oil
- 1 shallot, minced
- 3 garlic cloves, minced
- 2 large eggs, lightly beaten
- 6 ounces (3 cups) bean sprouts
- 4 scallions, sliced thin on bias
   Salt
- ¼ cup minced fresh cilantro
- 2 tablespoons dry-roasted unsalted peanuts, chopped
   Lime wedges

1. **FOR THE SAUCE:** Soak tamarind paste in boiling water until softened, about 10 minutes. Push mixture through fine-mesh strainer into bowl, removing seeds and fibers and extracting as much pulp as possible; discard solids. Whisk fish sauce, sugar, oil, vinegar, and cayenne into tamarind liquid.

2. **FOR THE NOODLES, TOFU, AND GARNISH:** Cover noodles with very hot tap water in large bowl and stir to

Making Vegetarian Pad Thai

1. MAKE SAUCE: Soak tamarind paste in boiling water, then strain. Whisk fish sauce, sugar, oil, vinegar, and cayenne into tamarind liquid.

2. SOAK NOODLES: Cover rice noodles with very hot tap water, stir to separate, and let soak until softened and pliable, about 20 minutes.

3. CRISP TOFU: Pat tofu cubes dry and toss with cornstarch. Add to skillet and cook until crisp and browned on all sides, 8 to 10 minutes. Set aside.

4. STIR-FRY: Cook shallot, garlic, and eggs in skillet, then add noodles, sauce, tofu, bean sprouts, and scallions and cook until tofu is heated through and noodles are tender.

separate. Let noodles soak until softened, pliable, and limp but not fully tender, about 20 minutes; drain. Spread tofu over paper towel–lined baking sheet and let drain for 20 minutes.

3. Gently pat tofu dry with paper towels, then toss with cornstarch in bowl. Transfer coated tofu to strainer and shake gently over bowl to remove excess cornstarch. Heat 3 tablespoons oil in 12-inch nonstick skillet over medium-high heat until just smoking. Add tofu and cook, turning as needed, until crisp and browned on all sides, 8 to 10 minutes; transfer to bowl.

4. Wipe out now-empty skillet with paper towels, add remaining 1 tablespoon oil, and return to medium heat until shimmering. Add shallot and garlic and cook until lightly browned, about 1½ minutes. Stir in eggs and cook, stirring vigorously, until eggs are scrambled but still moist, about 20 seconds.

NOTES FROM THE TEST KITCHEN

Tamarind

Sweet-tart, brownish-red tamarind is a necessary ingredient for a pad thai that looks and tastes authentic. It's commonly sold in paste (also called pulp) and in concentrate form. We prefer tamarind paste because it has the freshest, brightest flavor; it is firm, sticky, and filled with seeds and fibers. Tamarind concentrate looks more like a pomade than a food. It's black, thick, shiny, and gooey. Its flavor approximates that of tamarind paste, but it tastes less fruity and more "cooked," and it colors the pad thai a shade too dark. To use tamarind concentrate in the pad thai recipe, mix 1 tablespoon with ⅔ cup hot water. If neither product is available, you can also make an excellent pad thai using a substitute made with lime juice and water. Simply combine ⅓ cup lime juice and ⅓ cup water and use it in place of the tamarind paste, then use light brown sugar instead of granulated sugar to give the noodles some color and a faint molasses flavor. Because it will already contain a good hit of lime, do not serve this version with lime wedges.

---

5. Add drained noodles and sauce, increase heat to high, and cook, tossing gently, until noodles are evenly coated, about 1 minute. Add tofu, bean sprouts, and scallions to skillet and cook, tossing gently, until tofu is heated through and noodles are tender, about 2 minutes. Season with salt to taste and sprinkle with cilantro and peanuts. Serve with lime wedges.

Vegetable Lo Mein

SERVES 4 TO 6 VEGAN GF

✔ **WHY THIS RECIPE WORKS:** Most takeout versions of vegetable lo mein are disappointments, with oily noodles, a wan sauce, and a few sparse vegetables. We were after a bright, fresh-tasting lo mein with chewy noodles tossed in a salty-sweet sauce with a hefty amount of vegetables. We started with a full pound of meaty shiitakes and paired them with napa cabbage and sweet red bell peppers. We used a combination of classic Asian ingredients to make a simple, balanced sweet-and-savory sauce, then we stir-fried the vegetables in batches. A hit of Asian chili-garlic sauce at the end brightened this dish and gave it a nice kick of heat. When shopping for Chinese rice wine, look for one that is amber in color; if not available, sherry wine may be used as a substitute. If you cannot find fresh Chinese egg noodles, substitute 12 ounces dried spaghetti or linguine. It is important that the noodles are cooked at the last minute to avoid clumping. In order for this recipe to be gluten-free, you must use gluten-free spaghetti or linguine, gluten-free soy sauce or tamari, and gluten-free hoisin sauce.

SAUCE

- ½ cup vegetable broth
- 3 tablespoons soy sauce
- 2 tablespoons vegetarian oyster sauce
- 2 tablespoons hoisin sauce
- 1 tablespoon toasted sesame oil
- 1 teaspoon cornstarch
- ¼ teaspoon five-spice powder

NOODLES AND VEGETABLES

- 3 tablespoons vegetable oil
- 4 teaspoons grated fresh ginger
- 3 garlic cloves, minced
- 1 pound shiitake mushrooms, stemmed and halved if small or quartered if large
- 10 scallions, white parts sliced thin and green parts cut into 1-inch pieces
- 2 red bell peppers, stemmed, seeded, and sliced into ¼-inch-wide strips
- ½ small head napa cabbage, cored and sliced crosswise into ½-inch-thick pieces (4 cups)
- ¼ cup Chinese rice wine or dry sherry
- 1 pound fresh Chinese noodles
- 1 tablespoon Asian chili-garlic sauce

1. FOR THE SAUCE: Whisk all ingredients together in bowl.

2. FOR THE NOODLES AND VEGETABLES: Combine 1 tablespoon oil, ginger, and garlic in bowl. Heat 1 tablespoon oil in 12-inch nonstick skillet over high heat until just smoking. Add mushrooms and cook until lightly browned, 6 to 8 minutes. Stir in scallions and cook until wilted, 2 to 3 minutes; transfer to bowl.

3. Add remaining 1 tablespoon oil, bell peppers, and cabbage to now-empty skillet, and cook until spotty brown, about 8 minutes. Clear center of skillet, add garlic-ginger mixture, and cook, mashing mixture into skillet until fragrant, about 30 seconds; stir into vegetables.

4. Stir in wine and cook until liquid is nearly evaporated, 30 to 60 seconds. Stir in mushroom mixture and sauce and simmer until thickened, 1 to 2 minutes; cover and set aside.

5. Meanwhile, bring 4 quarts water to boil in large pot. Add noodles and cook, stirring often, until tender. Drain noodles and return them to pot. Add cabbage mixture and chili-garlic sauce and toss to combine. Serve.

Hot and Sour Ramen with Tofu, Shiitakes, and Spinach

SERVES 4 `FAST` `VEGAN`

⚓ **WHY THIS RECIPE WORKS:** In Japan, ramen shops line the streets, offering piping-hot bowls of noodles paired with meat and vegetables. For our vegetarian take on this dish, we wanted to swap out the meat for tofu. We started by browning the tofu (we selected extra-firm tofu, which held up best in the pan) and mushrooms, then turned to the sauce. We ditched the salty seasoning packets in favor of building our own sauce. To infuse our dish with a hot-and-sour flavor profile, we included Asian chili-garlic sauce, cider vinegar, and a bit of sugar. Vegetable broth contributed balancing sweetness and vegetal notes. We finished the dish by stirring in baby spinach just until wilted. To make the dish spicier, add extra Asian chili-garlic sauce. Do not substitute other types of noodles for the ramen noodles here. The sauce in this dish will seem a bit brothy when finished, but the liquid will be absorbed quickly by the noodles when serving.

- 14 ounces extra-firm tofu, cut into 1-inch cubes
  Salt and pepper
- 5 teaspoons vegetable oil
- 8 ounces shiitake mushrooms, stemmed and sliced thin
- 2 teaspoons Asian chili-garlic sauce
- 3 garlic cloves, minced
- 1 tablespoon grated fresh ginger
- 3½ cups vegetable broth
- 4 (3-ounce) packages ramen noodles, seasoning packets discarded
- 3 tablespoons cider vinegar
- 2 tablespoons soy sauce
- 2 teaspoons sugar
- 6 ounces (6 cups) baby spinach

1. Spread tofu over paper towel–lined baking sheet, let drain for 20 minutes, then gently press dry with paper towels. Season tofu with salt and pepper. Heat 2 teaspoons oil in 12-inch nonstick skillet over high heat until just smoking. Add tofu and cook, turning occasionally, until browned on all sides, 8 to 10 minutes; transfer to bowl.

2. Add remaining 1 tablespoon oil to now-empty skillet and heat over medium-high heat until shimmering. Add mushrooms and cook until browned, about 4 minutes. Stir in chili-garlic sauce, garlic, and ginger and cook until fragrant, about 30 seconds. Stir in broth.

3. Break ramen into chunks and add to skillet. Bring to simmer and cook, tossing ramen constantly with tongs to separate, until it is just tender but there is still liquid in pan, about 2 minutes.

4. Stir in vinegar, soy sauce, and sugar. Stir in spinach, 1 handful at a time, until spinach is wilted and sauce is thickened. Return tofu to skillet and heat until warmed through, about 30 seconds. Serve.

Spicy Basil Noodles with Crispy Tofu, Snap Peas, and Bell Peppers

SERVES 4 **VEGAN** **GF**

✓ **WHY THIS RECIPE WORKS:** This brightly flavored Thai dish combines tender rice noodles with fragrant fresh basil and a spicy, aromatic sauce. We infused our dish with heat by creating a paste of hot chiles, garlic, and shallots in the food processor. Cooking the mixture briefly deepened its flavor and mellowed the harshness of the raw aromatics. Fish sauce substitute, brown sugar, lime juice, and vegetable broth added sweet and savory flavors. A generous amount of basil gives this dish its trademark fresh flavor and color—we used a whopping 2 cups and stirred it in at the end to keep its flavor fresh. Pan-fried tofu, coated with a light layer of cornstarch, offered both creamy and crispy textures. Stir-fried snap peas and red bell pepper strips added some crunch. To make this dish spicier, add the chile seeds. Do not substitute other types of noodles for the rice noodles here; however, you can substitute (¼-inch-wide) dried flat rice noodles and reduce their soaking time to 20 minutes.

12	ounces (⅜-inch-wide) rice noodles
14	ounces extra-firm tofu, cut into 1-inch cubes
8	Thai, serrano, or jalapeño chiles, stemmed and seeded
6	garlic cloves, peeled
4	shallots, peeled
2	cups vegetable broth
¼	cup fish sauce substitute (page 60)
¼	cup packed brown sugar
3	tablespoons lime juice (2 limes)
	Salt and pepper
½	cup cornstarch
7	tablespoons vegetable oil
6	ounces sugar snap peas, strings removed
1	red bell pepper, stemmed, seeded, sliced into ¼-inch-wide strips, and halved crosswise
2	cups fresh Thai basil or sweet basil leaves

1. Cover noodles with very hot tap water in large bowl and stir to separate. Let noodles soak until softened, pliable, and

Soaking Rice Noodles

A. UNDERSOAKED: These noodles are undersoaked and are still too hard. They will take too long to stir-fry.

B. OVERSOAKED: These noodles are oversoaked and are too soft and gummy. They will overcook when stir-fried and stay tangled.

C. PROPERLY SOAKED: These noodles are perfectly soaked and just softened. They will turn tender when stir-fried and remain separated.

limp but not fully tender, 35 to 40 minutes; drain. Spread tofu over paper towel–lined baking sheet and let drain for 20 minutes.

2. Meanwhile, pulse chiles, garlic, and shallots in food processor into smooth paste, about 20 pulses, scraping down bowl as needed. In bowl, whisk broth, fish sauce, sugar, and lime juice together.

3. Adjust oven rack to upper-middle position and heat oven to 200 degrees. Gently pat tofu dry with paper towels, season with salt and pepper, then toss with cornstarch in bowl. Transfer coated tofu to strainer and shake gently over bowl to remove excess cornstarch. Heat 3 tablespoons oil in 12-inch nonstick skillet over medium-high heat until just smoking. Add tofu and cook, turning as needed, until crisp and browned on all sides, 8 to 10 minutes; transfer to paper towel–lined plate and keep warm in oven.

4. Wipe out now-empty skillet with paper towels, add 1 tablespoon oil, and heat over high heat until just smoking. Add snap peas and bell pepper and cook, stirring often, until vegetables are crisp-tender and beginning to brown, 3 to 5 minutes; transfer to bowl.

5. Add remaining 3 tablespoons oil to now-empty skillet and heat over medium-high heat until shimmering. Add processed chile mixture and cook until moisture evaporates and color deepens, 3 to 5 minutes. Add drained noodles and broth mixture and cook, tossing gently, until sauce has thickened and noodles are well coated and tender, 5 to 10 minutes.

6. Stir in cooked vegetables and basil and cook until basil wilts slightly, about 1 minute. Top individual portions with crispy tofu and serve.

Mee Goreng

SERVES 4 TO 6 **VEGAN** **GF**

✅ **WHY THIS RECIPE WORKS:** This one-dish Indonesian favorite features spicy pan-fried noodles with vegetables or meat and shrimp, a special sweet soy sauce, and a garnish of crispy shallots. For our vegetarian version, we kept the ingredients simple, featuring tofu and bok choy along with the traditional fried shallots. To give the dish plenty of spice, we used a hefty amount of sambal oelek (a sauce made from ground chiles without added flavorings). Typically, this dish is made with sweet soy sauce, but we found that using dark brown sugar, molasses, and regular soy sauce was a perfect substitute for the hard-to-find ingredient. Lastly, a squeeze of lime rounded out the spicy and sweet base we had created. Don't skip the limes here; they are important in balancing out this otherwise sweet dish. If you cannot find fresh Chinese egg noodles, substitute 12 ounces dried spaghetti or linguine. In order for this recipe to be gluten-free, you must use 12 ounces dried gluten-free spaghetti or linguine and gluten-free soy sauce or tamari.

- 1 **pound fresh Chinese noodles**
- ¼ **cup packed dark brown sugar**
- ¼ **cup molasses**
- ¼ **cup soy sauce**
- 4 **large shallots, 2 minced and 2 sliced thin**
- 3 **garlic cloves, minced**
- 2 **teaspoons sambal oelek**
- 14 **ounces extra-firm tofu, cut into 1-inch cubes**
  Salt and pepper
- 2 **tablespoons cornstarch**
- 5 **tablespoons vegetable oil**
- 1 **pound bok choy, stalks and greens separated and sliced ½ inch thick**
- 4 **scallions, sliced thin on bias**
  Lime wedges

1. Bring 4 quarts water to boil in large pot. Add noodles and cook, stirring often, until tender. Drain noodles and set aside.

Creamy tofu, tender bok choy, and crispy scallions pair nicely with chewy noodles in a sweet and spicy stir-fry sauce.

2. Whisk sugar, molasses, and soy sauce together in bowl. In separate bowl, combine minced shallots, garlic, and sambal oelek.

3. Spread tofu over paper towel–lined baking sheet and let drain for 20 minutes. Gently pat tofu dry with paper towels, season with salt and pepper, then toss with cornstarch in bowl. Transfer coated tofu to strainer and shake gently over bowl to remove excess cornstarch. Heat 3 tablespoons oil in 12-inch nonstick skillet over medium-high heat until just smoking. Add tofu and cook, turning as needed, until crisp and browned on all sides, 8 to 10 minutes; transfer to bowl.

4. Add 1 tablespoon oil to now-empty skillet and heat until shimmering. Add sliced shallots and cook until golden, about 5 minutes; transfer to paper towel–lined plate.

5. Add remaining 1 tablespoon oil to now-empty skillet and heat until shimmering. Add bok choy stalks and cook until crisp-tender, about 3 minutes. Clear center of skillet, add garlic mixture, and cook, mashing mixture into skillet until fragrant, about 30 seconds; stir into vegetables.

6. Stir in noodles, tofu, bok choy leaves, and scallions. Whisk sauce to recombine, add to skillet and cook, stirring constantly, until sauce is thickened, 1 to 2 minutes. Serve with lime wedges.

We stuff these traditional steamed dumplings with a flavorful filling featuring mushrooms, tofu, and pickled kimchi.

Steamed Chinese Dumplings (Shu Mai)

MAKES ABOUT 40 DUMPLINGS

✔ **WHY THIS RECIPE WORKS:** Steamed Chinese dumplings are usually filled with pork or shrimp, but we wanted a vegetarian version that was as satisfying as the original. We started with creamy ground tofu and pungent kimchi. Along with the traditional flavorings—cilantro, Chinese rice wine, ginger, and toasted sesame oil—we added soy sauce and dried shiitake mushrooms for extra savoriness. For the wrappers, we cut square egg roll skins into rounds. Finally, we garnished each dumpling with finely grated carrot in lieu of the traditional roe. After steaming them for just 6 minutes, we served them with a small dash of our very spicy homemade chili oil. We prefer our chili oil, but store-bought works too. A traditional bamboo steamer basket works best here; if you don't have one, you can use a collapsible metal steamer basket set inside a covered pot.

14 ounces extra-firm tofu, cut into 2-inch pieces

8 ounces vegetarian kimchi, drained

Assembling Shu Mai

1. Brush edges of wrapper lightly with water, then place heaping tablespoon of filling in center. Pinch opposite sides of wrapper with fingers, rotate dumpling 90 degrees, and repeat pinching.

2. Continue to pinch dumpling until you have 8 equidistant pinches around circumference of dumpling.

3. Gather up sides of dumpling and squeeze gently at top to create "waist."

4. Holding crimped dumpling firmly in hand, pack filling tightly with flat side of butter knife.

¾ ounce dried shiitake mushroom caps, soaked in hot water 30 minutes, squeezed dry, and cut into ¼-inch dice

2 tablespoons soy sauce

2 tablespoons cornstarch

2 tablespoons minced fresh cilantro

1 tablespoon toasted sesame oil

1 tablespoon Chinese rice wine or dry sherry

1 tablespoon rice vinegar

2 teaspoons sugar

2 teaspoons grated fresh ginger

½ teaspoon salt

½ teaspoon pepper

1 pound (5½-inch) square egg roll wrappers

¼ cup finely grated carrot

1 recipe Chili Oil (page 154)

1. Spread tofu over paper towel–lined baking sheet, let drain for 20 minutes, then gently pat dry with paper towels. Squeeze excess liquid from kimchi.

2. Place tofu and kimchi in food processor and pulse until coarsely chopped with pieces no larger than ¼ inch, about 5 pulses; transfer to bowl. Stir in mushrooms, soy sauce, cornstarch, cilantro, sesame oil, wine, vinegar, sugar, ginger, salt, and pepper until well combined.

3. Line baking sheet with parchment paper. Working with 6 or 7 wrappers at a time, cut two 3-inch rounds from each wrapper using 3-inch biscuit cutter; you should have 40 to 42 rounds. Keep wrappers covered with moist paper towels.

4. Working with 6 rounds at a time (cover others with moist paper towel), brush edges with water and place heaping tablespoon of filling in center. Pinch wrapper around sides of filling, leaving top exposed. Flatten pinched edges, squeeze top edge to create "waist," then pack filling using flat side of butter knife. Transfer to prepared baking sheet and cover with damp dish towel. Top each dumpling with pinch of grated carrot.

5. Cut piece of parchment slightly smaller than diameter of steamer basket and place in basket. Poke about 20 small holes in parchment and lightly coat with vegetable oil spray. Place batches of dumplings on parchment liner, making sure they are not touching. Set steamer over simmering water and cook, covered, until dumplings are tender, about 6 minutes. Serve with chili oil.

CHILI OIL

MAKES ABOUT ¼ CUP   **FAST** **VEGAN** **GF**

Although we prefer the flavor of peanut oil here, vegetable or canola oil can be substituted.

1½ teaspoons soy sauce
1 teaspoon sugar
¼ teaspoon salt
¼ cup peanut oil
2 tablespoons red pepper flakes
1 garlic clove, peeled

Combine soy sauce, sugar, and salt in bowl; set aside. Heat oil in small saucepan over medium heat until just shimmering and registers 300 degrees. Remove pan from heat and stir in pepper flakes, garlic, and soy sauce mixture. Let cool to room temperature, stirring occasionally, about 1 hour. Discard garlic and serve. (Oil can be refrigerated for up to 1 week.)

These classic pan-fried potstickers are stuffed with a cabbage and mushroom filling and dipped in a savory scallion sauce.

Cabbage and Mushroom Potstickers

MAKES 24 DUMPLINGS

✔ **WHY THIS RECIPE WORKS:** To make a hearty vegetarian version of Chinese potstickers, we decided to use a combination of cabbage and mushrooms for the filling. To start, we salted and drained the cabbage to get rid of excess moisture while we chopped the mushrooms in a food processor and sautéed them to drive off their moisture. We combined all the ingredients, then chilled the mixture to prevent it from leaking out when we filled and cooked the potstickers. However, the filling turned tough when cooked in the potstickers. To solve this, we added egg whites to the filling. As the potstickers cooked, the egg whites puffed up almost like a soufflé, making the otherwise compact filling light and tender. As for the wrapper, we turned to *gyoza* wrappers; made without egg, they are sturdy and hold up well when pan-fried. To cook the potstickers, we placed them in a cold, lightly oiled skillet before turning on the burner, then added water to the skillet and steamed them until tender. Finally, we removed the lid and continued to cook them until they developed a nice, flavorful crust. You will need a 12-inch skillet with a tight-fitting lid for this recipe. You can substitute wonton wrappers for the gyoza wrappers; wonton wrappers are smaller, so they will yield about 40 potstickers and you may need to reduce their steaming time slightly.

- 3 cups minced napa cabbage leaves
  Salt and pepper
- 8 ounces white mushrooms, trimmed and quartered
- 2 teaspoons plus 2 tablespoons vegetable oil
- 4 scallions, minced
- 2 large egg whites, lightly beaten
- 4 teaspoons soy sauce
- 1 teaspoon grated fresh ginger
- 1 garlic clove, minced
- 24 (3½-inch) round gyoza wrappers
- 1 cup water, plus extra for brushing
- 1 recipe Scallion Dipping Sauce

1. Toss cabbage with ¼ teaspoon salt in colander and let drain for 20 minutes; press gently to squeeze out excess moisture.

2. Meanwhile, pulse mushrooms in food processor until finely chopped, about 15 pulses. Heat 2 teaspoons oil in 12-inch nonstick skillet over medium-high heat until shimmering. Add mushrooms and ¼ teaspoon salt, and cook until liquid has evaporated and mushrooms clump and are starting to brown, 5 to 7 minutes. Transfer to large bowl and let cool for 15 minutes.

3. Stir drained cabbage, scallions, egg whites, soy sauce, ginger, garlic, and ⅛ teaspoon pepper into mushrooms. Cover and refrigerate until chilled, at least 30 minutes or up to 24 hours.

4. Working with 4 wrappers at a time (cover others with moist paper towel), brush edges of wrappers with water and place scant tablespoon of filling in center. Fold wrapper in half and pinch dumpling closed, pressing out any air pockets. Place dumpling on 1 side and gently flatten bottom. Transfer

---

to baking sheet and cover with damp dish towel. (Dumplings can be refrigerated for up to 24 hours or frozen for up to 1 month; if frozen, do not thaw before cooking.)

5. Brush 1 tablespoon oil over bottom of 12-inch nonstick skillet and arrange half of dumplings in skillet, flat side facing down (they may overlap). Cook over medium heat, without moving them, until golden brown on bottom, 3 to 4 minutes.

6. Reduce heat to low, add ½ cup water, and cover. Cook until most of water is absorbed and wrappers are slightly translucent, 8 to 10 minutes. Uncover, increase heat to medium, and cook, without stirring dumplings, until bottoms are well browned and crisp, 1 to 2 minutes; transfer to paper towel–lined plate.

7. Wipe out now-empty skillet with paper towels and repeat with remaining oil, dumplings, and water. Serve with Scallion Dipping Sauce.

Assembling Potstickers

1. Moisten edge of each wrapper, then place scant tablespoon of filling in center.

2. Fold wrapper in half around filling to make half-moon shape.

3. With forefinger and thumb, pinch dumpling closed, pressing out any air pockets.

4. Place dumpling on its side and press gently to flatten bottom.

CHAPTER 4

Rice and Grains

■ FAST (Less than 45 minutes start to finish)   ■ VEGAN   ■ GLUTEN-FREE
Photos: Curried Millet Pilaf; Almost Hands-Free Risotto with Parmesan

SIMPLE RICE RECIPES

Healthy, inexpensive, and conveniently shelf-stable, rice is a staple in many parts of the world and an essential ingredient in the vegetarian kitchen. A side of rice is a great way to bulk up a simple meal or temper a spicy curry or stir-fry. There are as many ways to cook rice as there are different types; here are a few of our favorite simple recipes.

Stovetop White Rice

SERVES 4 TO 6   `FAST` `VEGAN` `GF`

Basmati, jasmine, or Texmati rice can be substituted for the long-grain rice.

- 1 tablespoon unsalted butter or extra-virgin olive oil
- 2 cups long-grain white rice, rinsed
- 3 cups water
- 1 teaspoon salt

Melt butter in large saucepan over medium heat. Add rice and cook, stirring often, until edges begin to turn translucent, about 2 minutes. Add water and salt and bring to boil. Cover, reduce heat to low, and simmer until liquid is absorbed and rice is tender, about 20 minutes. Remove pot from heat, lay clean folded dish towel underneath lid, and let rice sit for 10 minutes. Fluff rice with fork and serve.

Basmati Rice Pilaf

SERVES 4   `FAST` `GF`

Long-grain white, jasmine, or Texmati rice can be substituted for the basmati.

- 2¼ cups water
- Salt and pepper
- 3 tablespoons unsalted butter
- ½ onion, chopped fine
- 1½ cups basmati rice, rinsed

Bring water to boil in small covered saucepan over medium-high heat. Add 1½ teaspoons salt and season with pepper; cover to keep hot. Meanwhile, melt butter in large saucepan over medium heat. Add onion and cook until softened but not browned, about 4 minutes. Stir in rice and cook until edges begin to

turn translucent, about 3 minutes. Stir in hot seasoned water and bring to brief boil. Reduce heat to low, cover, and simmer until liquid is absorbed, 16 to 18 minutes. Remove pot from heat, lay clean folded dish towel underneath lid, and let rice sit for 10 minutes. Fluff rice with fork and serve.

Sushi Rice

SERVES 4 TO 6   `FAST` `VEGAN` `GF`

You can substitute short-grain rice for the sushi rice. Regular rice vinegar can be substituted for the seasoned rice vinegar. Do not rinse the rice before cooking; the rice's exterior starch gives the finished dish the proper sticky texture.

- 2 cups sushi or short-grain white rice
- 2 cups water
- 2 teaspoons seasoned rice vinegar
- 1 teaspoon salt

Bring rice, water, vinegar, and salt to boil in medium saucepan over high heat. Cover, reduce heat to low, and cook until liquid is absorbed, 7 to 9 minutes. Remove rice from heat and let sit, covered, until tender, about 15 minutes. Fluff rice with fork and serve.

Foolproof Baked White Rice

SERVES 4   `FAST` `VEGAN` `GF`

For an accurate measurement of boiling water, bring a full kettle of water to a boil, then measure out the desired amount. Basmati, jasmine, or Texmati rice can be substituted for the long-grain rice.

- 2¾ cups boiling water
- 1⅓ cups long-grain white rice, rinsed
- 1 tablespoon extra-virgin olive oil
- Salt and pepper

Adjust oven rack to middle position and heat oven to 450 degrees. Combine boiling water, rice, oil, and ½ teaspoon salt in 8-inch square baking dish. Cover dish tightly with double layer of aluminum foil. Bake until liquid is absorbed and rice is tender, about 20 minutes. Remove dish from oven, uncover, and fluff rice with fork, scraping up any rice that has stuck to bottom. Re-cover dish with foil and let rice sit for 10 minutes. Season with salt and pepper to taste and serve.

Foolproof Baked Brown Rice

SERVES 4   `VEGAN` `GF`

Medium-grain or short-grain brown rice can be substituted for the long-grain rice.

- 2⅓ cups boiling water
- 1½ cups long-grain brown rice, rinsed
- 2 teaspoons extra-virgin olive oil
- Salt and pepper

Adjust oven rack to middle position and heat oven to 375 degrees. Combine boiling water, rice, oil, and ½ teaspoon salt in 8-inch square baking dish. Cover dish tightly with double layer of aluminum foil. Bake until liquid is absorbed and rice is tender, about 1 hour. Remove dish from oven, uncover, and fluff rice with fork, scraping up any rice that has stuck to bottom. Cover dish with clean dish towel and let rice sit for 5 minutes. Uncover and let rice sit 5 minutes longer. Season with salt and pepper to taste and serve.

Our Mexican rice gets intense flavor from the cooking liquid, a potent puree of fresh tomatoes, onion, and vegetable broth.

Mexican Rice

SERVES 6 TO 8   **VEGAN**   **GF**

WHY THIS RECIPE WORKS: Rice cooked the Mexican way should be a flavorful pilaf-style dish, but we've had our share of soupy or greasy versions. We wanted tender rice infused with fresh flavor. To keep the grains distinct, we rinsed the rice before cooking it to remove excess starch, then pan-fried it in oil before adding the liquid to give it a satisfying texture and a mild toasted flavor. For the rice cooking liquid, we pureed fresh tomatoes with an onion and combined the mixture with vegetable broth. For savory flavor and color, we added a little tomato paste. Baking the rice ensured even cooking. Cilantro, jalapeño, and lime juice complemented the richer tones of the cooked tomatoes, garlic, and onion. To keep the dish from being too spicy, we removed some of the jalapeño seeds. Use an ovensafe pot about 12 inches in diameter so that the rice cooks evenly and in the time indicated. We've successfully used both a straight-sided sauté pan and a Dutch oven. Whichever type of pot you use, it should have a tight-fitting, ovensafe lid.

Making Mexican Rice

1. MAKE TOMATO-ONION PUREE: Process tomatoes and onion in food processor until smooth, about 15 seconds. Measure out 2 cups.

2. FRY RICE: Heat oil in Dutch oven over medium-high heat for 1 to 2 minutes. Add rice and fry, stirring often, until rice is light golden and translucent, 6 to 8 minutes.

3. BAKE RICE: After adding liquid and more aromatics, bring mixture to boil, cover, and cook in 350-degree oven until rice is tender, 30 to 35 minutes, stirring well after 15 minutes.

4. FOLD IN CILANTRO AND JALAPEÑO: Gently fold in cilantro and reserved minced jalapeño with seeds to taste.

2   ripe tomatoes, cored and quartered
1   onion, root end trimmed, and quartered
3   jalapeño chiles, stemmed
⅓   cup vegetable oil
2   cups long-grain white rice, rinsed
4   garlic cloves, minced
2   cups vegetable broth
1   tablespoon tomato paste
1½   teaspoons salt
½   cup minced fresh cilantro
    Lime wedges

1. Adjust oven rack to middle position and heat oven to 350 degrees. Process tomatoes and onion in food processor until smooth, about 15 seconds. Transfer mixture to liquid measuring cup and spoon off excess until mixture measures 2 cups. Remove ribs and seeds from 2 jalapeños and discard; mince flesh and set aside. Mince remaining 1 jalapeño, including ribs and seeds; set aside.

2. Heat oil in Dutch oven over medium-high heat for 1 to 2 minutes. Drop 3 or 4 grains rice in oil; if grains sizzle, oil is ready. Add rice and cook, stirring often, until rice is light golden and translucent, 6 to 8 minutes.

3. Reduce heat to medium. Stir in garlic and reserved seeded jalapeños and cook, stirring constantly, until fragrant, about 1½ minutes. Stir in pureed tomato-onion mixture, broth, tomato paste, and salt. Increase heat to medium-high and bring to boil.

4. Cover pot, transfer to oven, and cook until liquid is absorbed and rice is tender, 30 to 35 minutes, stirring well after 15 minutes. Fold in cilantro and reserved jalapeño with seeds to taste. Serve with lime wedges.

VARIATION
Mexican Brown Rice VEGAN GF
Substitute long-grain brown rice for white rice; do not rinse rice and reduce rice frying to 3 to 3½ minutes. Increase broth to 2½ cups and increase oven cooking time to 1 to 1½ hours, stirring every 30 minutes.

Coconut Rice with Bok Choy and Lime
SERVES 4 TO 6 FAST VEGAN GF

 WHY THIS RECIPE WORKS: Rich, creamy coconut rice is served around the globe as a cooling accompaniment to spicy curries, stir-fries, and more. This dressed-up version features baby bok choy along with aromatic lemon grass, lime, and cilantro. Following the traditional method, we cooked basmati rice in coconut milk along with the aromatic lemon grass, which steeped in the liquid and lent its flavor as the rice simmered. To ensure the bok choy stalks turned tender by the time the rice was cooked, we sautéed them in the pan along with some minced shallot before adding the rice. When the rice was done, we stirred in fragrant lime zest and juice and cilantro along with the delicate bok choy greens. We prefer the flavor of basmati rice in this recipe, but long-grain white, jasmine, or Texmati rice can be substituted.

Smashing Lemon Grass

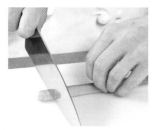

1. Trim dry top (this part is usually green) and tough bottom of each stalk.

2. Peel and discard dry outer layer until moist, tender inner stalk is exposed.

3. Smash peeled stalk with back of chef's knife or meat pounder to release maximum flavor.

2 teaspoons vegetable oil
2 heads baby bok choy (4 ounces each), stalks sliced ½ inch thick and greens chopped
1 shallot, minced
1½ cups basmati rice, rinsed
1½ cups water
¾ cup canned coconut milk
1 lemon grass stalk, trimmed to bottom 6 inches and smashed
Salt and pepper
2 tablespoons minced fresh cilantro
1 teaspoon grated lime zest plus 2 teaspoons juice

1. Heat oil in large saucepan over medium-high heat until shimmering. Add bok choy stalks and shallot and cook, stirring occasionally, until softened, about 2 minutes.

2. Stir in rice, water, coconut milk, lemon grass, and 2 teaspoons salt and bring to boil. Reduce heat to low, cover, and simmer gently until liquid is absorbed, 18 to 20 minutes.

3. Fold in cilantro, lime zest and juice, and bok choy greens, cover, and cook until rice is tender, about 3 minutes. Discard lemon grass. Season with salt and pepper to taste, and serve.

This uniquely sweet-and-savory dish features aromatic basmati rice studded with a variety of nuts and dried fruit.

Jeweled Rice

SERVES 4 TO 6 VEGAN GF

✓ **WHY THIS RECIPE WORKS:** Jeweled rice is a staple in Persian cuisine and features basmati rice perfumed with candied carrots, saffron, and cardamom; its name comes from the colorful dried fruit and nuts that traditionally stud its appealingly golden surface. We love the dish's subtle balance between sweet and savory, and we were inspired to re-create it while making it simpler and easier. With ingredients that are soaked, bloomed, parcooked, layered, and steamed, this dish typically uses almost every pot in the kitchen. We streamlined our version by cooking the rice using an easy pilaf method, adding the spices and some sautéed onion to the water to infuse the rice with rich flavor. While it simmered, we candied the orange zest and carrots. Once the rice was done, we sprinkled our candied mixture and some dried fruit on top and let it plump up while our rice rested off the heat. Finally, we stirred in the nuts just before serving so they'd retain their crunch. We prefer the flavor of basmati rice in this recipe, but long-grain white, jasmine, or Texmati rice can be substituted.

4¼ cups water
1 cup sugar
6 (2-inch) strips orange zest, sliced thin lengthwise
2 carrots, peeled and cut into ¼-inch pieces
2 tablespoons extra-virgin olive oil
1 onion, chopped fine
Salt and pepper
¾ teaspoon saffron threads, crumbled
½ teaspoon ground cardamom
1½ cups basmati rice, rinsed
½ cup currants
½ cup dried cranberries
¼ cup sliced almonds, toasted
¼ cup pistachios, toasted and chopped

1. Bring 2 cups water and sugar to boil in small saucepan over medium-high heat. Stir in orange zest and carrots, reduce heat to medium-low, and simmer until carrots are tender, 10 to 15 minutes. Drain well, transfer to plate, and let cool.

2. Meanwhile, heat oil in large saucepan over medium heat until shimmering. Add onion and 1½ teaspoons salt and cook until onion is softened, about 5 minutes. Stir in saffron and cardamom and cook until fragrant, about 30 seconds. Stir in rice and cook, stirring often, until grain edges begin to turn translucent, about 3 minutes. Stir in remaining 2¼ cups water and bring to simmer. Reduce heat to low, cover, and simmer gently until liquid is absorbed and rice is tender, 16 to 18 minutes.

3. Remove pot from heat and sprinkle candied carrots and orange zest, currants, and cranberries over rice. Cover, laying clean folded dish towel underneath lid, and let sit for 10 minutes. Add almonds and pistachios and fluff gently with fork to combine. Season with salt and pepper to taste, and serve.

Slicing Orange Zest Thinly

1. Using vegetable peeler, remove 2-inch-long strip orange zest from orange, avoiding bitter white pith just beneath.

2. Using chef's knife, cut zest strips lengthwise into long, thin pieces.

Baked Wild Rice

SERVES 4 TO 6 `VEGAN` `GF`

✔ **WHY THIS RECIPE WORKS:** We love wild rice, with its chewy outer husk and nutty, savory flavor, but it can take nearly an hour to become tender on the stovetop. We wanted to take advantage of the oven to make wild rice an easy, hands-off affair. We started with our recipe for baked brown rice, spreading the rice in a baking dish, pouring boiling water over the top, and baking it until tender. To get the hardier grains to cook through, we had to increase both the amount of water and the cooking time. After a little more than an hour, we had evenly cooked, tender grains with great chew. The recipe can be doubled easily using a 13 by 9-inch baking dish. Be sure to cover the pot when bringing the water to a boil in step 2; any water loss due to evaporation will affect how the rice cooks. Do not use quick-cooking or presteamed wild rice in this recipe; you may need to read the ingredient list on the package carefully to determine if the wild rice is presteamed.

1½ **cups wild rice, rinsed**
3 **cups water**
2 **teaspoons unsalted butter or extra-virgin olive oil**
¾ **teaspoon salt**

1. Adjust oven rack to middle position and heat oven to 375 degrees. Spread rice into 8-inch square glass baking dish.

2. Bring water, butter, and salt to boil in covered medium saucepan over high heat. Once boiling, stir to combine, then pour immediately over rice. Cover baking dish tightly with aluminum foil and bake until liquid is absorbed and rice is tender, 70 to 80 minutes.

3. Remove baking dish from oven, uncover, and fluff rice with fork. Re-cover dish with foil and let rice sit for 10 minutes before serving.

VARIATION

Baked Wild Rice with Almonds and Cranberries

SERVES 4 TO 6 `VEGAN` `GF`

The recipe can be doubled easily using a 13 by 9-inch baking dish. Be sure to cover the pot when bringing the water to a boil in step 2; any water loss due to evaporation will affect how the rice cooks. Finely chopping the cranberries ensures that they will soften in the steaming rice. Dried cherries can be substituted for the cranberries. Do not use quick-cooking or presteamed wild rice in this recipe; you may need to read the ingredient list on the package carefully to determine if the wild rice is presteamed.

NOTES FROM THE TEST KITCHEN

Shopping for Wild Rice

Wild rice is technically not in the same family as other rices; it's actually an aquatic grass. Wild rice is North America's only native grain. It grows naturally in lakes and also is cultivated in man-made paddies in Minnesota, California, and Canada. When we tasted five widely available brands, textural differences stood out the most; our top three, including our winner, cooked up springy and firm, while the other two blew out. What accounted for the difference? Processing. To create a shelf-stable product, manufacturers heat the grains, which gelatinizes their starches and drives out moisture, according to one of two methods: parching (the traditional approach) or parboiling. To parch, manufacturers load batches of rice into cylinders, which spin over a fire—an inexact process that produces less toothsome results. Parboiling, a newer method, steams the grains in a controlled pressurized environment. The result: more uniform and complete gelatinization, which translates into rice that cooks more evenly. Our favorite brand, **Goose Valley Wild Rice**, boasted grains that had a great crunchy exterior yet were tender inside.

1½ **cups wild rice, rinsed**
3 **tablespoons unsalted butter or extra-virgin olive oil**
1 **onion, chopped fine**
¾ **teaspoon salt**
3 **cups water**
¼ **cup dried cranberries, chopped fine**
¼ **cup sliced almonds, toasted**

1. Adjust oven rack to middle position and heat oven to 375 degrees. Spread rice into 8-inch square glass baking dish.

2. Melt butter in medium saucepan over medium heat. Add onion and salt and cook until onion is softened, 5 to 7 minutes. Stir in water. Cover pot, increase heat to high, and bring to boil. Once boiling, stir to combine, then pour mixture immediately over rice. Cover baking dish tightly with aluminum foil and bake until liquid is absorbed and rice is tender, 70 to 80 minutes.

3. Remove baking dish from oven, uncover, and fluff rice with fork. Stir in cranberries, re-cover dish with foil, and let rice sit for 10 minutes. Fold in sliced almonds before serving.

ALL ABOUT **COOKING RICE**

Here are three simple methods for basic rice cooking: boiling, pilaf-style (which we think yields the best results), and microwaving. Boiling and simmering the rice in ample amounts of water (like pasta) on the stovetop is easy. While some may argue it doesn't produce the best rice, we think it is a great (and foolproof) method when you want rice to round out a meal or fill a burrito. The best thing about simmering rice on the stovetop is that rinsing and measuring aren't even necessary. And microwaving rice? Well, after working on it for a while in the test kitchen, we can honestly say that not only does the microwave work, it works really well. Plus you can cook the rice right in the serving bowl.

If you want to make rice for a crowd, use the boiling method and double the amount of rice (there's no need to add more water or salt). We don't recommend cooking more than 1 cup of rice in the microwave.

BOILING DIRECTIONS: Bring the water to a boil in a large saucepan. Stir in the rice and 2½ teaspoons salt. Return to a boil, then reduce to a simmer and cook until the rice is tender, following the cooking times given in the chart below. Drain.

PILAF-STYLE DIRECTIONS: Rinse the rice (see page 165). Heat 1 tablespoon oil in a medium saucepan (preferably nonstick) over medium-high heat until shimmering. Stir in the rice and cook until the edges of the grains begin to turn translucent, about 3 minutes. Stir in the water and ¼ teaspoon salt. Bring the mixture to a simmer, then reduce the heat to low, cover, and continue to simmer until the rice is tender and has absorbed all the water, following the cooking times given in the chart below. Off the heat, place a clean folded dish towel under the lid and let the rice sit for 10 minutes. Fluff the rice with a fork.

MICROWAVE DIRECTIONS: Rinse the rice (see page 165). Combine the water, the rice, 1 tablespoon oil, and ¼ teaspoon salt in a bowl. Cover and microwave on high (full power) until the water begins to boil, 5 to 10 minutes. Reduce the microwave heat to medium (50 percent power) and continue to cook until the rice is just tender, following the cooking times given in the chart below. Remove from the microwave and fluff with a fork. Cover the bowl with plastic wrap, poke several vent holes in the plastic with the tip of a knife, and let sit until completely tender, about 5 minutes.

TYPE OF RICE	COOKING METHOD	AMOUNT OF RICE	AMOUNT OF WATER	COOKING TIME
Short- and Medium-Grain White Rice	Boiled	1 cup	4 quarts	10 to 15 minutes
	Pilaf-Style	1 cup	1¾ cups	10 to 15 minutes
	Microwave	X	X	X
Long-Grain White Rice	Boiled	1 cup	4 quarts	12 to 17 minutes
	Pilaf-Style	1 cup	1¾ cups	16 to 18 minutes
	Microwave	1 cup	2 cups	10 to 15 minutes
Short- and Medium-Grain Brown Rice	Boiled	1 cup	4 quarts	22 to 27 minutes
	Pilaf-Style	1 cup	1¾ cups	40 to 50 minutes
	Microwave	1 cup	2 cups	25 to 30 minutes
Long-Grain Brown Rice	Boiled	1 cup	4 quarts	25 to 30 minutes
	Pilaf-Style	1 cup	1¾ cups	40 to 50 minutes
	Microwave	1 cup	2 cups	25 to 30 minutes
Wild Rice	Boiled	1 cup	4 quarts	35 to 40 minutes
	Pilaf-Style	X	X	X
	Microwave	X	X	X
Basmati, Jasmine, or Texmati Rice	Boiled	1 cup	4 quarts	12 to 17 minutes
	Pilaf-Style	1 cup	1¾ cups	16 to 18 minutes
	Microwave	1 cup	2 cups	10 to 15 minutes

X = Not recommended

Hearty Baked Brown Rice

SERVES 4 TO 6 `GF`

✔ **WHY THIS RECIPE WORKS:** We set out to bulk up our Foolproof Baked Brown Rice, with aromatics and vegetables that would complement the hearty flavor and texture of the rice. For aromatic flavor that would permeate the dish, we sautéed two onions until well browned before adding the rice and water to the pot. Once the rice was tender, we stirred in chopped roasted red peppers and let them warm through as the rice rested off the heat. Then we stirred in some fresh parsley and black pepper, and we served the dish with grated Parmesan cheese and bright lemon wedges. Finally, we made some simple variations—a Greek-inspired version with peas, feta, and mint, and a Southwestern take with black beans, bell pepper, and cilantro. Medium-grain or short-grain brown rice can be substituted for the long-grain rice.

4	teaspoons vegetable oil
2	onions, chopped fine
2¼	cups water
1	cup vegetable broth
1½	cups long-grain brown rice, rinsed
1	teaspoon salt
¾	cup chopped jarred roasted red peppers
½	cup minced fresh parsley
¼	teaspoon pepper
1	ounce Parmesan cheese, grated (½ cup)
	Lemon wedges

1. Adjust oven rack to middle position and heat oven to 375 degrees. Heat oil in Dutch oven over medium heat until shimmering. Add onions and cook, stirring occasionally, until well browned, 12 to 14 minutes.

2. Add water and broth, cover, and bring to boil. Off heat, stir in rice and salt. Cover, transfer pot to oven, and bake until liquid is absorbed and rice is tender, 65 to 70 minutes.

3. Remove pot from oven and uncover. Fluff rice with fork and stir in red peppers. Replace lid and let rice sit for 5 minutes. Stir in parsley and pepper. Serve with Parmesan and lemon wedges.

VARIATIONS

Hearty Baked Brown Rice with Peas, Feta, and Mint `GF`

Reduce amount of oil to 1 tablespoon and omit 1 onion. Substitute 1 cup thawed frozen peas for roasted red peppers, ¼ cup minced fresh mint for parsley, ½ teaspoon grated lemon zest for pepper, and ½ cup crumbled feta for Parmesan.

Hearty Baked Brown Rice with Black Beans and Cilantro `VEGAN` `GF`

Substitute 1 finely chopped green bell pepper for 1 onion. Once vegetables are well browned in step 1, stir in 3 minced garlic cloves and cook until fragrant, about 30 seconds. Substitute 1 (15-ounce) can black beans for roasted red peppers and ¼ cup minced fresh cilantro for parsley. Omit Parmesan and substitute lime wedges for lemon wedges.

Skillet Brown Rice and Beans with Corn and Fresh Tomatoes

SERVES 6 `VEGAN` `GF`

✔ **WHY THIS RECIPE WORKS:** The sustaining combination of rice and beans is a staple in many cuisines. We wanted to make a simple weeknight version with bold Latin American flavor. White rice is traditional, but we preferred the texture, chew, and robust flavor of brown rice. After sautéing an onion, we added fresh corn and the uncooked rice to the skillet with garlic, cumin, and cayenne and sautéed them until fragrant. Then we stirred in broth and simmered the rice until tender. Canned black beans kept the dish quick; to keep them from getting mushy, we stirred them in partway through cooking. A flavorful salsa of grape tomatoes, scallions, cilantro, and lime juice added a fresh counterpoint to the rich, spicy rice and beans. We prefer the flavor of fresh corn; however, 1½ cups frozen corn, thawed and patted dry, can be substituted.

2	tablespoons extra-virgin olive oil
1	onion, minced
2	ears corn, kernels cut from cobs
1	cup long-grain brown rice, rinsed
4	garlic cloves, minced
1	teaspoon cumin
	Pinch cayenne pepper
3¼	cups vegetable broth
2	(15-ounce) cans black beans, rinsed
	Salt and pepper
12	ounces grape tomatoes, quartered
5	scallions, sliced thin
¼	cup minced fresh cilantro
1	tablespoon lime juice

1. Heat 1 tablespoon oil in 12-inch nonstick skillet over medium-high heat until shimmering. Add onion and cook until softened and lightly browned, 5 to 7 minutes. Stir in corn and cook until lightly browned, about 4 minutes. Stir in rice, garlic, cumin, and cayenne and cook until fragrant, about 30 seconds.

2. Stir in broth and bring to simmer. Cover, reduce heat to medium-low, and simmer gently, stirring occasionally, for 25 minutes.

3. Stir in beans, cover, and continue to simmer until liquid has been absorbed and rice is tender, 20 to 25 minutes. Season with salt and pepper to taste.

4. Combine remaining 1 tablespoon oil, tomatoes, scallions, cilantro, and lime juice in bowl and season with salt and pepper to taste. Sprinkle tomato mixture over rice and beans and serve.

VARIATIONS

Skillet Brown Rice and Chickpeas with Coconut Milk VEGAN GF

Substitute 2 finely chopped yellow bell peppers for corn, 1½ teaspoons garam masala for cumin, and canned chickpeas for black beans. Reduce amount of vegetable broth to 1¾ cups and add 1 (13.5-ounce) can light coconut milk to skillet with broth.

Spanish-Style Skillet Brown Rice and Chickpeas VEGAN GF

Substitute 2 finely chopped red bell peppers for corn, pinch of crumbled saffron for cumin, and canned chickpeas for black beans.

Rinsing Rice and Grains

Place rice or grains in fine-mesh strainer and rinse under cool water until water runs clear, occasionally stirring lightly with your hand. Let drain briefly.

Miso Brown Rice Cakes

SERVES 4 GF

✔ **WHY THIS RECIPE WORKS:** Easy, inexpensive, and substantial, rice cakes should have a permanent place on any vegetarian table. Here we aimed to use hearty long-grain brown rice and give the dish a flavorful Asian twist. We paired the rice with red miso and shiitake mushrooms for depth of flavor and meatiness. Ginger and garlic rounded out the flavors. Although we usually cook brown rice in the oven to ensure fluffy grains, that technique would work against us

here. Instead, we turned to the stovetop method to aid in releasing starches that would help hold the patties together when pan-fried. Once the rice was cool, we pulsed it in a food processor to help break down the starches for even better binding. Then we mixed the rice with egg, sesame oil, and the miso, plus scallions for some freshness, formed the mixture into patties, and chilled them briefly until firm. Just a few minutes in a hot skillet gave us crisp, browned rice patties. Although we prefer the flavor of red miso here, you can substitute white miso, but do not substitute "light" miso; its flavor is too mild. See page 55 for information about buying miso.

3	tablespoons vegetable oil
8	ounces shiitake mushrooms, stemmed and chopped
2	teaspoons grated fresh ginger
2	garlic cloves, minced
1½	cups long-grain brown rice
3¾	cups water
	Salt and pepper
4	scallions, chopped fine
1	large egg plus 1 yolk, lightly beaten
3	tablespoons red miso
1½	teaspoons sesame oil
1	recipe Sriracha Mayo (page 43)

1. Heat 1 tablespoon vegetable oil in large saucepan over medium heat until shimmering. Add mushrooms and cook until lightly browned, about 5 minutes. Stir in ginger and garlic and cook until fragrant, about 30 seconds. Add rice, water, and ½ teaspoon salt and bring to simmer. Reduce heat to low, cover, and cook until rice is tender, about 50 minutes, stirring occasionally. Spread rice mixture onto rimmed baking sheet and let cool for 15 minutes.

2. Pulse rice mixture in food processor until coarsely ground, about 10 pulses; transfer to large bowl. Stir in scallions, egg and yolk, miso, sesame oil, ½ teaspoon salt, and ¼ teaspoon pepper until well combined.

3. Line rimmed baking sheet with parchment paper and spray with vegetable oil spray. Using wet hands, divide rice mixture into 8 equal portions and pack firmly into ½-inch-thick patties; lay on prepared sheet. Refrigerate rice cakes, uncovered, until chilled and firm, about 30 minutes.

4. Heat 1 tablespoon vegetable oil in 12-inch nonstick skillet over medium-high heat until shimmering. Gently lay 4 rice cakes in skillet and cook until crisp and browned on both sides, about 4 minutes per side, turning gently halfway through cooking; transfer to plate and cover to keep warm. Repeat with remaining 1 tablespoon vegetable oil and remaining rice cakes. Serve with Sriracha Mayo.

We bake our hearty brown rice on one rack and roast carrots and kale on the other, then we top it all with a fried egg.

Brown Rice Bowls with Roasted Carrots, Kale, and Fried Eggs

SERVES 4 GF

✓ **WHY THIS RECIPE WORKS:** Rice bowls are a healthy, hearty dish in which a combination of flavorful components are arranged on a bed of rice. We were after a version that paired nutty brown rice with roasted vegetables. First we tossed sweet carrots with *za'atar*, a bold Middle-Eastern spice blend, and roasted them until they were tender and spotty brown. We started cooking them covered to soften them, then we uncovered them for the last 15 minutes to get a nice roasted flavor and some caramelization. When we uncovered the carrots, we also spread some chopped kale over the top. Briefly roasting the kale gave it great flavor and a crispy texture that provided the dish with nice contrast. Taking advantage of the time the vegetables spent in the oven, we baked the rice alongside, which was a conveniently hands-off method that gave us great results. To round out the rice and vegetables, we topped

each bowl with a fried egg, which, when broken, moistened the rice and added another layer of richness to the dish. A simple red wine vinegar and shallot vinaigrette finished the dish. Medium-grain or short-grain brown rice can be substituted for the long-grain rice.

2 cups boiling water
1 cup long-grain brown rice, rinsed
   Salt and pepper
5 carrots, peeled, halved crosswise, then halved or quartered lengthwise to create uniformly sized pieces
⅓ cup extra-virgin olive oil
2 teaspoons za'atar
8 ounces kale, stemmed and chopped into 1-inch strips
2 tablespoons red wine vinegar
1 small shallot, minced
4 large eggs

1. Adjust oven racks to upper-middle and lower-middle positions and heat oven to 375 degrees. Combine boiling water, rice, and ¾ teaspoon salt in 8-inch square baking dish and cover tightly with 2 layers of aluminum foil. Bake rice on lower rack until tender, 45 to 50 minutes. Remove rice from oven, uncover, and fluff with fork. Cover with dish towel and let sit for 5 minutes.

2. Meanwhile, toss carrots, 1 tablespoon oil, za'atar, ¼ teaspoon salt, and ⅛ teaspoon pepper together in bowl. Spread carrots onto parchment paper–lined baking sheet, cover with foil, and roast on upper rack for 20 minutes.

3. Toss kale, 1 tablespoon oil, ¼ teaspoon salt, and ⅛ teaspoon pepper together in bowl. Remove foil from carrots and spread kale on top. Continue to roast vegetables, uncovered, until carrots are spotty brown and tender and kale is crisp and edges are lightly browned, about 15 minutes.

4. Portion brown rice into individual bowls and top with roasted vegetables. Whisk vinegar, shallot, and 3 tablespoons oil together in bowl and season with salt and pepper to taste. Drizzle vinaigrette over rice and vegetables; cover and set aside.

5. Heat remaining 1 teaspoon oil in 12-inch nonstick skillet over low heat for 5 minutes. Crack eggs into 2 small bowls (2 eggs per bowl) and season with salt and pepper. Increase heat to medium-high and heat until oil is shimmering. Working quickly, pour eggs into skillet, cover, and cook for 1 minute. Remove skillet from burner and let sit, covered, 15 to 45 seconds for runny yolks, 45 to 60 seconds for soft but set yolks, and about 2 minutes for medium-set yolks. Top each bowl with fried egg, and serve.

Brown Rice Bowls with Crispy Tofu and Vegetables

SERVES 6 **VEGAN** **GF**

✔ **WHY THIS RECIPE WORKS:** Rice bowls are popular fare in Japan, so we wanted a version of our brown rice bowl inspired by Japanese flavors. We started by swapping out the long-grain rice for sticky short-grain brown rice, which is common in Japan. While it simmered on the stovetop, we made a potent dressing by briefly boiling rice vinegar, mirin, and sugar. We flavored some of the mixture with soy sauce, ginger, orange, and lime for serving and drizzled the rest over the rice to season it as it cooled. For the topping, we crisped fingers of tofu in a skillet and garnished them with crumbled nori seaweed, sliced radishes, avocado, cool cucumber, and scallions. To save time, prep the tofu and vegetables while the rice cooks. We prefer the creamier texture of soft tofu here, but firm, extra-firm, or light firm tofu will also work (light tofu won't taste as rich and will be drier). Nori is seaweed that has been dried and pressed into sheets used for rolling sushi; you can find nori in the international foods aisle of the supermarket. For this recipe to be gluten-free, you must use gluten-free soy sauce. For more information on cutting tofu into fingers, see page 224.

RICE AND DRESSING

- 3½ cups water
- 2⅓ cups short-grain brown rice, rinsed
- 6 tablespoons rice vinegar
- 6 tablespoons mirin
- ½ teaspoon sugar
- 3 tablespoons soy sauce
- 1 teaspoon grated fresh ginger
- ½ teaspoon grated orange zest plus 1 tablespoon juice
- ½ teaspoon grated lime zest plus 1 tablespoon juice

VEGETABLES AND TOFU

- 28 ounces soft tofu, patted dry and cut into 3-inch-long by ½-inch-thick fingers
  Salt and pepper
- ¾ cup cornstarch
- ¼ cup cornmeal
- 2 tablespoons vegetable oil
- 1 (8 by 7½-inch) sheet nori, crumbled (optional)
- 6 radishes, sliced thin
- 1 avocado, halved, pitted, and sliced thin
- 1 cucumber, peeled, halved lengthwise, seeded, and sliced thin
- 4 scallions, sliced thin

1. FOR THE RICE AND DRESSING: Bring water and rice to simmer in large saucepan over high heat. Reduce heat to low, cover, and continue to simmer until rice is tender and water is absorbed, 45 to 50 minutes. Remove pot from heat, lay clean folded dish towel underneath lid, and let sit for 10 minutes.

2. Bring vinegar, mirin, and sugar to boil in small saucepan, then remove from heat. Measure ⅓ cup vinegar mixture into small bowl and whisk in soy sauce, ginger, orange zest and juice, and lime zest and juice; set aside for serving. Transfer cooked rice to large bowl, sprinkle with remaining vinegar mixture, and let cool, gently tossing with wooden paddle or spoon occasionally, about 20 minutes.

3. FOR THE VEGETABLES AND TOFU: While rice cooks, spread tofu over paper towel–lined baking sheet and let drain for 20 minutes. Gently press tofu dry with paper towels and season with salt and pepper.

4. Adjust oven rack to middle position, place paper towel–lined plate on rack, and heat oven to 200 degrees. Place wire rack over rimmed baking sheet. Whisk cornstarch and cornmeal together in shallow dish. Working with several pieces of tofu at a time, coat thoroughly with cornstarch mixture, pressing to help coating adhere, and transfer to prepared wire rack.

5. Heat 1 tablespoon oil in 12-inch nonstick skillet over medium-high heat until shimmering. Carefully add half of tofu and cook until crisp and lightly golden on all sides, 10 to 12 minutes; transfer to plate in oven. Repeat with remaining 1 tablespoon oil and remaining tofu.

6. Portion rice into 6 individual serving bowls and sprinkle with some of nori, if using. Top with tofu, radishes, avocado, and cucumber. Sprinkle with scallions and drizzle with reserved dressing. Serve, passing remaining nori separately.

Indonesian-Style Fried Rice

SERVES 4 TO 6 **GF**

✔ **WHY THIS RECIPE WORKS:** *Nasi Goreng* is an Indonesian version of fried rice seasoned with chile paste and sweet soy sauce and garnished with fried shallots, egg, and vegetables. We wanted to make an approachable version that stayed true to the classic dish. We found that a sauce of molasses, dark brown sugar, soy sauce, and fish sauce substitute was a perfect alternative to the hard-to-find sweet soy sauce. We created our own chile paste by coarsely pureeing garlic, shallots, and fresh Thai chiles. To get distinct grains of rice, this dish is traditionally made with day-old rice, but we were able to mimic this effect by rinsing the rice thoroughly, coating it with oil, and chilling it in the fridge before cooking it. For the vegetables, we liked

Getting to Know Rice

A grain of rice is made up of endosperm, germ, bran, and a husk. Brown rice is simply husked; white rice also has the germ and bran removed. This makes the rice cook faster and softer, but also removes much of the nutrients, as well as flavor.

LONG-GRAIN WHITE RICE

This broad category includes generic long-grain rice as well as aromatic varieties such as basmati, Texmati, and jasmine. The grains are slender and cook up light, fluffy, and distinct, making them good for pilafs and salads.

MEDIUM-GRAIN WHITE RICE

This category includes rices used to make risotto (Arborio) and paella (Valencia), as well as many Japanese and Chinese varieties. The grains are fat and cook up a bit sticky, and when simmered, they clump together.

SHORT-GRAIN WHITE RICE

The grains of short-grain rice are almost round, and the texture is quite sticky and soft when cooked. Most of us are familiar with short-grain rice through its use in sushi.

BROWN RICE

As with white rice, brown rice comes in a variety of grain sizes: short, medium, and long. Long-grain brown rice, the best choice for pilafs, cooks up fluffy, with separate grains. Medium-grain brown rice is a bit more sticky, perfect for risotto, paella, and similar dishes. Short-grain brown rice is the most sticky, ideal for sushi and other Asian dishes.

BASMATI RICE

Prized for its nutty flavor and sweet aroma, basmati rice is eaten in pilafs and biryanis and with curries. Indian basmati is aged for a minimum of one year before being packaged. This dehydrates the rice so that, once cooked, it expand greatly.

RED RICE

Red rice is a special variety of rice with a red husk rather than the more common brown. It is usually unhulled or partially hulled and has a high nutritional value and a nutty flavor.

BLACK RICE

Like brown rice, black rice is sold unhulled. But only black rice contains anthocyanins, the same antioxidant compounds in blueberries and blackberries. These compounds are what turn the rice a deep purple as it cooks.

broccoli florets, steamed in the skillet until they were crisp-tender. Finally, we topped the dish with a simple omelet and more shallots, sliced thin and fried until golden. If Thai chiles are unavailable, substitute two serranos or two medium jalapeños. This dish is fairly spicy; to reduce the spiciness, remove the ribs and seeds from the chiles or use fewer chiles. This dish progresses very quickly at step 4, so it's important to have all of the ingredients ready to go. For this recipe to be gluten-free, you must use gluten-free soy sauce. We prefer the flavor of jasmine rice in this recipe, but long-grain white, basmati, or Texmati rice can be substituted. Serve with sliced cucumbers and tomato wedges.

RICE

- 2 tablespoons vegetable oil
- 2 cups jasmine rice, rinsed
- 2⅔ cups water

STIR-FRY

- 5 green or red Thai chiles, stemmed
- 7 large shallots, peeled (4 quartered, 3 sliced thin)
- 4 large garlic cloves, peeled
- 3 tablespoons dark brown sugar
- 3 tablespoons molasses
- 3 tablespoons soy sauce
- 3 tablespoons fish sauce substitute (see page 60)
  Salt
- 4 large eggs
- ½ cup vegetable oil
- 1 pound broccoli florets, cut into 1-inch pieces
- ¼ cup water
- 4 large scallions, sliced thin
  Lime wedges

1. FOR THE RICE: Heat oil in large saucepan over medium heat until shimmering. Add rice and stir to coat with oil, about 30 seconds. Stir in water and bring to boil. Reduce heat to low, cover, and continue to simmer until rice is tender and water is absorbed, 16 to 18 minutes. Remove pot from heat, lay clean folded dish towel underneath lid, and let sit for 10 minutes. Spread rice onto rimmed baking sheet and let cool for 10 minutes. Transfer to refrigerator and chill for 20 minutes.

2. FOR THE STIR-FRY: Pulse chiles, quartered shallots, and garlic in food processor to coarse paste, about 15 pulses, scraping down sides of bowl as needed; transfer to bowl. In separate bowl, stir sugar, molasses, soy sauce, fish sauce, and 1¼ teaspoons salt together. In third bowl, whisk eggs and ¼ teaspoon salt together.

3. Cook sliced shallots and oil in 12-inch nonstick skillet over medium heat, stirring constantly, until shallots are golden and crisp, 6 to 10 minutes. Using slotted spoon, transfer shallots to paper towel–lined plate and season with salt. Pour off oil and reserve. Wipe out skillet with paper towels.

4. Heat 1 teaspoon reserved oil in now-empty skillet over medium heat until shimmering. Add half of eggs to skillet, tilt pan to coat bottom, cover, and cook until bottom of omelet is spotty golden brown and top is just set, about 1½ minutes. Slide omelet onto cutting board, roll up into tight log, and cut crosswise into 1-inch-wide segments; leave segments rolled. Repeat with 1 teaspoon reserved oil and remaining eggs.

5. Break up any large clumps chilled rice with fingers. Combine broccoli and water in now-empty skillet, cover, and cook over medium-high heat until broccoli is crisp-tender and water is absorbed, 4 to 6 minutes; transfer to small bowl.

6. Heat 3 tablespoons reserved oil in now-empty skillet over medium heat until just shimmering. Add chile mixture and cook until mixture turns golden, 3 to 5 minutes. Whisk molasses mixture to recombine, clear center of skillet, add mixture to pan, and bring to simmer. Add rice and broccoli and cook, stirring and folding constantly, until rice is heated through, broccoli is tender, and mixture is evenly coated, about 3 minutes. Stir in scallions. Transfer to platter and garnish with omelet rolls, fried shallots, and lime wedges. Serve.

This aromatic biryani boasts complex flavor thanks to a mix of warm spices, saffron, and roasted cauliflower.

Cauliflower Biryani

SERVES 4 TO 6 **GF**

✔ **WHY THIS RECIPE WORKS:** The best biryani recipes place fragrant long-grain basmati center stage, enriching it with saffron and a variety of fresh herbs and pungent spices. However, most recipes take time to develop deep flavor by steeping whole spices and cooking each part of the dish on its own before marrying them. We decided to deconstruct this dish to make it easier and faster, while staying true to its warmth and homey appeal. We wanted to pair our rice with sweet, earthy roasted cauliflower. We cut the cauliflower into small florets to speed up roasting and tossed it with warm spices to give it deep flavor. While it roasted, we sautéed an onion until golden, then cooked jalapeño, garlic, and more spices until fragrant. We added the rice to this flavorful mixture and simmered it until tender. Once the rice finished cooking, we let the residual heat plump the currants and bloom the saffron while the rice rested. Lastly, we stirred in lots of bright mint and cilantro and our roasted cauliflower. Biryani is traditionally served with a cooling yogurt sauce; ideally, you should make it before starting the biryani to allow the flavors in the sauce to meld. We prefer the flavor of basmati rice in this recipe, but long-grain white, jasmine, or Texmati rice can be substituted.

1	head cauliflower (2 pounds), cored and cut into ½-inch florets
¼	cup extra-virgin olive oil
¼	teaspoon ground cardamom
¼	teaspoon ground cumin
	Salt and pepper
1	onion, sliced thin
4	garlic cloves, minced
1	jalapeño chile, stemmed, seeded, and minced
⅛	teaspoon ground cinnamon
⅛	teaspoon ground ginger
1½	cups basmati rice, rinsed
2¼	cups water
¼	cup dried currants or raisins
½	teaspoon saffron threads, lightly crumbled
2	tablespoons chopped fresh cilantro
2	tablespoons chopped fresh mint
1	recipe Yogurt-Herb Sauce (page 43)

1. Adjust oven rack to middle position and heat oven to 425 degrees. Toss cauliflower, 2 tablespoons oil, ⅛ teaspoon cardamom, ⅛ teaspoon cumin, ½ teaspoon salt, and ¼ teaspoon pepper together in bowl. Spread cauliflower onto rimmed baking sheet and roast until tender, 15 to 20 minutes.

2. Meanwhile, heat remaining 2 tablespoons oil in large saucepan over medium-high heat until shimmering. Add onion and cook, stirring often, until soft and dark brown around edges, 10 to 12 minutes.

3. Stir in garlic, jalapeño, cinnamon, ginger, remaining ⅛ teaspoon cardamom, and remaining ⅛ teaspoon cumin and cook until fragrant, about 1 minute. Stir in rice and cook until well coated, about 1 minute. Add water and ½ teaspoon salt and bring to simmer. Reduce heat to low, cover, and simmer until all liquid is absorbed, 16 to 18 minutes.

4. Remove pot from heat and sprinkle currants and saffron over rice. Cover, laying clean folded dish towel underneath lid, and let sit for 10 minutes. Fold in cilantro, mint, and roasted cauliflower. Season with salt and pepper to taste and serve with yogurt sauce.

Vegetable Paella
SERVES 6 `VEGAN` `GF`

✔ **WHY THIS RECIPE WORKS:** The challenge in developing a vegetarian paella recipe was making a dish that is usually centered on a variety of meat and seafood fit our vegetarian needs while still staying true to the dish's identity. We did this by using a variety of hearty vegetables that are common in Spanish culture: artichokes, bell peppers, fennel, and peas. We gave the artichokes and peppers extra flavor by roasting them and then tossing them with a bright, lemony sauce. We sautéed the fennel with chopped onion to give it a rich caramelized flavor that gave the dish aromatic backbone. And we cooked the rice with smoked paprika to imitate the smoky flavor that is the hallmark of this dish. To infuse the rice with complex flavor, we cooked the paprika with garlic until fragrant and browned diced tomatoes to deepen their flavor. Next, we coated the rice with this potent mixture before adding broth, wine, and saffron and simmering the rice until tender. You will need at least a 6-quart Dutch oven for this recipe. *Soccarat*, a layer of crusty browned rice that forms on the bottom of the pan, is a traditional part of paella. In our version, soccarat does not develop because most of the cooking is done in the oven; if desired, there are directions on how to make a soccarat before serving in step 5.

18 ounces frozen artichoke hearts, thawed and patted dry
2 red bell peppers, stemmed, seeded, and coarsely chopped
½ cup kalamata olives, pitted and chopped
9 garlic cloves, peeled (3 whole, 6 minced)

We swap the traditional sausage and seafood for bell peppers, fennel, artichoke hearts, and peas in our vegetable paella.

6 tablespoons extra-virgin olive oil
  Salt and pepper
3 tablespoons chopped fresh parsley
2 tablespoons lemon juice
1 onion, chopped fine
1 fennel bulb, stalks discarded, bulb halved, cored, and sliced thin
½ teaspoon smoked paprika
1 (14.5-ounce) can diced tomatoes, drained, minced, and drained again
2 cups Valencia or Arborio rice
3 cups vegetable broth
⅓ cup dry white wine or Pernod
½ teaspoon saffron threads, crumbled
½ cup frozen peas, thawed

1. Adjust oven rack to lower-middle position, place rimmed baking sheet on rack, and heat oven to 450 degrees. Toss artichokes, peppers, olives, whole garlic cloves, 2 tablespoons oil, ½ teaspoon salt, and ¼ teaspoon pepper together in bowl. Spread vegetables onto hot baking sheet and roast

Saffron

Sometimes known as "red gold," saffron is the world's most expensive spice. It's made from the dried stigmas of *Crocus sativus* flowers; the stigmas are so delicate they must be harvested by hand in a painstaking process. Luckily, a little saffron goes a long way, adding a distinct reddish-gold color, notes of honey and grass, and a slight hint of bitterness to dishes like paella and risotto. The saffron you find in the supermarket is usually Spanish. When shopping for saffron, what should you look for? We held a small tasting of broths infused with different saffron samples. The reddest threads yielded intensely flavorful, heady, perfumed broths. So, when shopping, look for red threads with no spots of yellow or orange. Or, to save money, a good-quality powdered saffron would be just as flavorful and fragrant as the threads.

until artichokes are browned around edges and peppers are browned, 20 to 25 minutes; let cool slightly.

2. Mince roasted garlic. In large bowl, whisk 2 tablespoons oil, 2 tablespoons parsley, lemon juice, and minced roasted garlic together. Add roasted vegetables and toss to combine. Season with salt and pepper to taste.

3. Reduce oven temperature to 350 degrees. Heat remaining 2 tablespoons oil in Dutch oven over medium heat until shimmering. Add onion and fennel and cook until softened, 10 to 15 minutes.

4. Stir in remaining minced garlic and paprika and cook until fragrant, about 30 seconds. Stir in tomatoes and cook until mixture begins to darken and thicken slightly, about 2 minutes. Stir in rice and cook until grains are well coated with tomato mixture, about 1 minute. Stir in broth, wine, saffron, and 1 teaspoon salt. Increase heat to medium-high and bring to boil, stirring occasionally. Cover pot, transfer to oven, and cook until liquid is absorbed and rice is tender, 25 to 35 minutes.

5. For optional soccarat, uncover, transfer to stovetop, and cook over medium-high heat for about 5 minutes, rotating pot as needed, until bottom layer of rice is well browned and crisp.

6. Sprinkle roasted vegetables and peas over top, cover, and let paella sit for 5 minutes. Sprinkle with remaining 1 table-spoon parsley and serve.

VARIATION

Vegetable Paella in a Paella Pan VEGAN GF

Substitute 14- to 15-inch paella pan for Dutch oven, increase broth to 3¼ cups, and increase wine to ½ cup. Before placing pan in oven, cover tightly with aluminum foil. For optional soccarat, reduce stovetop cooking time to 3 minutes.

Almost Hands-Free Risotto with Parmesan

SERVES 6 GF

✔ **WHY THIS RECIPE WORKS:** Classic risotto can demand half an hour of stovetop tedium for the best creamy results. Our goal was 5 minutes of stirring, tops. First, we swapped out the saucepan for a Dutch oven, which has a thick, heavy bottom, deep sides, and a tight-fitting lid—perfect for trapping and distributing heat evenly. Typical recipes dictate adding the broth in small increments after the wine has been absorbed and stirring constantly after each addition, but we added most of the broth at once and covered the pan, allowing the rice to simmer until almost all the broth had been absorbed, stirring just twice. After adding the second and final addition of broth, we stirred the pot and then turned off the heat. Without sitting over a direct flame, the sauce turned out perfectly creamy and the rice was thickened, velvety, and just barely chewy. Adding the Parmesan before the short rest gave it a chance to melt into the risotto. To finish, we simply stirred in butter and a squeeze of lemon juice. This more hands-off method requires precise timing, so we strongly recommend using a timer.

- 5 cups vegetable broth
- 1½ cups water
- 4 tablespoons unsalted butter
- 1 large onion, chopped fine
  Salt and pepper
- 1 garlic clove, minced
- 2 cups Arborio rice
- 1 cup dry white wine
- 2 ounces Parmesan cheese, grated (1 cup)
- 1 teaspoon lemon juice

1. Bring broth and water to boil in large saucepan over high heat. Cover and reduce heat to medium-low to maintain bare simmer.

2. Melt 2 tablespoons butter in Dutch oven over medium heat. Add onion and ¾ teaspoon salt and cook until onion is softened, 4 to 5 minutes. Stir in garlic and cook until fragrant, about 30 seconds. Stir in rice and cook, stirring often, until grain edges begin to turn translucent, about 3 minutes.

3. Stir in wine and cook, stirring constantly, until fully absorbed, 2 to 3 minutes. Stir in 5 cups hot broth mixture. Reduce heat to medium-low, cover, and simmer until almost all liquid has been absorbed and rice is just al dente, 18 to 19 minutes, stirring twice during cooking.

4. Add ¾ cup hot broth mixture and stir gently and constantly until risotto becomes creamy, about 3 minutes. Stir in Parmesan. Remove pot from heat, cover, and let sit for 5 minutes. Stir in remaining 2 tablespoons butter and lemon juice. Season with salt and pepper to taste. Before serving, stir in remaining broth mixture as needed to loosen consistency of risotto.

VARIATIONS

Almost Hands-Free Risotto with Herbs `GF`
Stir in 2 tablespoons minced fresh parsley and 2 tablespoons minced fresh chives before serving.

Almost Hands-Free Risotto with Fennel and Saffron `GF`
Add 1 fennel bulb, cored and chopped fine, to pot with onion and cook until softened, about 12 minutes. Add ¼ teaspoon ground coriander and large pinch crumbled saffron threads to pot with garlic.

Making Almost Hands-Free Risotto

1. HEAT BROTH AND WATER: Bring broth and water to boil. Cover and reduce heat to medium-low to maintain simmer.

2. SAUTÉ ONION AND TOAST RICE: Add onion to melted butter in Dutch oven and cook until softened. Stir in garlic. Add rice, stirring often, and cook until edges of grains are translucent.

3. ADD BROTH, COVER, AND SIMMER: Stir in wine and cook until absorbed. Stir in 5 cups hot broth mixture. Reduce heat to medium-low, cover, and simmer until rice is al dente, stirring twice.

4. LET SIT 5 MINUTES: Add ¾ cup broth mixture and stir until risotto becomes creamy. Stir in Parmesan. Remove from heat, cover, and let sit for 5 minutes. Stir in remaining butter and lemon juice.

Almost Hands-Free Risotto with Porcini `GF`
In order for this recipe to be gluten-free, you must use gluten-free soy sauce.

Add ¼ ounce dried porcini mushrooms, rinsed and minced, to pot with garlic. Substitute soy sauce for lemon juice.

Butternut Squash Risotto
SERVES 6 `GF`

✔ **WHY THIS RECIPE WORKS:** Butternut squash and risotto should make a perfect culinary couple, but often the squash and rice never become properly intertwined. We wanted a creamy, orange-tinted rice fully infused with deep squash flavor. We concentrated on developing the flavor of the squash and keeping it tender. First, we sautéed the squash to intensify its flavor. We also sautéed the seeds and fibers and steeped them in the vegetable broth, then used the liquid to cook the rice—this infused every bite with sweet, earthy squash flavor. Finally we found that adding the squash in two stages, half with the toasted rice and half just before serving, preserved its delicate texture. Parmesan cheese added richness, and sage and nutmeg lent woodsy, warm notes. This more hands-off method requires precise timing, so we strongly recommend using a timer.

2	tablespoons extra-virgin olive oil
1½	pounds butternut squash, peeled, seeded with fibers and seeds reserved, and cut into ½-inch cubes (4½ cups)
	Salt and pepper
4	cups vegetable broth
2	cups water
4	tablespoons unsalted butter
2	small onions, chopped fine
2	garlic cloves, minced
2	cups Arborio rice
1½	cups dry white wine
1½	ounces Parmesan cheese, grated (¾ cup)
2	tablespoons minced fresh sage
¼	teaspoon ground nutmeg

1. Heat oil in 12-inch nonstick skillet over medium-high heat until shimmering. Add 3½ cups squash, spread in even layer, and cook without stirring until golden brown, about 5 minutes. Season with ¼ teaspoon salt and ¼ teaspoon pepper and continue to cook, stirring occasionally, until squash is tender and browned, about 5 minutes; transfer to bowl.

2. Add remaining cubed squash and reserved squash fibers and seeds to now-empty skillet and cook over medium heat, stirring often, until lightly browned, about 4 minutes. Transfer to large saucepan and add broth and water. Cover pot, bring to boil over high heat, then reduce heat to medium-low and simmer gently for 10 minutes. Strain broth through fine-mesh strainer, pressing on solids to extract as much liquid as possible; discard solids. Return strained broth to saucepan, cover, and keep warm over low heat.

3. Melt 3 tablespoons butter in now-empty skillet over medium heat. Add onions, ½ teaspoon salt, and ½ teaspoon pepper and cook until onions are softened, 5 to 7 minutes. Add garlic and cook until fragrant, about 30 seconds. Stir in rice and cook, stirring often, until grain edges begin to turn translucent, about 3 minutes.

4. Stir in wine and cook, stirring constantly, until fully absorbed, 2 to 3 minutes. Stir in 5 cups hot broth mixture and half of browned squash cubes. Reduce heat to medium-low, cover, and simmer until almost all liquid has been absorbed and rice is just al dente, 18 to 19 minutes, stirring twice during cooking.

5. Add ¾ cup hot broth mixture and stir gently and constantly until risotto becomes creamy, about 3 minutes. Stir in Parmesan. Remove pot from heat, cover, and let sit for 5 minutes. Stir in sage, nutmeg, and remaining 1 tablespoon butter. Season with salt and pepper to taste and gently fold in remaining browned squash cubes. Before serving, stir in remaining broth mixture as needed to loosen consistency of risotto.

Spring Vegetable Risotto
SERVES 4 `GF`

✓ **WHY THIS RECIPE WORKS:** We love the combination of fresh spring vegetables and creamy risotto, but bland flavor and mushy vegetables can ruin this Italian classic. For a risotto primavera with perfectly al dente rice and flavorful vegetables, we started with a combination of asparagus and leeks. The leeks melted down beautifully, infusing the rice with their delicate flavor. Sautéing the asparagus spears and stirring them into the rice right before serving kept them from turning into mush. For a good backbone of flavor, we simmered the leek greens and the tough asparagus stems in the broth we used for cooking the rice. Then we topped the dish with a gremolata of parsley, mint, and lemon zest. To substitute onions for the leeks, use 1 roughly chopped onion in the broth and 2 finely chopped onions in the risotto. This more hands-off method requires precise timing, so we strongly recommend using a timer.

GREMOLATA
- 2 tablespoons minced fresh parsley, stems reserved
- 2 tablespoons minced fresh mint, stems reserved
- ½ teaspoon grated lemon zest

RISOTTO
- 1 pound asparagus, trimmed, tough ends reserved and chopped coarse, spears cut on bias into ½-inch lengths
- 2 leeks, white and light green parts halved lengthwise, sliced thin, and washed thoroughly; dark green parts chopped coarse
- 4 cups vegetable broth
- 3 cups water
- 5 tablespoons unsalted butter
  Salt and pepper
- ½ cup frozen peas
- 2 garlic cloves, minced
- 1½ cups Arborio rice
- 1 cup dry white wine
- 1½ ounces Parmesan cheese, grated (¾ cup)
- 2 teaspoons lemon juice

1. FOR THE GREMOLATA: Combine all ingredients in small bowl and set aside.

2. FOR THE RISOTTO: Bring chopped asparagus ends, chopped dark green leek parts, reserved parsley and mint stems, broth, and water to boil in large saucepan over high heat. Reduce heat to medium-low, partially cover, and simmer for 20 minutes. Strain broth through fine-mesh strainer into medium bowl, pressing on solids to extract as much liquid as possible. Return strained broth to saucepan, cover, and set over low heat to keep warm.

3. Melt 1 tablespoon butter in Dutch oven over medium heat. Add asparagus spears, pinch salt, and pinch pepper. Cook, stirring occasionally, until asparagus is crisp-tender, 4 to 6 minutes. Add peas and continue to cook for 1 minute. Transfer vegetables to plate.

4. Melt 3 tablespoons butter in now-empty Dutch oven over medium heat. Add white and light green leek parts, garlic, ½ teaspoon salt, and ½ teaspoon pepper. Cook, stirring occasionally, until leeks are softened, 5 to 7 minutes. Stir in rice and cook, stirring often, until grain edges begin to turn translucent, about 3 minutes.

5. Stir in wine and cook, stirring constantly, until fully absorbed, 2 to 3 minutes. Stir in 4 cups hot broth mixture. Reduce heat to medium-low, cover, and simmer until almost all liquid has been absorbed and rice is just al dente, 18 to 19 minutes, stirring twice during cooking.

6. Add ½ cup hot broth mixture and stir gently and constantly until risotto becomes creamy, about 3 minutes. Stir in Parmesan. Remove pot from heat, cover, and let sit for 5 minutes. Stir in lemon juice and remaining 1 tablespoon butter. Season with salt and pepper to taste and gently fold in asparagus and peas. Before serving, stir in remaining broth mixture as needed to loosen consistency of risotto and sprinkle individual servings with gremolata.

Spring Vegetable Risotto with Carrots and Watercress GF

Substitute 3 carrots, peeled and cut into ½-inch pieces, peels and trimmings chopped coarse, for asparagus; boil carrot peels and trimmings with dark green leek parts. Cook carrots in step 3 until crisp-tender, 8 to 10 minutes; transfer to plate. Substitute 4 cups chopped watercress for peas; add watercress to pot with cooked carrots in step 6.

Rice Salad with Oranges, Olives, and Almonds

SERVES 4 TO 6 VEGAN GF

✔ **WHY THIS RECIPE WORKS:** We wanted a rice salad recipe with rice that was tender, fluffy, and light, not dense, sticky, or mushy. To achieve that goal, we found a method for cooking long-grain rice that would preserve its fresh-from-the-pan tender texture once cooled: toasting the rice, boiling it (like pasta) in an abundant amount of water, draining it, then spreading it on a baking sheet to cool and dry. Toasting the rice helped to keep the grains distinct and separate, and boiling it in plenty of water washed away its excess starch, further preventing stickiness. To flavor the salad, we tossed the cooled rice with a simple orange vinaigrette and some fresh oranges, briny olives, and crunchy almonds. We let the salad sit for 20 minutes before serving to give the flavors time to meld. Taste the rice as it nears the end of its cooking time; it should be cooked through and toothsome, but not crunchy. Be careful not to overcook the rice or the grains will "blow out" and fray. We prefer the flavor of basmati rice in this recipe, but long-grain white, jasmine, or Texmati rice can be substituted.

1½ cups basmati rice
    Salt and pepper
 2 tablespoons extra-virgin olive oil
 2 teaspoons sherry vinegar
 1 small garlic clove, minced
 ¼ teaspoon grated orange zest plus 1 tablespoon juice
 2 oranges, peeled and cut into segments
 ⅓ cup green olives, chopped
 ⅓ cup slivered almonds, toasted
 2 tablespoons minced fresh oregano

1. Bring 4 quarts water to boil in Dutch oven. Meanwhile, toast rice in 12-inch skillet over medium heat until faintly fragrant and some grains turn opaque, 5 to 8 minutes. Stir 1½ teaspoons salt and toasted rice into boiling water and cook, stirring occasionally, until rice is tender but not soft, about 15 minutes. Drain rice, spread onto rimmed baking sheet, and let cool completely, about 15 minutes; transfer to large bowl.

2. Whisk oil, vinegar, garlic, orange zest and juice, 1 teaspoon salt, and ½ teaspoon pepper together in separate bowl, then drizzle over cooled rice. Add oranges, olives, almonds, and oregano and toss to combine. Let sit for 20 minutes before serving.

Rice Salad with Cauliflower, Cashews, and Mango

SERVES 4 TO 6 VEGAN GF

Taste the rice as it nears the end of its cooking time; it should be cooked through and toothsome, but not crunchy. Be careful not to overcook the rice or the grains will "blow out" and fray. We prefer the flavor of basmati rice in this recipe, but long-grain white, jasmine, or Texmati rice can be substituted.

1½ cups basmati rice
    Salt and pepper
 2 tablespoons vegetable oil
 ½ small head cauliflower, cut into small florets (about 2 cups)
 1 tablespoon curry powder
 ¼ cup currants
 ½ cup roasted cashews, chopped
 1 mango, peeled and diced fine
 3 tablespoons minced fresh chives

1. Bring 4 quarts water to boil in Dutch oven. Meanwhile, toast rice in 12-inch skillet over medium heat until faintly fragrant and some grains turn opaque, 5 to 8 minutes. Stir 1½ teaspoons salt and toasted rice into boiling water and cook, stirring occasionally, until rice is tender but not soft, about 15 minutes. Drain rice, spread onto rimmed baking sheet, and let cool completely, about 15 minutes; transfer to large bowl.

2. Heat oil in 12-inch skillet over high heat until shimmering. Add cauliflower, curry powder, and ½ teaspoon salt and cook, stirring constantly, until fragrant and curry powder adheres to cauliflower, about 1 minute. Stir in currants and ¼ cup water. Reduce heat to medium-high and cook until water evaporates and cauliflower is tender, about 3 minutes; transfer to bowl with rice.

3. Add cashews, mango, chives, ½ teaspoon salt, and ¼ teaspoon pepper to rice and toss to combine. Let sit for 20 minutes before serving.

Rice Salad with Pineapple, Jícama, and Pumpkin Seeds

SERVES 4 TO 6 `GF`

Taste the rice as it nears the end of its cooking time; it should be cooked through and toothsome, but not crunchy. Be careful not to overcook the rice or the grains will "blow out" and fray. We prefer the flavor of basmati rice in this recipe, but long-grain white, jasmine, or Texmati rice can be substituted.

1½ **cups basmati rice**
    Salt and pepper
 2 **tablespoons vegetable oil**
 1 **jalapeño chile, stemmed, seeded, and minced**
½ **teaspoon grated lime zest plus 1 tablespoon juice**
 1 **small garlic clove, minced**
 1 **teaspoon honey**
 1 **cup finely diced fresh pineapple**
 1 **cup peeled and finely diced jícama**
⅓ **cup pumpkin seeds, toasted**
 2 **scallions, sliced thin**
 3 **tablespoons minced fresh cilantro**

1. Bring 4 quarts water to boil in Dutch oven. Meanwhile, toast rice in 12-inch skillet over medium heat until faintly fragrant and some grains turn opaque, 5 to 8 minutes. Stir 1½ teaspoons salt and toasted rice into boiling water and cook, stirring occasionally, until rice is tender but not soft, about 15 minutes. Drain rice, spread onto rimmed baking sheet, and let cool completely, about 15 minutes; transfer to large bowl.

2. Whisk oil, jalapeño, lime zest and juice, garlic, honey, 1 teaspoon salt, and ½ teaspoon pepper together in separate bowl, then drizzle over cooled rice. Add pineapple, jícama, pumpkin seeds, scallions, and cilantro and toss to combine. Let sit for 20 minutes before serving.

Brown Rice Salad

SERVES 4 TO 6 `GF`

WHY THIS RECIPE WORKS: With its pleasantly chewy texture and nutty flavor, brown rice works perfectly in an easy salad. However, our favorite method for brown rice—baking—didn't work here; once it was cooled and drizzled with the dressing, the rice turned out gummy. To solve this problem, we tried the method we used for our white rice salad. We cooked the rice by boiling it in a large pot of water, which washed away its excess starches. Then we spread it out on a

To get the right texture for our brown rice salad, we boiled the rice like pasta, then spread it on a baking sheet to cool rapidly.

baking sheet to cool rapidly, preventing it from overcooking as it sat. To season the rice, we drizzled it with some lemon juice while it was still warm. Then we topped the rice with asparagus spears (cooked until tender and well browned), crunchy almonds, creamy goat cheese, and fresh parsley. A quick lemon dressing finished our simple rice salad.

1½ **cups long-grain brown rice**
    Salt and pepper
 1 **teaspoon grated lemon zest plus 3 tablespoons juice**
3½ **tablespoons extra-virgin olive oil**
 1 **pound asparagus, trimmed**
 1 **shallot, minced**
 4 **ounces goat cheese, crumbled (1 cup)**
½ **cup slivered almonds, toasted**
¼ **cup minced fresh parsley**

1. Bring 4 quarts water to boil in large pot. Add rice and 2 teaspoons salt and cook, stirring occasionally, until rice is tender, 22 to 25 minutes. Drain rice, spread onto rimmed baking sheet, and drizzle with 1 tablespoon lemon juice. Let rice cool completely, about 10 minutes; transfer to large bowl.

2. Heat 1 tablespoon oil in 12-inch skillet over medium-high heat until shimmering. Add asparagus, with half of tips pointed in 1 direction and half pointed in opposite direction. Shake pan gently to help distribute spears evenly (they will not quite fit in single layer). Cover and cook until asparagus is bright green and still crisp, about 5 minutes.

3. Uncover, increase heat to high, and season with salt and pepper. Cook, moving spears around with tongs as needed, until asparagus is tender and well browned on 1 side, 5 to 7 minutes. Transfer asparagus to cutting board, let cool, then cut into 1-inch pieces.

4. Whisk remaining 2½ tablespoons oil, shallot, lemon zest, remaining 2 tablespoons lemon juice, ½ teaspoon salt, and ½ teaspoon pepper together in small bowl, then drizzle over cooled rice. Add asparagus and all but 2 tablespoons goat cheese and toss to combine. Let sit for 10 minutes.

5. Add ⅓ cup almonds and 3 tablespoons parsley and toss to combine. Season with salt and pepper to taste. Sprinkle with remaining almonds, remaining goat cheese, and remaining parsley and serve.

VARIATIONS
Brown Rice Salad with Jalapeño, Tomatoes, and Avocado
SERVES 4 TO 6 `GF`
To make this salad spicier, add the chile seeds.

- 1½ **cups long-grain brown rice**
- **Salt and pepper**
- 1 **teaspoon grated lime zest plus**
- 3 **tablespoons juice (2 limes)**
- 2½ **tablespoons extra-virgin olive oil**
- 2 **teaspoons honey**
- 2 **garlic cloves, minced**
- ½ **teaspoon ground cumin**
- 10 **ounces cherry tomatoes, halved**
- 1 **avocado, halved, pitted, and cut into ½-inch pieces**
- 1 **jalapeño chile, stemmed, seeded, and minced**
- 5 **scallions, sliced thin**
- ¼ **cup minced fresh cilantro**

1. Bring 3 quarts water to boil in large pot. Add rice and 2 teaspoons salt and cook, stirring occasionally, until rice is tender, 22 to 25 minutes. Drain rice, spread onto rimmed

baking sheet, and drizzle with 1 tablespoon lime juice. Let rice cool completely, about 10 minutes; transfer to large bowl.

2. Whisk oil, honey, garlic, lime zest and remaining 2 tablespoons juice, cumin, ½ teaspoon salt, and ½ teaspoon pepper together in small bowl, then drizzle over cooled rice. Add tomatoes, avocado, and jalapeño and toss to combine. Let sit for 10 minutes.

3. Add ¼ cup scallions and cilantro and toss to combine. Season with salt and pepper to taste. Sprinkle with remaining scallions and serve.

Brown Rice Salad with Fennel, Mushrooms, and Walnuts
SERVES 4 TO 6 `VEGAN` `GF`
Cremini mushrooms can be substituted for the white mushrooms.

- 1½ **cups long-grain brown rice**
- **Salt and pepper**
- 3 **tablespoons white wine vinegar**
- ¼ **cup extra-virgin olive oil**
- 1 **pound white mushrooms, trimmed and quartered**
- 1 **large fennel bulb, stalks discarded, bulb halved, cored, and sliced thin**
- 1 **shallot, minced**
- ⅔ **cup walnuts, toasted and chopped coarse**
- 2 **tablespoons minced fresh tarragon**
- 2 **tablespoons minced fresh parsley**

1. Bring 3 quarts water to boil in large pot. Add rice and 2 teaspoons salt and cook, stirring occasionally, until rice is tender, 22 to 25 minutes. Drain rice, spread onto rimmed baking sheet, and drizzle with 1 tablespoon vinegar. Let rice cool completely, about 10 minutes; transfer to large bowl.

2. Heat 1 tablespoon oil in 12-inch skillet over medium-high heat until shimmering. Add mushrooms and ½ teaspoon salt and cook, stirring occasionally, until pan is dry and

Cooling Rice for Salad

After cooking and draining rice, spread onto rimmed baking sheet and drizzle with 1 tablespoon citrus juice or vinegar. Let rice cool completely, about 10 minutes; transfer to large bowl.

mushrooms are browned, 6 to 8 minutes; transfer to plate and let cool.

3. Heat 1 tablespoon oil in now-empty skillet over medium-high heat until shimmering. Add fennel and ¼ teaspoon salt and cook, stirring occasionally, until just browned and crisp-tender, 3 to 4 minutes; transfer to plate with mushrooms and let cool.

4. Whisk remaining 2 tablespoons oil, remaining 2 tablespoons vinegar, shallot, ½ teaspoon salt, and ½ teaspoon pepper together in small bowl, then drizzle over cooled rice. Add mushroom-fennel mixture and toss to combine. Let sit for 10 minutes.

5. Add ½ cup walnuts, tarragon, and 1 tablespoon parsley and toss to combine. Season with salt and pepper to taste. Sprinkle with remaining walnuts and remaining 1 tablespoon parsley and serve.

Red Rice and Quinoa Salad

SERVES 4 TO 6   VEGAN   GF

✓ **WHY THIS RECIPE WORKS:** For a rice and grain salad that was colorful, hearty, and a little out of the ordinary, we turned to a mix of nutty quinoa and red rice. Red rice is a variety of rice with a red husk; it has a nutty flavor and is highly nutritious. To combine the two ingredients in a salad, we decided to cook both in the same pot using the pasta method. We gave the rice a 15-minute head start and then added in the quinoa to ensure the grains were both done at the same time. Then we drained them, drizzled them with lime juice to add bright flavor, and let them cool. Next, we looked for ingredients that would make this salad fresh and sweet. We added in orange segments (and used some of their juice in our dressing) and dates for sweetness. Cilantro and red pepper flakes added a fresh bite and a bit of spiciness to round it out. We like the convenience of prewashed quinoa; rinsing removes the quinoa's bitter protective coating (called saponin). If you buy unwashed quinoa (or if you are unsure whether it's washed), rinse it before cooking. For how to segment an orange, see page 244.

¾ **cup red rice**
   Salt and pepper
¾ **cup prewashed white quinoa**
3 **tablespoons lime juice (2 limes)**
2 **oranges**
1 **small shallot, minced**
1 **tablespoon minced fresh cilantro plus 1 cup leaves**

Tender red rice and nutty quinoa perfectly complement the sweet oranges and dates in this fresh but hearty salad.

¼ **teaspoon red pepper flakes**
¼ **cup extra-virgin olive oil**
6 **ounces pitted dates, chopped (1 cup)**

1. Bring 4 quarts water to boil in large pot over high heat. Add rice and 1 tablespoon salt and cook, stirring occasionally, for 15 minutes. Add quinoa to pot and continue to cook until grains are tender, 12 to 14 minutes. Drain rice-quinoa mixture, spread onto rimmed baking sheet, and drizzle with 2 tablespoons lime juice. Let rice cool completely, about 20 minutes.

2. Meanwhile, cut away peel and pith from oranges. Holding fruit over bowl, use paring knife to slice between membranes to release segments. Cut segments in half crosswise. If needed, squeeze orange membranes to equal 2 tablespoons juice in bowl.

3. Whisk 2 tablespoons orange juice, remaining 1 tablespoon lime juice, shallot, minced cilantro, and pepper flakes in large bowl. Whisking constantly, drizzle in oil. Season with salt and pepper to taste. Add rice-quinoa mixture, dates, orange segments, and remaining 1 cup cilantro leaves and toss to combine. Season with salt and pepper to taste. Serve.

We feature the nutty, roasted flavor of black rice in a bright salad with snap peas and an Asian-inspired vinaigrette.

1½ cups black rice

Salt and pepper

3 tablespoons plus 1 teaspoon rice vinegar

2 teaspoons minced shallot

2 teaspoons honey

2 teaspoons Asian chili-garlic sauce

1 teaspoon grated fresh ginger

¼ cup extra-virgin olive oil

1 tablespoon toasted sesame oil

6 ounces sugar snap peas, strings removed and halved

5 radishes, trimmed, halved, and sliced thin

1 red bell pepper, stemmed, seeded, and chopped fine

¼ cup minced fresh cilantro

1. Bring 4 quarts water to boil in Dutch oven over medium-high heat. Add rice and 1 teaspoon salt and cook until rice is tender, 20 to 25 minutes. Drain rice, spread onto rimmed baking sheet, and drizzle with 1 teaspoon vinegar. Let rice cool completely, about 15 minutes.

2. Whisk remaining 3 tablespoons vinegar, shallot, honey, chili-garlic sauce, ginger, ¼ teaspoon salt, and ⅛ teaspoon pepper together in large bowl. Whisking slowly, drizzle in olive oil and sesame oil until combined. Add cooled rice, snap peas, radishes, bell pepper, and cilantro and toss to combine. Season with salt and pepper to taste, and serve.

Black Rice Salad with Snap Peas and Ginger-Sesame Vinaigrette

SERVES 4 TO 6 GF

✔ **WHY THIS RECIPE WORKS:** Black rice, also known as purple rice or forbidden rice, is an ancient grain that was once reserved for the emperors of China. It has a delicious roasted, nutty taste and is used in anything from salads to dessert puddings. We decided to use it in a simple salad, and, to stick with its decidedly Asian roots, we paired it with crunchy snap peas, peppery radishes, cilantro, and a ginger-sesame vinaigrette. Our major obstacle was finding the right method for cooking the rice, as it is easy to overcook. We discovered that the best way to keep it evenly cooked was to cook it like pasta, in lots of boiling water, giving it space to move around. Once it was cooked, we drizzled it with a little vinegar for a boost of flavor and let it cool completely on a baking sheet. This ensured perfectly cooked grains that had the expected chew of black rice without any mushiness.

Baked Barley

SERVES 4 TO 6

✔ **WHY THIS RECIPE WORKS:** With its nutty taste and substantial, chewy texture, barley offers a great alternative to rice. We started with easy-to-find pearl barley, which is processed to remove its hull and bran. For a simple method that would give us perfect results, we adapted the technique we created for simple baked brown rice. We brought the water to a boil to shorten the cooking time, poured it over the barley in a baking dish, and covered the dish tightly with foil before moving it to the oven. Settling on the right ratio of water to barley required some testing since barley can absorb two to three times its volume in cooking liquid. We finally settled on 3½ cups of water to 1½ cups of barley. After a little over an hour in the oven, followed by a 10-minute rest, the barley was perfectly cooked, with grains that were separate and fully cooked without being soggy. Be sure to cover the pot when bringing the water to a boil in step 2; any water loss due to evaporation will affect how the barley cooks. Do not substitute hulled, hull-less, quick-cooking, or presteamed barley for the pearl barley in this recipe; you may need to read the ingredient list on the package carefully to determine if the barley is presteamed.

- 1½ **cups pearl barley, rinsed**
- 3½ **cups water**
- 2 **teaspoons unsalted butter**
- 1 **teaspoon salt**

1. Adjust oven rack to middle position and heat oven to 375 degrees. Spread barley in 8-inch square glass baking dish.

2. Bring water, butter, and salt to boil in covered medium saucepan over high heat. Once boiling, stir to combine, then pour immediately over barley. Cover baking dish tightly with aluminum foil and bake until barley is tender and no water remains, 70 to 80 minutes.

3. Remove dish from oven, uncover, and fluff barley with fork. Re-cover dish and let barley sit for 10 minutes before serving.

VARIATION
Baked Barley with Porcini Mushrooms
SERVES 4 TO 6
Be sure to cover the pot when bringing the water to a boil in step 2; any water loss due to evaporation will affect how the barley cooks. Do not substitute hulled, hull-less, quick-cooking, or presteamed barley for the pearl barley in this recipe; you may need to read the ingredient list on the package carefully to determine if the barley is presteamed.

- 1½ **cups pearl barley, rinsed**
- 3 **tablespoons unsalted butter**
- 1 **onion, minced**
- 1 **teaspoon salt**
- ¼ **ounce dried porcini mushrooms, rinsed and minced**
- 1 **teaspoon minced fresh thyme**
- 3½ **cups water**

1. Adjust oven rack to middle position and heat oven to 375 degrees. Spread barley in 8-inch square glass baking dish.

2. Melt butter in medium saucepan over medium heat. Add onion and salt and cook until onion is softened, 5 to 7 minutes. Stir in mushrooms and thyme and cook until fragrant, about 1 minute. Stir in water, cover pot, increase heat to high, and bring to boil.

3. Once boiling, stir to combine, then pour immediately over barley. Cover baking dish tightly with aluminum foil and bake until barley is tender and no water remains, 70 to 80 minutes.

4. Remove dish from oven, uncover, and fluff barley with fork. Re-cover dish and let barley sit for 10 minutes before serving.

Barley Risotto
SERVES 4 TO 6

WHY THIS RECIPE WORKS: We found that preparing barley with a risotto cooking method was a great way to use this healthy grain. We used pearl barley in this dish because the hull and the bran are removed, leaving the starchy interior exposed. This helped to create a supple, velvety sauce when simmered—much the same as risotto made with Arborio rice. We used the classic risotto cooking method, with one minor change: We added more liquid, because barley takes a bit longer to cook and absorbs more liquid. To complement the hearty risotto, we sautéed an onion and a carrot before adding the barley and the cooking liquid to the pot. Finally, we finished the dish with fresh thyme, Parmesan cheese, and a little butter for richness. You may not need to use all of the broth when cooking the risotto. Do not substitute hulled, hull-less, quick-cooking, or presteamed barley for the pearl barley in this recipe; you may need to read the ingredient list on the package carefully to determine if the barley is presteamed. Serve with lemon wedges and extra grated Parmesan cheese.

- 4 **cups vegetable broth**
- 4 **cups water**
- 1 **tablespoon vegetable oil**
- 1 **onion, chopped fine**
- 1 **carrot, peeled and chopped fine**
- 1½ **cups pearl barley**
- 1 **cup dry white wine**
- 1 **teaspoon minced fresh thyme**
- 2 **ounces Parmesan cheese, grated (1 cup)**
- 1 **tablespoon unsalted butter**
  Salt and pepper

1. Bring broth and water to simmer in medium saucepan. Reduce heat to lowest setting and cover to keep warm.

2. Heat oil in large saucepan over medium heat until shimmering. Add onion and carrot and cook until vegetables are softened, 5 to 7 minutes. Stir in barley and cook, stirring often, until lightly toasted and aromatic, about 4 minutes. Stir in wine and cook until fully absorbed, about 2 minutes.

3. Stir in thyme and 3 cups warm broth. Simmer, stirring occasionally, until liquid is absorbed and bottom of pan is dry, 22 to 25 minutes. Stir in 2 cups warm broth and simmer, stirring occasionally, until liquid is absorbed and bottom of pan is dry, 15 to 18 minutes.

4. Continue to cook risotto, stirring often and adding remaining broth as needed to prevent pan bottom from becoming

ALL ABOUT **COOKING GRAINS**

From amaranth to wheat berries, the types of grains and the best methods for cooking them can vary tremendously. Some grains, such as bulgur, cook in minutes, while others, such as barley or oat berries, take much longer. Here in the test kitchen we have homed in on three basic methods for cooking grains. We then determined which are best for each type of grain. Of the three cooking methods for grains, pilaf-style is our favorite because it produces grains with a light and fluffy texture and a slightly toasted flavor.

BOILING DIRECTIONS: Bring the water to a boil in a large saucepan. Stir in the grain and ½ teaspoon salt. Return to a boil, then reduce to a simmer and cook until the grain is tender, following the cooking times given in the chart below. Drain.

PILAF-STYLE DIRECTIONS: Rinse and then dry the grains on a towel (see page 190). Heat 1 tablespoon oil in a medium saucepan (preferably nonstick) over medium-high heat until shimmering. Stir in the grain and toast until lightly golden and fragrant, 2 to 3 minutes. Stir in the water and ¼ teaspoon salt. Bring the mixture to a simmer, then reduce the heat to low, cover, and continue to simmer until the grain is tender and has absorbed all of the water, following the cooking times given below. Off the heat, let the grain stand for 10 minutes, then fluff with a fork.

MICROWAVE DIRECTIONS: Rinse the grain (see page 165). Combine the water, the grain, 1 tablespoon oil, and ¼ teaspoon salt in a bowl. Cover and cook following the times and temperatures given below. Remove from the microwave and fluff with a fork. Cover the bowl with plastic wrap, poke several vent holes with the tip of a knife, and let sit until completely tender, about 5 minutes.

TYPE OF GRAIN	COOKING METHOD	AMOUNT OF GRAIN	AMOUNT OF WATER	COOKING TIME
Amaranth *	Pilaf-Style	1 cup	1½ cups	20 to 25 minutes
	Boiled	X	X	X
	Microwave	1 cup	2 cups	5 to 10 minutes on high, then 15 to 20 minutes on medium
Pearl Barley	Pilaf-Style	X	X	X
	Boiled	1 cup	4 quarts	20 to 25 minutes
	Microwave	X	X	X
Buckwheat (Kasha)	Pilaf-Style	1 cup	2 cups	10 to 15 minutes
	Boiled	1 cup	2 quarts	10 to 12 minutes
	Microwave	X	X	X
Bulgur (medium- to coarse-grind)	Pilaf-Style **	1 cup	1 cup	16 to 18 minutes
	Boiled	1 cup	4 quarts	5 minutes
	Microwave	1 cup	1 cup	5 to 10 minutes on high
Farro	Pilaf-Style	X	X	X
	Boiled	1 cup	4 quarts	15 to 20 minutes
	Microwave	X	X	X
Millet	Pilaf-Style ***	1 cup	2 cups	15 to 20 minutes
	Boiled	X	X	X
	Microwave	X	X	X
Oat Berries	Pilaf-Style	1 cup	1⅓ cups	30 to 40 minutes
	Boiled	1 cup	4 quarts	30 to 40 minutes
	Microwave	X	X	X
Quinoa (any color)	Pilaf-Style	1 cup	1 cup + 3 tablespoons	18 to 20 minutes
	Boiled	X	X	X
	Microwave	1 cup	2 cups	5 minutes on medium, then 5 minutes on high
Wheat Berries	Pilaf-Style	X	X	X
	Boiled	1 cup	4 quarts	1 hour
	Microwave	X	X	X

* Do not rinse.

** For pilaf, do not rinse, and skip the toasting step, adding the grain to the pot with the liquid.

*** For pilaf, increase the toasting time until the grains begin to pop, about 12 minutes.

X = Not recommended

dry, until barley is cooked through but still somewhat firm in center, 15 to 20 minutes. Off heat, stir in Parmesan and butter. Season with salt and pepper to taste and serve.

VARIATIONS

Barley Risotto with Mushrooms and Red Wine

A medium-bodied dry red wine blend such as a Côtes du Rhône works nicely here.

Omit carrot. Substitute red wine for white wine and fresh rosemary for thyme. Before adding barley to pan, add 8 ounces cremini mushrooms, trimmed and cut into ½-inch pieces, and ½ ounce dried porcini mushrooms, rinsed and minced, and cook until just beginning to brown, about 4 minutes.

Barley Risotto with Roasted Butternut Squash

Omit carrot and thyme. Before adding barley to pan, add 2 cloves minced garlic and cook until fragrant, about 30 seconds. While barley cooks, toss 6 cups peeled and seeded butternut squash, cut into ½-inch pieces, with 1 tablespoon vegetable oil and season with salt and pepper; spread onto parchment paper–lined rimmed baking sheet and roast in 450-degree oven until tender and golden brown, about 30 minutes. Stir roasted squash, 1 teaspoon minced fresh sage, and ⅛ teaspoon ground nutmeg into barley before serving.

California Barley Bowl with Lemon-Yogurt Sauce

SERVES 4 **FAST**

✔ **WHY THIS RECIPE WORKS:** For a fresh, California-style take on the widely popular rice bowls, we swapped out the rice for hearty, substantial barley and paired it with snow peas, chunks of ripe avocado, and toasted, spiced sunflower seeds. To pull it all together, we created a zesty yogurt sauce infused with lemon and mint. To keep the cooking method easy, we simply boiled the barley until tender, then tossed it with a bright lemon-mint dressing. While the barley cooked, we sautéed the snow peas with some coriander and toasted the sunflower seeds with lots of warm spices. Lastly, we mixed together a quick yogurt sauce with more lemon and mint to drizzle over the top. Once the barley was cooked, we tossed it with the peas, topped it with the chunks of avocado and the sunflower seeds, and drizzled it with yogurt sauce. Do not substitute hulled or hull-less barley in this recipe. If using quick-cooking or presteamed barley (read the ingredient list on the package carefully to determine this), you will need to alter the barley cooking time in step 1.

In this west coast take on a rice bowl, we swap the rice for barley and top it with snow peas, avocado, and spiced seeds.

1 cup pearl barley
Salt and pepper
¼ cup extra-virgin olive oil
8 ounces snow peas, strings removed and halved lengthwise
1 teaspoon ground coriander
¾ cup sunflower seeds
½ teaspoon ground cumin
⅛ teaspoon ground cardamom
1 cup plain yogurt
2 teaspoons grated lemon zest plus 3 tablespoons juice
2 tablespoons minced fresh mint
2 avocados, halved, pitted, and cut into ½-inch pieces

1. Bring 4 quarts water to boil in large pot. Add barley and 1 tablespoon salt and cook until tender, 20 to 25 minutes; drain and transfer to large bowl.

2. Meanwhile, heat ½ tablespoon oil in 12-inch skillet over medium-high heat until just smoking. Add snow peas and

½ teaspoon coriander and cook until peas are spotty brown, about 3 minutes; transfer to plate.

3. Add ½ tablespoon oil to now-empty skillet and heat over medium heat until shimmering. Stir in sunflower seeds, cumin, cardamom, remaining ½ teaspoon coriander, and ½ teaspoon salt. Cook, stirring constantly, until seeds are toasted, about 2 minutes; remove from heat and let cool.

4. Whisk yogurt, 1 teaspoon lemon zest and 2 tablespoons juice, 1 tablespoon mint, ½ teaspoon salt, and ¼ teaspoon pepper together in small bowl; cover and refrigerate until needed.

5. Whisk remaining 3 tablespoons oil, remaining 1 teaspoon lemon zest and 1 tablespoon juice, and remaining 1 tablespoon mint together in separate bowl and season with salt and pepper to taste. Pour dressing over barley, add snow peas, and toss well to coat. Portion barley into individual bowls, top with avocados and spiced sunflower seeds, and drizzle with yogurt sauce. Serve.

Bulgur Pilaf with Cremini Mushrooms

SERVES 4 VEGAN

✔ **WHY THIS RECIPE WORKS:** We wanted to pair the nutty flavor and substantial texture of bulgur with earthy mushrooms in an easy pilaf-style dish. For big mushroom flavor, we chose widely available cremini mushrooms plus a quarter-ounce of dried porcini, which added nice earthiness and depth. But our real breakthrough came when we added a dash of soy sauce. Although it may sound odd for a Mediterranean dish, it amplified the mushroom flavor and gave the dish a rich mahogany color. First we sautéed the mushrooms with an onion, then we added the bulgur and the cooking liquid (a combination of water and vegetable broth) and simmered it until tender. Then we removed the pot from the heat, placed a dish towel underneath the lid, and let the bulgur steam gently for 10 minutes, which resulted in perfectly tender, chewy grains. When shopping, don't confuse bulgur with cracked wheat, which has a much longer cooking time and will not work in this recipe.

- 2 **tablespoons extra-virgin olive oil**
- 1 **onion, minced**
- ¼ **ounce dried porcini mushrooms, rinsed and minced**
  Salt and pepper
- 8 **ounces cremini or white mushrooms, trimmed, stemmed, and quartered if small or cut into 6 pieces if large**

- 2 **garlic cloves, minced**
- 1 **cup medium-grind bulgur, rinsed**
- ¾ **cup vegetable broth**
- ¾ **cup water**
- 1 **teaspoon soy sauce**
- ¼ **cup minced fresh parsley**

1. Heat 1 tablespoon oil in large saucepan over medium heat until shimmering. Add onion, porcini mushrooms, and ¼ teaspoon salt and cook until onion is softened, 5 to 7 minutes. Stir in remaining 1 tablespoon oil and cremini mushrooms. Increase heat to medium-high, cover, and cook until cremini have released their liquid and begin to brown, about 4 minutes.

2. Stir in garlic and cook until fragrant, about 30 seconds. Stir in bulgur, broth, water, and soy sauce and bring to simmer. Reduce heat to low, cover, and simmer until bulgur is tender, 16 to 18 minutes.

3. Remove pot from heat, lay clean folded dish towel underneath lid, and let bulgur sit for 10 minutes. Fluff bulgur with fork, stir in parsley, and season with salt and pepper to taste. Serve.

VARIATION

Bulgur Pilaf with Shiitake Mushrooms VEGAN

Substitute 8 ounces stemmed and thinly sliced shiitake mushrooms for cremini, and 2 thinly sliced scallions for parsley. Add 1 tablespoon grated fresh ginger to pot with garlic.

Tabbouleh

SERVES 4 VEGAN

✔ **WHY THIS RECIPE WORKS:** Tabbouleh is a traditional Middle Eastern salad made of bulgur, parsley, tomato, and onion steeped in a penetrating mint and lemon dressing. For our recipe, we started by salting the tomatoes to rid them of excess moisture that otherwise made our salad soggy. Soaking the bulgur in lemon juice and some of the drained tomato liquid, rather than in water, allowed it to soak up lots of flavor. A whole chopped onion overwhelmed the salad, but two mild scallions added just the right amount of oniony flavor. Bright parsley, mint, and a bit of cayenne pepper rounded out the dish. We added the herbs and vegetables while the bulgur was still soaking, so the components had time to mingle, resulting in a cohesive, balanced dish. When shopping, don't confuse bulgur with cracked wheat, which has a much longer cooking time and will not work in this recipe.

To give our tabbouleh bold flavor, we soak the bulgur in juice we drain from the tomatoes instead of plain water.

3 tomatoes, cored and cut into ½-inch pieces
  Salt and pepper
½ cup medium-grind bulgur, rinsed
¼ cup lemon juice (2 lemons)
6 tablespoons extra-virgin olive oil
⅛ teaspoon cayenne pepper
1½ cups minced fresh parsley
½ cup minced fresh mint
2 scallions, sliced thin

1. Toss tomatoes with ¼ teaspoon salt in fine-mesh strainer set over bowl and let drain, tossing occasionally, for 30 minutes; reserve 2 tablespoons drained tomato juice. Toss bulgur with 2 tablespoons lemon juice and reserved tomato juice in bowl and let sit until grains begin to soften, 30 to 40 minutes.

2. In large bowl, whisk remaining 2 tablespoons lemon juice, oil, cayenne, and ¼ teaspoon salt together. Add drained tomatoes, soaked bulgur, parsley, mint, and scallions and toss gently to combine. Cover and let sit at room temperature until flavors have blended and bulgur is tender, about 1 hour.

3. Before serving, toss to recombine and season with salt and pepper to taste.

VARIATION
Spiced Tabbouleh VEGAN
Add ¼ teaspoon ground cinnamon and ¼ teaspoon ground allspice to dressing with cayenne.

Bulgur Salad with Carrots and Almonds
SERVES 4 TO 6 VEGAN

✔ **WHY THIS RECIPE WORKS:** Bulgur may not be as trendy as quinoa, but it is almost as versatile. To make a simple, flavorful bulgur salad, we wanted to use the simple technique for making tabbouleh, but with some interesting new flavors. In keeping with bulgur's Middle Eastern roots, we used warm spices, lemon, shredded carrot, crunchy almonds, and lots of chopped fresh herbs. We softened the bulgur in a mixture of water, lemon juice, and salt for an hour and a half until it had the perfect toothsome chew. Fresh mint, cilantro, and scallions made our salad fresh and bright, and cumin and cayenne added depth of flavor. The sweet shredded carrots nicely accented the rich, nutty taste of the bulgur. When shopping, don't confuse bulgur with cracked wheat, which has a much longer cooking time and will not work in this recipe.

1½ cups medium-grind bulgur, rinsed
1 cup water
6 tablespoons lemon juice (2 lemons)
  Salt and pepper
⅓ cup extra-virgin olive oil
½ teaspoon ground cumin
⅛ teaspoon cayenne pepper
4 carrots, peeled and shredded
3 scallions, sliced thin
½ cup sliced almonds, toasted
⅓ cup chopped fresh mint
⅓ cup chopped fresh cilantro

1. Combine bulgur, water, ¼ cup lemon juice, and ¼ teaspoon salt in bowl. Cover and let sit at room temperature until grains are softened, about 1½ hours.

2. Whisk oil, remaining 2 tablespoons lemon juice, cumin, cayenne, and ½ teaspoon salt together in large bowl. Add soaked bulgur, carrots, scallions, almonds, mint, and cilantro and toss to combine. Season with salt and pepper to taste and serve.

Your typical natural foods store sells more than a dozen types of grain, and the supermarket sells almost as many. The following are our favorites. The list includes cornmeal and couscous, which aren't technically grains, but we include them here since they are prepared and served like grains.

Amaranth

Amaranth, a staple of the Incas and Aztecs, is second only to quinoa for protein content among grains. The tiny gold, black-flecked seeds are also high in vitamins and minerals. Amaranth has a complex flavor that's very nutty and earthy. It is often dry-toasted before being cooked and can be prepared like porridge or rice. The whole seeds can also be popped like popcorn.

Barley

While barley might be most familiar as a key ingredient in beer, it is a nutritious high-fiber, high-protein, and low-fat cereal grain with a nutty flavor that is similar to that of brown rice. It is great in soups and in salads, as risotto, and as a simple side dish. Barley is available in multiple forms. Hulled barley, which is sold with the hull removed and the fiber-rich bran intact, is considered a whole grain and is higher in nutrients compared with pearl (or pearled) barley, which is hulled barley that has been polished to remove the bran. There is a quick-cooking barley, which is available as kernels or flakes. Hulled barley takes a long time to cook and should be soaked prior to cooking. Pearl barley cooks much more quickly, making it a more versatile choice when you are adding it to soups or making risotto or a simple pilaf. Use it as a stand-in for dishes where you might ordinarily use rice, such as stir-fries or curry.

Buckwheat Groats and Kasha

Buckwheat, despite its name, is not related to wheat but is in fact an herb that is related to sorrel and rhubarb. Native to Russia, buckwheat appears in cuisines all over the globe, particularly in Eastern Europe and Japan (think soba noodles). Buckwheat has an assertive flavor and can be found in several forms. Hulled, crushed buckwheat seeds are known as buckwheat groats, and because of their high carbohydrate content they are generally treated like a grain. Grayish-green in color, groats have a mildly earthy flavor. They are often eaten as a staple like rice and are baked into puddings and porridges.

Kasha is buckwheat groats that have been roasted. This process gives kasha a darker color and a noticeably earthier and roasty flavor that some people love, and others don't. Kasha is often served pilaf-style and as a hot cereal, and it also is traditionally used in blintzes, combined with pasta to make a traditional Eastern European Jewish dish called *kasha varnishkes*, and included as part of a filling for pastries known as knishes.

Bulgur

Bulgur is made from parboiled or steamed wheat kernels/berries that are then dried, partially stripped of their outer bran layer, and coarsely ground. The result of this process is a relatively fast-cooking, highly nutritious grain that can be used in a variety of applications. Bulgur is perfect for tabbouleh and salads because it requires little more than a soak to become tender and flavorful. We especially like soaking it in flavorful liquids, such as lemon or lime juice, to imbue the whole grain with bright flavor. Coarse-grind bulgur, which requires simmering, is our top choice for making pilaf. Note that medium-grind bulgur can work in either application if you make adjustments to soaking or cooking times. Cracked wheat, on the other hand, often sold alongside bulgur, is not precooked and cannot be substituted for bulgur. Be sure to rinse bulgur, regardless of grain size, to remove excess starches that can turn the grain gluey.

Cornmeal

For many consumers, buying cornmeal used to mean picking up a container of Quaker, or perhaps (especially if you lived in the South) a stone-ground local variety. But at most supermarkets today, you've got a lot more options to sort through: fine-, medium-, and coarse-ground; instant and quick-cooking; and whole-grain, stone-ground, and regular. What do they all mean, which should you buy, and does it even matter? Yes, it definitely does matter. Whether you are making Southern-style cornbread, pancakes, polenta, or a rustic Italian-style cake, different recipes require different grinds and types of cornmeal. What you use can make a big difference. Make sure to read—and buy—carefully.

Couscous

Couscous is a starch made from durum semolina, the high-protein wheat flour that is also used to make Italian pasta. Traditional Moroccan couscous is made by rubbing coarse-ground durum semolina and water between the hands to form small granules. The couscous is then dried and cooked over a simmering stew in a steamer called a *couscoussier*. About the size of bread crumbs, the boxed couscous found in most supermarkets is a precooked version that needs only a few minutes of steeping in hot liquid in order to be fully cooked. Israeli couscous, also known as pearl couscous, is larger than traditional couscous (about the size of a caper) and is not precooked. It has a unique, nutty flavor.

Farro

A favorite ingredient in Tuscan cuisine, these hulled whole-wheat kernels boast a sweet, nutty flavor and a chewy bite. In Italy, the grain is available in three sizes—*farro piccolo*, *farro medio*, and *farro grande*—but the midsize type is most common in the United States. Although we usually turn to the absorption method for quicker-cooking grains, farro takes better to the pasta method because the abundance of water cooks the grains more evenly. When cooked, the grains will be tender but have a slight chew, similar to al dente pasta.

Millet

Believed to be the first domesticated cereal grain, this tiny cereal grass seed has a long history and is still a staple in a large part of the world, particularly in Asia and Africa. The seeds can be ground into flour or used whole. Millet has a mellow corn flavor that works well in both savory and sweet applications, including flatbreads, puddings, and pan-fried cakes. It can be cooked pilaf-style, or it can be turned into a creamy breakfast porridge or polenta-like dish by slightly overcooking the seeds, which causes them to burst and release starch. To add texture to baked goods, try incorporating a small amount of millet into the batter.

Oat Berries (Oat Groats)

Labeled either oat berries or oat groats, this whole grain is simply whole oats that have been hulled and cleaned. They are the least processed oat product (other forms are processed further, such as rolled flat, cut, or ground). Because they have hardly been processed, they retain a high nutritional value. They have an appealing chewy texture and a mildly nutty flavor. Oats are usually thought of as a breakfast cereal, but oat berries make a great savory side dish cooked pilaf-style.

Oats

From breakfast table to cookie jar, this nutritious cereal grass is a versatile grain. Rolled (or old-fashioned) oats are made by hulling, cleaning, steaming, and rolling whole oats. We love oats for their toasty flavor and hearty chew in cookies and in toppings for crisps and cobblers. Steel-cut oats are dense and chewy (too chewy for most baked goods), with a strong buttery flavor. These whole-grain oats are partially cooked and then cut into pieces with steel blades. Steel-cut oats take about 25 minutes longer to cook than rolled oats.

Quinoa

Quinoa originated in the Andes Mountains of South America, and while it is generally treated as a grain, it is actually the seed of the goosefoot plant. Sometimes referred to as a "super grain," quinoa is high in protein, and its protein is complete, which means it possesses all of the amino acids in the balanced amounts that our bodies require. Beyond its nutritional prowess, we love quinoa for its addictive crunchy texture, nutty taste, and ease of preparation. Cooked as a pilaf or for a salad, it can be ready in about 20 minutes. Unless labeled "prewashed," quinoa should always be rinsed before cooking to remove its protective layer (called saponin), which is unpleasantly bitter.

Wheat Berries

Wheat berries, often erroneously referred to as "whole wheat," are whole, unprocessed kernels of wheat. Since none of the grain has been removed, wheat berries are an excellent source of nutrition. Compared with more refined forms of wheat (cracked wheat, bulgur, and flour), wheat berries require a relatively long cooking time. In the test kitchen, we like to toast the dry wheat berries until they are fragrant, and then simmer them for about an hour until they are tender but still retain a good bite.

Bulgur Salad with Grapes and Feta

SERVES 4

✓ **WHY THIS RECIPE WORKS:** For another version of our light, flavorful bulgur salad, we swapped out the carrots for sweet, juicy grapes and tangy feta cheese. We softened the bulgur in a mixture of water, lemon juice, and salt for an hour and a half. Once the bulgur was tender and flavorful, we tossed it with more fresh lemon juice, cumin, and cayenne for depth of flavor, along with the grapes and feta. Quartering the grapes ensured we got some sweetness in every bite. Scallions and mint gave the salad plenty of bright, fresh flavor. Finally, for textural contrast, we added crunchy toasted slivered almonds. When shopping, don't confuse bulgur with cracked wheat, which has a much longer cooking time and will not work in this recipe.

- 1½ **cups medium-grind bulgur, rinsed**
- 1 **cup water**
- 5 **tablespoons lemon juice (2 lemons)**
  Salt and pepper
- ¼ **cup extra-virgin olive oil**
- ¼ **teaspoon ground cumin**
  Pinch cayenne pepper
- 6 **ounces seedless red grapes, quartered (1 cup)**
- ½ **cup slivered almonds, toasted**
- 2 **ounces feta cheese, crumbled (½ cup)**
- 2 **scallions, sliced thin**
- ¼ **cup chopped fresh mint**

1. Combine bulgur, water, ¼ cup lemon juice, and ¼ teaspoon salt in bowl. Cover and let sit at room temperature until grains are softened, about 1½ hours.

2. Whisk oil, remaining 1 tablespoon lemon juice, cumin, cayenne, and ¼ teaspoon salt together in large bowl. Add soaked bulgur, grapes, ⅓ cup almonds, ⅓ cup feta, scallions, and mint and toss to combine. Season with salt and pepper to taste. Sprinkle with remaining almonds and feta before serving.

Couscous

SERVES 4 TO 6 FAST VEGAN

✓ **WHY THIS RECIPE WORKS:** Couscous, a starch made from durum semolina, the high-protein wheat flour that is also used to make pasta, is one of the fastest and easiest side dishes to prepare. It is traditionally served under stews and braises to soak up the flavorful sauce, but it can also be a quick and tasty side dish for a variety of foods. We wanted to develop a classic version for saucy dishes as well as a handful of flavor-packed variations that would be as convenient as the box kind, but much fresher-tasting. Toasting the couscous grains in butter or olive oil deepened their flavor and helped them cook up light and separate. And to bump up the flavor even further, we replaced half of the cooking water with vegetable broth. After just 7 minutes of steeping, the couscous was fluffy and tender. For our dressed-up variations, dried fruit, nuts, and citrus juice added textural interest and sweet, bright notes.

- 2 **tablespoons unsalted butter or extra-virgin olive oil**
- 2 **cups couscous**
- 1 **cup water**
- 1 **cup vegetable broth**
  Salt and pepper

Melt butter in medium saucepan over medium-high heat. Add couscous and cook, stirring frequently, until grains are just beginning to brown, about 5 minutes. Stir in water, broth, and 1 teaspoon salt. Cover, remove pan from heat, and let sit until grains are tender, about 7 minutes. Uncover, fluff grains with fork, and season with pepper to taste. Serve.

VARIATIONS

Couscous with Dates and Pistachios FAST VEGAN

Increase butter (or oil) to 3 tablespoons. Add ½ cup chopped pitted dates, 1 tablespoon grated fresh ginger, and ½ teaspoon ground cardamom to pot with couscous. Increase water to 1¼ cups. Before serving, stir in ¾ cup coarsely chopped toasted pistachios, 3 tablespoons minced fresh cilantro, and 2 teaspoons lemon juice.

Couscous with Dried Cherries and Pecans FAST VEGAN

Increase butter (or oil) to 3 tablespoons. Add ½ cup coarsely chopped dried cherries, 2 cloves minced garlic, ¾ teaspoon garam masala, and ⅛ teaspoon cayenne pepper to pot with couscous, and increase water to 1¼ cups. Before serving, stir in ¾ cup coarsely chopped toasted pecans, 2 thinly sliced scallions, and 2 teaspoons lemon juice.

Couscous with Carrots, Raisins, and Pine Nuts FAST VEGAN

Increase butter (or oil) to 3 tablespoons. Before adding couscous to pot, add 2 peeled and grated carrots and ½ teaspoon ground cinnamon and cook until softened, about 2 minutes. Add ½ cup raisins to pot with couscous, and increase water to 1¼ cups. Before serving, stir in ¾ cup toasted pine nuts, 3 tablespoons minced fresh cilantro, ½ teaspoon grated orange zest, and 1 tablespoon orange juice.

Preparing Fennel

1. Cut off tops and feathery fronds.

2. Trim thin slice from base and remove any tough or blemished outer layers.

3. Cut bulb in half through base. Use small sharp knife to remove pyramid-shaped core.

4. Slice fennel halves into thin strips.

Tender baby spinach and aromatic sautéed fennel dress up hearty Israeli couscous in this simple weeknight dish.

Israeli Couscous with Caramelized Fennel and Spinach

SERVES 4 TO 6 **VEGAN**

🗸 **WHY THIS RECIPE WORKS:** In this simple dish, we used larger-grained Israeli couscous instead of the more traditional small-grain Moroccan couscous to give our dish a heartier texture and great visual appeal. Israeli couscous also has a unique nutty taste that we paired with baby spinach and thinly sliced anise-flavored fennel. Some lemon zest and fresh lemon juice brightened it up, and chives added freshness. Since Israeli couscous is larger than traditional couscous, it requires a slightly different cooking technique. Whereas traditional couscous can simply be soaked in boiling water to rehydrate and turn tender, the larger grains of Israeli couscous require boiling or simmering. Once the couscous was tender, we sautéed the fennel along with some sliced onion; the baby spinach just needed to be stirred in off the heat until it was lightly wilted. Do not substitute regular couscous in this dish, as it requires a different cooking method and will not work in this recipe. Serve with lemon wedges.

1½ cups Israeli couscous
    Salt and pepper
2 tablespoons extra-virgin olive oil
3 fennel bulbs, stalks discarded, bulbs halved, cored, and sliced thin
½ onion, halved and sliced ¼ inch thick
2 garlic cloves, minced
½ teaspoon grated lemon zest plus 1 tablespoon juice
4 ounces (4 cups) baby spinach
3 tablespoons minced fresh chives

1. Bring 4 quarts water to boil in Dutch oven. Stir in couscous and 1 tablespoon salt and cook until tender, about 5 minutes. Drain couscous, transfer to large bowl, and cover to keep warm.

2. Wipe now-empty pot dry, add 1½ tablespoons oil, and place over medium-low heat until shimmering. Add fennel, onion, and ¼ teaspoon salt, cover, and cook, stirring occasionally, until vegetables have softened and released their liquid, about 15 minutes. Uncover, increase heat to medium-high, and cook, stirring often, until lightly browned and liquid has evaporated, 15 to 20 minutes.

3. Stir in garlic and lemon zest and cook until fragrant, about 1 minute. Off heat, stir in spinach, cover, and let sit until spinach is wilted, about 2 minutes. Stir in couscous, lemon juice, chives, and remaining ½ tablespoon oil. Season with salt and pepper to taste and serve warm or at room temperature.

Farro with Mushrooms and Thyme

SERVES 4 `FAST` `VEGAN`

✔ **WHY THIS RECIPE WORKS:** Farro is a popular ingredient in Tuscan cuisine thanks to its sweet, nutty flavor and chewy bite. Although we usually turn to the absorption method for quicker-cooking grains, a few tests proved that the pasta method was a better choice for farro because the abundance of water cooked the grains more evenly. Mushrooms sautéed with shallot and thyme lent the dish plenty of meatiness, and using sherry to deglaze the pan after the mushrooms browned added some complexity to the dish. Finishing with sherry vinegar and a couple of tablespoons of fresh parsley added brightness and freshness that balanced the hearty, savory flavors. White mushrooms can be substituted for the cremini. Do not substitute pearled (*perlato*) farro for the whole farro in this recipe. If using quick-cooking or presteamed farro (read the ingredient list on the package carefully to determine this), you will need to alter the farro cooking time in step 1.

- 1 **cup whole farro**
  Salt and pepper
- 2 **tablespoons extra-virgin olive oil**
- 8 **ounces cremini mushrooms, trimmed and chopped coarse**
- 1 **shallot, minced**
- 1 **teaspoon minced fresh thyme**
- 2 **tablespoons dry sherry**
- 2 **tablespoons minced fresh parsley**
- 1 **teaspoon sherry vinegar**

1. Bring 4 quarts water to boil in Dutch oven. Stir in farro and 1 tablespoon salt and boil until tender, 15 to 20 minutes. Drain farro, transfer to large bowl, and cover to keep warm.

2. Meanwhile, heat oil in 12-inch skillet over medium-high heat until shimmering. Add mushrooms, shallot, thyme, and ¼ teaspoon salt and cook, stirring frequently, until moisture has evaporated and vegetables start to brown, 5 to 8 minutes. Stir in sherry and cook, scraping up any browned bits, until pan is almost dry, 1 to 2 minutes.

3. Add farro and cook, stirring constantly, until heated through, about 1 minute. Off heat, stir in parsley and vinegar. Season with salt and pepper to taste, and serve.

Farro and Broccoli Rabe Gratin

SERVES 6

✔ **WHY THIS RECIPE WORKS:** For this recipe, we set out to create a new kind of casserole, one featuring a whole grain that was both hearty and healthy. We chose Italian flavors, accenting the nutty farro with creamy white beans, slightly bitter broccoli rabe, and salty Parmesan. Toasting the farro in the aromatics and oil gave it some extra nuttiness and jump-started the cooking process, making the end result more evenly cooked. We liked small white beans in this dish, as they blended in nicely with the farro while giving it some creaminess and added protein. Blanching the broccoli rabe in salted water tamed its bitterness. We then sautéed it with garlic and pepper flakes for extra flavor. Sun-dried tomatoes gave us the extra pop of flavor we were after in this dish. All that was left was to combine all the ingredients in a casserole dish and stick it under the broiler to brown the Parmesan dusted over the top. Do not substitute pearled (*perlato*), quick-cooking, or presteamed farro for the whole farro in this recipe; you may need to read the ingredient list on the package carefully to determine if the farro is presteamed.

- 2 **tablespoons extra-virgin olive oil**
- 1 **onion, minced**
- 1½ **cups whole farro, rinsed**
- 2 **cups vegetable broth**
- 1½ **cups water**
- 4 **ounces Parmesan cheese, grated (2 cups)**
  Salt and pepper
- 1 **pound broccoli rabe, trimmed and cut into 2-inch lengths**
- 6 **garlic cloves, minced**
- ⅛ **teaspoon red pepper flakes**
- 1 **(15-ounce) can small white beans or navy beans, rinsed**
- ½ **cup oil-packed sun-dried tomatoes, chopped**

To make a modern whole-grain casserole, we combine farro with small white beans, broccoli rabe, and sun-dried tomatoes.

1. Heat 1 tablespoon oil in large saucepan over medium heat until shimmering. Add onion and cook until softened and lightly browned, 5 to 7 minutes. Stir in farro and cook until lightly toasted, about 2 minutes. Stir in broth and water and bring to simmer. Reduce heat to low and continue to simmer, stirring often, until farro is just tender and remaining liquid has thickened into creamy sauce, 20 to 25 minutes. Off heat, stir in 1 cup Parmesan and season with salt and pepper to taste.

2. Meanwhile, bring 4 quarts water to boil in Dutch oven. Add broccoli rabe and 1 tablespoon salt and cook until just tender, about 2 minutes. Drain broccoli rabe and transfer to bowl.

3. Wipe now-empty Dutch oven dry, add remaining 1 tablespoon oil, garlic, and pepper flakes, and cook over medium heat until fragrant and sizzling, 1 to 2 minutes. Stir in drained broccoli rabe and cook until hot and well coated, about 2 minutes. Off heat, stir in beans, farro mixture, and sun-dried tomatoes. Season with salt and pepper to taste.

4. Position oven rack 6 inches from broiler element and heat broiler. Pour bean-farro mixture into 3-quart broiler-safe casserole dish and sprinkle with remaining 1 cup Parmesan. Broil until lightly browned and hot, 3 to 5 minutes. Let cool 5 minutes before serving.

Storing Rice, Grains, and Beans

To prevent open boxes and bags of rice, grains, and beans from spoiling in the pantry, store them in airtight containers, and, if you have space, keep rice and grains in the freezer. This is especially important for whole grains, which turn rancid with oxidation. Use rice and grains within six months. Though beans are less susceptible to pests and spoilage than rice and grains, and can be kept up to a year, you will get the best results if you use beans within the first month or two of purchase.

Farro Risotto

SERVES 5   FAST   VEGAN

✔ **WHY THIS RECIPE WORKS:** Italians often prepare farro in much the same way that they cook risotto to make a rich, creamy dish called *farrotto*. We set out to come up with our own version. To keep it simple, we adopted our easy method for risotto. A few modifications were in order, however. Farro required more frequent stirring to ensure that the grains cooked evenly. We also found that we didn't need to warm the liquid before adding it to the pot—the farro cooked through just fine. As for flavorings, onion was a good start, and garlic, thyme, and sweet, earthy carrot made our farrotto even better. It's traditional to finish risotto with butter and Parmesan, but these additions masked the nutty grain. We preferred fresh parsley and lemon juice. For a creamy texture, be sure to stir the risotto often in step 2. Do not substitute pearled (*perlato*), quick-cooking, or presteamed farro for the whole farro in this recipe; you may need to read the ingredient list on the package carefully to determine if the farro is presteamed.

1 **onion, minced**
1 **carrot, peeled and chopped fine**
1 **tablespoon extra-virgin olive oil**
  Salt and pepper
3 **garlic cloves, minced**
1 **teaspoon minced fresh thyme**
1½ **cups whole farro**
2 **cups vegetable broth**
1½ **cups water**
2 **tablespoons minced fresh parsley**
1 **teaspoon lemon juice**

1. Combine onion, carrot, oil, and ¼ teaspoon salt in large saucepan. Cover and cook over medium-low heat, stirring

occasionally, until vegetables are softened, 8 to 10 minutes. Stir in garlic and thyme and cook until fragrant, about 30 seconds.

2. Stir in farro and cook until lightly toasted, about 2 minutes. Stir in broth and water and bring to simmer. Reduce heat to low and continue to simmer, stirring often, until farro is tender, 20 to 25 minutes.

3. Stir in parsley and lemon juice. Season with salt and pepper to taste and serve.

VARIATIONS

Farro Risotto with Arugula, Lemon, and Parmesan FAST

Omit carrot. Stir in 2 cups baby arugula, ½ cup grated Parmesan cheese, and ½ teaspoon grated lemon zest with parsley before serving.

Farro Risotto with Fennel, Radicchio, and Balsamic Vinegar FAST VEGAN

Substitute 1 fennel bulb, halved, cored, and finely chopped, for carrot, and 2 teaspoons balsamic vinegar for lemon juice. Stir in ½ small head thinly sliced radicchio with parsley.

Curried Millet Pilaf

SERVES 4 TO 6 FAST GF

✔ **WHY THIS RECIPE WORKS:** Since millet is a staple in Middle Eastern and Indian cuisines, we turned to that part of the world to inspire the flavor profile of this easy pilaf, adding basil, mint, raisins, almonds, and curry powder. Toasting the millet before simmering the seeds gave them nutty depth; we first dried the tiny, soggy seeds so they would toast properly. After some testing, we landed on a 2:1 ratio of liquid to millet, which ensured evenly cooked, fluffy seeds. We served it with a dollop of yogurt for richness and an appealing cooling counterpoint to the heat of the curry. We prefer whole-milk yogurt in this recipe, but low-fat yogurt can be substituted if desired. Unlike other grains, we have found that millet can become gluey if allowed to steam off the heat. Once all the liquid has been absorbed, use a gentle hand to stir in the basil, raisins, almonds, and scallion greens, then serve immediately.

1	tablespoon extra-virgin olive oil
3	scallions, white and green parts separated, sliced thin
1	teaspoon curry powder
1½	cups millet, rinsed and dried on towel
3	cups water
	Salt and pepper
½	cup chopped fresh basil and/or mint
¼	cup raisins
¼	cup sliced almonds, toasted
½	cup plain yogurt

1. Heat oil in large saucepan over medium heat until shimmering. Add scallion whites and curry powder and cook until fragrant, about 1 minute. Stir in millet and cook, stirring often, until lightly browned, about 2 minutes.

2. Stir in water and ¾ teaspoon salt and bring to boil. Reduce heat to low, cover, and simmer until liquid is absorbed, 15 to 20 minutes.

3. Off heat, fluff millet with fork and gently stir in basil, raisins, almonds, and scallion greens. Season with salt and pepper to taste. Serve, dolloping individual portions with yogurt.

Drying Grains

1. After rinsing grains, spread over rimmed baking sheet lined with clean dish towel and let dry for 15 minutes.

2. When grains are dry, pick up towel by corners and gently shake grains into bowl.

Creamy Cheesy Millet

SERVES 4 TO 6 GF

✔ **WHY THIS RECIPE WORKS:** We wanted to take advantage of millet's starchiness to turn it into a creamy, savory side dish similar to a polenta. However, it took some testing to find a method that gave us the silky consistency we were after. When we cooked the millet in the amount of liquid we'd normally use for polenta, it didn't break down enough, giving us a texture that was slightly set up, like oatmeal, not the loose consistency we wanted. To get better results, we had to start the millet in 5 cups of liquid (4 cups of water plus 1 cup of milk to lend some richness). This made all the difference. We also slightly overcooked the millet so that the seeds burst and released their starch, creating the right creamy consistency. Since millet is very mild, we toasted it briefly before cooking to bring out its flavor. We also stirred in a good amount of Parmesan and basil before serving to ensure this dish had plenty of flavor.

1 tablespoon extra-virgin olive oil

1 shallot, minced

2 garlic cloves, minced

1 cup millet, rinsed and dried on towel

4 cups water

1 cup whole milk

Salt and pepper

2 ounces Parmesan cheese, grated (1 cup)

2 tablespoons shredded fresh basil

1. Heat oil in large saucepan over medium heat until shimmering. Stir in shallot and cook until softened, about 2 minutes. Add garlic and cook until fragrant, about 30 seconds. Stir in millet and cook, stirring often, until fragrant and lightly browned, about 2 minutes.

2. Stir in water, milk, and 1 teaspoon salt and bring to boil. Reduce heat to low, cover, and simmer, stirring occasionally, until thick and porridgy, about 20 minutes. Uncover and continue to cook, stirring frequently, until millet is mostly broken down, 8 to 10 minutes.

3. Off heat, stir in Parmesan until melted. Sprinkle with basil and season with salt and pepper to taste. Serve.

Oat Berry Pilaf with Walnuts and Gorgonzola

SERVES 4 TO 6 `GF`

Unlike the oats we eat for breakfast, oat berries are whole oats with a hearty texture and chew—perfect for a simple pilaf.

✔ **WHY THIS RECIPE WORKS:** While we think of oats mostly as part of a wholesome breakfast, oat berries—whole oats that have been hulled and cleaned—have great flavor and a satisfying chew. We wanted to make a flavorful oat berry pilaf with hearty add-ins. To cook the oat berries, we sautéed some shallot for aromatic backbone, then added the water and oat berries to the pan. Because oat berries naturally have a nutty flavor, we skipped the step of toasting them. After testing various ratios of water to oat berries, we settled on 2 cups water to 1½ cups oat berries. Creamy, pungent Gorgonzola cheese provided a nice balance to the oat berries' earthy flavor. We tried stirring the Gorgonzola into the oat berries once they were cooked, but the result was a thick, gluey mixture. It was better to wait and simply sprinkle the cheese over the oat berries just before serving. Toasted, chopped walnuts added more richness and a nice crunch. Tart cherries and a drizzle of tangy balsamic vinegar cut through the richness, while parsley gave our pilaf the freshness it needed.

1 tablespoon extra-virgin olive oil

1 shallot, minced

2 cups water

1½ cups oat berries (groats), rinsed

Salt and pepper

¾ cup walnuts, toasted and chopped

½ cup dried cherries

2 tablespoons minced fresh parsley

1 tablespoon balsamic vinegar

2 ounces Gorgonzola cheese, crumbled (½ cup)

1. Heat oil in large saucepan over medium heat until shimmering. Add shallot and cook until softened, about 2 minutes. Stir in water, oat berries, and ¼ teaspoon salt and bring to simmer. Reduce heat to low, cover, and continue to simmer until oat berries are tender but still slightly chewy, 30 to 40 minutes.

2. Remove pot from heat and lay clean folded dish towel underneath lid. Let sit for 10 minutes. Fluff oat berries with fork and fold in walnuts, cherries, and parsley. Season with salt and pepper to taste and drizzle with vinegar. Serve, sprinkling individual portions with Gorgonzola.

This oat berry salad has a surprisingly deep flavor thanks to a bold dressing of lemon juice, cumin, paprika, and cayenne.

1 cup oat berries (groats), rinsed
   Salt and pepper
3 tablespoons extra-virgin olive oil
2 tablespoons lemon juice
2 tablespoons minced fresh cilantro
1 teaspoon honey
1 garlic clove, minced
¼ teaspoon ground cumin
⅛ teaspoon paprika
   Pinch cayenne pepper
1 (15-ounce) can chickpeas, rinsed
6 ounces (6 cups) baby arugula
½ cup jarred roasted red peppers, drained, patted dry, and chopped
2 ounces feta cheese, crumbled (½ cup)

1. Bring 2 quarts water to boil in large saucepan. Add oat berries and ½ teaspoon salt, partially cover, and cook, stirring often, until tender but still chewy, 45 to 50 minutes. Drain oat berries, rinse under cold running water until cool, then transfer to large bowl.

2. Whisk oil, lemon juice, cilantro, honey, garlic, cumin, paprika, cayenne, and ¼ teaspoon salt together in small bowl, then drizzle over oat berries. Stir in chickpeas, arugula, roasted red peppers, and feta. Season with salt and pepper to taste and serve.

Oat Berry, Chickpea, and Arugula Salad

SERVES 4 TO 6 **GF**

✔ **WHY THIS RECIPE WORKS:** We thought that chewy, nutty oat berries were worth highlighting in a main-course salad. To give the grains the perfect chewy, tender texture when served cold, we cooked the oat berries in a large amount of water, pasta style, then drained and rinsed them under cold water to stop the cooking so the grains wouldn't end up mushy. For the leafy component of our dinner salad, assertive, peppery arugula paired well with the nutty oat berries, and we added chickpeas for a little more heft and complementary buttery flavor and creamy texture. Roasted red peppers added sweetness, and creamy feta lent the right richness and salty bite. A simple lemon and cilantro dressing spiked with cumin, paprika, and cayenne provided the perfect amount of spice and brightness.

Savory Steel-Cut Oatmeal with Spinach and Mushrooms

SERVES 4 **GF**

✔ **WHY THIS RECIPE WORKS:** Although steel-cut oats are known for making stellar oatmeal, they also can be used to make a healthy, hearty, and savory main dish. For the oats, we started with the easy method from our Overnight Steel-Cut Oatmeal (page 201). To drastically shorten the hands-on cooking time, we stirred the oats into boiling water and let them sit for up to 12 hours. This enabled the grains to hydrate and partially soften hands-off; then, when we were ready for dinner, we added more water and simmered the mixture for just 4 to 6 minutes, until the oats were thickened. Because the creamy texture and consistency of the oatmeal were similar to a classic risotto, we decided to borrow the flavors of that dish. We added a flavorful combination of sautéed aromatics, cremini mushrooms, peas, and spinach and finished the dish with salty, nutty Parmesan cheese and fresh parsley. The oatmeal will continue to thicken as it cools. If you prefer a looser consistency, thin the oatmeal with boiling water. In order for this recipe to be gluten-free, you must use steel-cut oats that have been processed in a gluten-free facility (such as Bob's Red Mill).

4 cups water
1 cup steel-cut oats
   Salt and pepper
1 tablespoon vegetable oil
3 ounces cremini mushrooms, trimmed and sliced thin
¼ cup finely chopped onion
4 garlic cloves, minced
4 ounces (4 cups) baby spinach
¼ cup frozen peas, thawed
2 ounces Parmesan cheese, grated (1 cup)
3 tablespoons minced fresh parsley

1. Bring 3 cups water to boil in large saucepan over high heat. Remove pan from heat and stir in oats and ¼ teaspoon salt. Cover pan and let sit for at least 4 or up to 12 hours.

2. Stir remaining 1 cup water into oats and bring to boil over medium-high heat. Reduce heat to medium and cook, stirring occasionally, until oats are softened but still retain some chew and mixture thickens and resembles warm pudding, 4 to 6 minutes. Remove pan from heat and let sit for 5 minutes.

3. Meanwhile, heat oil in 12-inch nonstick skillet over medium heat until shimmering. Add mushrooms, onion, and 1 teaspoon salt and cook, stirring often, until vegetables are softened, about 5 minutes. Stir in garlic and cook until fragrant, about 30 seconds. Stir in spinach and peas and cook until spinach is wilted, about 2 minutes. Season with salt and pepper to taste. Stir vegetables, Parmesan, and parsley into oats and serve.

Creamy Parmesan Polenta
SERVES 4 `GF`

✓ **WHY THIS RECIPE WORKS:** Topped with flavorful sautéed or braised vegetables, polenta is a great option for a satisfying winter meal; however, if you don't stir polenta almost constantly to ensure even cooking, it forms intractable lumps, and it can take up to an hour to cook. We wanted to get creamy, smooth polenta with rich corn flavor—but without the fussy process. From the outset, we knew that the right type of cornmeal was essential. Coarse-ground degerminated cornmeal gave us the soft but hearty texture and nutty flavor we were looking for. Adding a pinch of baking soda to the pot helped to soften the cornmeal's endosperm, which cut down on the cooking time. The baking soda also encouraged the granules to break down and release their starch in a uniform way, creating a silky, creamy consistency with minimal stirring. Parmesan cheese and butter, stirred in at the last minute, ensured a satisfying, rich flavor. If the polenta bubbles or sputters even slightly after the first 10 minutes, the heat is too high and you may need a flame tamer (see page 195). To help turn this into a meal, we also created a few vegetable-based Hearty Toppings for Polenta (page 194), which can be prepared while the polenta cooks.

7½ cups water
   Salt and pepper
   Pinch baking soda
1½ cups coarse-ground cornmeal
4 ounces Parmesan cheese, grated (2 cups), plus extra for serving
2 tablespoons unsalted butter

Making Creamy Parmesan Polenta

1. BOIL WATER AND ADD BAKING SODA: Bring water to boil over medium-high heat. Stir in salt and pinch baking soda.

2. SLOWLY STIR IN CORNMEAL: Slowly pour in cornmeal, stirring constantly. Bring to boil, continuing to stir. Reduce heat to lowest setting and cover.

3. WHISK, COVER, AND COOK: After 5 minutes, whisk until smooth. Cover and continue to cook until grains are tender.

4. STIR IN CHEESE, THEN LET SIT: Remove pot from heat. Stir in cheese, butter, and pepper to taste. Cover and let sit for 5 minutes.

HEARTY TOPPINGS FOR POLENTA

Polenta makes a great base for sautéed, braised, or roasted vegetables or hearty ragouts, stews, or chilis. Here are a few of our favorite easy vegetable toppings to serve with polenta.

Sautéed Cherry Tomato and Fresh Mozzarella Topping

MAKES ENOUGH FOR 4 SERVINGS

FAST GF

Don't stir the cheese into the sautéed tomatoes or it will melt prematurely and turn rubbery.

- 3 tablespoons extra-virgin olive oil
- 2 garlic cloves, peeled and sliced thin
  Pinch red pepper flakes
  Pinch sugar
- 1½ pounds cherry tomatoes, halved
  Salt and pepper
- 6 ounces fresh mozzarella cheese, cut into ½-inch cubes
- 2 tablespoons shredded fresh basil

Cook oil, garlic, pepper flakes, and sugar in 12-inch nonstick skillet over medium-high heat until fragrant and sizzling, about 1 minute. Stir in tomatoes and cook until just beginning to soften, about 1 minute. Off heat, season with salt and pepper to taste. Spoon mixture over individual portions of polenta, top with mozzarella and basil, and serve.

Eggplant and Tomato Topping

MAKES ENOUGH FOR 4 SERVINGS

FAST GF

Leaving the skin on the eggplant helps keep the pieces intact during cooking.

- ¼ cup extra-virgin olive oil
- 1 pound eggplant, cut into ¾-inch chunks
  Salt and pepper
- 3 garlic cloves, minced
- 1 (28-ounce) can whole peeled tomatoes, drained with juice reserved, chopped
- ⅓ cup chopped fresh basil
- ¼ cup grated Parmesan cheese

Heat oil in 12-inch nonstick skillet over medium-high heat until shimmering. Add eggplant and ¼ teaspoon salt and cook until eggplant is beginning to brown, 5 to 7 minutes. Reduce heat to medium and cook, stirring occasionally, until tender, about 5 minutes. Stir in garlic and cook until fragrant, about 30 seconds. Stir in tomatoes and reserved juice and simmer until slightly thickened, 2 to 4 minutes. Season with salt and pepper to taste. Spoon mixture over individual portions of polenta, top with basil and Parmesan, and serve.

Broccoli Rabe, Sun-Dried Tomato, and Pine Nut Topping

MAKES ENOUGH FOR 4 SERVINGS

FAST GF

Broccolini can be substituted for the broccoli rabe.

- ½ cup oil-packed sun-dried tomatoes, chopped coarse
- 3 tablespoons extra-virgin olive oil
- 6 garlic cloves, minced
- ½ teaspoon red pepper flakes
  Salt
- 1 pound broccoli rabe, trimmed and cut into 1½-inch pieces
- ¼ cup vegetable broth
- 3 tablespoons pine nuts, toasted
- ¼ cup grated Parmesan cheese

Cook sun-dried tomatoes, oil, garlic, pepper flakes, and ½ teaspoon salt in 12-inch nonstick skillet over medium-high heat, stirring frequently, until garlic is fragrant and slightly toasted, about 1½ minutes. Add broccoli rabe and broth, cover, and cook until rabe turns bright green, about 2 minutes. Uncover and cook, stirring frequently, until most of broth has evaporated and rabe is just tender, 2 to 3 minutes. Season with salt to taste. Spoon mixture over individual portions of polenta, top with pine nuts and Parmesan, and serve.

Mushroom and Rosemary Topping

MAKES ENOUGH FOR 4 SERVINGS

FAST GF

Any type of mushroom can be used here, including white, cremini, shiitake, or oyster.

- 2 tablespoons unsalted butter
- 2 tablespoons extra-virgin olive oil
- 1 small onion, chopped fine
- 2 garlic cloves, minced
- 2 teaspoons minced fresh rosemary
- 1 pound mushrooms (such as cremini, shiitake, or oyster), stemmed and sliced thin
- ⅓ cup vegetable broth
  Salt and pepper
- ¼ cup grated Parmesan cheese

Heat butter and oil in 12-inch nonstick skillet over medium-high heat until butter is melted and hot. Add onion and cook until softened and beginning to brown, 5 to 7 minutes. Stir in garlic and rosemary and cook until fragrant, about 30 seconds. Stir in mushrooms and cook, stirring occasionally, until they release their moisture, about 6 minutes. Add broth and simmer briskly until sauce thickens, about 8 minutes. Season with salt and pepper to taste. Spoon mushroom mixture over individual portions of polenta, sprinkle with Parmesan, and serve.

Sorting Out Polenta

In the supermarket, cornmeal can be labeled anything from yellow grits to corn semolina. Forget the names. When shopping for the right product to make polenta, there are three things to consider: "instant" or "quick-cooking" versus the traditional style, degerminated or whole-grain meal, and grind size.

Instant and quick-cooking cornmeals are parcooked and comparatively bland—leave them on the shelf. Though we love the full corn flavor of whole-grain cornmeal, it remains slightly gritty no matter how long you cook it. We prefer degerminated cornmeal, in which the hard hull and germ are removed from each kernel (check the back label or ingredient list to see if your cornmeal is degerminated; if it's not explicitly labeled as such, you can assume it's whole-grain).

As for grind, we found coarser grains brought the most desirable and pillowy texture to our Creamy Parmesan Polenta. However, grind coarseness can vary dramatically from brand to brand since there are no standards to ensure consistency—one manufacturer's "coarse" may be another's "fine." To identify coarse polenta as really coarse, the grains should be about the size of couscous.

INSTANT VERSUS TRADITIONAL

1. Bring water to boil in large saucepan over medium-high heat. Stir in 1½ teaspoons salt and baking soda. Slowly pour cornmeal into water in steady stream while stirring back and forth with wooden spoon or rubber spatula. Bring mixture to boil, stirring constantly, about 1 minute. Reduce heat to lowest setting and cover.

2. After 5 minutes, whisk polenta to smooth out any lumps that may have formed, about 15 seconds. (Make sure to scrape down sides and bottom of pan.) Cover and continue to cook, without stirring, until polenta grains are tender but slightly al dente, about 25 minutes longer. (Polenta should be loose and barely hold its shape; it will continue to thicken as it cools.)

3. Remove from heat, stir in Parmesan and butter, and season with pepper to taste. Let sit, covered, for 5 minutes. Serve, passing extra Parmesan separately.

Making a Flame Tamer

A flame tamer keeps risotto, polenta, and sauces from simmering too briskly. To make one, shape a sheet of heavy-duty aluminum foil into a 1-inch-thick ring of even thickness the size of your burner.

Quinoa Pilaf with Herbs and Lemon

SERVES 4 TO 6 `VEGAN` `GF`

☑ **WHY THIS RECIPE WORKS:** In the span of a decade, quinoa has gone from obscurity to mass consumption in America. In theory quinoa has an appealingly nutty flavor and a crunchy texture; in practice it often turns into a mushy mess with washed-out flavor and an underlying bitterness. We wanted a simple quinoa pilaf with light, distinct grains and great flavor. We found that most recipes for quinoa pilaf turned out woefully overcooked because they call for far too much liquid. We cut the water back to ensure tender grains with a satisfying bite. We also toasted the quinoa in a dry skillet to develop its natural nutty flavor before simmering. We flavored our pilaf with some onion sautéed in butter and finished it with herbs and a squeeze of lemon juice. We like the convenience of prewashed quinoa; rinsing removes the quinoa's bitter protective coating (called saponin). If you buy unwashed quinoa (or if you are unsure whether it's washed), rinse it and then spread it out over a clean dish towel to dry for 15 minutes before cooking.

1½	cups prewashed white quinoa
2	tablespoons unsalted butter or extra-virgin olive oil
1	small onion, chopped fine
¾	teaspoon salt
1¾	cups water
3	tablespoons chopped fresh cilantro, parsley, chives, mint, or tarragon
1	tablespoon lemon juice

1. Toast quinoa in medium saucepan over medium-high heat, stirring frequently, until quinoa is very fragrant and makes continuous popping sound, 5 to 7 minutes; transfer to bowl.

2. Add butter to now-empty pan and melt over medium-low heat. Add onion and salt and cook until onion is softened and light golden, 5 to 7 minutes. Stir in water and toasted quinoa, increase heat to medium-high, and bring to simmer. Cover, reduce heat to low, and simmer until grains are just tender and liquid is absorbed, 18 to 20 minutes, stirring once halfway through cooking.

3. Remove pan from heat and let sit, covered, for 10 minutes. Fluff quinoa with fork, stir in herbs and lemon juice, and serve.

VARIATIONS

Quinoa Pilaf with Apricots, Aged Gouda, and Pistachios `GF`

Add ½ teaspoon grated lemon zest, ½ teaspoon ground coriander, ¼ teaspoon ground cumin, and ⅛ teaspoon pepper to pot with onion and salt. Stir in ½ cup coarsely chopped dried apricots before letting quinoa sit for 10 minutes in step 3. Substitute ½ cup shredded aged gouda, ½ cup shelled pistachios, toasted and chopped coarse, and 2 tablespoons chopped fresh mint for herbs.

Quinoa Pilaf with Chipotle, Queso Fresco, and Peanuts `GF`

Add 1 teaspoon chipotle chile powder and ¼ teaspoon ground cumin to pot with onion and salt. Substitute ½ cup crumbled queso fresco, ½ cup coarsely chopped dry-roasted unsalted peanuts, and 2 thinly sliced scallions for herbs. Substitute 4 teaspoons lime juice for lemon juice.

Quinoa Pilaf with Olives, Raisins, and Cilantro `VEGAN` `GF`

In order for this variation to be vegan, you must use olive oil. Add ¼ teaspoon ground cumin, ¼ teaspoon dried oregano, and ⅛ teaspoon ground cinnamon to pot with onion and salt. Stir in ¼ cup golden raisins halfway through cooking quinoa. Substitute ⅓ cup coarsely chopped pimento-stuffed green olives and 3 tablespoons chopped fresh cilantro for chopped fresh herbs. Substitute 4 teaspoons red wine vinegar for lemon juice.

Quinoa, Black Bean, and Mango Salad with Lime Dressing

SERVES 4 TO 6   `VEGAN` `GF`

WHY THIS RECIPE WORKS: We wanted to feature the delicate texture and nutty flavor of quinoa in a fresh-tasting salad hearty enough for a main course. We started by toasting the quinoa to bring out its flavor before adding liquid to the pan and simmering the seeds until nearly tender. We then spread the quinoa over a rimmed baking sheet so that the residual heat would finish cooking it gently as it cooled, giving us perfectly cooked, fluffy grains. Black beans, mango, and bell pepper lent the salad heartiness, bright flavor, and color. A simple but intense dressing with lime juice, jalapeño, cumin, and cilantro gave this dish the acidity needed to keep its flavors fresh. We also added scallions and avocado for bite and creaminess. We like the convenience of prewashed quinoa; rinsing removes the quinoa's bitter protective coating (called saponin). If you buy unwashed quinoa (or if you are unsure whether it's washed), rinse it and then spread it out over a clean dish towel to dry for 15 minutes before cooking.

1½ **cups prewashed white quinoa**
2¼ **cups water**
    Salt and pepper
5   **tablespoons lime juice**
½   **jalapeño chile, stemmed, seeded, and chopped**
¾   **teaspoon ground cumin**
½   **cup extra-virgin olive oil**
⅓   **cup fresh cilantro leaves**
1   **red bell pepper, stemmed, seeded, and chopped**
1   **mango, peeled, pitted, and cut into ¼-inch pieces**
1   **(15-ounce) can black beans, rinsed**
2   **scallions, sliced thin**
1   **avocado, halved, pitted, and sliced thin**

Preparing a Mango

1. Cut thin slice from one end of mango so that it sits flat on counter.

2. Rest mango on trimmed bottom, then cut off skin in thin strips, top to bottom.

3. Cut down along each side of flat pit to remove flesh.

4. Trim around pit to remove any remaining flesh. Cut flesh into ¼-inch pieces.

1. Toast quinoa in large saucepan over medium-high heat, stirring often, until quinoa is very fragrant and makes continuous popping sound, 5 to 7 minutes. Stir in water and ½ teaspoon salt and bring to simmer. Cover, reduce heat to low, and simmer gently until most of water has been absorbed and quinoa is nearly tender, about 15 minutes. Spread quinoa onto rimmed baking sheet and let cool for 20 minutes; transfer to large bowl.

2. Process lime juice, jalapeño, cumin, and 1 teaspoon salt in blender until jalapeño is finely chopped, about 15 seconds. With blender running, add oil and cilantro; continue to process until smooth and emulsified, about 20 seconds.

3. Add bell pepper, mango, beans, scallions, and lime-jalapeño dressing to cooled quinoa and toss to combine. Season with salt and pepper to taste. Serve, topping individual portions with avocado.

Mediterranean Lettuce Cups with Quinoa, Olives, and Feta

SERVES 4 TO 6 GF

✔ **WHY THIS RECIPE WORKS:** Whatever the filling, lettuce cups make a perfect light lunch. We chose to fill our version with an easy, flavorful quinoa salad. We thought that Mediterranean flavors would complement the nuttiness of the quinoa, so we paired it with salty feta, briny olives, and fresh mint and oregano. While the quinoa was cooking, we blended up the feta with some yogurt and lots of herbs and vinegar to make a bold dressing. Once the quinoa cooled, we tossed it with cucumber, tomatoes, olives, shallot, and a bit of the dressing. We reserved the rest of the dressing for drizzling once we portioned our salad into the lettuce leaves. The large, crisp leaves of Bibb lettuce made perfectly sized cups. We like the convenience of prewashed quinoa; rinsing removes the quinoa's bitter protective coating (called saponin). If you buy unwashed quinoa (or if you are unsure whether it's washed), rinse it and then spread it out over a clean dish towel to dry for 15 minutes before cooking.

1½	cups prewashed white quinoa
2¼	cups water
	Salt and pepper
4	ounces feta cheese, crumbled (1 cup)
½	cup plain yogurt
¼	cup minced fresh mint
3	tablespoons red wine vinegar
2	tablespoons minced fresh oregano or 1½ teaspoons dried
½	cup extra-virgin olive oil
2	tomatoes, cored, seeded, and cut into ¼-inch pieces

This flavorful mix of quinoa, vegetables, and olives is spooned into crisp lettuce cups and dolloped with a yogurt-mint sauce.

1	cucumber, peeled, halved lengthwise, seeded, and cut into ¼-inch pieces
1	shallot, minced
¼	cup pitted black olives, chopped
2	heads Bibb lettuce (8 ounces each), leaves separated

1. Toast quinoa in medium saucepan over medium-high heat, stirring frequently, until quinoa is very fragrant and makes continuous popping sound, 5 to 7 minutes. Stir in water and ½ teaspoon salt and bring to simmer. Cover, reduce heat to low, and simmer gently until most of water has been absorbed and quinoa is nearly tender, about 15 minutes. Spread quinoa onto rimmed baking sheet and let cool for 20 minutes; transfer to large bowl.

2. Meanwhile, process feta, yogurt, mint, vinegar, oregano, ½ teaspoon salt, and ¼ teaspoon pepper in blender until smooth, about 15 seconds. With blender running, slowly add oil until incorporated, about 30 seconds.

3. Add tomatoes, cucumber, shallot, olives, and ⅔ cup feta dressing to cooled quinoa and toss to combine. Season with salt and pepper to taste. Spoon quinoa mixture into lettuce leaves (about ⅓ cup each), drizzle with remaining dressing, and serve.

To ensure our quinoa patties hold together in the pan, we skip toasting the grains and chill the patties before cooking.

Quinoa Patties with Spinach and Sun-Dried Tomatoes

SERVES 4 GF

WHY THIS RECIPE WORKS: For these appealing quinoa patties, we used classic white quinoa, which softened enough for us to shape, and skipped the usual toasting step, which caused the grains to separate. One whole egg plus one yolk and melty Monterey Jack cheese bound the grains together perfectly; chilling the patties for 30 minutes further ensured that they stayed together in the pan. Cooking the patties on the stovetop over medium heat created a crisp, flavorful crust on the outside while keeping the interiors moist. To give the patties interesting flavor, we mixed in chopped sun-dried tomatoes, scallions, delicate baby spinach, and a little lemon zest and juice. Sautéing the aromatics in some of the tomatoes' packing oil infused them with even more flavor. We like the convenience of prewashed quinoa; rinsing removes the quinoa's bitter protective coating (called saponin). If you buy unwashed quinoa (or if you are unsure whether it's washed), rinse it before cooking.

The Colors of Quinoa

White quinoa is the most commonly found variety of these tiny seeds native to South America, but red and black varieties are increasingly available. To see if color made a difference, we put together batches of our quinoa pilaf recipe using all three types.

White quinoa, the largest seeds of the three, had a slightly nutty, vegetal flavor with a hint of bitterness; it also had the softest texture of the three quinoas. The medium-size red seeds offered a heartier crunch, thanks to their additional seed coat, and a predominant nuttiness. Black quinoa seeds, the smallest of the three, have the thickest seed coat. They were notably crunchy in our recipe and retained their shape the most during cooking, but many tasters disliked their slightly sandy texture. These seeds had the mildest flavor, with a hint of molasses-like sweetness.

Our conclusion? You can use white and red quinoa interchangeably in our quinoa pilaf recipes and other side dishes or salads. However, white quinoa is best for dishes like cakes and patties because it is starchier and will hold together better. Black quinoa is better off in recipes specifically tailored to its distinctive texture and flavor.

½ cup oil-packed sun-dried tomatoes, chopped coarse, plus 1 tablespoon oil
4 scallions, chopped fine
4 garlic cloves, minced
2 cups water
1 cup prewashed white quinoa
1 teaspoon salt
1 large egg plus 1 large yolk, lightly beaten
2 ounces (2 cups) baby spinach, chopped
2 ounces Monterey Jack cheese, shredded (½ cup)
½ teaspoon grated lemon zest plus 2 teaspoons juice
2 tablespoons vegetable oil

1. Heat tomato oil in large saucepan over medium heat until shimmering. Add scallions and cook until softened, 3 to 5 minutes. Stir in garlic and cook until fragrant, about 30 seconds. Stir in water, quinoa, and salt and bring to simmer. Reduce heat to medium-low, cover, and continue to simmer until quinoa is tender, 16 to 18 minutes.

2. Remove pot from heat and let sit, covered, until liquid is fully absorbed, about 10 minutes. Transfer quinoa to large bowl and let cool for 15 minutes. Stir in sun-dried tomatoes, egg and yolk, spinach, Monterey Jack, and lemon zest and juice.

3. Line rimmed baking sheet with parchment paper. Divide quinoa mixture into 8 equal portions and pack firmly into 3½-inch-wide patties; place on prepared sheet. Refrigerate, uncovered, until patties are chilled and firm, about 30 minutes.

4. Heat 1 tablespoon vegetable oil in 12-inch nonstick skillet over medium heat until shimmering. Gently lay 4 patties in skillet and cook until set and well browned on both sides, 16 to 20 minutes, turning gently halfway through cooking; transfer to plate and cover to keep warm. Repeat with remaining 1 tablespoon vegetable oil and patties. Serve.

Quinoa Albondigas

SERVES 4 `GF`

☑ **WHY THIS RECIPE WORKS:** *Albondigas* are traditional Spanish meatballs frequently featured in tapas dishes. They are usually served in a flavorful saffron-infused tomato sauce. Our goal was to re-create this dish for the vegetarian table. For the base of our vegetarian meatballs, we decided that nutty, hearty quinoa would provide the best flavor and texture. We cooked it until it was slightly blown out so that the grains would be sticky and cohesive, then we added an egg, an extra yolk, and cheese to bind the quinoa together. Traditionally albondigas are browned in a pan, but we found that our delicate quinoa albondigas were best baked in the oven. A light coating of oil and 20 minutes in a 400-degree oven gave them a crisp, browned exterior. The Spanish often use a *picada*, a paste made from ground bread, almonds, and sometimes garlic and herbs, to flavor and thicken their sauces. We added saffron, parsley, paprika, and garlic along with the almonds to deepen its flavor. We like the convenience of prewashed quinoa; rinsing removes the quinoa's bitter protective coating (called saponin). If you buy unwashed quinoa (or if you are unsure whether it's washed), rinse it before cooking.

MEATBALLS

2 tablespoons extra-virgin olive oil
1 onion, chopped fine
4 garlic cloves, minced
½ teaspoon paprika
1¾ cups water
1 cup prewashed white quinoa
1 teaspoon salt
2 ounces Monterey Jack cheese, shredded (½ cup)
1 ounce Manchego or Parmesan cheese, grated (½ cup)
1 large egg plus 1 large yolk, lightly beaten
3 tablespoons minced fresh parsley
1 teaspoon grated lemon zest

For our vegetarian take on Spanish meatballs, we bind quinoa with cheese and egg and serve them in a saffron-tomato sauce.

SAUCE

2 tablespoons extra-virgin olive oil
1 onion, chopped fine
1 tablespoon tomato paste
2 tomatoes, cored, seeded, and chopped
1 cup vegetable broth
½ cup dry white wine
2 tablespoons minced fresh parsley
2 tablespoons finely chopped almonds
2 garlic cloves, minced
¼ teaspoon saffron threads, crumbled
¼ teaspoon paprika
Salt and pepper

1. FOR THE MEATBALLS: Heat 1 tablespoon oil in large saucepan over medium heat until shimmering. Add onion and cook until softened, about 5 minutes. Stir in garlic and paprika and cook until fragrant, about 30 seconds. Stir in water, quinoa, and salt and bring to simmer. Cover, reduce heat to low, and simmer gently until quinoa is tender, 16 to 18 minutes.

2. Remove pot from heat and let quinoa sit, covered, until liquid is fully absorbed, about 10 minutes. Spread quinoa onto rimmed baking sheet and let cool, about 15 minutes.

3. Line separate rimmed baking sheet with parchment paper and spray with vegetable oil spray. Mix cooled quinoa, Monterey Jack, Manchego, egg and yolk, parsley, and lemon zest together in large bowl until thoroughly combined. Portion and shape mixture into twenty-four ¾-inch balls and place on prepared baking sheet. Refrigerate balls, uncovered, until chilled and firm, about 30 minutes.

4. Adjust oven rack to middle position and heat oven to 400 degrees. Gently brush balls with remaining 1 tablespoon oil and bake until browned and slightly crisp, about 20 minutes.

5. FOR THE SAUCE: Meanwhile, heat oil in 12-inch nonstick skillet over medium heat until shimmering. Add onion and tomato paste and cook until onion is softened and lightly browned, 5 to 7 minutes. Stir in tomatoes and cook for 1 minute. Stir in broth and wine, cover, and cook until flavors meld, 8 to 10 minutes.

6. Mash parsley, almonds, garlic, saffron, paprika, ¼ teaspoon salt, and ⅛ teaspoon pepper together in bowl, then stir into sauce. Continue to simmer sauce until slightly thickened, about 2 minutes. Season with salt and pepper to taste. Transfer meatballs to platter, pour sauce over top, and serve.

A classic champagne vinaigrette ties together this salad of sweet blueberries, wheat berries, and endive.

Wheat Berry Salad with Blueberries and Goat Cheese

SERVES 4 TO 6

✔ **WHY THIS RECIPE WORKS:** The earthy, nutty flavor and firm chew of wheat berries make them an ideal choice for a hearty summer salad. We found it easiest to cook the wheat berry kernels like pasta, simply simmering them in a large pot of water until they were tender but still chewy. After an hour of simmering, the hearty grains had just the right texture. For the dressing, we chose a simple bright vinaigrette made with champagne vinegar, shallot, chives, and mustard. Juicy fresh blueberries added the perfect amount of sweetness and tang to our chewy grains. Endive provided an interesting bitter note, and creamy goat cheese was the perfect rich complement to finish off this summery salad. Just ¼ teaspoon of salt boosted the flavor of the grains in our boiling water, but be careful not to add any more than that. We found that with higher amounts, the salinity of the water prevented the wheat berries from absorbing the water, making the grains hard and crunchy. If using quick-cooking or presteamed wheat berries (read the ingredient list on the package carefully to determine this), you will need to adjust the wheat berry cooking time in step 1.

1½ cups wheat berries
 Salt and pepper
2 tablespoons champagne vinegar
1 tablespoon minced shallot
1 tablespoon minced fresh chives
1 teaspoon Dijon mustard
6 tablespoons extra-virgin olive oil
2 heads Belgian endive (4 ounces each), halved, cored, and sliced crosswise ¼ inch thick
7½ ounces (1½ cups) blueberries
¾ cup pecans, toasted and chopped coarse
4 ounces goat cheese, crumbled (1 cup)

1. Bring 4 quarts water to boil in large pot. Add wheat berries and ¼ teaspoon salt, partially cover, and cook, stirring often, until wheat berries are tender but still chewy, 50 to 70 minutes. Drain and rinse under cold running water until cool; drain well.

2. Whisk vinegar, shallot, chives, mustard, ½ teaspoon salt, and ¼ teaspoon pepper together in large bowl. Whisking constantly, drizzle in oil. Add wheat berries, endive, blueberries, and pecans and toss to combine. Season with salt and pepper to taste, sprinkle with goat cheese, and serve.

Hearty, filling whole grains flavored with warm spices, sweet fruit or maple syrup, and/or rich, crunchy nuts are an ideal start to a busy day. Here are a few quick and easy recipes for oatmeal, porridge, and hot cereal.

Millet Porridge with Maple Syrup

SERVES 4 **FAST** **GF**

We prefer this porridge made with whole milk, but low-fat or skim milk can be substituted.

- 3 **cups water**
- 1 **cup millet, rinsed**
- ⅛ **teaspoon ground cinnamon**
- ⅛ **teaspoon salt**
- 1 **cup whole milk**
- 3 **tablespoons maple syrup**

1. Bring water, millet, cinnamon, and salt to boil in medium saucepan over high heat. Reduce heat to low, cover, and cook until millet has absorbed all water and is almost tender, about 20 minutes.

2. Uncover and increase heat to medium, add milk, and simmer, stirring frequently, until millet is fully tender and mixture is thickened, about 10 minutes. Stir in maple syrup and serve.

Hot Quinoa Cereal

SERVES 6 **FAST** **GF**

We like the convenience of prewashed quinoa; rinsing removes the quinoa's bitter protective coating (called saponin). If you buy unwashed quinoa (or if you are unsure whether it's washed), rinse it before cooking.

- 1 **cup prewashed white quinoa**
- 1 **cup water**
- ⅛ **teaspoon salt**
- 1 **cup almond milk, plus extra for serving**
- 5 **ounces (1 cup) blueberries**
- ½ **cup whole almonds, toasted and chopped**
- 1 **tablespoon honey**

1. Bring quinoa, water, and salt to simmer in medium saucepan. Reduce heat to low, cover, and continue to simmer until quinoa is just tender, 15 to 17 minutes.

2. Uncover, stir in milk, and cook, stirring often, until milk is mostly absorbed and quinoa has consistency of porridge, about 10 minutes. Stir in blueberries, almonds, and honey. Serve, adding additional milk as needed to adjust consistency.

Overnight Steel-Cut Oatmeal

SERVES 4 **VEGAN** **GF**

The oatmeal will continue to thicken as it cools. If you prefer a looser consistency, thin the oatmeal with boiling water. In order for this recipe to be gluten-free, you must use steel-cut oats that have been processed in a gluten-free facility (such as Bob's Red Mill).

- 4 **cups water**
- 1 **cup steel-cut oats**
- ¼ **teaspoon salt**

1. Bring 3 cups water to boil in large saucepan over high heat. Remove pan from heat and stir in oats and salt. Cover pan and let sit overnight.

2. Stir remaining 1 cup water into oats and bring to boil over medium-high heat. Reduce heat to medium and cook, stirring occasionally, until oats are softened but still retain some chew and mixture thickens and resembles warm pudding, 4 to 6 minutes. Remove pan from heat and let sit for 5 minutes before serving.

VARIATIONS

APPLE-CINNAMON OVERNIGHT STEEL-CUT OATMEAL **GF**

Substitute ½ cup apple cider and ½ cup whole milk for water in step 2. Stir ½ cup

Cranberry-Orange Overnight Steel-Cut Oatmeal

peeled and grated sweet apple, 2 tablespoons packed dark brown sugar, and ½ teaspoon ground cinnamon into oatmeal with cider and milk. Sprinkle each serving with 2 tablespoons coarsely chopped toasted walnuts.

CRANBERRY-ORANGE OVERNIGHT STEEL-CUT OATMEAL **GF**

Substitute ½ cup orange juice and ½ cup whole milk for water in step 2. Stir ½ cup dried cranberries, 3 tablespoons packed dark brown sugar, and ⅛ teaspoon ground cardamom into oatmeal with orange juice and milk. Sprinkle each serving with 2 tablespoons toasted sliced almonds.

CARROT SPICE OVERNIGHT STEEL-CUT OATMEAL **GF**

Substitute ½ cup carrot juice and ½ cup whole milk for water in step 2. Stir ½ cup finely grated carrot, ¼ cup packed dark brown sugar, ⅓ cup dried currants, and ½ teaspoon ground cinnamon into oatmeal with carrot juice and milk. Sprinkle each serving with 2 tablespoons coarsely chopped toasted pecans.

CHAPTER 5

Beans and Soy

■ FAST (Less than 45 minutes start to finish)　■ VEGAN　▦ GLUTEN-FREE
Photos: Lentil Salad with Olives, Mint, and Feta; Shepherd's Pie

The trick to this humble dish is cooking the rice in the same liquid we use to cook the beans to infuse it with flavor.

The Science of Salt-Soaking Beans

Most people think of brining as a way to keep lean meat juicy and tender, but brining isn't just for meat. When you soak dried beans in salted water, they cook up with softer skins and are less likely to blow out and disintegrate. Why? It has to do with how the sodium ions in salt interact with the cells of the bean skins. As the beans soak, the sodium ions replace some of the calcium and magnesium ions in the skins. Because sodium ions are more weakly charged than calcium and magnesium ions, they allow more water to penetrate into the skins, leading to a softer texture. During soaking, the sodium ions will filter only partway into the beans, so their greatest effect is on the cells in the outermost part of the beans. Softening the skins also makes them less likely to split as the beans cook, keeping the beans intact. For 1 pound of dried beans, dissolve 3 tablespoons of table salt in 4 quarts of cold water. Soak the beans at room temperature for 8 to 24 hours. Drain and rinse them well before using.

FOR A QUICK SALT-SOAK

If you are pressed for time you can "quick-soak" your beans. Simply combine the salt, water, and beans in a large Dutch oven and bring to a boil over high heat. Remove the pot from the heat, cover, and let stand for 1 hour. Drain and rinse the beans well before using.

Cuban-Style Black Beans and Rice

SERVES 6 TO 8 **VEGAN** **GF**

✔ **WHY THIS RECIPE WORKS:** Beans and rice is a familiar combination the world over, but Cuban black beans and rice (known as *moros y cristianos*) is unique in that the rice is cooked in the inky concentrated liquid left over from cooking the beans, which renders the grains just as flavorful. For our own version, we reserved half of the ingredients for the *sofrito* (the traditional combination of sautéed garlic, bell pepper, and onion) and added them to the cooking liquid to infuse the beans with aromatic flavor. Lightly browning the remaining sofrito vegetables along with spices and tomato paste added complex flavor to this simple dish. Once the beans were soft, we combined them with the sofrito and rice to finish cooking. Baking the rice and beans eliminated the crusty bottom that can form when the dish is cooked on the stovetop. You will need a Dutch oven with a tight-fitting lid for this recipe. For more information on the science behind salt-soaking beans, and how to speed up the process if you're tight on time, see The Science of Salt-Soaking Beans.

Salt
1 **cup dried black beans, picked over and rinsed**
2 **large green bell peppers, halved, stemmed, and seeded**
1 **large onion, peeled and halved crosswise**
1 **head garlic (5 cloves minced, remaining head halved crosswise and left unpeeled)**
2 **bay leaves**
2 **tablespoons vegetable oil**
4 **teaspoons ground cumin**
1 **tablespoon minced fresh oregano or 1 teaspoon dried**
1 **tablespoon tomato paste**
1½ **cups long-grain white rice, rinsed**
2 **tablespoons red wine vinegar**
2 **scallions, sliced thin**
Lime wedges

1. Dissolve 1½ tablespoons salt in 2 quarts cold water in large container. Add beans and soak at room temperature for at least 8 hours or up to 24 hours. Drain and rinse well.

2. In Dutch oven, combine drained beans, 4 cups water, 1 bell pepper half, 1 onion half (with root end), halved garlic head, bay leaves, and 1 teaspoon salt. Bring to simmer over medium-high heat, cover, and reduce heat to low. Cook until beans are just soft, 30 to 40 minutes.

3. Discard pepper, onion, garlic, and bay leaves. Drain beans in colander set over large bowl, reserving 2½ cups bean cooking liquid. (If you don't have enough cooking liquid, add water as needed to measure 2½ cups.) Do not wash pot.

4. Adjust oven rack to middle position and heat oven to 350 degrees. Cut remaining bell peppers and onion into 2-inch pieces and pulse in food processor until chopped into rough ¼-inch pieces, about 8 pulses, scraping down sides of bowl as needed.

5. Add oil to now-empty pot and heat over medium heat until shimmering. Add processed peppers and onion, cumin, oregano, and tomato paste and cook, stirring often, until vegetables are softened and beginning to brown, 10 to 15 minutes. Stir in minced garlic and cook until fragrant, about 1 minute. Stir in rice and cook for 30 seconds.

6. Stir in beans, reserved bean cooking liquid, vinegar, and 1½ teaspoons salt. Increase heat to medium-high and bring to simmer. Cover, transfer to oven, and cook until liquid is absorbed and rice is tender, about 30 minutes. Fluff rice with fork and let rest, uncovered, for 5 minutes. Serve with scallions and lime wedges.

Southwestern Black Bean Salad

SERVES 6 TO 8   `FAST` `GF`

WHY THIS RECIPE WORKS: For a black bean salad with bold but balanced flavors, we wanted to avoid falling into the trap of piling on an endless array of ingredients. We found that a judicious mixture of black beans, corn, avocado, tomato, and cilantro gave us just the right combination of flavors and textures. Sautéing the corn (both fresh and frozen worked well) in a skillet until it was toasty and just starting to brown added a pleasant nuttiness to the kernels. We wanted a dressing with plenty of kick, so we made a concentrated dressing with lots of lime juice plus spicy chipotle chile. A teaspoon of honey balanced the bright citrus. Raw onion was too harsh in the dressing, but thinly sliced scallions lent a mild onion flavor. You will need 3 to 4 ears of corn in order to yield 2 cups of fresh kernels. If using frozen corn, be sure to thaw and drain it before cooking.

¼ cup extra-virgin olive oil
2 cups fresh or frozen corn
4 scallions, sliced thin
⅓ cup lime juice (3 limes)
1 tablespoon minced canned chipotle chile in adobo sauce
1 teaspoon honey
  Salt and pepper
2 (15-ounce) cans black beans, rinsed
2 ripe avocados, halved, pitted, and chopped
2 tomatoes, cored and chopped
¼ cup minced fresh cilantro

Making Cuban-Style Black Beans and Rice

1. SALT-SOAK BEANS: Dissolve 1½ tablespoons salt in 2 quarts cold water in large container. Add beans and soak at room temperature for at least 8 hours. Drain beans and rinse well.

2. SIMMER BEANS: Combine beans, water, bell pepper half, onion half, halved garlic head, bay leaves, and salt in Dutch oven. Bring to simmer, cover, and cook until beans are just soft. Drain beans, reserving 2½ cups cooking liquid.

3. COOK SOFRITO: Add chopped peppers and onion, cumin, oregano, and tomato paste. Cook until beginning to brown. Add garlic and cook until fragrant. Add rice, beans, reserved bean cooking liquid, vinegar, and salt.

4. BAKE: Bring mixture to simmer, cover pot, and transfer to oven. Cook until liquid is absorbed and rice is tender, about 30 minutes. Fluff rice and beans with fork, then let rest, uncovered, for 5 minutes.

1. Heat 2 tablespoons oil in 12-inch skillet over medium-high heat until shimmering. Add corn and cook until spotty brown, about 5 minutes; let cool slightly.

2. Whisk scallions, lime juice, chipotle, honey, ½ teaspoon salt, and ½ teaspoon pepper together in large bowl. Slowly whisk in remaining 2 tablespoons oil until incorporated. Add toasted corn, beans, avocados, tomatoes, and cilantro and toss to combine. Season with salt and pepper to taste, and serve.

Black Bean Chilaquiles
SERVES 4 `GF`

✔ WHY THIS RECIPE WORKS: Traditionally, the Mexican dish known as *chilaquiles* features fried tortillas covered in a chile sauce and simmered until softened. They're topped with shredded meat, cheese, and *crema* (the Mexican version of sour cream) and served with refried beans. We wanted to add the beans into the dish for a hearty vegetarian version. We opted to bake, not fry, our tortillas. Poblano peppers, garlic, onions, and whole peeled tomatoes, briefly simmered and then pureed until smooth, formed our sauce. Adding in a good amount of smoky chipotle chiles lent the right amount of heat and gave our dish depth. Mashing the black beans in the sauce before combining everything in a baking dish and heating it through gave our dish a thick, creamy consistency. Crumbled *queso fresco* contributed a salty, tangy bite, and a mixture of lime juice and sour cream worked well as a stand-in for the hard-to-find crema. If you cannot find poblano chiles, substitute 2 green bell peppers. To make this dish spicier, add the chile seeds. You can substitute feta cheese for the queso fresco.

- 10 (6-inch) corn tortillas, each cut into 8 wedges
- 3 tablespoons vegetable oil
- 2 poblano chiles, stemmed, seeded, and chopped coarse
- 2 onions, chopped fine
  Salt and pepper
- ¼ cup minced fresh cilantro
- 6 garlic cloves, minced
- 2 teaspoons minced canned chipotle chile in adobo sauce
- 1 cup water
- 1 (14.5-ounce) can whole peeled tomatoes
- 2 (15-ounce) cans black beans, rinsed
- 4 ounces queso fresco, crumbled (1 cup)
- ¼ cup sour cream
- 1 tablespoon lime juice
- 1 tomato, cored and chopped

1. Adjust oven racks to upper-middle and lower-middle positions and heat oven to 350 degrees. Toss tortillas with 2 tablespoons oil, then spread over 2 rimmed baking sheets and bake until brown and dry, 16 to 24 minutes, flipping tortillas halfway through baking; let cool. Increase oven temperature to 500 degrees.

2. Heat remaining 1 tablespoon oil in 12-inch skillet until shimmering. Add poblanos, half of onions, and ½ teaspoon salt and cook until vegetables are softened and lightly browned, 6 to 8 minutes.

3. Stir in 2 tablespoons cilantro, garlic, and chipotle and cook until fragrant, about 30 seconds. Stir in water and canned tomatoes and their juice, and cook until flavors have melded and sauce is slightly thickened, 10 to 15 minutes.

4. Transfer sauce to blender and process until smooth, about 1 minute. Return sauce to now-empty skillet, season with salt and pepper to taste, and bring to simmer over medium heat. Stir in beans and cook until warmed through, about 5 minutes. Mash beans with potato masher until coarsely mashed. Stir in baked tortillas and cook until they begin to soften, about 2 minutes.

5. Transfer mixture to 8-inch square baking dish and sprinkle with cheese. Bake on lower-middle rack until hot throughout, 5 to 10 minutes. Let casserole cool slightly. Combine sour cream and lime juice and drizzle over top. Sprinkle with chopped tomato, remaining onions, and remaining 2 tablespoons cilantro. Serve.

Black-Eyed Peas and Greens
SERVES 6 TO 8 `VEGAN` `GF`

✔ WHY THIS RECIPE WORKS: A big pot of black-eyed peas and greens is quintessential Southern food, and there are about as many versions as there are Southern cooks. The method is simple—put the ingredients in a pot, cover, and simmer. We decided to brown an onion first, deciding that the richer flavor justified the extra step. To boost the flavor further, we added garlic, red pepper flakes, and cumin (unorthodox, but good) with the softened onion. The traditional choice of collard greens was a clear winner. We went with canned black-eyed peas for their availability and convenience, but in the 30-some minutes that the dish needed to simmer, they disintegrated into near mush. The solution was to add the black-eyed peas for only the last 15 minutes of cooking and stir them in gently. Once the beans were warm, the greens were silken, and the rustic flavors had melded, we removed the lid and upped the heat to let the liquid reduce and concentrate. Vinegar for brightness and a little sugar stirred in at the end balanced the dish.

1 tablespoon vegetable oil

1 onion, halved and sliced thin

Salt and pepper

4 garlic cloves, minced

½ teaspoon ground cumin

¼ teaspoon red pepper flakes

2 cups water

1 (14.5-ounce) can diced tomatoes

1 pound collard greens, stemmed and chopped

2 (15-ounce) cans black-eyed peas, rinsed

1 tablespoon cider vinegar

1 teaspoon sugar

1. Heat oil in Dutch oven over medium heat until shimmering. Add onion and 2 teaspoons salt and cook, stirring frequently, until onion is golden brown, about 10 minutes. Stir in garlic, cumin, ½ teaspoon pepper, and pepper flakes and cook until fragrant, about 30 seconds.

2. Stir in water and tomatoes and their juice and bring to boil. Stir in greens, cover, and reduce heat to low. Simmer until greens are just tender, about 15 minutes.

3. Stir in beans gently, cover, and cook, stirring occasionally, until greens are silky and completely tender, about 15 minutes.

4. Uncover, increase heat to medium-high, and cook until liquid is nearly evaporated, about 5 minutes. Stir in vinegar and sugar and season with salt and pepper to taste. Serve.

Sweet, juicy peaches and rich pecans balance the spicy frisée and creamy black-eyed peas in this bright, fresh bean salad.

Black-Eyed Pea Salad with Peaches and Pecans

SERVES 4 TO 6 `FAST` `GF`

✔ **WHY THIS RECIPE WORKS:** With their delicate skins and creamy interiors, black-eyed peas are great in salads paired with a tart dressing and crunchy vegetables. They're most popular in the South, so we looked to Southern cuisine for inspiration. Peaches added sweet juiciness, while pecans lent crunch and richness. For a little spice, we stemmed, seeded, and finely chopped a jalapeño so its heat wouldn't overwhelm its sharp, fruity flavor. Greens were necessary, but we weren't interested in humdrum romaine. Instead, we turned to frisée, a delicate but slightly bitter-tasting lettuce. Finely chopped red onion added a sharp bite, and basil added fresh flavor. To tame any lingering heat of the jalapeño and the bitter flavor of the greens, we added a little honey to the dressing, plus lime juice for bright acidity. If you can't find peaches, you can substitute 1 orange, peeled and chopped into ½-inch pieces.

1 teaspoon grated lime zest plus
2½ tablespoons juice (2 limes)

1 teaspoon honey

1 small garlic clove, minced

Salt and pepper

2 tablespoons extra-virgin olive oil

2 (15-ounce) cans black-eyed peas, rinsed

2 peaches, halved, pitted, and chopped coarse

3 ounces frisée, trimmed and chopped into 2-inch pieces

¼ cup red onion, chopped fine

¼ cup pecans, toasted and chopped

¼ cup fresh basil leaves, torn into ½-inch pieces

1 jalapeño chile, stemmed, seeded, and chopped fine

Whisk lime zest and juice, honey, garlic, and ¾ teaspoon salt together in large bowl. Slowly whisk in oil until incorporated. Add beans, peaches, frisée, onion, pecans, basil, and jalapeño and toss to combine. Season with salt and pepper to taste and serve.

Cannellini Beans with Roasted Red Peppers and Kale

SERVES 4 **FAST** **GF**

✔ **WHY THIS RECIPE WORKS:** Some of the most inspired Mediterranean beans and greens dishes come from Italy. For this full-flavored one-pot take on the classic combination, we chose Italian flavors and paired cannellini beans and kale with jarred roasted red peppers. We sautéed garlic and onion with some hot red pepper flakes; the subtle spiciness balanced the sweetness of the beans and roasted peppers. We sliced the kale into thin ribbons and added it to the skillet a handful at a time to allow it to wilt. Choosing canned beans and jarred red peppers meant this dish could come together quickly. For the liquid, we used a combination of water and white wine to brighten the dish. We served the dish with savory Parmesan, bright lemon wedges, and a drizzle of olive oil. Swiss chard can be substituted for the kale.

¼ cup extra-virgin olive oil,
  plus extra for serving
4 garlic cloves, minced
¼ teaspoon red pepper flakes
1 small red onion, halved and sliced thin
  Salt and pepper
1 cup jarred roasted red peppers,
  sliced thin lengthwise
1 pound kale, stemmed and sliced
  thin crosswise
2 (15-ounce) cans cannellini beans, rinsed
½ cup dry white wine
½ cup water
1 ounce Parmesan cheese, grated (½ cup)
  Lemon wedges

1. Cook oil, garlic, and pepper flakes in 12-inch skillet over medium-high heat until garlic turns golden brown, about 2 minutes. Stir in onion and ¼ teaspoon salt, reduce heat to medium, and cook until onion is softened, about 5 minutes. Stir in red peppers and cook until softened and glossy, about 3 minutes.

2. Stir in kale, 1 handful at a time, and cook until wilted, about 3 minutes. Stir in beans, wine, and water and bring to simmer. Reduce heat to medium-low, cover, and cook until flavors have melded and kale is tender, 15 to 20 minutes. Season with salt and pepper to taste. Serve with Parmesan, lemon wedges, and extra oil.

Cannellini Bean Gratin

SERVES 6 TO 8 **GF**

✔ **WHY THIS RECIPE WORKS:** Tuscan-style white bean gratins are elegant yet homey casseroles featuring warm, saucy beans under a golden crust of cheese. We opted for convenient canned beans over dried. First we caramelized some onions, then we deglazed the pot with a little white wine and spread the onions in the bottom of a casserole dish, forming a flavorful base for our gratin. We then briefly simmered the beans in vegetable broth, along with rosemary, to jump-start the cooking and to infuse the beans with subtle flavor. After stirring in some nutty Parmesan, we poured our bean mixture on top of the onions. For a cheesy crust, we needed a melting cheese with big impact. Gruyère fit the bill; sprinkled over the top, it added a complex, earthy flavor that perfectly complemented the creamy beans below. Make sure to cook the onions until they are well caramelized and darkly colored in step 1.

3 tablespoons extra-virgin olive oil
3 onions, halved and sliced thin through root end
½ teaspoon brown sugar
6 garlic cloves, minced
⅛ teaspoon red pepper flakes
½ cup dry white wine
4 (15-ounce) cans cannellini beans, rinsed
1 cup vegetable broth
1 teaspoon minced fresh rosemary or ¼ teaspoon dried
2 ounces Parmesan cheese, grated (1 cup)
  Salt and pepper
4 ounces Gruyère cheese, shredded (1 cup)
2 tablespoons minced fresh parsley

1. Adjust oven rack to middle position and heat oven to 375 degrees. Heat 2 tablespoons oil in Dutch oven over medium-high heat until shimmering. Add onions and sugar and cook, stirring frequently, until softened, about 5 minutes. Reduce heat to medium-low and continue to cook, stirring often, until onions are dark golden and caramelized, 20 to 25 minutes.

2. Stir in garlic and pepper flakes and cook until fragrant, about 30 seconds. Stir in wine and cook until nearly evaporated, about 1 minute. Transfer onions to 13 by 9-inch baking dish and spread into even layer.

3. Add beans, broth, and rosemary to now-empty pot and bring to brief simmer, about 1 minute. Off heat, gently stir in remaining 1 tablespoon oil and Parmesan. Season with salt and pepper to taste, spread evenly over onions, then sprinkle with Gruyère.

4. Bake, uncovered, until cheese is lightly golden and bubbling around edges, 15 to 20 minutes. Sprinkle with parsley and serve.

Sicilian Escarole with Cannellini Beans

SERVES 4 | FAST | VEGAN | GF

✓ WHY THIS RECIPE WORKS: This dish combines the buttery texture of cannellini beans with tender, slightly bitter escarole. To make this tasty side quick enough for a weeknight, we chose convenient canned beans over dried. Sautéed onions gave the dish a rich, deep flavor base without requiring too much time at the stove. Red pepper flakes lent a slight heat without overwhelming the other ingredients. A combination of vegetable broth and water provided a savory backbone without making the dish too salty or sweet. We added the escarole and beans along with the liquid, and then we cooked the greens just until the leaves were wilted before cranking up the heat so the liquid would quickly evaporate. This short stint on the heat prevented the beans from breaking down and becoming mushy. Once we took the pot off the heat, we stirred in lemon juice for a bright finish and drizzled on some extra olive oil for richness. Chicory can be substituted for the escarole; however, its flavor is stronger.

1 tablespoon extra-virgin olive oil, plus extra for serving
2 onions, chopped fine
  Salt and pepper
4 garlic cloves, minced
⅛ teaspoon red pepper flakes
1 head escarole (1 pound), trimmed and sliced 1 inch thick
1 (15-ounce) can cannellini beans, rinsed
1 cup vegetable broth
1 cup water
2 teaspoons lemon juice

1. Heat oil in Dutch oven over medium-high heat until shimmering. Add onions and ½ teaspoon salt and cook, stirring frequently, until onions are softened and lightly browned, 5 to 7 minutes. Stir in garlic and pepper flakes and cook until fragrant, about 30 seconds.

2. Stir in escarole, beans, broth, and water and cook, stirring often, until escarole is wilted, about 5 minutes. Increase heat to high and cook until liquid is nearly evaporated, 10 to 15 minutes.

3. Off heat, stir in lemon juice. Drizzle with extra oil and season with salt and pepper to taste. Serve.

NOTES FROM THE TEST KITCHEN

The Importance of Rinsing Beans

Canned beans are made by pressure-cooking dried beans directly in the can with water, salt, and preservatives. As the beans cook, starches and proteins leach into the liquid, thickening it. We generally call for canned beans to be rinsed to remove this starchy liquid, but is the extra step really necessary? To find out, we did a side-by-side taste test of chickpea salad and bean chili. In the chili, there are so many bold flavors that rinsing the beans didn't matter. However, tasters detected notable differences in the salad; the version with rinsed beans was brighter in flavor and less pasty than the version with unrinsed beans. So while rinsing the beans isn't always necessary, the thick, salty bean liquid does have the potential to throw a simpler recipe off-kilter. And since rinsing beans takes only a few seconds, we recommend doing so.

Greek-Style Chickpea Salad

SERVES 6 TO 8 | FAST | GF

✓ WHY THIS RECIPE WORKS: With their buttery flavor and ability to soak up flavor, chickpeas are a perfect choice for a hearty bean salad. We decided to pair convenient canned chickpeas with Greek flavors. We started with a simple dressing of lemon juice, olive oil, and garlic and added Dijon mustard and finely chopped kalamata olives. For the vegetables, we liked red onion and chopped cucumber plus fresh mint and parsley. Tasters loved the contrast of the creamy chickpeas, the fresh herbs, and the crisp, cool cucumber. A sprinkling of tangy crumbled feta added some richness. This refreshing salad is excellent served over a bed of greens with Olive Oil–Sea Salt Pita Chips (page 424).

3 tablespoons lemon juice
2 tablespoons pitted kalamata olives, chopped fine
1 tablespoon Dijon mustard
1 small garlic clove, minced
1 tablespoon extra-virgin olive oil
2 (15-ounce) cans chickpeas, rinsed
½ small red onion, chopped fine
½ large cucumber, peeled, halved lengthwise, seeded, and chopped fine
¼ cup minced fresh mint
1 ounce feta cheese, crumbled (¼ cup)
1 tablespoon minced fresh parsley
  Salt and pepper

Whisk lemon juice, olives, mustard, and garlic together in large bowl. Slowly whisk in oil until incorporated. Add chickpeas, onion, cucumber, mint, feta, and parsley and toss to combine. Season with salt and pepper to taste, and serve.

VARIATION

North African–Style Chickpea Salad

SERVES 6 TO 8 **FAST** **VEGAN** **GF**

This salad is excellent served over a bed of greens with Olive Oil–Sea Salt Pita Chips (page 424).

1½ tablespoons lemon juice

1 small garlic clove, minced

½ teaspoon ground cumin

½ teaspoon paprika

2 tablespoons extra-virgin olive oil

2 (15-ounce) cans chickpeas, rinsed

1 carrot, peeled and shredded

½ cup raisins

2 tablespoons minced fresh mint

Salt and pepper

Whisk lemon juice, garlic, cumin, and paprika together in large bowl. Slowly whisk in oil until incorporated. Add chickpeas, carrot, raisins, and mint and toss to combine. Season with salt and pepper to taste, and serve.

A bold marinade infuses this salad of blanched cauliflower and creamy chickpeas with incredibly deep, complex flavor.

Marinated Chickpea and Cauliflower Salad

SERVES 6 TO 8 **VEGAN** **GF**

✅ **WHY THIS RECIPE WORKS:** For this outstanding bean salad, we marinated earthy cauliflower and creamy chickpeas, which are robust enough to absorb the marinade without turning mushy. First we blanched the cauliflower for a few minutes, softening its exterior so that the dressing could be absorbed more readily. Heating the marinade before tossing it with the salad also helped it to absorb. To make the marinade, we bloomed saffron in hot water to coax out more of its distinct, complex flavors. Then we heated smashed garlic cloves in olive oil to infuse the oil with flavor and tame the garlic's harsh edge. Along with the saffron, smoked paprika and a sprig of rosemary gave the marinade a vibrant brick-red hue and earthy, aromatic flavor. Thin slices of lemon lent bright citrus flavor. Letting the chickpeas and cauliflower rest in the marinade for at least 4 hours allowed the flavors to meld and deepen. Use a small sprig of rosemary, or its flavor will be overpowering. This dish can be served cold or at room temperature.

1 head cauliflower (2 pounds), cored and cut into 1-inch florets

Salt and pepper

¼ teaspoon saffron threads, crumbled

¾ cup extra-virgin olive oil

10 garlic cloves, peeled and smashed

3 tablespoons sugar

1 tablespoon smoked paprika

1 small sprig fresh rosemary

¼ cup sherry vinegar

1 (15-ounce) can chickpeas, rinsed

1 lemon, sliced thin

2 tablespoons minced fresh parsley

1. Bring 2 quarts water to boil in large saucepan. Add cauliflower and 1 tablespoon salt and cook until florets begin to soften, about 3 minutes. Drain florets and transfer to paper towel–lined baking sheet.

2. Combine ½ cup hot water and saffron in bowl; set aside. Heat oil and garlic in small saucepan over medium-low heat until fragrant and beginning to sizzle but not browned, 4 to

6 minutes. Stir in sugar, paprika, and rosemary and cook until fragrant, about 30 seconds. Off heat, stir in saffron mixture, vinegar, 2 teaspoons salt, and ¼ teaspoon pepper.

3. In large bowl, combine florets, saffron mixture, chickpeas, and lemon. Transfer mixture to gallon-size zipper-lock bag and refrigerate for at least 4 hours or up to 3 days, flipping bag occasionally. To serve, transfer cauliflower and chickpeas to serving bowl with slotted spoon and sprinkle with parsley.

Chickpeas with Garlic and Parsley

SERVES 6 TO 8   FAST   VEGAN   GF

✔ **WHY THIS RECIPE WORKS:** With their buttery, nutty flavor and creamy texture, canned chickpeas can make a terrific dish when simply sautéed with a few flavorful ingredients. In search of easy kitchen staples that would transform our canned chickpeas, we reached for garlic and red pepper flakes. Instead of mincing the garlic like usual, we cut it into thin slices and sautéed them in extra-virgin olive oil to mellow their flavor. The thin slivers maintained their presence in the finished dish. We softened an onion along with this aromatic base, then added the chickpeas with vegetable broth, which imparted a rich, savory backbone to the dish without overpowering it. As final touches, parsley and lemon juice gave our chickpeas a burst of freshness. Serve with rice or couscous.

¼ cup extra-virgin olive oil
4 garlic cloves, sliced thin
⅛ teaspoon red pepper flakes
1 onion, chopped fine
 Salt and pepper
2 (15-ounce) cans chickpeas, rinsed
1 cup vegetable broth
2 tablespoons minced fresh parsley
2 teaspoons lemon juice

1. Combine 3 tablespoons oil, garlic, and pepper flakes in 12-inch skillet and cook over medium heat, stirring occasionally, until garlic is light golden brown, 3 to 5 minutes. Stir in onion and ¼ teaspoon salt and cook until onion is softened and lightly browned, 5 to 7 minutes. Stir in chickpeas and broth and bring to simmer. Cover and cook until chickpeas are warmed through and flavors have melded, about 7 minutes.

2. Uncover, increase heat to high, and simmer until nearly all liquid has evaporated, about 3 minutes. Off heat, stir in parsley and lemon juice. Season with salt and pepper to taste, drizzle with remaining 1 tablespoon oil, and serve.

VARIATIONS
Chickpeas with Red Bell Pepper, Scallions, and Basil   FAST   VEGAN   GF
Add 1 stemmed, seeded, and chopped red bell pepper to pan with onion and salt. Substitute chopped fresh basil for parsley, and stir in 2 thinly sliced scallions before serving.

Chickpeas with Smoked Paprika and Cilantro   FAST   VEGAN   GF
Omit red pepper flakes. Add ½ teaspoon smoked paprika to skillet after onion has softened; cook until fragrant, about 30 seconds. Substitute minced fresh cilantro for parsley, and sherry vinegar for lemon juice.

Curried Chickpeas with Yogurt   FAST   GF
Omit red pepper flakes. Add 1 teaspoon curry powder to skillet after onion has softened; cook until fragrant, about 30 seconds. Add ⅓ cup raisins to skillet with chickpeas. Substitute lime juice for lemon juice, and stir in ¼ cup plain yogurt before serving.

Chickpea Cakes

SERVES 6   FAST

✔ **WHY THIS RECIPE WORKS:** Like black beans, chickpeas make great veggie burgers. We found that unlike black beans, however, heartier chickpeas needed to go into the food processor to help them break down, and getting the right texture took a bit of trial and error. If underprocessed, the beans were too coarse and didn't hold together; if overprocessed, we ended up with hummus. We wanted a combination of two textures: some finely chopped chickpeas to help bind the patties, along with some larger pieces for texture. To bind the patties, two eggs and some panko bread crumbs did the trick, and for richness we added yogurt and olive oil. A combination of garam masala, cayenne pepper, scallions, and cilantro ensured these patties were anything but bland. Avoid overmixing the chickpea mixture in step 1 or the cakes will have a mealy texture. A fresh and cooling cucumber-yogurt sauce helps brighten the dish. Serve with lime wedges.

2 (15-ounce) cans chickpeas, rinsed
2 large eggs
6 tablespoons extra-virgin olive oil
1 teaspoon garam masala
⅛ teaspoon cayenne pepper
⅛ teaspoon salt
1 cup panko bread crumbs

½ cup plain Greek yogurt
2 scallions, sliced thin
3 tablespoons minced fresh cilantro
1 shallot, minced
1 recipe Cucumber-Yogurt Sauce (page 43)

1. Pulse chickpeas in food processor until coarsely ground, about 8 pulses. Whisk eggs, 2 tablespoons oil, garam masala, cayenne, and ⅛ teaspoon salt together in medium bowl. Gently stir in processed chickpeas, panko, yogurt, scallions, cilantro, and shallot until just combined. Divide into 6 equal portions and gently pack into 1-inch-thick patties.

2. Heat 2 tablespoons oil in 12-inch nonstick skillet over medium heat until shimmering. Carefully lay 3 patties in skillet and cook until well browned and firm on both sides, 4 to 5 minutes per side.

3. Transfer cakes to plate and tent with aluminum foil. Return now-empty skillet to medium heat and repeat with remaining 2 tablespoons oil and remaining 3 patties. Serve with Cucumber-Yogurt Sauce.

Cranberry Beans with Tequila, Green Chiles, and Pepitas

SERVES 4 TO 6 **GF**

✔ **WHY THIS RECIPE WORKS:** Cranberry beans possess a delicate flavor and creamy texture not unlike those of pinto or cannellini. Originally from South America, they have become popular in Mexico as well, so we decided to pair them with bold Mexican flavors. Cranberry beans are rarely ever found canned, so we knew we'd start with dried beans. To help the beans cook up creamy and tender, we soaked them overnight in salt water. Then we sautéed some onion and garlic with lots of paprika, some cumin seeds, and dried oregano. Once the mixture was fragrant, we added a little tequila to the pot to give the beans some kick. Cooking it until evaporated prevented the dish from tasting too boozy. Next we stirred in the brined beans and water and transferred the pot to the oven, where the beans could cook gently without constant monitoring. Once the beans were tender, we stirred in some convenient canned chiles to give the dish great spice and some brightness, then we cooked the beans uncovered for 15 minutes more to allow the sauce to thicken. A garnish of rich sour cream, crunchy pepitas, and quick pickled shallots and radishes nicely balanced the rich, warm flavors of the cranberry beans. If cranberry beans are not available, you can substitute pinto beans. For more information on the science behind salt-soaking beans, and how to speed up the process if you're tight on time, see page 204.

We showcase the delicate flavor and texture of cranberry beans in a bold Mexican-inspired sauce with chiles and tequila.

Salt and pepper
1 pound (2½ cups) dried cranberry beans, picked over and rinsed
¼ cup extra-virgin olive oil
1 onion, chopped fine
6 garlic cloves, minced
1 tablespoon paprika
½ teaspoon cumin seeds
½ teaspoon dried oregano
¼ cup tequila
5 cups water
1 tablespoon packed brown sugar
1 bay leaf
½ cup canned chopped green chiles
½ cup roasted pepitas
½ cup sour cream or queso fresco
1 recipe Quick Pickled Shallots and Radishes (page 366)

1. Dissolve 3 tablespoons salt in 4 quarts cold water in large container. Add beans and soak at room temperature for at least 8 hours or up to 24 hours. Drain and rinse well.

2. Adjust oven rack to middle position and heat oven to 325 degrees. Heat oil in Dutch oven over medium heat until shimmering. Add onion and 1 teaspoon salt and cook until onion is softened, about 5 minutes. Stir in garlic, paprika, cumin, and oregano and cook until fragrant, about 1 minute. Stir in tequila and cook until evaporated, about 30 seconds. Stir in water, sugar, bay leaf, and cranberry beans; bring to simmer. Cover, transfer pot to oven, and cook until beans are tender, stirring once halfway through cooking, about 1¼ hours.

3. Add green chiles, stirring vigorously. Return pot to oven uncovered, and cook until sauce is thickened slightly, about 15 minutes. Season with salt and pepper to taste and serve with pepitas, sour cream, and pickles.

Edamame Salad

SERVES 4   **FAST**   **GF**

✅ **WHY THIS RECIPE WORKS:** Edamame are a great base for salads because their bright, fresh flavor and satisfying pop of texture pair perfectly with leafy greens and vegetables. However, keeping the focus on the edamame proved to be a challenge, as tart vinaigrettes or bold-flavored vegetables easily overpowered the beans' mild flavor. Baby arugula served as the perfect base thanks to its subtle peppery flavor and delicate, tender leaves. Lots of mint and basil helped to bring a light, summery flavor to the salad. Thinly sliced shallot added mild onion flavor, and just a couple of radishes added crunch and color. For the vinaigrette, we chose to use rice vinegar for its mild acidity and added a little honey for sweetness and to help emulsify the dressing. One small clove of garlic added flavor without taking over the dish. The finishing touch was a sprinkling of roasted sunflower seeds, which added nuttiness and depth to our bright salad.

2	tablespoons rice vinegar
1	tablespoon honey
1	small garlic clove, minced
	Salt and pepper
3	tablespoons extra-virgin olive oil
20	ounces frozen shelled edamame beans, thawed and patted dry
2	ounces (2 cups) baby arugula
½	cup shredded fresh basil
½	cup chopped fresh mint
2	radishes, trimmed, halved, and sliced thin
1	shallot, halved and thinly sliced
¼	cup roasted sunflower seeds

Peppery radish and arugula and a simple herb vinaigrette are the perfect complements to satisfying edamame.

Whisk vinegar, honey, garlic, and 1 teaspoon salt together in large bowl. Slowly whisk in oil until incorporated. Add edamame, arugula, basil, mint, radishes, and shallot and toss to combine. Sprinkle with sunflower seeds and season with salt and pepper to taste. Serve.

Lentil Salad with Olives, Mint, and Feta

SERVES 4 TO 6   **GF**

✅ **WHY THIS RECIPE WORKS:** The main challenge in making a lentil salad is cooking the lentils so that they maintain their shape and firm-tender bite. We found this required two key steps. The first was to salt-soak the lentils, which softened their skins, leading to fewer blowouts. The second was to cook the lentils in the oven, which heated them gently and uniformly. Then all we had to do was to pair the earthy beans with a tart vinaigrette and boldly flavored mix-ins. We mixed bright white wine vinegar with extra-virgin olive oil, then added fresh mint, minced shallot, and chopped kalamata olives. A sprinkle of rich

Getting to Know Lentils

Lentils come in dozens of sizes and colors, and the variations in flavor and color are considerable. We evaluated the most commonly available types of lentils in terms of taste, texture, and appearance. Here's what we found.

BROWN AND GREEN LENTILS

These larger lentils are what you'll find in every supermarket. They are a uniform drab brown or green. They have a mild yet light and earthy flavor and creamy texture. They hold their shape well when cooked and have tender insides. These are all-purpose lentils, great in soups and salads or tossed with olive oil and herbs.

LENTILLES DU PUY

These French lentils are smaller than the common brown and green varieties. They are a dark olive-green, almost black. We love them for their rich, earthy, complex flavor and firm yet tender texture. They keep their shape and look beautiful on the plate when cooked, so they're perfect for salads and dishes where the lentils take center stage.

RED AND YELLOW LENTILS

These small, split orange-red or golden-yellow lentils completely disintegrate when cooked. If you are looking for a lentil that will quickly break down into a thick puree, this is the one to use.

BLACK LENTILS

Like *lentilles du Puy*, black lentils are slightly smaller than the standard brown lentils. They have a deep black hue similar to the color of caviar. In fact, some markets refer to them as beluga lentils. They have a robust, earthy flavor and hold their shape well when cooked, but their skins can make dishes dark and muddy.

WHITE LENTILS

White lentils are simply skinned and split black lentils. They have a unique flavor similar to that of mung beans. Like red and yellow lentils, they disintegrate as they cook, and they boast a particularly viscous, starchy texture that makes for a great soup.

feta finished the dish. French green lentils, or *lentilles du Puy*, are our preferred choice for this recipe, but it works with any type of lentil except red or yellow. Salt-soaking helps keep the lentils intact, but if you don't have time, they'll still taste good. You will need an ovensafe medium saucepan for this recipe. The salad can be served warm or at room temperature.

> Salt and pepper
> 1 cup lentils, picked over and rinsed
> 5 garlic cloves, lightly crushed and peeled
> 1 bay leaf
> 5 tablespoons extra-virgin olive oil
> 3 tablespoons white wine vinegar
> ½ cup pitted kalamata olives, coarsely chopped
> ½ cup chopped fresh mint
> 1 large shallot, minced
> 1 ounce feta cheese, crumbled (¼ cup)

1. Dissolve 1 teaspoon salt in 4 cups warm water (about 110 degrees) in bowl. Add lentils and soak at room temperature for 1 hour. Drain well.

2. Adjust oven rack to middle position and heat oven to 325 degrees. Combine drained lentils, 4 cups water, garlic, bay leaf, and ½ teaspoon salt in medium saucepan. Cover, transfer to oven, and cook until lentils are tender but remain intact, 45 to 60 minutes.

3. Drain lentils well, discarding garlic and bay leaf. In large bowl, whisk oil and vinegar together. Add drained lentils, olives, mint, and shallot and toss to combine. Season with salt and pepper to taste. Transfer to serving dish and sprinkle with feta. Serve warm or at room temperature.

VARIATIONS

Lentil Salad with Hazelnuts and Goat Cheese GF

Substitute red wine vinegar for white wine vinegar, and add 2 teaspoons Dijon mustard to dressing. Omit olives and substitute ¼ cup chopped fresh parsley for mint. Substitute ½ cup crumbled goat cheese for feta, and sprinkle with ⅓ cup coarsely chopped toasted hazelnuts before serving.

Lentil Salad with Carrots and Cilantro VEGAN GF

Substitute lemon juice for white wine vinegar. Toss 2 carrots, peeled and cut into 2-inch-long matchsticks, with 1 teaspoon ground cumin, ½ teaspoon ground cinnamon, and ⅛ teaspoon cayenne pepper in bowl; cover and microwave until carrots are tender but still crisp, 2 to 4 minutes. Substitute carrots for olives, and ¼ cup chopped fresh cilantro for mint. Omit shallot and feta.

Lentil Salad with Spinach, Walnuts, and Parmesan Cheese `GF`

Substitute sherry vinegar for white wine vinegar. Place 4 cups baby spinach and 2 tablespoons water in bowl. Cover and microwave until spinach is wilted and volume is halved, 3 to 4 minutes. Remove bowl from microwave and keep covered for 1 minute. Transfer spinach to colander; gently press to release liquid. Transfer spinach to cutting board and roughly chop. Return to colander and press again. Substitute chopped spinach for olives and mint, and ¾ cup coarsely grated Parmesan cheese for feta. Sprinkle with ⅓ cup coarsely chopped toasted walnuts before serving.

French Lentils

SERVES 6 TO 8   `VEGAN` `GF`

✓ **WHY THIS RECIPE WORKS:** Smaller and firmer than the more common brown and green varieties, French lentils, or *lentilles du Puy*, are a favorite in the test kitchen thanks to their rich, complex flavor and tender texture. For a simple side dish that highlights their sweet, earthy flavors, we began by slowly cooking them with carrots, onion, and celery (a classic combination called a *mirepoix*). Garlic and thyme added aromatic flavors that complemented the lentils. Vegetable broth lent the dish an overwhelming sweetness, but water let the flavors of the vegetables and lentils come through. We cooked the lentils until they became completely tender, and then finished the dish with a splash of olive oil along with some parsley and lemon juice. French green lentils are our preferred choice for this recipe, but it works with any type of lentil except red or yellow.

- 2 **carrots, peeled and chopped fine**
- 1 **onion, chopped fine**
- 1 **celery rib, chopped fine**
- 2 **tablespoons extra-virgin olive oil**
  Salt and pepper
- 2 **garlic cloves, minced**
- 1 **teaspoon minced fresh thyme or ¼ teaspoon dried**
- 2½ **cups water**
- 1 **cup lentilles du Puy, picked over and rinsed**
- 2 **tablespoons minced fresh parsley**
- 2 **teaspoons lemon juice**

1. Combine carrots, onion, celery, 1 tablespoon oil, and ½ teaspoon salt in large saucepan. Cover and cook over medium-low heat, stirring occasionally, until vegetables are softened, 8 to 10 minutes. Stir in garlic and thyme and cook until fragrant, about 30 seconds.

Sweet golden raisins and aromatic curry powder bring another layer of flavor to our classic French lentils.

2. Stir in water and lentils and bring to simmer. Reduce heat to low, cover, and continue to simmer, stirring occasionally, until lentils are mostly tender but still slightly crunchy, 40 to 50 minutes.

3. Uncover and continue to cook, stirring occasionally, until lentils are completely tender, about 8 minutes. Stir in remaining 1 tablespoon oil, parsley, and lemon juice. Season with salt and pepper to taste and serve.

VARIATIONS

French Lentils with Swiss Chard `VEGAN` `GF`

This variation yields a little extra and serves 8.

Omit carrots, celery, and parsley. Separate stems and leaves from 12 ounces Swiss chard; finely chop stems and chop leaves into ½-inch pieces. Add chard stems to pot with onion and stir chard leaves into pot after uncovering in step 3.

Curried French Lentils with Golden Raisins `VEGAN` `GF`

Add 1 teaspoon curry powder to pot with onion. Stir ½ cup golden raisins into pot after uncovering in step 3. Substitute minced fresh cilantro for parsley.

Mujaddara is a Middle-Eastern peasant dish of tender lentils, basmati rice, and a contrasting garnish of crispy fried onions.

Lentils, Rice, and Crispy Onions (Mujaddara)

SERVES 4 TO 6 **GF**

✔ **WHY THIS RECIPE WORKS:** This classic Middle Eastern dish is a spectacular example of how a few humble ingredients can add up to a dish that's satisfying and complex. Tender basmati rice and lentils are seasoned with warm spices and minced garlic and topped with deeply flavorful fried onions. To give the onions the best crispy texture, we microwaved them briefly to remove some of their liquid, then fried them in oil to a deep golden brown. We used a pilaf method to cook the rice and lentils; giving the lentils a 15-minute head start ensured that they finished cooking at the same time as the rice. Soaking the rice in hot water gave it a fluffy, not sticky, texture. Blooming the spices and toasting the rice in oil left over from frying the onions deepened the flavor of the spices and garlic and enhanced the rice's nutty flavor. Finished with a bracing garlicky yogurt sauce, this pilaf is comfort food at its best. Large green or brown lentils both work well in this recipe; do not substitute French green lentils, or *lentilles du Puy*. It is crucial

to thoroughly dry the microwaved onions after rinsing. The best way to accomplish this is to use a salad spinner.

YOGURT SAUCE

- 1 cup plain whole-milk yogurt
- 2 tablespoons lemon juice
- ½ teaspoon garlic, minced
- ½ teaspoon salt

RICE AND LENTILS

- 2 pounds onions, halved and sliced ¼ inch thick
  Salt and pepper
- 1½ cups vegetable oil
- 8½ ounces (1¼ cups) green or brown lentils, picked over and rinsed
- 1¼ cups basmati rice
- 3 garlic cloves, minced
- 1 teaspoon ground coriander
- 1 teaspoon ground cumin
- ½ teaspoon ground cinnamon
- ½ teaspoon ground allspice
- ⅛ teaspoon cayenne pepper
- 1 teaspoon sugar
- 3 tablespoons minced fresh cilantro

1. FOR THE YOGURT SAUCE: Whisk all ingredients together in bowl and refrigerate until serving time.

2. FOR THE RICE AND LENTILS: Toss onions with 2 teaspoons salt in bowl and microwave for 5 minutes. Rinse thoroughly, drain, and pat dry with paper towels. Cook onions and oil in Dutch oven over high heat, stirring often, until golden brown, 25 to 30 minutes. Drain onions in colander set in large bowl, reserving 3 tablespoons oil. Transfer onions to paper towel–lined baking sheet. Do not wash pot.

3. Meanwhile, bring lentils, 4 cups water, and 1 teaspoon salt to boil in medium saucepan over high heat. Reduce heat to low and cook until lentils are tender, 15 to 17 minutes. Drain and set aside.

4. While onions and lentils cook, place rice in medium bowl, add hot tap water to cover by 2 inches, and let stand 15 minutes. Using hands, gently swish grains to release excess starch. Carefully pour off water, leaving rice in bowl. Add cold tap water to rice and pour off water. Repeat adding and pouring off cold water 4 to 5 times, until water runs almost clear. Drain rice in fine-mesh strainer.

5. Heat 3 tablespoons reserved onion oil, garlic, coriander, cumin, cinnamon, allspice, ¼ teaspoon pepper, and cayenne in now-empty Dutch oven over medium heat until fragrant, about 2 minutes. Stir in rice and cook, stirring occasionally, until edges of rice begin to turn translucent, about 3 minutes.

Stir in 2¼ cups water, sugar, and 1 teaspoon salt and bring to boil. Stir in lentils, reduce heat to low, cover, and cook until all liquid is absorbed, about 12 minutes.

6. Remove pot from heat, lay clean folded dish towel underneath lid, and let sit for 10 minutes. Fluff rice and lentils with fork and stir in cilantro and half of onions. Transfer to serving platter and top with remaining onions. Serve with yogurt sauce.

Spiced Red Lentils (Masoor Dal)
SERVES 4 GF

✔ **WHY THIS RECIPE WORKS:** Dals are heavily spiced lentil stews common throughout India. Split red lentils give the dish a mild, slightly nutty taste, and as the stew slowly simmers, they break down to a smooth consistency. We wanted our dal to be simple yet still embody the complex flavors of Indian cuisine, so we started with the spices. We created a balanced blend of warm spices with just a subtle layer of heat. Blooming the spices in oil until they were fragrant boosted and deepened their flavors. Onion, garlic, and ginger rounded out the aromatic flavor. Authentic dal should have a porridge-like consistency, bordering on a puree (without the need for a blender). Getting this consistency required cooking the lentils with just the right amount of water: We finally settled on 4 cups water to 1¼ cups lentils for a dal that was smooth but not thin. Before serving, we added cilantro for color and freshness, diced raw tomato for sweetness and acidity, and a pat of butter for richness. You cannot substitute other types of lentils for the red lentils here; they have a very different texture. Serve over rice.

1	tablespoon vegetable oil
½	teaspoon ground coriander
½	teaspoon ground cumin
½	teaspoon ground cinnamon
½	teaspoon ground turmeric
⅛	teaspoon ground cardamom
⅛	teaspoon red pepper flakes
1	onion, chopped fine
4	garlic cloves, minced
1½	teaspoons grated fresh ginger
4	cups water
8½	ounces (1¼ cups) red lentils, picked over and rinsed
1	pound plum tomatoes, cored, seeded, and chopped
½	cup minced fresh cilantro
2	tablespoons unsalted butter
	Salt and pepper
	Lemon wedges

1. Heat oil in large saucepan over medium-high heat until shimmering. Add coriander, cumin, cinnamon, turmeric, cardamom, and pepper flakes and cook until fragrant, about 10 seconds. Stir in onion and cook until softened, about 5 minutes. Stir in garlic and ginger and cook until fragrant, about 30 seconds.

2. Stir in water and lentils and bring to boil. Reduce heat to low and simmer, uncovered, until lentils are tender and resemble coarse puree, 20 to 25 minutes.

3. Stir in tomatoes, cilantro, and butter and season with salt and pepper to taste. Serve with lemon wedges.

Baked Navy Beans
SERVES 4 TO 6 VEGAN GF

✔ **WHY THIS RECIPE WORKS:** Authentic Boston baked beans are always a hit, but we don't often have the 5 to 6 hours they require, and classic versions are not vegetarian-friendly picnic fare: Salt pork, and sometimes bacon as well, is often the first ingredient in the pot. To get the same creamy-textured beans in a lot less time, first we simmered dried beans with a little baking soda. The alkaline soda weakened the cell structure of the beans, helping them to become tender more quickly and allowing us to shave the baking time down to 2 hours. We started by adding traditional flavorings—molasses, brown sugar, mustard, and cider vinegar—but we needed to find a way to deepen the flavor and amp up the meatiness of the dish. Adding soy sauce and smoked paprika proved to be the solution; the umami-rich soy sauce gave the dish more savory flavor, and the paprika added great smoky depth. In order for this recipe to be gluten-free, you must use gluten-free soy sauce or tamari.

1	pound (2½ cups) dried navy beans, picked over and rinsed
1	tablespoon baking soda
1	tablespoon vegetable oil
1	onion, chopped fine
¼	cup molasses
2	tablespoons packed dark brown sugar
2	tablespoons soy sauce
4	teaspoons Dijon mustard
2	teaspoons smoked paprika
	Salt and pepper
2	teaspoons cider vinegar

All About Dried Beans

Canned beans are undeniably convenient, but when the beans are the star of a dish, we prefer the superior flavor and texture of dried beans.

BUYING

When shopping for beans, it's essential to select "fresh" dried beans. Buy those that are uniform in size and have a smooth exterior. When dried beans are fully hydrated and cooked, they should be plump, with taut skins, and have creamy insides; spent beans will have wrinkled skin and a dry, almost gritty texture.

STORING

Uncooked beans should be stored in a cool, dry place in a sealed plastic or glass container. Beans are less susceptible than rice and grains to pests and spoilage, but it is still best to use them within a month or two. Always pick over dried beans to remove stones and debris, and rinse them before cooking to wash away any dust or impurities.

SUBSTITUTING CANNED BEANS FOR DRIED

Most recipes that call for dried beans require the beans to cook slowly with the other ingredients so that they release their starches and thicken the dish. When you replace the dried beans with canned beans and shorten the cooking time (canned beans are fully cooked and need to cook only long enough to warm through and soak up flavor), you sacrifice both the flavor and the texture of the finished dish. But if you're short on time and want to swap in canned beans, a general rule of thumb is that 1 cup of dried beans equals 3 cups of canned beans.

1. Adjust oven rack to middle position and heat oven to 350 degrees. Bring 3 quarts water, beans, and baking soda to boil in Dutch oven over high heat. Reduce heat to medium-high and simmer vigorously for 20 minutes. Drain and rinse beans and pot. Dry pot.

2. Heat oil in now-empty pot over medium heat until shimmering. Add onion and cook until softened, about 5 minutes. Stir in 4½ cups water, rinsed beans, molasses, sugar, soy sauce, 1 tablespoon mustard, paprika, ¾ teaspoon salt, and ¼ teaspoon pepper and bring to boil. Cover pot, transfer to oven, and cook until beans are nearly tender, about 1½ hours.

3. Uncover and continue to bake until beans are completely tender, about 30 minutes. Stir in remaining 1 teaspoon mustard and vinegar. Season with salt and pepper to taste. Serve.

Refried Pinto Beans

MAKES 2½ CUPS   FAST   VEGAN   GF

✔ **WHY THIS RECIPE WORKS:** Authentic refried beans, or *frijoles refritos*, are leftover stewed beans cooked in a generous amount of lard until they are softened enough to mash. We wanted to achieve the same lush texture and rich, savory flavor with less fuss and without the lard. To start, we found that dried beans weren't essential—rinsed canned pinto beans worked just fine and saved us the hassle of cooking beans from scratch—the whole recipe came together in just 30 minutes. For authentic flavor, we reached for smoky chipotle chile powder, cumin, oregano, and several cloves of garlic. Two tablespoons of umami-rich tomato paste added even more savory depth. Processing a portion of the beans with some water in the food processor created the silky, creamy texture we were after, and pulsing the remaining beans ensured some chunky bites remained in the final dish. Cilantro and lime juice at the end gave our beans some brightness.

- 2 (15-ounce) cans pinto beans, rinsed
- 1 cup water, plus extra as needed
- 1 tablespoon vegetable oil
- 1 onion, chopped fine
- Salt and pepper
- 2 tablespoons tomato paste
- 3 garlic cloves, minced
- 1 teaspoon ground cumin
- ½ teaspoon chipotle chile powder
- ½ teaspoon dried oregano
- 1 tablespoon minced fresh cilantro
- 2 teaspoons lime juice

1. Process all but 1 cup of beans and water in food processor until smooth, about 30 seconds, scraping down sides of bowl as needed. Add remaining beans and pulse until coarsely ground, about 5 pulses.

2. Heat oil in 12-inch nonstick skillet over medium heat until shimmering. Add onion and ½ teaspoon salt and cook until onion is softened, about 5 minutes. Stir in tomato paste, garlic, cumin, chile powder, and oregano and cook until fragrant, about 1 minute. Stir in bean mixture and cook, stirring constantly, until well combined and thickened slightly, about 3 minutes. Off heat, stir in cilantro and lime juice and season with salt and pepper to taste. Add additional hot water as needed to adjust consistency and serve.

Sorting Dried Beans

Before cooking dried beans, you should pick them over for any small stones or debris and then rinse them. The easiest way to check for small stones is to spread the beans out over a large plate or rimmed baking sheet.

Red Beans and Rice

SERVES 6 TO 8 `GF`

✔ **WHY THIS RECIPE WORKS:** Eating red beans and rice on Mondays is a tradition in New Orleans, where for decades custom held that the first day of the workweek be devoted to laundry. Doing laundry took all day, and having a pot of beans simmering on the stove was a way to accomplish dinner at the same time. Our goal was to make a vegetarian version of this traditional recipe with widely available ingredients. We substituted small red beans for the local Camellia-brand dried red beans and replaced the smoky, meaty flavor of tasso (traditional Cajun ham) with a combination of chipotle chile in adobo sauce and smoked paprika. We started by sautéing green pepper, onion, and celery, then we added garlic, thyme, bay leaves, and cayenne pepper to give the beans complex aromatic flavor. In keeping with tradition, we served the saucy beans over white rice to soak up every bit of flavor. In order for the starch from the beans to thicken the cooking liquid, it is important to maintain a vigorous simmer in step 2. For more information on the science behind salt-soaking beans, and how to speed up the process if you're tight on time, see page 204.

RED BEANS

- Salt and pepper
- 1 pound (2 cups) small dried red beans, picked over and rinsed
- 3 tablespoons unsalted butter
- 1 onion, chopped fine
- 1 green bell pepper, stemmed, seeded, and chopped fine
- 1 celery rib, chopped fine
- 3 garlic cloves, minced
- 2 teaspoons minced canned chipotle chile in adobo sauce

Spicy chipotle chile, smoked paprika, and plenty of aromatics give our Cajun red beans and rice bold, authentic flavor.

- 1½ teaspoons smoked paprika
- 1 teaspoon minced fresh thyme or ¼ teaspoon dried
- 2 bay leaves
- ⅛ teaspoon cayenne pepper
- 1 teaspoon red wine vinegar, plus extra as needed
- 3 scallions, sliced thin
- Hot sauce

RICE

- 1 tablespoon unsalted butter
- 2 cups long-grain white rice, rinsed
- 3 cups water
- 1 teaspoon salt

1. FOR THE RED BEANS: Dissolve 3 tablespoons salt in 4 quarts cold water in large container. Add beans and soak at room temperature for at least 8 hours or up to 24 hours. Drain and rinse well.

2. Melt 1 tablespoon butter in Dutch oven over medium heat. Add onion, bell pepper, celery, and ½ teaspoon salt and cook, stirring often, until vegetables are softened, 6 to 7 minutes. Stir in garlic, chipotle, paprika, thyme, bay leaves, cayenne, and ¼ teaspoon pepper and cook until fragrant, about 30 seconds. Stir in beans and 9 cups water and bring to boil over high heat. Reduce heat to medium-low and simmer vigorously, stirring occasionally, until beans are just soft and liquid begins to thicken, 45 to 60 minutes.

3. Stir in vinegar and 1 teaspoon salt and cook until liquid is thick and beans are fully tender and creamy, about 30 minutes.

4. FOR THE RICE: Melt butter in large saucepan over medium heat. Add rice and cook, stirring often, until edges begin to turn translucent, about 2 minutes. Add water and salt and bring to boil. Cover, reduce heat to low, and simmer until liquid is absorbed and rice is tender, about 20 minutes. Remove pot from heat, lay clean folded dish towel underneath lid, and let rice sit for 10 minutes. Fluff rice with fork.

5. Discard bay leaves from beans and stir in remaining 2 tablespoons butter. Season with salt and extra vinegar to taste. Portion rice into individual bowls, top with beans, and sprinkle with scallions. Serve with hot sauce.

Homemade Tofu

MAKES 14 OUNCES VEGAN GF

✔ **WHY THIS RECIPE WORKS:** In Japan, tofu is made at dawn, like bread, for early morning distribution, and it boasts a silky-smooth texture and a clean, delicate taste. Unfortunately, truly fresh tofu is hard to come by in American grocery stores. Happily, tofu is no harder to make than yogurt. The process is simple: Curdle hot soy milk with a mineral salt called *nigari*, then press out the whey to create the desired texture. We found it best to start with dried beans and make our own soy milk to ensure the tofu would coagulate properly. To make the milk, we soaked the soybeans until they split apart easily, then blended them with water until smooth. Next, we brought the mixture to a boil, simmered it until thickened, then drained it through cheesecloth. To make the tofu, we brought our soy milk back to a boil, then added the nigari in two stages. Once the milk started to form curds, we transferred the curds to a tofu mold and pressed them until the tofu reached our desired firmness.

8   **ounces (1¼ cups) dried soybeans, picked over and rinsed**
2   **teaspoons liquid nigari**

1. Place beans in large container, cover by 2 inches water, and soak until beans are pale yellow and split apart when rubbed between fingertips, 12 to 18 hours.

2. Drain and rinse beans; you should have about 3 cups. Working in 3 batches, process 1 cup soaked soybeans with 3 cups water in blender until mostly smooth, about 3 minutes; transfer to Dutch oven. (You will use 9 cups water total.)

3. Bring soybean mixture to boil over medium-high heat, stirring often with rubber spatula to prevent scorching and boiling over. Reduce heat to medium-low and simmer, stirring often, until slightly thickened, about 10 minutes. Meanwhile, line colander with butter muslin or triple layer of cheesecloth and set over large bowl.

4. Pour soybean mixture into prepared colander. Being careful of hot liquid, pull edges of muslin together and twist to form tight pouch, then firmly squeeze with tongs to help extract as much liquid as possible. You should have about 8 cups of soy milk; discard soybean pulp or reserve for another use.

5. Transfer strained milk to clean Dutch oven and bring to boil over medium-high heat, stirring often; remove from heat. Combine ½ cup water and nigari in measuring cup.

6. While stirring soy milk in fast figure-8 motion with rubber spatula, add half of nigari mixture, about 6 stirs. Cover pot and let sit undisturbed for 2 minutes. Uncover, sprinkle remaining ¼ cup nigari mixture over top and gently stir using figure-8 motion, about 6 stirs. Cover pot and let sit undisturbed until curds form and whey is pooling on top and around sides of pot, about 20 minutes.

7. Line tofu mold with butter muslin or triple layer of cheesecloth and place in colander set over large bowl. Using skimmer or large slotted spoon, gently transfer soy milk curds to prepared mold, trying not to break up curds. Cover with excess muslin, add top of press, and weight with 2-pound weight until desired firmness is reached: 20 minutes for soft; 30 minutes for medium; 40 to 50 minutes for firm.

8. Gently remove tofu from mold and place in baking dish. Fill with cold water to cover and let sit until tofu is slightly firmer, about 10 minutes. (Tofu can be refrigerated in airtight container filled with water for up to 1 week; change water daily.)

What You Need to Make Tofu

Dried soybeans are available at Asian markets and some supermarkets, and online. Liquid *nigari* can be found online at culturesforhealth.com and at Asian supermarkets. You can find tofu molds online, but if you don't want to invest in one, poke three even holes in the bottom of a quart-size plastic berry container, then cut off the lid and trim it down to fit just inside the container. Line the container with muslin or cheesecloth and scoop the curds into the container just as you would with a mold, then cover with the muslin/cheesecloth and place the trimmed plastic lid on top.

How to Make Homemade Tofu

1. SOAK BEANS: Place beans in large container, cover by 2 inches water, and soak for 12 to 18 hours. Beans will more than double in size and turn from beige to pale yellow. Drain and rinse beans.

2. PUREE BEANS: Process beans in blender with water until mostly smooth, about 3 minutes. Transfer to Dutch oven and bring to boil over medium-high heat, stirring often with rubber spatula to prevent scorching and boiling over. Reduce heat to medium-low and simmer, stirring often, until slightly thickened, about 10 minutes.

3. DRAIN SOY MILK: Strain cooked soy mixture into colander lined with butter muslin or triple layer of cheesecloth and set over large bowl. Pull edges of muslin together and twist to form tight pouch, then firmly squeeze with tongs to help extract as much liquid as possible.

4. MAKE CURDS: Bring soy milk to boil, then remove from heat. While stirring with rubber spatula, stir in half of nigari-water mixture. Cover pot and let sit for 2 minutes. Sprinkle remaining nigari mixture over top and gently stir using figure-8 motion. Cover pot and let sit until curds form, about 20 minutes.

5. TRANSFER CURDS TO MOLD: Using skimmer or large slotted spoon, gently transfer soy milk curds to tofu mold lined with butter muslin or triple layer of cheesecloth and placed in colander over bowl, trying not to break up curds.

6. PRESS TOFU: Cover with excess muslin, add top of press, and weight with 2-pound weight until desired firmness is reached: 20 minutes for soft; 30 minutes for medium; 40 to 50 minutes for firm.

Japanese Seaweed

Seaweed has long played a role in the cuisine of Japan. It is used to flavor stocks and soups, as a garnish for rice and noodle dishes, and as a key ingredient for *maki*, commonly referred to as rolled sushi. Three types of seaweed are the most common: nori, kombu, and wakame. You can find seaweed in the international aisle of well-stocked supermarkets, in Asian and natural foods markets, and online.

NORI

Nori is the Japanese word for seaweed and is the only variety used for maki (rolled sushi). It is also crumbled and used as a garnish for rice and noodles. Nori is available plain, seasoned with a mixture of soy sauce, sugar, and spices, or seasoned with sesame oil and salt (Korean-style). Nori is often toasted before being added to a dish to release its flavor and to make it more pliable for rolling sushi.

KOMBU

Kombu is a key ingredient in dashi, a broth essential to Japanese cuisine. When purchasing kombu, take note of the chalky, white powder on the exterior. This is an indication of the glutamic acid content and translates to increased flavor. Kombu is primarily sold in dried whole sheets that are quite thick. It is often simmered in soups or broths to impart flavor, and the softened kombu can then be eaten as part of the meal.

WAKAME

Wakame is a traditional garnish in miso soup and many Japanese salads. It is available dried in thin sheets, shreds (or flakes), or fresh-salted. Both dried and fresh varieties are used to flavor soups or can be made into salads. Dried wakame must be rehydrated in water for at least 3 to 5 minutes before using, while fresh-salted wakame should be rinsed briefly to remove the excess salt, then soaked in water for 1 to 2 minutes.

To play up the delicate texture of raw tofu, we steep it in an intensely flavored salty, sweet, and savory marinade.

Chilled Marinated Tofu

SERVES 4 TO 6   VEGAN   GF

✔ **WHY THIS RECIPE WORKS:** Marinated raw tofu is served throughout Japan during the sticky summer months as a cool and refreshing appetizer or snack. In the best renditions, a flavorful marinade and a few choice garnishes amplify the tofu's delicate sweet-soy flavor. The marinade for this dish is typically a soy sauce–enhanced dashi, the ubiquitous Japanese broth prepared from kombu seaweed and bonito (skipjack tuna) flakes. We replaced the bonito with a glutamate-rich combination of wakame seaweed, fish sauce substitute, mirin, and sugar. This mixture produced a well-rounded marinade: sweet, salty, and robust—almost meaty in its intensity. A splash of rice wine vinegar, added off the heat after the broth had steeped, provided a bit of balance. For the garnishes, we liked a sprinkle of crumbled nori, sliced scallions, and a drizzle of toasted sesame oil. A sprinkling of *shichimi togarishi* (a common Japanese spice mix) tastes good on this tofu. For an accurate measurement of boiling water, bring a full kettle of water to a boil and then measure out the desired amount.

14 ounces firm tofu, halved lengthwise, then
   cut crosswise into ½-inch-thick squares
   Salt and pepper

2 cups boiling water

¼ cup fish sauce substitute (page 60)

¼ cup mirin

4 teaspoons sugar

¼ ounce wakame seaweed

¼ ounce kombu seaweed

4 teaspoons rice vinegar

2 sheets toasted nori seaweed, crumbled

2 scallions, sliced thin on bias
   Toasted sesame oil

1. Spread tofu over paper towel–lined baking sheet, let drain for 20 minutes, then gently press dry with paper towels. Season with salt and pepper.

2. Meanwhile, combine boiling water, fish sauce, mirin, sugar, wakame, and kombu in bowl. Cover and let sit for 15 minutes. Strain liquid through fine-mesh strainer, discarding solids, then return broth to now-empty bowl.

3. Add tofu and vinegar, cover, and refrigerate until cool, at least 2 hours or up to 2 days. To serve, use slotted spoon to transfer tofu to platter, top with nori and scallions, and drizzle with sesame oil to taste.

A combination of crisp, crunchy vegetables is the perfect complement to the silky tofu in this bright Asian salad.

Tofu and Vegetable Salad

SERVES 4 TO 6 GF

 **WHY THIS RECIPE WORKS:** Our goal for this recipe was a light and easy Asian-inspired salad that boasted plenty of vegetables in a fresh, bright vinaigrette. First we sought out a mix of vegetables that, along with the tofu, would give our salad enough heft to make it a main course. We settled on napa cabbage, snow peas, red bell pepper, bean sprouts, and carrots. Next we considered the tofu. We preferred soft tofu here for its creamy, custardlike texture, and we pan-fried it to give it a slightly crispy outside. Draining the tofu on a paper towel–lined baking sheet before cooking helped to give it the light golden crust we were after and kept the tofu's liquid from watering down the dressing. For a vinaigrette with plenty of punch, we combined mild rice vinegar and lime juice with honey, fish sauce substitute, fresh ginger, nutty toasted sesame oil, and spicy, garlicky Sriracha sauce. A sprinkling of cilantro and toasted sesame seeds provided the perfect accents. Firm or extra-firm tofu will also work here, but it will taste drier.

28 ounces soft tofu, cut into ¾-inch cubes
   Salt and pepper

3 tablespoons lime juice (2 limes)

3 tablespoons honey

2 tablespoons rice vinegar

2 tablespoons fish sauce substitute (page 60),
   plus extra as needed

1 tablespoon grated fresh ginger

1½ teaspoons Sriracha sauce

6 tablespoons vegetable oil

3 tablespoons toasted sesame oil

4 cups shredded napa cabbage

6 ounces snow peas, strings removed,
   cut in half lengthwise

2 carrots, peeled and shredded

1 red bell pepper, stemmed, seeded,
   and cut into ½-inch pieces

1 cup bean sprouts

2 scallions, sliced thin on bias

3 tablespoons minced fresh cilantro

1 tablespoon sesame seeds, toasted

Tofu is a great food choice for vegetarians because it is high in protein as well as iron and calcium. We love it in the test kitchen because it is an ideal canvas for bold or aromatic sauces. It also takes to a wide variety of preparations from stir-frying and sautéing to roasting, braising, grilling, and scrambling. There are many recipes that include tofu throughout this book.

So what is tofu, exactly? Tofu is the result of a process that is similar to cheese making: Curds, the result of coagulating soy milk, are set in a mold and pressed to extract as much, or as little, of the liquid whey as desired. Depending on how long the tofu is pressed, and how much coagulant is used, the amount of whey released will vary, creating a range of textures from soft to firm.

Choosing the Right Tofu

Tofu is available in a variety of textures: extra-firm, firm, medium-firm, soft, and silken. We use all these varieties throughout this book, and reaching for the right variety will be key to the success of any given recipe. In general, firmer varieties hold their shape when cooking, while softer varieties do not, so it follows that each type of tofu is best when used in specific ways.

EXTRA-FIRM AND FIRM TOFU

We prefer extra-firm or firm tofu for stir-fries and noodle dishes, as they hold their shape in high heat cooking applications and when tossed with pasta. These two varieties of tofu are also great marinated (they absorb marinade better compared with softer varieties) or tossed raw into salads.

MEDIUM AND SOFT TOFU

Medium and soft tofu boast a creamy texture; we love to pan-fry these kinds of tofu, often coated with cornstarch, to achieve a crisp outside, which makes a nice textural contrast to the silky interior. Soft tofu is great scrambled like eggs.

SILKEN TOFU

Silken tofu has a soft, ultracreamy texture and is often used as a base for smoothies and dips, in desserts such as puddings, or as an egg replacement in vegan baked goods.

Storing Tofu

Tofu is highly perishable and has the best flavor and texture when it is fresh, so look for a package with the latest expiration date possible. To store an opened package, cover the tofu with water and store, refrigerated, in a covered container, changing the water daily. Any hint of sourness means the tofu is past its prime.

Cutting Tofu

Draining and pressing tofu before cooking helps to remove excess moisture and prevent watery dishes. Cutting the tofu before draining it exposes more surface area for draining.

TO CUT TOFU INTO SLABS:
Slice block of tofu crosswise into ¾-inch slabs.

TO CUT TOFU INTO FINGERS:
Cut tofu crosswise into slabs, then slice each slab into fingers of desired size.

TO CUT TOFU INTO CUBES:
Cut tofu into fingers, then cut each finger into cubes of desired size.

Drying Tofu

Spread tofu pieces evenly over rimmed baking sheet lined with paper towels, and let sit for 20 minutes to drain. Gently press tofu dry with paper towels.

1. Spread tofu over paper towel–lined baking sheet, let drain for 20 minutes, then gently press dry with paper towels. Season with salt and pepper. Meanwhile, whisk lime juice, honey, vinegar, fish sauce, ginger, and Sriracha together in medium bowl. Slowly whisk in ¼ cup vegetable oil and sesame oil until incorporated. Measure out and reserve ¼ cup vinaigrette separately for salad.

2. Heat 1 tablespoon vegetable oil in 12-inch nonstick skillet over medium-high heat until shimmering. Add half of tofu and brown lightly on all sides, about 5 minutes; transfer to bowl with remaining vinaigrette. Repeat with remaining 1 tablespoon vegetable oil and remaining tofu. Gently toss tofu to coat with vinaigrette, then let cool to room temperature, about 10 minutes.

3. Combine cabbage, snow peas, carrots, bell pepper, bean sprouts, and scallions in large bowl. Drizzle with reserved vinaigrette and toss to combine. Add tofu mixture and toss gently to combine. Season with fish sauce to taste. Sprinkle with cilantro and sesame seeds, and serve.

Warm Cabbage Salad with Crispy Tofu

SERVES 4 TO 6 `FAST` `VEGAN` `GF`

✔ **WHY THIS RECIPE WORKS:** Paired with crispy pan-fried tofu and a zesty dressing, bagged coleslaw mix transforms into an impressive entrée. We gave the dressing extra punch, mixing together oil, vinegar, soy sauce, sugar, and Asian chili-garlic sauce, and heating it in the microwave. Then we tossed it with the coleslaw mix, crunchy chopped peanuts, scallions, cilantro, and mint. For the tofu, draining it, dredging it in a mixture of cornmeal and cornstarch, and pan-frying it created the perfect light, crispy crust to contrast with its creamy interior. We prefer the texture of soft or medium-firm tofu here. Firm or extra-firm tofu will also work, but they will taste drier. Bags of coleslaw mix can vary in size, but a few ounces more or less won't make a difference here. To make the dish spicier, use the higher amount of Asian chili-garlic sauce. In order for this recipe to be gluten-free, you must use gluten-free soy sauce or tamari.

28 ounces soft tofu, halved lengthwise and sliced
   crosswise into 3-inch-long by ½-inch-thick fingers
   Salt and pepper
¾ cup plus 3 tablespoons vegetable oil
5 tablespoons rice vinegar
2 tablespoons soy sauce
2 tablespoons sugar
1–2 teaspoons Asian chili-garlic sauce
1 (14-ounce) bag green coleslaw mix

Golden fried tofu fingers contrast with a warm cabbage salad tossed with a tangy, subtly spicy dressing.

¾ cup dry-roasted peanuts, chopped
4 scallions, sliced thin
½ cup fresh cilantro leaves
½ cup chopped fresh mint
¾ cup cornstarch
¼ cup cornmeal

1. Spread tofu over paper towel–lined baking sheet, let drain for 20 minutes, then gently press dry with paper towels. Season with salt and pepper.

2. Meanwhile, whisk 3 tablespoons oil, vinegar, soy sauce, sugar, and chili-garlic sauce together in bowl, cover, and microwave until simmering, 1 to 2 minutes. Measure out and reserve 2 tablespoons dressing separately for drizzling over tofu. Toss remaining dressing with coleslaw mix, peanuts, scallions, cilantro, and mint.

3. Combine cornstarch and cornmeal in shallow dish. Working with several tofu pieces at a time, coat thoroughly with cornstarch mixture, pressing gently to adhere; transfer to wire rack set in rimmed baking sheet.

4. Heat remaining ¾ cup oil in 12-inch nonstick skillet over medium-high heat until shimmering. Working in 2 batches,

DIPPING SAUCES FOR TOFU FINGERS

HONEY-MUSTARD DIPPING SAUCE

MAKES ABOUT ¾ CUP **FAST** **GF**

- ½ cup yellow mustard
- ⅓ cup honey
- Salt and pepper

Mix mustard and honey together in bowl, season with salt and pepper to taste, and serve.

RANCH DIPPING SAUCE

MAKES ABOUT ¾ CUP **FAST** **GF**

Fresh herbs are essential for the flavor of this sauce; do not substitute dried herbs.

- ⅓ cup sour cream
- ⅓ cup mayonnaise
- 2 tablespoons water or buttermilk
- 1 tablespoon minced fresh cilantro
- 1 teaspoon lemon juice
- ¾ teaspoon minced fresh dill
- ⅛ teaspoon garlic powder
- Salt and pepper

Mix all ingredients together in bowl, season with salt and pepper to taste, and serve.

SWEET ORANGE DIPPING SAUCE

MAKES ABOUT ¾ CUP **FAST** **GF**

Freshly squeezed orange juice is especially good here.

- ¾ cup orange juice
- ¼ cup orange marmalade
- 1 tablespoon honey
- 2 teaspoons cornstarch
- Pinch ground ginger
- Pinch garlic powder
- Lemon juice
- Salt

Whisk orange juice, marmalade, honey, cornstarch, ginger, and garlic powder together in small saucepan. Bring to simmer over medium-high heat, whisking constantly. Reduce heat to medium-low and cook, stirring occasionally, until slightly thickened, 3 to 5 minutes. Off heat, season with lemon juice and salt to taste. Let cool to room temperature before serving.

Fried Tofu Fingers

SERVES 4 **FAST**

✔ **WHY THIS RECIPE WORKS:** The satisfying contrast between the crispy, browned exterior and silky interior is what makes these fried tofu fingers an instant favorite. To get the best possible crust on the tofu, we drained it on paper towels and patted it dry. This kept it from becoming soggy or breaking apart when fried. For the breading, we stuck with a traditional technique. We dipped the tofu in flour, then in beaten egg to help the coating stick. Finally, we dredged the tofu in extra-crisp panko bread crumbs to get a great crunchy texture. Working in batches, we shallow-fried the tofu in vegetable oil until it was golden brown on the outside and soft and velvety on the inside. Finally, we came up with a variety of addictive sauces for dipping. You can use either firm or extra-firm tofu in this recipe. Serve with your favorite dipping sauce.

- 14 ounces firm tofu, cut into 3-inch-long by ½-inch-thick fingers
- Salt and pepper
- 3 cups panko bread crumbs
- 1 cup all-purpose flour
- 2 large eggs
- ¾ cup vegetable oil

1. Spread tofu over paper towel–lined baking sheet, let drain for 20 minutes, then gently press dry with paper towels. Season with salt and pepper.

2. Adjust oven rack to middle position, place paper towel–lined plate on rack, and heat oven to 200 degrees. Spread panko in shallow dish. Spread flour in second shallow dish. Beat eggs in third shallow dish.

3. Working with several tofu pieces at a time, dredge in flour, dip in egg, then coat with panko, pressing gently to adhere; transfer to wire rack set in rimmed baking sheet.

4. Heat oil in 12-inch skillet over medium-high heat until shimmering. Working in 2 batches, cook tofu until light golden brown on all sides, about 4 minutes. Lift tofu from oil, letting excess oil drip back into skillet, then transfer to plate in oven. Serve.

A light coating of cornstarch and cornmeal gives our tofu a crisp crust and helps the sweet chili glaze to cling.

Sweet Chili Glazed Tofu

SERVES 4 TO 6 `VEGAN` `GF`

✓ **WHY THIS RECIPE WORKS:** For tofu with a crispy outer coating and bold, spicy-sweet flavor, we made crispy tofu fingers and tossed them with a sweet and spicy chili glaze. We wanted the coating for our tofu to be light, crispy, and nicely browned; to achieve this, we found that a combination of ¾ cup of cornstarch and ¼ cup of cornmeal was just right. Cutting our tofu into fingers gave us a greater coating-to-tofu ratio, which provided the right balance of crispy crust to creamy interior along with plenty of surface area for the clingy glaze to adhere. Soft tofu gave us a nice textural contrast between the crisp outside and the silky interior. To keep the light coating from getting greasy, we swapped the traditional skillet for nonstick so we could use less oil, resulting in tofu that was light and crispy. Firm or extra-firm tofu will also work, but it will taste drier. To make the dish spicier, use the higher amount of Asian chili-garlic sauce.

TOFU

28 ounces soft tofu, cut into 3-inch-long by ½-inch-thick fingers
    Salt and pepper
 ¾ cup cornstarch
 ¼ cup cornmeal
 ¼ cup vegetable oil

GLAZE

 ½ cup water
 ½ cup rice vinegar
 ⅓ cup sugar
 4 garlic cloves, minced
2–3 teaspoons Asian chili-garlic sauce
 2 teaspoons cornstarch
 ¼ cup minced fresh cilantro
    Salt

1. FOR THE TOFU: Spread tofu over paper towel–lined baking sheet, let drain for 20 minutes, then gently press dry with paper towels. Season with salt and pepper.

2. Adjust oven rack to middle position, place paper towel–lined plate on rack, and heat oven to 200 degrees. Combine cornstarch and cornmeal in shallow dish. Working with several tofu pieces at a time, coat thoroughly with cornstarch mixture, pressing gently to adhere; transfer to wire rack set in baking sheet.

3. Heat 2 tablespoons oil in 12-inch nonstick skillet over medium-high heat until shimmering. Cook half of tofu until crisp and lightly golden on all sides, 10 to 12 minutes. Lift tofu from oil, letting excess oil drip back into skillet, then transfer to plate in oven. Repeat with remaining 2 tablespoons oil and remaining tofu.

4. FOR THE GLAZE: Whisk water, vinegar, sugar, garlic, chili-garlic sauce, and cornstarch together in bowl. Wipe out now-empty skillet with paper towels, add glaze, and simmer over medium heat until syrupy and reduced to 1¼ cups, 2 to 3 minutes.

5. Off heat, stir in cilantro. Add tofu and turn to coat with glaze. Season with salt to taste and serve.

VARIATION

Honey-Mustard Glazed Tofu `GF`

Substitute orange juice for rice vinegar, ⅓ cup honey for sugar, 3 tablespoons Dijon mustard for Asian chili-garlic sauce, and 3 thinly sliced scallions for cilantro.

Grilled Soy-Ginger Glazed Tofu

SERVES 4 TO 6 `VEGAN` `GF`

✔ **WHY THIS RECIPE WORKS:** Tofu has a soft, silky texture that contrasts nicely with the crisp, browned crust that results from a quick stint on the grill, and its mild flavor gets a boost from the sweet-and-sour flavors of this Asian-style glaze. First we made the glaze by simmering soy sauce, sugar, mirin, fresh ginger, garlic, and chili-garlic sauce. Some cornstarch helped to thicken the sauce so it would cling to the tofu. We found the key to successfully grilled tofu was cutting it to the right shape and handling it carefully on the grill. We tried grilling tofu that had been cut into planks, strips, and cubes, and found that tofu cut lengthwise into 1-inch-thick planks fared best. This shape maximized surface contact, and the larger pieces were easier to turn. Using two spatulas provided the best leverage for flipping the delicate tofu. You can use either firm or extra-firm tofu in this recipe. In order for this recipe to be gluten-free, you must use gluten-free soy sauce or tamari. Dry sherry or white wine can be substituted for the mirin in this recipe. Be sure to handle the tofu gently on the grill, or it may break apart.

GLAZE

- ⅓ cup soy sauce
- ⅓ cup water
- ⅓ cup sugar
- ¼ cup mirin
- 1 tablespoon grated fresh ginger
- 2 garlic cloves, minced
- 2 teaspoons cornstarch
- 1 teaspoon Asian chili-garlic sauce

TOFU

- 28 ounces firm tofu, sliced lengthwise into 1-inch-thick planks
- 2 tablespoons vegetable oil
- Salt and pepper
- ¼ cup minced fresh cilantro

1. FOR THE GLAZE: Simmer soy sauce, water, sugar, mirin, ginger, garlic, cornstarch, and chili-garlic sauce in small saucepan over medium-high heat until thickened and reduced to ¾ cup, 5 to 7 minutes; transfer to bowl.

2. FOR THE TOFU: Spread tofu over paper towel–lined baking sheet, let drain for 20 minutes, then gently press dry with paper towels. Brush tofu with oil and season with salt and pepper.

3A. FOR A CHARCOAL GRILL: Open bottom vent completely. Light large chimney starter filled with charcoal briquettes (6 quarts). When top coals are partially covered with ash, pour two-thirds evenly over half of grill, then pour remaining coals

Taking tofu to the grill is a great way to get a crisp crust and lots of flavorful browning to contrast with the silky centers.

over other half of grill. Set cooking grate in place, cover, and open lid vent completely. Heat grill until hot, about 5 minutes.

3B. FOR A GAS GRILL: Turn all burners to high, cover, and heat grill until hot, about 15 minutes. Leave all burners on high.

4. Clean and oil cooking grate. Gently place tofu on grill, perpendicular to grate bars (on hotter part of grill if using charcoal). Cook (covered if using gas) until lightly browned on both sides, 6 to 10 minutes, gently flipping tofu halfway through cooking using 2 spatulas.

5. Turn all burners to medium if using gas, or slide tofu to cooler part of grill if using charcoal. Brush tofu with ¼ cup glaze and cook until well browned, 1 to 2 minutes. Flip tofu, brush with ¼ cup glaze, and cook until well browned, 1 to 2 minutes. Transfer tofu to platter, brush with remaining ¼ cup glaze, and sprinkle with cilantro. Serve.

VARIATION

Grilled Asian Barbecue Glazed Tofu `VEGAN` `GF`
In order for this recipe to be gluten-free, you must use gluten-free soy sauce or tamari.

Substitute following mixture for glaze: Simmer ⅓ cup hoisin sauce, ⅓ cup ketchup, 2 tablespoons rice vinegar,

1½ tablespoons soy sauce, 1½ tablespoons toasted sesame oil, 1 tablespoon grated fresh ginger, and 1 minced scallion in small saucepan over medium-high heat until thickened and reduced to ¾ cup, 5 to 7 minutes.

Caramel Tofu

SERVES 4 `VEGAN` `GF`

✓ **WHY THIS RECIPE WORKS:** For a tofu recipe that would convince even the most reluctant diner, we tossed cubes of tofu with cornstarch, lightly pan-fried them, and served them with a traditional Vietnamese salty-sweet caramel sauce. It is satisfying, surprisingly savory, and addictive. To achieve the tricky balance of sweet and savory in our sauce, we kept our caramel base simple and added a healthy dose of savory garlic, fish sauce substitute, and pepper. To ensure our caramel sauce was sweet but still had depth, we added a thinly sliced onion to caramelize in the sauce. Tossing the tofu with cornstarch and pan-frying it gave it an appealing crisp, browned exterior, then we drizzled it with the caramel sauce and topped it with some chopped peanuts for textural contrast and a sprinkling of cilantro and scallions for a fresh finish. You can use either firm or extra-firm tofu in this recipe. The caramel can go from amber-colored to burnt quickly, so it's important to have the cup and a half of water at the ready to stop the caramelization. Serve over rice.

With crisp, fried crusts, creamy centers, and a sweet and salty caramel sauce, this dish will appeal even to tofu skeptics.

21	ounces firm tofu, cut into ¾-inch cubes
	Salt and pepper
1¾	cups water
⅓	cup sugar
6	tablespoons vegetable oil
5	garlic cloves, minced
1	onion, halved and sliced thin
3	tablespoons fish sauce substitute (page 60)
½	cup plus 2 teaspoons cornstarch
½	cup fresh cilantro leaves
¼	cup dry-roasted peanuts, chopped
3	scallions, green parts only, sliced thin on bias

1. Spread tofu over paper towel–lined baking sheet, let drain for 20 minutes, then gently press dry with paper towels. Season with salt and pepper.

2. Meanwhile, pour ¼ cup water into medium saucepan, then sprinkle sugar evenly over top. Cook over medium heat, gently swirling pan occasionally (do not stir), until sugar melts and mixture turns color of maple syrup, 7 to 10 minutes.

3. Stir in 3 tablespoons oil and garlic and cook until fragrant, about 30 seconds. Off heat, slowly whisk in remaining 1½ cups water (sauce will sizzle). Stir in onion, fish sauce, 2 teaspoons cornstarch, and 1 teaspoon pepper. Return pan to medium-low heat and simmer vigorously until onions are

Making Caramel for Caramel Sauce

1. Pour water into medium saucepan, then sprinkle sugar evenly over top.

2. Cook over medium heat, gently swirling pan occasionally (do not stir), until sugar melts and mixture turns color of maple syrup, 7 to 10 minutes.

softened and sauce has thickened, 10 to 15 minutes. Remove from heat and cover to keep warm.

4. Spread remaining ½ cup cornstarch in shallow dish. Working with several tofu pieces at a time, coat thoroughly with cornstarch, pressing gently to adhere; transfer to plate.

5. Heat remaining 3 tablespoons oil in 12-inch nonstick skillet over high heat until just smoking. Add tofu and cook, turning as needed, until all sides are crisp and well browned, 10 to 15 minutes; transfer to paper towel–lined plate to drain. Transfer tofu to platter, drizzle with sauce, and sprinkle with cilantro, peanuts, and scallions. Serve.

Chile Braised Tofu

SERVES 4 `GF`

♥ **WHY THIS RECIPE WORKS:** Braising is a technique most often employed for cooking large, tough cuts of meat, because the low-and-slow, moist cooking method aids in breaking down the meat's collagen. So it may seem counterintuitive to braise tender, delicate tofu. But we found that the longer cooking time was perfect for infusing tofu with flavor as it cooked gently in a highly seasoned sauce, turning mild tofu into a boldly flavorful dish. For the sauce, we used dried ancho chiles to make a potent, Tex-Mex-inspired sauce. Soaking the dried chiles in boiling water for 15 minutes softened them so they easily broke down to a paste in the blender. The chiles alone, however, were too bitter and one-dimensional. Adding aromatic onion, garlic, and cumin made our sauce taste more well rounded, while a teaspoon of sugar helped to soften the bitter ancho flavor without making our sauce taste sweet. Tomato paste thickened the sauce and gave it more savory depth. Finishing the sauce with some butter gave it a silky richness, and a little lime juice brightened up the overall flavor of our dish. You can use either firm or extra-firm tofu in this recipe. Serve over rice.

- 3 **dried ancho chiles, stemmed, seeded, and torn into 1-inch pieces**
- 1 **onion, chopped**
- 1 **tablespoon tomato paste**
- 2 **garlic cloves, crushed and peeled**
- 1 **teaspoon ground cumin**
- 1 **teaspoon sugar**
  Salt
- 3 **tablespoons unsalted butter**
- 21 **ounces extra-firm tofu, sliced crosswise into ¾-inch-thick slabs**

Tofu is ideal for soaking up flavors—it needs just a 30-minute braise in a bold chile sauce to transform into a savory dinner.

- 1 **tablespoon lime juice plus lime wedges for serving**
- 2 **tablespoons minced fresh cilantro**

1. Pour 2 cups boiling water over anchos in bowl and let sit until very soft, about 15 minutes; drain anchos, discarding liquid. Process softened anchos, onion, ¼ cup water, tomato paste, garlic, cumin, sugar, and 1 teaspoon salt in blender until mixture forms thick but smooth puree, about 1 minute, stopping to scrape down sides of blender jar as needed,

2. Melt 1 tablespoon butter in 12-inch skillet over medium heat. Add ancho puree and cook, stirring often, until mixture is fragrant and thickens slightly, about 3 minutes. Whisk in 1¾ cups water until smooth.

3. Lay tofu in skillet in even layer and bring to simmer. Reduce heat to low and simmer gently until tofu is warmed through and flavors have melded, about 30 minutes.

4. Transfer tofu to platter. Stir remaining 2 tablespoons butter and lime juice into sauce and season with salt and pepper to taste. Pour sauce over tofu, sprinkle with cilantro, and serve with lime wedges.

Teriyaki Tofu

SERVES 4 TO 6 `VEGAN` `GF`

✔ WHY THIS RECIPE WORKS: Teriyaki sauce and tofu are a perfect match: Teriyaki sauce is easy to make from a few pantry ingredients, and the mild tofu readily soaks up the potent teriyaki flavors. First we made our teriyaki sauce from scratch with soy sauce, sugar, mirin, garlic, ginger, and some cornstarch for thickening. To encourage the tofu to absorb as much flavor as possible, we turned to the slow, gentle heat of the oven and cut the tofu into slabs. But when we pulled the tofu out of the oven, we were disappointed to find that the liquid released from the tofu during cooking had watered down the sauce, even after draining the tofu for a full 20 minutes. Since it was impossible to drain the tofu of all its liquid, we decided to account for the released liquid by overreducing the sauce to start. As the tofu baked, it released water into the concentrated sauce, diluting it to just the right flavor and thickness. You can use either firm or extra-firm tofu in this recipe. In order for this recipe to be gluten-free, you must use gluten-free soy sauce or tamari. Serve over rice.

½ cup water
½ cup soy sauce
½ cup sugar
2 tablespoons mirin
1 garlic clove, minced
1 teaspoon cornstarch
½ teaspoon grated fresh ginger
28 ounces extra-firm tofu, sliced crosswise into ¾-inch-thick slabs
Pepper
2 scallions, green parts only, sliced thin
Lime wedges

1. Adjust oven rack to middle position and heat oven to 350 degrees. Whisk water, soy sauce, sugar, mirin, garlic, cornstarch, and ginger together in small saucepan until smooth. Bring sauce to boil over medium-high heat, whisking occasionally, then reduce heat to medium-low and simmer vigorously until sauce is thickened and reduced to ¾ cup, 12 to 15 minutes.

2. Arrange tofu in even layer in 13 by 9-inch baking dish and pour sauce evenly over top. Cover with aluminum foil and bake until flavors have melded and tofu is warmed through, about 30 minutes, flipping tofu halfway through cooking.

3. Transfer tofu to platter. Season sauce with pepper to taste, pour over tofu, and sprinkle with scallions. Serve with lime wedges.

Asian Braised Tofu with Winter Squash and Coconut Milk

SERVES 4 `VEGAN` `GF`

✔ WHY THIS RECIPE WORKS: Nothing is better in the colder months than a hearty braised dish with layers of flavor, but most braising recipes are centered around meat. We wanted a vegetarian braise with satisfying and rich Asian flavors. We turned to tofu plus a combination of butternut squash and eggplant, which we browned first in a skillet. To build a flavorful base for our braise, we sautéed onion, garlic, ginger, and lemon grass until softened and fragrant. For the braising liquid, we combined vegetable broth plus coconut milk, which added richness and a creamy texture. The vegetables needed only 20 minutes to cook through and lend their flavors to the sauce, which we finished with some cilantro, lime juice, and soy sauce. You can use either firm or extra-firm tofu in this recipe. In order for this recipe to be gluten-free, you must use gluten-free soy sauce or tamari. For more information on how to prepare lemon grass, see page 160. Serve with rice.

14 ounces extra-firm tofu, cut into ¾-inch cubes
Salt and pepper
3 tablespoons vegetable oil
1½ pounds butternut squash, peeled, seeded, and cut into ½-inch pieces (4½ cups)
1 pound eggplant, cut into ½-inch pieces
1 onion, chopped fine
8 garlic cloves, minced
2 tablespoons grated fresh ginger
1 lemon grass stalk, trimmed to bottom 6 inches and bruised with back of chef's knife
1 (13.5-ounce) can coconut milk
½ cup vegetable broth
½ cup minced fresh cilantro
4 teaspoons lime juice
Soy sauce
2 scallions, sliced thin

1. Spread tofu over paper towel–lined baking sheet, let drain for 20 minutes, then gently press dry with paper towels. Season with salt and pepper.

2. Meanwhile, heat 1 tablespoon oil in 12-inch nonstick skillet over medium-high heat until shimmering. Add squash and cook until golden brown, 8 to 10 minutes; transfer to large bowl.

3. Add 1 tablespoon oil to now-empty skillet and heat over medium-high heat until shimmering. Add eggplant and cook until golden brown, 5 to 7 minutes; transfer to bowl with squash.

4. Add remaining 1 tablespoon oil to skillet and heat over medium heat until shimmering. Add onion and cook until softened and lightly browned, 5 to 7 minutes. Stir in garlic, ginger, and lemon grass and cook until fragrant, about 30 seconds. Stir in coconut milk, broth, browned squash-eggplant mixture, and drained tofu. Bring to simmer, reduce heat to medium-low, and cook until vegetables are softened and sauce is slightly thickened, 15 to 20 minutes.

5. Off heat, discard lemon grass. Stir in cilantro and lime juice. Season with soy sauce and pepper to taste. Sprinkle with scallions and serve.

Thai-Style Tofu and Basil Lettuce Cups

SERVES 4 ⬛ FAST ⬛ VEGAN ⬛ GF

✔ **WHY THIS RECIPE WORKS:** We took inspiration from the sweet, savory, and spicy flavors of Thai cuisine and made a stir-fried tofu filling to serve in crisp, cool lettuce cups. The key to the Thai-style low-temperature method is to sauté the aromatics slowly over medium-low heat. The aromatics infuse the oil as they cook, which gives the finished dish deep, complex flavor. We thought this technique would be perfect for infusing mild tofu with great flavor. For the aromatics, we combined garlic, basil, and Thai chiles. We reserved a portion of this mixture and added fish sauce substitute, vegetarian oyster sauce, sugar, and vinegar to make a balanced, savory stir-fry sauce. We added the oil, remaining aromatics, sliced shallot, and tofu (which we pulsed in a food processor, then pressed dry) to a cold skillet and cooked everything over medium heat until the tofu and shallots turned golden brown. At the end, we stirred in the sauce and more fresh basil leaves until wilted, then added some crunchy peanuts. You can use either firm or extra-firm tofu in this recipe. If fresh Thai chiles are unavailable, substitute two serranos or one jalapeño. For a milder version of the dish, remove the seeds and ribs from the chiles. Serve with steamed rice, if desired.

14 ounces extra-firm tofu, cut into 2-inch pieces
   Salt and pepper
2 cups fresh basil leaves
3 garlic cloves, peeled
6 green or red Thai chiles, stemmed
2 tablespoons fish sauce substitute (page 60), plus extra as needed
1 tablespoon vegetarian oyster sauce

To make a flavorful filling for Thai-style lettuce cups, we punch up mild tofu with basil, garlic, and spicy Thai chiles.

1 tablespoon sugar
1 teaspoon distilled white vinegar, plus extra as needed
3 shallots, halved and sliced thin
2 tablespoons vegetable oil
¼ cup dry-roasted peanuts, chopped
2 heads Bibb lettuce (1 pound), leaves separated
   Red pepper flakes

1. Spread tofu over paper towel–lined baking sheet, let drain for 20 minutes, then gently press dry with paper towels. Season with salt and pepper.

2. Meanwhile, process 1 cup basil, garlic, and chiles in food processor until finely chopped, 6 to 10 pulses, scraping down sides of bowl as needed. Transfer 1 tablespoon basil mixture to small bowl and stir in fish sauce, oyster sauce, sugar, and vinegar. Transfer remaining basil mixture to 12-inch nonstick skillet.

3. Pulse tofu in now-empty food processor until coarsely chopped, 3 to 4 pulses. Line baking sheet with clean paper towels. Spread processed tofu over prepared baking sheet and press gently with paper towels to dry.

4. Stir dried tofu, shallots, and oil into skillet with basil mixture and cook over medium heat, stirring occasionally, until tofu and shallots are browned, 10 to 15 minutes. (Mixture should start to sizzle after about 1½ minutes; adjust heat as needed.)

5. Add reserved basil mixture and continue to cook, stirring constantly, until well coated, about 1 minute. Stir in remaining 1 cup basil and cook, stirring constantly, until wilted, 30 to 60 seconds. Off heat, stir in peanuts. Transfer mixture to platter and serve with lettuce leaves, pepper flakes, extra fish sauce, and extra vinegar.

Glazed Caribbean Tofu with Rice and Pigeon Peas

SERVES 4 TO 6   VEGAN   GF

✔ **WHY THIS RECIPE WORKS:** A glaze made with curry and pineapple preserves, and brightened with a little lime juice, ensures this tofu is anything but mild mannered. While the tofu drained, we started cooking rice to serve with the tofu. Enriching the rice's cooking liquid with coconut milk made it a creamy, rich companion for the spicy-sweet tofu, and adding onion, jalapeño, and pigeon peas lent complementary flavor, texture, and heartiness. Canned pigeon peas (popular in West Indian cooking) can be found in most supermarkets; however, black-eyed peas or kidney beans can be substituted if necessary. You can use either firm or extra-firm tofu in this recipe. For more heat, include the jalapeño seeds and ribs.

28 ounces firm tofu, halved lengthwise, then cut crosswise into ¾-inch-thick squares
    Salt and pepper
1   tablespoon curry powder
1   onion, chopped
2   jalapeño chiles, stemmed, seeded, and minced
¼   cup vegetable oil
1½ cups long-grain white rice
1   (15-ounce) can pigeon peas, rinsed
1   (13.5-ounce) can coconut milk
1   cup plus 3 tablespoons water
½   cup pineapple preserves
2   tablespoons lime juice
¼   teaspoon red pepper flakes

1. Spread tofu over paper towel–lined baking sheet, let drain for 20 minutes, then gently press dry with paper towels. Season with salt and pepper and sprinkle evenly with curry powder.

2. Meanwhile, cook onion, jalapeños, and 2 tablespoons oil in large saucepan over medium-high heat until vegetables are softened, about 3 minutes. Stir in rice and cook until opaque, about 1 minute. Stir in peas, coconut milk, 1 cup water, and 1 teaspoon salt. Bring to boil, then reduce heat to low, cover, and cook until rice is tender, about 20 minutes. Season with salt and pepper to taste.

3. Microwave pineapple preserves in bowl until bubbling, about 1 minute, then whisk in remaining 3 tablespoons water, lime juice, and pepper flakes.

4. Heat remaining 2 tablespoons oil in 12-inch nonstick skillet over medium-high heat until just smoking. Add half of tofu and cook until golden and crisp on all sides, about 5 minutes; transfer to paper towel–lined plate. Repeat with remaining tofu using oil left in pan, then return all tofu to skillet. Add pineapple mixture and simmer, turning tofu to coat, until glaze thickens, about 1 minute. Serve with rice.

Shepherd's Pie

SERVES 4 TO 6

✔ **WHY THIS RECIPE WORKS:** Shepherd's pie has universal appeal as a hearty, homey meal. To make a satisfying vegetarian version, we looked to the gravy to provide rich, meaty flavor. First, we sautéed umami-rich mushrooms and tomato paste with onion and garlic to create lots of flavor-boosting fond, then we deglazed the pan with Madeira wine before adding the broth. But the real key to ensuring rich flavor turned out to be veggie protein crumbles. When crumbled apart and cooked in our rich gravy, we found their texture and flavor added depth and appealing chew. To round out our pie, we added chopped carrots, thyme, and a bay leaf to the gravy, then we whipped up some mashed potatoes, with an egg yolk for added structure, for the traditional topping. Piping the mashed potatoes on top of the filling turned out to be far easier and neater than trying to spread them over the wet, saucy base. Using a fork to create ridges that would pick up good browning under the broiler was the perfect final touch. If using frozen veggie protein crumbles, do not thaw them before adding them to the skillet.

2½ pounds russet potatoes, peeled and cut into 1-inch pieces
    Salt and pepper
4   tablespoons unsalted butter, melted
½   cup milk
1   large egg yolk
8   scallions, green parts only, sliced thin

Topping Shepherd's Pie

1. Place mashed potatoes in large zipper-lock bag and snip off 1 corner to make 1-inch opening.

2. Pipe potatoes evenly over filling, covering entire surface.

3. Smooth potatoes with back of spoon, then make ridges over surface using fork.

NOTES FROM THE TEST KITCHEN

Getting to Know Veggie Protein Crumbles

Made of seasoned, textured soy protein, veggie protein crumbles make a great vegetarian stand-in for ground meat. They readily soak up flavor and have a firm, chewy texture that adds a satisfying meatiness to dishes like pasta sauces, casseroles, chilis, and stir-fries. With lots of protein and little to no fat or sugar, they're also a healthy choice. Veggie protein crumbles come in several forms—you can find them frozen, refrigerated, and dehydrated (with instructions to reconstitute them before using). While the textures can vary pretty widely from brand to brand, we found that all types worked well in our recipes. We have had good luck with **Lightlife Smart Ground Original**. If you are vegan or gluten-free, be sure to check the ingredients carefully and look for a vegan or gluten-free brand. Veggie protein crumbles tend to be a bit salty, so season your recipe with a light hand.

2 teaspoons vegetable oil
1 onion, chopped
4 ounces white mushrooms, trimmed and chopped
1 tablespoon tomato paste
2 garlic cloves, minced
2 tablespoons Madeira or ruby port
2 tablespoons all-purpose flour
2½ cups vegetable broth
2 teaspoons vegetarian Worcestershire sauce
2 sprigs fresh thyme
1 bay leaf
2 carrots, peeled and chopped
12 ounces veggie protein crumbles, broken into small pieces

1. Place potatoes, 1 tablespoon salt, and enough water to cover in medium saucepan. Bring to boil over high heat, then reduce heat to medium-low and simmer until potatoes are tender and tip of paring knife inserted into potato meets no resistance, 8 to 10 minutes.

2. Drain potatoes, return to saucepan, and cook over low heat, shaking pot occasionally, until surface moisture on potatoes has evaporated, about 1 minute. Off heat, mash potatoes well, then stir in melted butter. Whisk milk and egg yolk together in small bowl, then stir into potatoes. Stir in scallions and season with salt and pepper to taste. Cover and set aside.

3. Heat oil in broiler-safe 10-inch skillet over medium heat until shimmering. Add onion, mushrooms, and ¼ teaspoon pepper and cook until vegetables begin to soften, 4 to 6 minutes. Stir in tomato paste and garlic and cook until bottom of skillet is dark brown, about 2 minutes.

4. Stir in Madeira and cook, scraping up any browned bits, until evaporated, about 1 minute. Stir in flour and cook for 1 minute. Stir in broth, Worcestershire, thyme sprigs, bay leaf, and carrots and bring to boil, scraping up any browned bits. Reduce heat to medium-low and simmer gently until carrots and mushrooms are tender, 10 to 15 minutes. Discard thyme sprigs and bay leaf. Stir in veggie protein crumbles and season with salt and pepper to taste.

5. Adjust oven rack 5 inches from broiler element and heat broiler. Place mashed potatoes in large zipper-lock bag and snip off bottom corner to make 1-inch opening. Pipe potatoes evenly over filling, covering entire surface. Smooth potatoes with back of spoon, then make ridges over surface using fork. Place skillet on rimmed baking sheet and broil until potatoes are golden and filling is bubbly, 10 to 15 minutes. Let cool for 10 minutes before serving.

Pan-Seared Tempeh Steaks with Chimichurri Sauce

SERVES 4 VEGAN GF

✓ **WHY THIS RECIPE WORKS:** Made from whole fermented soybeans and a mix of grains, tempeh has a firmer, chewier texture than tofu, but it is just as good at soaking up flavor. Looking for an easy but impressive tempeh recipe, we gave it a similar treatment to steak. Marinating the tempeh in a highly seasoned base infused it with flavor, then patting the tempeh dry and pan-searing it created a crispy edge and made the texture more cohesive. Next, we wanted to balance the tempeh's earthy flavor by serving it with a bright herb sauce. Chimichurri sauce is a traditional condiment for steak that combines parsley, wine vinegar, oil, lots of garlic, oregano, and a good dose of red pepper flakes. It paired perfectly with our tempeh, lending bright flavor and richness to the seared "steaks." In order for this recipe to be gluten-free, you must use gluten-free tempeh.

- ¼ cup water
- 6 tablespoons red wine vinegar
- 6 garlic cloves, minced
- 2 teaspoons dried oregano
- ½ teaspoon red pepper flakes
- 1 pound tempeh, cut into 3½-inch-long by ⅜-inch-thick slabs
- 1 cup fresh parsley leaves
- ¾ cup extra-virgin olive oil
  Salt and pepper

1. Combine water, ¼ cup vinegar, half of garlic, 1 teaspoon oregano, and ¼ teaspoon pepper flakes in 1-gallon zipper-lock bag. Add tempeh, press out air, seal, and toss to coat. Refrigerate tempeh for at least 1 hour or up to 24 hours, flipping bag occasionally.

2. Pulse parsley, ½ cup oil, remaining 2 tablespoons vinegar, remaining garlic, remaining 1 teaspoon oregano, remaining ¼ teaspoon pepper flakes, and ½ teaspoon salt in food processor until coarsely chopped, about 10 pulses. Transfer to bowl and season with salt and pepper to taste.

3. Remove tempeh from marinade and pat dry with paper towels. Heat 2 tablespoons oil in 12-inch nonstick skillet over medium heat until shimmering. Add 4 pieces tempeh and cook until golden brown on first side, 2 to 4 minutes.

4. Flip tempeh, reduce heat to medium-low, and continue to cook until golden brown on second side, 2 to 4 minutes; transfer to platter. Wipe out skillet with paper towels and repeat with remaining 2 tablespoons oil and remaining tempeh. Serve with parsley sauce.

We take advantage of tempeh's hearty texture by marinating and pan-searing it, then topping it with a bright herb sauce.

VARIATION

Pan-Seared Tempeh Steaks with Chermoula Sauce VEGAN GF

Omit oregano. Substitute lemon juice for red wine vinegar, ¼ teaspoon cayenne for red pepper flakes, and cilantro for parsley. Add ½ teaspoon ground cumin and ½ teaspoon paprika to tempeh marinade. Add ½ teaspoon ground cumin and ½ teaspoon paprika to sauce.

Cutting Tempeh into Slabs

1. Cut each piece crosswise into two 3½-inch-long pieces.

2. Next cut each piece horizontally into ⅜-inch-thick slabs.

Getting to Know Tempeh

While tofu has hit the mainstream, tempeh might not be as familiar. Tempeh is made by fermenting cooked soybeans, then forming the mixture into a firm, dense cake. Some versions also contain beans, grains, and flavorings. It serves as a good meat substitute and is a mainstay of many vegetarian diets—it's particularly popular in Southeast Asia. It has a strong nutty flavor, but it also will absorb flavors easily. And because it's better than tofu at holding its shape when cooked, it's a versatile choice for many dishes from sandwiches and tacos to curry. It's also a healthy choice, since it's high in protein, cholesterol-free, and low in fat and contains many essential vitamins and minerals. Tempeh is sold in most supermarkets and can be found with different grain and flavoring combinations. We use five-grain tempeh in our recipes, but any plain variety will work. If you are gluten-free, be sure to look for a gluten-free brand of tempeh.

Curried Tempeh with Cauliflower and Peas

SERVES 4 TO 6   VEGAN   GF

✔ **WHY THIS RECIPE WORKS:** With its deep, intense flavors, curry makes a perfect pairing for strong-tasting tempeh. To create truly complex curry flavor, we started by toasting curry powder and garam masala in a dry skillet. A serrano chile delivered the right combination of flavor and spice. Blooming glutamate-rich tomato paste with our seasonings added a meaty, savory element to our curry. Canned diced tomatoes pulsed in a food processor formed the base of the sauce. Simmering the tempeh in the curry for 15 minutes helped to infuse it with the curry's flavor. To round out our curry, we added cauliflower, simmering it in the sauce until tender, and convenient frozen peas. Finishing our tempeh curry with a dash of coconut milk imparted a little extra richness. For more heat, use the higher amount of serranos and/or include the serrano seeds and ribs. In order for this recipe to be gluten-free, you must use gluten-free tempeh. Serve over rice.

2 tablespoons curry powder
1½ teaspoons garam masala
1 (14.5-ounce) can diced tomatoes
¼ cup vegetable oil

2 onions, chopped fine
3 garlic cloves, minced
1 tablespoon grated fresh ginger
1–1½ serrano chiles, stemmed, seeded, and minced
1 tablespoon tomato paste
½ head cauliflower (1 pound), cored and cut into 1-inch florets
8 ounces tempeh, cut into 1-inch pieces
1¼ cups water
Salt
1 cup frozen peas
¼ cup coconut milk or heavy cream
2 tablespoons minced fresh cilantro

1. Toast curry powder and garam masala in 10-inch skillet over medium-high heat, stirring constantly, until spices darken slightly and become fragrant, about 1 minute. Transfer to bowl. Pulse tomatoes and their juice in food processor until coarsely chopped, 3 to 4 pulses.

2. Heat 3 tablespoons oil in Dutch oven over medium-high heat until shimmering. Add onions and cook, stirring occasionally, until caramelized, about 10 minutes.

3. Reduce heat to medium. Clear center of pot and add remaining 1 tablespoon oil, garlic, ginger, serrano, and tomato paste. Cook, mashing mixture into skillet, until fragrant, about 1 minute. Add cauliflower and tempeh and cook, stirring constantly, until well coated with spices.

4. Stir in processed tomatoes, water, and 1 teaspoon salt, scraping up any browned bits. Increase heat to medium-high and bring to simmer. Cover, reduce heat to medium, and cook, stirring occasionally, until vegetables are tender, 10 to 15 minutes. Stir in peas and coconut milk and cook until heated through, about 2 minutes. Off heat, season with salt to taste and sprinkle with cilantro. Serve.

Grating Ginger

Although we love the floral pungency of fresh ginger, it has a distractingly fibrous texture when minced or coarsely grated. To prevent this, we use a rasp-style grater to grate the ginger to a fine pulp.

To grate fresh ginger finely, peel small section of large knob of ginger, then carefully grate peeled portion, using rest of ginger as handle.

The key to our tempeh tacos is a bold taco seasoning of chili powder, oregano, onion, garlic, lime juice, and brown sugar.

Making Your Own Taco Shells

1. In 8-inch skillet, heat ¾ cup vegetable oil to 350 degrees. Using tongs, slip half of corn tortilla into hot oil and submerge it with metal spatula. Fry until just set, but not brown, about 30 seconds.

2. Flip tortilla. Hold tortilla open about 2 inches while keeping bottom submerged in oil. Fry until golden brown, about 1½ minutes. Flip again and fry other side until golden brown.

3. Transfer shell, upside down, to paper towel–lined baking sheet to drain. Repeat with remaining tortillas, keeping oil between 350 and 375 degrees. For best results, use homemade taco shells immediately.

Tempeh Tacos

SERVES 4 TO 6 `FAST` `VEGAN` `GF`

✔ **WHY THIS RECIPE WORKS:** Much more than just a stand-in for more traditional beef or chicken versions, these tempeh tacos have their own nutty flavor and tender but firm texture. Rather than rely on questionable supermarket seasoning packets, we created our own taco mix to complement the tempeh. Chili powder and dried oregano added the right depth without overpowering the tempeh. To make their flavor fuller and rounder, we bloomed the spices briefly in hot oil. This simple step gave the filling a rich, deep flavor that was markedly better than stirring the spices in raw. For a light sauce to carry the flavors of the spices and keep the filling cohesive, we used a combination of tomato sauce and vegetable broth. To give the sauce sweet-and-sour balance, we added brown sugar and lime juice. In order for this recipe to be gluten-free, you must use gluten-free tempeh and taco shells. You can use store-bought taco shells or make your own following the instructions. If you use store-bought shells, warm them in the oven before serving. Serve with your favorite taco toppings.

1 tablespoon vegetable oil
1 onion, chopped fine
3 tablespoons chili powder
4 garlic cloves, minced
1 teaspoon dried oregano
1 pound tempeh, crumbled into ¼-inch pieces
1 (8-ounce) can tomato sauce
1 cup vegetable broth
1 teaspoon packed brown sugar
2 tablespoons minced fresh cilantro
1 tablespoon lime juice
Salt and pepper
12 taco shells

1. Heat oil in 12-inch skillet over medium heat until shimmering. Add onion and cook until softened, about 5 minutes. Stir in chili powder, garlic, and oregano and cook until fragrant, about 30 seconds. Stir in tempeh and cook until lightly browned, about 5 minutes.

2. Stir in tomato sauce, broth, and sugar and simmer until thickened, about 2 minutes. Off heat, stir in cilantro and lime juice and season with salt and pepper to taste. Divide filling evenly among taco shells, and serve.

CHAPTER 6

Salads Big and Small

For salads with rice and grains, see page 157.
For salads with beans and soy, see page 203.

■ FAST (Less than 45 minutes start to finish) ■ VEGAN ■ GLUTEN-FREE

Photos: Grilled Vegetable and Bread Salad; French Potato Salad with Dijon Mustard and Fines Herbes

FOOLPROOF VINAIGRETTES

For a well-balanced vinaigrette that wouldn't separate, we whisked the oil and vinegar together with a little mayonnaise, which acted as an emulsifier. You can use red wine, white wine, or champagne vinegar here; however, it is important to use high-quality ingredients. These vinaigrettes each make about ¼ cup, enough to dress about 8 to 10 cups of greens.

Classic Vinaigrette

MAKES ¼ CUP `FAST` `GF`

This dressing works well with all types of greens.

- 1 **tablespoon wine vinegar**
- 1½ **teaspoons minced shallot**
- ½ **teaspoon regular or light mayonnaise**
- ½ **teaspoon Dijon mustard**
- ⅛ **teaspoon salt**
   Pinch pepper
- 3 **tablespoons extra-virgin olive oil**

Whisk vinegar, shallot, mayonnaise, mustard, salt, and pepper together in small bowl until smooth. Whisking constantly, slowly drizzle in oil until emulsified. (Vinaigrette can be refrigerated for up to 2 weeks.)

Lemon Vinaigrette

MAKES ¼ CUP `FAST` `GF`

This is best for dressing mild greens.

- ¼ **teaspoon grated lemon zest plus 1 tablespoon juice**
- ½ **teaspoon regular or light mayonnaise**
- ½ **teaspoon Dijon mustard**
- ⅛ **teaspoon salt**
   Pinch pepper
   Pinch sugar
- 3 **tablespoons extra-virgin olive oil**

Whisk lemon zest and juice, mayonnaise, mustard, salt, pepper, and sugar together in small bowl until smooth. Whisking constantly, slowly drizzle in oil until emulsified. (Vinaigrette can be refrigerated for up to 2 weeks.)

Balsamic-Mustard Vinaigrette

MAKES ¼ CUP `FAST` `GF`

This is best for dressing assertive greens.

- 1 **tablespoon balsamic vinegar**
- 2 **teaspoons Dijon mustard**
- 1½ **teaspoons minced shallot**
- ½ **teaspoon regular or light mayonnaise**
- ½ **teaspoon minced fresh thyme**
- ⅛ **teaspoon salt**
   Pinch pepper
- 3 **tablespoons extra-virgin olive oil**

Whisk vinegar, mustard, shallot, mayonnaise, thyme, salt, and pepper together in small bowl until smooth. Whisking constantly, slowly drizzle in oil until emulsified. (Vinaigrette can be refrigerated for up to 2 weeks.)

Herb Vinaigrette

MAKES ¼ CUP `FAST` `GF`

Serve this vinaigrette immediately.

- 1 **tablespoon wine vinegar**
- 1 **tablespoon minced fresh parsley or chives**
- 1½ **teaspoons minced shallot**
- ½ **teaspoon minced fresh thyme, tarragon, marjoram, or oregano**
- ½ **teaspoon regular or light mayonnaise**
- ½ **teaspoon Dijon mustard**
- ⅛ **teaspoon salt**
   Pinch pepper
- 3 **tablespoons extra-virgin olive oil**

Whisk vinegar, parsley, shallot, thyme, mayonnaise, mustard, salt, and pepper together in small bowl until smooth. Whisking constantly, slowly drizzle in oil until emulsified.

Classic Vinaigrette

Walnut Vinaigrette

MAKES ¼ CUP `FAST` `GF`

- 1 **tablespoon wine vinegar**
- 1½ **teaspoons minced shallot**
- ½ **teaspoon regular or light mayonnaise**
- ½ **teaspoon Dijon mustard**
- ⅛ **teaspoon salt**
   Pinch pepper
- 1½ **tablespoons roasted walnut oil**
- 1½ **tablespoons extra-virgin olive oil**

Whisk vinegar, shallot, mayonnaise, mustard, salt, and pepper together in small bowl until smooth. Whisking constantly, slowly drizzle in oils until emulsified. (Vinaigrette can be refrigerated for up to 2 weeks.)

BOLD SALAD DRESSINGS

The bright, bold flavors of these dressings are perfect whether you want to dress up a simple side salad or make a satisfying salad worthy of the dinner table. For the Miso-Sesame, Orange-Lime, and Tahini-Lemon dressings, you will need about 1 tablespoon of dressing for every 2 cups of greens. For the thicker Creamy Garlic Dressing, you will need about 2 tablespoons of dressing for every 2 cups of greens.

Orange-Lime Dressing

MAKES ABOUT 1 CUP `VEGAN` `GF`

Although fresh-squeezed orange juice will taste best, any store-bought orange juice will work here. To avoid off-flavors, make sure to reduce the orange juice in a nonreactive stainless steel pan.

- 2 **cups orange juice**
- 3 **tablespoons lime juice**
- 2 **tablespoons extra-virgin olive oil**
- 1 **tablespoon honey**
- 1 **tablespoon minced shallot**
- ½ **teaspoon salt**
- ½ **teaspoon pepper**

Simmer orange juice in small saucepan over medium heat until slightly thickened and reduced to ⅔ cup, about 30 minutes. Transfer to medium bowl and refrigerate until cool, about 15 minutes. Whisk in remaining ingredients until smooth. (Dressing can be refrigerated for up to 4 days.)

Tahini-Lemon Dressing

MAKES ABOUT 1 CUP
`FAST` `VEGAN` `GF`

- 3 **tablespoons lemon juice**
- 2 **tablespoons tahini**
- 1 **scallion, minced**
- 1 **garlic clove, minced**
- ¾ **teaspoon salt**
- ¼ **teaspoon pepper**
- ¾ **cup extra-virgin olive oil**

Whisk lemon juice, tahini, scallion, garlic, salt, and pepper together in small bowl until smooth. Whisking constantly, slowly drizzle in oil until emulsified. (Dressing can be refrigerated for up to 4 days.)

Miso-Sesame Dressing

MAKES ABOUT 1 CUP
`FAST` `VEGAN` `GF`

We prefer the flavor of red miso in this dressing. Do not use powdered miso or the dressing will be overly salty and have a watery texture. See page 55 for information about buying miso. This vinaigrette also tastes great on cooked green beans. In order for this recipe to be gluten-free, you must use gluten-free soy sauce or tamari.

- 6 **tablespoons water**
- ¼ **cup rice vinegar**
- 7 **teaspoons red miso**
- 1 **tablespoon soy sauce**
- 1½ **teaspoons honey**
- 1 **(2-inch) piece ginger, peeled and chopped coarse**
- 1 **small garlic clove, chopped coarse**
- ¼ **cup canola oil**
- 1 **tablespoon toasted sesame oil**

Process water, vinegar, miso, soy sauce, honey, ginger, and garlic together in blender until ginger and garlic are finely chopped, about 15 seconds. With blender running, add oils in steady stream until incorporated, then continue to process until smooth, about 15 seconds. (Dressing can be refrigerated for up to 1 week.)

Miso-Sesame Dressing

Creamy Garlic Dressing

MAKES ABOUT 1½ CUPS `FAST` `GF`

Do not substitute low-fat or nonfat sour cream or mayonnaise here—the dressing will become harsh. This creamy, assertive dressing pairs well with bitter greens like escarole or chicory.

- ¾ **cup extra-virgin olive oil**
- 6 **tablespoons sour cream or mayonnaise**
- 3 **tablespoons lemon juice**
- 4 **teaspoons Dijon mustard**
- 1 **tablespoon white wine vinegar**
- 3 **garlic cloves, minced**
- ½ **teaspoon salt**
- ½ **teaspoon pepper**

Whisk all ingredients together in bowl until smooth. (Dressing can be refrigerated for up to 1 week.)

The Simplest Green Salad

SERVES 4 FAST VEGAN GF

✔ **WHY THIS RECIPE WORKS:** This quick and easy way to make a simple salad requires no measuring, no whisking, and (virtually) no thought. And you need only three ingredients: greens, extra-virgin olive oil, and vinegar. We also like to rub the bowl with a cut garlic clove to impart just a hint of flavor, and we season the salad with salt and pepper before serving. It is important to use high-quality ingredients, as there are no bells or whistles to camouflage old lettuce, flavorless oil, or harsh vinegar. Be sure to use interesting leafy greens, such as mesclun, arugula, or Bibb lettuce, rather than those with a more neutral flavor, such as iceberg lettuce.

Making the Simplest Green Salad

1. RUB BOWL WITH GARLIC: To impart subtle garlic flavor, rub inside of salad bowl with half clove of peeled garlic before adding lettuce.

2. ADD WASHED GREENS: Add washed and dried salad greens to bowl. We suggest 2 lightly packed cups per person for side salad.

3. DRIZZLE WITH OIL: Slowly drizzle greens with extra-virgin olive oil. Toss greens gently and repeat drizzling and tossing as needed until greens are lightly coated.

4. SEASON WITH VINEGAR, SALT, AND PEPPER: Finally, sprinkle greens with small amounts of vinegar, salt, and pepper to taste and toss gently to coat until salad tastes just right.

½ garlic clove, peeled
8 ounces (8 cups) lettuce, torn into bite-size pieces if necessary
Extra-virgin olive oil
Vinegar
Salt and pepper

Rub inside of salad bowl with garlic. Add lettuce. Holding thumb over mouth of olive oil bottle to control flow, slowly drizzle lettuce with small amount of oil. Toss greens very gently. Continue to drizzle with oil and toss gently until greens are lightly coated and just glistening. Sprinkle with small amounts of vinegar, salt, and pepper to taste and toss gently to coat. Serve.

Asparagus and Spinach Salad with Sherry Vinegar and Goat Cheese

SERVES 4 TO 6 FAST GF

✔ **WHY THIS RECIPE WORKS:** For a bright, fresh-flavored asparagus salad, the cooking method was paramount. Blanching and steaming both produced bland and sometimes mushy spears, while sautéing the asparagus over high heat delivered deep flavor and tender texture (and was quicker than bringing a pot of water to a boil). Strips of red pepper sautéed with the asparagus gave the salad a sweet, roasted flavor and bright color. Then we tossed the tender vegetables with baby spinach to round out the fresh, crisp composition. A zesty sherry vinegar dressing gave the asparagus bold flavor, and the addition of creamy, delicate goat cheese made our salad richer and more substantial.

6 tablespoons extra-virgin olive oil
1 red bell pepper, stemmed, seeded, and cut into 1 by ¼-inch strips
1 pound asparagus, trimmed and cut on bias into 1-inch lengths
Salt and pepper
1 shallot, sliced thin
1 tablespoon plus 1 teaspoon sherry vinegar
1 garlic clove, minced
6 ounces (6 cups) baby spinach
4 ounces goat cheese, cut into small chunks

1. Heat 2 tablespoons oil in 12-inch nonstick skillet over high heat until just smoking. Add bell pepper and cook until lightly browned, about 2 minutes. Stir in asparagus, ¼ teaspoon salt, and ⅛ teaspoon pepper and cook until asparagus is browned and almost tender, about 2 minutes. Stir in shallot and cook until softened and asparagus is crisp-tender, about 1 minute. Transfer to large plate and let cool for 5 minutes.

2. Meanwhile, whisk vinegar, garlic, ¼ teaspoon salt, and ⅛ teaspoon pepper together in bowl. Whisking constantly, drizzle in remaining 4 tablespoons oil.

3. Toss spinach with 2 tablespoons dressing in bowl, and divide among salad plates. Toss asparagus mixture with remaining dressing in now-empty bowl and arrange over spinach. Sprinkle with goat cheese and serve.

How to Measure Salad Greens

To lightly pack greens, drop handfuls into large glass measuring cup, then gently pat down using your fingertips.

VARIATIONS

Asparagus and Mesclun Salad with Cornichons and Hard-Cooked Eggs

SERVES 4 TO 6 [FAST] [GF]

5 tablespoons extra-virgin olive oil
1 pound asparagus, trimmed and cut on bias into 1-inch lengths
  Salt and pepper
2 tablespoons white wine vinegar
2 tablespoons minced cornichons
1 small shallot, minced
2 teaspoons chopped fresh tarragon
1 teaspoon chopped capers
6 ounces (6 cups) mesclun
3 Foolproof Hard-Cooked Eggs (page 379), peeled and chopped

1. Heat 1 tablespoon oil in 12-inch nonstick skillet over high heat until just smoking. Add asparagus, ¼ teaspoon salt, and ¼ teaspoon pepper and cook, stirring occasionally, until asparagus is browned and crisp-tender, about 4 minutes. Transfer to large plate and let cool for 5 minutes.

2. Meanwhile, whisk vinegar, cornichons, shallot, tarragon, capers, and ¼ teaspoon pepper together in bowl. Whisking constantly, drizzle in remaining 4 tablespoons oil.

3. Toss mesclun with 2 tablespoons dressing in bowl, and divide among salad plates. Toss asparagus with remaining dressing and arrange over mesclun. Garnish with chopped eggs and serve.

Asparagus and Watercress Salad with Thai Flavors

SERVES 4 TO 6 [FAST] [VEGAN] [GF]
The asparagus in this salad tastes best when well chilled. Five minutes in the freezer makes quick work of cooling down the just-cooked asparagus.

2 tablespoons lime juice
2 tablespoons fish sauce substitute (see page 60)
2 tablespoons water
2 teaspoons sugar
1 small garlic clove, minced
1 small jalapeño chile, stemmed, seeded, and minced
2 carrots, peeled and cut into 2-inch-long matchsticks
1 tablespoon vegetable oil
1 pound asparagus, trimmed and cut on bias into 1-inch lengths
6 ounces (6 cups) watercress
¼ cup chopped fresh mint
⅓ cup unsalted dry-roasted peanuts, chopped

1. Whisk lime juice, fish sauce, water, sugar, garlic, and jalapeño together in bowl until sugar dissolves. Measure out and reserve 1 tablespoon dressing separately in large bowl. Add carrots to remaining dressing and let sit.

2. Heat oil in 12-inch nonstick skillet over high heat until just smoking. Add asparagus and cook, stirring occasionally, until browned and crisp-tender, about 4 minutes. Transfer to large plate and place in freezer 5 minutes.

3. Toss watercress with reserved 1 tablespoon dressing in bowl, and divide among salad plates. Toss asparagus and mint with carrot mixture and arrange over watercress. Sprinkle with peanuts and serve.

Cutting Asparagus on the Bias

After trimming tough ends from asparagus, cut on bias into 1-inch lengths.

Arugula Salad with Grapes, Fennel, Gorgonzola, and Pecans

SERVES 6 `FAST` `GF`

✔ **WHY THIS RECIPE WORKS:** Arugula has a lively, peppery bite, so it's important to choose accompaniments that can stand up to its assertive character. We found that the sweet and salty notes of fruits and cheeses worked well as supporting players to arugula; tasters especially liked a combination of red grapes and bold Gorgonzola cheese. Thinly sliced fennel gave the salad more substance, and chopped pecans added a crunch that provided a nice counterpoint. As for the dressing, we started with oil, white wine vinegar, and shallot and added a spoonful of apricot jam for some fruity sweetness, pulling the flavors of the salad right in line.

4 teaspoons apricot jam

3 tablespoons white wine vinegar

1 small shallot, minced

Salt and pepper

3 tablespoons extra-virgin olive oil

½ small fennel bulb, fronds minced, stalks discarded, bulb halved, cored, and sliced thin

5 ounces (5 cups) baby arugula

6 ounces red seedless grapes, halved lengthwise (1 cup)

3 ounces Gorgonzola cheese, crumbled (¾ cup)

½ cup pecans, toasted and chopped

1. Whisk jam, vinegar, shallot, ¼ teaspoon salt, and ¼ teaspoon pepper together in large bowl. Whisking constantly, drizzle in oil. Stir in sliced fennel and let stand for 15 minutes.

2. Add arugula, grapes, and fennel fronds and toss gently to coat. Season with salt and pepper to taste and divide among salad plates. Sprinkle with Gorgonzola and pecans and serve.

VARIATION

Arugula Salad with Oranges, Feta, and Sugared Pistachios

SERVES 6 `FAST` `GF`

Chopped toasted pistachios can be substituted for the sugared pistachios if desired.

SUGARED PISTACHIOS

½ cup shelled pistachios

1 large egg white, lightly beaten

⅓ cup sugar

SALAD

2 oranges

2 tablespoons plus 2 teaspoons lemon juice

5 teaspoons orange marmalade

1 small shallot, minced

1 tablespoon minced fresh mint

Salt and pepper

3 tablespoons extra-virgin olive oil

5 ounces (5 cups) baby arugula

3 ounces feta cheese, crumbled (¾ cup)

1. **FOR THE SUGARED PISTACHIOS:** Adjust oven rack to middle position and heat oven to 325 degrees. Toss pistachios with egg white in bowl. Using slotted spoon, transfer nuts to 8-inch square baking dish lined with parchment paper; discard excess egg white. Stir in sugar until nuts are completely coated. Bake, stirring mixture every 5 to 10 minutes, until coating turns nutty brown, 25 to 30 minutes; transfer to plate and let cool.

2. **FOR THE SALAD:** Cut away peel and pith from oranges. Holding fruit over bowl, use paring knife to slice between membranes to release segments. Cut segments in half widthwise and let drain in fine-mesh strainer.

3. Whisk lemon juice, marmalade, shallot, mint, ¼ teaspoon salt, and ⅛ teaspoon pepper in large bowl. Whisking constantly, drizzle in oil. Add arugula and oranges and toss gently to combine. Season with salt and pepper to taste and divide among salad plates. Sprinkle with feta and sugared pistachios and serve.

Segmenting an Orange

1. Using paring knife, cut away peel and pith from orange.

2. Holding fruit over bowl, slice between membranes to release individual orange segments.

Citrus Salad with Watercress, Dried Cranberries, and Pecans

SERVES 4 TO 6 **FAST** **GF**

✔ WHY THIS RECIPE WORKS: Savory salads made with oranges and grapefruit are an impressive way to showcase colorful winter fruit—but only if you can tame the bitterness of the grapefruit and prevent the fruit's ample juice from drowning the other components. We started by treating the fruit with salt to counter the grapefruits' bitter notes (a technique we've used in the past with coffee and eggplant). Draining the seasoned fruit enabled us to preemptively remove the excess juice, and reserving some to use in the dressing for the salad greens helped to make the salad more cohesive. Toasted, salted nuts added richness that contrasted nicely with the fruit and the assertively flavored greens, and dried fruit added texture and sweetness. We prefer to use navel oranges, tangelos, or Cara Caras in this salad. Blood oranges can also be used, but because they are smaller you'll need four of them.

2 red grapefruits
3 oranges
1 teaspoon sugar
   Salt and pepper
1 teaspoon unsalted butter
½ cup pecans, chopped coarse
3 tablespoons extra-virgin olive oil
1 small shallot, minced
1 teaspoon Dijon mustard
4 ounces (4 cups) watercress, torn into
   bite-size pieces
⅔ cup dried cranberries

1. Cut away peel and pith from grapefruits and oranges. Cut each fruit in half from pole to pole, then slice crosswise into ¼-inch-thick pieces. Transfer fruit to bowl, toss with sugar and ½ teaspoon salt, and let sit for 15 minutes.

2. Melt butter in 8-inch skillet over medium heat. Add pecans and ½ teaspoon salt and cook, stirring often, until pecans are lightly browned and fragrant, 2 to 4 minutes; transfer to paper towel–lined plate.

3. Drain fruit in colander set over bowl, reserving 2 tablespoons juice. Arrange fruit on platter and drizzle with oil. Whisk reserved juice, shallot, and mustard together in medium bowl. Add watercress, ⅓ cup cranberries, and ¼ cup pecans and toss to coat. Arrange watercress mixture over fruit, leaving 1-inch border of fruit around edges. Sprinkle with

Cutting Up Citrus for Salad

1. Cut away peel and pith from fruit, then halve fruit from pole to pole.

2. Slice each half crosswise into ¼-inch-thick pieces.

NOTES FROM THE TEST KITCHEN

Buying Salad Greens

Not only is there a dizzying array of greens available at the supermarket now, but in a good market you can buy the same greens more than one way: full heads, prewashed in a bag, in a plastic clamshell, and loose in bulk bins. Which is the right choice for you? A sturdy lettuce like romaine can be washed and stored for up to a week, making it a good option for many nights' worth of salads. Prewashed bags of baby spinach, arugula, and mesclun mix offer great convenience, but be sure to turn over the bags and inspect the greens as closely as you can; the sell-by date alone doesn't ensure quality, so if you see moisture in the bag or hints of blackened leaf edges, move on.

Don't buy bags of already-cut lettuce that you can otherwise buy as whole heads, like romaine or Bibb or red leaf. Precut lettuce will be inferior in quality because the leaves begin to spoil once they are cut (bagged hearts of romaine are fine, but stay away from bags of cut romaine). Endive and radicchio are always sold in heads, and because they are sturdy and will last a while, they are nice to have on hand to complement other greens and just to add more interest to a salad. And when a special salad is planned for company, for the best results you should buy the greens either the day of the party or the day before.

remaining ⅓ cup cranberries and remaining ¼ cup pecans. Season with salt and pepper to taste and serve.

VARIATIONS

Citrus Salad with Arugula, Golden Raisins, and Walnuts FAST GF

Substitute coarsely chopped walnuts for pecans, arugula for watercress, and ½ cup golden raisins for cranberries.

Citrus Salad with Napa Cabbage, Dried Cherries, and Cashews FAST VEGAN GF

Substitute coarsely chopped salted roasted cashews for pecans, omitting butter and step 2. Substitute ½ small head napa cabbage, cored and sliced thin (4 cups), for watercress, and dried cherries for cranberries.

Citrus Salad with Radicchio, Dates, and Smoked Almonds FAST VEGAN GF

Substitute coarsely chopped smoked almonds for pecans, omitting butter and step 2. Substitute 1 small head radicchio, halved, cored, and sliced thin, for watercress, and chopped pitted dates for cranberries.

Salad with Crispy Spiced Chickpeas and Honey-Mustard Vinaigrette

SERVES 4 TO 6 GF

✔ **WHY THIS RECIPE WORKS:** For this salad, we put a vegetarian spin on the classic flavors of caramelized onions, smoky bacon, and creamy mustard dressing. To replace the salty, smoky flavor of the bacon, we fried protein-rich chickpeas in oil until they were toasty and crisp, then tossed them with smoked paprika, cumin, sugar, salt, and cayenne pepper. Crushing some of the chickpeas ensured that they clung to the lettuce. A scant teaspoon of mayonnaise whisked with a combination of sweet, viscous honey, seedy whole-grain mustard, and apple cider vinegar gave us a vinaigrette that was creamy yet not so heavy that it weighed down the delicate mesclun leaves. Charring sliced red onions under the broiler brought out their sweetness and added an extra layer of smoke to this hearty salad. Mesclun is typically a mixture of such specialty greens as arugula, Belgian endive, and radicchio.

SALAD

- 1 teaspoon smoked paprika
- 1 teaspoon sugar
- ½ teaspoon ground cumin
    Salt

We dress up a simple mesclun salad with a honey-mustard vinaigrette and a topping of spiced pan-fried chickpeas.

- ¼ teaspoon cayenne pepper
- ¾ cup plus 1 tablespoon vegetable oil
- 1 (15-ounce) can chickpeas, rinsed and thoroughly dried
- 1 red onion, halved and sliced through root end
- 6 ounces (6 cups) mesclun

DRESSING

- 1½ tablespoons apple cider vinegar
- 1 tablespoon whole-grain mustard
- 2 teaspoons honey
- 1½ teaspoons grated lemon zest
- ¾ teaspoon mayonnaise
- ¼ teaspoon salt
- ¼ cup extra-virgin olive oil

1. FOR THE SALAD: Combine paprika, sugar, cumin, ½ teaspoon salt, and cayenne in large bowl; set aside. Heat ¾ cup oil in large Dutch oven over high heat until just smoking. Add chickpeas, partially cover (to prevent splattering), and cook, stirring occasionally, until deep golden brown and crisp, 10 to 12 minutes.

2. Using slotted spoon, transfer chickpeas to paper towel–lined plate and let drain briefly. Toss chickpeas in large bowl with reserved spices, let cool slightly, then crush about half of chickpeas into coarse crumbs with fork.

3. Adjust oven rack 6 inches from broiler element and heat broiler. Toss onion with remaining 1 tablespoon oil and ¼ teaspoon salt and spread over aluminum foil–lined rimmed baking sheet. Broil onions, checking often, until edges are charred, 6 to 8 minutes, stirring halfway through cooking. Let onions cool slightly, then add to spiced chickpeas along with mesclun and toss to combine.

4. FOR THE DRESSING: Whisk vinegar, mustard, honey, lemon zest, mayonnaise, and salt together in bowl. Whisking constantly, drizzle in oil. Drizzle dressing over salad and toss to combine. Serve.

Salad with Herbed Baked Goat Cheese and Vinaigrette

SERVES 6

✔ **WHY THIS RECIPE WORKS:** Warm goat cheese salad, a French classic, can easily misfire, becoming nothing more than flavorless, oozing cheese melted onto limp greens. We wanted creamy cheese infused with the flavor of fresh herbs, surrounded by crisp, golden breading, all cradled in lightly dressed greens. For cheese rounds with an exceptionally crisp crust, we found that white Melba toast crumbs beat out fresh bread crumbs and other cracker crumbs. Freezing the breaded goat cheese rounds for 30 minutes before baking them ensured a crunchy coating and a smooth, but not melted, interior. Just like in the finest French bistros, we served our warm breaded goat cheese on hearty greens, lightly dressed with a classic vinaigrette. Prepare the salad components while the cheese is in the freezer, then toss the greens and vinaigrette while the cheese cools a bit after baking. Hearty salad greens, such as a mix of arugula and frisée, work best here.

- 2 **tablespoons red wine vinegar**
- 1 **tablespoon Dijon mustard**
- 1 **teaspoon minced shallot**
   Salt and pepper
- 6 **tablespoons extra-virgin olive oil**
- 14 **ounces (14 cups) mixed hearty salad greens**
- 1 **recipe Herbed Baked Goat Cheese**

Combine vinegar, mustard, shallot, and ¼ teaspoon salt in large bowl. Whisking constantly, drizzle in oil. Season with pepper to taste. Add greens, toss gently to coat, then divide among salad plates. Arrange warm goat cheese on greens and serve.

HERBED BAKED GOAT CHEESE

MAKES 12 ROUNDS
The baked goat cheese should be served warm.

- 3 **ounces (2 cups) white Melba toasts**
- 1 **teaspoon pepper**
- 3 **large eggs**
- 2 **tablespoons Dijon mustard**
- 1 **tablespoon minced fresh thyme**
- 1 **tablespoon minced fresh chives**
- 12 **ounces firm goat cheese**
   Extra-virgin olive oil

1. Process Melba toasts in food processor to fine, even crumbs, about 1½ minutes; transfer to medium bowl and stir in pepper. In separate medium bowl, whisk eggs and mustard together. In third medium bowl, combine thyme and chives.

2. Using cheese wire or dental floss, slice cheese into 12 evenly sized pieces. Roll each piece cheese into ball, then roll in herbs to coat lightly. Working with 6 pieces at a time, roll in egg mixture, then coat with crumbs, pressing to help coating adhere. Flatten each ball into 1-inch-thick disk and lay on large plate. Freeze cheese until firm, at least 30 minutes or up to 1 week.

3. Adjust oven rack to top position and heat oven to 475 degrees. Brush tops and sides of cheese evenly with olive oil. Bake until crumbs are golden brown and cheese is slightly soft, 7 to 12 minutes. Using thin metal spatula, transfer cheese to paper towel–lined plate and let cool 3 minutes before serving.

VARIATION

Salad with Apples, Walnuts, Dried Cherries, and Herbed Baked Goat Cheese

SERVES 6
Hearty salad greens, such as a mix of arugula and frisée, work best here.

- 1 **cup dried cherries**
- 2 **tablespoons cider vinegar**
- 1 **tablespoon Dijon mustard**
- 1 **teaspoon minced shallot**
   Salt and pepper
- ¼ **teaspoon sugar**
- 6 **tablespoons extra-virgin olive oil**
- 14 **ounces (14 cups) mixed hearty salad greens**

2 Granny Smith apples, cored, quartered, and sliced ⅛ inch thick

½ cup walnuts, toasted and chopped

1 recipe Herbed Baked Goat Cheese (page 247)

1. Soak cherries in ½ cup hot water in bowl until plump, about 10 minutes; drain.

2. Combine vinegar, mustard, shallot, ¼ teaspoon salt, and sugar in large bowl. Whisking constantly, drizzle in oil. Season with pepper to taste. Add greens, toss gently to coat, then divide among salad plates. Sprinkle with cherries, apples, and walnuts. Arrange warm goat cheese on top and serve.

NOTES FROM THE TEST KITCHEN

Putting Together a Perfect Salad

PAIRING LEAFY GREENS WITH VINAIGRETTES

Vinaigrettes are the best choice for dressing leafy greens; heavier, creamier dressings are best on sturdy lettuce such as romaine or iceberg. Most salad greens fall into one of two categories: mellow or assertive. When you're making a green salad, it's important to choose your vinaigrette recipe carefully to complement the greens you are using.

MELLOW-FLAVORED

Boston, Bibb, mâche, mesclun, red and green leaf, red oak, and flat-leaf spinach. Their mild flavors are easily overpowered and are best complemented by a simple dressing such as a classic red wine vinaigrette.

ASSERTIVE OR SPICY GREENS

Arugula, escarole, chicory, Belgian endive, radicchio, frisée, and watercress. These greens can easily stand up to strong flavors like mustard, shallots, and balsamic vinegar and can also be paired with a slightly sweet or creamy vinaigrette.

HOW TO DRESS A SALAD

Getting a properly dressed salad requires a few simple steps. You never want to dump a set amount of dressing over greens and assume they will be perfectly coated. Once you have overdressed your salad, there is no going back, so it's best to lightly drizzle and toss the salad with tongs a couple of times, tasting as you go. Generally, ¼ cup vinaigrette dresses 8 to 10 cups of lightly packed greens, enough for 4 to 6 side salads or 2 to 3 dinner salads. For the freshest salad, make sure to dress your greens just before serving. Also, for just a hint of garlic flavor, rub the inside of the salad bowl with half a clove of peeled garlic before adding the lettuce.

Greek Salad

SERVES 6 TO 8 FAST GF

✔ **WHY THIS RECIPE WORKS:** Most versions of Greek salad consist of iceberg lettuce, chunks of green pepper, and a few pale wedges of tomato, sparsely dotted with cubes of feta and garnished with one forlorn olive. For our Greek salad, we aimed a little higher: We wanted a salad with crisp ingredients and bold flavors, highlighted by briny kalamata olives and tangy feta, all blended together with a bright-tasting dressing infused with fresh herbs. For a dressing with balanced flavor, we used a combination of lemon juice and red wine vinegar and added fresh oregano, olive oil, and a small amount of garlic. We poured the dressing over fresh vegetables, including romaine lettuce, tomatoes, onions, and cucumbers, as well as fresh mint and parsley, roasted peppers, and a generous sprinkling of feta and olives. For efficiency, prepare the other salad ingredients while the onion and cucumber marinate. Use a salad spinner to dry the lettuce thoroughly after washing; any water left clinging to the leaves will dilute the dressing.

VINAIGRETTE

3 tablespoons red wine vinegar

2 teaspoons minced fresh oregano

1½ teaspoons lemon juice

1 garlic clove, minced

½ teaspoon salt

⅛ teaspoon pepper

6 tablespoons extra-virgin olive oil

SALAD

1 cucumber, peeled, halved lengthwise, seeded, and sliced ⅛ inch thick

½ red onion, sliced thin

2 romaine lettuce hearts (12 ounces), torn into 1½-inch pieces

2 large tomatoes, cored, seeded, and cut into wedges

1 cup jarred roasted red peppers, cut into ½ by 2-inch strips

¼ cup fresh parsley leaves, torn

¼ cup fresh mint leaves, torn

20 pitted kalamata olives, quartered lengthwise

5 ounces feta cheese, crumbled (1¼ cups)

1. **FOR THE VINAIGRETTE:** Whisk vinegar, oregano, lemon juice, garlic, salt, and pepper together in large bowl. Whisking constantly, drizzle in oil.

2. **FOR THE SALAD:** Stir cucumber and onion into vinaigrette and let stand for 20 minutes. Add lettuce, tomatoes, red peppers, parsley, and mint and toss gently to coat. Transfer salad to wide, shallow serving bowl and sprinkle with olives and feta. Serve.

Caramelized sweet potatoes and a bright pomegranate vinaigrette are the perfect complement to earthy, hearty kale.

Kale Salad with Sweet Potatoes and Pomegranate Vinaigrette

SERVES 4 GF

✔ **WHY THIS RECIPE WORKS:** We love the earthy flavor of uncooked kale, but the texture of raw kale can be a little tough. Many recipes call for tossing it with dressing and letting it tenderize in the fridge overnight. This method didn't deliver the tender leaves we were after, and the long sitting time wasn't very convenient. Luckily, we found another technique that worked better and faster: massaging. Squeezing and massaging the kale broke down the cell walls in much the same way that heat would, darkening the leaves and turning them silky. Caramelized roasted sweet potatoes, shredded radicchio, crunchy pecans, a sprinkling of Parmesan cheese, and a sweet pomegranate vinaigrette turned our salad into a hearty meal. Pomegranate molasses can be found in the international aisle of well-stocked supermarkets; if you can't find it, substitute 2 tablespoons of lemon juice, 2 teaspoons of mild molasses, and 1 teaspoon of honey. Tuscan kale (also known as dinosaur or Lacinato kale) is more tender than curly-leaf and red kale; if using curly-leaf or red kale, increase the massaging time to 5 minutes. Do not use baby kale.

SALAD

1½ pounds sweet potatoes, peeled, quartered lengthwise, and cut crosswise into ½-inch pieces
1 tablespoon extra-virgin olive oil
   Salt and pepper
12 ounces Tuscan kale, stemmed and sliced crosswise into ½-inch-wide strips (7 cups)
½ head radicchio (5 ounces), cored and sliced thin
½ cup pecans, toasted and chopped
   Shaved Parmesan cheese

VINAIGRETTE

2 tablespoons water
1½ tablespoons pomegranate molasses
1 small shallot, minced
1 tablespoon honey
1 tablespoon cider vinegar
¼ teaspoon salt
¼ teaspoon pepper
⅓ cup extra-virgin olive oil

1. FOR THE SALAD: Adjust oven rack to middle position and heat oven to 400 degrees. Toss sweet potatoes with oil and season with salt and pepper. Lay potatoes in single layer on rimmed baking sheet and roast until bottom edges are browned on both sides, 25 to 30 minutes, flipping potatoes halfway through roasting time. Transfer potatoes to plate and let cool for 20 minutes.

2. Meanwhile, vigorously squeeze and massage kale with hands until leaves are uniformly darkened and slightly wilted, about 1 minute.

3. FOR THE VINAIGRETTE: Whisk water, pomegranate molasses, shallot, honey, vinegar, salt, and pepper together in large bowl. Whisking constantly, drizzle in oil.

4. Add roasted potatoes, kale, and radicchio to vinaigrette and toss gently to coat. Transfer to platter and sprinkle with pecans and shaved Parmesan to taste. Serve.

Massaging Kale

Vigorously squeeze and massage kale with hands on counter or in large bowl until leaves are uniformly darkened and slightly wilted, about 1 minute for flat-leaf kale (or 5 minutes for curly-leaf or red kale).

Our modern take on Caesar salad features a combination of kale and spinach and a creative vegetarian Caesar dressing.

Kale Caesar Salad

SERVES 4 AS A MAIN DISH OR 6 AS A SIDE DISH

✓ **WHY THIS RECIPE WORKS:** We wanted a hearty kale salad with a classic Caesar dressing, but this dressing relies on anchovies to add the salty, umami backbone that defines its flavor. To mimic this flavor, we opened a jar of pickles—not for the spears, but for the juice. With a balance of acid, salt, and spice, the pickle brine lent depth to our dressing. We also cut the extra-virgin olive oil with canola oil, which made for a less harsh flavor. Squeezing and massaging the raw kale broke down its cellular structure, giving it an appealing tenderness, and adding a little baby spinach lightened the dish. For crisp but not rock-hard croutons, we tossed bread cubes with water, then browned them in a skillet with olive oil and a little garlic. Some Parmesan gave the croutons a cheesy outer crunch. A rasp-style grater makes quick work of turning the garlic into a paste. Tuscan kale (also known as dinosaur or Lacinato kale) is more tender than curly-leaf and red kale; if using curly-leaf or red kale, increase the massaging time to 5 minutes. Do not use baby kale.

Making Kale Caesar Salad

1. MAKE CROUTONS: For crisp croutons, toss cubed bread with water and salt, then add to nonstick skillet with oil and cook until browned and crisp. Toss with garlic paste and Parmesan.

2. MAKE DRESSING: After whisking in egg yolks and seasonings, add olive oil and canola oil in slow, steady stream while whisking constantly until dressing is creamy and fully emulsified.

3. TENDERIZE KALE: To tenderize raw kale quickly, vigorously squeeze and massage leaves with hands until darkened and slightly wilted, about 1 minute.

4. TOSS, DRIZZLE WITH DRESSING, AND TOSS AGAIN: Toss kale, spinach, and croutons together in large bowl. Drizzle with dressing, toss gently to coat, and serve.

CROUTONS

- 5 tablespoons extra-virgin olive oil
- ½ teaspoon garlic, minced to paste
- ½ loaf ciabatta, cut into ¾-inch cubes (4½ cups)
- ¼ cup water
- ¼ teaspoon salt
- 2 tablespoons finely grated Parmesan cheese

SALAD

- 2 tablespoons dill pickle juice
- ½ teaspoon garlic, minced to paste
- 2 large egg yolks
- 2 tablespoons lemon juice
- ½ teaspoon vegetarian Worcestershire sauce
  Salt and pepper

- 6 tablespoons extra-virgin olive oil
- ¼ cup canola or vegetable oil
- 1 ounce finely grated Parmesan cheese (½ cup)
- 12 ounces Tuscan kale, stemmed and sliced crosswise into ½-inch-wide strips (7 cups)
- 4 ounces (4 cups) baby spinach

1. FOR THE CROUTONS: Combine 1 tablespoon oil and garlic paste in bowl. In separate bowl, toss bread cubes with water and salt, squeezing to help bread absorb water. Combine remaining 4 tablespoons oil and bread in 12-inch nonstick skillet and cook over medium-high heat, stirring often, until browned and crisp, 7 to 10 minutes.

2. Off heat, clear center of skillet, add garlic mixture, and cook using residual heat until fragrant, about 10 seconds. Transfer crouton mixture to clean bowl, sprinkle with Parmesan, and toss until well combined.

3. FOR THE SALAD: Whisk pickle juice and garlic paste together in medium bowl and let sit for 10 minutes. Whisk in egg yolks, lemon juice, Worcestershire, and ¼ teaspoon salt. Whisking constantly, slowly drizzle in olive oil and canola oil. Whisk in Parmesan and season with pepper to taste.

4. Vigorously squeeze and massage kale with hands until leaves are uniformly darkened and slightly wilted, about 1 minute. Toss kale, spinach, and croutons together in large bowl. Drizzle with dressing, toss gently to coat, and serve.

Mâche and Mint Salad with Cucumber

SERVES 6 TO 8 FAST VEGAN GF

✓ **WHY THIS RECIPE WORKS:** This simple and refreshing salad makes an easy but interesting side—the perfect salad for having with company. The combination of delicate mâche and thinly sliced cucumber is light and elegant, and mint and crunchy pine nuts reinforce the dish's theme. We kept the dressing traditional with just lemon juice, fresh parsley, thyme, and garlic, plus briny capers for bursts of bold flavor. Mâche is a baby lettuce with sweet, nutty flavor. It is a very delicate green, so be sure to handle it gently and make sure it is dried thoroughly before tossing with the vinaigrette. If you can't find mâche, you can substitute either baby spinach or mesclun.

- 12 ounces (12 cups) mâche
- ½ cup chopped fresh mint
- 1 cucumber, sliced thin
- ⅓ cup pine nuts, toasted

Storing and Preparing Salad Greens

HOW TO STORE SALAD GREENS

For crisp lettuce, such as iceberg and romaine, core the lettuce, wrap it in moist paper towels, and refrigerate in a partially open plastic produce bag or zipper-lock bag.

For leafy greens, such as arugula, baby spinach, and mesclun, store in the original plastic container or bag if prewashed. If not prewashed, wash and dry thoroughly in a salad spinner and store directly in the spinner between layers of paper towels, or lightly roll in paper towels and store in a zipper-lock bag left slightly open.

For tender lettuce, such as Boston and Bibb, if the lettuce comes with the roots attached, leave the lettuce portion attached to the roots and store in the original plastic container, a plastic produce bag, or a zipper-lock bag left slightly open. If the lettuce is without roots, wrap it in moist paper towels and refrigerate in a plastic produce bag or a zipper-lock bag left slightly open.

HOW TO WASH AND DRY SALAD GREENS

Nothing ruins a salad faster than biting into gritty leaves, and trying to dress a salad while the greens are still wet is a losing battle—the dressing will slide off and the water from the greens will dilute the dressing. To wash salad greens, fill a sink or salad spinner bowl with cool water, add the cut greens, and gently swish them around. Let the grit settle to the bottom of the sink or bowl, then lift the greens out and drain the water. Repeat until the greens no longer release any dirt. Dry the greens in a salad spinner, stopping several times to dump out excess moisture from the bottom of the spinner. Keep spinning the greens until no more moisture accumulates in the spinner.

- 1 tablespoon lemon juice
- 1 tablespoon minced fresh parsley
- 1 tablespoon capers, rinsed and minced
- 1 teaspoon minced fresh thyme
- 1 garlic clove, minced
- ¼ teaspoon salt
- ¼ teaspoon pepper
- ¼ cup extra-virgin olive oil

Gently toss mâche, mint, cucumber, and pine nuts together in large bowl. In small bowl, whisk lemon juice, parsley, capers, thyme, garlic, salt, and pepper together. Whisking constantly, drizzle in oil. Drizzle dressing over salad and toss gently to coat. Serve.

Here are some of the most common salad greens you'll find at the market. With such a wide array of greens to choose from, it's good to know how to mix and match them to build interesting salads. Many are great on their own, but others are generally best used to add texture or color to other salads. No matter what type of greens you buy, make sure to select the freshest ones possible and avoid any that are wilted, bruised, or discolored.

TYPE/DESCRIPTION	YIELD	SERVING SUGGESTIONS
Arugula (also called Rocket or Roquette) Delicate dark green leaves with a peppery bite; sold in bunches, usually with roots attached, or prewashed in cellophane bags; bruises easily and can be very sandy, so wash thoroughly in several changes of water before using.	5-ounce bag (5 cups) 6-ounce bunch (3 cups)	Serve alone for a full-flavored salad, or add to romaine, Bibb, or Boston lettuce to give a spicy punch; for a classic salad, combine with Belgian endive and radicchio.
Belgian Endive Small, compact head of firm white or pale yellow leaves; should be completely smooth and blemish-free; slightly bitter flavor and crisp texture; one of the few salad greens we routinely cut rather than tear; remove whole leaves from the head and slice crosswise into bite-size pieces.	4-ounce head (1 cup sliced)	Add to watercress or to Bibb, Boston, or loose-leaf lettuce; combine with diced apples, blue cheese, and walnuts; use whole leaves in place of crackers with dips and flavorful soft cheeses.
Bibb Lettuce Small, compact heads; pale- to medium-green leaves; soft, buttery outer leaves; inner leaves have a surprising crunch and a sweet, mild flavor.	8-ounce head (8 cups)	Combine with watercress or endive, or with Boston, loose-leaf, or romaine lettuce; great tossed with fresh herbs (whole parsley leaves, chives, or dill).
Boston Lettuce Loose, fluffy head, ranging in color from pale green to red-tipped; similar in texture and flavor to Bibb lettuce, but with softer leaves.	8-ounce head (8 cups)	Combine with baby spinach, watercress, or endive, or with Bibb or romaine lettuce; terrific as a bed for fritters and pan-fried veggie cakes.
Chicory (also called Curly Endive) Loose, feathery head of bright green, bitter leaves; texture is somewhat chewy.	10-ounce head (10 cups)	Add to bitter green salads or use sparingly to add punch to mild mixed greens; great with Balsamic-Mustard or Walnut Vinaigrette or Creamy Garlic Dressing (see pages 240–241).
Escarole A kind of chicory with tough, dark green leaves and a mildly bitter flavor; inner leaves are slightly milder.	15-ounce head (15 cups)	Use as an accent to romaine; serve on its own with Balsamic-Mustard Vinaigrette (page 240).
Frisée A kind of chicory; milder in flavor than other chicories, but with similar feathery leaves; pale green to white in color.	10-ounce head (4 cups)	Combine with arugula or watercress, or with Boston or Bibb lettuce; serve on its own with warm balsamic vinaigrette; great when paired with toasted walnuts and herbed goat cheese.

	TYPE/DESCRIPTION	YIELD	SERVING SUGGESTIONS
	Iceberg A large, round, tightly packed head of pale green leaves; very crisp and crunchy, with minimal flavor.	1-pound head (12 cups)	Cut into wedges and top with creamy dressing; tear into chunks and toss with Bibb, Boston, or loose-leaf lettuce.
	Loose-Leaf Lettuces (specifically Red Leaf and Green Leaf) Ruffled dark red or green leaves that grow in big, loose heads; versatile, with a soft yet crunchy texture; green leaf is crisp and mild; red leaf is earthier.	12-ounce head (12 cups)	Pair red leaf with romaine lettuce or watercress; pair green leaf with arugula, radicchio, or watercress; great on sandwiches and veggie burgers, or as a bed for prepared salads.
	Mâche (also called Lamb's Tongue or Lamb's Lettuce) Small heads of three or four stems of small, sweet, deep green leaves; very delicate; usually sold prewashed in bags; if buying heads, wash thoroughly, can be sandy.	4-ounce bag (4 cups)	Combine with arugula or watercress; perfect on its own with crumbled goat cheese and Classic Vinaigrette (page 240).
	Mesclun (also called Mesclune, Spring Mix, Field Greens) A mix of up to 14 different baby greens, including spinach, red leaf, oak leaf, frisée, radicchio, green leaf; delicate leaves; flavors range from mild to slightly bitter depending on the blend.	4 ounces bagged or loose (4 cups)	Great as a delicate salad; terrific paired with goat cheese and Lemon Vinaigrette (page 240).
	Radicchio Tight heads of red or deep purple leaves streaked with white ribs; bitter flavor.	10-ounce head (3 cups)	Cut into ribbons and mix with arugula, endive, or watercress, or with red or green leaf, Boston, or Bibb lettuce; adds color to any salad.
	Romaine Long, full heads with stiff and deep green leaves; crisp, crunchy leaves with a mild, earthy flavor; also sold in bags of three romaine hearts; tough outer leaves should be discarded from full heads.	6-ounce heart (4 cups) 14-ounce head (9 cups)	A great all-purpose lettuce; mix with spinach, watercress, arugula, endive, or radicchio, or with Boston, Bibb, or red leaf lettuce; good on sandwiches and veggie burgers.
	Spinach (Flat-Leaf, Curly-Leaf, and Baby) All varieties are vibrant green with an earthy flavor; choose tender flat-leaf or baby spinach for raw salads; tough curly-leaf spinach is better steamed and sautéed; rinse loose spinach well to remove dirt; varieties available prewashed in bags.	5-ounce bag (5 cups) 11-ounce bunch (5 cups)	Delicious mixed with arugula, watercress, or napa cabbage, or with romaine, Bibb, Boston, or loose-leaf lettuce; classic as a wilted salad with creamy dressing or warm lemon vinaigrette.
	Watercress Delicate dark green leaves with tough, bitter stems; refreshing mustardlike flavor similar to arugula; usually sold in bunches, sometimes available prewashed in bags; if buying watercress in bunches, take care to wash thoroughly.	2-ounce bunch (2 cups)	Adds flavorful punch and texture to mildly flavored or tender greens such as Bibb or Boston lettuce; delicious on its own with tart green apples, blue cheese, and a mustard-based dressing.

Pan-Roasted Pear Salad with Watercress, Parmesan, and Pecans

SERVES 4 TO 6 `GF`

✓ **WHY THIS RECIPE WORKS:** For our pear salad recipe, we wanted a simple technique for caramelizing pears that wouldn't overcook the fruit. We sautéed the quartered pears over medium-high heat, which prevented the interiors from softening too much, tossing them with sugar before cooking to encourage better browning. Since we were already using balsamic vinegar in the vinaigrette (its fruity flavor accentuated the pear flavor), we tried adding a couple of extra tablespoons to the hot pan with the roasted pears. The result gave us our best pear salad recipe: The extra vinegar instantly reduced to form a glazy coating on the pears, perfectly matching the flavor of the salad. We prefer Bartlett pears for this recipe, but Bosc pears can also be used. The pears should be ripe but firm; the flesh at the neck of the pear should give slightly when pressed gently with a finger. If using Bartletts, look for pears that are starting to turn from green to yellow. Romaine lettuce may be substituted for the green leaf.

 3 pears (8 ounces each), quartered and cored
2½ teaspoons sugar
 Salt and pepper
 2 tablespoons plus 2 teaspoons extra-virgin olive oil
 ¼ cup balsamic vinegar
 1 small shallot, minced
 ½ head green leaf lettuce (6 ounces), torn into 1-inch pieces
 4 ounces (4 cups) watercress
 ¾ cup pecans, toasted and chopped
 Shaved Parmesan cheese

1. Toss pears, 2 teaspoons sugar, ¼ teaspoon salt, and ⅛ teaspoon pepper in bowl. Heat 2 teaspoons oil in 12-inch nonstick skillet over medium-high heat until just smoking. Add pears, either cut side down, in single layer and cook until golden brown on first side, 2 to 4 minutes. Using fork, tip each pear onto second cut side and cook until light brown, 2 to 4 minutes.

2. Turn off heat, leave skillet on burner, and add 2 tablespoons vinegar. Gently stir until vinegar becomes glazy and coats pears, about 30 seconds. Transfer pears to large plate and let cool to room temperature, about 45 minutes. Cut each pear quarter crosswise into ½-inch pieces.

3. Whisk remaining 2 tablespoons vinegar, remaining ½ teaspoon sugar, and shallot together in large bowl. Whisking constantly, drizzle in remaining 2 tablespoons oil. Add lettuce, watercress, and pears to bowl and toss gently to coat. Season with salt and pepper to taste and divide among salad plates. Sprinkle with pecans and top with shaved Parmesan to taste. Serve.

VARIATIONS

Pan-Roasted Pear Salad with Radicchio, Blue Cheese, and Walnuts `GF`

Substitute 1 large head radicchio, quartered, cored, and cut crosswise into ½-inch pieces (4 cups), for watercress; 1 cup crumbled Gorgonzola or Stilton cheese for Parmesan; and toasted and chopped walnuts for pecans.

Pan-Roasted Pear Salad with Frisée, Goat Cheese, and Almonds `GF`

Substitute 1 head frisée, torn into 1-inch pieces (4 cups), for watercress; 1 cup crumbled goat cheese for Parmesan; and toasted sliced almonds for pecans.

Pan-Roasting Pears

Cook pears in nonstick skillet until golden brown on first side, 2 to 4 minutes. Using fork, tip each pear onto second cut side and cook until light brown, 2 to 4 minutes.

Warm Spinach Salad with Feta and Pistachios

SERVES 6 `FAST` `GF`

✓ **WHY THIS RECIPE WORKS:** We wanted a foolproof recipe for a warm spinach salad that would provide a nice alternative to basic greens. We experimented with various types of spinach and found that flat-leaf and baby spinach became soft and mushy, but hardier curly-leaf spinach stood up to the heat. To make the dressing, we began by heating 2 tablespoons of fruity extra-virgin olive oil in a Dutch oven along with some minced shallot. For bright citrus flavor, we also simmered a strip of lemon zest in the oil, then we added fresh lemon juice before tossing in the spinach off the heat. The residual heat in the pot steamed the spinach until it was warm and just wilted. Peppery sliced radishes, crumbled feta, and toasted pistachios rounded out our updated spinach salad. Be sure to cook the spinach just until it begins to wilt; any longer and the leaves will overcook and clump. Be sure to use curly-leaf spinach here; do not substitute flat-leaf or baby spinach.

1½ ounces feta cheese, crumbled (⅓ cup)

3 tablespoons extra-virgin olive oil

1 (2-inch) strip lemon zest plus 1½ tablespoons juice

1 shallot, minced

2 teaspoons sugar

10 ounces curly-leaf spinach, stemmed and torn into bite-size pieces

6 radishes, trimmed and sliced thin

3 tablespoons chopped unsalted pistachios, toasted

Salt and pepper

1. Place feta on plate and freeze until slightly firm, about 15 minutes.

2. Cook oil, lemon zest, shallot, and sugar in Dutch oven over medium-low heat until shallot is softened, about 5 minutes. Off heat, discard zest and stir in lemon juice. Add spinach, cover, and let steam off heat until it just begins to wilt, about 30 seconds.

3. Transfer spinach mixture and liquid left in pot to large bowl. Add radishes, pistachios, and chilled feta and toss to combine. Season with salt and pepper to taste, divide among salad plates, and serve.

VARIATIONS

Warm Spinach Salad with Apple, Blue Cheese, and Pecans FAST GF

Use any sweet apple here such as Fuji, Jonagold, Pink Lady, Jonathan, Macoun, or Gala.

Substitute orange zest and juice for lemon, ½ chopped sweet apple for radishes, crumbled blue cheese for feta, and pecans for pistachios.

Warm Spinach Salad with Strawberries, Goat Cheese, and Almonds FAST GF

We recommend using Ruby Red grapefruit in this salad.

Substitute grapefruit zest and juice for lemon, 6 thinly sliced strawberries for radishes, and almonds for pistachios.

Making Lemon Zest Strips

Using vegetable peeler, remove strips of zest from lemon, making sure to avoid bitter-tasting white pith.

This perfectly simple salad features buttery avocados, sweet cherry tomatoes, sliced shallot, and shaved ricotta salata.

Avocado Salad with Tomato and Radish

SERVES 6 FAST GF

WHY THIS RECIPE WORKS: In salad, buttery avocados demand an acidic dressing to cut their richness. Using a little mayonnaise as an emulsifier allowed us to make a creamy dressing with equal parts vinegar and olive oil. To add flavor and textural contrast, we steered clear of leafy greens and relied on crunchier vegetables like fennel and radishes and sweet, juicy fruits like cherry tomatoes and mango. A garnish of salty cheese was the perfect finishing touch to complement the creamy avocado. Arranging the dressed avocado chunks below the other ingredients maximized visual appeal by preventing the avocado from turning the salad a murky army green. Crumbled feta cheese can be substituted for the ricotta salata. Don't skip the step of soaking the shallot—the ice water helps tame its oniony bite.

All About Avocados

The flesh of this rich fruit has a creamy, buttery texture and a delicate flavor. Here are our tips for buying and storing avocados.

BUYING AVOCADOS

Although there are many varieties of avocado, in the United States small, rough-skinned Hass avocados are the most common, and we prefer them in the test kitchen. When they're ripe, their skin turns from green to dark purply black, and the fruit yields to a gentle squeeze. However, when selecting avocados, keep in mind that a soft avocado may be a bruised fruit rather than a ripe one. A good test is to try to flick the small stem off the avocado. If it comes off easily and you can see green underneath it, the avocado is ripe. If you see brown underneath after prying it off, the avocado is not usable. If it does not come off easily, the avocado is still unripe. Because these fruits ripen off the tree, that's not a problem; you just have to plan ahead when buying them and allow time for them to ripen.

RIPENING AND STORING AVOCADOS

At room temperature, rock-hard avocados generally ripen within two days, but they may ripen unevenly. Once ripe, they will last two days, on average, if kept at room temperature. Avocados may take up to four days to ripen in the refrigerator, but they will ripen more evenly. Ripe avocados last about five days when refrigerated, though some discoloration may occur. Store them toward the front of the refrigerator, on the middle to bottom shelves, where temperatures are more moderate. Avocado flesh does not freeze well; as the water in the fruit crystallizes, it destroys the avocado's creamy texture, leaving it mushy and watery when defrosted.

KEEPING LEFTOVER AVOCADO GREEN

Avocado flesh turns brown very quickly once it is exposed to air. To minimize the effect, it's best to prepare avocados at the last moment whenever possible. However, if you need to use only half of an avocado, you can store the leftover half by rubbing 1 tablespoon of olive oil on all of the exposed avocado flesh, allowing the excess oil to drip into a shallow bowl, then placing the avocado half, cut side down, in the center of the oil puddle, creating a "seal." Store the avocado in the refrigerator.

1   large shallot, sliced thin
3   tablespoons red wine vinegar
1   garlic clove, minced
½   teaspoon mayonnaise
     Salt and pepper
3   tablespoons extra-virgin olive oil
3   avocados, halved, pitted, and cut into ¾-inch pieces
12   ounces cherry tomatoes, quartered
3   radishes, trimmed, sliced thin
½   cup chopped fresh basil
3   ounces ricotta salata, shaved thin

1. Place shallot in 2 cups ice water and let stand for 30 minutes; drain and pat dry.

2. Whisk vinegar, garlic, mayonnaise, ¼ teaspoon salt, and ¼ teaspoon pepper together in medium bowl. Whisking constantly, drizzle in oil. Gently toss avocados with 2 tablespoons dressing and ½ teaspoon salt in separate bowl, then transfer to platter. Toss shallot, tomatoes, radishes, and basil in bowl with remaining dressing and spoon over avocados. Sprinkle with ricotta salata and serve.

VARIATIONS

Avocado Salad with Orange and Fennel

SERVES 6   FAST   GF

High-quality green olives work best here. We prefer to use navel oranges, tangelos, or Cara Caras in this salad. Blood oranges can also be used, but since they are smaller you'll need four of them.

1   large shallot, sliced thin
3   oranges
3   tablespoons sherry vinegar
1   garlic clove, minced
½   teaspoon mayonnaise
½   teaspoon hot paprika
     Salt and pepper
3   tablespoons extra-virgin olive oil
3   avocados, halved, pitted, and cut into ¾-inch pieces
1   fennel bulb, stalks discarded, bulb halved, cored, and sliced thin
⅓   cup slivered almonds, toasted
¼   cup chopped fresh parsley
¼   cup pitted green olives, sliced

1. Place shallot in 2 cups ice water and let stand for 30 minutes; drain and pat dry.

2. Grate 1 teaspoon orange zest from oranges. Cut away peel and pith from oranges. Quarter oranges, then slice crosswise into ¼-inch-thick pieces.

3. Whisk orange zest, vinegar, garlic, mayonnaise, paprika, and ¼ teaspoon salt together in medium bowl. Whisking constantly, drizzle in oil. Gently toss avocados with 2 tablespoons dressing and ½ teaspoon salt in separate bowl, then transfer to platter. Toss shallot, oranges, fennel, almonds, and parsley in bowl with remaining dressing and spoon over avocados. Sprinkle with olives and serve.

Avocado Salad with Mango and Jícama

SERVES 6 ▪ FAST ▪ GF

Feta can be substituted for the *queso fresco.*

- ½ teaspoon lemon zest plus 3 tablespoons juice
- 1 small shallot, minced
- 1 garlic clove, minced
- ½ teaspoon mayonnaise
- Salt
- Pinch cayenne
- 3 tablespoons extra-virgin olive oil
- 3 avocados, halved, pitted, and cut into ¾-inch pieces
- 2 mangos, peeled, pitted, and cut into ½-inch pieces
- 1 small head jícama, peeled and cut into 2-inch-long matchsticks
- ¼ cup chopped fresh basil
- ¼ cup chopped fresh mint
- 3 ounces queso fresco cheese, crumbled (¾ cup)

Whisk lemon zest and juice, shallot, garlic, mayonnaise, ¼ teaspoon salt, and cayenne together in medium bowl. Whisking constantly, drizzle in oil. Gently toss avocados with 2 tablespoons dressing and ½ teaspoon salt in separate bowl, then transfer to platter. Toss mangos, jícama, basil, and mint in bowl with remaining dressing and spoon over avocados. Sprinkle with queso fresco and serve.

Roasted Beet Salad with Goat Cheese and Pistachios

SERVES 4 ▪ GF

✔ **WHY THIS RECIPE WORKS:** With a sweet, earthy flavor, juicy texture, and ruby-red hue, beets are a real showstopper. To make them the star of a simple yet elegant salad, we had to find the easiest way to prepare them. Boiling and steaming diluted their flavor, but when wrapped in foil and roasted, the beets were juicy and tender with a concentrated sweetness. Peeling was easier when the beets were still warm—the skins slid off effortlessly. We also tossed the sliced beets with the dressing while still warm, allowing them to absorb maximum flavor. Crumbled goat cheese, peppery arugula, and toasted pistachios rounded out the dish. When buying beets, look for bunches that have the most uniformly sized beets so that they will roast in the same amount of time. If the beets are different sizes, remove the smaller ones from the oven as they become tender. You can use either golden or red beets (or a mix of each) in this recipe.

- 2 pounds beets, trimmed
- 2 tablespoons extra-virgin olive oil
- 4 teaspoons sherry vinegar
- Salt and pepper
- 2 ounces (2 cups) baby arugula
- 2 ounces goat cheese, crumbled (½ cup)
- 2 tablespoons chopped unsalted pistachios, toasted

1. Adjust oven rack to middle position and heat oven to 400 degrees. Wrap beets individually in aluminum foil and place on rimmed baking sheet. Roast beets until skewer

Cutting Up an Avocado

1. After slicing avocado in half around pit, lodge edge of chef's knife into pit and twist to remove.

2. Do not try to pull pit off with your hands; instead, use large wooden spoon to pry pit safely off knife.

3. Using dish towel to hold avocado steady, make cross-hatch incisions in flesh of each avocado half with knife, without cutting through skin.

4. Using soupspoon, gently scrape diced avocado out of skin.

Removing Skins from Roasted Beets

When beets are cool enough to handle, carefully rub off skins using paper towel.

inserted into center meets little resistance (you will need to unwrap beets to test them), 45 to 60 minutes.

2. Remove beets from oven and carefully open foil packets. When beets are cool enough to handle, carefully rub off skins using paper towel. Slice beets into ½-inch-thick wedges, and, if large, cut in half crosswise.

3. Whisk oil, vinegar, ¼ teaspoon salt, and ¼ teaspoon pepper together in large bowl. Add beets, toss to coat, and let cool to room temperature, about 20 minutes. Add arugula and gently toss to coat. Season with salt and pepper to taste. Transfer to platter, sprinkle with goat cheese and pistachios, and serve.

VARIATION

Roasted Beet Salad with Blood Oranges and Almonds GF

Navel oranges, tangelos, or Cara Caras can be substituted for the blood oranges, but since they are larger you'll need to use just one of them.

Substitute 1 cup shaved ricotta salata for goat cheese, and sliced toasted almonds for pistachios. Cut away peel and pith from 2 blood oranges; quarter oranges, then slice each quarter crosswise into ½-inch-thick pieces and add to salad with arugula.

Broccoli Salad with Raisins and Walnuts

SERVES 4 TO 6 FAST GF

✔ **WHY THIS RECIPE WORKS:** Most recipes for this potluck classic leave the broccoli raw, but we found that cooking it briefly in boiling water improved both its flavor and its appearance. Adding the hardier stems to the cooking water before the florets levels the playing field, so both are tender at the same time. Drying the broccoli in a salad spinner gets rid of excess moisture, so the dressing—a tangy mayo-and-vinegar mixture—doesn't get watered down. Toasted walnuts and golden raisins bring crunch and salty-sweet balance to this salad. When prepping the broccoli, keep the stems and florets separate. If you don't own a salad spinner, lay the broccoli on a clean dish towel to dry in step 2.

½ **cup golden raisins**
1½ **pounds broccoli, florets cut into 1-inch pieces, stalks peeled and sliced ¼ inch thick**
½ **cup mayonnaise**
1 **tablespoon balsamic vinegar**
  Salt and pepper
½ **cup walnuts, toasted and chopped coarse**
1 **large shallot, minced**

1. Bring 3 quarts water to boil in Dutch oven. Meanwhile, fill large bowl with ice water. Combine ½ cup of boiling water and raisins in small bowl, cover, and let sit for 5 minutes; drain.

2. Meanwhile, add broccoli stalks to pot of boiling water and cook for 1 minute. Add florets and cook until slightly tender, about 1 minute. Drain broccoli, then transfer to bowl of ice water. Drain again, transfer to salad spinner, and spin dry.

3. Whisk mayonnaise, vinegar, ½ teaspoon salt, and ¼ teaspoon pepper together in large bowl. Add broccoli, raisins,

Preparing Broccoli for Salad

1. Place head of broccoli upside down on cutting board and cut florets off stems.

2. Slice larger florets into 1-inch pieces by slicing them through stems.

3. Cut away tough outer peel and square off stalks.

4. Slice stalks crosswise into ¼-inch-thick pieces.

walnuts, and shallot and toss to combine. Season with salt and pepper to taste and serve. (Salad can be refrigerated for up to 6 hours.)

VARIATIONS

Broccoli Salad with Currants and Pine Nuts FAST GF

Substitute currants for raisins and toasted pine nuts for walnuts.

Broccoli Salad with Cherries and Pecans FAST GF

Substitute dried cherries for raisins and toasted pecans for walnuts.

Broccoli Salad with Cranberries and Almonds FAST GF

Substitute dried cranberries for raisins and toasted, sliced almonds for walnuts.

Brussels Sprout and Kale Slaw with Herbs and Peanuts

SERVES 4 FAST VEGAN GF

☑ **WHY THIS RECIPE WORKS:** Raw Brussels sprouts and kale leaves may sound like an odd combination for a salad, but these two cabbage-like vegetables are perfect together; since the uncooked leaves hold up well for hours, they're ideal for picnics and making ahead. To keep our slaw crisp and light, we left the Brussels sprouts raw and marinated them in the dressing to soften them just slightly. A vigorous massage tenderized the kale leaves in just a minute. A simple cider and coriander vinaigrette, fresh cilantro and mint, chopped peanuts, plus a squeeze of lime juice gave this slaw a refreshing Southeast Asian profile. Tuscan kale (also known as dinosaur or Lacinato kale) is more tender than curly-leaf and red kale; if using curly-leaf or red kale, increase the massaging time to 5 minutes. Do not use baby kale. For more information on thinly slicing Brussels sprouts, see page 260.

- ⅓ **cup cider vinegar**
- 3 **tablespoons sugar**
- ½ **teaspoon ground coriander**
  Salt and pepper
- 2 **tablespoons extra-virgin olive oil**

For a crisp, crunchy slaw that won't end up waterlogged, we combine sliced, marinated Brussels sprouts and Tuscan kale.

- 1 **pound Brussels sprouts, trimmed, halved, and sliced very thinly**
- 8 **ounces Tuscan kale, stemmed and sliced into ¼-inch strips (4½ cups)**
- ¼ **cup dry-roasted, salted peanuts, roughly chopped**
- 1 **tablespoon chopped fresh cilantro**
- 1 **tablespoon chopped fresh mint**
  Lime juice

1. Whisk vinegar, sugar, coriander, ½ teaspoon salt, and ¼ teaspoon pepper together in large bowl. Whisking constantly, drizzle in oil. Add Brussels sprouts and toss to combine. Cover and let sit at room temperature for at least 30 minutes or up to 2 hours.

2. Vigorously squeeze and massage kale with hands until leaves are uniformly darkened and slightly wilted, about 1 minute. Add kale, peanuts, cilantro, and mint to bowl with Brussels sprouts and toss to combine. Season with salt and lime juice to taste and serve.

Brussels Sprout Salad with Pecorino and Pine Nuts

SERVES 8 `FAST` `GF`

✔ **WHY THIS RECIPE WORKS:** To make Brussels sprouts shine in a salad, we needed to get rid of some of their vegetal rawness. Rather than cooking the sprouts, we sliced them very thin and then marinated them in a bright vinaigrette made with lemon juice and Dijon mustard. The 30-minute soak in the acidic dressing softened and seasoned the sprouts, bringing out and balancing their flavor. Adding toasted pine nuts and shredded Pecorino Romano to our salad just before serving added a layer of crunch and nutty richness. Slice the sprouts as thinly as possible. Shred the Pecorino Romano on a coarse grater.

- 3 tablespoons lemon juice
- 2 tablespoons Dijon mustard
- 1 small shallot, minced
- 1 garlic clove, minced
  Salt and pepper
- 6 tablespoons extra-virgin olive oil
- 2 pounds Brussels sprouts, trimmed, halved, and sliced very thin
- 3 ounces Pecorino Romano cheese, shredded (1 cup)
- ½ cup pine nuts, toasted

1. Whisk lemon juice, mustard, shallot, garlic, and ½ teaspoon salt together in large bowl. Whisking constantly, drizzle in oil. Add Brussels sprouts, toss to combine, and let sit for at least 30 minutes or up to 2 hours.

2. Stir in Pecorino and pine nuts. Season with salt and pepper to taste and serve.

VARIATIONS

Brussels Sprout Salad with Cheddar, Hazelnuts, and Apple `FAST` `GF`

See page 431 for more information on toasting and skinning hazelnuts.

Substitute 1 cup shredded sharp cheddar for Pecorino and ½ cup hazelnuts, toasted, skinned, and chopped, for pine nuts. Add 1 Granny Smith apple, cored and cut into ½-inch pieces, with cheese and nuts.

Brussels Sprout Salad with Smoked Gouda, Pecans, and Dried Cherries `FAST` `GF`

Substitute 1 cup shredded smoked gouda for Pecorino and ½ cup pecans, toasted and chopped, for pine nuts. Add ½ cup chopped dried cherries with cheese and nuts.

Sweet and Sour Cabbage Salad with Apple and Fennel

SERVES 6 TO 8 `VEGAN` `GF`

✔ **WHY THIS RECIPE WORKS:** Cabbage salads dressed with bright vinaigrettes are a nice change of pace from heavier, mayonnaise-based slaws. Their natural spicy-sweetness and crunchy texture work well with strong and unconventional flavors, highlighting the leaves' taste without overpowering it. But cabbage tends to become watery and bland once dressed and allowed to sit, because the cabbage itself exudes water. We solved this problem by salting and draining the cabbage to draw out the liquid. A lively honey-mustard vinaigrette and fresh, crisp apple and fennel rounded out the salad's flavor and texture.

- ½ head green cabbage, cored and shredded (6 cups)
  Salt and pepper
- ½ small red onion, chopped fine
- 2 tablespoons rice vinegar
- 1 tablespoon honey
- 2 teaspoons minced fresh tarragon
- 1 teaspoon Dijon mustard
- 2 tablespoons extra-virgin olive oil
- 1 large Granny Smith apple, peeled, cored, and cut into ¼-inch pieces
- 1 fennel bulb, stalks discarded, bulb halved, cored, and sliced thin

1. Toss shredded cabbage with 1 teaspoon salt and let drain in colander for at least 1 hour or up to 4 hours.

2. Rinse cabbage under cold running water (or in large bowl of ice water if serving immediately). Press cabbage, but do not squeeze, to drain, then pat dry with paper towels. (Cabbage can be refrigerated for up to 24 hours.)

Slicing Brussels Sprouts

Slice halved Brussels sprouts thinly using chef's knife.

3. Whisk onion, vinegar, honey, tarragon, and mustard together in medium bowl. Whisking constantly, drizzle in oil. Add cabbage, apple, and fennel and toss to coat. Season with salt and pepper to taste. Cover and refrigerate for at least 1 hour or up to 1 day.

VARIATIONS

Cabbage and Red Pepper Salad with Lime-Cumin Vinaigrette

SERVES 6 TO 8 `VEGAN` `GF`

½ head green cabbage, cored and shredded (6 cups)
  Salt and pepper
1 teaspoon grated lime zest plus 2 tablespoons juice
1 tablespoon rice vinegar or sherry vinegar
1 tablespoon honey
1 teaspoon ground cumin
  Pinch cayenne pepper
2 tablespoons extra-virgin olive oil
1 red bell pepper, stemmed, seeded, and cut into thin strips

1. Toss shredded cabbage with 1 teaspoon salt and let drain in colander for at least 1 hour or up to 4 hours.

2. Rinse cabbage under cold running water (or in large bowl of ice water if serving immediately). Press cabbage, but do not squeeze, to drain, then pat dry with paper towels. (Cabbage can be refrigerated for up to 24 hours.)

3. Whisk lime zest and juice, vinegar, honey, cumin, and cayenne together in medium bowl. Whisking constantly, drizzle in oil. Add cabbage and bell pepper and toss to coat. Season with salt and pepper to taste. Cover and refrigerate for at least 1 hour or up to 1 day.

Confetti Cabbage Salad with Spicy Peanut Dressing

SERVES 6 TO 8 `VEGAN` `GF`

Grate the carrot on a coarse grater. In order for this recipe to be gluten-free, you must use gluten-free soy sauce or tamari.

½ head green cabbage, cored and shredded (6 cups)
1 large carrot, peeled and grated
  Salt and pepper
2 tablespoons smooth peanut butter
2 tablespoons peanut or vegetable oil
2 tablespoons rice vinegar
1 tablespoon soy sauce
2 garlic cloves, chopped coarse
1 teaspoon honey
1 tablespoon grated fresh ginger
½ jalapeño chile, stemmed, halved, and seeded
4 radishes, trimmed, halved lengthwise, and sliced thin
4 scallions, sliced thin

1. Toss shredded cabbage and carrot with 1 teaspoon salt and let drain in colander for at least 1 hour or up to 4 hours.

2. Rinse cabbage mixture under cold running water (or in large bowl of ice water if serving immediately). Press cabbage mixture, but do not squeeze, to drain, then pat dry with paper towels. (Cabbage mixture can be refrigerated for up to 24 hours.)

3. Process peanut butter, oil, vinegar, soy sauce, garlic, honey, ginger, and jalapeño in food processor to smooth paste, about 30 seconds. Toss cabbage mixture, radishes, scallions, and dressing together in medium bowl. Season with salt and pepper to taste. Cover and refrigerate for at least 1 hour or up to 1 day.

Shredding Cabbage

1. Cut cabbage into quarters, then trim and discard core.

2. Separate cabbage into small stacks of leaves that flatten when pressed.

3. Using chef's knife, cut each stack of cabbage leaves into thin shreds.

Celery Root Salad with Apple and Parsley

SERVES 4 TO 6 FAST GF

✔ **WHY THIS RECIPE WORKS:** Unlike cooked celery root purees or gratins, a celery root salad maintains the vegetable's pristine white appearance, its crunchy, coleslaw-like texture, and (most important) its refreshing herbal flavor. For easy peeling, we removed the top and bottom from the celery root and then used a paring knife to remove the outer layer of flesh. For thin pieces of celery root that would retain their crunch, we grated it coarsely. We dressed the celery root with a vinaigrette finished with sour cream, which lent the salad creamy, tangy richness. Tart Granny Smith apple complemented the celery root nicely, and we freshened it up with sliced scallions and a combination of fresh parsley and tarragon. Add a teaspoon or so more oil to the dressed salad if it seems a bit dry.

2	tablespoons lemon juice
1½	tablespoons Dijon mustard
1	teaspoon honey
	Salt and pepper
3	tablespoons vegetable oil
3	tablespoons sour cream
1	celery root (14 ounces), peeled
½	Granny Smith apple, peeled and cored
2	scallions, sliced thin
2	teaspoons minced fresh parsley
2	teaspoons minced fresh tarragon (optional)

1. Whisk lemon juice, mustard, honey, and ½ teaspoon salt together in medium bowl. Whisking constantly, drizzle in oil. Whisk in sour cream.

2. Grate celery root and apple using food processor fitted with shredding disk or coarse grater, then stir immediately into dressing (to prevent browning). Stir in scallions, parsley, and tarragon, if using. Season with salt and pepper to taste. Cover and refrigerate for at least 30 minutes or up to 1 day.

VARIATIONS

Celery Root Salad with Apple, Caraway, and Horseradish FAST GF

Add ½ teaspoon caraway seeds and 1½ teaspoons prepared horseradish to salad with herbs.

Celery Root Salad with Red Onion, Mint, Orange, and Fennel Seeds FAST GF

Add ½ teaspoon grated orange zest and 1 teaspoon fennel seeds to dressing. Substitute 2 tablespoons finely chopped red onion for scallion and mint for tarragon.

Celery Root Salad with Pear and Hazelnuts FAST GF

See page 431 for information on toasting and skinning hazelnuts.

Substitute ½ pear for apple. Add ¼ cup hazelnuts, toasted, skinned, and chopped, to salad with herbs.

Moroccan-Style Carrot Salad

SERVES 6 FAST VEGAN GF

✔ **WHY THIS RECIPE WORKS:** This classic Moroccan salad combines grated carrots with olive oil, lemon juice, and spices. We tried grating the carrots both with a coarse grater and with a food processor and found that the coarse grater worked best. To complement the earthy carrots, we added juicy orange segments, reserving some of the orange juice to add to the salad dressing. We balanced the sweet orange juice with a squeeze of lemon juice and warm spices—cumin, cayenne, and cinnamon. The musty aroma and slight nuttiness of the cumin nicely complemented the sweetness of the carrots. A touch of honey provided a pleasing floral note. To add color and freshness, we stirred in some minced cilantro before serving.

2	oranges
1	pound carrots, peeled
1	tablespoon lemon juice
1	teaspoon honey
¾	teaspoon ground cumin
⅛	teaspoon cayenne pepper
⅛	teaspoon ground cinnamon
	Salt and pepper
3	tablespoons minced fresh cilantro
3	tablespoons extra-virgin olive oil

1. Cut away peel and pith from oranges. Holding fruit over bowl, use paring knife to slice between membranes to release segments. Cut segments in half widthwise and let drain in fine-mesh strainer, reserving juice.

2. Grate carrots on coarse grater into large bowl. Whisk lemon juice, honey, cumin, cayenne, cinnamon, and ½ teaspoon salt into reserved orange juice. Add drained oranges and orange juice mixture to carrots and toss gently to coat. Let salad sit until liquid starts to pool in bottom of bowl, 3 to 5 minutes.

3. Drain salad in fine-mesh strainer; return to bowl. Stir in cilantro and oil, season with salt and pepper to taste, and serve.

Salting the vegetables and making an extra-potent dressing prevents our fresh chopped salad from getting watered down.

Summer Vegetable Chopped Salad

SERVES 4 **FAST** VEGAN GF

✓ **WHY THIS RECIPE WORKS:** Chopped salads should be lively, thoughtfully chosen compositions of lettuce and vegetables. Too often, though, the salad is a bland mix of watery vegetables. To avoid a soggy salad, we salted the vegetables to draw out their excess moisture. Seeding the cucumbers and quartering tomatoes exposed more surface area to the salt for even better results. Then we made an extra-potent dressing with equal parts oil and vinegar to give the salad bright acidic flavor. Letting the vegetables marinate in the vinaigrette for a few minutes before adding the lettuce intensified their flavor. Along with the cucumbers and tomatoes, we chose sweet yellow bell pepper, red onion, and crisp, peppery radishes and tossed them all with chopped romaine lettuce hearts. Be sure to add the lettuce just before serving, or it will turn soggy.

3 cucumbers, peeled, halved lengthwise, seeded, and cut into ½-inch pieces

1½ pounds cherry tomatoes, quartered
Salt and pepper

¼ cup red wine vinegar

1 garlic clove, minced

¼ cup extra-virgin olive oil

1 yellow bell pepper, stemmed, seeded, and cut into ½-inch pieces

1 small red onion, chopped fine

8 ounces radishes, trimmed and sliced thin

¾ cup chopped fresh parsley

1 romaine lettuce heart (6 ounces), cut into 1-inch pieces

1. Toss cucumbers and tomatoes with 1 teaspoon salt and let drain in colander for 15 minutes.

2. Whisk vinegar, garlic, ¼ teaspoon salt, and ⅛ teaspoon pepper together in large bowl. Whisking constantly, drizzle in oil. Add drained cucumbers and tomatoes, bell pepper, onion, radishes, and parsley and toss to coat. Let salad sit for at least 5 minutes or up to 20 minutes.

3. Add lettuce and gently toss to combine. Season with salt and pepper to taste and serve.

VARIATIONS

Mediterranean Chopped Salad

SERVES 4 **FAST** GF

Cherry tomatoes can be substituted for the grape tomatoes.

1 cucumber, peeled, halved lengthwise, seeded, and cut into ½-inch pieces

10 ounces grape tomatoes, quartered
Salt and pepper

3 tablespoons red wine vinegar

1 garlic clove, minced

3 tablespoons extra-virgin olive oil

1 (15-ounce) can chickpeas, rinsed

½ cup pitted kalamata olives, chopped

½ small red onion, chopped fine

½ cup chopped fresh parsley

1 romaine lettuce heart (6 ounces), cut into ½-inch pieces

4 ounces feta cheese, crumbled (1 cup)

1. Toss cucumber and tomatoes with 1 teaspoon salt and let drain in colander for 15 minutes.

2. Whisk vinegar and garlic together in large bowl. Whisking constantly, drizzle in oil. Add drained cucumber and tomatoes, chickpeas, olives, onion, and parsley and toss to coat. Let salad sit for at least 5 minutes or up to 20 minutes.

3. Add lettuce and feta and toss to combine. Season with salt and pepper to taste and serve.

Fennel and Apple Chopped Salad

SERVES 4 **FAST** **GF**

Pecans can be substituted for the walnuts. We like Braeburn, Jonagold, or Red Delicious apples in this salad.

- 1 cucumber, peeled, halved lengthwise, seeded, and cut into ½-inch pieces
  Salt and pepper
- 3 tablespoons extra-virgin olive oil
- 3 tablespoons white wine vinegar
- 1 fennel bulb, stalks discarded, bulb halved, cored, and cut into ¼-inch pieces
- 2 apples, cored and cut into ¼-inch pieces
- ½ small red onion, chopped fine
- ¼ cup chopped fresh tarragon
- 1 romaine lettuce heart (6 ounces), cut into ½-inch pieces
- ½ cup walnuts, toasted and chopped
- 4 ounces goat cheese, crumbled (1 cup)

1. Toss cucumber with ½ teaspoon salt and let drain in colander for 15 minutes.

2. Whisk oil and vinegar together in large bowl. Add drained cucumber, fennel, apples, onion, and tarragon and toss to coat. Let salad sit for at least 5 minutes or up to 20 minutes.

3. Add lettuce and walnuts and gently toss to combine. Season with salt and pepper to taste. Sprinkle portions with goat cheese before serving.

Pear and Cranberry Chopped Salad

SERVES 4 **FAST** **GF**

If you prefer to use a very mild and mellow blue cheese, we recommend Danish blue; if you prefer a sharp one, try Stilton.

- 1 cucumber, peeled, halved lengthwise, seeded, and cut into ½-inch pieces
  Salt and pepper
- 3 tablespoons extra-virgin olive oil
- 3 tablespoons sherry vinegar

- 1 red bell pepper, stemmed, seeded, and cut into ¼-inch pieces
- 1 ripe but firm pear, cut into ¼-inch pieces
- ½ small red onion, chopped fine
- ½ cup dried cranberries
- 1 romaine lettuce heart (6 ounces), cut into ½-inch pieces
- 4 ounces blue cheese, crumbled (1 cup)
- ½ cup shelled pistachios, toasted and chopped

1. Toss cucumber with ½ teaspoon salt and let drain in colander for 15 minutes.

2. Whisk oil and vinegar together in large bowl. Add drained cucumber, bell pepper, pear, onion, and cranberries and toss to coat. Let salad sit for at least 5 minutes or up to 20 minutes.

3. Add lettuce, blue cheese, and pistachios and toss to combine. Season with salt and pepper to taste and serve.

Cutting Up a Bell Pepper

1. Slice off top and bottom of pepper and remove seeds.

2. Slice down through side of pepper.

3. Lay pepper flat on cutting board, trim away remaining ribs and seeds, then cut into pieces as desired.

Cucumber Salad with Chile, Mint, and Basil

SERVES 4 TO 6 `FAST` `VEGAN` `GF`

✔ **WHY THIS RECIPE WORKS:** Cucumbers can make a cool, crisp salad—but not if they're soggy from their own moisture and swimming in a watery dressing. For a cucumber salad with good crunch, we drained the sliced cucumbers on paper towels while we prepared the dressing. To prevent the dressing from getting watered down, we made a concentrated version with ⅓ cup of vinegar (which we reduced to 2 tablespoons) and just 2 teaspoons of oil. When tossed with the cucumbers, this potent mixture retained its bright flavor. Spicy Thai chiles, fresh basil and mint, and crunchy chopped peanuts nicely complemented the cool cucumber. Be sure to slice the cucumbers ⅛ to ³⁄₁₆ inch thick. This salad is best served within 1 hour of being dressed.

        4   cucumbers, peeled, halved lengthwise,
            seeded, and sliced very thin
        ⅓   cup white wine vinegar
        2   Thai chiles, stemmed, seeded, and minced
        1   tablespoon lime juice
        1   tablespoon fish sauce substitute (page 60)
        2   teaspoons vegetable oil
        2   teaspoons sugar
        1   teaspoon salt
        ¼   cup chopped fresh mint
        ¼   cup chopped fresh basil
        ¼   cup dry-roasted peanuts, toasted and
            chopped coarse

1. Spread cucumber slices evenly on paper towel–lined baking sheet. Refrigerate while preparing dressing.

2. Bring vinegar to simmer in small saucepan over medium-low heat and cook until reduced to 2 tablespoons, 4 to 6 minutes. Transfer to large bowl and let cool to room temperature, about 10 minutes. Whisk in chiles, lime juice, fish sauce, oil, sugar, and salt.

3. Just before serving, add cucumbers, mint, and basil to dressing and gently toss to combine. Let salad sit for at least 5 minutes, then toss again. Sprinkle with peanuts and serve.

VARIATIONS
Cucumber Salad with Jalapeños, Cilantro, and Pepitas

SERVES 4 TO 6 `FAST` `VEGAN` `GF`

To make this salad spicier, reserve and add the chile seeds to the dressing.

`NOTES FROM THE TEST KITCHEN`

All About Vinegars

Bright, acidic vinegar is essential to making many salad dressings. We also frequently reach for vinegar to add acidity and flavor to sauces, stews, soups, and bean dishes. Because different vinegars have distinctly different flavors, you will want to stock several varieties in your pantry.

BALSAMIC VINEGAR

Traditional Italian balsamic vinegars are aged for years to develop complex flavor—but they're pricey. They're best saved to drizzle over finished dishes. For vinaigrettes and glazes and to finish dishes, we use commercial balsamic vinegars, which are younger wine vinegars with added sugar and coloring. **Lucini Gran Riserva Balsamico** is our favorite.

CIDER VINEGAR

This vinegar has a bite and a fruity sweetness perfect for vinaigrettes; it pairs well in salads tossed with apple or dried fruits. It also works well in bread-and-butter pickles, barbecue sauce, and coleslaw. Our favorite is **Spectrum Naturals**.

RED WINE VINEGAR

Use this slightly sweet, sharp vinegar for bold vinaigrettes and rich sauces. With an acidity level as high as 7 percent, it works particularly well with potent flavors. We prefer red wine vinegars made from a blend of wine grapes and Concord grapes; our favorite brand is **Laurent du Clos**.

WHITE WINE VINEGAR

This vinegar's refined, fruity bite makes it perfect for light vinaigrettes and buttery sauces. We also use it in dishes like potato salad and hollandaise sauce where the color of red wine vinegar would detract from the presentation. **Spectrum Naturals Organic White Wine Vinegar** is our favorite.

RICE VINEGAR

Also referred to as rice wine vinegar, this vinegar is made from steamed rice. Since rice vinegar has lower acidity than that in other vinegars—just 4 percent—we use it to add gentle balance to Asian-influenced dishes. Avoid cooking with seasoned rice vinegar, as it can taste overly sweet.

DISTILLED WHITE VINEGAR

White vinegar has no added flavor and is therefore the harshest—and yet most pure—vinegar. Avoid using it in vinaigrettes; we use it most often to make pickles and, diluted with water, as a cleaning agent.

4 cucumbers, peeled, halved lengthwise, seeded, and sliced very thin
⅓ cup white wine vinegar
2 teaspoons grated lime zest plus 1 tablespoon juice
1 jalapeño chile, stemmed, seeded, and minced
2 teaspoons extra-virgin olive oil
1½ teaspoons sugar
1 teaspoon salt
1 cup chopped fresh cilantro
3 tablespoons pepitas, toasted and chopped coarse

1. Spread cucumber slices evenly on paper towel–lined baking sheet. Refrigerate while preparing dressing.

2. Bring vinegar to simmer in small saucepan over medium-low heat and cook until reduced to 2 tablespoons, 4 to 6 minutes. Transfer to large bowl and let cool to room temperature, about 10 minutes. Whisk in lime zest and juice, jalapeño, oil, sugar, and salt.

3. Just before serving, add cucumbers and cilantro to dressing and gently toss to combine. Let salad sit for at least 5 minutes, then toss again. Sprinkle with pepitas and serve.

Cucumber Salad with Ginger, Sesame, and Scallions
SERVES 4 TO 6 FAST VEGAN GF

Look for nori along with other Japanese ingredients in the international aisle of the grocery store.

4 cucumbers, peeled, halved lengthwise, seeded, and sliced very thin
⅓ cup white wine vinegar
1 tablespoon lime juice
2 teaspoons grated fresh ginger
2 teaspoons toasted sesame oil
2 teaspoons sugar
1 teaspoon salt
5 scallions, sliced thin
1 toasted and crumbled sheet of nori
3 tablespoons toasted sesame seeds

1. Spread cucumber slices evenly on paper towel–lined baking sheet. Refrigerate while preparing dressing.

2. Bring vinegar to simmer in small saucepan over medium-low heat and cook until reduced to 2 tablespoons, 4 to 6 minutes. Transfer to large bowl and let cool to room temperature, about 10 minutes. Whisk in lime juice, ginger, oil, sugar, and salt.

3. Just before serving, add cucumbers, scallions, and nori to dressing and gently toss to combine. Let salad sit for at least 5 minutes, then toss again. Sprinkle with sesame seeds and serve.

Roasted Fennel and Mushroom Salad with Radishes
SERVES 4 VEGAN GF

✓ **WHY THIS RECIPE WORKS:** Roasting can give new life to tired produce, but it can also make for a limp, soggy salad. We wanted a simple, flavorful salad built on a base of roasted vegetables with compatible flavors and colors. We chose a combination of fennel and mushrooms; both kept their structure when roasted and cooked to a firm yet tender consistency. First we tossed the vegetables with a little olive oil and seasoned them with salt and pepper, plus a pinch of sugar to aid in caramelization. To guarantee maximum browning, we placed them on a preheated baking sheet in a 500-degree oven. Tossing the roasted vegetables with a simple vinaigrette while they were still hot allowed for better flavor absorption. To freshen up our hearty roasted vegetable salad, we added crisp, raw radishes and some of the minced fennel fronds to the mix. If fennel fronds (the delicate greenery attached to the fennel stems) are unavailable, substitute 1 tablespoon chopped fresh tarragon.

2 fennel bulbs, fronds minced, stalks discarded, bulbs halved, cored, and cut crosswise into ½-inch-thick slices
20 ounces cremini mushrooms, trimmed, quartered if large or halved if medium
3 tablespoons extra-virgin olive oil
Salt and pepper
¼ teaspoon sugar
2 tablespoons lemon juice
1 teaspoon Dijon mustard
6 radishes, trimmed, halved, and sliced thin

1. Adjust oven rack to lowest position, place large rimmed baking sheet on rack, and heat oven to 500 degrees. Toss fennel and mushrooms with 2 tablespoons oil, ½ teaspoon salt, ¼ teaspoon pepper, and sugar in bowl. Working quickly, carefully spread fennel and mushrooms over hot baking sheet in even layer. Roast until vegetables are tender and well browned on 1 side, 20 to 25 minutes (do not stir during roasting).

2. Meanwhile, whisk lemon juice, mustard, ¼ teaspoon salt, and ⅛ teaspoon pepper together in now-empty bowl. Whisking constantly, drizzle in remaining 1 tablespoon oil.

3. Add hot vegetables to bowl with vinaigrette, toss, and let cool to room temperature, about 30 minutes. Stir in radishes and transfer to serving platter. Sprinkle with fronds and serve.

Algerian-Style Fennel, Orange, and Olive Salad

SERVES 4 TO 6 `FAST` `VEGAN` `GF`

✔ WHY THIS RECIPE WORKS: In Algeria and Tunisia, raw fennel is often used to make distinctive crisp, light salads. We liked the fennel best when it was sliced as thin as possible; this kept the texture from being too tough or chewy. Sweet, juicy oranges were the perfect match for the crisp fennel. To ensure they were evenly distributed in the salad, we cut the oranges into bite-size pieces and tossed the salad gently to keep the segments from falling apart. To finish off the salad, we added some oil-cured black olives, which are ubiquitous in the region, plus some fresh mint, lemon juice, good extra-virgin olive oil, salt, and pepper. Because this dish is so simple, using high-quality ingredients is essential. Blood oranges are traditional in this dish; navel oranges, tangelos, or Cara Caras can also be used, but since they are larger, you'll need just three of them.

- 4 blood oranges
- 2 fennel bulbs, stalks discarded, bulbs halved, cored, and sliced thin
- ½ cup pitted oil-cured black olives, slivered
- ¼ cup roughly chopped fresh mint
- 2 tablespoons lemon juice
  Salt and pepper
- ¼ cup extra-virgin olive oil

1. Cut away peel and pith from oranges. Quarter oranges, then slice each quarter crosswise into ¼-inch-thick pieces. Combine oranges, fennel, olives, and mint in large bowl.

2. In small bowl, whisk lemon juice, ¼ teaspoon salt, and ⅛ teaspoon pepper together. Whisking constantly, drizzle in oil. Drizzle dressing over salad and toss gently to coat. Season with salt and pepper to taste and serve. (Salad can be refrigerated for up to 2 days.)

Green Bean Salad with Cilantro Sauce

SERVES 6 TO 8 `FAST` `VEGAN` `GF`

✔ WHY THIS RECIPE WORKS: To dress up a simple green bean salad, we came up with a fresh take on pesto that swapped the traditional basil for bright, grassy cilantro. A single scallion brightened the green color of the sauce, and walnuts and garlic cloves, briefly toasted in a skillet, added nutty depth. We liked regular olive oil rather than the traditional extra-virgin olive oil in this recipe because its milder flavor allowed the cilantro to really shine through. Finally, a touch of lemon juice rounded out the flavors and helped to loosen the sauce to just the right consistency. We blanched and shocked the beans to set their vibrant green color and ensure they were evenly cooked. Don't worry about drying the beans before tossing them with the sauce; any water that clings to the beans will help to thin out the sauce.

- ¼ cup walnuts
- 2 garlic cloves, unpeeled
- 2½ cups fresh cilantro leaves and stems, tough stem ends trimmed (about 2 bunches)
- ½ cup olive oil
- 4 teaspoons lemon juice
- 1 scallion, sliced thin
  Salt and pepper
- 2 pounds green beans, trimmed

1. Cook walnuts and garlic in 8-inch skillet over medium heat, stirring often, until toasted and fragrant, 5 to 7 minutes; transfer to bowl. Let garlic cool slightly, then peel and roughly chop.

2. Process walnuts, garlic, cilantro, oil, lemon juice, scallion, ½ teaspoon salt, and ⅛ teaspoon pepper in food processor, scraping down bowl as needed, until smooth, about 1 minute. Season with salt and pepper to taste. (Sauce can be refrigerated for up to 2 days.)

3. Bring 3 quarts water to boil in Dutch oven over high heat. Meanwhile, fill large bowl with ice water. Add 1 tablespoon salt and green beans to boiling water and cook until crisp-tender, about 4 minutes. Drain beans, transfer to ice water, and let sit until chilled, about 2 minutes.

4. Drain beans and transfer to bowl. Add cilantro sauce and toss to coat. Season with salt and pepper to taste and serve. (Salad can be refrigerated for up to 4 hours.)

VARIATION
Green Beans and Potatoes with Cilantro Sauce `VEGAN` `GF`
Before cooking beans, place 1 pound red potatoes, unpeeled and sliced ¼ inch thick, in large saucepan and add water to cover by 1 inch water; bring to boil, then reduce to simmer and cook until tender, about 5 minutes. Drain potatoes, spread out over rimmed baking sheet, and drizzle with some of cilantro sauce. Reduce amount of beans to 1 pound and cut into 2-inch lengths; cook as directed. Toss beans and potatoes with remaining sauce, season with salt and pepper to taste, and serve.

We season roasted butternut squash with a bold blend of Middle Eastern spices for a complexly flavored squash salad.

Roasted Butternut Squash Salad with Za'atar and Parsley

SERVES 4 TO 6 VEGAN GF

✔ **WHY THIS RECIPE WORKS:** The sweet, nutty flavor of roasted butternut squash pairs best with flavors that are bold enough to balance that sweetness. To fill this role in our roasted butternut squash salad, we chose the traditional Middle Eastern spice blend *za'atar* (a pungent combination of toasted sesame seeds, thyme, marjoram, and sumac). We found that using high heat and placing the rack in the lowest position produced perfectly browned squash with a firm center in about 30 minutes. Dusting the za'atar over the hot squash worked much like toasting the spice, boosting its flavor. For a foil to the tender squash, we considered a host of nuts before landing on toasted pumpkin seeds. They provided the textural accent the dish needed and reinforced the squash's flavor. Pomegranate seeds added a burst of tartness and color.

Pepitas, or pumpkin seeds, are available at most supermarkets and natural foods stores. You can substitute chopped red grapes or small blueberries for the pomegranate seeds.

3–3½	pounds butternut squash, peeled, seeded, and cut into ½-inch pieces (8–10 cups)
¼	cup extra-virgin olive oil
	Salt and pepper
1	teaspoon za'atar spice blend
1	small shallot, minced
2	tablespoons lemon juice
2	tablespoons honey
¾	cup fresh parsley leaves
⅓	cup unsalted pepitas, toasted
½	cup pomegranate seeds

1. Adjust oven rack to lowest position and heat oven to 450 degrees. Toss squash with 1 tablespoon oil in bowl and season with salt and pepper. Lay squash in single layer on rimmed baking sheet and roast until well browned and tender, 30 to 35 minutes, stirring halfway through roasting time. Remove squash from oven, sprinkle with za'atar, and let cool for 15 minutes.

2. Whisk shallot, lemon juice, honey, and ¼ teaspoon salt together in large bowl. Whisking constantly, drizzle in remaining 3 tablespoons oil. Add squash, parsley, and pepitas and toss gently to combine. Arrange on platter, sprinkle with pomegranate seeds, and serve.

NOTES FROM THE TEST KITCHEN

Toasting Nuts and Seeds

Toasting nuts and seeds maximizes their flavor, so whether you are adding them to a salad or tossing them into a pasta dish or baked good it pays to spend a few minutes toasting them.

To toast a small amount (less than 1 cup) of nuts or seeds, put them in a dry skillet over medium heat. Toast until they are lightly browned and fragrant, shaking the skillet occasionally to prevent scorching, 3 to 8 minutes. Watch the nuts closely because they can go from golden to burnt very quickly. To toast a large quantity of nuts, spread the nuts in a single layer on a rimmed baking sheet and toast in a 350-degree oven. To promote even toasting, shake the baking sheet every few minutes, and toast until the nuts are lightly browned and fragrant, 5 to 10 minutes.

Indonesian Vegetable Salad with Peanut Sauce (Gado Gado)

SERVES 4 GF

 WHY THIS RECIPE WORKS: Literally translated as "mix-mix," *Gado gado* is a classic Indonesian salad that pairs a variety of steamed, seasonal vegetables, cabbage, and hard-cooked eggs with a creamy coconut milk–based peanut sauce. We wanted to streamline the cooking process for the myriad salad components and come up with convenient substitutes for the hard-to-find specialty ingredients. To make the peanut sauce, we combined coconut milk with sautéed minced garlic and red curry paste, which packs the traditional flavorings of lemon grass, shallots, kaffir lime, and chile in a convenient package. A fish sauce substitute along with brown sugar approximated the flavor of fermented shrimp paste and sweetened soy sauce, two more traditional ingredients. A little Sriracha provided the requisite heat and chile flavor, and tamarind paste lent a tart fruitiness. To give the sauce plenty of peanut flavor, we used chunky peanut butter, then added a garnish of freshly chopped peanuts for texture. Finally, for the vegetables, we kept things simple by simmering small red potatoes in a saucepan until tender, then blanching green beans and cauliflower in the same water. Shredded cabbage and sliced cucumber, plus the traditional hard-cooked eggs, rounded out the salad.

This Indonesian classic features a variety of fresh vegetables generously drizzled with a spicy, creamy peanut sauce.

DRESSING

- 2 tablespoons red curry paste
- 1 tablespoon vegetable oil
- 3 garlic cloves, minced
- ½ cup coconut milk
- ⅓ cup water
- ¼ cup chunky peanut butter
- 2 tablespoons fish sauce substitute (page 60)
- 4 teaspoons dark brown sugar
- 1 tablespoon tamarind paste
- 2 teaspoons Sriracha sauce
- ¼ cup dry-roasted peanuts, chopped

SALAD

- 12 ounces small red potatoes, unpeeled
- 1 tablespoon salt
- 8 ounces green beans, trimmed
- 8 ounces cauliflower florets, cut into 1-inch pieces
- ½ small green cabbage, cored and sliced thin (6 cups)
- 1 cucumber, peeled and sliced ½ inch thick
- 4 Foolproof Hard-Cooked Eggs (page 379), halved lengthwise

1. FOR THE DRESSING: Cook curry paste, oil, and garlic in small saucepan over medium-high heat, stirring often, until mixture begins to stick to pan bottom, 2 to 3 minutes. Whisk in coconut milk, water, peanut butter, fish sauce, sugar, tamarind, and Sriracha. Bring to simmer, then reduce heat to low and cook until slightly thickened, 5 to 8 minutes. Transfer to bowl and let cool to room temperature, about 30 minutes. Stir in peanuts.

2. FOR THE SALAD: Place potatoes and salt in large saucepan and add water to cover by 1 inch. Bring to boil over high heat, reduce heat to medium-low, and simmer until potatoes are just tender and paring knife can be slipped in and out of potatoes with little resistance, 10 to 15 minutes. Using slotted spoon, transfer potatoes to baking sheet lined with several layers of paper towels and let drain.

3. Return cooking water to boil over high heat, add green beans, and cook until just tender, 4 to 8 minutes. Using slotted spoon, transfer beans to colander and rinse under cold running water to cool; transfer to baking sheet with potatoes.

4. Return cooking water to boil over high heat, add cauliflower, and cook until just tender, 6 to 8 minutes. Using slotted spoon, transfer cauliflower to colander and rinse under cold running water to cool; transfer to baking sheet with potatoes and beans.

5. Divide cabbage among individual plates. Cut potatoes into ½-inch wedges. Arrange potatoes, beans, cauliflower, cucumbers, and eggs over cabbage and drizzle liberally with dressing. Serve with remaining dressing.

French Potato Salad with Dijon Mustard and Fines Herbes

SERVES 4 TO 6   **FAST** **VEGAN** **GF**

✔ **WHY THIS RECIPE WORKS:** French potato salad should be pleasing not only to the eye but also to the palate. The potatoes (small red potatoes are traditional) should be tender but not mushy, and the flavor of the vinaigrette should penetrate the relatively bland potatoes. To eliminate torn skins and broken slices, a common pitfall in boiling skin-on red potatoes, we sliced the potatoes before boiling them. To evenly infuse the potatoes with the garlicky mustard vinaigrette, we spread the warm potatoes out on a baking sheet and poured the vinaigrette over the top. Gently folding in fresh herbs just before serving helped keep the potatoes intact. If fresh chervil isn't available, substitute an additional ½ tablespoon of minced parsley and an additional ½ teaspoon of tarragon. Use small red potatoes measuring 1 to 2 inches in diameter for this recipe.

2	pounds small red potatoes, unpeeled, sliced ¼ inch thick
2	tablespoons salt
1	garlic clove, peeled and threaded on skewer
¼	cup extra-virgin olive oil
1½	tablespoons champagne vinegar or white wine vinegar
2	teaspoons Dijon mustard
½	teaspoon pepper
1	small shallot, minced
1	tablespoon minced fresh chervil
1	tablespoon minced fresh parsley
1	tablespoon minced fresh chives
1	teaspoon minced fresh tarragon

1. Place potatoes and salt in large saucepan and add water to cover by 1 inch. Bring to boil over high heat, reduce heat to medium-low, and simmer until potatoes are just tender and paring knife can be slipped in and out of potatoes with little resistance, 5 to 6 minutes.

2. While potatoes are cooking, lower skewered garlic into simmering water and blanch for 45 seconds. Run garlic under cold running water, then remove from skewer and mince.

3. Drain potatoes, reserving ¼ cup cooking water. Arrange hot potatoes close together in single layer on rimmed baking sheet. Whisk oil, minced garlic, vinegar, mustard, pepper, and reserved potato cooking water together in bowl, then drizzle evenly over potatoes. Let potatoes sit at room temperature until flavors meld, about 10 minutes. (Potatoes can be refrigerated for up to 8 hours; return to room temperature before serving.)

Making French Potato Salad

1. COOK SLICED POTATOES: Combine sliced potatoes and salt in large saucepan and cover with 1 inch water. Bring to boil over high heat, reduce heat to medium-low, and simmer until potatoes are just tender, 5 to 6 minutes.

2. BLANCH GARLIC: While potatoes are cooking, lower skewered garlic into simmering water and blanch for 45 seconds. Run garlic under cold running water, then remove from skewer and mince.

3. POUR DRESSING OVER WARM POTATOES: Arrange hot potatoes close together in single layer on rimmed baking sheet. Drizzle evenly with dressing and let sit at room temperature until flavors meld, about 10 minutes.

4. ADD HERBS BEFORE SERVING: Combine shallot and herbs in small bowl, then sprinkle over potatoes and combine gently using rubber spatula. Serve.

4. Transfer potatoes to large bowl. Combine shallot and herbs in small bowl, then sprinkle over potatoes and combine gently using rubber spatula. Serve.

VARIATIONS

French Potato Salad with Fennel, Tomato, and Olives FAST VEGAN GF

If desired, chop 1 tablespoon of the fennel fronds and add it to the salad with the parsley.

Omit chervil, chives, and tarragon. Increase parsley to 3 tablespoons. Add ½ bulb thinly sliced fennel, 1 cored and chopped tomato, and ¼ cup pitted oil-cured black olives, quartered, to salad with shallots and parsley.

French Potato Salad with Radishes, Cornichons, and Capers FAST VEGAN GF

Omit chervil, chives, tarragon, and parsley. Substitute 2 table-spoons minced red onion for shallot. Add 2 thinly sliced red radishes, ¼ cup rinsed capers, and ¼ cup thinly sliced cornichons to salad with onion.

Sweet and Red Potato Salad

SERVES 6 TO 8 FAST GF

WHY THIS RECIPE WORKS: For a sweet take on classic potato salad, we added in sweet potatoes and Granny Smith apples with the usual potatoes and swapped out the mayo dressing for a light vinaigrette. We found that chunks of red potatoes held their shape better than other types when simmered. To balance the sweetness of the apples, we added a bit of hot sauce for kick. Cider vinegar nicely accentuated the flavor of the apples, and whole-grain mustard and honey rounded out the dressing. We prefer the mild flavor of regular olive oil in this dressing instead of the stronger flavor of extra-virgin olive oil. While any variety of apple will work here, we prefer the tartness and crunch of Granny Smiths in this recipe.

SALAD
- 2 **pounds sweet potatoes, peeled and cut into ¾-inch pieces**
- 1 **pound red potatoes, unpeeled, cut into ¾-inch pieces**
- 2 **tablespoons salt**
- 3 **Granny Smith apples, peeled, cored, and cut into ¾-inch chunks**
- 2 **ounces (2 cups) baby arugula**
- 4 **scallions, sliced thin**

For a lighter take on potato salad, we combine crisp apples, sweet potatoes, and red potatoes with a flavorful vinaigrette.

DRESSING
- ¼ **cup cider vinegar**
- 3 **tablespoons whole-grain mustard**
- 2 **tablespoons honey**
- 1 **tablespoon hot sauce**
- ½ **cup olive oil**
  Salt and pepper

1. FOR THE SALAD: Place sweet potatoes, red potatoes, and salt in large saucepan and add water to cover by 1 inch. Bring to boil over high heat, reduce heat to medium-low, and simmer until potatoes are just tender and paring knife can be slipped in and out of potatoes with little resistance, about 8 minutes.

2. Drain potatoes and let cool to room temperature, 15 to 30 minutes. When cool, combine potatoes with apples, arugula, and scallions in large bowl.

3. FOR THE DRESSING: Meanwhile, combine vinegar, mustard, honey, and hot sauce together in small bowl. Whisking constantly, drizzle in oil. Drizzle dressing over salad and toss gently to coat. Season with salt and pepper to taste and serve.

Sweet Potato Salad

SERVES 4 TO 6   **VEGAN**   **GF**

✔ WHY THIS RECIPE WORKS: For a picnic-worthy sweet potato salad, we had to rethink our typical potato salad protocol. Unlike their starchy white counterparts, sweet potatoes quickly become waterlogged and mushy when they are boiled. Instead, we steamed the sweet potatoes to get a perfect tender texture without turning them soggy. Adding crisp bell pepper to the steaming basket during the final minutes of cooking helped to temper its raw crunch. Then we tossed the vegetables with a seasoned vinegar mixture to ensure that they were well flavored throughout. Chilling the sweet potatoes in the refrigerator before finishing the salad with vinaigrette, some scallions, and a sprinkling of parsley also prevented them from having a mushy texture. Cilantro can be substituted for the parsley.

- 2 **pounds sweet potatoes, peeled and cut into ¾-inch pieces**
- 1 **red bell pepper, stemmed, seeded, and chopped fine**
- 2½ **tablespoons cider vinegar**
- 1½ **tablespoons Dijon mustard**
  Salt and pepper
  Pinch cayenne pepper
- ¼ **cup extra-virgin olive oil**
- 2 **scallions, sliced thin**
- 2 **tablespoons minced fresh parsley**

1. Fill Dutch oven with 1 inch water and bring to boil over high heat. Reduce heat to medium-low and carefully lower steamer basket into pot. Add sweet potatoes to basket, cover, and cook until potatoes are nearly tender, about 15 minutes.

2. Add bell pepper to basket, cover, and cook until sweet potatoes and pepper are tender, 2 to 4 minutes. Transfer vegetables to large bowl.

3. Whisk vinegar, mustard, ½ teaspoon salt, ¼ teaspoon pepper, and cayenne together in small bowl. Drizzle half of vinegar mixture over vegetables, toss gently to combine, and refrigerate until vegetables are cool, about 45 minutes.

4. Whisking constantly, drizzle oil into remaining vinegar mixture, then gently stir into vegetables. Stir in scallions and parsley, season with salt and pepper to taste, and serve.

Greek Cherry Tomato Salad

SERVES 4 TO 6   **GF**

✔ WHY THIS RECIPE WORKS: Cherry tomatoes can make a great salad, but they exude lots of liquid when cut, quickly turning a salad into a soup. To get rid of some of the tomato juice without throwing away flavor, we quartered and salted the tomatoes before whirling them in a salad spinner to separate the seeds and jelly from the flesh. After we strained the juice and discarded the seeds, we reduced the tomato jelly to a flavorful concentrate (adding garlic, oregano, shallot, olive oil, and vinegar) and reunited it with the tomatoes. Feta cheese added richness and another layer of flavor to this great all-season salad. If cherry tomatoes are unavailable, substitute grape tomatoes cut in half along the equator. If you don't have a salad spinner, wrap the bowl tightly with plastic wrap after the salted tomatoes have stood for 30 minutes and gently shake to remove seeds and excess liquid. Strain the liquid and proceed with the recipe as directed. If you have less than

Preventing Soggy Cherry Tomato Salad

1. Toss tomatoes, ½ teaspoon sugar, and ¼ teaspoon salt together in bowl and let sit for 30 minutes.

2. Transfer tomatoes to salad spinner and spin until seeds and excess liquid have been removed, 45 to 60 seconds, stopping to redistribute tomatoes during spinning.

3. Strain ½ cup tomato liquid through fine-mesh strainer into liquid measuring cup; discard any extra liquid.

4. Bring tomato liquid, shallot, garlic, vinegar, and oregano to simmer in small saucepan over medium heat and cook until reduced to 3 table-spoons, 6 to 8 minutes.

½ cup of juice after spinning, proceed with the recipe using the entire amount of juice and reduce it to 3 tablespoons as directed (the cooking time will be shorter).

- 1½   **pounds cherry tomatoes, quartered**
- ½   **teaspoon sugar**
-    **Salt and pepper**
- 1   **shallot, minced**
- 2   **garlic cloves, minced**
- 1   **tablespoon red wine vinegar**
- ½   **teaspoon dried oregano**
- 2   **tablespoons extra-virgin olive oil**
- 1   **small cucumber, peeled, halved lengthwise, seeded, and cut into ½-inch dice**
- ½   **cup pitted kalamata olives, chopped**
- 4   **ounces feta cheese, crumbled (1 cup)**
- 3   **tablespoons chopped fresh parsley**

1. Toss tomatoes, sugar, and ¼ teaspoon salt together in bowl and let sit for 30 minutes. Transfer tomatoes to salad spinner and spin until seeds and excess liquid have been removed, 45 to 60 seconds, stopping to redistribute tomatoes several times during spinning. Return tomatoes to bowl. Strain ½ cup tomato liquid through fine-mesh strainer into liquid measuring cup; discard any extra liquid.

2. Bring tomato liquid, shallot, garlic, vinegar, and oregano to simmer in small saucepan over medium heat and cook until reduced to 3 tablespoons, 6 to 8 minutes. Transfer to small bowl and let cool to room temperature, about 5 minutes. Whisking constantly, drizzle in oil. Season with salt and pepper to taste.

3. Add cucumber, olives, feta, and parsley to bowl with tomatoes. Drizzle with dressing and toss gently to coat. Serve.

VARIATIONS

Cherry Tomato Salad with Basil and Fresh Mozzarella GF

Omit garlic, oregano, cucumbers, olives, feta, and parsley. Substitute balsamic vinegar for red wine vinegar. Add 1½ cups fresh basil, roughly torn, and 8 ounces fresh mozzarella, cut into ½-inch cubes and patted dry, to tomatoes with dressing.

Cherry Tomato Salad with Tarragon and Blue Cheese GF

Omit garlic, oregano, cucumbers, olives, feta, and parsley. Substitute cider vinegar for red wine vinegar and add 4 teaspoons honey and 2 teaspoons Dijon mustard to tomato liquid before cooking. Add ½ cup roughly chopped toasted pecans, ½ cup crumbled blue cheese, and 1½ tablespoons chopped fresh tarragon to tomatoes before dressing.

Cherry Tomato Salad with Mango and Lime Curry Vinaigrette GF

Omit garlic, oregano, cucumber, olives, and parsley. Add 4 teaspoons lime juice and ¼ teaspoon curry powder to tomato liquid before cooking. Add 1 mango, peeled, pitted, and cut into ½-inch dice; ½ cup toasted slivered almonds; and 3 tablespoons chopped fresh cilantro to tomatoes before dressing.

Cherry Tomato Salad with Watermelon and Feta Cheese GF

Omit garlic, oregano, cucumber, olives, and parsley. Substitute white wine vinegar for red wine vinegar and vegetable oil for olive oil. Add 1 cup watermelon, cut into ½-inch cubes, and 3 tablespoons chopped fresh mint to tomatoes before dressing.

Caprese Salad

SERVES 4 TO 6   FAST   GF

✔ **WHY THIS RECIPE WORKS:** Italy is famous for *insalata caprese*, its simple salad highlighting fresh mozzarella, ripe tomatoes, and fragrant basil. Despite its simplicity, we wondered if there were any tricks to making a foolproof version. We found that the most important step was to start with fully ripened tomatoes and a good-quality fresh mozzarella packed in water. We tried several different proportions, and tasters preferred the salad made with 3 parts tomato to 2 parts mozzarella. Some recipes call for minced red onion and red wine vinegar; however, we liked the salad simply drizzled with oil and seasoned with salt and pepper so that the acidity of the tomatoes and the delicate flavor of the mozzarella shone through. As for the basil, it was best when roughly chopped and sprinkled over the top; layering whole leaves among the slices of mozzarella and tomato looked appealing, but the leaves were simply too big and too chewy. Lastly, we noted the importance of using a high-quality extra-virgin olive oil and coarse salt. Both regular olive oil and table salt tasted too heavy and dense for this light, aromatic salad. Serve with crusty bread to help sop up the tasty tomato-flavored liquid that pools in the bottom of the platter.

- 1½   **pounds very ripe tomatoes, cored and cut into ¼-inch-thick slices**
- 1   **pound fresh mozzarella cheese, cut into ¼-inch-thick slices**
- 2   **tablespoons coarsely chopped fresh basil**
- ¼   **teaspoon kosher salt or sea salt**
- ⅛   **teaspoon pepper**
- ¼   **cup extra-virgin olive oil**

Buying and Storing Fresh Tomatoes

Buying tomatoes at the height of summer won't guarantee juicy, flavorful fruit, but keeping these guidelines in mind will help.

CHOOSE LOCALLY GROWN TOMATOES

If at all possible, this is the best way to ensure a flavorful tomato. The shorter the distance a tomato has to travel, the riper it can be when it's picked. And commercial tomatoes are engineered to be sturdier, with thicker walls and less of the flavorful jelly and seeds.

LOOKS AREN'T EVERYTHING

When selecting tomatoes, oddly shaped tomatoes are fine, and even cracked skin is OK. Avoid tomatoes that are overly soft or leaking juice. Choose tomatoes that smell fruity and feel heavy. And consider trying heirloom tomatoes; grown from naturally pollinated plants and seeds, they are some of the best local tomatoes you can find.

BUY SUPERMARKET TOMATOES ON THE VINE

If supermarket tomatoes are your only option, look for tomatoes sold on the vine. Although this does not mean that they were fully ripened on the vine, they are better than regular supermarket tomatoes, which are picked when still green and blasted with ethylene gas to develop texture and color.

STORING TOMATOES

Once you've brought your tomatoes home, proper storage is important to preserve their fresh flavor and texture for as long as possible. Here are the rules we follow in the test kitchen:

- Never refrigerate tomatoes; the cold damages enzymes that produce flavor compounds, and it ruins their texture, turning the flesh mealy. Even when cut, tomatoes should be kept at room temperature (wrap them tightly in plastic wrap).
- If the vine is still attached, leave it on and store the tomatoes stem end up. Tomatoes off the vine should be stored stem side down. We have found that this prevents moisture from escaping and bacteria from entering, and thus prolongs shelf life.
- To quickly ripen hard tomatoes, store them in a paper bag with a banana or apple, both of which emit ethylene gas, which hastens ripening.

Layer tomatoes and mozzarella alternately, in concentric circles, over platter. Sprinkle with basil, salt, and pepper, then drizzle with oil. Let salad sit until flavors meld, 5 to 10 minutes. Serve.

Tomato and Burrata Salad with Pangrattato and Basil

SERVES 4 TO 6

✔ **WHY THIS RECIPE WORKS:** Burrata is a deluxe version of fresh mozzarella in which the supple cheese is bound around a filling of cream and bits of cheese. We wanted to create a Caprese-inspired salad in which this decadent cheese could star alongside summer's best tomatoes. We quickly realized that just tomatoes, basil, and good extra-virgin olive oil weren't enough to bring out the best in the cheese as they do in Caprese; the richness of the Burrata overwhelmed the components. To maximize the flavor of the tomatoes, we used a combination of standard tomatoes and sweet cherry tomatoes, and we found that salting them and letting them sit for 30 minutes helped draw out their watery juices, intensifying the tomato flavor. Blending the olive oil with a little minced shallot and mild sweet-tart white balsamic vinegar gave us a simple but bold vinaigrette. Finally, we found that adding a topping of Italian *pangrattato* (garlicky bread crumbs) helped bring the dish together, soaking up both the tomato juices and the Burrata cream. The success of this dish depends on using ripe, flavorful tomatoes and fresh, high-quality Burrata. Be ready to serve this dish immediately after it is assembled.

- 3 ounces rustic white bread, torn into rough pieces (1½ cups)
- 6 tablespoons extra-virgin olive oil
  Salt and pepper
- 1 garlic clove, minced
- 1½ pounds very ripe tomatoes, cored and cut into 1-inch pieces
- ½ pound cherry or grape tomatoes, halved
- 1 shallot, halved and sliced thin
- 1½ tablespoons white balsamic vinegar
- ½ cup chopped fresh basil
- 8-10 ounces Burrata cheese, room temperature

This decadent take on *insalata caprese* features fresh summer tomatoes, Burrata cheese, basil, and garlicky bread crumbs.

1. Pulse bread in food processor into large crumbs measuring between ⅛ and ¼ inch, about 10 pulses. Combine crumbs, 2 tablespoons oil, pinch salt, and pinch pepper in 12-inch nonstick skillet. Cook over medium heat, stirring often, until crumbs are crisp and golden, about 10 minutes. Clear center of skillet, add garlic, and cook, mashing it into skillet, until fragrant, about 30 seconds. Stir garlic into crumbs. Transfer to plate and let cool.

2. Meanwhile, spread tomatoes out over baking sheet lined with several layers of paper towels. Sprinkle with ¼ teaspoon salt and let sit for 30 minutes.

3. Combine shallot, vinegar, and ¼ teaspoon salt in large bowl. Whisking constantly, drizzle in remaining 4 tablespoons oil. Add tomatoes and basil, toss gently to combine, then arrange on platter. Place Burrata on clean plate and cut into 1-inch pieces, collecting creamy liquid. Sprinkle Burrata evenly over tomatoes and drizzle with creamy liquid. Sprinkle with bread crumbs and serve immediately.

Grilled Vegetable and Bread Salad

SERVES 2

✔ **WHY THIS RECIPE WORKS:** Grilled vegetables are the perfect basis for a summer supper, when all kinds of produce are at the height of ripeness. We wanted to pair nicely charred vegetables with chunks of rustic bread, fresh herbs, and a bright vinaigrette for a summery take on Italian-style vegetable and bread salad. To keep with our Mediterranean theme, we chose zucchini, red bell pepper, and sweet red onion for the vegetables. After 10 minutes on the grill, the vegetables were perfectly browned and tender and full of smoky flavor. We brushed slices of rustic French bread with oil and quickly toasted them over the grill. Then we simply tossed everything with a vinaigrette of basil, lemon, garlic, and mustard. A rustic round loaf, or a baguette sliced on the extreme bias, works best for this recipe. Be sure to use high-quality bread. You will need one 12-inch metal skewer for this recipe. This recipe can be doubled; you may need to cook the vegetables and bread in separate batches depending on the size of your grill.

¼   cup extra-virgin olive oil
1   tablespoon chopped fresh basil
½   teaspoon grated lemon zest plus 2 teaspoons juice
1   small garlic clove, minced
½   teaspoon Dijon mustard
    Salt and pepper
1   small red onion, sliced into ¾-inch-thick rounds
1   red bell pepper, stemmed, seeded, and quartered
1   zucchini, halved lengthwise
3   ounces French or Italian bread, cut into 1-inch-thick slices
2   ounces goat cheese, crumbled (½ cup)

1. Whisk 2 tablespoons oil, basil, lemon zest and juice, garlic, mustard, ⅛ teaspoon salt, and ⅛ teaspoon pepper together in large bowl. Thread onion rounds from side to side

Skewering Onion for Grilling

For easy grilling, skewer onion slices from side to side.

onto 12-inch metal skewer. Brush onion, bell pepper, zucchini, and bread with remaining 2 tablespoons oil and season with salt and pepper.

2A. FOR A CHARCOAL GRILL: Open bottom vent completely. Light large chimney starter half-filled with charcoal briquettes (3 quarts). When top coals are partially covered with ash, pour evenly over grill. Set cooking grate in place, cover, and open lid vent completely. Heat grill until hot, about 5 minutes.

2B. FOR A GAS GRILL: Turn all burners to high, cover, and heat grill until hot, about 15 minutes. Turn all burners to medium.

3. Clean and oil cooking grate. Place vegetables and bread on grill. Cook, covered if using gas, flipping as needed, until bread is well toasted, about 4 minutes, and vegetables are spottily charred, 10 to 15 minutes. Transfer bread and vegetables to cutting board as they finish cooking.

4. Carefully remove onion from skewer. Cut vegetables and bread into 1-inch pieces and toss gently in bowl with vinaigrette. Divide among salad plates, sprinkle with goat cheese, and serve.

NOTES FROM THE TEST KITCHEN

The Best Extra-Virgin Olive Oil

For most cooked dishes, we're perfectly happy reaching for an inexpensive olive oil, but in vinaigrettes or for drizzling over dishes, only a good-quality olive oil will do. Extra-virgin oils range wildly in price, color, and quality, so it's hard to know which to buy. While many things can affect the quality and flavor of olive oil, the type of olive, the time of harvest (earlier means greener, more bitter, and pungent; later, more mild and buttery), and the processing are the most important factors. The best-quality olive oil comes from olives pressed as quickly as possible without heat (which coaxes more oil from the olives at the expense of flavor). Out of those we tasted, our favorites oils were produced from a blend of olives and, thus, were well rounded. Made of a blend of intense Picual, mild Hojiblanca, Ocal, and Arbequina olives, **Columela Extra Virgin Olive Oil** took top honors for its buttery, fruity flavor and excellent balance.

We toast the bread and salt the tomatoes to make a panzanella salad with lightly moistened, not soggy, chunks of rustic bread.

Panzanella

SERVES 4   VEGAN

☑ **WHY THIS RECIPE WORKS:** When the rustic Italian bread and tomato salad, *panzanella*, is done well, the sweet juice of the tomatoes mixes with a bright-tasting vinaigrette, moistening chunks of thick-crusted bread until they're soft and just a little chewy—but the line between lightly moistened and unpleasantly soggy is very thin. Toasting fresh bread in the oven, rather than using the traditional day-old bread, was a good start. The bread lost enough moisture in the oven to absorb the dressing without getting waterlogged. A 10-minute soak in the flavorful dressing yielded perfectly moistened, nutty-tasting bread ready to be tossed with the tomatoes, which we salted to intensify their flavor. A thinly sliced cucumber and shallot for crunch and bite plus a handful of chopped fresh basil perfected our salad. The success of this recipe depends on high-quality ingredients, including ripe, in-season tomatoes and fruity olive oil. Fresh basil is also a must. Your bread may vary in density, so you may not need the entire loaf for this recipe. Be ready to serve this dish immediately after it is assembled.

    1   (1-pound) loaf rustic Italian or French bread,
        cut or torn into 1-inch pieces (6 cups)
    ½   cup extra-virgin olive oil
        Salt and pepper
    1½ pounds ripe tomatoes, cored, seeded,
        and cut into 1-inch pieces
    3   tablespoons red wine vinegar
    1   cucumber, peeled, halved lengthwise, seeded,
        and sliced thin
    1   shallot, sliced thin
    ¼   cup chopped fresh basil

1. Adjust oven rack to middle position and heat oven to 400 degrees. Toss bread pieces with 2 tablespoons oil and ¼ teaspoon salt in bowl and spread in single layer on rimmed baking sheet. Toast bread until just starting to turn light golden, 15 to 20 minutes, stirring halfway through baking. Let cool to room temperature.

2. Meanwhile, gently toss tomatoes with ½ teaspoon salt in large bowl. Transfer to colander set over now-empty bowl and let drain for 15 minutes, tossing occasionally.

3. Whisk remaining 6 tablespoons oil, vinegar, and ¼ teaspoon pepper into drained tomato juices. Add toasted bread, toss to coat, and let stand for 10 minutes, tossing occasionally. Add drained tomatoes, cucumber, shallot, and basil, and toss to coat. Season with salt and pepper to taste and serve immediately.

VARIATIONS

Panzanella with Garlic and Capers `VEGAN`

Whisk 1 minced garlic clove and 2 tablespoons rinsed capers into dressing before adding toasted bread.

Panzanella with Olives and Feta

Add ⅓ cup coarsely chopped kalamata olives and ½ cup crumbled feta cheese to salad with vegetables before serving.

Panzanella with Peppers and Arugula `VEGAN`

Substitute 1 thinly sliced stemmed and seeded red bell pepper for cucumber and 1 cup coarsely chopped baby arugula for basil.

Pita Bread Salad with Olives and Feta (Fattoush)

SERVES 4 TO 6 `FAST`

WHY THIS RECIPE WORKS: Traditionally, *fattoush* consists of small bites of days-old pita bread mixed with cucumbers and tomatoes and dressed with lemon juice, mint, and fruity olive oil. The dry bread should hold up to the dressing and vegetables without becoming soggy. To prevent the bread from turning soggy under the vinaigrette, we crisped the pita bread in the oven. For the tomatoes, we decided to use cherry tomatoes since they are consistently sweet year round. We also added some romaine lettuce to ensure the salad had plenty of crisp, fresh crunch. A lemony vinaigrette with a generous amount of mint and parsley kept the flavors in the salad fresh and bright. Finally, crumbled feta cheese and kalamata olives added bursts of great flavor.

    4   (8-inch) pita breads, torn into ½-inch pieces
    ½   cup extra-virgin olive oil
    ¼   cup fresh mint leaves
    ¼   cup fresh parsley leaves
    ¼   cup lemon juice (2 lemons)
        Salt and pepper
    1   small head romaine lettuce (10 ounces),
        torn into 1-inch pieces
    12 ounces cherry tomatoes, halved
    1   cucumber, peeled, halved lengthwise, seeded,
        and cut into ½-inch pieces
    3   scallions, sliced thin
    ½   cup pitted kalamata olives, sliced thin
    4   ounces feta cheese, crumbled (1 cup)

1. Adjust oven rack to middle position and heat oven to 375 degrees. Spread pita out evenly over rimmed baking sheet and bake until crisp but not brown, 7 to 10 minutes, stirring halfway through baking. Let cool to room temperature.

2. Pulse oil, mint, parsley, lemon juice, and ¼ teaspoon salt in blender (or mini food processor) until herbs are finely chopped, about 20 pulses. Toss cooled pita, dressing, lettuce, tomatoes, cucumber, scallions, and olives together in large bowl. Season with salt and pepper to taste, sprinkle with feta, and serve.

CHAPTER 7

Vegetable Sides

■ FAST (Less than 45 minutes start to finish)   ▪ VEGAN   ▦ GLUTEN-FREE

Photos: Roasted Winter Squash Halves; Spinach with Garlic and Lemon

Roasted Artichokes

SERVES 4 `VEGAN` `GF`

✓ **WHY THIS RECIPE WORKS:** Steaming artichokes washes out their delicate nuttiness. We wanted to roast artichokes for concentrated flavor and great caramelization. First we prepped the artichokes for the oven, trimming the leaves, halving the artichokes, and removing the fuzzy chokes. Submerging the prepped artichokes in water and lemon juice kept them from oxidizing. Because they have so much surface area, artichokes can quickly dry out and toughen in the oven, so we covered them with aluminum foil to let them steam in their own juices. This gave us tender inner leaves and hearts, perfectly softened outer leaves, and a great nutty flavor. Tossing the artichokes with oil and roasting them cut side down encouraged flavorful browning. If your artichokes are larger than 8 to 10 ounces, strip away another layer or two of the toughest outer leaves. The tender inner leaves, heart, and stem are entirely edible. To eat the tough outer leaves, use your teeth to scrape the flesh out from the underside of each leaf. These artichokes taste great warm or at room temperature.

Roasting fresh artichokes in a covered dish lets them steam in their own juices, concentrating their delicate, nutty flavor.

> 1   **lemon, plus lemon wedges for serving**
> 4   **artichokes (8 to 10 ounces each)**
> 3   **tablespoons extra-virgin olive oil**
> ¾   **teaspoon salt**
>   **Pinch pepper**

1. Adjust oven rack to lower-middle position and heat oven to 475 degrees. Cut lemon in half, squeeze halves into container filled with 2 quarts water, then add spent halves.

2. Working with 1 artichoke at a time, trim stem about ¾ inch long and cut off top quarter of artichoke. Break off bottom 3 or 4 rows of tough outer leaves by pulling them downward. Using paring knife, trim outer layer of stem and base, removing any dark green parts. Cut artichoke in half lengthwise, then remove fuzzy choke and any tiny inner purple-tinged leaves using small spoon. Submerge prepped artichokes in lemon water.

3. Brush 13 by 9-inch baking dish with 1 tablespoon oil. Remove artichokes from lemon water and shake off some of water, leaving some water clinging to leaves. Toss artichokes

Preparing Artichokes for Roasting

1. Using sharp chef's knife, trim stem about ¾ inch long and cut off top quarter of artichoke.

2. Break off bottom 3 or 4 rows of tough outer leaves by pulling them downward.

3. Using paring knife, trim outer layer of stem and base, removing any dark green parts.

4. Halve artichoke lengthwise, then remove fuzzy choke and any inner tiny purple-tinged leaves using small spoon.

Assessing Artichokes

When selecting fresh artichokes at the market, examine the leaves for some clues that will help you pick the best specimens. The leaves should look tight, compact, and bright green; they should not appear dried out or feathery at the edges. If you give an artichoke a squeeze, its leaves should squeak as they rub together (evidence that the artichoke still possesses much of its moisture). The leaves should also snap off cleanly; if they bend, the artichoke is old.

with remaining 2 tablespoons oil, salt, and pepper in bowl; gently rub oil and seasonings between leaves. Arrange artichokes, cut side down, in baking dish and cover tightly with aluminum foil.

4. Roast artichokes until cut sides begin to brown and bases and leaves are tender when poked with tip of paring knife, 25 to 30 minutes. Transfer artichokes to platter and serve with lemon wedges.

VARIATION

Roasted Artichokes with Lemon Vinaigrette VEGAN GF

Trim ends off 2 lemons, halve them crosswise, and arrange, cut side up, next to artichokes in baking dish; roast as directed. Let roasted lemons cool slightly, then squeeze into fine-mesh strainer set over bowl, extracting as much juice and pulp as possible; press firmly on solids to yield 1½ tablespoons juice. Whisk ½ teaspoon finely grated garlic, ½ teaspoon Dijon mustard, and ½ teaspoon salt into juice and season with pepper to taste. Whisking constantly, gradually drizzle in 6 tablespoons extra-virgin olive oil until emulsified. Whisk in 2 tablespoons minced fresh parsley. Serve with artichokes.

Pan-Roasted Asparagus

SERVES 4 TO 6 FAST GF

✔ **WHY THIS RECIPE WORKS:** Pan roasting is a simple stovetop cooking method that delivers crisp, evenly browned asparagus spears without the fuss of having to rotate each spear individually. We started with thicker spears because thin ones overcooked before they browned. To help the asparagus release moisture, which encouraged caramelization and better flavor, we parcooked it, covered, with butter and oil before browning it. The water evaporating from the butter helped to steam the asparagus, producing bright green, crisp-tender

spears. At this point, we removed the lid and cranked up the heat until the spears were evenly browned on the bottom. We found there was no need to brown the asparagus all over; tasters preferred the flavor of spears browned on only one side, and, as a bonus, the partially browned spears never had a chance to go limp. This recipe works best with asparagus that is at least ½ inch thick near the base. If using thinner spears, reduce the covered cooking time to 3 minutes and the uncovered cooking time to 5 minutes. Do not use pencil-thin asparagus; it overcooks too easily. You will need a 12-inch skillet with a tight-fitting lid for this recipe.

1 tablespoon extra-virgin olive oil
1 tablespoon unsalted butter
2 pounds thick asparagus, trimmed
  Salt and pepper
1 tablespoon lemon juice (optional)

1. Heat oil and butter in 12-inch skillet over medium-high heat. When butter has melted, add half of asparagus with tips pointed in one direction and remaining asparagus with tips pointed in opposite direction. Shake pan gently to help distribute spears evenly (they will not quite fit in single layer). Cover and cook until asparagus is bright green and still crisp, about 5 minutes.

2. Uncover, increase heat to high, and season with salt and pepper. Cook, moving spears around with tongs as needed, until asparagus is tender and well browned on 1 side, 5 to 7 minutes. Transfer asparagus to platter, sprinkle with lemon juice, if using, and serve.

VARIATIONS

Pan-Roasted Asparagus with Toasted Garlic and Parmesan FAST GF

Before cooking asparagus, cook 2 tablespoons extra-virgin olive oil and 3 thinly sliced garlic cloves in 12-inch skillet over medium heat, stirring occasionally, until garlic is crisp and golden, about 5 minutes. Using slotted spoon, transfer garlic to paper towel–lined plate. Add butter to oil left in skillet and cook asparagus as directed. Sprinkle asparagus with toasted garlic and 2 tablespoons grated Parmesan cheese before serving.

Pan-Roasted Asparagus with Cherry Tomatoes and Kalamata Olives FAST GF

Before cooking asparagus, cook 1 tablespoon extra-virgin olive oil and 2 minced garlic cloves in 12-inch skillet over medium heat until lightly golden, 2 to 3 minutes. Stir in 2 cups halved cherry tomatoes and ½ cup pitted and chopped kalamata olives and cook until tomatoes begin to break down, 1 to 2 minutes;

transfer mixture to bowl. Rinse and dry skillet, then cook asparagus as directed. Top asparagus with tomato mixture, ¼ cup chopped fresh basil, and ½ cup grated Parmesan cheese before serving.

Trimming Asparagus

1. Remove 1 stalk of asparagus from bunch and bend at thicker end until it snaps.

2. With broken asparagus as guide, trim tough ends from remaining asparagus bunch using chef's knife.

Broiled Asparagus

SERVES 2 TO 3 `FAST` `VEGAN` `GF`

✔ **WHY THIS RECIPE WORKS:** Broiling asparagus concentrates its flavor, helps to lightly caramelize its exterior, and, perhaps best of all, can be done in just minutes. We started with a bunch of asparagus of even thickness to be sure the spears would cook through evenly, then we tossed them with extra-virgin olive oil and seasoned them simply with salt and pepper. In just 10 minutes under the intense heat of the broiler, the spears were tender and lightly browned. And while we enjoyed the spears as is, we also came up with a simple balsamic glaze and an Asian vinaigrette, which we could prepare while the asparagus cooked. To ensure even cooking, choose asparagus that is roughly ½ inch thick. This asparagus can be served warm, at room temperature, or even chilled if desired.

 1 **pound asparagus, trimmed**
 1 **tablespoon extra-virgin olive oil**
   Salt and pepper
 1 **teaspoon lemon juice (optional)**

Adjust oven rack 6 inches from broiler element and heat broiler. Toss asparagus with oil in bowl and season with salt and pepper. Lay asparagus in single layer on rimmed baking sheet. Broil, shaking pan occasionally, until asparagus is tender and lightly browned, about 10 minutes. Transfer asparagus to serving dish and sprinkle with lemon juice, if using. Serve.

Broiled Asparagus with Balsamic Glaze `FAST` `VEGAN` `GF`

Simmer ¾ cup balsamic vinegar in 8-inch skillet over medium heat until reduced to ¼ cup, 15 to 20 minutes. Off heat, stir in ¼ cup extra-virgin olive oil; drizzle over broiled asparagus before serving.

Broiled Asparagus with Soy-Ginger Vinaigrette `FAST` `VEGAN` `GF`

In order for this recipe to be gluten-free, you must use gluten-free soy sauce or tamari.

Substitute vegetable oil for olive oil. Whisk ¼ cup lime juice (2 limes), 3 tablespoons toasted sesame oil, 3 tablespoons soy sauce, 2 thinly sliced scallions, 2 minced garlic cloves, 1 tablespoon grated fresh ginger, and 1 tablespoon honey together in bowl; drizzle over broiled asparagus before serving.

Braised Beets with Lemon and Almonds

SERVES 4 TO 6 `VEGAN` `GF`

✔ **WHY THIS RECIPE WORKS:** We sought a streamlined recipe for beets that maximized their sweet, earthy flavor—with minimal mess. Roasting the beets took over an hour, and boiling washed away their flavor, but braising worked perfectly. We partially submerged the beets in just 1¼ cups of water so that they partially simmered and partially steamed. Halving the beets cut down our cooking time even further. In just 45 minutes, the beets were tender and their skins slipped off easily. To further amplify their flavor, we reduced the braising liquid and added brown sugar and vinegar to make a glossy sauce. Shallot, toasted almonds, fresh mint and thyme, and a little lemon zest finished the dish. Look for beets that are roughly 2 to 3 inches in diameter. The beets can be served warm or at room temperature. If serving at room temperature, add the nuts, seeds, and fresh herbs right before serving.

 1½ **pounds beets, trimmed and halved horizontally**
 1¼ **cups water**
    Salt and pepper
  3 **tablespoons distilled white vinegar**
  1 **tablespoon packed light brown sugar**
  1 **shallot, sliced thin**
  1 **teaspoon grated lemon zest**
  ½ **cup almonds, toasted and chopped**
  2 **tablespoons chopped fresh mint**
  1 **teaspoon chopped fresh thyme**

For sweet, earthy braised beets, we submerge the beets in water partway so they partially simmer and partially steam.

1. Place beets, cut side down, in single layer in 11-inch straight-sided sauté pan or Dutch oven. Add water and ¼ teaspoon salt and bring to simmer over high heat. Reduce heat to low, cover, and simmer until beets are tender and tip of paring knife inserted into beets meets no resistance, 45 to 50 minutes.

2. Transfer beets to cutting board. Increase heat to medium-high and reduce cooking liquid, stirring occasionally, until pan is almost dry, 5 to 6 minutes. Add vinegar and sugar, return to boil, and cook, stirring constantly with heat-resistant spatula, until spatula leaves wide trail when dragged through glaze, 1 to 2 minutes. Remove pan from heat.

3. When beets are cool enough to handle, rub off skins with paper towel and cut into ½-inch wedges. Add beets, shallot, lemon zest, ½ teaspoon salt, and ¼ teaspoon pepper to glaze and toss to coat. Transfer to platter, sprinkle with almonds, mint, and thyme, and serve.

VARIATIONS

Beets with Lime and Pepitas VEGAN GF
Omit thyme. Substitute lime zest for lemon zest, toasted pepitas for almonds, and cilantro for mint.

Making Braised Beets

1. BRAISE HALVED BEETS: Place halved beets, cut side down, in sauté pan or Dutch oven with 1¼ cups water, and braise gently until beets are tender.

2. COOL, SKIN, AND CUT BEETS: Remove beets from pot, let cool, then rub off skins. Cut into ½-inch wedges.

3. REDUCE COOKING LIQUID TO MAKE GLAZE: Reduce braising liquid until pan is almost dry. Add vinegar and sugar and simmer until spatula leaves wide trail when dragged through glaze.

4. TOSS BEETS WITH GLAZE: Return beets to pot with shallot, lemon zest, salt, and pepper, and toss gently to coat.

NOTES FROM THE TEST KITCHEN

Beating Beet Stains

When cut, beets can bleed onto your cutting board, making a mess. To ensure easy cleanup, give the surface a light coat of vegetable oil spray before chopping. This thin coating will allow you to quickly wipe the board clean with a paper towel before proceeding with your next task.

Beets with Orange and Walnuts VEGAN GF
Substitute orange zest for lemon zest, walnuts for almonds, and parsley for mint.

Sesame-Glazed Baby Bok Choy

SERVES 4   **FAST**   **VEGAN**   **GF**

✔ **WHY THIS RECIPE WORKS:** When cooked properly, bok choy boasts crisp, celery-like stalks with an almost creamy texture and tender, earthy leaves. But bok choy can easily turn mushy and pallid. We wanted a cooking method that would give us perfectly cooked stalks and leaves every time. Steaming and blanching both made the bok choy limp and watery. We had better luck with stir-frying, which gave us crisp-tender stalks and flavorful browning. We got the best results with baby bok choy; its more delicate stalks cooked through by the time the leaves softened. To get great browning, we halved the heads and cooked them cut side down, without stirring, in a hot pan. Once they were perfectly tender, we set them aside and made a quick garlicky stir-fry sauce in the skillet. A sprinkling of toasted sesame seeds before serving added a pleasant crunch. Look for baby bok choy weighing no more than 4 ounces. If your market sells slightly larger baby bok choy, remove a layer or two of large outer stalks so that the vegetable will cook through properly. In order for this recipe to be gluten-free, you must use gluten-free soy sauce or tamari.

    2 tablespoons soy sauce
    2 tablespoons vegetable broth
    1 tablespoon rice vinegar
    2 teaspoons toasted sesame oil
    1 teaspoon sugar
    3 tablespoons vegetable oil
    3 garlic cloves, minced
    1 tablespoon grated fresh ginger
    2 scallions, sliced thin
    4 heads baby bok choy (4 ounces each), halved lengthwise
    1 tablespoon sesame seeds, toasted

1. Combine soy sauce, broth, vinegar, sesame oil, and sugar in bowl. In separate bowl, combine 1 tablespoon vegetable oil, garlic, ginger, and scallions.

2. Heat remaining 2 tablespoons vegetable oil in 12-inch nonstick skillet over high heat until just smoking. Place bok choy, cut side down, in skillet in single layer. Cook without moving until lightly browned, about 3 minutes. Turn bok choy and cook until lightly browned on second side, about 2 minutes. Transfer to platter.

3. Add garlic mixture to now-empty skillet and cook, stirring constantly, until fragrant, about 20 seconds. Add soy sauce mixture and simmer until thickened, about 20 seconds.

4. Return bok choy to skillet and cook, turning to coat with sauce, about 1 to 2 minutes. Return bok choy to platter, sprinkle with sesame seeds, and serve.

Skillet Broccoli with Olive Oil and Garlic

SERVES 4   **FAST**   **VEGAN**   **GF**

✔ **WHY THIS RECIPE WORKS:** The problem with sautéing broccoli florets is getting the toothsome core to cook through before the delicate outer buds overcook and begin to fall apart. A quick solution is to use a stir-fry method. First the broccoli is browned for color, then it's quickly steamed to cook through, and finally it's sautéed with some aromatics for a boost in flavor. The best thing about the stir-fry method is that you can do all three steps in quick succession in a 12-inch skillet with a tight-fitting lid. Either a traditional or a nonstick 12-inch skillet will work for this recipe. Using broccoli florets, rather than a bunch of broccoli, can save valuable prep time for this side dish. If buying broccoli in a bunch instead, you will need about 1½ pounds of broccoli in order to yield 1 pound of florets.

    3 tablespoons extra-virgin olive oil
    2 garlic cloves, minced
    ½ teaspoon minced fresh thyme
    1 pound broccoli florets, cut into 1-inch pieces
       Salt and pepper
    3 tablespoons water

1. Combine 1 tablespoon oil, garlic, and thyme in bowl. Heat remaining 2 tablespoons oil in 12-inch skillet over medium-high heat until just smoking. Add broccoli and ¼ teaspoon salt and cook, without stirring, until beginning to brown, about 2 minutes.

2. Add water, cover, and cook until broccoli is bright green but still crisp, about 2 minutes. Uncover and continue to cook until water has evaporated and broccoli is crisp-tender, about 2 minutes.

3. Clear center of pan, add garlic mixture, and cook, mashing mixture into skillet, until fragrant, about 30 seconds. Stir garlic mixture into broccoli. Transfer broccoli to serving dish and season with salt and pepper to taste. Serve.

VARIATION

Skillet Broccoli with Sesame Oil and Ginger   **FAST**   **VEGAN**   **GF**

Omit thyme. In garlic mixture, substitute 1 tablespoon toasted sesame oil for olive oil, and add 1 tablespoon grated fresh ginger. Substitute 2 tablespoons vegetable oil for olive oil when cooking broccoli.

Roasted Broccoli

SERVES 4 `FAST` `VEGAN` `GF`

✔ **WHY THIS RECIPE WORKS:** Roasting is a great way to deepen the flavor of vegetables, but broccoli can be tricky to roast given its awkward shape, dense, woody stalks, and shrubby florets. We wanted a roasted broccoli recipe that would give us evenly cooked broccoli—stalks and florets—and add concentrated flavor and dappled browning. The way we prepared the broccoli was the key. We sliced the crown in half, then cut each half into uniform wedges. We cut the stalks into rectangular pieces slightly smaller than the more delicate wedges. This promoted even cooking and great browning by maximizing contact with the hot baking sheet. Preheating the baking sheet on the lowest rack of the oven gave us even better browning. Tossing a scant ½ teaspoon of sugar over the broccoli along with salt, pepper, and a splash of olive oil gave us crisp-tipped florets and blistered and browned stalks that were sweet and full-flavored. Make sure to trim away the outer peel from the broccoli stalks as directed; otherwise, it will turn tough when cooked.

1¾ pounds broccoli
3 tablespoons extra-virgin olive oil
½ teaspoon sugar
½ teaspoon salt
Pinch pepper
Lemon wedges

1. Adjust oven rack to lowest position, place rimmed baking sheet on rack, and heat oven to 500 degrees. Cut broccoli horizontally at juncture of crowns and stalks. Cut crowns into 4 wedges if 3 to 4 inches in diameter or 6 wedges if 4 to

Cutting Broccoli Crowns into Wedges

1. Cut broccoli horizontally at juncture of crown and stalk, then cut crown in half through central stalk.

2. Cut crowns that measure 3 to 4 inches in diameter into 4 wedges, and crowns that measure 4 to 5 inches in diameter into 6 wedges.

For perfectly cooked roasted broccoli, we cut the crown into uniform wedges and the hearty stalks into smaller matchsticks.

5 inches in diameter. Trim tough outer peel from stalks, then cut into ½-inch-thick planks about 2 to 3 inches long.

2. Toss broccoli with oil, sugar, salt, and pepper in bowl. Working quickly, lay broccoli in single layer, flat sides down, on hot baking sheet. Roast until stalks are well browned and tender and florets are lightly browned, 9 to 11 minutes. Transfer to platter and serve with lemon wedges.

VARIATIONS

Roasted Broccoli with Garlic `FAST` `VEGAN` `GF`
Stir 1 tablespoon minced garlic into oil before tossing it with raw broccoli.

Roasted Broccoli with Shallots, Fennel Seeds, and Parmesan `FAST` `GF`
While broccoli roasts, heat 1 tablespoon extra-virgin olive oil in 8-inch skillet over medium heat until shimmering. Add 3 thinly sliced shallots and cook, stirring often, until shallots soften and are beginning to brown, 5 to 6 minutes. Stir in 1 teaspoon coarsely chopped fennel seeds and cook until

All About Garlic

The pungent, aromatic flavor of garlic is great in everything from pasta sauces to vinaigrettes to steamed vegetables. Here's everything you need to know about buying, storing, and cooking with garlic.

BUYING GARLIC

When shopping for garlic, look for unpackaged loose garlic heads so you can examine them closely. Pick heads without spots, mold, or sprouting. Squeeze them to make sure they are not rubbery, have no soft spots, and aren't missing cloves. The garlic shouldn't have much of a scent; if it does, you're risking spoilage. Of the various garlic varieties, your best bet is soft-neck garlic, since it stores well and is heat-tolerant. This variety features a circle of large cloves surrounding a small cluster at the center. Hard-neck garlic has a stiff center staff surrounded by large, uniform cloves and boasts a more intense, complex flavor. But since it's easily damaged and doesn't store as well as soft-neck garlic, wait to buy it at the farmers' market.

STORING GARLIC

With proper storage, whole heads of garlic should last at least a few weeks. Store heads in a cool, dark place with plenty of air circulation to prevent spoiling and sprouting. (A small basket in the pantry is ideal.)

PREPARING GARLIC

When preparing garlic, keep in mind that garlic's pungency emerges only after its cell walls are ruptured, triggering the creation of a compound called allicin. The more a clove is broken down, the more allicin is produced. Thus you can control the amount of bite garlic contributes to a recipe by how fine or coarse you cut it. It's also best not to cut garlic in advance; the longer cut garlic sits, the harsher its flavor.

COOKING GARLIC

Garlic's flavor is sharpest when raw. Once heated above 150 degrees, its enzymes are destroyed and no new flavor is produced. This is why roasted garlic, which is cooked slowly and takes longer to reach 150 degrees, has a mellow, slightly sweet flavor. Alternatively, garlic browned at very high temperatures (300 to 350 degrees) results in a more bitter flavor. To avoid the creation of bitter compounds, wait to add garlic to the pan until other aromatics or ingredients have softened. And don't cook garlic over high heat for much longer than 30 seconds; you want to cook it, stirring constantly, only until it turns fragrant.

shallots are golden brown, 1 to 2 minutes; remove from heat. Toss cooked broccoli with shallot mixture and garnish with shaved Parmesan before serving.

Roasted Broccoli with Olives, Garlic, Oregano, and Lemon FAST VEGAN GF

While broccoli roasts, cook 2 tablespoons extra-virgin olive oil, 5 thinly sliced garlic cloves, and ½ teaspoon red pepper flakes in 8-inch skillet over medium-low heat, stirring often, until garlic softens and is beginning to brown, 5 to 7 minutes. Off heat, stir in 2 tablespoons finely chopped pitted black olives, 1 teaspoon minced fresh oregano, and 2 teaspoons lemon juice. Toss cooked broccoli with olive mixture before serving.

Broccoli Rabe with Garlic and Red Pepper Flakes

SERVES 4 FAST VEGAN GF

✔ WHY THIS RECIPE WORKS: Some people prefer to eat broccoli rabe in its naturally bitter state, but for others, that bitterness is overwhelming. We wanted to develop a quick and dependable method of cooking this aggressive vegetable that would deliver less bitterness and rounder, more balanced flavor. We found that blanching the rabe in a large amount of salted water tamed its bitterness. Then we sautéed the blanched rabe with garlic and red pepper flakes, which complemented the vegetable's strong flavor. Using a salad spinner makes easy work of drying the cooled blanched broccoli rabe. You can reduce the amount of red pepper flakes if you prefer to make this dish less spicy.

14 ounces broccoli rabe, trimmed and cut into 1-inch pieces
   Salt
2 tablespoons extra-virgin olive oil
3 garlic cloves, minced
¼ teaspoon red pepper flakes

1. Bring 3 quarts water to boil in large saucepan. Fill large bowl with ice water. Add broccoli rabe and 2 teaspoons salt to boiling water and cook until wilted and tender, about 2½ minutes. Drain rabe, then transfer to bowl of ice water. Drain again and thoroughly pat dry.

2. Heat oil, garlic, and pepper flakes in 10-inch skillet over medium heat until garlic begins to sizzle, 3 to 4 minutes. Increase heat to medium high, add broccoli rabe, and cook, stirring to coat with oil, until heated through, about 1 minute. Season with salt to taste, transfer to platter, and serve.

VARIATION

Broccoli Rabe with Sun-Dried Tomatoes and Pine Nuts FAST VEGAN GF

Add ¼ cup oil-packed sun-dried tomatoes, cut into thin strips, to pan with garlic and red pepper flakes. Sprinkle broccoli rabe with 3 tablespoons toasted pine nuts before serving.

Garlicky Broccolini

SERVES 4 FAST GF

✔ **WHY THIS RECIPE WORKS:** With its crisp yet tender stalks and delicate tips, broccolini—a cross between broccoli and Chinese broccoli—has a lot of appeal. We wanted a foolproof method for preparing it. We tried sautéing the broccolini before adding a little water to let it steam through, but the delicate broccolini tips scorched during the sauté. Instead, we brought salted water to a boil in a skillet, added the broccolini, and covered the pan to trap the steam. A few minutes later, we removed the lid to reveal tender, emerald-green broccolini stalks. Another minute over the heat evaporated any remaining water. Halving the bottom 2 inches of the thicker stalks lengthwise ensured the stalks cooked evenly. A simple combination of minced garlic and red pepper flakes, plus a sprinkling of Parmesan cheese before serving, was all the broccolini needed. Broccolini is also sold as baby broccoli or asparation. You will need a 12-inch nonstick skillet with a tight-fitting lid for this recipe.

2 tablespoons extra-virgin olive oil
2 garlic cloves, minced
⅛ teaspoon red pepper flakes
⅓ cup water
½ teaspoon salt
1 pound broccolini, trimmed, bottom 2 inches of stems thicker than ½ inch halved lengthwise
2 tablespoons grated Parmesan cheese

1. Combine oil, garlic, and pepper flakes in bowl. Bring water and salt to boil in 12-inch nonstick skillet. Add broccolini, cover, reduce heat to medium-low, and cook until bright green and tender, about 5 minutes.

2. Uncover and cook until liquid evaporates, about 30 seconds. Clear center of skillet, add garlic mixture, and cook, mashing mixture into skillet, until fragrant, about 30 seconds. Stir garlic mixture into broccolini. Transfer to platter, sprinkle with Parmesan, and serve.

Trimming Broccolini

1. Trim only tough, dry ends from broccolini.

2. To ensure stems cook evenly, split thicker stalks in half through bottom 2 inches.

Braised Brussels Sprouts

SERVES 4 FAST GF

✔ **WHY THIS RECIPE WORKS:** Brussels sprouts probably have the worst reputation of any vegetable—kids and adults alike flee at the sight of them. But we think this is simply because they are almost always poorly prepared, and overcooking turns them limp and bitter. When done right, Brussels sprouts are crisp, tender, and nutty-flavored. Braising is the quickest method to cook these little cabbages, and we've found that using a skillet on the stovetop works best. As for the braising liquid, a combination of vegetable broth along with a quickly sautéed shallot was easy and added depth. We started the cooking in a covered skillet to quickly steam the sprouts, then removed the lid to let the broth reduce to a flavorful glaze during the final few minutes of cooking. When trimming the Brussels sprouts, be careful not to cut too much off the stem end or the leaves will fall away from the core. You will need a 12-inch nonstick skillet with a tight-fitting lid for this recipe.

2 tablespoons unsalted butter
1 shallot, minced
  Salt and pepper
1 pound Brussels sprouts, trimmed and halved
1 cup vegetable broth

1. Melt butter in 12-inch nonstick skillet over medium heat. Add shallot and ¼ teaspoon salt and cook until shallot is softened, about 2 minutes. Add Brussels sprouts, broth, and

⅛ teaspoon pepper and bring to simmer. Cover and cook until sprouts are bright green, about 9 minutes.

2. Uncover and continue to cook until sprouts are tender and liquid is slightly thickened, about 2 minutes. Season with salt and pepper to taste, transfer to platter, and serve.

VARIATIONS

Curried Brussels Sprouts with Currants FAST GF

Add 1½ teaspoons curry powder to pan with shallot. Add 3 tablespoons currants to pan with sprouts.

Cream-Braised Brussels Sprouts FAST GF

Substitute heavy cream for broth. Add pinch nutmeg to pan with sprouts. Sprinkle Brussels sprouts with 2 tablespoons minced fresh parsley or chives before serving.

Halving Brussels Sprouts

Cut sprouts in half through stem end so that leaves stay intact.

Roasted Brussels Sprouts

SERVES 6 TO 8   FAST VEGAN GF

✔ **WHY THIS RECIPE WORKS:** Roasting is an easy way to produce Brussels sprouts that are caramelized on the outside and tender on the inside. To ensure we achieved this balance, we started by roasting them covered with foil, tossing in a little bit of water to create a steamy environment, which cooked them through. We then removed the foil and roasted them for another 10 minutes to allow their exteriors to dry out and caramelize. If you are buying loose Brussels sprouts, select those that are about 1½ inches long. Quarter Brussels sprouts longer than 2½ inches; don't cut sprouts that are shorter than 1 inch.

2¼ pounds Brussels sprouts, trimmed and halved
3 tablespoons extra-virgin olive oil
1 tablespoon water
   Salt and pepper

1. Adjust oven rack to upper-middle position and heat oven to 500 degrees. Toss Brussels sprouts, oil, water, ¾ teaspoon salt, and ¼ teaspoon pepper in bowl until sprouts are coated. Transfer sprouts to rimmed baking sheet and arrange so cut sides are facing down.

2. Cover sheet tightly with aluminum foil and roast for 10 minutes. Remove foil and continue to cook until Brussels sprouts are well browned and tender, 10 to 12 minutes. Transfer to platter, season with salt and pepper to taste, and serve.

VARIATIONS

Roasted Brussels Sprouts with Garlic, Red Pepper Flakes, and Parmesan FAST GF

While Brussels sprouts roast, cook 3 tablespoons extra-virgin olive oil, 2 minced garlic cloves, and ½ teaspoon red pepper flakes in 8-inch skillet over medium heat until garlic is golden and fragrant, 1 to 2 minutes; remove from heat. Toss roasted Brussels sprouts with garlic oil before transferring to platter, then sprinkle with ¼ cup grated Parmesan cheese.

Roasted Brussels Sprouts with Walnuts and Lemon FAST GF

Toss roasted Brussels sprouts with ⅓ cup finely chopped toasted walnuts, 3 tablespoons melted unsalted butter, and 1 tablespoon lemon juice before transferring to platter.

Simple Cream-Braised Cabbage

SERVES 4   FAST GF

✔ **WHY THIS RECIPE WORKS:** The French have been cooking cabbage in cream for ages, and when we tried it, tasters loved the subtle mix of flavors, complemented by a slight residual crunch. We cut the richness of the cream with lemon juice (for its acidity) and shallot (for its subtle, sweet onion flavor). The cabbage needed only minutes to braise in a covered pan before it was ready to serve. You will need a 12-inch skillet with a tight-fitting lid for this recipe.

¼ cup heavy cream
1 teaspoon lemon juice
1 shallot, minced
½ head green cabbage, cored and shredded (4 cups)
   Salt and pepper

Heat cream, lemon juice, and shallot in 12-inch skillet over medium heat. Add cabbage and toss to coat. Cover and simmer, stirring occasionally, until cabbage is wilted but still bright green, 7 to 9 minutes. Season with salt and pepper to taste, transfer to bowl, and serve.

Shredding Cabbage

1. Cut cabbage into quarters, then cut away hard piece of core attached to each quarter.

2. Flatten small stacks of leaves on cutting board and use chef's knife to cut each stack crosswise into ¼-inch-wide shreds.

Roasted Carrots

SERVES 4 TO 6 `GF`

✅ **WHY THIS RECIPE WORKS:** Roasting carrots draws out their natural sugars and intensifies their flavor—if you can prevent them from coming out dry, shriveled, and jerkylike. Cutting the carrots into large batons about ½ inch thick gave us evenly cooked results with the best browning, and precooking the carrots before roasting kept their moisture in and minimized withering. We avoided dirtying a second pan by precooking the carrots (which we'd buttered and seasoned) right on the baking sheet, covered with foil. When the carrots were tender, we uncovered the baking sheet and returned it to the oven, where we roasted the carrots until their surface moisture evaporated and they took on caramelized streaks. While cutting the carrots into uniformly sized pieces is key for even cooking, it's the large size of the pieces that makes the recipe work, so make sure not to cut them too small.

1½ **pounds carrots, peeled**
 2 **tablespoons unsalted butter, melted**
   Salt and pepper

1. Adjust oven rack to middle position and heat oven to 425 degrees. Cut carrots in half crosswise, then cut them lengthwise into halves or quarters as needed to create

SAUCES FOR STEAMED OR ROASTED VEGETABLES

A quick sauce is a great way to add some interest and variety to simple steamed or roasted vegetables.

CURRY-YOGURT SAUCE WITH CILANTRO
MAKES ABOUT 1 CUP `FAST` `GF`

 1 **tablespoon vegetable oil**
 1 **shallot, minced**
 2 **teaspoons curry powder**
 ¼ **teaspoon red pepper flakes**
 ⅓ **cup water**
 ¼ **cup plain whole-milk yogurt**
 2 **tablespoons minced fresh cilantro**
 1 **teaspoon lime juice**
   Salt and pepper

Heat oil in 8-inch skillet over medium-high heat until shimmering. Add shallot and cook until softened, about 2 minutes. Stir in curry powder and pepper flakes and cook until fragrant, about 1 minute. Off heat, whisk in water, yogurt, cilantro, and lime juice. Season with salt and pepper to taste. Drizzle over vegetables before serving.

SOY-GINGER SAUCE WITH SCALLION
MAKES ABOUT ¾ CUP `FAST` `VEGAN` `GF`

In order for this recipe to be gluten-free, you must use gluten-free soy sauce or tamari. Mirin is a sweet Japanese cooking wine; sherry can be substituted if necessary.

 2 **teaspoons vegetable oil**
 1 **tablespoon grated fresh ginger**
 2 **garlic cloves, minced**
 ¼ **cup water**
 2 **tablespoons soy sauce**
 2 **tablespoons mirin**
 1 **tablespoon rice vinegar**
 1 **teaspoon toasted sesame oil**
 1 **scallion, sliced thin**

Heat vegetable oil in 8-inch skillet over medium-high heat until shimmering. Add ginger and garlic and cook until fragrant, about 1 minute. Reduce heat to medium-low, add water, soy sauce, mirin, and vinegar, and simmer until slightly syrupy, 4 to 6 minutes. Drizzle sauce and sesame oil over vegetables and sprinkle with scallion before serving.

uniformly sized pieces. Toss carrots, melted butter, ½ teaspoon salt, and ¼ teaspoon pepper together in bowl.

2. Transfer carrots to parchment paper–lined rimmed baking sheet and spread into single layer. Cover baking sheet tightly with aluminum foil and cook for 15 minutes. Remove foil and roast, stirring twice, until carrots are well browned and tender, 30 to 35 minutes. Transfer to platter, season with salt and pepper to taste, and serve.

VARIATIONS
Roasted Carrots and Fennel with Toasted Almonds and Lemon GF
Reduce amount of carrots to 1 pound. Add 1 small fennel bulb, stalks discarded and bulb cored and sliced ½ inch thick, to bowl with carrots; roast as directed. Toss vegetables with ¼ cup toasted sliced almonds, 2 teaspoons minced fresh parsley, and 1 teaspoon lemon juice before serving.

Roasted Carrots and Parsnips with Rosemary GF
Reduce amount of carrots to 1 pound. Add 8 ounces parsnips, peeled, halved crosswise, and cut lengthwise into halves or quarters as needed to create uniformly sized pieces, and 1 teaspoon minced fresh rosemary to bowl with carrots; roast as directed. Toss vegetables with 2 teaspoons minced fresh parsley before serving.

Roasted Carrots and Shallots with Lemon and Thyme GF
Reduce amount of carrots to 1 pound. Add 6 shallots, peeled and halved lengthwise, and 1 teaspoon minced fresh thyme to bowl with carrots; roast as directed. Toss vegetables with 1 teaspoon lemon juice before serving.

Cutting Carrots for Roasting

1. First, cut carrots in half crosswise.

2. Then, cut each half lengthwise into halves or quarters as needed to create uniformly sized pieces.

Glazed Carrots
SERVES 4 FAST GF

✔ **WHY THIS RECIPE WORKS:** For well-seasoned carrots with a glossy and clingy yet modest glaze, we started by slicing the carrots on the bias to maximize their surface area for the glaze. Most glazed carrot recipes start by steaming, parboiling, or blanching the carrots prior to glazing. To make glazed carrots a one-pot operation, we steamed them directly in the skillet, and we used vegetable broth (along with some salt and sugar) rather than water for fuller flavor. When the carrots were almost tender, we removed the lid and turned up the heat to reduce the cooking liquid. Then we added butter and a bit more sugar, and finally finished with a sprinkling of fresh lemon juice and a bit of black pepper to balance the dish. You will need a 12-inch nonstick skillet with a tight-fitting lid for this recipe.

1 pound carrots, peeled and sliced ¼ inch thick on bias
½ cup vegetable broth
3 tablespoons sugar
   Salt and pepper
1 tablespoon unsalted butter, cut into 4 pieces
2 teaspoons lemon juice

1. Bring carrots, broth, 1 tablespoon sugar, and ½ teaspoon salt to boil in 12-inch nonstick skillet. Reduce to simmer, cover, and cook, stirring occasionally, until carrots are almost tender, about 5 minutes.

2. Uncover, return to boil, and cook until liquid has thickened and reduced to about 2 tablespoons, about 2 minutes.

3. Stir in butter and remaining 2 tablespoons sugar. Cook, stirring frequently, until carrots are completely tender and glaze is lightly golden, about 3 minutes. Off heat, stir in lemon juice and season with salt and pepper to taste. Transfer to platter and serve.

VARIATIONS
Glazed Carrots with Orange and Cranberries FAST GF
Dried cherries can be used in place of the cranberries if you prefer.

Substitute ¼ cup orange juice for ¼ cup of broth. Add ¼ cup dried cranberries and ½ teaspoon grated orange zest to skillet with carrots. Omit 2 tablespoons sugar in step 3.

Glazed Curried Carrots with Currants and Almonds FAST GF
Add 1½ teaspoons curry powder to skillet with carrots. Add ¼ cup currants to skillet with butter. Sprinkle carrots with ¼ cup toasted sliced or slivered almonds before serving.

Honey-Glazed Carrots with Lemon and Thyme FAST GF

Substitute honey for sugar. Add ½ teaspoon grated lemon zest and ½ teaspoon minced fresh thyme to skillet with butter.

Slicing Carrots on the Bias

Cut carrots on bias into pieces about ½ inch thick and 2 inches long.

Roasted Cauliflower

SERVES 4 TO 6 VEGAN GF

✔ **WHY THIS RECIPE WORKS:** We wanted to add flavor to cauliflower without drowning it in a heavy blanket of cheese sauce, so we developed a recipe for roasted cauliflower with golden, nutty, well-browned edges and a sweet, tender interior. Since browning took place only where the cauliflower was in direct contact with the hot baking sheet, we sliced the head of cauliflower into wedges, creating more flat surface area than you'd get with florets. To keep the cauliflower from drying out in a hot oven, we started it covered and allowed it to steam until barely tender. Then we removed the foil and returned the pan to the oven to caramelize and brown the wedges. Flipping each wedge halfway through roasting ensured even cooking and color. Thanks to its natural sweetness and flavor, our roasted cauliflower needed little enhancement—just a drizzle of olive oil and a sprinkle of salt and pepper.

 1 head cauliflower (2 pounds)
 ¼ cup extra-virgin olive oil
    Salt and pepper

Cutting Cauliflower for Roasting

After trimming away any leaves and cutting stem flush with bottom of head, carefully slice into 8 equal wedges, keeping core and florets intact.

Cutting cauliflower into 8 wedges creates lots of surface area for nutty, caramelized edges and sweet, creamy interiors.

1. Adjust oven rack to lowest position and heat oven to 475 degrees. Trim outer leaves off cauliflower and cut stem flush with bottom. Cut head into 8 equal wedges. Place wedges, with either cut side down, on aluminum foil–lined rimmed baking sheet. Drizzle with 2 tablespoons oil and season with salt and pepper. Gently rub oil and seasonings into cauliflower. Gently flip cauliflower and repeat on second cut side with remaining 2 tablespoons oil, salt, and pepper.

2. Cover baking sheet tightly with foil and cook for 10 minutes. Remove foil and continue to roast until bottoms of cauliflower wedges are golden, 8 to 12 minutes.

3. Remove baking sheet from oven, carefully flip wedges using spatula, and continue to roast until cauliflower is golden all over, 8 to 12 minutes. Transfer to platter, season with salt and pepper to taste, and serve.

VARIATION
Spicy Roasted Cauliflower VEGAN GF

Stir 2 teaspoons curry powder or chili powder into oil in bowl before seasoning cauliflower in step 1.

Browned and Braised Cauliflower with Garlic, Ginger, and Soy

SERVES 4 TO 6 `FAST` `VEGAN` `GF`

✔ **WHY THIS RECIPE WORKS:** We wanted a method for properly cooking this often overcooked vegetable, then we wanted to dress it up with bold flavors. We settled on a combination of sautéing and braising, since braising alone took too long and resulted in soggy cauliflower. Sautéing concentrated its flavor, then we added liquid and flavorings to the pan and cooked the cauliflower, covered, until it was just crisp-tender. The deep flavor of the browned cauliflower held up well to bolder, more complex flavor combinations, so we used bright Asian-inspired flavors for one version and rich Indian spices for another. You will need a 12-inch nonstick skillet with a tight-fitting lid for this recipe. In order for this recipe to be gluten-free, you must use gluten-free soy sauce or tamari.

- 2 tablespoons grated fresh ginger
- 2 garlic cloves, minced
- 1 teaspoon toasted sesame oil
- 1½ tablespoons vegetable oil
- 1 head cauliflower (2 pounds), cored and cut into 1-inch florets
- ¼ cup water
- 2 tablespoons soy sauce
- 2 tablespoons rice vinegar
- 1 tablespoon dry sherry
- 2 scallions, minced
  Pepper

1. Combine ginger, garlic, and sesame oil in bowl. Heat vegetable oil in 12-inch nonstick skillet over medium-high heat until just smoking. Add cauliflower and cook, stirring occasionally, until beginning to brown, 6 to 7 minutes.

2. Clear center of skillet, add ginger mixture, and cook, mashing mixture into skillet, until fragrant, about 30 seconds. Stir ginger mixture into cauliflower.

3. Reduce heat to low and add water, soy sauce, vinegar, and sherry. Cover and cook until florets are crisp-tender, 4 to 5 minutes. Off heat, stir in scallions and season with pepper to taste. Transfer to platter and serve.

VARIATION

Browned and Braised Cauliflower with Indian Spices `FAST` `GF`

Cooking the spices for a minute or two removes their raw edge and allows their flavors to deepen. You will need a 12-inch nonstick skillet with a tight-fitting lid for this recipe.

- 1½ tablespoons vegetable oil
- 1 head cauliflower (2 pounds), cored and cut into 1-inch florets
- ½ onion, sliced thin
- 1 teaspoon ground coriander
- 1 teaspoon ground cumin
- 1 teaspoon ground turmeric
- ¼ teaspoon red pepper flakes
- ¼ cup water
- ¼ cup plain yogurt
- 1 tablespoon lime juice
- ¼ cup minced fresh cilantro
  Salt and pepper

1. Heat oil in 12-inch nonstick skillet over medium-high heat until just smoking. Add cauliflower and cook, stirring occasionally, until just softened, 2 to 3 minutes. Stir in onion and cook until florets begin to brown and onion softens, about 4 minutes.

2. Stir in coriander, cumin, turmeric, and pepper flakes; cook until spices are fragrant, 1 to 2 minutes. Reduce heat to low and add water, yogurt, and lime juice. Cover and cook until florets are crisp-tender, about 6 minutes. Stir in cilantro and season with salt and pepper to taste. Transfer to platter and serve.

Cutting Cauliflower into Florets

1. Pull off any leaves, then cut out core of cauliflower using paring knife.

2. Separate florets from inner stem using tip of knife.

3. Cut larger florets into smaller pieces by slicing through stem end.

We flavor our simple Swiss chard dish with plenty of sautéed garlic, bright white wine vinegar, and hot red pepper flakes.

Garlicky Swiss Chard

SERVES 4 TO 6 `FAST` `VEGAN` `GF`

✔ **WHY THIS RECIPE WORKS:** We wanted a one-pot approach to cooking hearty, flavorful Swiss chard. To avoid watery, overcooked chard, we started cooking the greens in a covered pot just until they wilted down. Then we uncovered the pot and continued to cook the greens until all the liquid evaporated. Cutting the tough stems smaller than the tender leaves meant that we could throw both in the pot at the same time and still get evenly cooked results. Plenty of garlic, sautéed in olive oil before the chard was added, gave this simple side a big hit of flavor, while a splash of mild white wine vinegar and red pepper flakes added brightness and subtle heat. You can use any variety of chard for this recipe. The recipe is easily doubled and cooked in two batches.

- 2 tablespoons plus 1 teaspoon extra-virgin olive oil
- 6 garlic cloves, minced

Prepping Chard

1. Cut leafy green portion away from either side of stalk using chef's knife.

2. Stack several leaves on top of one another and slice or chop into pieces (as directed in recipe). Wash and dry leaves after they've been cut, using salad spinner.

3. Recipes for chard often include stems. Wash stems thoroughly, then trim and cut them into small pieces (as directed in each recipe).

- 2 pounds Swiss chard, stems sliced crosswise ¼ inch thick, leaves sliced into ½-inch-wide strips
  Salt and pepper
- ⅛ teaspoon red pepper flakes
- 1 teaspoon white wine vinegar

1. Heat 2 tablespoons oil and garlic in Dutch oven over medium-low heat, stirring occasionally, until garlic is lightly golden, about 3 minutes. Stir in chard, ¼ teaspoon salt, and pepper flakes. Increase heat to high, cover, and cook, stirring occasionally, until chard is wilted but still bright green, 2 to 4 minutes.

2. Uncover and continue to cook, stirring often, until liquid evaporates, 4 to 6 minutes. Stir in vinegar and remaining 1 teaspoon oil, and season with salt and pepper to taste. Transfer to bowl and serve.

VARIATIONS

Garlicky Swiss Chard with Walnuts and Feta `FAST` `GF`

Sprinkle with ⅓ cup crumbled feta cheese and ¼ cup chopped, toasted walnuts before serving.

Garlicky Swiss Chard with Golden Raisins and Goat Cheese `FAST` `GF`

Add ¼ cup golden raisins to pot with chard. Sprinkle with ⅓ cup crumbled goat cheese and ¼ cup chopped, toasted hazelnuts before serving.

Asian-Style Swiss Chard `FAST` `VEGAN` `GF`

In order for this recipe to be gluten-free, you must use gluten-free soy sauce or tamari.

Add 1 tablespoon grated fresh ginger to pot with chard. In step 2, substitute 1 tablespoon sesame oil for olive oil and substitute 4 teaspoons soy sauce for vinegar. Sprinkle with 3 tablespoons sliced scallion and ¼ cup chopped, salted, dry-roasted peanuts before serving.

Quick Collard Greens

SERVES 4 TO 6 `FAST` `VEGAN` `GF`

✔ **WHY THIS RECIPE WORKS:** Collard greens are typically braised for at least an hour to soften their tough leaves, but we wanted a quick recipe that would give us the same results. Stemming the greens was a necessary first step, and blanching the leaves in salt water tenderized them and removed their bitterness in minutes. However, blanching left us with waterlogged greens, so we used a spatula to press out excess water, and then we rolled the greens up in a dish towel to dry them further. We chopped the compressed collards into thin slices perfect for sautéing. And since we weren't infusing the greens with flavor during a long braise, we added some aromatic garlic and spicy red pepper flakes to the hot oil for a quick, well-seasoned dish. You can substitute mustard or turnip greens for the collards; reduce their boiling time to 2 minutes.

Salt and pepper
2½ pounds collard greens, stemmed, leaves halved lengthwise
3 tablespoons extra-virgin olive oil
2 garlic cloves, minced
¼ teaspoon red pepper flakes

1. Bring 4 quarts water to boil in large pot over medium-high heat. Stir in 1 tablespoon salt, then add collard greens, 1 handful at a time. Cook until tender, 4 to 5 minutes. Drain and rinse with cold water until greens are cool, about 1 minute.

Making Quick Collard Greens

1. BLANCH GREENS: Add greens to boiling water, 1 handful at a time, and cook until tender, 4 to 5 minutes. Drain and rinse with cold water.

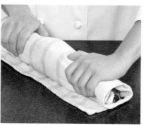

2. PRESS GREENS DRY: Press greens with rubber spatula to release excess liquid, then roll up inside clean dish towel and compress into 10-inch log.

3. SLICE LOG CROSSWISE: Remove collards from towel and cut crosswise into ¼-inch slices.

4. SAUTÉ GREENS: Cook greens in skillet until just beginning to brown, 3 to 4 minutes. Stir in garlic and pepper flakes and cook until greens are spotty brown, 1 to 2 minutes.

Press greens with rubber spatula to release excess liquid. Place greens on dish towel and compress into 10-inch log. Roll up towel tightly, then remove greens from towel. Cut greens crosswise into ¼-inch slices. (Greens can be refrigerated for up to 2 days before continuing.)

2. Heat oil in 12-inch nonstick skillet over medium-high heat until just smoking. Scatter greens in skillet and cook, stirring frequently, until just beginning to brown, 3 to 4 minutes. Stir in garlic and pepper flakes and cook until greens are spotty brown, 1 to 2 minutes. Season with salt and pepper to taste, transfer to bowl, and serve.

Sautéed Corn with Cherry Tomatoes, Ricotta Salata, and Basil

SERVES 4 TO 6 `FAST` `GF`

✓ **WHY THIS RECIPE WORKS:** To take advantage of the summer corn season, we wanted a quick recipe for sautéed corn bursting with fresh flavor. First we cut the kernels from the raw ears. To replicate the lightly charred, smoky flavor and satisfying texture of grilled corn, we seared the corn, without stirring it, in a little oil in a skillet. This caramelized the corn, contributing a rich sweetness and a deep toasted quality while ensuring the corn retained some crunch. Then, to balance the sweetness, we added toasted garlic chips, ricotta salata, and lemon juice. Cherry tomatoes and basil freshened the dish. We call for a range of lemon juice because fresh corn can vary in sweetness. If ricotta salata is unavailable, substitute a mild feta cheese.

- 2 **tablespoons vegetable oil**
- 3 **garlic cloves, sliced thin**
- 4 **ears corn, kernels cut from cobs (4 cups)**
  Salt and pepper
- 6 **ounces cherry tomatoes, halved**
- 1½ **ounces ricotta salata cheese, crumbled (⅓ cup)**
- ¼ **cup shredded fresh basil**
- 1–2 **tablespoons lemon juice**

1. Cook oil and garlic in 12-inch nonstick skillet over medium heat, stirring frequently, until garlic is light golden brown and fragrant, 2 to 3 minutes. Using slotted spoon, transfer garlic to large bowl, leaving oil in skillet.

2. Return skillet to medium-high heat and heat until shimmering. Add corn and sprinkle with ½ teaspoon salt. Cook, without stirring, until corn is browned on bottom and beginning to pop, about 3 minutes. Stir and continue to cook, stirring once or twice, until corn is spotty brown all over, 2 to 3 minutes. Transfer corn to bowl with garlic.

3. Stir in tomatoes, half of ricotta salata, basil, 1 tablespoon lemon juice, and ¼ teaspoon pepper. Season with salt, pepper, and remaining lemon juice to taste. Sprinkle with remaining ricotta salata and serve.

VARIATIONS

Sautéed Corn with Black Beans and Bell Pepper

SERVES 4 TO 6 `FAST` `VEGAN` `GF`

We call for a range of lime juice because fresh corn can vary in sweetness. To make this dish spicier, add in the chile seeds.

- 2 **tablespoons vegetable oil**
- ½ **red onion, chopped fine**

Keeping Side Dishes Warm

MAKE USE OF YOUR SLOW COOKER

Mashed potatoes seem to cool off faster than anything else you serve. Simply transfer the potatoes to a slow cooker set to low; adjust the consistency with hot cream or milk as needed before serving.

USE YOUR FONDUE POT

Keep sauces hot by transferring them to a fondue pot set to low. This method is also great for creamy dishes like creamed onions, candied sweet potatoes, and macaroni and cheese.

USE KITCHEN APPLIANCES TO YOUR ADVANTAGE

If your cooktop has an oven located just underneath, the oven's vents are typically located just behind the back burners. You can make use of the hot air coming out of the oven vent to warm up serving dishes and dinner plates by stacking them on top of one of the back burners. Make sure that the burner itself is cold and clean and that the stack of plates is stable.

PREWARM SERVING DISHES

Prewarming serving dishes can keep sides warm for an extra 10 to 20 minutes. Briefly heat your empty serving dishes in a warm oven or the microwave, or you can even use the drying cycle of the dishwasher.

- ½ **red bell pepper, stemmed, seeded, and cut into ¼-inch pieces**
- 1 **jalapeño chile, stemmed, seeded, and minced**
- 1 **garlic clove, minced**
- ½ **teaspoon ground cumin**
  Salt
- 1 **(15-ounce) can black beans, rinsed**
- 3 **ears corn, kernels cut from cobs (3 cups)**
- ½ **cup minced fresh cilantro**
- 2–3 **tablespoons lime juice**

1. Heat 1 tablespoon oil in 12-inch nonstick skillet over medium heat. Add onion, bell pepper, and jalapeño and cook, stirring occasionally, until onion is softened, 4 to 6 minutes. Add garlic, cumin, and ¼ teaspoon salt and cook until fragrant, about 1 minute. Add beans and cook until warmed through, about 1 minute; transfer mixture to large bowl and wipe out skillet.

2. Heat remaining 1 tablespoon oil in now-empty skillet over medium-high heat until shimmering. Add corn and sprinkle with ½ teaspoon salt. Cook, without stirring, until corn is browned on bottom and beginning to pop, about 3 minutes.

Stir and continue to cook, stirring once or twice, until corn is spotty brown all over, 2 to 3 minutes. Transfer corn to bowl with black bean mixture.

3. Stir in cilantro and 2 tablespoons lime juice. Season with salt and remaining lime juice to taste. Serve.

Sautéed Corn with Miso and Scallions

SERVES 4 TO 6 · FAST · VEGAN · GF

See page 55 for information about buying miso. Mirin is a sweet Japanese cooking wine; sherry can be substituted for the mirin if necessary. We call for a range of vinegar because fresh corn can vary in sweetness.

2	tablespoons vegetable oil
6	scallions, white parts minced, green parts sliced thin on bias
1	teaspoon grated fresh ginger
2	tablespoons white miso
1–2	tablespoons rice vinegar
4	ears corn, kernels cut from cobs (4 cups)
	Salt
1	tablespoon mirin
1	tablespoon toasted sesame seeds

1. Heat 1 tablespoon oil in 12-inch nonstick skillet over medium heat. Add scallion whites and ginger and cook, stirring frequently, until softened, 1 to 2 minutes. Transfer mixture to large bowl and whisk in miso and 1 tablespoon vinegar. Wipe out skillet.

2. Heat remaining 1 tablespoon oil in now-empty skillet over medium-high heat until shimmering. Add corn and sprinkle with ¼ teaspoon salt. Cook, without stirring, until corn is browned on bottom and beginning to pop, about 3 minutes. Stir and continue to cook, stirring once or twice, until corn is spotty brown all over, 2 to 3 minutes. Add mirin and cook until evaporated, about 1 minute. Transfer corn to bowl with scallion mixture.

3. Stir in scallion greens. Season with salt and remaining vinegar to taste. Sprinkle with sesame seeds and serve.

Removing Corn from the Cob

Stand corn upright inside large bowl and carefully cut kernels off cob using paring knife.

To make classic Mexican street corn at home, we swap a tangy mix of mayonnaise and sour cream for the traditional *crema*.

Mexican-Style Street Corn

SERVES 6 · FAST · GF

✔ **WHY THIS RECIPE WORKS:** In Mexico, vendors sell this messy, cheesy, utterly delicious grilled corn from street carts; we wanted to duplicate it at home. Tossing the corn with oil before grilling kept it from drying out or sticking to the grill grate, and spiking the oil with chili powder gave the corn deep, spicy flavor. Traditionally, the base of the creamy sauce is made with Mexican *crema*, but it's rarely available outside of Mexico. Luckily, we found that a mixture of mayonnaise and sour cream flavored with cilantro, garlic, lime juice, and a little more chili powder made a good substitute. We mixed the cheese (*queso fresco* and Cotija both worked well) into the mayonnaise mixture to keep it from crumbling off the corn. Once the corn was lightly charred, we coated the ears all over with the creamy cheese-mayonnaise mixture. If both queso fresco and Cotija cheese are unavailable, substitute ½ cup grated Pecorino Romano.

¼	cup mayonnaise
3	tablespoons sour cream

3 tablespoons minced fresh cilantro

1 garlic clove, minced

¾ teaspoon chili powder

¼ teaspoon pepper

¼ teaspoon cayenne pepper (optional)

4 teaspoons lime juice

2 ounces queso fresco or Cotija cheese, crumbled (½ cup)

4 teaspoons vegetable oil

¼ teaspoon salt

6 large ears corn, husks and silk removed

1. Combine mayonnaise, sour cream, cilantro, garlic, ¼ teaspoon chili powder, pepper, cayenne (if using), lime juice, and queso fresco in large bowl. In second large bowl, combine oil, salt, and remaining ½ teaspoon chili powder, then add corn and toss to coat.

2A. FOR A CHARCOAL GRILL: Open bottom vent completely. Light large chimney starter filled with charcoal briquettes (6 quarts). When top coals are partially covered with ash, pour evenly over half of grill. Set cooking grate in place, cover, and open lid vent completely. Heat grill until hot, about 5 minutes.

2B. FOR A GAS GRILL: Turn all burners to high, cover, and heat grill until hot, about 15 minutes. Leave all burners on high.

3. Clean and oil cooking grate. Place corn on grill (on hot side if using charcoal). Cook (covered if using gas), turning as needed, until lightly charred on all sides, 7 to 12 minutes. Transfer corn to bowl with mayonnaise mixture and toss to coat. Serve.

Broiled Eggplant with Basil

SERVES 4 FAST VEGAN GF

WHY THIS RECIPE WORKS: The biggest challenge when cooking eggplant is its excess moisture. If you try to simply slice and broil eggplant, it will steam in its own juices rather than brown. So to get broiled eggplant with great color and texture, we started by salting the eggplant to draw out its moisture. After 30 minutes, we patted the eggplant slices dry, moved them to a baking sheet (lined with aluminum foil for easy cleanup), and brushed them with oil. With the excess moisture taken care of, all the eggplant needed was a few minutes per side under the blazing hot broiler to turn a beautiful, flavorful mahogany color. With its concentrated roasted flavor, all the accompaniment the eggplant needed was a sprinkling of fresh basil. Make sure to slice the eggplant thin so that the slices will cook through by the time the exterior is browned.

NOTES FROM THE TEST KITCHEN

How to Grill Vegetables

To easily grill a simple vegetable to serve alongside dinner, use this chart as a guide. Brush or toss the vegetables with oil and season with salt and pepper before grilling. Grill vegetables over a medium-hot fire (you can comfortably hold your hand 5 inches above the cooking grate for 3 to 4 seconds).

VEGETABLE	PREPARATION	GRILLING DIRECTIONS
Asparagus	Snap off tough ends.	Grill, turning once, until streaked with light grill marks, 5 to 7 minutes.
Bell Pepper	Core, seed, and cut into large wedges.	Grill, turning often, until streaked with dark grill marks, 8 to 10 minutes.
Corn	Remove all but last layer of husk and snip off silk.	Grill, turning every 2 minutes, until husk chars and peels away at tip, 8 to 10 minutes.
Endive	Halve lengthwise through stem end.	Grill, flat side down, until streaked with dark grill marks, 5 to 7 minutes.
Eggplant	Remove ends. Cut into ¾-inch-thick rounds or strips.	Grill, turning once, until flesh is darkly colored, 8 to 10 minutes.
Fennel	Slice bulb through base into ¼-inch-thick pieces.	Grill, turning once, until streaked with dark grill marks and quite soft, 7 to 9 minutes.
Portobello Mushrooms	Discard stems and wipe caps clean.	Grill, turning once, until streaked with dark grill marks and quite soft, 7 to 9 minutes.
White or Cremini Mushrooms	Trim thin slice from stems then thread onto skewers.	Grill, turning several times, until golden brown, 6 to 7 minutes.
Onions	Peel, cut into ½-inch-thick slices, and skewer.	Grill, turning occasionally, until lightly charred, 10 to 12 minutes.
Cherry Tomatoes	Remove stems then thread onto skewers.	Grill, turning often, until streaked with dark grill marks, 3 to 6 minutes.
Plum Tomatoes	Halve lengthwise and seed.	Grill, turning once, until streaked with dark grill marks, about 6 minutes.
Zucchini or Summer Squash	Remove ends. Slice lengthwise into ½-inch-thick strips.	Grill, turning once, until streaked with dark grill marks, 8 to 10 minutes.

1½ pounds eggplant, sliced into ¼-inch-thick rounds

1 tablespoon kosher salt

3 tablespoons extra-virgin olive oil

   Pepper

2 tablespoons chopped fresh basil

1. Spread eggplant out over baking sheet lined with paper towels, sprinkle both sides with salt, and let stand for 30 minutes.

2. Adjust oven rack 4 inches from broiler element and heat broiler. Thoroughly pat eggplant dry, arrange on aluminum foil–lined baking sheet, and brush both sides with oil. Broil eggplant until tops are mahogany brown, 3 to 4 minutes. Flip eggplant over and broil until second side is brown, 3 to 4 minutes.

3. Transfer eggplant to platter, season with pepper to taste, and sprinkle with basil. Serve.

VARIATION

Broiled Eggplant with Sesame-Miso Glaze FAST VEGAN GF

See page 55 for information about buying miso. Any type of miso will work well here. Mirin is a sweet Japanese cooking wine; sherry can be substituted for the mirin if necessary.

Substitute vegetable oil for olive oil and 1 sliced scallion for basil. Whisk 1 tablespoon miso, 3 tablespoons mirin, and 1 tablespoon tahini together in bowl. After browning second side, brush with miso mixture, sprinkle with 1 tablespoon sesame seeds, and continue to broil until miso and seeds are browned, about 2 minutes.

Stir-Fried Eggplant

SERVES 4 FAST VEGAN GF

✔ **WHY THIS RECIPE WORKS:** For a boldly flavored eggplant stir-fry easy enough for a weeknight, we used an aromatic combination of fresh ginger, garlic, soy sauce, sesame oil, and vegetable broth. We started by sautéing the eggplant over high heat to drive off its excess moisture and give it good browning, then we cooked the garlic and ginger in more oil just until fragrant. Finally, we added the broth mixture to the skillet; in just a few minutes, the sauce was thickened and glossy and the eggplant was softened and infused with flavor. A sprinkling of sliced scallions before serving added color and freshness. Choose small eggplants (preferably those weighing about 8 ounces each) for this recipe. In order for this recipe to be gluten-free, you must use gluten-free soy sauce or tamari.

To get stir-fried eggplant with the perfect texture, we sauté it to drive off moisture, then simmer it in a flavorful sauce.

¼ cup vegetable broth

2 tablespoons soy sauce

1½ teaspoons toasted sesame oil

1 garlic clove, minced

1 teaspoon grated fresh ginger

1 teaspoon plus 1 tablespoon vegetable oil

2 small eggplants (8 ounces each), halved lengthwise and sliced crosswise ½ inch thick

2 scallions, sliced thin

1. Combine broth, soy sauce, and sesame oil in bowl. In separate bowl, combine garlic, ginger, and 1 teaspoon vegetable oil. Heat remaining 1 tablespoon vegetable oil in 12-inch non-stick skillet over high heat until just smoking. Add eggplant and cook, stirring often, until browned, about 3 minutes.

2. Clear center of skillet, add garlic mixture, and cook, mashing mixture into skillet, until fragrant, about 30 seconds. Stir garlic mixture into eggplant. Add broth mixture, cover, and reduce heat to medium. Cook until sauce is thickened and eggplant is softened, about 3 minutes. Transfer to platter, sprinkle with scallions, and serve.

Braised Belgian Endives

SERVES 4   `FAST` `GF`

✔ **WHY THIS RECIPE WORKS:** The right cooking method transforms sharp, bitter endives into a side dish of uncommonly complex flavor—at once mellow, sweet, and rich, yet still faintly bitter. Our challenge was to develop the deep flavor, richness, and gentle sweetness necessary to balance the endives' natural bite. We browned the endives in butter and sugar for maximum richness and sweetness, then braised them quickly in white wine and vegetable broth for a deep yet brightly flavored vegetable side dish. To avoid discoloration, do not cut the endives far in advance of cooking. Cooked endives can fall apart easily if not handled gently; use tongs and a spatula when handling them. You will need a 12-inch nonstick skillet with a tight-fitting lid for this recipe.

3 tablespoons unsalted butter

½ teaspoon sugar

Salt and pepper

4 heads Belgian endive (4 ounces each), halved lengthwise

¼ cup dry white wine

¼ cup vegetable broth

½ teaspoon minced fresh thyme

1 tablespoon minced fresh parsley

1 teaspoon lemon juice

1. Melt 2 tablespoons butter in 12-inch nonstick skillet over medium-high heat. Sprinkle sugar and ¼ teaspoon salt evenly into skillet, then lay endives, cut sides down, in single layer in skillet. Cook, shaking skillet occasionally, until first side is golden, about 5 minutes (reduce heat if endives brown too quickly). Turn endives over and cook until curved sides are golden, about 3 minutes.

2. Turn endives cut sides down and add wine, broth, and thyme. Reduce heat to low, cover, and simmer, checking occasionally, until leaves open up slightly and endives are tender throughout when poked with paring knife, 13 to 15 minutes. (If pan appears dry, add 2 tablespoons water.)

3. Transfer endives to platter. Simmer liquid left in skillet until reduced to syrupy consistency, 1 to 2 minutes. Off heat, whisk in remaining 1 tablespoon butter, parsley, and lemon juice. Season with salt and pepper to taste. Spoon sauce over endives and serve.

VARIATION

Cider-Braised Belgian Endives with Apples   `FAST` `GF`

Because the apples absorb some of the braising liquid, more cider is added to the pan before the sauce is reduced.

Omit lemon juice. Add 1 Granny Smith apple, peeled, cored, and cut into ¼-inch-thick wedges, to skillet with endives. Substitute ½ cup apple cider for vegetable broth and wine. Add 2 tablespoons cider to skillet before simmering to syrupy consistency in step 3.

Sautéed Escarole and White Beans

SERVES 4 TO 6   `FAST` `VEGAN` `GF`

✔ **WHY THIS RECIPE WORKS:** Greens and beans stewed together make a hearty, filling side dish; we wanted to come up with a quick and easy version of this classic combination. We started with leafy escarole and chose mild, tender white beans to balance the escarole's slightly bitter flavor. Canned beans kept our recipe simple, and once we simmered them briefly in vegetable broth, they had great flavor. We simmered the escarole and beans gently until the greens were wilted, then we increased the heat and reduced the liquid to a light glaze. For rich, aromatic flavor, we sautéed some onions, garlic, and red pepper flakes in oil beforehand. A squeeze of fresh lemon juice before serving added a balancing brightness. Chicory can be substituted for the escarole, though it will have a much stronger flavor.

3 tablespoons extra-virgin olive oil

2 onions, minced

Salt and pepper

4 garlic cloves, minced

⅛ teaspoon red pepper flakes

1 head escarole (1 pound), trimmed and cut into 1-inch pieces

2 cups vegetable broth

1 cup canned white beans, rinsed

2 teaspoons lemon juice

1. Heat oil in large Dutch oven over medium-high heat until shimmering. Add onions and ½ teaspoon salt and cook, stirring often, until onion is softened and lightly browned, 5 to 7 minutes. Stir in garlic and pepper flakes and cook until fragrant, about 30 seconds. Stir in escarole, broth, and beans and cook, stirring often, until escarole has wilted, about 5 minutes.

2. Increase heat to high and continue to cook until liquid has reduced to light glaze, 10 to 15 minutes. Off heat, stir in lemon juice and season with salt and pepper to taste. Serve.

Braised Fennel with White Wine and Parmesan

SERVES 4 `FAST` `GF`

✔ **WHY THIS RECIPE WORKS:** While fennel is excellent served raw in salads and antipasti, its crisp anise flavor turns mild and sweet once cooked. We wanted a recipe for braised fennel that would infuse the fennel with rich, savory flavor. The problem with cooking fennel lies in trying to achieve uniformly tender pieces. A combination of proper vegetable prep and cooking technique turned out to be the key to evenly cooked fennel. Fan-shaped wedges proved good for braising, because the thin slices cooked through quickly and evenly. It was important to cook the fennel slowly to deliver uniformly tender but not mushy results. A combination of butter, white wine, and Parmesan gave the fennel rich, balanced flavor. You will need a 12-inch nonstick skillet with a tight-fitting lid for this recipe. For more information on preparing fennel, see page 187.

- 3 tablespoons unsalted butter
- 2 fennel bulbs, stalks discarded, bulbs halved, cored, and cut crosswise into ½-inch-thick slices
- Salt and pepper
- ⅓ cup dry white wine
- ¼ cup grated Parmesan cheese

1. Melt butter in 12-inch nonstick skillet over medium heat. Add fennel and sprinkle with salt and pepper. Add wine, cover, and simmer for 15 minutes.

2. Turn slices over and continue to simmer, covered, until fennel is nearly tender, has absorbed most of liquid, and starts to turn golden, about 10 minutes.

3. Turn fennel again and continue to cook until golden on second side, about 4 minutes. Transfer to platter, sprinkle with Parmesan, and serve.

Sautéed Green Beans with Garlic and Herbs

SERVES 4 `FAST` `GF`

✔ **WHY THIS RECIPE WORKS:** To get tender, lightly browned, fresh-tasting green beans using just one pan, we turned to sautéing. But simply sautéing raw beans in hot oil resulted in blackened exteriors and undercooked interiors. Cooking the beans in water in a covered pan, then removing the lid to evaporate the liquid and brown the beans was better, but not foolproof. For the best results, we sautéed the beans until spotty brown, then added water to the pan and covered

it so the beans could cook through. Once the beans were bright green but still crisp, we lifted the lid to evaporate the water and promote additional browning. A little softened butter (or olive oil, in one of the variations) added to the pan at this stage lent richness and promoted even more browning. A few additional ingredients, such as garlic and herbs, added flavor without overcomplicating our recipe. This recipe yields crisp-tender beans. If you prefer a slightly more tender texture (or you are using large, tough beans), increase the water by 1 tablespoon and increase the covered cooking time by 1 minute. You will need a 12-inch nonstick skillet with a tight-fitting lid for this recipe.

- 1 tablespoon unsalted butter, softened
- 3 garlic cloves, minced
- 1 teaspoon minced fresh thyme
- 1 teaspoon vegetable oil
- 1 pound green beans, trimmed and cut into 2-inch lengths
- Salt and pepper
- ¼ cup water
- 2 teaspoons lemon juice

1. Combine butter, garlic, and thyme in bowl. Heat oil in 12-inch nonstick skillet over medium heat until just smoking. Add beans, ¼ teaspoon salt, and ⅛ teaspoon pepper and cook, stirring occasionally, until spotty brown, 4 to 6 minutes. Add water, cover, and cook until beans are bright green and still crisp, about 2 minutes.

2. Uncover, increase heat to high, and cook until water evaporates, 30 to 60 seconds. Add butter mixture and cook, stirring often, until beans are crisp-tender, lightly browned, and beginning to wrinkle, 1 to 3 minutes. Off heat, stir in lemon juice and season with salt and pepper to taste. Transfer to platter and serve.

VARIATIONS

Sautéed Green Beans with Smoked Paprika and Almonds `FAST` `GF`

Omit thyme. Add ¼ teaspoon smoked paprika to softened butter with garlic. Sprinkle beans with ¼ cup toasted slivered almonds before serving.

Spicy Sautéed Green Beans with Ginger and Sesame `FAST` `VEGAN` `GF`

Substitute following mixture for butter mixture: Combine 1 teaspoon toasted sesame oil, 1 teaspoon grated fresh ginger, and 1 tablespoon Asian chili-garlic sauce in bowl. Increase amount of oil in step 1 to 2 teaspoons. Sprinkle beans with 2 teaspoons toasted sesame seeds before serving.

To braise 2 pounds of kale, we sauté half until wilted, then stir in the rest with broth and water and simmer until tender.

Braised Kale

SERVES 4 TO 6 VEGAN GF

✓ **WHY THIS RECIPE WORKS:** We wanted a one-pot approach to turning kale tender, without spending hours watching a pot or leaving the greens awash in liquid. To fit a generous 2 pounds of kale in the pot, we sautéed half of the greens before adding the rest, then we stirred in a little liquid and covered the pot. In less than half an hour, the hearty greens had almost the tender-firm texture we wanted. We removed the lid to allow the liquid to evaporate as the greens finished cooking. With the texture right where we wanted it, all we had to do was come up with a few flavorful ingredients to add to the pot. We liked a simple combination of garlic, onions, and red pepper flakes, with a squeeze of fresh lemon juice to balance the dish. You can substitute collard greens for the kale here. For the best results, be sure the greens are fully cooked and tender in step 1 before moving on to step 2.

3 tablespoons extra-virgin olive oil
1 onion, chopped fine
5 garlic cloves, minced
⅛ teaspoon red pepper flakes
2 pounds kale, stemmed and chopped into 3-inch pieces
1 cup vegetable broth
1 cup water
  Salt and pepper
2 teaspoons lemon juice

1. Heat 2 tablespoons oil in Dutch oven over medium heat until shimmering. Add onion and cook until softened and beginning to brown, 4 to 5 minutes. Stir in garlic and pepper flakes and cook until fragrant, about 1 minute. Stir in half of kale and cook until beginning to wilt, about 1 minute. Stir in remaining kale, broth, water, and ¼ teaspoon salt. Quickly cover pot and reduce heat to medium-low. Cook, stirring occasionally, until greens are tender, 25 to 35 minutes.

2. Remove lid and increase heat to medium-high. Cook, stirring occasionally, until most of liquid has evaporated (bottom of pot will be almost dry and greens will begin to sizzle), 8 to 12 minutes. Off heat, stir in lemon juice and remaining 1 tablespoon oil. Season with salt and pepper. Transfer to bowl and serve.

VARIATION

Braised Kale with Coconut and Curry VEGAN GF
Substitute 2 teaspoons grated fresh ginger and 1 teaspoon curry powder for red pepper flakes, and 1 (13.5-ounce) can coconut milk for water. Substitute lime juice for lemon juice, and sprinkle kale with ¼ cup toasted and chopped cashews before serving.

Creamed Kale

SERVES 4 FAST GF

✓ **WHY THIS RECIPE WORKS:** We've all heard of creamed spinach, but with the increasing popularity of kale we wanted to put a new twist on this classic dish by developing a recipe for creamed kale. To keep our recipe streamlined, we eschewed making a separate béchamel sauce in favor of simply simmering the greens with cream until the sauce thickened. We started by wilting the greens in vegetable broth a handful at a time; this ensured that we could fit a generous amount of greens into our pot, and the broth lent the greens savory flavor. Once the greens were wilted, we built up the flavor by sautéing shallots, garlic, and red pepper flakes in some butter, then we added in the cream and kale and simmered everything until the sauce was thickened and clingy. A little Parmesan and

ALL ABOUT **HEARTY GREENS**

No longer just a farmers' market specialty item, hearty greens are now widely available in grocery stores across the country. Their sturdy leaves offer earthy flavor and texture as well as an abundance of nutrients—iron, fiber, vitamins K, A, and C, and magnesium, just to name a few. The season for hearty greens spans from early fall until late spring, sometimes stretching into summer. In this book you'll find these greens layered into gratins, tossed into pasta dishes and grain salads, and featured in side dishes and more. A large bunch of greens will reduce dramatically when cooked, so don't be intimidated if the greens initially dominate the pan.

Selecting Greens

There are many types of hearty greens, but the ones we use most often are Swiss chard, collard greens, kale, and mustard greens. Here is some basic information on each.

SWISS CHARD

Swiss chard has dark, ruffled leaves and a tough stem that can be crimson red, orange, yellow, or white. The leaves and stems need to be cooked separately, as the stems take much longer to soften. Look for bunches with bright-stemmed leaves that are firm and undamaged.

COLLARD GREENS

Collard greens have dark green, very wide leaves and a thick stem. Look for bunches with trimmed stems and no sign of yellowing or wilting. Unless you plan to slice the leaves thinly, it is best to braise collard greens until tender. They pair well with strongly flavored ingredients. Be sure to strip the leaves from the stems, which are tough and woody.

KALE

Kale is the darling of the vegetarian world and comes in many varieties: curly green kale, red kale, more delicate Tuscan kale, and baby kale. Its hearty leaves have a surprisingly sweet undertone. Kale is easy to find both in bunches and in prewashed bags. Tender baby kale can be eaten raw in salads without any special treatment, but mature kale is tougher. To eat it raw, cut it into pieces, then vigorously knead it for about 5 minutes.

MUSTARD GREENS

There are many varieties of mustard greens, but the most common has crisp, bright green leaves and thin stems. These greens have a medium-hot flavor with a fairly strong bite, which makes them especially well suited to spicy Asian noodle dishes.

Storing Greens

To preserve freshness, store greens loosely in a dry plastic bag in the refrigerator. Kept this way, the greens can last five to seven days.

Prepping Greens

1A. Hold leaf at base of stem and use knife to slash leafy portion from either side of tough stem.

1B. Alternatively, fold each leaf in half and cut along edge of rib to remove thickest part of rib and stem.

2. After separating leaves, stack several and either cut into strips or roll pile into cigar shape and coarsely chop.

3. Fill salad spinner bowl with cool water, add cut greens, and gently swish them around. Let grit settle to bottom of bowl, then lift greens out and drain water. Repeat until greens no longer release any dirt.

nutmeg rounded out the flavors nicely. You will need approximately three bunches of kale for this recipe, because it cooks down considerably.

1½ cups vegetable broth
1¾ pounds curly kale, stemmed and chopped
2 tablespoons unsalted butter
2 large shallots, sliced thin
2 garlic cloves, minced
¼ teaspoon red pepper flakes
¾ cup heavy cream
1 ounce Parmesan cheese, grated (½ cup)
⅛ teaspoon ground nutmeg
Pinch pepper
Lemon wedges

1. Bring 1 cup broth to boil in large Dutch oven over high heat. Gradually add kale, covering pot to let each addition wilt slightly, before stirring and adding more, about 4 minutes. When all kale has been added to pot, reduce heat to medium-high, cover, and cook, stirring occasionally, until kale is fully wilted and bottom of pot is nearly dry, 5 to 10 minutes. Transfer kale to bowl.

2. Wipe out now-empty pot with paper towels, add butter, and melt over medium heat. Stir in shallots and cook until shallots are softened, 5 to 7 minutes. Stir in garlic and pepper flakes and cook until fragrant, about 30 seconds. Add remaining ½ cup broth and bring to boil, scraping up any browned bits. Stir in cream and return to boil.

3. Stir in kale and cook, stirring occasionally, until sauce has thickened slightly and clings to kale, 7 to 10 minutes. Off heat, stir in Parmesan, nutmeg, and pepper. Transfer to bowl and serve with lemon wedges.

Braised Leeks

SERVES 4 FAST GF

✔ **WHY THIS RECIPE WORKS:** The unique onionlike sweetness of leeks makes them a delicious side dish, especially when braised, which gives them a tender, creamy texture and deep flavor. The key to this dish was cooking the leeks to the ideal doneness, so they'd be nicely caramelized on the outside and soft but not mushy on the inside. Selecting large leeks made things easier; they held together better in the pan and were less likely to overcook. To get better browning, we halved the leeks lengthwise and set them in the skillet cut side down; a sprinkling of sugar gave us even more caramelization.

Finally, we added wine, broth, and thyme to the skillet, simmered the leeks until tender, then reduced the cooking liquid to a flavorful glaze. Look for leeks about 1 inch in diameter and trim them to fit easily in the skillet. Leave enough of the root intact to hold the layers together. The leeks can fall apart easily when cooking, so be sure to handle them gently. You will need a 12-inch nonstick skillet with a tight-fitting lid for this recipe.

3 tablespoons unsalted butter
½ teaspoon sugar
Salt and pepper
4 large leeks, white and light green parts only, root ends trimmed, halved lengthwise
¼ cup dry white wine
¼ cup vegetable broth
½ teaspoon minced fresh thyme
1 tablespoon minced fresh parsley
1 teaspoon lemon juice

1. Melt 2 tablespoons butter in 12-inch nonstick skillet over medium-high heat. Sprinkle sugar and ¼ teaspoon salt evenly into skillet, then lay leeks cut side down in single layer in skillet. Cook, shaking skillet occasionally, until cut sides are golden, about 5 minutes (reduce heat if leeks brown too quickly).

2. Add wine, broth, and thyme. Reduce heat to low, cover, and simmer until leeks turn translucent and paring knife inserted into root end meets little resistance, about 10 minutes.

3. Transfer leeks to platter. Simmer liquid left in skillet until reduced to syrupy consistency, 1 to 2 minutes. Off heat, whisk in remaining 1 tablespoon butter, parsley, and lemon juice. Season with salt and pepper to taste. Spoon sauce over leeks and serve.

Trimming Leeks

1. Using chef's knife, trim away any small roots, leaving base intact to hold leek layers together.

2. Trim away dark green leaves. Cut leek in half lengthwise through base.

All About Onions

Many supermarkets stock a half-dozen types of onions. They don't all look the same or taste the same. Here are the onions and their close relatives that you will find in most markets.

YELLOW ONIONS

These strong-flavored onions maintain their potency when cooked, making them our first choice for cooking.

WHITE ONIONS

These pungent onions are similar to yellow onions but lack some of their complexity.

RED ONIONS

These crisp onions have a sweet, peppery flavor when raw and are often used in salads and for pickling.

SWEET ONIONS

Vidalia, Maui, and Walla Walla are three common sweet varieties. Their texture can become stringy when cooked, so these sugary onions are best used raw.

PEARL ONIONS

These crunchy small onions are generally used in soups, stews, and side dishes. Peeling them is a chore, so we recommend buying frozen pearl onions that are already peeled.

SHALLOTS

Shallots have a complex, subtly sweet flavor. When cooked, they become very soft and almost melt away, making them the perfect choice for sauces.

SCALLIONS

Scallions have an earthy flavor and a delicate crunch that work best in dishes that involve little or no cooking.

BUYING ONIONS

Choose onions with dry, papery skins. They should be rock-hard, with no soft spots or powdery mold on the skin. Avoid onions with green sprouts.

STORING ONIONS

Store onions and shallots at cool room temperature, away from light. Delicate scallions are the exception; they belong in the refrigerator. Stand them up in 1 inch of water in a tall container and cover them loosely with a plastic bag.

For tender, not shriveled, sautéed mushrooms, we crowd the skillet, then extend the cooking time to ensure they brown.

Sautéed Mushrooms with Shallots and Thyme

SERVES 4 **FAST** **GF**

✅ **WHY THIS RECIPE WORKS:** Supermarket mushrooms tend to shrink and shrivel when sautéed. We wanted to develop a quick sauté method that delivered enough white mushrooms to make a delicious, ample side dish. To get more flavor and less shriveling, we discovered that overloading the skillet and extending the cooking time allowed the mushrooms to give up just enough liquid to eventually fit in a single layer without shrinking to nothing. They browned nicely after we added a little oil or butter, and from there it was easy to enhance the dish with shallot, thyme, and Marsala, a classic combination for complementing the earthy flavor of mushrooms.

- 1 **tablespoon vegetable oil**
- 1½ **pounds white mushrooms, trimmed and halved if small or quartered if large**
- 1 **tablespoon unsalted butter**
- 1 **shallot, minced**

1 tablespoon minced fresh thyme
¼ cup dry Marsala
  Salt and pepper

1. Heat oil in 12-inch nonstick skillet over medium-high heat until shimmering. Add mushrooms and cook, stirring occasionally, until they release their liquid, about 5 minutes. Increase heat to high and cook, stirring occasionally, until liquid has evaporated, about 8 minutes.

2. Stir in butter, reduce heat to medium, and cook, stirring often, until mushrooms are dark brown, about 8 minutes.

3. Stir in shallot and thyme and cook until shallot is softened, about 3 minutes. Add Marsala and cook until evaporated, about 2 minutes. Season with salt and pepper to taste, transfer to platter, and serve.

VARIATION
Sautéed Mushrooms with Sesame and Ginger
SERVES 4 FAST VEGAN GF

We like to use a rasp-style grater for grating ginger quickly, though the small holes of a box grater also work well. Mirin is a sweet Japanese cooking wine; sherry can be substituted for the mirin if necessary. In order for this recipe to be gluten-free, you must use gluten-free soy sauce or tamari.

2 tablespoons vegetable oil
1½ pounds white mushrooms, trimmed and halved if small or quartered if large
1 tablespoon sesame seeds, toasted
1 tablespoon grated fresh ginger
2 tablespoons mirin
2 tablespoons soy sauce
1 teaspoon toasted sesame oil
2 scallions, sliced thin on bias

1. Heat 1 tablespoon vegetable oil in 12-inch nonstick skillet over medium-high heat until shimmering. Add mushrooms and cook, stirring occasionally, until they release their liquid,

about 5 minutes. Increase heat to high and cook, stirring occasionally, until liquid has evaporated, about 8 minutes.

2. Add remaining 1 tablespoon vegetable oil, reduce heat to medium, and cook, stirring often, until mushrooms are dark brown, about 8 minutes.

3. Stir in sesame seeds and ginger and cook until ginger is fragrant, about 30 seconds. Add mirin and soy sauce and cook until evaporated, about 30 seconds. Off heat, stir in sesame oil. Transfer to platter, sprinkle with scallions, and serve.

Roasted Portobello Mushrooms
SERVES 4 TO 6 VEGAN GF

✔ **WHY THIS RECIPE WORKS:** Portobello mushrooms are delicious when simply sautéed or grilled, but slow-cooking them really brings out their rich, earthy flavor. Mushrooms are composed of 80 percent water; what better way to draw out their moisture and concentrate their flavor than by roasting? However, our first attempts produced tough, rubbery mushrooms by the time we had cooked off enough water to get good browning. We found the trick was to score the mushroom caps before roasting; this helped wick away moisture, shortening the cooking time, so the mushrooms emerged from the oven tender and deeply flavorful. Preheating the baking sheet and brushing the mushrooms with oil gave us great browning, then we whisked together a simple balsamic vinaigrette to toss with the mushrooms before serving. These mushrooms can be served warm or at room temperature.

8 large portobello mushroom caps
¼ cup extra-virgin olive oil
  Salt and pepper
1 tablespoon balsamic vinegar
1 tablespoon minced fresh parsley
2 teaspoons minced fresh thyme
1 small garlic clove, minced

Trimming Mushrooms

White mushrooms have tender stems that can be cooked along with the mushroom caps. Simply trim off a thin slice from the bottom of the stem.

Scoring Portobello Mushrooms

Using tip of paring knife, lightly score top of each mushroom cap in ½-inch crosshatch pattern, about ⅛ inch deep.

1. Line rimmed baking sheet with aluminum foil. Adjust oven rack to upper-middle position, place prepared sheet on rack, and heat oven to 400 degrees. Cut ⅛-inch-deep slits in ½-inch crosshatch pattern on top of each mushroom cap. Brush both sides of caps with 2 tablespoons oil and sprinkle with 1 teaspoon salt.

2. Working quickly, remove baking sheet from oven and carefully arrange caps, gill side up, on preheated sheet. Roast mushrooms until they have released some of their liquid and are beginning to brown around edges, 10 to 12 minutes.

3. Flip caps over and continue to roast until liquid has completely evaporated and caps are golden brown, 10 to 12 minutes.

4. Transfer mushrooms to cutting board and let cool slightly. Meanwhile, whisk vinegar, parsley, thyme, garlic, and ¼ teaspoon pepper together in large bowl. Whisking constantly, drizzle in remaining 2 tablespoons oil.

5. Slice mushrooms into ½-inch strips, toss with vinaigrette, and season with salt and pepper to taste. Transfer to platter and serve.

VARIATION
Roasted Portobello Mushrooms with Greek Flavors VEGAN GF
Substitute 2 tablespoons lemon juice for vinegar and oregano for thyme. Toss 12 pitted and coarsely chopped kalamata olives with cooked mushrooms and vinaigrette before serving.

Roasted Red Potatoes
SERVES 4 VEGAN GF

✓ **WHY THIS RECIPE WORKS:** To arrive at our ideal roasted potatoes—ones with deep golden, crisp crusts and creamy, soft interiors—we took advantage of the naturally high moisture content of red potatoes. Covering them for part of the cooking time allowed the trapped moisture to steam the potatoes, giving them creamy flesh and allowing us to skip the extra step of parboiling, a welcome timesaver. Finishing the potatoes uncovered crisped the outsides to a perfect golden brown. Contact with the baking sheet was important to browning, so we flipped the potatoes partway through the browning process to achieve multisided crispness. We made these simple potatoes even easier by lining the baking sheet with foil, making for quick cleanup. If using very small potatoes, cut them in half instead of into wedges and flip them cut side up during the final 10 minutes of roasting.

2 **pounds red potatoes, unpeeled, cut into ¾-inch wedges**
3 **tablespoons extra-virgin olive oil**
   Salt and pepper

1. Adjust oven rack to middle position and heat oven to 425 degrees. Line rimmed baking sheet with aluminum foil. Toss potatoes with oil in bowl and season with salt and pepper. Arrange potatoes in single layer on prepared sheet, with either cut side facing down. Cover with foil and roast for 20 minutes.

2. Remove foil and continue to roast until sides of potatoes touching pan are crusty and golden, about 15 minutes. Flip potatoes over using metal spatula and continue to roast until crusty and golden on second side, about 8 minutes. Season with salt and pepper to taste, transfer to platter, and serve.

VARIATIONS
Roasted Red Potatoes with Garlic and Rosemary VEGAN GF
During final 3 minutes of roasting, sprinkle 2 tablespoons minced fresh rosemary over potatoes. Toss roasted potatoes with 1 garlic clove, minced to paste, before serving.

Roasted Red Potatoes with Feta, Olives, and Oregano GF
During final 3 minutes of roasting, sprinkle 1 tablespoon minced fresh oregano over potatoes. Combine ½ cup crumbled feta cheese, 12 pitted and chopped kalamata olives, 1 tablespoon lemon juice, and 1 garlic clove, minced to paste, in bowl. Toss roasted potatoes with feta mixture before serving.

Braised Red Potatoes with Lemon and Chives
SERVES 4 TO 6 GF

✓ **WHY THIS RECIPE WORKS:** What if you could make red potatoes with the creamy interiors you get from steaming and the crispy, browned exteriors you get from roasting—without doing either? That's the result promised by recipes for braised red potatoes, but they rarely deliver. To make good on the promise, we combined halved small red potatoes, butter, and salted water (plus thyme for flavoring) in a 12-inch skillet and simmered the spuds until their interiors were perfectly creamy and the water was fully evaporated. Then we let the potatoes continue to cook in the dry skillet until their cut sides browned in the butter, giving them the rich flavor and crisp edges of roasted potatoes. These crispy, creamy potatoes were so good they needed only a minimum of seasoning. We simply tossed them with some garlic (which we softened in the simmering

For crispy, creamy braised potatoes, we add butter to the braising liquid and simmer them until the water evaporates.

water along with the potatoes and then minced to a paste), lemon juice, chives, and pepper. Use small red potatoes measuring about 1½ inches in diameter.

1½ pounds small red potatoes, unpeeled, halved

2 cups water

3 tablespoons unsalted butter

3 garlic cloves, peeled

3 sprigs fresh thyme

¾ teaspoon salt

1 teaspoon lemon juice

¼ teaspoon pepper

2 tablespoons minced fresh chives

1. Arrange potatoes in single layer, cut side down, in 12-inch nonstick skillet. Add water, butter, garlic, thyme sprigs, and salt and bring to simmer over medium-high heat. Reduce heat to medium, cover, and simmer until potatoes are just tender, about 15 minutes.

2. Remove lid and use slotted spoon to transfer garlic to cutting board; discard thyme sprigs. Increase heat to medium-high and simmer vigorously, swirling pan occasionally, until

water evaporates and butter starts to sizzle, 15 to 20 minutes. When cool enough to handle, mince garlic to paste. Transfer paste to bowl and stir in lemon juice and pepper.

3. Continue to cook potatoes, swirling pan frequently, until butter browns and cut sides of potatoes turn spotty brown, 4 to 6 minutes longer. Off heat, add chives and garlic mixture and toss to coat thoroughly. Serve.

Braised Red Potatoes with Dijon and Tarragon GF

Substitute 2 teaspoons Dijon mustard for lemon juice and 1 tablespoon minced fresh tarragon for chives.

Braised Red Potatoes with Miso and Scallions GF

See page 55 for information about buying miso.

Reduce salt to ½ teaspoon. Substitute 1 tablespoon red miso for lemon juice and 3 thinly sliced scallions for chives.

Best Baked Potatoes

SERVES 4 **VEGAN** **GF**

✔ **WHY THIS RECIPE WORKS:** The best baked potatoes have a thick, chewy skin and a light, fluffy interior, and we wanted to find the best way to make them. After baking all-purpose, Yukon Gold, and russet potatoes, we determined only russets produced the fluffy, dry texture we were looking for. We also discovered that traditional slow baking was the best method, mainly because of the effect it has on the potato's skin. A substantial brown layer developed just under the skin when the potato was baked at 350 degrees for 1 hour and 15 minutes, and it added incredible flavor. In addition, we found that cooking the potatoes right on the oven rack was the best way to promote even browning and skin that was perfectly cooked all the way around, not just on top. The most important step to a fluffy potato was opening it wide while it was still steaming hot; if the steam stayed trapped inside, it made the interior

Releasing Steam from Baked Potatoes

Pierce baked potato several times with fork to create dotted X. Press in at ends of potato to push flesh up and out.

Understanding Potato Types

Since potatoes have varying textures (determined by starch level), you can't just reach for any potato and expect great results. Potatoes fall into three main categories—baking, boiling, or all-purpose—depending on texture.

BAKING POTATOES

These dry, floury potatoes contain more total starch (20 to 22 percent) than that in other categories, giving these varieties a dry, mealy texture. These potatoes are the best choice when baking and frying. In our opinion, they are also the best potatoes for mashing because they can drink up butter and cream. They work well when you want to thicken a stew or soup, but not when you want distinct chunks of potatoes. Common varieties: russet, Russet Burbank, and Idaho.

ALL-PURPOSE POTATOES

These potatoes contain less total starch (18 to 20 percent) than that in dry, floury potatoes but more than the total starch in firm boiling potatoes. Although they are considered "in-between" potatoes, in comparison to boiling potatoes their texture is more mealy, putting them closer to dry, floury potatoes. All-purpose potatoes can be mashed or baked but won't be as fluffy as dry, floury potatoes. They can be used in salads and soups but won't be quite as firm as boiling potatoes. Common varieties: Yukon Gold, Yellow Finn, Purple Peruvian, Kennebec, and Katahdin.

BOILING POTATOES

These potatoes contain a relatively low amount of total starch (16 to 18 percent), which means they have a firm, smooth, and waxy texture. Often they are called "new" potatoes because they are less-mature potatoes harvested in late spring and summer. They are less starchy than "old" potatoes because they haven't had time to convert their sugar to starch. They also have thinner skins. Firm, waxy potatoes are perfect when you want the potatoes to hold their shape, as with potato salad. They are also a good choice when roasting or boiling. Common varieties: Red Bliss, French Fingerling, Red Creamer, and White Rose.

soggy. You can bake as many potatoes as you like without altering the cooking time.

> 4 russet potatoes (8 ounces each), unpeeled
> Vegetable oil

Adjust oven rack to middle position and heat oven to 350 degrees. Rub potatoes lightly with oil, place directly on oven rack, and bake until paring knife easily pierces flesh, about 1¼ hours. Remove potatoes from oven and pierce with fork several times to create dotted X. Press in at ends of potato to push flesh up and out. Serve.

Oven Fries

SERVES 3 TO 4   `VEGAN`   `GF`

✔ **WHY THIS RECIPE WORKS:** The ease and neatness of oven frying—as opposed to deep frying in a pot of hot oil—is such an engaging proposition that we were determined to make oven fries worth eating on their own terms. We were after fries with a golden, crisp crust and a richly creamy interior. We soaked peeled russet potatoes, cut into wedges, in hot water for 10 minutes to remove excess starch. To further prevent the potatoes from sticking, we poured oil, salt, and pepper on the baking sheet, instead of on the potatoes, which elevated them just enough off of the pan. We covered the potatoes with aluminum foil to steam them for the first 5 minutes of cooking and then uncovered them and continued to bake until they were golden and crisp. Take care to cut the potatoes into evenly sized wedges so that all of the pieces will cook at about the same rate. A nonstick baking sheet works particularly well for this recipe. Use a heavy-duty baking sheet; the intense heat of the oven may cause lighter pans to warp. If you prefer not to peel the potatoes, just scrub them well before cutting.

> 2¼ pounds russet potatoes, peeled and cut lengthwise into 10 to 12 even wedges
> 5 tablespoons vegetable oil
> Salt and pepper

1. Adjust oven rack to lowest position and heat oven to 475 degrees. Place potatoes in large bowl, cover with hot tap water, and soak for 10 minutes. Meanwhile, coat 18 by 12-inch heavy-duty rimmed baking sheet with 4 tablespoons oil and sprinkle evenly with ¾ teaspoon salt and ¼ teaspoon pepper.

2. Drain potatoes, then spread out over paper towel–lined baking sheet and thoroughly pat dry. Rinse and wipe out

Cutting Oven Fries

1. Quarter potato lengthwise using chef's knife.

2. Cut each quarter into evenly sized wedges; 1 large potato should make 10 to 12 wedges.

now-empty bowl. Return potatoes to bowl and toss with remaining 1 tablespoon oil. Arrange potatoes in single layer on oiled and seasoned baking sheet, cover tightly with aluminum foil, and bake 5 minutes.

3. Remove foil and continue to bake until bottoms of potatoes are spotty golden brown, 15 to 20 minutes, rotating sheet halfway through roasting time.

4. Using metal spatula and tongs, scrape to loosen potatoes from pan, then flip each wedge, keeping potatoes in single layer. Continue baking until fries are golden and crisp, 5 to 15 minutes, rotating pan as needed if fries are browning unevenly. Transfer baked fries to paper towel–lined baking sheet and let drain. Season with salt and pepper to taste, transfer to platter, and serve.

Classic Mashed Potatoes

SERVES 4 **FAST** **GF**

✔ **WHY THIS RECIPE WORKS:** Many people would never consider consulting a recipe when making mashed potatoes, instead adding chunks of butter and glugs of cream to cooked spuds until their conscience tells them to stop. Little wonder, then, that mashed potatoes made this way are consistent only in their mediocrity. We wanted mashed potatoes that were perfectly smooth and creamy, with great potato flavor and plenty of buttery richness every time. We began by cutting starchy russets into chunks and simmering them until tender. For smooth, velvety potatoes, we discovered that there is a bit of science involved. If the half-and-half is stirred into the potatoes before the butter, the water in the half-and-half combines with the starch in the potatoes to make them gummy and heavy. But when the butter is added first, the fat coats the starch molecules and prevents them from reacting with the water in the half-and-half, making for smoother, more velvety mashed potatoes. Melting rather than merely softening the butter enabled it to coat the starch molecules quickly and easily, so that the potatoes turned out creamy and light. For the smoothest mashed potatoes, use a food mill or potato ricer.

2 pounds russet potatoes, peeled, quartered, and cut into 1-inch chunks
8 tablespoons unsalted butter, melted
1 cup half-and-half, hot
 Salt and pepper

1. Place potatoes in large saucepan and add water to cover by 1 inch. Bring water to boil, then reduce to simmer and cook until potatoes are tender and paring knife can be inserted into potatoes with no resistance, 20 to 25 minutes.

2. Drain potatoes in colander, tossing to remove any excess water. Wipe now-empty saucepan dry with paper towels. Return potatoes to pot and mash to uniform consistency, or process through food mill or ricer and back into dry pot.

3. Using rubber spatula, fold in melted butter until just incorporated. Fold in ¾ cup half-and-half, then add remaining ¼ cup as needed to adjust consistency. Season with salt and pepper to taste and serve.

VARIATIONS
Garlic Mashed Potatoes **FAST** **GF**
Toasting the garlic is essential for mellowing its harsh flavor. Avoid using unusually large garlic cloves, as they will not soften adequately during toasting.

Toast about 20 unpeeled garlic cloves in 8-inch skillet over lowest possible heat until spotty dark brown and slightly softened, about 22 minutes. Remove pan from heat, cover, and let stand until garlic is completely soft, 10 to 15 minutes. Peel and mince garlic, then fold it into potatoes with butter in step 3. (If using food mill or potato ricer, process softened, peeled cloves whole, along with potatoes.)

Mashed Potatoes with Scallions and Horseradish **FAST** **GF**
Fold ¼ cup drained prepared horseradish and 3 minced scallions into potatoes with half-and-half in step 3.

Mashed Potatoes with Smoked Cheddar and Whole-Grain Mustard **FAST** **GF**
Fold 2 tablespoons whole-grain mustard and 1 cup shredded smoked cheddar cheese into potatoes with half-and-half in step 3.

Smashed Potatoes

SERVES 4 GF

✓ **WHY THIS RECIPE WORKS:** Bold flavors and a rustic, chunky texture make smashed potatoes a satisfying side dish that pairs well with a range of entrées. We were after a good contrast of textures, with chunks of potato bound by a rich, creamy puree. Low-starch, high-moisture red potatoes were the best choice, as their compact structure held up well under pressure and their red skins provided nice contrasting color. For the best chunky texture, we cooked the potatoes whole in salted water with a bay leaf, then smashed them with a rubber spatula or the back of a wooden spoon. Giving the cooked potatoes a few minutes to dry ensured the skins weren't too slippery, making the job even easier. A combination of cream cheese, melted butter, and a little reserved potato cooking water gave our potatoes a unified creamy consistency. White potatoes can be used instead of red, but the dish won't be as colorful. We prefer to use small potatoes, 2 inches in diameter, in this recipe. Try to get potatoes of equal size; if that's not possible, test the larger potatoes for doneness. If only larger potatoes are available, increase the cooking time by about 10 minutes.

- 2 **pounds small red potatoes, unpeeled**
  Salt and pepper
- 1 **bay leaf**
- 4 **ounces cream cheese, room temperature**
- 4 **tablespoons unsalted butter, melted**
- 3 **tablespoons minced fresh chives (optional)**

1. Place potatoes in large saucepan and add water to cover by 1 inch. Add 1 teaspoon salt and bay leaf. Bring to boil over high heat, then reduce heat to medium-low and simmer gently until paring knife can be inserted into potatoes with no resistance, 35 to 45 minutes. Reserve ½ cup cooking water, then drain potatoes. Return potatoes to pot, discard bay leaf, and let potatoes sit in pot, uncovered, until surfaces are dry, about 5 minutes.

2. While potatoes dry, whisk softened cream cheese and melted butter together in bowl until smooth and fully incorporated. Add ¼ cup of reserved cooking water, chives, if using, ½ teaspoon salt, and ½ teaspoon pepper. Using rubber spatula or back of wooden spoon, smash potatoes just enough to break skins. Fold in cream cheese mixture until most of liquid has been absorbed and chunks of potatoes remain. Add more cooking water as needed, 1 tablespoon at a time, until potatoes are slightly looser than desired (potatoes will thicken slightly while sitting). Season with salt and pepper to taste and serve.

Mashed Potatoes and Root Vegetables

SERVES 4 GF

✓ **WHY THIS RECIPE WORKS:** Root vegetables like carrots, parsnips, turnips, and celery root can add an earthy flavor to mashed potatoes, but because root vegetables and potatoes have different starch levels and water content, treating them the same way creates a bad mash. We found that a 1:3 ratio of root vegetables to potatoes gave us an optimal creamy consistency, and caramelizing the root vegetables in a little butter helped bring out their natural earthy sweetness and boosted the overall flavor of the dish. To use just one pot, we first sautéed the root vegetables, and then added the potatoes with a little vegetable broth. To avoid a gluey texture, we rinsed the peeled, sliced potatoes in several changes of water before cooking them. Russet potatoes will yield a slightly fluffier, less creamy mash, but they can be used in place of the Yukon Gold potatoes if desired. It is important to cut the potatoes and root vegetables into evenly sized pieces so they cook at the same rate. This recipe can be doubled; use a large Dutch oven and increase the simmering time in step 2 to 40 minutes.

- 1½ **pounds Yukon Gold potatoes, peeled, quartered lengthwise, and cut crosswise into ¼-inch-thick slices**
- 4 **tablespoons unsalted butter**
- 8 **ounces carrots, parsnips, turnips, and/or celery root, peeled, carrots and parsnips cut into ¼-inch-thick half-moons, turnips and celery root cut into ½-inch dice**
- ⅓ **cup vegetable broth**
  Salt and pepper
- ¾ **cup half-and-half, warmed**
- 3 **tablespoons minced fresh chives**

1. Rinse potatoes using 3 or 4 changes of cold water, then drain well. Melt butter in large saucepan over medium heat. Add root vegetables and cook, stirring occasionally, until butter is browned and vegetables are dark brown and caramelized, 10 to 12 minutes. (If after 4 minutes vegetables have not started to brown, increase heat to medium-high.)

2. Stir in potatoes, broth, and ¾ teaspoon salt, cover, and reduce heat to low. Simmer gently, stirring occasionally and adjusting heat as needed, until potatoes fall apart easily when poked with fork and all liquid has been absorbed, 25 to 30 minutes. Remove pan from heat, remove lid, and allow steam to escape for 2 minutes.

3. Gently mash potatoes and root vegetables in saucepan with potato masher (do not mash vigorously). Gently fold in warm half-and-half and chives. Season with salt and pepper to taste, transfer to bowl, and serve.

VARIATION

Mashed Potatoes and Root Vegetables with Paprika and Parsley `GF`

This variation is particularly nice with carrots.

Toast 1½ teaspoons smoked or sweet paprika in 8-inch skillet over medium heat until fragrant, about 30 seconds. Substitute parsley for chives and fold toasted paprika into potatoes with parsley.

Sautéed Snow Peas with Lemon and Parsley

SERVES 4 `FAST` `VEGAN` `GF`

✔ **WHY THIS RECIPE WORKS:** We wanted to create a dish in which sweet, grassy snow peas would be the star component. To highlight and amplify the delicate flavor of the peas, we knew we needed to brown them to caramelize their flavor. We tried a traditional stir-fry technique, but the constant stirring gave us greasy, overcooked pods without any browning. Adding a sprinkle of sugar and cooking the peas without stirring for a short time helped to achieve a flavorful sear, then we continued to cook them, stirring constantly, until they were just crisp-tender. To boost flavor, we cleared the center of the pan and quickly sautéed a mixture of minced shallot, oil, and lemon zest before stirring everything together. A squeeze of lemon juice and a sprinkling of parsley added just before serving kept this dish fresh and bright. Chives, tarragon, cilantro, or basil can be substituted for the parsley.

1   **tablespoon vegetable oil**
1   **small shallot, minced**
1   **teaspoon finely grated lemon zest plus 1 teaspoon juice**
     Salt and pepper
⅛   **teaspoon sugar**
¾   **pound snow peas, strings removed**
1   **tablespoon minced fresh parsley**

Removing Strings from Snow Peas

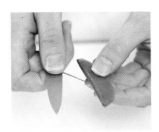

Using paring knife and your thumb, snip off tip of pea, then pull along flat side of pod to remove string.

A briefly sautéed aromatic mixture of minced shallot, lemon zest, and oil gives our crisp-tender snow peas great flavor.

1. Combine 1 teaspoon oil, shallot, and lemon zest in bowl. In separate bowl, combine ¼ teaspoon salt, ⅛ teaspoon pepper, and sugar.

2. Heat remaining 2 teaspoons oil in 12-inch nonstick skillet over high heat until just smoking. Add snow peas, sprinkle with salt mixture, and cook, without stirring, for 30 seconds. Stir briefly, then cook, without stirring, for 30 seconds. Continue to cook, stirring constantly, until peas are crisp-tender, 1 to 2 minutes.

3. Clear center of skillet, add shallot mixture, and cook, mashing mixture into skillet, until fragrant, about 30 seconds. Stir shallot mixture into peas. Stir in lemon juice and parsley and season with salt and pepper to taste. Transfer to bowl and serve.

VARIATIONS

Sautéed Snow Peas with Ginger, Garlic, and Scallion `FAST` `VEGAN` `GF`

Substitute 2 minced garlic cloves, 2 teaspoons grated fresh ginger, and 2 minced scallion whites for shallot and lemon zest, and red pepper flakes for black pepper. Substitute rice vinegar for lemon juice, and 2 sliced scallion greens for parsley.

Sautéed Snow Peas with Garlic, Cumin, and Cilantro `FAST` `VEGAN` `GF`

Add 2 minced garlic cloves and ½ teaspoon toasted and lightly crushed cumin seeds to shallot mixture in step 1. Substitute ½ teaspoon lime zest for lemon zest, lime juice for lemon juice, and cilantro for parsley.

Sautéed Snow Peas with Shallot, Lemon Grass, and Basil `FAST` `VEGAN` `GF`

Substitute 2 teaspoons minced fresh lemon grass for lemon zest, lime juice for lemon juice, and basil for parsley.

Spinach with Garlic and Lemon
SERVES 4 `FAST` `VEGAN` `GF`

✔ **WHY THIS RECIPE WORKS:** Overcooked spinach, bitter burnt garlic, and pallid lemon flavor are all too often the hallmarks of this simple side dish. Instead, we sought tender sautéed spinach seasoned with a perfect balance of garlic and lemon. For the spinach, we found that we greatly preferred the hearty flavor and texture of curly-leaf spinach over baby spinach, which wilted down into mush. We cooked the spinach in extra-virgin olive oil and, once cooked, used tongs to squeeze the spinach in a colander over the sink to get rid of all the excess moisture. Lightly toasted minced garlic, cooked after the spinach, added a sweet nuttiness. As for seasoning, all the spinach needed was salt and a squeeze of lemon juice. Leave some water clinging to the spinach leaves after rinsing to help encourage steam when cooking. Two pounds of flat-leaf spinach (about three bunches) can be substituted for the curly-leaf spinach, but do not use baby spinach because it is much too delicate.

Stemming Spinach

Holding leaf with one hand, use other hand to pull down and remove stem.

3 tablespoons extra-virgin olive oil
20 ounces curly-leaf spinach, stemmed
2 garlic cloves, minced
    Salt
    Lemon juice

1. Heat 1 tablespoon oil in Dutch oven over high heat until shimmering. Add spinach 1 handful at a time, stirring and tossing each handful to wilt slightly before adding more. Cook spinach, stirring constantly, until uniformly wilted, about 1 minute. Transfer spinach to colander and squeeze between tongs to release excess liquid.

2. Wipe now-empty pot dry with paper towels. Add garlic and remaining 2 tablespoons oil to pot and cook over medium heat until fragrant, about 30 seconds. Add squeezed spinach and toss to coat. Off heat, season with salt and lemon juice to taste. Transfer to bowl and serve.

VARIATION
Spinach with Shallots and Goat Cheese `FAST` `GF`

Substitute 2 thinly sliced shallots for garlic; cook shallots until softened, about 2 minutes. Sprinkle spinach with ⅓ cup crumbled goat cheese before serving.

Pureed Butternut Squash
SERVES 4 TO 6 `FAST` `GF`

✔ **WHY THIS RECIPE WORKS:** With its silky-smooth texture and earthy, lightly sweetened flavor, pureed butternut squash is a serious crowd-pleaser, but what's the best way to cook it? Most recipes for pureed squash cook the squash until tender, then puree it with some butter and/or heavy cream in a food processor. We tested a variety of squash cooking methods, including roasting, steaming, braising, and microwaving, and found that the microwave worked best. Not only was it one of the easiest cooking methods, but tasters far preferred the clean, sweet squash flavor that the microwave produced. The surprising thing about microwaving the squash was the amount of liquid released while cooking—we drained nearly ½ cup of squash liquid out of the bowl before pureeing. (We tasted the liquid and found it had a slightly bitter flavor, which is why we did not opt to include it in the puree.) The squash puree needed only 2 tablespoons of half-and-half and 2 tablespoons of butter to help round out its flavor and add some richness.

2 pounds butternut squash, peeled, seeded, and cut into 1½-inch pieces (6 cups)
2 tablespoons half-and-half
2 tablespoons unsalted butter
1 tablespoon packed brown sugar
Salt and pepper

1. Microwave squash in covered bowl until tender and easily pierced with fork, 15 to 20 minutes, stirring halfway through cooking time.

2. Drain squash in colander, then transfer to food processor. Add half-and-half, butter, sugar, and 1 teaspoon salt and process until squash is smooth, about 20 seconds, stopping to scrape down bowl as needed. Transfer to serving bowl, season with salt and pepper to taste, and serve.

Cutting Up Butternut Squash

1. After peeling squash, trim off top and bottom and cut squash in two between narrow neck and wide curved bottom.

2. Cut squash neck into evenly sized planks, then cut planks into evenly sized pieces, according to recipe.

3. Cut squash base in half lengthwise, then scoop out and discard seeds and fibers.

4. Slice each base half into evenly sized lengths. Cut lengths into evenly sized pieces, according to recipe.

VARIATIONS

Pureed Butternut Squash with Sage and Toasted Almonds FAST GF

While squash microwaves, cook 1 tablespoon unsalted butter with ½ teaspoon minced fresh sage in 8-inch skillet over medium-low heat until fragrant, about 2 minutes. Substitute sage butter for butter added to food processor. Sprinkle with ¼ cup toasted sliced almonds before serving.

Pureed Butternut Squash with Orange FAST GF

Add 2 tablespoons orange marmalade to food processor with butter.

Pureed Butternut Squash with Honey and Chipotle Chile FAST GF

Substitute honey for sugar. Add 1½ teaspoons minced canned chipotle chile in adobo sauce to food processor with butter.

Roasted Winter Squash Halves

SERVES 4 VEGAN GF

✓ **WHY THIS RECIPE WORKS:** Winter squashes, such as acorn and butternut, with their tough skin and dense interior, are ideal for slow cooking and are best when roasted until well done, which helps develop the sweetest flavor and smoothest texture. Though varieties of winter squash vary significantly in size and texture, we were hoping to develop a one-recipe-fits-all approach. After some experimentation, we found that roasting the unpeeled and seeded halves cut side down gave a slightly better texture than roasting them cut side up. We found it best to cook the squash on an aluminum foil–lined baking sheet that had been oiled. The oil promoted better browning and reduced the risk of sticking, and the foil made cleanup easy. This recipe can be made with butternut, acorn, buttercup, kabocha, or delicata squash. The roasting time will vary depending on the kind of squash you use.

2 tablespoons extra-virgin olive oil
2 pounds winter squash, halved lengthwise and seeded
Salt and pepper

1. Adjust oven rack to middle position and heat oven to 400 degrees. Line rimmed baking sheet with aluminum foil and grease foil with 1 tablespoon oil. Brush cut sides of squash with remaining 1 tablespoon oil and place, cut side down, on

Halving Winter Squash

To keep fingers safe when cutting open squash, pound very lightly on back of knife with rubber mallet to drive blade slowly through squash.

All About Squash

Generally, squash is divided into two categories: winter squash and summer squash. Zucchini and yellow squash are the most common varieties of summer squash. They both have thin, edible skins and a high moisture content, so they cook quickly whether steamed, baked, or sautéed. Winter squashes have hard, thick peels and firm flesh that requires longer cooking to turn tender. The flesh can vary from deep yellow to orange in color. The most common varieties of winter squash are acorn, butternut, and spaghetti.

BUYING WINTER SQUASH

Whether acorn, butternut, delicata, or another variety, winter squash should feel hard; soft spots are an indication that the squash has been mishandled. Squash should also feel heavy for its size, a sign that the flesh is moist and ripe. Most supermarkets sell butternut squash that has been completely or partially prepped. Whole squash you peel yourself has the best flavor and texture, but if you are looking to save a few minutes of prep, we have found that the peeled and halved squash is fine. We don't like the butternut squash sold in chunks; while it's a timesaver, the flavor is wan and the texture stringy.

BUYING ZUCCHINI AND SUMMER SQUASH

Choose zucchini and summer squash that are firm and without soft spots. Smaller squashes are more flavorful and less watery than larger specimens; they also have fewer seeds. Look for zucchini and summer squash no heavier than 8 ounces, and preferably just 6 ounces.

STORING SQUASH

You can store winter squash in a cool, well-ventilated spot for several weeks. Zucchini and summer squash are more perishable; store them in the refrigerator in a partially sealed zipper-lock bag for up to five days.

prepared baking sheet. Roast until fork inserted into center meets little resistance, 30 to 50 minutes.

2. Remove squash from oven and flip cut side up. If necessary, cut large pieces in half to yield 4 pieces. Season with salt and pepper to taste, transfer to platter, and serve.

VARIATIONS
Roasted Winter Squash Halves with Soy Sauce and Maple Syrup VEGAN GF
In order for this recipe to be gluten-free, you must use gluten-free soy sauce or tamari.

Substitute vegetable oil for olive oil. While squash roasts, combine 3 tablespoons maple syrup, 2 tablespoons soy sauce, and ½ teaspoon grated fresh ginger in bowl. After flipping cooked squash cut side up in step 2, brush with maple mixture and return to oven until well caramelized, 5 to 10 minutes.

Roasted Winter Squash Halves with Browned Butter and Sage GF
While squash roasts, melt 6 tablespoons unsalted butter in 8-inch skillet over medium heat. Add 6 thinly sliced fresh sage leaves and cook, swirling pan often, until butter is golden and sage is crisp, 4 to 5 minutes. Drizzle sage butter over squash before serving.

Spaghetti Squash with Garlic and Parmesan
SERVES 4 GF

✔ **WHY THIS RECIPE WORKS:** The delicate flavor and creamy flesh of spaghetti squash make it a great addition to any meal, but many recipes bury the squash underneath too many competing flavors. We kept our recipe simple so the delicate and earthy flavor of the squash would shine through. Brushing the squash halves with oil, seasoning them with salt and pepper, and roasting them cut side down brought out the sweetness of the flesh. Once the squash was cooked, shredding it was as simple as holding the halves over a bowl and scraping them with a fork. After draining the excess liquid, we dressed the squash with Parmesan, fresh basil, lemon juice, and garlic for an easy, flavorful side dish that tasted like summer. Choose a firm squash with an even pale-yellow color. Avoid greenish-tinged squashes, which are immature, and those that yield to gentle pressure, which are old.

1 **spaghetti squash (2½ pounds),**
   halved lengthwise and seeded
2 **tablespoons extra-virgin olive oil**
   Salt and pepper
¼ **cup grated Parmesan cheese**
1 **tablespoon chopped fresh basil**
1 **teaspoon lemon juice**
1 **garlic clove, minced**

1. Adjust oven rack to middle position and heat oven to 450 degrees. Brush cut sides of squash with 1 tablespoon oil and season with salt and pepper. Lay squash cut side down in 13 by 9-inch baking dish. Roast squash until just tender and tip of paring knife can be slipped into flesh with slight resistance, 25 to 30 minutes.

2. Flip squash over and let cool slightly. Holding squash with clean dish towel over large bowl, use fork to scrape squash flesh from skin while shredding it into fine pieces.

3. Drain excess liquid from bowl, then gently stir in Parmesan, basil, lemon juice, garlic, and remaining 1 tablespoon oil. Season with salt and pepper to taste and serve.

VARIATION

Spaghetti Squash with Asian Flavors VEGAN GF
In order for this recipe to be gluten-free, you must use gluten-free soy sauce or tamari.

Omit Parmesan, basil, lemon juice, garlic, and remaining 1 tablespoon oil in step 3. Toss shredded squash with 2 thinly sliced scallions, 1 tablespoon soy sauce, 2½ teaspoons vegetable oil, 1 teaspoon rice vinegar, ½ teaspoon toasted sesame oil, and ½ teaspoon toasted sesame seeds before serving.

Shredding Spaghetti Squash

Holding roasted squash half with clean dish towel over large bowl, use fork to scrape squash flesh from skin, shredding flesh into fine pieces.

Roasted Sweet Potatoes
SERVES 4 TO 6 VEGAN GF

WHY THIS RECIPE WORKS: Too often, roasted sweet potatoes turn out starchy and wan. We wanted a method that gave us potatoes with a nicely caramelized exterior, a smooth, creamy interior, and an earthy sweetness. Cutting them into ¾-inch-thick rounds and laying them flat on a baking sheet ensured even cooking. A few experiments proved a lower roasting temperature resulted in a sweeter potato, so we started the sliced potatoes in a cold (versus preheated) oven and covered them with aluminum foil, which allowed plenty of time for their starches to convert to sugars. We removed the foil after 30 minutes and continued to roast the potatoes until their edges were crisp. Choose potatoes that are as even in width as possible; trimming the small ends prevents them from burning. If you prefer not to peel the potatoes, just scrub them well before cutting.

Making Roasted Sweet Potatoes

1. CUT POTATOES INTO ROUNDS: Rinse peeled sweet potatoes and cut into ¾-inch-thick rounds.

2. START COVERED IN COLD OVEN: Cover baking sheet tightly with foil and place in cold oven. Turn oven to 425 degrees and cook potatoes for 30 minutes.

3. UNCOVER: Remove top layer of foil and return potatoes to oven to continue roasting until bottom edges are golden brown, 15 to 25 minutes.

4. FLIP AND FINISH ROASTING: Flip slices over with spatula and continue to roast until bottom edges are golden brown, 18 to 22 minutes. Let cool before serving.

3 **pounds sweet potatoes, peeled, ends trimmed, rinsed, and cut into ¾-inch-thick rounds**
2 **tablespoons vegetable oil**
   Salt and pepper

1. Line 18 by 13-inch heavy-duty rimmed baking sheet with aluminum foil and coat with vegetable oil spray. Toss potatoes with oil and 1 teaspoon salt in bowl and season with pepper. Arrange potatoes in single layer on prepared baking sheet and cover tightly with foil.

2. Adjust oven rack to middle position and place potatoes in cold oven. Turn oven to 425 degrees and cook potatoes for 30 minutes.

3. Remove baking sheet from oven and remove top layer of foil. Return potatoes to oven and cook until bottom edges of potatoes are golden brown, 15 to 25 minutes.

4. Remove baking sheet from oven and, using thin metal spatula, flip slices over. Continue to roast until bottom edges of potatoes are golden brown, 18 to 22 minutes. Let roasted potatoes cool for 5 to 10 minutes, then transfer to serving dish. Serve.

VARIATIONS

Roasted Sweet Potatoes with Maple-Thyme Glaze GF
Whisk ¼ cup maple syrup, 2 tablespoons melted unsalted butter, and 2 teaspoons minced fresh thyme together in bowl. Brush mixture over both sides of partially cooked potatoes when flipping in step 4; continue to roast potatoes as directed.

NOTES FROM THE TEST KITCHEN

Sweet Potato or Yam?

You often hear "yam" and "sweet potato" used interchangeably, but they actually belong to completely different botanical families. Yams, generally sold in Latin and Asian markets, are often sold in chunks (they can grow to be several feet long) and can be found in dozens of varieties, with flesh ranging from white to light yellow to pink, and skin from off-white to brown. They all have very starchy flesh. Sweet potatoes are also found in several varieties and can have firm or soft flesh, but it's the soft varieties that have in the past been mislabeled as "yams," and the confusion continues to this day. In an attempt to remedy this, the U.S. Department of Agriculture now requires labels with the term "yam" to be accompanied by the term "sweet potato" when appropriate. We typically buy the conventional sweet potato, a longish, knobby tuber with dark orange-brown skin and vivid flesh that cooks up moist and sweet. The buttery sweet Beauregard is our favorite variety.

Roasted Sweet Potatoes with Spiced Brown Sugar Glaze GF
Cook ¼ cup packed light brown sugar, 2 tablespoons apple juice, 2 tablespoons unsalted butter, ¼ teaspoon ground cinnamon, ¼ teaspoon ground ginger, and ⅛ teaspoon ground nutmeg in small saucepan over medium heat until butter has melted and sugar is dissolved, 2 to 4 minutes. Brush mixture over both sides of partially cooked potatoes when flipping in step 4; continue to roast potatoes as directed.

Mashed Sweet Potatoes
SERVES 4 GF

✔ **WHY THIS RECIPE WORKS:** We wanted a method for making mashed sweet potatoes that would push their deep, earthy sweetness to the fore and produce a silky puree with enough body to hold its shape on a fork. We braised sliced sweet potatoes in a mixture of butter and heavy cream to impart a smooth richness. Adding salt brought out the potatoes' delicate flavor, and just a teaspoon of sugar bolstered their sweetness. Once the potatoes were tender, we mashed them in the saucepan with a potato masher. We skipped the typical pumpkin pie seasoning and instead let the simple sweet potato flavor shine through. Cutting the sweet potatoes into slices of even thickness is important in getting them to cook at the same rate. A potato masher will yield slightly lumpy sweet potatoes; a food mill will make a perfectly smooth puree.

2 **pounds sweet potatoes, peeled, quartered lengthwise, and cut crosswise into ¼-inch-thick slices**
4 **tablespoons unsalted butter, cut into 4 pieces**
2 **tablespoons heavy cream**
1 **teaspoon sugar**
   Salt and pepper

1. Combine potatoes, butter, cream, sugar, and ½ teaspoon salt in large saucepan and cook, covered, over low heat, stirring occasionally, until potatoes fall apart when poked with fork, 35 to 45 minutes.

2. Off heat, mash potatoes in saucepan with potato masher until smooth. Season with salt and pepper to taste and serve.

VARIATIONS

Maple-Orange Mashed Sweet Potatoes GF
Stir in 2 tablespoons maple syrup and ½ teaspoon grated orange zest before serving.

Garlic Mashed Sweet Potatoes with Coconut Milk and Cilantro VEGAN GF

Substitute ½ cup coconut milk for butter and cream, and add 1 small minced garlic clove and ¼ teaspoon red pepper flakes to pot with potatoes. Stir in 1 tablespoon minced fresh cilantro before serving.

Sweet Potato Fries with Spicy Dipping Sauce

SERVES 4 TO 6 GF

✔ **WHY THIS RECIPE WORKS:** Too often, sweet potato fries simply don't do justice to their namesake vegetable. We wanted thick-cut sweet potato fries with crispy exteriors and creamy, sweet interiors. Taking a cue from commercial frozen fries, which rely on a starchy coating to encourage crispness, we dunked the potato wedges in a slurry of water and cornstarch. Blanching the potatoes with salt and baking soda before dipping them in the slurry helped the coating stick to the potatoes, giving the fries a supercrunchy crust that stayed crispy. To keep the fries from sticking to the pan, we used a nonstick skillet, which had the added benefit of allowing us to use less oil. We prefer peanut oil for frying, but vegetable oil may be used instead. For a finishing touch to complement the natural sweetness of the fries, we made a spicy Belgian-style dipping sauce; however, they also taste good on their own.

SPICY SAUCE

- 6 tablespoons mayonnaise
- 2 teaspoons Asian chili-garlic sauce, plus extra as needed
- 2 teaspoons distilled white vinegar

FRIES

- ½ cup cornstarch
  Kosher salt
- 1 teaspoon baking soda
- 3 pounds sweet potatoes, peeled and cut lengthwise into ¾-inch-thick wedges, wedges cut in half crosswise
- 3 cups peanut oil

1. FOR THE SPICY SAUCE: Whisk mayonnaise, chili-garlic sauce, and vinegar together in bowl. Add extra chili-garlic sauce to taste.

2. FOR THE FRIES: Adjust oven rack to middle position and heat oven to 200 degrees. Set wire rack in rimmed baking sheet. Whisk cornstarch and ½ cup cold water together in large bowl.

For an ultracrunchy coating, we blanch sweet potato wedges with salt and baking soda, which ensures the coating sticks.

3. Bring 2 quarts water, ¼ cup salt, and baking soda to boil in Dutch oven. Add potatoes, return to boil, then reduce to simmer and cook until exteriors turn slightly mushy (centers will remain firm), 3 to 5 minutes.

4. Whisk cornstarch slurry to recombine. Using wire skimmer or slotted spoon, transfer potatoes to bowl with slurry.

Cutting Sweet Potatoes into Fries

1. Peel potatoes (if desired), then cut lengthwise into ¾-inch-thick wedges.

2. Cut wedges in half crosswise (if potatoes are shorter than 4 inches in length, do not cut in half).

Using rubber spatula, fold potatoes with slurry until slurry turns light orange, thickens to paste, and clings to potatoes.

5. Heat oil in 12-inch nonstick skillet over high heat to 325 degrees. Using tongs, carefully add one-third of potatoes. Fry until crisp and lightly browned, 7 to 10 minutes, using tongs to flip potatoes halfway through frying (adjust heat as needed to maintain oil temperature between 280 and 300 degrees).

6. Using wire skimmer or slotted spoon, transfer fries to prepared wire rack, using fork to separate any that stick together. Season with salt to taste and transfer to oven to keep warm. Return oil to 325 degrees and repeat in 2 more batches with remaining potatoes. Serve.

Slow-Roasted Tomatoes

SERVES 4   VEGAN   GF

✓ **WHY THIS RECIPE WORKS:** Slow roasting is a great way to use up an abundance of garden tomatoes or to improve wan supermarket tomatoes, as it produces a sweet, concentrated flavor with little effort. We started by cutting the tomatoes into thick slices and layering them into a baking dish. Drizzling them with plenty of extra-virgin olive oil infused them with bright, fruity flavor as they cooked. Thin slices of garlic mellowed and softened during the long cooking time, lending a rich, nutty flavor. A sprinkle of salt and pepper was all the seasoning this summery dish needed. Leftover tomato oil can be used to make salad dressings or as a dipping oil for bread.

  ½ **cup extra-virgin olive oil**
  4 **garlic cloves, sliced thin**
  2 **pounds ripe tomatoes, cored and
     cut crosswise into ½-inch-thick slices
     Salt and pepper**

1. Adjust oven rack to middle position and heat oven to 325 degrees. Brush bottom of 13 by 9-inch baking dish with 2 tablespoons oil and sprinkle with half of garlic. Arrange tomato slices in pan, overlapping edges as needed to fit. Pour remaining 6 tablespoons oil over tomatoes, then sprinkle with salt and remaining garlic. Roast tomatoes until slightly shriveled and most of juices have been replaced with oil, 1½ to 2 hours.

2. Remove dish from oven and let tomatoes cool in oil for at least 15 minutes or up to 4 hours. To serve, remove tomatoes from oil with slotted spoon and season with salt and pepper to taste. (Cooled tomatoes and oil can be refrigerated for up to 2 weeks; return to room temperature before serving.)

Sautéed Cherry Tomatoes

SERVES 4   FAST   VEGAN   GF

✓ **WHY THIS RECIPE WORKS:** Cherry tomatoes usually play more of a supporting role in salads or sides, but they can make a terrific side dish on their own. We found that the key was to cook them for just a minute in a hot skillet to soften their texture and bring out their flavorful juices. As an added bonus, this technique meant that our dish came together in less than 10 minutes. We seasoned the tomatoes simply, with just some olive oil, basil, garlic, and a little sugar to bring out their natural flavor. Pear or grape tomatoes can be substituted for the cherry tomatoes. If the cherry tomatoes are especially sweet, you may want to reduce or omit the sugar. A combination of red and yellow cherry tomatoes makes this an especially attractive side dish.

  1 **tablespoon extra-virgin olive oil**
 1½ **pounds cherry tomatoes, halved**
  2 **teaspoons sugar**
  1 **garlic clove, minced**
  2 **tablespoons chopped fresh basil
     Salt and pepper**

Heat oil in 12-inch nonstick skillet over medium-high heat until just smoking. Add tomatoes and sugar and cook, tossing often, until tomatoes begin to soften, about 1 minute. Stir in garlic and cook until fragrant, about 30 seconds. Off heat, stir in basil and season with salt and pepper to taste. Serve.

Zucchini Ribbons with Shaved Parmesan

SERVES 6 TO 8   FAST   GF

✓ **WHY THIS RECIPE WORKS:** This elegant alternative to salad is also a unique way to serve zucchini without softening its crunchy texture or altering its fresh flavor by cooking. Slicing the zucchini lengthwise into thin ribbons maximized its surface area for dressing to cling to and was more visually appealing than cutting the zucchini into rounds. A vegetable peeler or mandoline made quick work of this step. Then we dressed the zucchini simply with extra-virgin olive oil, lemon juice, mint, and shaved Parmesan cheese. Using in-season zucchini, good olive oil, and high-quality Parmesan is crucial in this simple side dish. Be ready to serve this dish shortly after it is assembled.

Dressed with just olive oil, lemon juice, mint, and Parmesan, delicate zucchini ribbons make a perfect summery side dish.

1½ **pounds zucchini**
   Salt and pepper
½   **cup extra-virgin olive oil**
¼   **cup lemon juice (2 lemons)**
2   **tablespoons minced fresh mint**
6   **ounces Parmesan cheese, shaved**

Using vegetable peeler, slice zucchini lengthwise into very thin ribbons. Gently toss zucchini ribbons in bowl with salt and pepper to taste, then arrange attractively on platter. Drizzle with olive oil and lemon juice, sprinkle with mint and Parmesan, and serve.

Making Zucchini Ribbons

Using vegetable peeler or mandoline, slice zucchini lengthwise into very thin ribbons.

Sautéed Zucchini or Yellow Summer Squash
SERVES 4   VEGAN   GF

✔ **WHY THIS RECIPE WORKS:** Because zucchini and summer squash are so watery, they often cook up soggy and bland. We wanted to find a way to make sautéed zucchini or summer squash with concentrated flavor and an appealing texture. The key was to remove water by salting and draining the squash for 30 minutes and then patting it dry. We sautéed an onion first for some depth, then we added the squash, along with some lemon zest, to the hot skillet, where the squash became tender and lightly browned with minimal stirring. A little lemon juice and parsley stirred in off the heat lent bright flavors. Do not add more salt when cooking, or the dish will be too salty. Basil, mint, tarragon, or chives can be substituted for the parsley.

1½ **pounds zucchini or yellow summer squash,**
   sliced ¼ inch thick
   Kosher salt and pepper
3   **tablespoons extra-virgin olive oil**
1   **small onion, chopped fine**
1   **teaspoon grated lemon zest plus**
   1 tablespoon juice
1   **tablespoon minced fresh parsley**

1. Toss zucchini with 1 tablespoon salt in colander set over bowl and let drain until roughly ⅓ cup water drains from zucchini, about 30 minutes. Pat zucchini dry with paper towels and carefully wipe away any residual salt.

2. Heat oil in 12-inch nonstick skillet over medium heat until shimmering. Add onion and cook until almost softened, about 3 minutes. Increase heat to medium-high, add zucchini and lemon zest, and cook, stirring occasionally, until zucchini is golden brown, about 10 minutes.

3. Off heat, stir in lemon juice and parsley and season with pepper to taste. Transfer to platter and serve.

VARIATION
Sautéed Zucchini or Yellow Summer Squash with Olives and Oregano   VEGAN   GF
Substitute 1 teaspoon minced fresh oregano for parsley. Add ¼ cup pitted and chopped kalamata olives to zucchini with lemon juice.

CHAPTER 8

Savory Flatbreads, Pizza, Tarts, and More

■ FAST (Less than 45 minutes start to finish)   ■ VEGAN   ■ GLUTEN-FREE
Photos: Classic Cheese Pizza; Vegetable Torta with Asiago and Herbs

Naan with Ricotta, Sun-Dried Tomatoes, and Olive Tapenade

SERVES 2 TO 3 **FAST**

✔ **WHY THIS RECIPE WORKS:** We used naan, a traditional Indian flatbread, as a convenient prebaked crust on which we could build a quick and easy savory flatbread. To top our convenient crust, we combined the concentrated flavors of salty kalamata olives against a backdrop of sweet sun-dried tomatoes and crunchy pine nuts. To add richness and to hold everything together, we mixed ricotta with Parmesan, garlic, and lemon juice and spread the mixture over the naan. The toppings needed only a brief stint in the oven to warm through, so we brushed the baking sheet with olive oil and baked the naan on the lowest rack in a 500-degree oven to help it crisp up during the short baking time. We recommend using either whole-milk or part-skim ricotta; do not use fat-free ricotta here.

- ¼ cup extra-virgin olive oil
- 2 (8-inch) naan breads
- 4 ounces (½ cup) whole-milk ricotta cheese
- ¼ cup Parmesan cheese, grated
- 1½ teaspoons lemon juice
- 1 garlic clove, minced
- ¼ teaspoon salt

NOTES FROM THE TEST KITCHEN

Naan and Lavash

Naan and lavash are two traditional flatbreads that have recently become widely available in supermarkets. Naan is an Indian yeast bread traditionally baked in a tandoor oven. With its great chewy texture and puffed, lightly charred crust, it makes a perfect prebaked pizza or tart crust. Of course, you can also just warm them plain and serve them as a simple flatbread alongside dinner.

Lavash is a soft, thin, round or rectangular flatbread popular in the Middle East. Lavash makes a great sandwich wrap, but we discovered that it also bakes up beautifully with an appealingly crisp, crackerlike crust, making it a great stand-in for a traditional pizza crust. We brush it with oil, bake it, then sprinkle it with toppings and bake it again for a simple but sophisticated meal. Look for it near the deli counter among the pita breads, tortillas, and other wrap options.

- ⅛ teaspoon pepper
- 3 tablespoons oil-packed sun-dried tomatoes, rinsed, patted dry, and chopped fine
- 3 tablespoons finely chopped pitted kalamata olives
- 1½ tablespoons pine nuts
- 1 scallion, sliced thin

1. Adjust oven rack to lowest position and heat oven to 500 degrees. Brush baking sheet with 1 tablespoon oil and lay naan breads on sheet. Combine ricotta, Parmesan, 1 tablespoon oil, lemon juice, garlic, salt, and pepper in bowl. In separate bowl, combine tomatoes, olives, pine nuts, and remaining 2 tablespoons oil.

2. Spread ricotta mixture evenly over each naan, leaving ½-inch border around edge. Scatter tomato-olive mixture evenly over top. Bake until naan are golden brown around edges, 8 to 10 minutes, rotating baking sheet halfway through baking. Sprinkle with scallion, cut into wedges, and serve.

VARIATION

Naan with Roasted Red Peppers, Feta, and Olives

SERVES 2 TO 3 **FAST**

Be sure to rinse and dry the roasted red peppers, as the brine can impart a sour or acidic aftertaste.

- 3 tablespoons extra-virgin olive oil
- 2 (8-inch) naan breads
- ½ cup jarred roasted red peppers, rinsed and patted dry
  Salt and pepper
- 2 ounces feta cheese, crumbled (½ cup)
- 3 tablespoons finely chopped pitted kalamata olives
- 2 tablespoons fresh parsley leaves

1. Adjust oven rack to lowest position and heat oven to 500 degrees. Brush baking sheet with 1 tablespoon oil and lay naan breads on sheet. Process red peppers and remaining 2 tablespoons oil in food processor, scraping down sides of processor bowl as needed, until smooth, about 30 seconds. Season with salt and pepper to taste.

2. Spread red pepper puree evenly over each naan, leaving ½-inch border around edge. Scatter feta and olives evenly over top. Bake until naan are golden brown around edges, 8 to 10 minutes, rotating baking sheet halfway through baking. Sprinkle with parsley, cut into wedges, and serve.

We use convenient store-bought lavash to make a crisp, crackerlike base for this easy flatbread.

Lavash with Spinach, Tomatoes, and Olives

SERVES 4 FAST

✔ **WHY THIS RECIPE WORKS:** Lavash is a Middle Eastern flatbread that, when baked, has a crisp, crackerlike texture that makes a great base for a simple yet sophisticated dinner. To get the lavash crisp enough to add toppings, we brushed them with oil and toasted them quickly in the oven. Then we spread them with a flavorful mixture of thawed frozen spinach, fresh tomato, fontina cheese, and fruity green olives. We sprinkled the topping with a little Parmesan and returned the lavash to the oven for a few minutes to melt and brown the cheese. If you cannot fit both lavash on a single baking sheet, use two baking sheets and bake on the upper-middle and lower-middle racks, rotating the baking sheets halfway through baking.

- 2 tablespoons extra-virgin olive oil
- 2 pieces lavash bread
- 10 ounces frozen spinach, thawed and squeezed dry
- 4 ounces fontina cheese, shredded (1 cup)
- 1 tomato, cored and cut into ½-inch pieces
- ½ cup chopped pitted large green olives
- 3 garlic cloves, minced
- ¼ teaspoon red pepper flakes
- ¼ teaspoon salt
- ¼ teaspoon pepper
- 1 ounce Parmesan cheese, grated (½ cup)

1. Adjust oven rack to middle position and heat oven to 475 degrees. Brush oil over both sides of lavash and lay on baking sheet. Bake lavash until golden brown, about 5 minutes, flipping halfway through baking.

2. Combine spinach, fontina, tomato, olives, garlic, pepper flakes, salt, and pepper in bowl. Spread mixture evenly over each lavash and sprinkle Parmesan over top. Bake until cheese is melted and spotty brown, 6 to 8 minutes. Serve.

VARIATION
Lavash with Curried Cauliflower and Fennel FAST

Omit spinach, tomato, and olives. Melt 2 tablespoons unsalted butter in 12-inch skillet over medium-high heat. Add 2 cups chopped cauliflower, 1 chopped fennel bulb, 3 tablespoons water, ½ teaspoon salt, and ½ teaspoon curry powder. Cover and cook, stirring occasionally, until vegetables are tender, 6 to 8 minutes; let cool slightly. Combine cauliflower mixture with fontina, garlic, and spices before topping lavash. Substitute ½ cup crumbled goat cheese for Parmesan. Sprinkle with 2 thinly sliced scallions before serving.

Multigrain Flatbread with Roasted Tomatoes and Zucchini

MAKES THREE 16 BY 8-INCH FLATBREADS, SERVES 6

✔ **WHY THIS RECIPE WORKS:** To make a flatbread with rustic multigrain flavor, we used a combination of whole-wheat flour and high-protein bread flour (which contributes great chew), plus seven-grain hot cereal mix, which gave us a variety of grains in one convenient package. To mimic the golden color and charred flavor flatbreads traditionally get from clay or wood-burning ovens, we relied on a preheated baking stone. For the topping, we combined roasted cherry tomatoes and zucchini with tangy feta cheese. For an accurate measurement of boiling water, bring a full kettle of water to a boil, then measure out the desired amount. You can substitute all-purpose flour for the bread and/or whole-wheat flour; however, the resulting crust will be a little less chewy. If you do not have a baking stone, you can use a preheated rimless (or inverted) baking sheet.

DOUGH

1¾ cups boiling water

1 cup (5 ounces) seven-grain hot cereal mix

2–2¼ cups (11 to 12⅓ ounces) bread flour

1 cup (5½ ounces) whole-wheat flour

2¼ teaspoons instant or rapid-rise yeast

1½ teaspoons salt

3 tablespoons olive oil

TOPPING

2 pounds cherry tomatoes, halved

2 zucchini, cut into ½-inch pieces

2 shallots, peeled, halved, and sliced thin

3 garlic cloves, sliced thin

5 tablespoons olive oil

1 tablespoon balsamic vinegar

1 teaspoon sugar

⅛ teaspoon red pepper flakes

Salt and pepper

8 ounces feta cheese, crumbled (2 cups)

3 tablespoons chopped fresh basil

1. FOR THE DOUGH: Stir boiling water and cereal mix together in medium bowl, cover, and let stand, stirring occasionally, until mixture resembles thick porridge and is just warm (about 110 degrees), about 30 minutes.

2. Pulse 2 cups bread flour, whole-wheat flour, yeast, and salt in food processor to combine. Dollop porridge mixture over top and drizzle in oil. Process until rough ball forms, 30 to 40 seconds. Let dough rest for 2 minutes, then process for 30 seconds longer. If dough is sticky and clings to blade, add remaining ¼ cup bread flour, 1 tablespoon at a time; pulse to incorporate.

3. Turn dough out onto lightly floured counter and knead into smooth, round ball. Place dough in large lightly oiled bowl and cover with greased plastic wrap. Let rise in warm place until nearly doubled in size, 1 to 1½ hours.

4. FOR THE TOPPING: Meanwhile, adjust oven racks to lower-middle and upper-middle positions and heat oven to 350 degrees. Toss tomatoes, zucchini, shallots, garlic, 2 tablespoons oil, vinegar, sugar, pepper flakes, ½ teaspoon salt, and ¼ teaspoon pepper in bowl.

5. Spread vegetables out over 2 rimmed baking sheets. Roast, without stirring, until tomato skins have shriveled slightly but tomatoes still retain their shape, 35 to 40 minutes, switching and rotating sheets halfway through baking. Let cool slightly.

6. Place baking stone on lower-middle rack and increase oven temperature to 500 degrees. Let baking stone heat for at least 30 minutes or up to 1 hour.

7. Turn dough out onto lightly floured counter, divide into 3 equal pieces, and cover with greased plastic wrap. Working

with 1 piece of dough at a time (keep other pieces covered), press and roll dough into 16 by 8-inch oval, flouring counter as needed. Transfer dough to rimless (or inverted) baking sheet lined with parchment paper and reshape as needed.

8. Lightly brush dough with 1 tablespoon oil. Scatter one-third of roasted vegetables evenly over dough and sprinkle with ⅔ cup feta, leaving ½-inch border at edge.

9. Slide parchment paper and flatbread onto hot baking stone. Bake flatbread until edges are brown and crisp, 8 to 13 minutes, rotating flatbread halfway through baking. (Prepare remaining flatbreads while first bakes.)

10. Remove flatbread from oven by sliding parchment paper back onto baking sheet. Transfer flatbread to cutting board. Sprinkle with 1 tablespoon basil, then slice and serve. Let stone reheat for 5 minutes before baking other flatbreads.

VARIATIONS

Multigrain Flatbread with Roasted Tomatoes and Eggplant

Omit vinegar. Substitute 1 eggplant, cut into ½-inch pieces, for zucchini, and 1 tablespoon chopped fresh mint for basil (use 1 teaspoon of mint per flatbread).

Multigrain Flatbread with Roasted Tomatoes and Corn

Omit vinegar. Substitute 2 cups corn kernels for zucchini, and 2 thinly sliced scallions for basil.

Multigrain Flatbread with Roasted Tomatoes and Mushrooms

Omit vinegar. Substitute 1 pound trimmed and quartered white mushrooms for zucchini.

Multigrain Flatbread with Roasted Tomatoes and Fennel

Substitute 1 thinly sliced fennel bulb for zucchini.

Caramelized Onion Flatbread with Blue Cheese and Walnuts

MAKES TWO 14 BY 8-INCH TARTS, SERVES 4 TO 6

✔ **WHY THIS RECIPE WORKS:** We wanted a simple recipe for a rustic flatbread that featured sweet, sticky caramelized onions. To get the best caramelized onions, we started the onions over medium-low heat and cooked them until they had released their moisture, then we turned up the heat and continued to cook them until they were deeply browned. Adding some brown sugar helped the onions to caramelize more

Sweet, sticky caramelized onions and pungent blue cheese give this savory flatbread bold, balanced flavor.

quickly and brought out their sweet flavors. Once we had our onions perfected, we rolled out a piece of pizza dough, brushed it with oil, and scattered them over the top. Rich, pungent blue cheese and crunchy walnuts were the perfect complements. To get a nicely crisp, browned crust, we baked the flatbreads on a preheated baking stone. A garnish of fresh scallions added bright flavor and color. We like to use our One-Pound Classic Pizza Dough (page 331); however, you can use store-bought pizza dough. If you do not have a baking stone, you can use a preheated rimless (or inverted) baking sheet.

2 tablespoons extra-virgin olive oil,
   plus extra for brushing
2 pounds onions, halved and sliced
   through root end ¼ inch thick
1 teaspoon packed brown sugar
   Salt and pepper
1 pound pizza dough
1 cup walnuts, toasted and chopped coarse
4 ounces blue cheese, crumbled (1 cup)
2 scallions, sliced thin

1. Adjust oven rack to lower-middle position, place baking stone on rack, and heat oven to 500 degrees. Let baking stone heat for at least 30 minutes or up to 1 hour.

2. Heat oil in 12-inch nonstick skillet over medium-low heat until shimmering. Stir in onions, brown sugar, and ½ teaspoon salt. Cover and cook, stirring occasionally, until onions are softened and have released their juices, about 10 minutes. Remove lid, increase heat to medium-high, and continue to cook, stirring often, until onions are deeply browned, 10 to 15 minutes.

3. Transfer dough to lightly floured counter, divide in half, and cover with greased plastic wrap. Working with 1 piece of dough at a time (keep other piece covered), press and roll dough into 14 by 8-inch oval. Transfer dough to parchment paper–lined rimless (or inverted) baking sheet and reshape as needed. Gently dimple surface of dough with your fingertips.

4. Brush dough liberally with oil and season with pepper. Scatter half of caramelized onions, ½ cup walnuts, and ½ cup blue cheese evenly over dough, leaving ½-inch border around edge. Slide parchment paper and flatbread onto hot baking stone.

5. Bake until flatbread is deep golden brown, about 10 minutes, rotating flatbread halfway through baking. (Prepare second tart while first bakes.) Remove flatbread from oven by sliding parchment paper back onto baking sheet. Transfer flatbread to cutting board, discarding parchment. Sprinkle with half of scallions, then slice and serve. Let stone reheat for 5 minutes before baking second flatbread.

VARIATIONS

Caramelized Onion Flatbread with Potato, Goat Cheese, and Rosemary

Omit walnuts, blue cheese, and scallions. Toss 1 pound very thinly sliced unpeeled small red potatoes with 1 tablespoon water in large bowl. Cover tightly with plastic wrap and microwave until potatoes are just tender, 3 to 7 minutes. Let potatoes cool. In step 4, scatter half of potatoes and ½ cup crumbled goat cheese over each flatbread, then sprinkle each with ¼ teaspoon minced fresh rosemary.

Caramelized Onion Flatbread with Shaved Brussels Sprouts, Fontina, and Hazelnuts

Omit walnuts, blue cheese, and scallions. Toss 10 ounces trimmed and thinly sliced Brussels sprouts with 2 teaspoons extra-virgin olive oil and ¼ teaspoon salt. In step 4, scatter half of Brussels sprouts, ½ cup shredded fontina, and 2 tablespoons toasted, skinned, and chopped hazelnuts over each flatbread.

Tart, fruity sumac and a whole-wheat crust lend a distinctive flavor to this Middle Eastern–inspired flatbread.

Mushroom Musakhan

MAKES TWO 15-INCH FLATBREADS, SERVES 4 TO 6

✓ WHY THIS RECIPE WORKS: *Musakhan* is a popular Palestinian dish featuring chewy flatbread topped with roasted chicken, caramelized onions, pine nuts, and tart sumac—a deep purple-red, tangy, fruity spice. We wanted a vegetarian version that still had the distinctive flavor of the original dish. First we swapped in sautéed portobello mushrooms for the chicken. Their earthy, robust flavor and juicy flesh made our musakhan taste and feel as meaty as the original. Next we made a sticky-sweet caramelized onion jam spiced with sumac, allspice, and cardamom. The traditional base, *taboon* bread, is a thick, slightly chewy, and crispy flatbread. We found that our recipe for Thin-Crust Whole-Wheat Pizza Dough made an perfect stand-in thanks to its wheaty flavor and crisp, chewy edges. Our recommended baking stone, by Old Stone Oven, can handle the heat of the broiler, but thinner baking stones can crack; if you use another stone, be sure to check the manufacturer's website. If you do not have a baking stone, you can use a preheated rimless (or inverted) baking sheet. Serve with yogurt.

1 recipe Thin-Crust Whole-Wheat Pizza Dough (page 335)
½ cup extra-virgin olive oil
2 tablespoons minced fresh oregano or 2 teaspoons dried
4 garlic cloves, minced
1½ tablespoons sumac
¼ teaspoon ground allspice
⅛ teaspoon ground cardamom
2 teaspoons packed light brown sugar
Salt and pepper
2 pounds onions, halved and sliced through root end into ¼-inch-thick pieces
¼ cup pine nuts
2 pounds portobello mushroom caps, gills removed, caps halved and sliced ½ inch thick
2 tablespoons minced fresh chives

1. Remove dough from refrigerator and divide in half. Shape each half into smooth, tight ball. Place on lightly oiled baking sheet, spaced at least 3 inches apart, cover loosely with greased plastic wrap, and let stand for 1 hour. Adjust oven rack to lower-middle position, place baking stone on rack, and heat oven to 500 degrees. Let baking stone heat for at least 30 minutes or up to 1 hour.

2. Meanwhile, combine 1 tablespoon oil, oregano, garlic, sumac, allspice, and cardamom in bowl. Heat 2 tablespoons oil in 12-inch nonstick skillet over high heat until shimmering. Stir in brown sugar and ½ teaspoon salt. Add onions and stir to coat. Cook, stirring occasionally, until onions begin to soften and release some moisture, about 5 minutes. Reduce heat to medium and cook, stirring frequently, until onions are deeply browned and slightly sticky, 35 to 40 minutes. (If onions are sizzling or scorching, reduce heat. If onions are not browning after 15 to 20 minutes, increase heat.) Clear center of skillet, add oregano-garlic mixture, and cook, mashing mixture into skillet, until fragrant, about 30 seconds. Stir oregano-garlic mixture into onions.

3. Transfer onion mixture to food processor and pulse to jamlike consistency, about 5 pulses. Transfer to bowl, stir in pine nuts, and season with salt and pepper to taste.

4. Wipe now-empty skillet clean with paper towels. Heat 2 tablespoons oil over medium-high heat until shimmering. Add half of mushrooms and ½ teaspoon salt and cook, stirring occasionally, until evenly browned, 8 to 10 minutes; transfer to separate bowl. Repeat with 2 tablespoons oil, remaining mushrooms, and ½ teaspoon salt.

5. Heat broiler for 10 minutes. Meanwhile, coat 1 ball of dough generously with flour and place on well-floured counter. Using fingertips, gently flatten dough into 8-inch disk. Using hands, gently stretch dough into 12 by 8-inch oval, working along edges as you go. Transfer dough to well-floured peel and stretch into 15 by 8-inch oval.

6. Spread half of onion mixture evenly over dough, edge to edge, and scatter half of mushrooms over top.

7. Slide flatbread carefully onto stone and return oven to 500 degrees. Bake until crust is well browned, about 10 minutes, rotating flatbread halfway through baking. Transfer flatbread to wire rack and let cool for 5 minutes. Drizzle with 1½ teaspoons oil and sprinkle with 1 tablespoon chives. Slice and serve.

8. Heat broiler for 10 minutes. Repeat steps 5 through 7 with remaining ingredients to make second flatbread, returning oven to 500 degrees when flatbread is placed on stone.

Huaraches with Poblanos, Red Peppers, and Queso Fresco

MAKES 6 HUARACHES, SERVES 4 TO 6   `GF`

✓ **WHY THIS RECIPE WORKS:** A popular dish in Mexico City, *huaraches* are thick, oblong corn cakes topped with beans, lettuce, and salsa. The huaraches themselves are easy to make: A simple masa-based dough is pressed into cakes and cooked on both sides to create a golden-brown, crisp exterior. We liked the base of flavorful refried beans but wanted a more substantial vegetable component than a simple salsa. We found that we liked sautéed red bell peppers paired with mildly spicy poblano chiles. Quick pickled shallots and radishes provided the perfect crispness that we needed for textural contrast, and their fresh, bright flavor cut through the richness of the beans. A sprinkle of *queso fresco* was the perfect finish. Masa harina is an instant corn masa flour. We've had good luck using Maseca, Goya Masarica, and Bob's Red Mill brands; if using Goya brand, do not confuse it with a similar looking cornmeal product called *masarepa*. You can use canned vegetarian refried pinto beans or our Refried Pinto Beans (page 218). Serve with shredded lettuce and Mexican Crema (page 366).

> 3 tablespoons vegetable oil
> 2 poblano chiles, stemmed, seeded, and cut into ¼-inch-wide strips
> 2 red bell peppers, stemmed, seeded, and cut into ¼-inch-wide strips
>   Salt
> 2 cups (8 ounces) masa harina
> 1¾ cups hot tap water
> ¾ cup vegetarian refried pinto beans, warmed
> 1½ ounces queso fresco, crumbled (⅓ cup)
> 1 recipe Quick Pickled Shallots and Radishes (page 366)

These Mexican masa cakes are made with just corn flour, salt, and water and cooked to a deep golden brown.

1. Heat 1 tablespoon oil in 12-inch nonstick skillet over medium-high heat until shimmering. Add poblanos, bell peppers, and ½ teaspoon salt and cook, stirring occasionally, until peppers are softened and lightly browned, 10 to 12 minutes. Transfer peppers to bowl and cover to keep warm. Wipe out skillet with paper towels.

2. Mix masa harina and 1 teaspoon salt in medium bowl, then stir in water with rubber spatula. Using hands, knead mixture in bowl until soft, sticky dough forms, 1 to 2 minutes. Cover dough with wet dish towel and let sit for 5 minutes.

3. Adjust oven rack to middle position and heat oven to 200 degrees. Set wire rack in rimmed baking sheet and place in oven. Line second baking sheet with parchment paper. Cut quart-size zipper-lock bag into 2 equal-size plastic squares. Transfer dough to clean counter and form into ball, then portion dough evenly into 6 pieces. Roll each piece into 5-inch-long rope and place on prepared sheet. Cover dough with wet dish towel.

4. Working with 1 piece of dough at a time, press dough flat into ⅛-inch-thick oval between prepared plastic squares using flat-bottomed pot or pie plate. Remove plastic, return shaped dough to prepared sheet, and cover with wet dish towel while shaping remaining dough.

5. Heat 2 teaspoons oil in now-empty skillet over medium-high heat until shimmering, and swirl to coat pan. Place 2 pieces dough in single layer in skillet and cook until dark spotty brown on first side, 4 to 6 minutes. Flip and continue to cook until second side is crisp, 2 to 4 minutes. Transfer to wire rack in oven and repeat with remaining oil and dough in 2 more batches.

6. Spread 2 tablespoons beans in even layer over each huarache, leaving ¼-inch border around edge. Distribute chilepepper mixture evenly among huaraches and sprinkle evenly with queso fresco. Serve with pickled shallots and radishes.

Forming Huaraches

1. Form dough into ball, then portion dough evenly into 6 pieces. Roll each piece into 5-inch-long rope and place on prepared sheet. Cover dough with wet dish towel.

2. Working with 1 piece of dough at a time, press dough flat into ⅛-inch-thick oval between prepared plastic squares using flat-bottomed pot or pie plate.

Socca with Swiss Chard, Pistachios, and Apricots

MAKES 5 FLATBREADS, SERVES 4 VEGAN GF

✔ **WHY THIS RECIPE WORKS:** *Socca* is a savory flatbread made with chickpea flour and is popular in southern France. The loose, pancakelike batter comes together in less than a minute—simply whisk together chickpea flour, water, olive oil, salt, and pepper. Traditionally the batter is poured into a cast-iron skillet and baked in a wood-burning oven to make a large socca with a blistered top and a smoky flavor. But in a home oven, this technique produced socca that was dry and limp. So we ditched the oven for the higher heat of the stovetop, which gave us crispy, golden-brown socca. But flipping the skillet-size socca wasn't as easy as we'd hoped. We solved this problem by making several smaller flatbreads instead. As an added bonus, the smaller flatbreads had a higher ratio of crunchy crust to tender interior. To complement our savory flatbreads, we came

We top these hearty chickpea flatbreads with a sweet and savory topping of Swiss chard, apricots, and pistachios.

up with a flavorful topping of Swiss chard, dried apricots, and toasted pistachios. Warm spices like cumin and allspice balanced the bright notes of the chickpea flour. Chickpea flour is also sold as garbanzo bean flour and is available in most well-stocked supermarkets.

BATTER

1½ cups (6¾ ounces) chickpea (garbanzo bean) flour
½ teaspoon salt
½ teaspoon pepper
½ teaspoon turmeric
1½ cups water
6 tablespoons plus 1 teaspoon extra-virgin olive oil

TOPPING

1 tablespoon extra-virgin olive oil
1 onion, chopped fine
2 garlic cloves, minced
¾ teaspoon ground cumin
Salt and pepper
⅛ teaspoon allspice

12 ounces Swiss chard, stemmed and chopped

3 tablespoons finely chopped dried apricots

2 tablespoons finely chopped toasted pistachios

1 teaspoon white wine vinegar

1. FOR THE BATTER: Adjust oven rack to middle position and heat oven to 200 degrees. Set wire rack in rimmed baking sheet and place in oven. Whisk chickpea flour, salt, pepper, and turmeric together in bowl. Slowly whisk in water and 3 tablespoons oil until combined and smooth.

2. Heat 2 teaspoons oil in 8-inch nonstick skillet over medium-high heat until shimmering. Add ½ cup batter to skillet, tilting pan to coat bottom evenly. Reduce heat to medium and cook until crisp at edges and golden brown on bottom, 3 to 5 minutes. Flip socca and continue to cook until second side is browned, 2 to 3 minutes. Transfer to wire rack in preheated oven and repeat with remaining oil and batter.

3. FOR THE TOPPING: Heat oil in 12-inch nonstick skillet over medium heat until shimmering. Add onion and cook until softened, about 5 minutes. Stir in garlic, cumin, ¼ teaspoon salt, and allspice and cook until fragrant, about 30 seconds. Stir in Swiss chard and apricots and cook until chard is wilted, 4 to 6 minutes. Off heat, stir in pistachios and vinegar, and season with salt and pepper to taste. Top each cooked socca with ⅓ cup chard mixture, slice, and serve.

VARIATION

Socca with Caramelized Onion and Rosemary

MAKES 5 FLATBREADS, SERVES 4　GF

BATTER

1½ cups (6¾ ounces) chickpea (garbanzo bean) flour

1½ teaspoons minced fresh rosemary

½ teaspoon salt

½ teaspoon pepper

1½ cups water

6 tablespoons plus 1 teaspoon extra-virgin olive oil

5 tablespoons Parmesan cheese, finely grated

TOPPING

1 tablespoon extra-virgin olive oil

½ teaspoon light brown sugar

Salt and pepper

3 onions, halved and sliced thin

1 teaspoon sherry vinegar

1. FOR THE BATTER: Adjust oven rack to middle position and heat oven to 200 degrees. Set wire rack in rimmed baking sheet and place in oven. Whisk chickpea flour, rosemary,

salt, and pepper together in bowl. Slowly whisk in water and 3 tablespoons oil until combined and smooth.

2. Heat 2 teaspoons oil in 8-inch nonstick skillet over medium-high heat until shimmering. Add ½ cup batter to skillet, tilting pan to coat bottom evenly. Reduce heat to medium and cook until crisp at edges and golden brown on bottom, 3 to 5 minutes. Flip socca and sprinkle 1 tablespoon Parmesan evenly over top. Continue to cook until second side is browned, 2 to 3 minutes. Transfer to wire rack in preheated oven and repeat with remaining oil, batter, and Parmesan.

3. FOR THE TOPPING: Heat oil in 12-inch nonstick skillet over high heat until shimmering. Stir in brown sugar and ¼ teaspoon salt. Add onions and stir to coat. Cook, stirring occasionally, until onions begin to soften and release some moisture, about 5 minutes. Reduce heat to medium and continue to cook, stirring often, until onions are well caramelized, 30 to 35 minutes. (If onions are sizzling or scorching, reduce heat. If onions are not browning after 15 to 20 minutes, increase heat.) Off heat, stir in vinegar and season with salt and pepper to taste. Top each cooked socca with scant ¼ cup onion mixture, slice, and serve.

Classic Cheese Pizza

MAKES TWO 14-INCH PIZZAS, SERVES 4 TO 6

✔ **WHY THIS RECIPE WORKS:** Homemade pizza really is far better than frozen or delivery, and our easy recipe results in a pie as good as any you could get at a pizzeria. Leaving the outer edge of the pizza slightly thicker than the center ensured a chewy yet crisp crust. To make it easy to get the pizza into the oven, we transferred the rolled-out dough to a parchment paper–lined baking sheet. After spreading a light layer of sauce on the dough and sprinkling it with two cheeses, we used the parchment to slide the pizza onto a preheated baking stone. We like to use our Classic Pizza Dough (page 331) and Easy Pizza Sauce (page 331); however, you can substitute store-bought pizza dough and sauce. For the crispiest crust, we use a baking stone. If you do not have a baking stone, you can use a preheated rimless (or inverted) baking sheet. You can also use a semolina flour– or cornmeal-dusted pizza peel in place of the parchment paper.

2 pounds pizza dough

1 tablespoon extra-virgin olive oil

2 cups pizza sauce

12 ounces mozzarella cheese, shredded (3 cups)

¼ cup grated Parmesan cheese

Making Pizza at Home

Here are some of our favorite tips for easy, parlor-worthy pizza at home.

EASY CHEESE SHREDDING

Use a clean plastic bag (a large zipper-lock bag works best) to hold the grater and the cheese. By placing the bag around both, you can grate without getting your hands dirty or worrying about rogue pieces flying off into your kitchen. The best part? Leftover shredded cheese is ready for storage, no transfer needed.

KEEP TOPPINGS ON HAND

Homemade pizza is a blank canvas that can be creatively covered with myriad toppings. To have topping options on hand, try this simple solution: Whenever cooking something such as roasted red peppers or caramelized onions, reserve some in a plastic container, label it, and freeze it. The next time you're making pizza, simply defrost and top away.

NO PEEL? NO STONE? NO PROBLEM

A baking stone is a terrific investment if you enjoy making bread and pizza, and a peel makes the process easier. But you can make do with rimless or inverted baking sheets for both the stone and the peel. To improvise a baking stone, preheat a baking sheet for 30 minutes. For an improvised peel, cover a rimless or an inverted rimmed baking sheet with parchment paper, shape and top the pizza on the parchment, and slide parchment and pizza directly onto the preheated stone or baking sheet.

TWO WAYS TO REHEAT

Reheating pizza in the microwave turns it soggy, and just throwing it into a hot oven can dry it out. Here's a reheating method that really works: Place the cold slices on a rimmed baking sheet, cover the sheet tightly with aluminum foil, and place it on the lowest rack of a cold oven. Then set the oven temperature to 275 degrees and let the pizza warm for 25 to 30 minutes. This approach leaves the interior of the crust soft, the cheese melty, and the toppings hot and bottom crust crisp. For just a slice or two, place a nonstick skillet over medium heat and add dried oregano. Place the pizza in the skillet and reheat, covered, for about 5 minutes. The pizza will come out hot and crisp, and with an irresistible aroma.

1. Adjust oven rack to lower-middle position, place baking stone on rack, and heat oven to 500 degrees. Let baking stone heat for at least 30 minutes or up to 1 hour.

2. Transfer dough to lightly floured counter, divide in half, and cover with greased plastic wrap. Working with 1 piece of dough at a time (keep other piece covered), use fingertips to gently flatten into 8-inch disk, leaving 1 inch of outer edge slightly thicker than center. Using hands, gently stretch dough into 14-inch round, working along edges and giving dough quarter turns as you stretch. Transfer dough to parchment-lined rimless (or inverted) baking sheet and reshape as needed.

3. Lightly brush outer ½-inch edge of dough with ½ tablespoon oil. Using back of spoon, spread 1 cup pizza sauce evenly over dough, leaving ½-inch border. Sprinkle 1½ cups mozzarella and 2 tablespoons Parmesan evenly over sauce.

4. Slide parchment paper and pizza onto hot baking stone. Bake pizza until edges are brown and cheese is golden in spots, 8 to 13 minutes, rotating pizza halfway through baking. Prepare second pizza while first bakes.

5. Remove pizza from oven by sliding parchment paper back onto baking sheet. Transfer pizza to wire rack, discarding parchment. Let pizza cool for 5 minutes, then slice and serve. Let stone reheat for 5 minutes before baking second pizza.

VARIATIONS

Classic Pizza Margherita

Substitute following mixture for pizza sauce: Pulse 1 (28-ounce) can diced tomatoes with their juice in food processor until crushed, about 3 pulses; transfer to fine-mesh strainer and let drain for 30 minutes. Combine drained tomatoes with 1 tablespoon chopped fresh basil, 1 small minced garlic clove, ½ teaspoon sugar, and ¼ teaspoon salt in bowl. Substitute 12 ounces fresh mozzarella cheese, cut into 1-inch chunks, for shredded mozzarella and Parmesan. Sprinkle pizza with additional chopped fresh basil and sea salt to taste before serving.

Pizza with Caramelized Onions, Arugula, and Ricotta

Heat 2 teaspoons extra-virgin olive oil in 12-inch nonstick skillet over medium heat until shimmering. Stir in 3 onions, halved and sliced thin, ½ teaspoon light brown sugar, and ¼ teaspoon salt and cook until onions begin to soften, about 5 minutes. Reduce heat to medium-low and continue to cook, stirring often, until onions are caramelized, 20 to 25 minutes. Season with salt and pepper to taste and transfer to bowl. In separate bowl, season 1 cup whole-milk ricotta cheese with salt and pepper to taste. Reduce mozzarella to 2 cups. In step 3, sprinkle 1 cup mozzarella evenly over sauce with Parmesan, dollop half of seasoned ricotta evenly over top, and sprinkle with half of

EASY PIZZA SAUCE

MAKES 2 CUPS `FAST` `VEGAN` `GF`

While it is convenient to use jarred pizza sauce, we think it is almost as easy, and a lot tastier, to whip up your own.

- 1 (28-ounce) can whole peeled tomatoes, drained with juice reserved
- 1 tablespoon extra-virgin olive oil
- 2 garlic cloves, minced
- 1 teaspoon red wine vinegar
- 1 teaspoon dried oregano
- ½ teaspoon salt
- ¼ teaspoon pepper

Process tomatoes, oil, garlic, vinegar, oregano, salt, and pepper in food processor until smooth, about 30 seconds. Transfer mixture to liquid measuring cup and add reserved tomato juice until sauce measures 2 cups. (Sauce can be refrigerated for up to 1 week or frozen for up to 1 month.)

---

onion mixture. While pizza bakes, toss 2 cups baby arugula with 2 teaspoons extra-virgin olive oil and 1 teaspoon red wine vinegar in bowl, and season with salt and pepper to taste. Sprinkle each pizza with half of dressed arugula before serving.

Pizza with Garlicky Broccoli and Sun-Dried Tomatoes

Heat 2 teaspoons extra-virgin olive oil in 12-inch nonstick skillet over medium heat until shimmering. Add 8 ounces broccoli florets, cut into 1-inch pieces, and cook until lightly browned, about 5 minutes. Stir in 3 minced garlic cloves and cook until fragrant, about 30 seconds. Add ¼ cup water, cover, and cook for 3 minutes. Uncover and add ½ cup oil-packed sun-dried tomatoes, rinsed, patted dry, and sliced thin; cook until broccoli is tender and water is evaporated, about 2 minutes. Season with salt and pepper to taste and transfer to bowl. Top each pizza with half of broccoli mixture before baking.

Pizza with Mushrooms, Spinach, and Goat Cheese

Heat 2 teaspoons extra-virgin olive oil in 12-inch nonstick skillet over medium heat until shimmering. Add 2 (4- to 5-inch) portobello mushroom caps sliced ¼ inch thick. Cover and cook until wilted and wet, about 5 minutes. Uncover and continue to cook until mushrooms are dry and browned, 5 to 10 minutes. Stir in 3 minced garlic cloves and cook until

fragrant, about 30 seconds. Season with salt and pepper to taste and transfer to bowl. Reduce mozzarella to 2½ cups. After spreading sauce over dough, sprinkle each pizza with 10 ounces frozen spinach, thawed, squeezed dry, and chopped coarse; 1¼ cups mozzarella; ¼ cup crumbled goat cheese; Parmesan; and half of mushroom mixture.

Classic Pizza Dough

MAKES 2 POUNDS `VEGAN`

✔ **WHY THIS RECIPE WORKS:** With a homemade pizza dough waiting in the refrigerator, you're already halfway to an easy dinner. Great pizza crust doesn't require the amount of kneading that other types of dough require, and while you can certainly use a stand mixer to make it, a food processor does a great job in a matter of minutes. We use bread flour because its relatively high protein content gives the pizza dough great elasticity and chew. Once the dough comes together, it needs only an hour or so to rise before you can assemble the pizzas. All-purpose flour can be substituted for the bread flour, but the resulting crust will be a little less chewy.

- 4¼ cups (23⅓ ounces) bread flour
- 2¼ teaspoons instant or rapid-rise yeast
- 1½ teaspoons salt
- 2 tablespoons olive oil
- 1½ cups warm water (110 degrees)

1. Pulse flour, yeast, and salt together in food processor to combine, about 5 pulses. With processor running, add oil, then water; process until rough ball forms, 30 to 40 seconds. Let dough rest for 2 minutes, then process for 30 seconds longer. (If after 30 seconds dough is very sticky and clings to blade, add extra flour as needed.)

2. Transfer dough to lightly floured counter and knead until smooth, about 1 minute. Shape dough into tight ball, place in large lightly oiled bowl, and cover tightly with plastic wrap. (Dough can be refrigerated for up to 16 hours; let sit at room temperature for 30 minutes before using.)

3. Place in warm spot and let dough rise until doubled in size, 1 to 1½ hours.

VARIATION

One-Pound Classic Pizza Dough `VEGAN`

Reduce amounts of all ingredients by half; mix, knead, and let rise as directed.

The exceptionally crisp, chewy crust of *pizza bianca* is so good, it needs hardly any topping—just oil, rosemary, and salt.

Pizza Bianca

MAKES ONE 17 BY 12-INCH PIZZA, SERVES 6 TO 8   `VEGAN`

✔ **WHY THIS RECIPE WORKS:** The Roman version of pizza has a crisp but extraordinarily chewy crust, and it's so good on its own that it's usually topped with just olive oil, rosemary, and kosher salt. A superhydrated dough is the secret to its chewy texture, but the extra-wet dough usually requires more kneading. Instead, we let the dough rest for 20 minutes, which let us get away with just 10 minutes of kneading. After an initial rise, the dough was to sticky to roll out, but it was easy to pour out and then press flat onto a baking sheet. We gave the dough another brief rest before baking it with the traditional olive oil, rosemary, and salt. Place a damp dish towel under the mixer and watch it during kneading to prevent it from wobbling off the counter. Handle the dough with lightly oiled hands to prevent sticking. If using a baking sheet smaller than 18 by 13 inches, the pizza will be thicker and the baking time will be longer. If you do not have a baking stone, you can use a preheated rimless (or inverted) baking sheet. Serve the pizza by itself as a snack, or with soup or salad as a light entrée.

3 cups (15 ounces) all-purpose flour

1⅔ cups water, room temperature

1¼ teaspoons salt

1½ teaspoons instant or rapid-rise yeast

1¼ teaspoons sugar

5 tablespoons extra-virgin olive oil

1 teaspoon kosher salt

2 tablespoons fresh rosemary leaves

1. Using stand mixer fitted with dough hook, mix flour, water, and salt together on low speed until no areas of dry flour remain, 3 to 4 minutes, scraping down bowl as needed. Turn off mixer and let dough rest for 20 minutes.

2. Sprinkle yeast and sugar over dough. Knead on low speed until fully combined, 1 to 2 minutes. Increase mixer speed to high and knead until dough is glossy and smooth and pulls away from sides of bowl, 6 to 10 minutes. (Dough will pull away from sides only while mixer is on. When mixer is off, dough will fall back to sides.)

3. Using fingers, coat large bowl with 1 tablespoon oil, rubbing excess oil from fingers onto blade of rubber spatula. Using oiled spatula, transfer dough to prepared bowl and pour 1 tablespoon oil over top. Flip dough over once so that it is well coated with oil; cover bowl tightly with plastic wrap and let dough rise at room temperature until nearly tripled in volume and large bubbles have formed, 2 to 2½ hours. (Dough can be refrigerated for up to 24 hours. Bring dough to room temperature, 2 to 2½ hours, before proceeding with step 4.)

4. One hour before baking, adjust oven rack to middle position, place baking stone on rack, and heat oven to 450 degrees. Coat rimmed baking sheet with 2 tablespoons oil. Using rubber spatula, turn dough out onto prepared baking sheet along with any oil in bowl. Using fingertips, press dough out toward edges of baking sheet, taking care not to tear dough. (Dough will not fit snugly into corners. If dough resists stretching, let it relax for 5 to 10 minutes before trying to stretch it again.) Let dough rest until slightly bubbly, 5 to 10 minutes. Using dinner fork, poke surface of dough 30 to 40 times and sprinkle with kosher salt.

5. Bake until golden brown, 20 to 30 minutes, sprinkling rosemary over top and rotating baking sheet halfway through baking. Using metal spatula, transfer pizza to cutting board. Brush dough lightly with remaining 1 tablespoon oil. Slice and serve immediately.

VARIATIONS

Pizza Bianca with Tomatoes and Mozzarella

Place 1 (28-ounce) can crushed tomatoes in fine-mesh strainer set over medium bowl. Let sit for 30 minutes, stirring 3 times to allow juices to drain. Combine ¾ cup tomato solids,

1 tablespoon extra-virgin olive oil, and ⅛ teaspoon salt in small bowl. (Save remaining solids and juice for another use.) Omit kosher salt and rosemary. In step 5, bake pizza until spotty brown, 15 to 17 minutes. Remove pizza from oven, spread tomato mixture evenly over surface, and sprinkle with 1½ cups shredded mozzarella (do not brush pizza with remaining 1 tablespoon oil). Return pizza to oven and continue to bake until cheese begins to brown in spots, 5 to 10 minutes longer.

Pizza Bianca with Caramelized Onions and Gruyère

1. Heat 1 tablespoon butter and 1 tablespoon vegetable oil in 12-inch nonstick skillet over high heat until butter is melted. Stir in 1 teaspoon packed light brown sugar and ½ teaspoon salt, then add 2 pounds onions, halved and sliced ¼ inch thick; stir to coat. Cook, stirring occasionally, until onions begin to soften and release some moisture, about 5 minutes. Reduce heat to medium and cook, stirring often, until onions are deeply browned and slightly sticky, 35 to 40 minutes longer. (If onions are sizzling or scorching, reduce heat. If onions are not browning after 15 to 20 minutes, increase heat.)

2. Off heat, stir in 1 tablespoon water and season with pepper to taste. Transfer to large plate and let cool to room temperature. In step 5, bake pizza until spotty brown, 15 to 17 minutes. Remove pizza from oven, spread caramelized onions evenly over surface, and sprinkle with 2 cups shredded Gruyère and 2 teaspoons minced fresh thyme (do not brush pizza with remaining 1 tablespoon oil). Return pizza to oven and continue to bake until cheese begins to brown in spots, 5 to 10 minutes longer.

Shaping Pizza Bianca

1. Coat rimmed baking sheet with 2 tablespoons oil. Using rubber spatula, turn dough out onto prepared baking sheet along with any oil in bowl.

2. Using fingertips, press dough out toward edges of baking sheet, taking care not to tear dough. (Dough will not fit snugly into corners. If dough resists stretching, let it relax for 5 to 10 minutes before trying to stretch it again.)

To complement the flavor of our whole-wheat pizza crust, we pair a bold garlic oil with basil and three kinds of cheese.

Whole-Wheat Pizza with Garlic Oil, Three Cheeses, and Basil

MAKES TWO 13-INCH PIZZAS, SERVES 4 TO 6

✔ **WHY THIS RECIPE WORKS:** We wanted to build a pizza on our thin-crust whole-wheat pizza dough. A traditional tomato-based sauce clashed with the whole-wheat flavor, so we opted for an oil-based sauce. To give it intense aromatic flavor, we heated the oil with garlic, oregano, and red pepper flakes. We spread the garlic oil over the dough rounds, then topped them with cheese and fresh basil. To get the best flavor, we chose a combination of three cheeses: bold Pecorino Romano, melty mozzarella, and dollops of creamy ricotta (which we added after baking to keep it from breaking in the high heat). Our recommended baking stone, by Old Stone Oven, can handle the heat of the broiler, but thinner baking stones can crack; if you use another stone, be sure to check the manufacturer's website. If you do not have a baking stone, you can use a preheated rimless (or inverted) baking sheet. Shape the second dough ball while the first pizza bakes, but don't top the pizza until right before you bake it.

All About Flour

ALL-PURPOSE FLOUR

All-purpose flour is by far the most versatile flour available. Its protein content (10 to 11.7 percent, depending on the brand: King Arthur is close to 11.7 percent, Pillsbury and Gold Medal around 10.5 percent) provides enough structure to make good sandwich bread, yet it's light enough to use for cakes of a medium to coarse crumb. We prefer unbleached flour. Bleached flours sometimes taste flat or have off-flavors.

BREAD FLOUR

With a protein content of 12 percent to 14 percent, bread flour develops a lot of gluten, providing strong, chewy structure for rustic breads, flatbreads, and pizza crusts. For sandwich breads we prefer using all-purpose flour for a softer crumb.

WHOLE-WHEAT FLOUR

Whole-wheat flour is made from all three parts of the wheat kernel—the endosperm as well as the fiber-rich bran, or outer shell, and the tiny, vitamin-packed germ. The presence of the germ and bran in whole-wheat flour makes it not only more nutritious and more flavorful, but also more dense and less able to rise. We generally don't like breads or pizza crusts made with 100 percent whole-wheat flour; they are too dense and can be sour-tasting. Instead, we rely on a combination of all-purpose flour and whole-wheat flour.

MEASURING FLOUR

The way you measure flour can make a big difference in your recipe. Weighing flour is the most accurate, but the dip-and-sweep method is also reliable. Spooning flour into a measuring cup and then leveling it off is significantly less accurate. For the dip-and-sweep method, simply dip the measuring cup into the container of flour and sweep away the excess with a straight-edged object like the back of a butter knife.

STORING FLOUR

Refined flours, including all-purpose and bread flour, can be stored in airtight containers in your pantry for up to one year. A wide-mouthed plastic container allows you to scoop out what you need without spilling. A tight-fitting lid is also essential. Whole-wheat flour and others made from whole grains contain more fat than that in refined flours and can turn rancid quickly at room temperature. We recommend storing these flours in the freezer. It's best to bring chilled flour to room temperature before baking.

1½ pounds Thin-Crust Whole-Wheat Pizza Dough (page 335)
¼ cup extra-virgin olive oil
2 garlic cloves, minced
½ teaspoon pepper
½ teaspoon dried oregano
⅛ teaspoon red pepper flakes
⅛ teaspoon salt
   Whole-wheat or bread flour for counter
1 cup fresh basil leaves
1 ounce Pecorino Romano cheese, grated (½ cup)
8 ounces whole-milk mozzarella cheese, shredded (2 cups)
6 ounces (¾ cup) whole-milk ricotta cheese

1. Remove dough from refrigerator and divide in half. Shape each half into smooth, tight ball. Place on lightly oiled baking sheet, spaced at least 3 inches apart, cover loosely with greased plastic wrap, and let stand for 1 hour. Adjust oven rack 4½ inches from broiler element, set baking stone on rack, and heat oven to 500 degrees. Let baking stone heat for at least 30 minutes or up to 1 hour.

2. Meanwhile, heat oil in 8-inch skillet over medium-low heat until shimmering. Add garlic, pepper, oregano, pepper flakes, and salt and cook, stirring constantly, until fragrant, about 30 seconds. Transfer to bowl and let cool.

3. Heat broiler for 10 minutes. Meanwhile, coat 1 ball of dough generously with flour and place on well-floured counter. Using fingertips, gently flatten dough into 8-inch disk, leaving 1 inch of outer edge slightly thicker than center. Using hands, gently stretch dough into 12-inch round, working along edges and giving dough quarter turns as you stretch. Transfer dough to well-floured peel and stretch into 13-inch round.

4. Using back of spoon, spread half of garlic oil evenly over dough, leaving ¼-inch border. Layer ½ cup basil leaves evenly over sauce, then sprinkle with ¼ cup Pecorino and 1 cup mozzarella.

5. Slide pizza carefully onto stone and return oven to 500 degrees. Bake until crust is well browned and cheese is bubbly and partially browned, 8 to 10 minutes, rotating pizza halfway through baking. Transfer pizza to wire rack and dollop half of ricotta evenly over top. Let cool for 5 minutes, then slice and serve.

6. Heat broiler for 10 minutes. Repeat steps 3 through 5 with remaining ingredients to make second pizza, returning oven to 500 degrees when pizza is placed on stone.

VARIATION

Whole-Wheat Pizza with Pesto and Goat Cheese

Process 2 cups basil leaves, 7 tablespoons extra-virgin olive oil, ¼ cup pine nuts, 3 minced garlic cloves, and ½ teaspoon salt in food processor until smooth, scraping down sides of bowl as needed, about 1 minute. Stir in ¼ cup finely grated Parmesan or Pecorino Romano cheese and season with salt and pepper to taste. Substitute pesto for garlic oil. In step 4, omit basil leaves, Pecorino Romano, and mozzarella. In step 5, omit ricotta. Top each pizza with ½ cup crumbled goat cheese before baking.

Thin-Crust Whole-Wheat Pizza Dough
MAKES 1½ POUNDS

✔ **WHY THIS RECIPE WORKS:** Most whole-wheat pizza crust is as dry and dense as cardboard. We wanted to find a way to make it as crisp and chewy as traditional pizza crust and highlight its nutty, wheaty flavor. For balanced whole-wheat flavor, we used a combination of 60 percent whole-wheat flour and 40 percent bread flour. To help hydrate the hearty whole-wheat flour, we increased the amount of water. Our highly hydrated dough helped strengthen the gluten network, and using ice water kept the dough from overheating as it was kneaded in the food processor. Giving the dough a long rest gave the enzymes in the dough time to slightly weaken the gluten strands, increasing the dough's ability to stretch; the rest also allowed for more flavor-boosting fermentation. Finally, because our dough was so wet, preheating the pizza stone under the broiler's high heat was key for getting a nicely browned crust. King Arthur brand bread flour works best in this recipe.

    1½ cups (8¼ ounces) whole-wheat flour
    1   cup (5½ ounces) bread flour
    2   teaspoons honey
    ¾   teaspoon instant or rapid-rise yeast
    1¼ cups ice water
    2   tablespoons extra-virgin olive oil
    1¾ teaspoons salt

1. Pulse whole-wheat flour, bread flour, honey, and yeast in food processor to combine, about 5 pulses. With processor running, slowly add ice water and process until dough is just combined and no dry flour remains, about 10 seconds. Let dough rest for 10 minutes.

2. Add oil and salt to dough and process until it forms satiny, sticky ball that clears sides of workbowl, 45 to 60 seconds. Transfer dough to lightly oiled counter and knead until smooth, about 1 minute. Shape dough into tight ball and place in large lightly oiled bowl. Cover bowl tightly with plastic wrap and refrigerate for at least 18 hours or up to 2 days.

Our perfectly sealed calzones feature a rich spinach and ricotta filling that won't ooze or leak during baking.

Ricotta and Spinach Calzones
SERVES 4

✔ **WHY THIS RECIPE WORKS:** With soggy fillings and bready crusts, bad calzones are found everywhere. The best recipe should result in a satisfying balance of crisp crust with plenty of chew and a healthy proportion of rich and flavorful filling. We started with an easy-to-make filling featuring ricotta and spinach, with some Parmesan and oil for richness and an egg yolk to thicken the mixture. We spread the filling onto the bottom halves of two rolled-out pizza rounds and brushed egg wash over the edges before folding the top halves over. Cutting vents in the tops allowed steam to escape while baking. The calzones needed only 15 minutes in the oven and a few minutes to cool before serving. We like to use our One-Pound Classic Pizza Dough (page 331); however, you can use store-bought pizza dough. Be sure to let the dough sit out at room temperature while preparing the remaining ingredients and heating the oven, or it will be difficult to stretch. Serve with your favorite marinara or tomato pasta sauce.

10 ounces frozen chopped spinach,
   thawed and squeezed dry

8 ounces (1 cup) whole-milk ricotta cheese

4 ounces mozzarella cheese, shredded (1 cup)

1 ounce Parmesan cheese, grated (½ cup)

1 tablespoon extra-virgin olive oil

1 large egg, lightly beaten with 2 tablespoons
   water, plus 1 large yolk

2 garlic cloves, minced

1½ teaspoons minced fresh oregano

⅛ teaspoon red pepper flakes

1 pound pizza dough

1. Adjust oven rack to lower-middle position and heat oven to 500 degrees. Cut two 9-inch square pieces of parchment paper. Combine spinach, ricotta, mozzarella, Parmesan, oil, egg yolk, garlic, oregano, and pepper flakes in bowl.

2. Place dough on lightly floured counter, divide in half, and cover with greased plastic wrap. Working with 1 piece of dough at a time (keep other piece covered), use rolling pin to flatten dough into 9-inch round. Transfer each piece of dough to parchment square and reshape as needed.

3. Spread half of spinach filling evenly over half of each dough round, leaving 1-inch border at edge. Brush edge with egg wash. Fold other half of dough over filling, leaving ½-inch border of bottom half uncovered. Press edges of dough together and crimp to seal.

4. Using sharp knife, cut 5 steam vents, about 1½ inches long, in top of calzones. Brush tops with remaining egg wash. Transfer calzones (still on parchment) onto baking sheet, trimming parchment as needed to fit. Bake until golden brown, about 15 minutes, rotating baking sheet halfway through baking. Transfer calzones to wire rack and let cool for 5 minutes before serving.

VARIATION

Cheesy Broccoli Calzones

Omit spinach. Reduce ricotta to ½ cup and increase shredded mozzarella to 1½ cups. Add ½ cup crumbled feta cheese and 10 ounces frozen broccoli florets, thawed and chopped, to ricotta mixture.

Fennel, Olive, and Goat Cheese Tarts

SERVES 4

✔ **WHY THIS RECIPE WORKS:** We wanted to make elegant yet easy tarts inspired by the flavors of the Mediterranean. Using convenient store-bought puff pastry for the tart crust kept the recipe simple. For the filling, fresh anise-flavored fennel and briny cured olives made a light but bold combination. Tangy goat cheese thinned with olive oil and brightened with fresh basil contrasted nicely with the rich, flaky pastry and helped bind the vegetables and pastry together. Parbaking the pastry without the weight of the filling allowed it to puff up nicely. To keep the filling firmly in place, we cut a border

Assembling a Calzone

1. Spread half of spinach filling evenly over half of each dough round, leaving 1-inch border at edge.

2. Brush edge of dough with egg wash. Fold other half of dough over filling, leaving ½-inch border of bottom half uncovered.

3. Press edges of dough together, pressing out any air. Start at 1 end and place index finger diagonally across edge; pull bottom layer of dough over finger and press to seal.

4. Cut 5 steam vents, about 1½ inches long, across top of each calzone. Cut through only top layer of dough.

around the edges of the baked crusts and lightly pressed down on the centers to make neat beds for the cheese and vegetables. Just 5 minutes more in the oven heated the filling through and browned the crusts beautifully. To thaw frozen puff pastry, let it sit either in the refrigerator for 1 day or on the counter for 30 minutes to 1 hour.

1 (9½ by 9-inch) sheet puff pastry, thawed and cut in half

3 tablespoons extra-virgin olive oil

1 large fennel bulb, stalks discarded, bulb halved, cored, and sliced thin

3 garlic cloves, minced

½ cup dry white wine

½ cup pitted oil-cured black olives, chopped

1 teaspoon grated lemon zest plus 1 tablespoon juice

Salt and pepper

8 ounces goat cheese, softened

5 tablespoons chopped fresh basil

1. Adjust oven rack to middle position and heat oven to 425 degrees. Lay puff pastry halves on parchment paper–lined baking sheet and poke all over with fork. Bake pastry until puffed and golden brown, about 15 minutes, rotating baking sheet halfway through baking. Using tip of paring knife, cut ½-inch-wide border around top edge of each pastry, then press centers down with fingertips.

2. Meanwhile, heat 1 tablespoon oil in 12-inch skillet over medium-high heat until shimmering. Add fennel and cook until softened and browned, about 10 minutes. Stir in garlic and cook until fragrant, 30 seconds. Add wine, cover, and cook for 5 minutes. Uncover and cook until liquid has evaporated and fennel is very soft, 3 to 5 minutes. Off heat, stir in olives and lemon juice and season with salt and pepper to taste.

3. Mix goat cheese, ¼ cup basil, remaining 2 tablespoons oil, lemon zest, and ¼ teaspoon pepper together in bowl, then spread evenly over center of pastry shells. Spoon fennel mixture over top. (Tarts can be held at room temperature for 2 hours before baking.)

4. Bake tarts until cheese is heated through and crust is deep golden, 5 to 7 minutes. Sprinkle with remaining 1 table-spoon basil and serve.

VARIATION

Artichoke, Shallot, and Goat Cheese Tarts
Substitute 1 (9-ounce) box frozen artichoke hearts, thawed and patted dry, for fennel. Add 1 shallot, halved and sliced thin, and ½ teaspoon salt to skillet with artichokes; cook until

Store-bought puff pastry makes this elegant fennel and goat cheese tart surprisingly simple to prepare.

artichokes are tender and spotty brown, 3 to 5 minutes. After adding wine, do not cover skillet. Cook until wine evaporates, about 3 minutes. Omit olives and lemon zest. Substitute 2 teaspoons balsamic vinegar for lemon juice.

Making a Puff Pastry Tart Shell

1. Lay pastry rectangles on parchment paper–lined baking sheet and poke all over with fork. Bake pastry until puffed and golden, about 15 minutes.

2. Using tip of paring knife, cut ½-inch-wide border around top edge of each baked pastry and press center down with fingertips to create bed for filling.

Fresh versus Supermarket Mozzarella

For such a mild-mannered cheese, mozzarella sure is popular. Most supermarkets stock two main varieties: fresh (usually packed in brine) and supermarket, or low-moisture (available either as a block or preshredded).

WHAT'S THE DIFFERENCE?

Both varieties are made by stretching and pulling the curds by hand or machine, which aligns the proteins into long chains and gives the cheese its elasticity. However, the final products differ considerably when it comes to water weight. According to federal standards, fresh mozzarella must have a moisture content between 52 percent and 60 percent, which makes it highly perishable. Drier, firmer low-moisture mozzarella hovers between 45 percent and 52 percent and is remarkably shelf-stable—it can last in the fridge for weeks.

WHEN TO USE FRESH

We prefer the sweet richness and tender bite of the fresh stuff for snacking, sandwiches, and Caprese salad but tend not to use it in cooked applications, since heat can destroy its delicate flavor and texture.

WHEN TO USE SUPERMARKET

For most baked dishes, we turn to the low-moisture kind. It offers mellow flavor that blends seamlessly with bolder ingredients and melts nicely in everything from lasagna to pizza. The test kitchen's top-rated supermarket mozzarella is block-style Sorrento Whole Milk Mozzarella. Its gooey creaminess and clean dairy flavor are exactly what we want on pizza. It is so good that we even have found ourselves snacking on it straight out of the package.

STORING MOZZARELLA

Storing supermarket mozzarella presents a conundrum: As it sits, it releases moisture. If this moisture evaporates too quickly, the cheese dries out. But if the moisture stays on the cheese's surface, it encourages mold. To find the best storage method, we wrapped mozzarella in various materials, refrigerated the samples for six weeks, and monitored them for mold and dryness. The best method: first wrapping the cheese in waxed or parchment paper, and then loosely wrapping the paper in aluminum foil. The paper wicks moisture away, while the foil cover traps enough water to keep the cheese from drying out. Fresh mozzarella does not store well and is best eaten within a day or two.

To keep excess moisture from ruining the crust of our showstopping tomato tart, we salt and drain the tomatoes.

Tomato Tart

SERVES 4 TO 6

♡ **WHY THIS RECIPE WORKS:** Tomato tarts sound promising, but often recipes yield soggy crusts and fillings with very little flavor. We set out to develop a simple recipe with a flavorful and foolproof crust, a creamy base, and a topping of fragrant sliced tomatoes. To ensure that the tomatoes didn't leach moisture into the tart, we salted them and let them drain for half an hour on paper towels. We combined a trio of cheeses— Parmesan, ricotta, and mozzarella—with olive oil into a base layer to go under the tomatoes. Then all we had to do was spread the cheese mixture over the bottom of the baked tart shell, shingle the tomatoes on top, and bake the tart until the tomatoes were slightly wilted. Drizzling the tomatoes with a mixture of olive oil and minced garlic before baking kept them from drying out and infused them with flavor. We prefer the light flavor of part-skim ricotta here, but whole-milk ricotta can be substituted; do not use fat-free ricotta.

3 plum tomatoes, cored and
  sliced ¼ inch thick
  Salt and pepper
3 tablespoons extra-virgin olive oil
1 garlic clove, minced
1 ounce Parmesan cheese, grated (½ cup)
4 ounces (½ cup) part-skim ricotta cheese
1 ounce mozzarella cheese, shredded (¼ cup)
1 recipe All-Butter Press-In Tart Dough
  (page 340), baked and cooled
2 tablespoons chopped fresh basil

1. Spread tomatoes out over several layers of paper towels, sprinkle with ½ teaspoon salt, and let drain for 30 minutes. Combine 2 tablespoons oil and garlic in small bowl. In separate bowl, combine Parmesan, ricotta, mozzarella, and remaining 1 tablespoon oil, and season with salt and pepper to taste.

2. Adjust oven rack to middle position and heat oven to 425 degrees. Spread ricotta mixture evenly over bottom of tart shell. Blot tomatoes dry with paper towels and shingle attractively on top of ricotta in concentric circles. Drizzle with garlic-oil mixture. (Tart can be held at room temperature for up to 2 hours before baking.)

3. Bake tart on rimmed baking sheet until bubbling and tomatoes are slightly wilted, 20 to 25 minutes, rotating sheet halfway through baking.

4. Let tart cool on baking sheet for at least 10 minutes or up to 2 hours. To serve, remove outer metal ring of tart pan, slide thin metal spatula between tart and tart pan bottom, and carefully slide tart onto serving platter or cutting board. Sprinkle with basil before serving.

VARIATIONS
Zucchini Tart
Substitute 1 large zucchini, sliced into ¼-inch-thick rounds, for tomatoes. Salt zucchini as directed in step 1.

Mushroom Tart
Omit tomatoes and garlic-oil mixture. Heat 1 tablespoon extra-virgin olive oil in 12-inch nonstick skillet over medium-high heat until shimmering. Add 1 pound white button mushrooms, sliced thin, and ½ teaspoon salt and cook until lightly browned, about 15 minutes. Stir in 2 teaspoons minced fresh thyme and 1 minced garlic clove and cook until fragrant, about 1 minute longer. Spoon mushroom mixture over ricotta mixture and bake tart as directed.

Making a Tomato Tart

1. SALT AND DRAIN TOMATOES: Spread tomatoes out over several layers of paper towels, sprinkle with ½ teaspoon salt, and let drain for 30 minutes. Blot tomatoes dry with paper towels.

2. SPREAD RICOTTA MIXTURE OVER TART SHELL: Combine Parmesan, ricotta, mozzarella, and 1 tablespoon oil, and season with salt and pepper to taste. Spread ricotta mixture evenly over bottom of baked tart shell.

3. SHINGLE TOMATOES: Shingle tomatoes attractively in concentric circles, starting at outside edge and working inward. Drizzle tomatoes with garlic-oil mixture.

4. BAKE TART: Bake tart in 425-degree oven until bubbling and tomatoes are slightly wilted, 20 to 25 minutes, rotating sheet halfway through baking. Let tart cool on baking sheet for at least 10 minutes or up to 2 hours before serving.

All-Butter Press-In Tart Dough

MAKES ONE 9-INCH TART

✓ **WHY THIS RECIPE WORKS:** Tart dough is notoriously tricky to work with; it contains less moisture than pie dough and bakes up with a firmer, crisper, more cookielike texture. As with pie dough, overworking the dough can quickly make it tough. But without that little bit of extra moisture, it's even harder to roll out. Enter press-in tart dough. Rather than being rolled out and transferred to a tart pan, press-in tart dough is mixed just until it comes together, then simply sprinkled in clumps into a tart pan and gently pressed down into an even layer. This easy method makes tricky tart dough foolproof. To make our dough even easier, we mixed it in the food processor, which cut the butter into the dough quickly and evenly and prevented our warm hands from melting the butter as it was worked. This method also meant that we could skip the usual step of chilling the dough before forming the crust, so we could whip up a batch in no time. This dough does not need to be chilled before pressing it into the tart pan; however, if it becomes too soft to work with, let it firm up in the refrigerator for a few minutes.

1¼   **cups (6¼ ounces) all-purpose flour**
 1   **tablespoon sugar**
½   **teaspoon salt**
 8   **tablespoons unsalted butter,**
      cut into ¼-inch pieces and chilled
 3   **tablespoons ice water**

1. Process flour, sugar, and salt together in food processor until combined. Scatter butter pieces over top and pulse until mixture resembles coarse cornmeal, about 15 pulses. Add 2 tablespoons ice water and continue to process until large clumps of dough form and no powdery bits remain, about 5 seconds. If dough doesn't clump, add remaining 1 tablespoon water and pulse to incorporate, about 4 pulses. (Dough can be refrigerated for up to 2 days or frozen for up to 1 month. Let refrigerated or frozen dough sit on counter until very soft before using.)

2. Sprinkle walnut-size clumps of dough evenly into 9-inch tart pan. Working outward from center, press dough into even layer, sealing any cracks. Working around edge, press dough firmly into corners of pan with fingers. Go around edge once more, pressing dough up sides and into fluted ridges. Use thumb to level off top edge. Use excess dough to patch any holes. Lay plastic wrap over dough and smooth out any

Shaping a Press-In Tart Shell

1. Sprinkle walnut-size clumps of dough evenly into tart pan.

2. Working outward from center, press dough into even layer, sealing any cracks. Working around edge, press dough firmly into corners of pan with your fingers.

3. Go around edge once more, pressing dough up sides and into fluted ridges. Use your thumb to level off top edge.

4. Use excess dough to patch any holes. Lay plastic wrap over dough and smooth out any bumps using palm of hand.

bumps using palm of hand. Leaving plastic on top of dough, place tart pan on large plate and freeze tart shell until firm, about 30 minutes.

3. Adjust oven rack to middle position and heat oven to 375 degrees. Set tart pan on large baking sheet. Press double layer of aluminum foil into frozen tart shell and over edges of pan and fill with pie weights. Bake until tart shell is golden brown and set, about 30 minutes, rotating baking sheet halfway through baking. Transfer baking sheet to wire rack and carefully remove weights and foil. Let tart shell cool on baking sheet.

Wedges of Camembert cheese are the star of this tart; as the tart bakes, the cheese melts and binds together the filling.

Camembert, Sun-Dried Tomato, and Potato Tart

SERVES 4 TO 6

✓ **WHY THIS RECIPE WORKS:** The inspiration for this tart came from a French dish of cheese, bacon, and potatoes called *tartiflette*. A wheel of soft, melty cheese is the star of this dish. The wheel is sliced through the middle, cut into wedges, then arranged cut side down over the tart. As the tart bakes, the rind forms a crisp crust and the cheese melts out over the filling and into the crevices, binding the potatoes and crust together. We chose creamy, pungent Camembert for the cheese and swapped out the usual bacon for sun-dried tomatoes. Their concentrated, salty-sweet flavor and satisfying texture worked perfectly with the rich cheese and buttery crust. For the potatoes, we sliced Yukon Gold potatoes and browned them in a skillet before spreading them in the tart shell and topping them with the cheese. If you can't find a wheel of Camembert, look for wedges that you can slice in half. Depending on the ripeness and style of the cheese used, the cheese may melt less and range in mildness of flavor.

NOTES FROM THE TEST KITCHEN

Storing Butter

When stored in the fridge, even when wrapped, butter can pick up odors and turn rancid within just a few weeks. When you buy a pound of butter, store it in the freezer for up to four months and transfer it to the fridge one stick at a time as needed. Place the butter in the back of the fridge, where it's coldest, and not in the door, where temperatures are higher.

The temperature of butter makes a difference in many recipes and can dramatically affect the texture of finished baked goods. Pie dough made with warm or room-temperature butter rather than chilled butter will be nearly impossible to roll out, and the resulting crust will be hard and tough rather than tender and flaky. Generally, recipes will call for butter chilled, softened, or melted and cooled. Chilled butter (about 35 degrees) should be cold and unyielding when pressed with a finger. To chill butter quickly, cut it into small pieces and freeze until very firm, 10 to 15 minutes. Softened butter (65 to 67 degrees) will bend easily without breaking and will give slightly when pressed. To soften butter quickly, you can place cold butter in a plastic bag and use a rolling pin to pound it to the desired consistency, or you can cut the butter into small pieces and let it sit until softened. For melted and cooled butter (85 to 90 degrees), melt the butter on the stovetop or in the microwave, then let it cool for about 5 minutes.

2 tablespoons unsalted butter

1 onion, halved and sliced ¼ inch thick

1 pound (2 to 3 medium) Yukon Gold potatoes, peeled and sliced ¼ inch thick

2 teaspoons minced fresh thyme
   Salt and pepper

½ cup oil-packed sun-dried tomatoes, rinsed, patted dry, and chopped coarse

1 recipe All-Butter Press-In Tart Dough (page 340), baked and cooled

1 (8-ounce) wheel Camembert cheese

1. Adjust oven rack to middle position and heat oven to 375 degrees. Melt butter in 12-inch nonstick skillet over medium heat. Add onion and cook, stirring often, until golden brown, about 10 minutes. Stir in potatoes, thyme, 1 teaspoon salt, and ¼ teaspoon pepper. Increase heat to medium-high and continue to cook, stirring occasionally, until potatoes are tender and lightly browned, 6 to 8 minutes. Stir in sun-dried tomatoes.

2. Spread potato mixture evenly into tart shell. Cut Camembert wheel in half through middle to make 2 thin wheels, then cut each half into 4 wedges. Arrange wedges of cheese, rind side up, over top of tart.

3. Bake tart on baking sheet until golden and cheese is melted and bubbling, 25 to 35 minutes, rotating sheet halfway through baking. Let tart cool on sheet for 10 minutes. To serve, remove outer metal ring of tart pan, slide thin metal spatula between tart and tart pan bottom, and carefully slide tart onto serving platter or cutting board. Serve warm.

Cutting Camembert into Wedges

1. Cut wheel of Camembert in half horizontally to form 2 rounds.

2. Cut each round into 4 equal pieces.

Mushroom and Leek Galette

MAKES TWO 12-INCH GALETTES, SERVES 4 TO 6

✔ **WHY THIS RECIPE WORKS:** Many free-form vegetable tart recipes simply borrow a standard pastry dough intended for fruit, but vegetables are more prone to leaking liquid into the crust or falling apart when the tart is sliced. We needed a crust that was extra-sturdy and boasted a complex flavor of its own. We also wanted a robust-tasting filling featuring the classic combination of meaty mushrooms and sweet leeks. To give the crust earthy flavor and a hearty crumb, we added in some whole-wheat flour. To keep the dough tender, we took a hands-off approach to mixing; we just barely mixed the dry and wet ingredients together, and then rested the dough briefly before rolling it out. To punch up its flaky texture and create more structure, we gave the dough a series of folds to create numerous interlocking layers. To remove moisture from the vegetables, we microwaved and drained the mushrooms and browned the leeks on the stovetop. Finally, we made a rich binder with crème fraîche, Dijon mustard, and crumbled Gorgonzola. An equal amount of rye flour can be substituted for the whole-wheat flour. Cutting a few small holes in the dough prevents it from lifting off the pan as it bakes. If you do not have a baking stone, you can use a preheated rimless (or inverted) baking sheet.

A combination of meaty, savory mushrooms and sweet leeks makes the perfect filling for our vegetable galette.

DOUGH

1¼ cups (6¼ ounces) all-purpose flour
½ cup (2¾ ounces) whole-wheat flour
1 tablespoon sugar
¾ teaspoon salt
10 tablespoons unsalted butter, cut into ½-inch pieces and chilled
7 tablespoons ice water
1 teaspoon distilled white vinegar

FILLING

1¼ pounds shiitake mushrooms, stemmed and sliced thin
5 teaspoons extra-virgin olive oil
1 pound leeks, white and light green parts only, sliced ½ inch thick and washed thoroughly (3 cups)
1 teaspoon minced fresh thyme
2 tablespoons crème fraîche
1 tablespoon Dijon mustard
  Salt and pepper
3 ounces Gorgonzola cheese, crumbled (¾ cup)

1 large egg, lightly beaten
  Kosher salt
2 tablespoons minced fresh parsley

1. FOR THE DOUGH: Pulse all-purpose flour, whole-wheat flour, sugar, and salt in food processor until combined, 2 to 3 pulses. Add butter and pulse until pea-size pieces form, about 10 pulses. Transfer mixture to medium bowl.

2. Sprinkle water and vinegar over mixture. With rubber spatula, use folding motion to mix until loose, shaggy mass forms with some dry flour remaining (do not overwork). Transfer mixture to center of large sheet of plastic wrap, press gently into rough 4-inch square, and wrap tightly. Refrigerate for at least 45 minutes.

3. Transfer dough to lightly floured counter. Roll into 11 by 8-inch rectangle, with short side of rectangle parallel to edge of counter. Using bench scraper, bring bottom third of dough up over middle third, then fold upper third over it, folding like business letter into 8 by 4-inch rectangle. Turn dough 90 degrees counterclockwise. Roll out dough again into 11 by 8-inch rectangle and fold into thirds again. Turn dough 90 degrees counterclockwise and repeat rolling and folding into thirds. After last fold, fold dough in half to create 4-inch square. Press top of dough gently to seal. Wrap in plastic wrap and refrigerate for at least 45 minutes or up to 2 days.

4. FOR THE FILLING: Microwave mushrooms in covered bowl until just tender, 3 to 5 minutes. Transfer to colander to drain, then return to bowl. Meanwhile, heat 1 tablespoon oil in 12-inch skillet over medium heat until shimmering. Add leeks and thyme, cover, and cook, stirring occasionally, until leeks are tender and beginning to brown, 5 to 7 minutes. Transfer to bowl with mushrooms. Stir in crème fraîche and mustard and season with salt and pepper to taste. Set aside.

5. Adjust oven rack to lower-middle position, place baking stone on rack, and heat oven to 400 degrees. Remove dough from refrigerator and let stand at room temperature for 15 to 20 minutes. Roll out on generously floured (up to ¼ cup) counter to 14-inch circle about ⅛ inch thick. (Trim edges as needed to form rough circle.) Transfer dough to parchment paper–lined rimmed baking sheet. With tip of paring knife, cut five ¼-inch circles in dough (1 at center and 4 evenly spaced midway from center to edge of dough). Brush top of dough with 1 teaspoon oil.

6. Spread half of filling evenly over dough, leaving 2-inch border around edge. Sprinkle with half of Gorgonzola, cover with remaining filling, and top with remaining Gorgonzola. Drizzle remaining 1 teaspoon oil over filling. Grasp 1 edge of dough and fold up outer 2 inches over filling. Repeat around circumference of tart, overlapping dough every 2 to 3 inches; gently pinch pleated dough to secure but do not press dough into filling. Brush dough with egg and sprinkle evenly with kosher salt.

7. Lower oven temperature to 375 degrees. Bake until crust is deep golden brown and filling is beginning to brown, 35 to 45 minutes, rotating sheet halfway through baking. Cool tart on baking sheet on wire rack for 10 minutes. Using offset or wide metal spatula, loosen tart from parchment and carefully slide tart off parchment and onto cutting board. Sprinkle with parsley, cut into wedges, and serve.

VARIATIONS

Potato and Shallot Galette with Goat Cheese
Substitute following for mushroom filling in step 4: Microwave 1 pound Yukon Gold potatoes, sliced ¼ inch thick, in covered bowl until just tender, 4 to 8 minutes; drain and return to bowl. Heat 1 tablespoon oil in 12-inch skillet over medium heat until shimmering. Add 4 ounces thinly sliced shallots and 1 teaspoon minced fresh rosemary, cover, and cook until beginning to brown, 5 to 7 minutes; add to potatoes. Stir in ¼ cup crème fraîche, ¼ cup chopped kalamata olives, and 1 teaspoon grated lemon zest; season with salt and pepper to taste. Substitute ¾ cup crumbled goat cheese for Gorgonzola cheese.

Butternut Squash Galette with Gruyère
Substitute following for mushroom filling in step 4: Microwave 6 cups baby spinach and ¼ cup water in covered bowl until wilted by half, 3 to 4 minutes; let stand, covered, for 1 minute. Drain thoroughly, chop coarsely, then drain again while pressing with rubber spatula to remove excess liquid; return to bowl. Microwave 3 cups butternut squash, cut into ½-inch cubes, in covered bowl until just tender, about 8 minutes; drain and add to spinach. Heat 1 tablespoon oil in 12-inch skillet over medium heat until shimmering. Add 1 thinly sliced red onion and ½ teaspoon minced fresh oregano, cover, and cook until beginning to brown, 5 to 7 minutes; add to spinach and squash. Stir in ¾ cup shredded Gruyère cheese, 2 tablespoons crème fraîche, and 1 teaspoon sherry vinegar and season with salt and pepper to taste. Omit Gorgonzola cheese when assembling tart.

Pleating a Free-Form Tart

Gently grasp 1 edge of dough and make 2-inch-wide fold over filling. Lift and fold another segment of dough over first fold to form pleat. Repeat every 2 to 3 inches.

Vegetable Torta with Asiago and Herbs

SERVES 6 TO 8

✓ **WHY THIS RECIPE WORKS:** Vegetable tortas should be eye-catching showstoppers, but they often turn out to be piles of soggy, bland vegetables. For a four-star, make-ahead vegetable torta showcasing late-summer vegetables, we knew we would have to figure out the best approach for removing as much moisture as possible from the vegetables to concentrate their flavors. We began by salting and pressing the eggplant, zucchini, and tomatoes. The eggplant and zucchini required precooking—we roasted the eggplant in a 450-degree oven until browned and dry, and microwaved the more delicate zucchini between paper towels weighted with a plate. The salted and drained tomatoes, however, could be baked right on top of the torta. A simple egg custard bound the vegetables together, and a bread-crumb crust protected the edges from sticking and burning. Roasting the eggplant slices on wire racks set in rimmed baking sheets kept them from sticking to the pans. Alternatively, they can be roasted directly on well-oiled baking sheets; after roasting, use a thin spatula to carefully remove the slices. Hard Italian Asiago is too mild for this recipe—use a domestic Asiago (available in supermarkets) that yields to pressure when pressed. The torta is best served warm or at room temperature.

FILLING

- 3 pounds eggplant, peeled, halved crosswise, and cut lengthwise into ½-inch-thick slices
  Kosher salt and pepper
- 3 tablespoons extra-virgin olive oil
- 2 red bell peppers
- 1 garlic head, top quarter cut off to expose garlic cloves
- 2 large tomatoes, cored and sliced ¼ inch thick
- 4 zucchini, sliced ¼ inch thick on steep bias
- 3 large eggs
- ¼ cup heavy cream
- 2 teaspoons minced fresh thyme
- 2 tablespoons lemon juice
- 3 ounces Asiago cheese, grated fine (1½ cups)
- 2 tablespoons shredded fresh basil

CRUST

- 4 slices hearty white sandwich bread, torn into quarters
- 2 ounces Asiago cheese, grated fine (1 cup)
- 3 tablespoons unsalted butter, melted

1. FOR THE FILLING: Grease 2 wire racks and set inside 2 rimmed baking sheets. Adjust oven racks to upper-middle and lower-middle positions and heat oven to 450 degrees. Toss eggplant with 1 tablespoon salt and drain in colander for 30 minutes; wipe and press firmly with paper towels to dry and to remove salt. Brush with 2 tablespoons oil, season with pepper, and arrange on prepared racks.

2. Rub bell peppers with ½ tablespoon oil and lay on racks with eggplant. Place garlic, cut side up, on 12-inch piece of aluminum foil, drizzle with remaining ½ tablespoon oil, and wrap securely. Roast vegetables until eggplant is well browned and peppers are blistered, 30 to 35 minutes, switching and

Assembling Vegetable Torta

1. Press 1 cup crumbs evenly over pan bottom using bottom of dry measuring cup. Press remaining crumbs into sides of pan to form thick walls that stop ¼ inch from top of pan.

2. Cover pan bottom with single layer of eggplant, tearing pieces as needed to fit. Layer cheese, zucchini, remaining eggplant, and red peppers into pan.

3. After adding custard, tilt pan from side to side and shake gently back and forth to ensure even distribution.

4. Arrange tomatoes in attractive circular pattern on top of torta, partially overlapping them. Press gently on tomatoes, then sprinkle with reserved crumbs.

rotating sheets and turning peppers halfway through baking. Meanwhile, roast garlic on lower rack until cloves are very soft, 40 to 50 minutes. Transfer peppers to bowl, cover, and let steam until cool; remove skin, stems, and seeds and slice peppers lengthwise into 3 pieces. Let eggplant cool on racks, and let garlic cool in foil.

3. While vegetables roast, spread tomatoes out over paper towel–lined baking sheet, sprinkle with 1 teaspoon salt, and let sit for 30 minutes; press firmly with paper towels to dry. Toss zucchini with 1 tablespoon salt and let drain in colander for 30 minutes; pat dry with paper towels. Layer and stack zucchini on plate between multiple layers of paper towels. Top with second plate, press firmly to compress, and microwave until steaming, about 10 minutes; let cool for 5 minutes, then remove top plate. (Cooked vegetables can be refrigerated separately for up to 1 day.)

4. FOR THE CRUST: Thoroughly grease 9-inch springform pan. Pulse bread to coarse crumbs in food processor, about 10 pulses. Sprinkle cheese and melted butter over crumbs and pulse to combine, about 5 pulses. Reserve 3 tablespoons crumbs for topping. Press 1 cup crumbs evenly over pan bottom using bottom of dry measuring cup. Press remaining crumbs into sides of pan to form thick walls that stop ¼ inch from top of pan.

5. Unwrap roasted garlic, squeeze cloves from skin into bowl, and mash with fork. Without cleaning food processor, process garlic paste, eggs, cream, thyme, and lemon juice until thoroughly combined, about 30 seconds. Heat oven to 375 degrees.

6. Cover pan bottom with single layer of eggplant, tearing pieces as needed to fit, then sprinkle with 2 tablespoons cheese. Repeat with layer of zucchini and 2 tablespoons cheese. Repeat with another layer of eggplant and 2 tablespoons cheese. Repeat with all of red peppers and 2 tablespoons cheese. Pour half of custard over top; tilt and shake pan to distribute. Repeat layering of remaining eggplant and zucchini, sprinkling each layer with 2 tablespoons cheese (about 4 more layers). Pour remaining custard over top; tilt and shake pan.

7. Shingle tomato slices attractively over top, starting at edge and working toward center. Press gently on tomatoes, then sprinkle with reserved crumbs. Set torta on baking sheet and bake on lower-middle rack until crumb topping is lightly browned and torta registers 175 degrees, 1¼ to 1½ hours.

8. Let torta cool in pan for 10 minutes. Run thin knife around inside of springform pan ring to loosen, then remove ring and let torta cool for 20 minutes. Sprinkle with basil before serving. (Torta can be refrigerated overnight; let sit at room temperature for 1 hour before serving.)

Tender, flaky, and subtly savory pastry shells encase a hearty filling of poblano chiles, pinto beans, and pepper Jack cheese.

Poblano and Corn Hand Pies

MAKES 16 PIES, SERVES 6 TO 8

✔ **WHY THIS RECIPE WORKS:** Empanadas are a perennial Latin American favorite; we wanted a simpler version that we could make at home. To get dough that was easy to work with and sturdy enough to fill while baking up tender and flaky, we found that vegetable shortening was essential. To give it a subtle savory flavor, we used vegetable broth for the liquid and added a generous dose of salt. For the filling, we chose a combination of poblano chiles, hearty pinto beans, and warm spices. Pepper Jack cheese added more heat and richness, and sliced scallions added freshness. Mashing a portion of the pinto beans with some of their liquid created a moist binder for the filling. By oiling and preheating the baking sheets, we created a searing-hot cooking surface for the hand pies, which helped to give them crisp, golden-brown crusts without the mess and hassle of deep frying. Poking each hand pie with the tines of a fork before baking created a vent for the steam to escape, which kept the hand pies from inflating as they baked. Serve the hand pies with Mexican Crema (page 366).

FILLING

- 1 (15-ounce) can pinto beans, 3 tablespoons liquid reserved, beans rinsed
- 1½ cups frozen corn, thawed
- 6 ounces pepper Jack cheese, shredded (1½ cups)
- 3 scallions, white parts minced, green parts sliced thin
- 2 tablespoons vegetable oil
- 3 poblano chiles, stemmed, seeded, and cut into ¼-inch pieces
- 2 garlic cloves, minced
- 2 teaspoons minced fresh oregano or ½ teaspoon dried
- 1½ teaspoons ground cumin
- 1½ teaspoons ground coriander
- Salt and pepper

DOUGH

- 4 cups (20 ounces) all-purpose flour
- 2 teaspoons salt
- 1 teaspoon baking powder
- 8 tablespoons vegetable shortening, cut into ½-inch pieces
- 1 cup vegetable broth
- 2 large eggs, lightly beaten
- 5 tablespoons vegetable oil

1. FOR THE FILLING: Place one-quarter of beans in large bowl, add bean liquid, and, using back of wooden spoon, mash until coarsely mashed. Stir in remaining beans, corn, cheese, and scallion greens.

2. Heat oil in 12-inch nonstick skillet over medium-high heat until shimmering. Add poblanos and scallion whites, and cook, stirring occasionally, until softened, 3 to 5 minutes. Stir in garlic, oregano, cumin, coriander, ½ teaspoon salt, and ¼ teaspoon pepper and cook until fragrant, about 30 seconds. Transfer poblano mixture to bowl with beans and stir well to combine. Season with salt and pepper to taste and let cool slightly. Refrigerate until completely cool, 45 minutes to 1 hour. (Filling can be refrigerated for up to 2 days.)

3. FOR THE DOUGH: Meanwhile, process flour, salt, and baking powder in food processor until combined, about 3 seconds. Add shortening and pulse until mixture resembles coarse cornmeal, 6 to 8 pulses. Add broth and eggs and pulse

until dough just comes together, about 5 pulses. Transfer dough to lightly floured counter and knead until dough forms smooth ball, about 20 seconds. Divide dough into 16 equal pieces. With cupped hands, form each piece into a smooth, tight ball. (Dough can be covered and refrigerated for up to 24 hours.)

4. Adjust oven racks to upper-middle and lower-middle positions, place 1 rimmed baking sheet on each rack, and heat oven to 425 degrees. Working with 1 piece of dough at a time, roll into 6-inch circle on lightly floured counter. Place heaping ¼ cup cooled filling in center of dough round. Brush edges of dough with water and fold dough over filling. Press to seal, trim any ragged edges, and crimp edges with tines of fork. Pierce top of each hand pie once with fork.

5. Drizzle 2 tablespoons oil onto each hot sheet, then return to oven for 2 minutes. Gently brush tops of shaped and filled pies with remaining 1 tablespoon oil. Carefully place 8 pies on each prepared sheet and cook until golden brown, 20 to 25 minutes, switching and rotating sheets halfway through baking. Transfer hand pies to wire rack and let cool to room temperature, about 30 minutes. Serve.

TO MAKE AHEAD: Hand pies can be frozen for up to 1 month. Transfer baked and cooled pies to zipper-lock freezer bags, press out air, and seal. To serve, do not thaw before reheating. Adjust oven rack to middle position and heat oven to 350 degrees. Place pies on wire rack set in rimmed baking sheet and bake until heated through, 20 to 30 minutes. Serve.

Sealing Hand Pies

1. Brush edges of each dough round with water and fold 1 side over filling to form half-moon. For tidy pies, trim any ragged edges with pastry wheel.

2. Use tines of fork to make decorative crimp that tightly seals pies. Pierce top of each pie once with fork.

Samosas

MAKES 24 TURNOVERS, SERVES 8 TO 10

⚑ **WHY THIS RECIPE WORKS:** Samosas are Indian-style turnovers that boast a pungently spiced vegetable filling in a thin, crispy pastry shell. To make our own version, we started with a simple potato filling. We built a fragrant flavor base of fennel, cumin, mustard seed, fenugreek, turmeric, and pepper flakes in a skillet. We added an onion, ginger, and garlic, then stirred in softened chunks of potato to let their edges crisp and brown. Fresh peas, cilantro, and lemon juice rounded out the warm flavors. Making the dough with a generous amount of vegetable oil gave us crusts that turned out crispy and golden when fried. Adding some yogurt made the dough extra-elastic so we could easily pack the samosas with plenty of stuffing. We prefer the texture of whole fennel and cumin seeds in this filling; however, you can substitute ½ teaspoon ground fennel and ½ teaspoon ground cumin. We prefer whole-milk yogurt here, but low-fat or nonfat yogurt can be substituted. You will need at least a 6-quart Dutch oven for this recipe. A wire spider comes in handy when frying the samosas. Serve with Cilantro-Mint Chutney (page 43).

FILLING

- 2 pounds russet potatoes, peeled and cut into 1-inch chunks
  Salt and pepper
- 3 tablespoons vegetable oil
- 1 teaspoon fennel seeds
- 1 teaspoon cumin seeds
- 1 teaspoon brown mustard seeds
- ¼ teaspoon ground fenugreek
- ¼ teaspoon ground turmeric
- ⅛ teaspoon red pepper flakes
- 1 onion, chopped fine
- 3 garlic cloves, minced
- 1½ teaspoons grated fresh ginger
- ½ cup frozen peas, thawed
- ¼ cup minced fresh cilantro
- 1½ teaspoons lemon juice

DOUGH

- 2 cups (10 ounces) all-purpose flour
- ½ teaspoon salt
- 2 tablespoons plain whole-milk yogurt
- 3 tablespoons vegetable oil
- 6 tablespoons cold water

- 3 quarts vegetable oil

Shaping Samosas

1. Working with 1 half-moon piece of dough, moisten straight side with wet finger, then fold in half. Crimp with fork to seal seam on straight side only; leave rounded edge open and unsealed.

2. Hold dough gently in cupped hand, with open, unsealed edge facing up; gently open dough into cone shape. Pack with 2 tablespoons of filling, leaving ¼-inch rim at top.

3. Moisten inside rim of cone with wet finger and pinch top edge together to seal. Lay samosa on flat surface and crimp sealed edge with fork to secure.

1. FOR THE FILLING: Place potatoes and 1 tablespoon salt in large saucepan and add water to cover by 1 inch. Bring water to boil, then reduce to simmer and cook until potatoes are tender and paring knife can be inserted into potatoes with little resistance, 12 to 15 minutes. Drain potatoes and set aside to cool slightly.

2. Heat oil in 12-inch nonstick skillet over medium-high heat until shimmering. Add fennel seeds, cumin seeds, mustard seeds, fenugreek, turmeric, and pepper flakes and cook until fragrant, about 10 seconds. Stir in onion and 1 teaspoon salt and cook until onion is softened, 5 to 7 minutes. Stir in garlic and ginger and cook until fragrant, about 30 seconds. Stir in cooled potatoes and cook until beginning to brown around edges, 5 to 7 minutes. Stir in peas.

3. Transfer mixture to bowl, cool to room temperature, then refrigerate until completely cool, about 1 hour. Stir in cilantro and lemon juice and season with salt and pepper to taste. (Filling can be refrigerated for up to 2 days; reserve cilantro and lemon juice and stir in before serving)

4. FOR THE DOUGH: Pulse flour and salt in food processor until combined, about 4 pulses. Drizzle yogurt and 3 tablespoons oil over flour mixture and process until mixture resembles coarse cornmeal, about 5 seconds. With machine running, slowly add 4 tablespoons water until dough forms ball. If dough doesn't come together, add remaining 2 tablespoons water, 1 tablespoon at a time, with processor running, until dough ball forms. Dough should feel very soft and malleable.

5. Transfer dough to floured counter and knead by hand until slightly firm, about 2 minutes. Wrap dough in plastic wrap and let rest for at least 20 minutes, or refrigerate for up to 24 hours.

6. Divide dough into 12 equal pieces and cover with greased plastic wrap. Working with 1 piece of dough at a time, roll dough into 5-inch round. Cut each dough round in half to form 24 half-moons.

7. Working with 1 half-moon piece of dough, moisten straight side with wet finger, then fold in half. Press to seal seam on straight side only and crimp with fork to secure; leave rounded edge open and unsealed. Pick up piece of dough and hold gently in cupped hand, with open, unsealed edge facing up; gently open dough into cone shape. Fill dough cone with 2 tablespoons filling and pack filling in tightly, leaving ¼-inch rim at top. Moisten inside rim of cone with wet finger and pinch top edge together to seal. Lay samosa on flat surface and crimp sealed edge with fork to secure. Repeat with remaining dough and remaining filling.

8. Adjust oven rack to middle position and heat oven to 200 degrees. Line baking sheet with several layers of paper towels and set aside. Heat remaining 3 quarts oil in large Dutch oven over medium-high heat to 375 degrees. Add 8 samosas and fry until golden brown and bubbly, 2½ to 3 minutes, adjusting heat as needed to maintain 375 degrees. Using slotted spoon, transfer samosas to prepared baking sheet and keep warm in oven. Return oil to 375 degrees and repeat frying remaining samosas in 2 more batches. Serve.

Stuffed Naan

MAKES 4 STUFFED NAAN, SERVES 4

✔ **WHY THIS RECIPE WORKS:** *Keema naan* is an Indian dish of crisp, chewy naan bread stuffed with juicy ground lamb flavored with bold, warm spices. To create a vegetarian version, we used veggie protein crumbles to mimic the texture of the ground meat and added a mix of bold aromatics—garam masala, chili powder, and coriander—and tomato puree for the perfect balance of depth, warmth, spice, and sweetness. To create a soft naan that was pleasantly chewy, we started with a moist dough with a fair amount of fat. However, when we tried to roll it out, the dough snapped back like a rubber band. To help the dough relax, we gave it plenty of resting time and folded it over itself several times as it proofed. Cooking the naan in a covered skillet delivered heat to both sides of the bread at once, producing naan that were nicely charred but still moist. High-protein bread flour helped to make a dough substantial enough to support our hearty filling. Do not use nonfat yogurt in this recipe. A 12-inch nonstick skillet may be used in place of the cast-iron skillet. For efficiency, stretch and fill the next ball of dough while each naan is cooking. If using frozen veggie protein crumbles, do not thaw them before adding them to the skillet. Serve with Cilantro-Mint Chutney (page 43) or Yogurt-Herb Sauce (page 43).

DOUGH

½ **cup ice water**

⅓ **cup plain whole-milk yogurt**

3 **tablespoons vegetable oil**

1 **large egg yolk**

Stuffing Naan

1. Transfer 1 dough ball to lightly floured counter. Flatten ball using hands or rolling pin and roll out to 6-inch disk. Place generous ¼ cup filling in center.

2. Bring up sides of dough around filling and pinch top to seal. Roll and shape into ball again and sprinkle with flour.

3. Using hands and rolling pin, press and roll stuffed dough into 7-inch round of even thickness, sprinkling dough and counter with flour as needed to prevent sticking. Using fork, poke entire surface of round, about 15 times.

2 cups (11 ounces) bread flour

1¼ teaspoons sugar

½ teaspoon instant or rapid-rise yeast

1¼ teaspoons salt

FILLING

2 tablespoons plus 1 teaspoon vegetable oil

1 small onion, finely chopped

3 garlic cloves, minced

¾ teaspoon ground coriander

½ teaspoon chili powder

½ teaspoon garam masala

Salt and pepper

5 ounces veggie protein crumbles

1½ tablespoons tomato puree

2 tablespoons water

2 tablespoons minced fresh cilantro

1. FOR THE DOUGH: In measuring cup or small bowl, combine water, yogurt, oil, and egg yolk. Process flour, sugar, and yeast in food processor until combined, about 2 seconds. With processor running, slowly add water mixture; process until dough is just combined and no dry flour remains, about 10 seconds. Let dough stand for 10 minutes.

2. Add salt to dough and process until dough forms satiny, sticky ball that clears sides of workbowl, 30 to 60 seconds. Transfer dough to lightly floured counter and knead until smooth, about 1 minute. Shape dough into tight ball and place in large lightly oiled bowl. Let dough rise at room temperature for 30 minutes.

3. Fold partially risen dough over itself 8 times by gently lifting and folding edge of dough toward middle, turning bowl 90 degrees after each fold. Cover with plastic wrap and let rise for 30 minutes. Repeat folding, turning, and rising 1 more time, for total of three 30-minute rises.

4. Adjust oven rack to middle position and heat oven to 350 degrees. Set wire rack in rimmed baking sheet. Transfer dough to lightly floured counter and divide into 4 equal pieces. Shape each piece into smooth, tight ball. Place dough balls on lightly oiled baking sheet, at least 2 inches apart; cover loosely with greased plastic wrap. Let stand for 15 to 20 minutes.

5. FOR THE FILLING: Meanwhile, heat 2 tablespoons oil in 12-inch cast-iron skillet over medium heat until shimmering. Add onion and cook until softened, 5 to 7 minutes. Stir in garlic, coriander, chili powder, garam masala, ½ teaspoon salt, and ¼ teaspoon pepper and cook until fragrant, about 30 seconds. Add veggie protein crumbles, tomato puree, and water and cook, stirring to break up crumbles, until liquid has evaporated, about 1 minute. Stir in cilantro and transfer to bowl. Wipe out skillet with paper towels.

For foolproof stuffed naan, we make the dough easy to work with by folding it over itself several times during proofing.

6. Transfer 1 dough ball to lightly floured counter. Flatten ball using hands or rolling pin and roll out to 6-inch round. Place generous ¼ cup filling in center and pull edges of dough up, seal, shape into ball again, and sprinkle with flour. Using hands and rolling pin, press and roll stuffed dough into 7-inch round of even thickness, sprinkling dough and counter with flour as needed to prevent sticking. (Small rips in dough are OK; for larger tears, pinch dough closed.) Using fork, poke entire surface of round, about 15 times.

7. Heat remaining 1 teaspoon oil in now-empty skillet over medium heat until shimmering. Wipe oil out of skillet completely with paper towels. Mist top of dough lightly with water. Place dough in pan, moistened side down; mist top surface of dough lightly with water; and cover. Cook until bottom is browned in spots across surface, 2 to 4 minutes. Flip naan, cover, and continue to cook on second side until lightly browned, 2 to 3 minutes. (If naan puffs up, gently poke with fork to deflate.) Transfer to prepared wire rack and repeat filling, rolling, and cooking remaining 3 dough balls. Once last naan is cooked and placed on wire rack, transfer sheet to oven and bake until edges of stuffed naan no longer look doughy and are light golden in color, 10 to 15 minutes. Serve immediately.

CHAPTER 9

Sandwiches, Wraps, Burgers, and More

■ FAST (Less than 45 minutes start to finish)   ■ VEGAN   ■ GLUTEN-FREE
Photos: Grilled Cheese Sandwiches with Cheddar and Shallot; Grilled Portobello Burgers

BRUSCHETTA

This classic Italian antipasto starts with slices of simple toasted garlic bread. A combination of chopped tomatoes and olive oil is the most traditional topping, but there are endless variations. Here are a few of our favorites.

Toasted Bread for Bruschetta

SERVES 8 TO 10 `FAST` `VEGAN`

Toast the bread just before assembling the bruschetta. If you prefer, the bread can be toasted on a grill.

- 1 loaf country bread with thick crust (about 10 by 5 inches), ends discarded, sliced crosswise into ¾-inch-thick pieces
- ½ garlic clove, peeled
  Extra-virgin olive oil
  Salt

Adjust oven rack 4 inches from broiler element and heat broiler. Place bread on aluminum foil–lined baking sheet. Broil until bread is deep golden on both sides, 1 to 2 minutes per side. Lightly rub 1 side of each bread slice with garlic and brush with oil. Season with salt to taste.

Bruschetta with Black Olive Pesto, Ricotta, and Basil

SERVES 8 TO 10 `FAST`

- ½ cup pitted kalamata olives
- 1 small shallot, minced
- 2 tablespoons extra-virgin olive oil, plus extra for drizzling
- 1½ teaspoons lemon juice
- 1 garlic clove, minced
- 12 ounces whole-milk ricotta cheese
  Salt and pepper
- 1 recipe Toasted Bread for Bruschetta
- 2 tablespoons shredded fresh basil

Process olives, shallot, oil, lemon juice, and garlic in food processor until uniform paste forms, about 10 seconds. Season ricotta with salt and pepper to taste. Spread olive pesto evenly on toasts. Carefully spread ricotta over pesto. Drizzle with extra oil to taste, sprinkle with basil, and serve.

Bruschetta with Grape Tomatoes, Arugula Pesto, and Goat Cheese

SERVES 8 TO 10 `FAST`

- 12 ounces grape tomatoes, quartered
  Salt and pepper
- ¼ teaspoon sugar
- 7 tablespoons extra-virgin olive oil
- 1 tablespoon red wine vinegar
- 3 ounces (3 cups) baby arugula
- 1 recipe Toasted Bread for Bruschetta
- 2 ounces goat cheese, crumbled
- 1 tablespoon minced shallot

1. Combine tomatoes, ½ teaspoon salt, and sugar in bowl and let sit 30 minutes. Spin tomatoes in salad spinner until excess liquid has been removed, 45 to 60 seconds, redistributing tomatoes several times during spinning. Return to bowl and toss with 3 tablespoons oil, vinegar, and ¼ teaspoon pepper.

2. Process arugula, remaining 4 tablespoons oil, ½ teaspoon salt, and ¼ teaspoon pepper in food processor until smooth, about 1 minute. Spread pesto evenly on toasts. Top with tomatoes, goat cheese, and shallot. Serve.

Bruschetta with Grape Tomatoes, White Bean Puree, and Rosemary

SERVES 8 TO 10 `FAST`

- 12 ounces grape tomatoes, quartered
  Salt and pepper
- ¼ teaspoon sugar
- 6 tablespoons extra-virgin olive oil
- 1 tablespoon red wine vinegar
- 1 (15-ounce) can cannellini beans, rinsed
- 2 tablespoons water
- 1 recipe Toasted Bread for Bruschetta
- 1 ounce Parmesan cheese, shaved
- 2 teaspoons minced fresh rosemary

1. Combine tomatoes, ½ teaspoon salt, and sugar in bowl and let sit 30 minutes. Spin tomatoes in salad spinner until excess liquid has been removed, 45 to 60 seconds, redistributing tomatoes several times during spinning. Return to bowl and toss with 3 tablespoons oil, vinegar, and ¼ teaspoon pepper.

2. Process beans, water, ½ teaspoon salt, and ¼ teaspoon pepper in food processor until smooth, about 1 minute. With processor running, slowly add remaining 3 tablespoons oil until incorporated. Spread bean mixture evenly on toasts. Top with tomatoes and Parmesan and sprinkle with rosemary. Serve.

Bruschetta with Artichoke Hearts and Parmesan

SERVES 8 TO 10 `FAST`

Use artichoke hearts packed in water.

- 1 (14-ounce) can artichoke hearts, rinsed and patted dry
- 2 tablespoons extra-virgin olive oil, plus extra for drizzling
- 2 tablespoons chopped fresh basil
- 2 teaspoons lemon juice
- 1 garlic clove, minced
  Salt and pepper
- 2 ounces Parmesan cheese, 1 ounce grated fine, 1 ounce shaved
- 1 recipe Toasted Bread for Bruschetta

Pulse artichoke hearts, oil, basil, lemon juice, garlic, ¼ teaspoon salt, and ¼ teaspoon pepper in food processor until coarsely pureed, about 6 pulses, scraping down bowl once during pulsing. Add grated Parmesan and pulse to combine, about 2 pulses. Spread artichoke mixture evenly on toasts. Top toasts with shaved Parmesan, season with pepper to taste, and drizzle with extra oil to taste. Serve.

For the simplest and most flavorful sandwich we spread creamy avocado seasoned with lemon vinaigrette on toast.

Avocado Toast

SERVES 4 `FAST` `VEGAN`

✔ WHY THIS RECIPE WORKS: Some dishes are so simple that they are not even worth talking about. But avocado toast definitely is. Avocado toast is having its moment; it's healthy, delicious, and it's one of the simplest things to make for a quick breakfast or lunch. We took ours up a notch by whisking together a lemony vinaigrette and mixing it in as we mashed one of the avocados, giving our dish a distinct citrusy punch. Smeared on toasted rustic country bread, topped with sliced avocado, then sprinkled with a little coarse sea salt and red pepper flakes, our version of this dish is spectacularly tasty. Topping it with a fried egg just takes it over the top.

2 tablespoons extra-virgin olive oil
1 teaspoon finely grated lemon zest
   plus 1 tablespoon juice
   Coarse sea salt or kosher salt and pepper
2 ripe avocados, halved and pitted, 1 avocado
   chopped and 1 avocado sliced thin

4 (½-inch-thick) slices crusty bread
¼ teaspoon red pepper flakes (optional)

1. Whisk oil, lemon zest and juice, ¼ teaspoon salt, and ⅛ teaspoon pepper together in small bowl. Add chopped avocado and mash into dressing with fork.

2. Adjust oven rack 4 inches from broiler element and heat broiler. Place bread on aluminum foil–lined baking sheet. Broil until bread is deep golden on both sides, 1 to 2 minutes per side.

3. Spread mashed avocado mixture evenly on toasts. Arrange avocado slices evenly over top. Sprinkle with ¼ teaspoon salt and pepper flakes, if using, and serve.

VARIATION

Avocado Toast with Fried Eggs `FAST`

Cut 2 teaspoons unsalted butter into 4 pieces; keep chilled. Crack 4 eggs into 2 small bowls (2 eggs per bowl) and season with salt and pepper. Heat 2 teaspoons vegetable oil in 12-inch nonstick skillet over low heat for 5 minutes. Increase heat to medium-high and heat until oil is shimmering. Add butter and swirl to coat pan. Working quickly, add eggs to pan from opposite sides, cover, and cook for 1 minute. Remove skillet from burner and let stand, covered, for 15 to 45 seconds for runny yolks (white around edge of yolk will be barely opaque), 45 to 60 seconds for soft but set yolks, and about 2 minutes for medium-set yolks. Top avocado toasts with fried eggs and serve.

Grilled Cheese Sandwiches with Cheddar and Shallot

SERVES 4 `FAST`

✔ WHY THIS RECIPE WORKS: Melty American cheese on fluffy white bread is a childhood classic, but we wanted a grilled cheese for adults that offered more robust flavor. Aged cheddar gave us the complexity we were after, but it made for a greasy sandwich with a grainy filling. Adding a splash of wine and some Brie boosted the flavor even further and helped the aged cheddar melt evenly without separating or becoming greasy. Using a food processor to combine the ingredients ensured our cheese-and-wine mixture was easy to spread. A little bit of shallot ramped up the flavor without detracting from the cheese, and a smear of mustard butter livened up the bread. Look for a cheddar aged for about one year (avoid cheddar aged for longer; it won't melt well). To bring the cheddar to room temperature quickly, microwave the pieces until warm, about 30 seconds.

7 ounces aged cheddar cheese, cut into
   24 equal pieces, room temperature
2 ounces Brie cheese, rind removed
2 tablespoons dry white wine
4 teaspoons minced shallot
3 tablespoons unsalted butter, softened
1 teaspoon Dijon mustard
8 slices hearty white sandwich bread

1. Adjust oven rack to middle position and heat oven to 200 degrees. Set wire rack in rimmed baking sheet. Process cheddar, Brie, and wine in food processor until smooth paste forms, 20 to 30 seconds. Add shallot and pulse to combine, 3 to 5 pulses; transfer cheese mixture to bowl. In separate bowl, combine butter and mustard.

NOTES FROM THE TEST KITCHEN

Gluten-Free Sandwich Bread

When you're avoiding gluten, it's tough to give up toast and sandwiches. Enter gluten-free bread: a multi-billion-dollar industry that's rapidly expanding as the trend of avoiding gluten for dietary reasons continues to grow. Hoping to find a loaf that was a serviceable alternative to (not a sacrifice compared with) regular sandwich bread, we tasted eight national brands of gluten-free white sandwich bread, both plain and toasted with butter. Unfortunately, almost all of the breads were unappealing when eaten plain. Toasting and buttering turned a few inedible samples palatable, but most were still subpar by our sandwich bread standards. The exception: our winning bread, whose light wheaty taste and yielding chew were impressively close to that of regular white bread.

Udi's Gluten Free White Sandwich Bread has a clean, yeasty flavor and a moderate amount of chew, making it the best—and only worthwhile—alternative to regular sandwich bread. It contains far more protein than the competing breads—as much as 72 percent more—thanks to protein-rich egg whites. Like gluten, egg whites build structure by trapping air in the baking bread. Udi's also adds chemical leaveners and, of course, yeast, which contribute more lift, along with a generous amount of salt, which boosts flavor. You can find it in the freezer case at the supermarket (most gluten-free sandwich breads are sold frozen to prevent staling, which happens more quickly because the breads are high in moisture—as much as 55 percent compared with roughly 36 percent for regular sandwich bread).

2. Brush butter-mustard mixture evenly over 1 side of each slice of bread. Flip 4 slices over and spread processed cheese mixture evenly over second side. Top with remaining 4 slices bread, buttered side up, and press down gently.

3. Heat 12-inch nonstick skillet over medium heat for 2 minutes. Place 2 sandwiches in skillet, reduce heat to medium-low, and cook until both sides are crisp and golden brown, 6 to 9 minutes per side.

4. Transfer sandwiches to prepared wire rack and keep warm in oven. Wipe out skillet with paper towels and cook remaining 2 sandwiches. Serve.

VARIATIONS
Grilled Cheese Sandwiches with Gruyère and Chives FAST
Substitute room-temperature Gruyère cheese, cut into 24 equal pieces, for cheddar, hearty rye sandwich bread for white bread, and 4 teaspoons minced fresh chives for shallot.

Grilled Cheese Sandwiches with Asiago and Dates FAST
Substitute room-temperature Asiago cheese, cut into 24 equal pieces, for cheddar, hearty oatmeal sandwich bread for white bread, and 4 teaspoons finely chopped dates for shallot.

Portobello Panini
SERVES 4 FAST

✔ **WHY THIS RECIPE WORKS:** The meaty, hearty texture of portobello mushrooms makes them perfect for panini. Add melty fontina cheese, roasted red peppers, and an herbed mayonnaise, and you are guaranteed an irresistible meal. To ensure the mushrooms were tender, we precooked them in the grill pan before assembling and toasting the sandwiches. Shredding the fontina helped speed up the melting process and guaranteed an even layer of gooey cheese. To mimic the signature grill marks of a panini press, we used a nonstick grill pan and weighted the sandwiches down with a Dutch oven while they toasted on each side. The Dutch oven worked so well that we used it to weight the portobellos while they cooked as well. We like to use rustic, artisanal bread for this recipe; rather than a narrow baguette, look for a wide loaf that will yield big slices. We like the attractive grill marks that a grill pan gives the panini, but you can substitute a 12-inch nonstick skillet.

½ cup mayonnaise
4 garlic cloves, minced
1 teaspoon minced fresh rosemary or ¼ teaspoon dried

We use a grill pan and a heavy Dutch oven to get the crisp, browned crust that's essential to good panini.

6   **large portobello mushroom caps, halved**
6   **tablespoons extra-virgin olive oil**
¼   **teaspoon salt**
¼   **teaspoon pepper**
8   **(½-inch-thick) slices crusty bread**
8   **ounces fontina cheese, shredded (2 cups)**
½   **cup jarred roasted red peppers,**
    patted dry and sliced ½ inch thick

1. Adjust oven rack to middle position and heat oven to 200 degrees. Set wire rack in rimmed baking sheet. Combine mayonnaise, garlic, and rosemary in bowl. In separate bowl, toss mushrooms with ¼ cup oil, salt, and pepper.

2. Heat 12-inch nonstick grill pan over medium heat for 1 minute. Place mushrooms, gill side up, in pan and place Dutch oven on top. Cook until mushrooms are well browned on both sides, about 5 minutes per side. Transfer mushrooms to plate and wipe out pan with paper towels.

3. Brush remaining 2 tablespoons oil evenly over 1 side of each slice of bread. Flip bread over and spread mayonnaise mixture evenly over second side. Assemble 4 sandwiches by layering ingredients as follows between prepared bread (with

mayonnaise mixture inside sandwich): half of fontina, cooked mushrooms, red peppers, and remaining fontina. Press gently on sandwiches to set.

4. Return grill pan to medium heat for 1 minute. Place 2 sandwiches in pan, place Dutch oven on top, and cook until bread is golden and crisp on first side, about 4 minutes. Flip sandwiches, replace Dutch oven, and cook until second side is crisp and cheese is melted, about 4 minutes.

5. Transfer sandwiches to prepared wire rack and keep warm in oven. Wipe out grill pan with paper towels and cook remaining 2 sandwiches. Serve.

Cooking Panini in a Grill Pan

Place sandwiches in grill pan, place Dutch oven on top, and cook until bread is golden and crisp on first side, about 4 minutes. Flip sandwiches and cook until second side is crisp and cheese is melted, about 4 minutes.

Roasted Eggplant and Mozzarella Panini

SERVES 4   **FAST**

✓ **WHY THIS RECIPE WORKS:** With such a simple ingredient list, this classic Italian sandwich should be easy to make. But most versions have too much grease and not enough flavor. We wanted to punch up the flavor while staying true to the simplicity of the dish. To cut back on the greasiness, we chose to broil the eggplant instead of pan-frying it. Traditionally, the eggplant is layered with fresh tomatoes, mozzarella, and basil. But since we were already broiling the eggplant, we opted to broil the tomatoes as well, along with some garlic, deepening and rounding out their flavors. Once the tomatoes were nicely charred and had split open, we mashed them together with the roasted garlic and some red wine vinegar to make a chunky, bright tomato sauce. We layered the broiled eggplant with the tomato sauce, shredded mozzarella, and chopped fresh basil to make a bold, balanced eggplant panini that's even better than the classic.

1   **pound eggplant, sliced into ½-inch-thick rounds**
10   **ounces grape tomatoes**
2   **garlic cloves, peeled**
5   **tablespoons extra-virgin olive oil**

Salt and pepper
1   tablespoon red wine vinegar
8   (½-inch-thick) slices crusty bread
6   ounces mozzarella cheese, shredded (1½ cups)
½   cup coarsely chopped fresh basil

1. Adjust 1 oven rack 4 inches from broiler element and second rack to middle position, and heat broiler. Line rimmed baking sheet with aluminum foil and spray with vegetable oil spray. Spread eggplant, tomatoes, and garlic evenly over baking sheet and drizzle with 3 tablespoons oil. Sprinkle with ½ teaspoon salt and ¼ teaspoon pepper. Broil until vegetables are browned and tomatoes have split open, 8 to 10 minutes, flipping eggplant once during broiling.

2. Transfer tomatoes to small bowl and mash with fork. Mince roasted garlic and stir into tomatoes. Stir in vinegar, ½ teaspoon salt, and ¼ teaspoon pepper.

3. Reduce oven temperature to 200 degrees. Set wire rack in clean rimmed baking sheet. Brush remaining 2 tablespoons oil evenly over 1 side of each slice of bread. Assemble 4 sandwiches by layering ingredients as follows between prepared bread (with oiled sides outside sandwich): half of mozzarella, tomato sauce, eggplant, basil, and remaining mozzarella. Press gently on sandwiches to set.

4. Heat 12-inch nonstick grill pan over medium heat for 1 minute. Place 2 sandwiches in pan, place Dutch oven on top, and cook until bread is golden and crisp on first side, about 4 minutes. Flip sandwiches, replace Dutch oven, and cook until second side is crisp and cheese is melted, about 4 minutes.

5. Transfer sandwiches to prepared wire rack and keep warm in oven. Wipe out grill pan with paper towels and cook remaining 2 sandwiches. Serve.

NOTES FROM THE TEST KITCHEN

Storing Bread

Storing bread in the refrigerator to extend its shelf life may seem like a good idea, but this actually shortens it. The cool temperature of the fridge speeds up the staling process, and a loaf of refrigerated bread will go stale more quickly than an unrefrigerated loaf. Bread will last a few days stored in a bread box or simply cut side down on the counter. Do not store bread in plastic (the trapped moisture encourages mold). For longer storage, wrap the bread tightly in aluminum foil, place it in a zipper-lock bag, and store in the freezer for up to one month. To serve, bake the frozen foil-wrapped loaf directly on the rack of a 450-degree oven until warm and crisp, 10 to 30 minutes.

To give these French sandwiches a bright flavor, we add a green olive tapenade to the roasted zucchini and goat cheese.

French Summer Sandwiches with Zucchini and Olive Tapenade

SERVES 4   **FAST**

✔ **WHY THIS RECIPE WORKS:** To make an interesting summer vegetable sandwich, we put a twist on the ubiquitous combination of pesto, tomato, and mozzarella. We kept the focus on fresh summer vegetables by pairing tender mesclun with zucchini and mint. We tried simply adding the zucchini to the sandwich without cooking it, but no matter how thinly we shaved it, it tasted raw, so we roasted it to get it softened and nicely caramelized. While the zucchini roasted, we made the fastest-ever olive tapenade by pulsing fruity green olives, lemon juice, shallot, garlic, and capers in the food processor. We spread some rich, creamy goat cheese over a baguette, drizzled it with our superflavorful tapenade, and layered in the roasted zucchini. Finally, we tossed the mesclun and mint with oil and lemon juice and topped our sandwich. The end result was a nuanced but simple summer vegetable sandwich.

2 zucchini, cut in half crosswise, then sliced lengthwise into ¼-inch-thick planks

5 tablespoons extra-virgin olive oil
  Salt and pepper

10 pitted green olives

1 tablespoon minced shallot

1 tablespoon lemon juice

1 small garlic clove, minced

1 teaspoon capers, drained

1½ ounces (1½ cups) mesclun

⅓ cup minced fresh mint

4 ounces goat cheese, softened

1 (24-inch) baguette, cut crosswise into 4 equal lengths and sliced in half lengthwise

1. Adjust oven rack to middle position and heat oven to 425 degrees. Toss zucchini with 2 tablespoons oil, ½ teaspoon salt, and ¼ teaspoon pepper, then spread in single layer on aluminum foil–lined rimmed baking sheet. Bake until zucchini are spotty brown on both sides, about 15 minutes, flipping halfway through baking.

2. Meanwhile, pulse olives, 2 tablespoons oil, shallot, 1 teaspoon lemon juice, garlic, and capers in food processor until mixture forms slightly chunky paste, about 10 pulses (do not overprocess). Whisk remaining 1 tablespoon oil and remaining 2 teaspoons lemon juice together in medium bowl. Add mesclun and mint and toss to coat. Season with salt and pepper to taste.

3. Spread goat cheese evenly over cut sides of each baguette. Assemble 4 sandwiches by layering ingredients as follows between prepared baguettes: olive tapenade, zucchini, and mesclun mixture. Press gently on sandwiches to set. Serve.

VARIATION

French Summer Sandwiches with Roasted Tomatoes and Olive Tapenade FAST

Substitute 4 plum tomatoes, cored and cut in half lengthwise, for zucchini, and basil for mint.

Philly-Style Broccoli Rabe, Portobello, and Cheese Sandwiches

SERVES 4 FAST

✔ WHY THIS RECIPE WORKS: We wanted to make a vegetarian version of Philly's famous cheesesteak. First we swapped out the steak for meaty, umami-rich portobellos. To give the sandwich a more complex and satisfying texture, we added subtly bitter, hearty broccoli rabe. We sautéed the broccoli rabe with some garlic and pepper flakes for heat and then

We stuff our Philly-style sandwiches with meaty portobello mushrooms, crisp-tender broccoli rabe, and American cheese.

tossed it with vinegar before letting it sit while we cooked the mushrooms. To mimic the traditional thinly shaved steak, we cut the mushrooms into thin slices and sautéed them until they were nicely browned and flavorful. Once the mushrooms were cooked, we stirred in the broccoli rabe. To bind it all together, we let slices of American cheese melt into the vegetables to make a rich, cohesive filling that we piled high on toasted sub rolls.

3 tablespoons vegetable oil

2 garlic cloves, sliced thin

⅛ teaspoon red pepper flakes

¾ pound broccoli rabe, trimmed and cut into ½-inch pieces

2 tablespoons water
  Salt and pepper

2 tablespoons balsamic vinegar

6 portobello mushroom caps, gills removed, halved, and sliced thin

10 slices (10 ounces) deli American cheese

4 (8-inch) Italian sub rolls, split lengthwise and toasted

1. Heat 1 tablespoon oil in 12-inch nonstick skillet over medium heat until shimmering. Add garlic and pepper flakes and cook for 1 minute. Stir in broccoli rabe, water, and ½ teaspoon salt. Cover and cook until broccoli rabe is bright green and crisp-tender, 3 to 4 minutes. Off heat, stir in vinegar, then transfer to bowl.

2. Heat remaining 2 tablespoons oil in now-empty skillet over medium-high heat until shimmering. Add mushrooms (skillet will be very full), cover, and cook, stirring occasionally, until mushrooms release their liquid, 6 to 8 minutes. Uncover and continue to cook until moisture has evaporated and mushrooms begin to brown, 6 to 8 minutes.

3. Stir broccoli rabe back into skillet and season with salt and pepper to taste. Reduce heat to low and shingle cheese over vegetables. Cook until cheese is melted, about 2 minutes. Fold melted cheese thoroughly into mushroom mixture. Divide mixture evenly among toasted rolls. Serve.

Tofu Banh Mi

SERVES 4 **FAST**

👨‍🍳 **WHY THIS RECIPE WORKS:** In Vietnam, *banh mi* is simply a term for all kinds of bread, but in the United States most people recognize it as a Vietnamese-style sandwich featuring chicken, pork, or tofu and crunchy pickled vegetables. For our own version, we started by making crispy, flavorful tofu. We sliced the tofu into sandwich-size slabs and drained them on paper towels to make it easier to get a crispy crust. Then we dredged the slabs in cornstarch and seared them in a hot skillet until they were nicely browned. For the vegetables, we quick-pickled cucumber slices and shredded carrot in lime juice and our vegetarian fish sauce substitute. Sriracha-spiked mayonnaise gave the sandwich a spicy kick, while a sprinkling of fresh cilantro added an authentic garnish.

Our Vietnamese-style *banh mi* sandwiches feature crispy tofu, fresh cilantro, and pickled carrots and cucumber.

14   ounces firm tofu, sliced crosswise into
      ½-inch-thick slabs
      Salt and pepper
⅓   cup cornstarch
2   carrots, peeled and shredded
½   cucumber, peeled, halved lengthwise,
      seeded, and sliced thin
1   teaspoon grated lime zest plus 1 tablespoon juice
1   tablespoon fish sauce substitute (see page 60)
¼   cup mayonnaise
1   tablespoon Sriracha sauce
3   tablespoons vegetable oil
4   (8-inch) Italian sub rolls, split lengthwise and
      toasted
⅓   cup fresh cilantro leaves

1. Spread tofu over paper towel–lined baking sheet, let drain for 20 minutes, then gently press dry with paper towels and season with salt and pepper. Spread cornstarch in shallow dish. Dredge tofu in cornstarch and transfer to plate.

2. Meanwhile, combine carrots, cucumber, lime juice, and fish sauce in bowl and let sit for 15 minutes. Whisk mayonnaise, Sriracha, and lime zest together in separate bowl.

3. Heat oil in 12-inch nonstick skillet over medium-high heat until just smoking. Add tofu and cook until both sides are crisp and browned, about 4 minutes per side. Transfer to paper towel–lined plate.

4. Spread mayonnaise mixture evenly over cut sides of each roll. Assemble 4 sandwiches by layering ingredients as follows between prepared rolls: tofu, pickled vegetables (leaving liquid in bowl), and cilantro. Press gently on sandwiches to set. Serve.

Tempeh Reubens

SERVES 4

✔ **WHY THIS RECIPE WORKS:** Because a good Reuben is all about the combination of corned beef, Russian dressing, Swiss cheese, and rye bread, we needed a clever solution when replacing the corned beef with a vegetarian option. We chose hearty tempeh for its firm texture and its ability to stand up to strong flavors. To impart the tempeh with the true flavor of corned beef, we decided to "corn" it. Compared with traditional corned beef, which takes upward of 4 hours, corning tempeh was remarkably easy—just a 10-minute simmer in a traditional corning brine was enough to impart the distinctive flavor without making the tempeh too salty. Then we browned the tempeh in a skillet to give it a nice crust. To make a quick Russian dressing, we started with prepared cocktail sauce and mixed it with creamy mayonnaise, crunchy pickles, and some tart pickle juice. The result was a dressing with great flavor and a satisfying crunch. We topped the sandwiches with sauerkraut and Swiss cheese and toasted them in a skillet until the cheese was melted and the bread was crisp and golden brown. For more information on cutting tempeh into slabs, see page 235.

10 tablespoons cider vinegar
½ cup water
2 teaspoons ground allspice
1½ teaspoons salt
1 teaspoon black peppercorns, cracked
1 teaspoon dried thyme
1 teaspoon paprika
1 pound tempeh, cut into 3½-inch-long by ⅜-inch-thick slabs
1 cup sauerkraut, drained and rinsed
1 teaspoon packed brown sugar
¼ cup vegetable oil
¼ cup mayonnaise
¼ cup finely chopped sweet pickles plus 1 teaspoon pickle brine
2 tablespoons cocktail sauce
4 tablespoons unsalted butter, melted
8 slices hearty rye bread
4 ounces Swiss cheese, shredded (1 cup)

1. Combine ½ cup vinegar, water, allspice, salt, peppercorns, thyme, and paprika in large saucepan and bring to simmer over medium heat. Add tempeh, cover, reduce heat to medium-low, and simmer until liquid is mostly absorbed, 10 to 15 minutes, turning tempeh halfway through cooking. Transfer tempeh to plate and let cool for 10 minutes.

2. Meanwhile, cook sauerkraut, remaining 2 tablespoons vinegar, and sugar in 12-inch nonstick skillet over medium-high heat, stirring occasionally, until liquid evaporates,

Making Tempeh Reubens

1. CORN TEMPEH: Combine vinegar, water, allspice, salt, peppercorns, thyme, and paprika in large saucepan and bring to simmer over medium heat. Add tempeh, cover, reduce heat to medium-low, and simmer until liquid is mostly absorbed, 10 to 15 minutes, turning tempeh halfway through cooking.

2. COOK SAUERKRAUT AND MAKE DRESSING: Cook sauerkraut, vinegar, and sugar in 12-inch nonstick skillet over medium-high heat, stirring occasionally, until liquid evaporates, about 3 minutes; transfer to bowl. Whisk mayonnaise, pickles and brine, and cocktail sauce together in bowl.

3. BROWN TEMPEH: Heat 2 tablespoons oil in now-empty skillet over medium heat until shimmering. Add tempeh and cook until golden brown on first side, 2 to 4 minutes. Flip tempeh, reduce heat to medium-low, and continue to cook until golden brown on second side, 2 to 4 minutes.

4. ASSEMBLE REUBENS AND TOAST: Assemble sandwiches by layering half of Swiss, tempeh, sauerkraut, and remaining Swiss between prepared bread. Cook sandwiches over medium-low heat until golden brown on first side, about 2 minutes. Flip sandwiches, cover skillet, and cook until second side is golden brown and cheese is melted, about 2 minutes.

about 3 minutes; transfer to bowl. Wipe out skillet with paper towels.

3. Heat 2 tablespoons oil in now-empty skillet over medium heat until shimmering. Add 4 pieces tempeh and cook until golden brown on first side, 2 to 4 minutes. Flip tempeh, reduce heat to medium-low, and continue to cook until golden brown on second side, 2 to 4 minutes; transfer to clean plate. Wipe out skillet with paper towels and repeat with remaining 2 tablespoons oil and remaining tempeh. Wipe out skillet with paper towels.

4. Whisk mayonnaise, pickles and brine, and cocktail sauce together in bowl. Brush melted butter evenly over 1 side of each slice of bread. Flip bread over and spread mayonnaise mixture evenly over second side. Assemble 4 sandwiches by layering ingredients as follows between prepared bread (with mayonnaise mixture inside sandwich): half of Swiss, tempeh, sauerkraut, remaining Swiss. Press gently on sandwiches to set.

5. Heat now-empty skillet over medium-low heat for 2 minutes. Place 2 sandwiches in pan and cook until golden brown on first side, about 2 minutes. Flip sandwiches, cover skillet, and cook until second side is golden brown and cheese is melted, about 2 minutes. Transfer sandwiches to serving platter. Wipe out skillet with paper towels and cook remaining 2 sandwiches. Serve.

Veggie Wraps with Hummus

SERVES 4 **FAST** **VEGAN**

✔ **WHY THIS RECIPE WORKS:** Often the only vegetarian sandwich option at a deli is a disappointing veggie wrap with bleak lettuce and tomatoes, and bland hummus. We wanted to reinvent this simple sandwich with plenty of fresh veggies and balanced flavors. We started by tossing peppery sliced radishes and sweet shredded carrots with a simple lemon and parsley dressing. For the bread, we mixed things up by swapping out the usual tortilla for lavash, a soft, thin Middle Eastern flatbread. We spread a hefty amount of creamy hummus on each wrap, then added the carrots and radishes. Topped with juicy tomatoes, buttery sliced avocados, and crunchy alfalfa sprouts, this sandwich makes a perfect light, healthy lunch. We like to use our Classic Hummus (page 406) here; however, you can use store-bought hummus.

- 2 tablespoons minced fresh parsley
- 1 teaspoon grated lemon zest plus
  2 tablespoons juice
- ¼ teaspoon salt
- ¼ teaspoon pepper

- 3 tablespoons extra-virgin olive oil
- 2 carrots, peeled and shredded
- 4 radishes, trimmed, halved, and sliced thin
- 4 pieces lavash bread
- 1⅓ cups plain hummus
- 2 tomatoes, cored and sliced thin
- 2 avocados, halved, pitted, and sliced thin
- 4 ounces alfalfa sprouts

1. Whisk parsley, lemon zest and juice, salt, and pepper together in bowl. Whisking constantly, slowly drizzle in oil until emulsified. Add carrots and radishes and toss to coat.

2. Lay lavash on counter and spread ⅓ cup hummus over each piece. Divide tomatoes, avocados, alfalfa sprouts, and carrot mixture evenly among lavash. Fold sides of lavash over filling, fold bottom of lavash over sides and filling, and roll tightly into wrap. Slice in half and serve.

Korean Barbecue Tempeh Wraps

SERVES 4 **FAST** **VEGAN**

✔ **WHY THIS RECIPE WORKS:** With bold flavors and sweet, sticky sauce, barbecue chicken wraps are always a hit. We decided to translate those winning flavors into a vegetarian wrap. For the protein, we chose tempeh, which has a great firm, chewy texture that stood out from the vegetables in the wrap. To give the tempeh a flavorful browned crust, we seared it in a skillet before tossing it with the barbecue sauce. Store-bought barbecue sauces are often too sweet and one-note, so we decided to make our own. To balance the flavor of the tempeh with both sweetness and a little heat, we chose a Korean-style barbecue sauce. A combination of soy sauce, sugar, and spicy Sriracha sauce paired perfectly with the flavor of the tempeh. Adding some cornstarch and simmering the sauce for 5 minutes gave it a thick, luscious consistency that clung nicely to the tempeh. We tossed half of the barbecue sauce with the tempeh, then we drizzled the other half over the vegetables so the wrap would have great flavors throughout. Thinly sliced baby bok choy, whole cilantro leaves, sliced radishes, and scallions lent bright flavor and freshness.

- ¾ cup sugar
- 6 tablespoons soy sauce
- 6 tablespoons water
- 5 garlic cloves, minced
- 1½ tablespoons rice vinegar
- 1½ teaspoons Sriracha sauce
- 1½ teaspoons cornstarch

To give this simple tempeh wrap great flavor, we make our own sweet and spicy Korean-style barbecue sauce.

¼   cup vegetable oil
1   pound tempeh, cut crosswise into
     ½-inch-thick strips
4   (10-inch) flour tortillas
2   heads baby bok choy (4 ounces each),
     sliced thin crosswise
1   cup fresh cilantro leaves
3   radishes, trimmed, halved, and sliced thin
2   scallions, sliced thin

1. Whisk sugar, soy sauce, water, garlic, rice vinegar, Sriracha, and cornstarch together in bowl; set aside. Heat 2 tablespoons oil in 12-inch nonstick skillet over medium heat until shimmering. Add half of tempeh and cook until golden brown on both sides, 2 to 4 minutes per side. Transfer to paper towel–lined plate. Repeat with remaining 2 tablespoons oil and remaining tempeh.

2. Add sugar-soy mixture to now-empty skillet and bring to simmer over medium-low heat. Cook until thickened and reduced to about 1 cup, about 5 minutes. Transfer tempeh to bowl, add half of sauce, and toss to coat. Lay tortillas on counter, then divide tempeh evenly among tortillas. Top evenly with

bok choy, cilantro, radishes, and scallions, then drizzle each wrap with 1 tablespoon sauce. Fold sides of tortilla over filling, fold bottom of tortilla over sides and filling, and roll tightly. Slice in half and serve, passing remaining sauce separately.

Falafel

MAKES 20 TO 25 FALAFEL, SERVES 4   **VEGAN**   **GF**

✔ **WHY THIS RECIPE WORKS:** Falafel are a Middle Eastern specialty of savory fried chickpea balls or patties generously seasoned with herbs and spices. The best falafel have a moist, light interior and a well-browned, crisp crust. Traditionally, the chickpeas aren't precooked, but rather are soaked overnight in a saltwater solution; the salt weakens the cell structure of the chickpea skins, allowing the chickpeas to absorb more water and giving them a softer texture. Once the chickpeas were softened, we ground them with fresh herbs and warm spices: scallions, parsley, cilantro, garlic, cumin, and cinnamon. Then we shaped and fried the falafel. We found that smaller falafel (about 1 tablespoon each) had the perfect ratio of crispy crust to tender interior. They fit nicely into a sandwich, and they were also just the right size—two bites—for an appetizer. We served the falafel with a simple creamy tahini sauce. The chickpeas in this recipe must be soaked overnight; you cannot substitute canned beans or quick-soaked chickpeas because their texture will be soggy. Serve the falafel in lavash or pita bread with lettuce, pickled vegetables, and chopped tomatoes or cucumbers, or as hors d'oeuvres with the tahini sauce as a dip.

     Salt and pepper
1   cup dried chickpeas, picked over and rinsed
5   scallions, chopped coarse
½   cup fresh parsley leaves
½   cup fresh cilantro leaves
3   garlic cloves, minced
¼   teaspoon ground cumin
⅛   teaspoon ground cinnamon
2   cups vegetable oil
1   recipe Tahini Sauce (page 362)

1. Dissolve 1½ tablespoons salt in 2 quarts cold water in large container. Add chickpeas and soak at room temperature for at least 8 hours or up to 24 hours. Drain and rinse well.

2. Process chickpeas, scallions, parsley, cilantro, garlic, cumin, cinnamon, ½ teaspoon salt, and ½ teaspoon pepper in food processor until smooth, about 1 minute, scraping down sides of bowl as needed. Form mixture into 1 tablespoon–size disks, about ½ inch thick and 1 inch wide, and place on

TAHINI SAUCE

MAKES ABOUT 1¼ CUPS `FAST` `VEGAN` `GF`

½ cup tahini
½ cup water
¼ cup lemon juice (2 lemons)
2 garlic cloves, minced
   Salt

Process tahini, water, lemon juice, and garlic in food processor until smooth, about 20 seconds. Season with salt to taste and serve. (Sauce can be refrigerated for up to 4 days. Bring to room temperature and stir to combine before serving.)

We toss the rice noodles and vegetables for our fresh spring rolls with a mix of lime juice, fish sauce substitute, and sugar.

parchment paper–lined baking sheet. (Falafel can be refrigerated for up to 2 hours.)

3. Adjust oven rack to middle position and heat oven to 200 degrees. Set wire rack in rimmed baking sheet. Heat oil in 12-inch skillet over medium-high heat to 375 degrees. Fry half of falafel, flipping halfway through cooking and adjusting heat as needed to maintain 375 degrees, until deep brown, about 5 minutes. Transfer to prepared sheet and keep warm in oven. Return oil to 375 degrees and repeat with remaining falafel. Serve with Tahini Sauce.

Fresh Vegetable Spring Rolls

MAKES 8 SPRING ROLLS `FAST` `VEGAN` `GF`

✔ **WHY THIS RECIPE WORKS:** Fresh spring rolls should offer a pleasing contrast in texture (soft wrapper, chewy noodles, and crunchy vegetables) and in flavor (fresh mint, basil, and cilantro; peanuts, spicy chiles, and salty sauce). But too often, spring rolls disappoint, with gummy noodles and bland vegetables. We set out to develop a recipe for foolproof spring rolls with fresh, bright flavors. We started by boiling the rice noodles, then we tossed them with carrots, peanuts, and jalapeño in a combination of lime juice, fish sauce substitute, and sugar. Before rolling the filling up in the rice paper wrappers, we soaked the wrappers in water just long enough to make them pliable. Finally, we made a spicy, not-too-sweet hoisin-peanut sauce for dipping. If you can't find Thai basil, do not substitute regular basil; its flavor is too gentle to stand up to the other, more assertive flavors in the filling. Mint makes a better substitute. Be sure to make only one spring roll at a time to keep the wrappers moist and pliable.

2½ tablespoons lime juice (2 limes)
1½ tablespoons fish sauce substitute (see page 60)
1 teaspoon sugar
3 ounces rice vermicelli
1 teaspoon salt
1 large carrot, peeled and shredded
⅓ cup chopped dry-roasted peanuts
1 jalapeño chile or 2 Thai chiles, stemmed, seeded, and minced
1 large cucumber, peeled, halved lengthwise, seeded, and cut into matchsticks
4 leaves red leaf lettuce or Boston lettuce, halved lengthwise
8 (8-inch) round rice paper wrappers
½ cup fresh Thai basil or mint, small leaves left whole, medium and large leaves torn into ½-inch pieces
½ cup fresh cilantro leaves
1 recipe Hoisin-Peanut Dipping Sauce (page 363)

1. Combine lime juice, fish sauce, and sugar in bowl.
2. Bring 4 quarts water to boil in large pot. Remove from heat, stir in rice vermicelli and salt, and let sit, stirring

occasionally, until noodles are tender but not mushy, about 10 minutes. Drain noodles, transfer to medium bowl, and toss with 2 tablespoons fish sauce mixture.

3. Toss carrot, peanuts, and jalapeño with 1 tablespoon fish sauce mixture in small bowl. Toss cucumber with remaining 1 tablespoon fish sauce mixture in separate bowl.

4. Arrange lettuce on platter. Spread clean, damp dish towel on counter. Fill 9-inch pie plate with 1 inch room-temperature water. Submerge each wrapper in water until just pliable, about 2 minutes; lay softened wrapper on towel. Scatter about 6 basil leaves and 6 cilantro leaves over wrapper. Arrange 5 cucumber sticks horizontally on wrapper, leaving 2-inch border at bottom. Top with 1 tablespoon carrot mixture, then arrange about 2½ tablespoons noodles on top of carrot mixture. Fold bottom of wrapper up over filling. Fold sides of wrapper over filling, then roll wrapper up into tight spring roll. Set spring roll on 1 lettuce piece on platter. Cover with second damp dish towel.

5. Repeat with remaining wrappers and filling. Serve with peanut dipping sauce, wrapping lettuce around exterior of each roll. (Spring rolls are best eaten immediately but can be covered with clean, damp dish towel and refrigerated for up to 4 hours.)

Assembling Spring Rolls

1. Fill 9-inch pie plate with 1 inch room-temperature water. Submerge wrapper in water until just pliable, about 2 minutes; lay softened wrapper on towel.

2. After layering herbs, cucumber, carrot mixture, and noodles on rice paper wrapper, fold up bottom 2-inch border of wrapper over filling.

3. Fold sides of wrapper over filling and roll wrapper up into tight spring roll.

HOISIN-PEANUT DIPPING SAUCE

MAKES ABOUT ¾ CUP **FAST** **VEGAN** **GF**

In order for this recipe to be gluten-free, you must use gluten-free hoisin sauce.

- ¼ **cup creamy peanut butter**
- ¼ **cup hoisin sauce**
- ¼ **cup water**
- 2 **tablespoons tomato paste**
- 1 **teaspoon Asian chili-garlic sauce (optional)**
- 2 **teaspoons vegetable oil**
- 2 **garlic cloves, minced**
- 1 **teaspoon red pepper flakes**

Whisk peanut butter, hoisin, water, tomato paste, and chili-garlic sauce, if using, together in bowl. Heat oil, garlic, and pepper flakes in small saucepan over medium heat until fragrant, 1 to 2 minutes. Stir in peanut butter mixture and bring to simmer. Reduce heat to medium-low and cook, stirring occasionally, until flavors meld, about 3 minutes. (Sauce should have ketchup-like consistency; if too thick, add water, 1 teaspoon at a time, until proper consistency is reached.) Transfer sauce to bowl and let cool to room temperature. (Sauce can be refrigerated for up to 3 days. Bring to room temperature before serving.)

NOTES FROM THE TEST KITCHEN

Juicing Lemons and Limes

We've tried countless methods and gizmos for juicing lemons and limes and have dismissed most of them. However, we do endorse rolling lemons vigorously on a hard surface before slicing them open to be juiced. Why? Rolling a lemon on a hard surface bruises, breaks up, and softens the rind's tissues while it tears the membranes of the juice vesicles (the tear-shaped juice sacs), filling the inside of the lemon with juice before it is cut and squeezed. Once the lemon is rolled, we recommend either a wooden reamer or a juicer, which we have found to be especially easy and fast, and equally effective.

However you squeeze them, we strongly recommend that you squeeze lemon or lime juice at the last minute; our testing has proven that the flavor mellows quickly and the juice will taste bland in a short time.

Sizzling Saigon Crêpes (Banh Xeo)

MAKES 9 CRÊPES, SERVES 8 `VEGAN` `GF`

✔ **WHY THIS RECIPE WORKS:** Named for the sound these crêpes make when the batter hits a hot wok, sizzling Saigon crêpes are best described as paper-thin Vietnamese omelets. These crispy yellow rice-flour crêpes, usually stuffed with pork and shrimp, are wrapped with lettuce and herbs and dipped into a sweet-tart dipping sauce. For our vegetarian version, we chose a simple filling of shredded carrots, onions, and bean sprouts. The batter for the crêpes is simple: just water, rice flour, and coconut milk. To give them a subtle savory flavor, we added scallions and turmeric. To make the flipping and folding of these delicate crêpes easier, we cooked them in a 10-inch nonstick skillet instead of a traditional wok. For the dressing, we combined fish sauce substitute with lime juice, sugar, minced fresh chiles, and garlic. Rice flour is available at some supermarkets and can also be found in natural foods stores; you cannot substitute regular flour or cornstarch for the rice flour. Make sure to stir the coconut milk thoroughly before measuring out the desired amount. To make this dish spicier, add in the chile ribs and seeds. If you can't find Thai basil, you can substitute regular basil. To allow for practice, the recipe yields one extra crêpe.

DRESSING AND GARNISH
- ⅓ cup fish sauce substitute (see page 60)
- ¼ cup warm water
- 3 tablespoons lime juice (2 limes)
- 2 tablespoons sugar
- 2 Thai, serrano, or jalapeño chiles, stemmed, seeded, and minced
- 1 garlic clove, minced
- 2 heads red or green leaf lettuce, leaves separated and left whole
- 1 cup fresh Thai basil leaves
- 1 cup fresh cilantro leaves

CRÊPES
- 2¾ cups water
- 1¾ cups rice flour
- ½ cup coconut milk
- 4 scallions, sliced thin
- Salt
- 1 teaspoon ground turmeric
- ¼ cup vegetable oil
- 1 onion, halved and sliced thin
- 1 pound carrots, peeled and shredded
- 6 ounces (3 cups) bean sprouts

1. FOR THE DRESSING AND GARNISH: Whisk fish sauce, water, lime juice, sugar, chiles, and garlic together in bowl until sugar dissolves. Divide dressing among 6 small dipping bowls. Arrange lettuce, basil, and cilantro on serving platter.

2. FOR THE CRÊPES: Adjust oven rack to middle position and heat oven to 200 degrees. Set wire rack in rimmed baking sheet. Whisk water, flour, coconut milk, scallions, 1 teaspoon salt, and turmeric together in bowl until combined.

3. Heat 1 tablespoon oil in 10-inch nonstick skillet over medium-high heat until shimmering. Add onion and ½ teaspoon salt and cook until onion is softened, 5 to 7 minutes.

Cooking Saigon Crêpes

1. Quickly stir batter to recombine, then pour ½ cup batter into skillet while swirling pan gently to distribute evenly over pan bottom.

2. Reduce heat to medium and cook crêpe until edges pull away from sides and are deep golden, 3 to 5 minutes. Gently slide spatula underneath edge of crêpe, grasp edge with fingertips, and flip crêpe.

3. Slide crêpe out of skillet and onto wire rack set in rimmed baking sheet; transfer to 200-degree oven to keep warm.

We stuff crisp rice-flour crêpes with a savory filling then wrap wedges of them in lettuce for dipping in a sweet-tart sauce.

Transfer to bowl. Add carrots to skillet and cook until tender, about 2 minutes. Transfer to bowl with onions and let cool slightly. Stir in bean sprouts.

4. Wipe out skillet with paper towels. Heat 1 teaspoon oil in now-empty skillet over medium-high heat until just smoking. Quickly stir batter to recombine, then pour ½ cup batter into skillet while swirling pan gently to distribute it evenly over pan bottom. Reduce heat to medium and cook crêpe until edges pull away from sides and are deep golden, 3 to 5 minutes.

5. Gently slide spatula underneath edge of crêpe, grasp edge with fingertips, and flip crêpe. Cook until spotty brown on second side, 2 to 3 minutes. Slide crêpe out of skillet and onto prepared wire rack and transfer to oven to keep warm. Repeat with remaining oil and remaining batter.

6. Divide carrot mixture evenly among crêpes and fold crêpes in half. Serve crêpes with dipping sauce, passing garnish platter separately. (To eat, slice off wedge of crêpe, wrap in lettuce leaf, sprinkle with basil and cilantro, and dip into sauce.)

Soft Corn Tacos with Sweet Potato, Poblanos, and Corn

SERVES 4 TO 6 **GF**

✅ **WHY THIS RECIPE WORKS:** Whether it's chicken, steak, pork, or fish, tacos are usually focused on the meat. We wanted to make a great-tasting taco that was all about the vegetables. We started by testing a wide variety of vegetables to find the best combination. Spring vegetables like asparagus and peas didn't feel right here, and vegetables like carrots and celery were too crunchy to make a soft taco filling. We had better success with sweet vegetables that blended nicely with heat and warm spices. Our favorite combination turned out to be sweet potatoes, poblano peppers, and corn. To balance their sweet flavors, we seasoned the vegetables with plenty of garlic, cumin, coriander, and oregano. Then we spread all of the vegetables out on baking sheets and roasted them to get crunchy, caramelized exteriors and tender interiors. Finally, we piled the warm vegetables in soft tacos and topped them with crumbled *queso fresco,* tangy pickled shallots and radishes, and a rich Mexican crema. Crumbled feta can be substituted for the queso fresco.

3 tablespoons extra-virgin olive oil
3 garlic cloves, minced
1½ teaspoons ground cumin
1½ teaspoons ground coriander
1 teaspoon minced fresh oregano
or ¼ teaspoon dried
1 teaspoon salt
½ teaspoon pepper
1 pound sweet potatoes, peeled and
cut into ½-inch pieces
4 poblano chiles, stemmed, seeded,
and cut into ½-inch-wide strips
3 ears corn, kernels cut from cobs
1 large onion, halved and sliced ½ inch thick
¼ cup minced fresh cilantro
12 (6-inch) corn tortillas, warmed
2 ounces queso fresco, crumbled (½ cup)
1 recipe Quick Pickled Shallots and
Radishes (page 366)
1 recipe Mexican Crema (page 366)

1. Adjust oven racks to upper-middle and lower middle-positions and heat oven to 450 degrees. Whisk oil, garlic, cumin, coriander, oregano, salt, and pepper together in large bowl. Add potatoes, poblanos, corn, and onion to bowl and toss to coat.

2. Spread vegetable mixture in even layer over 2 rimmed baking sheets. Bake vegetables until tender and golden brown, about 30 minutes, stirring vegetables and switching and rotating sheets halfway through baking.

3. Return vegetables to now-empty large bowl, add cilantro, and toss to combine. Divide vegetables evenly among tortillas and top with queso fresco, pickles, and crema. Serve.

Warming Tortillas

Toast tortillas on gas stove over medium flame until charred around edges, 30 seconds per side. Or toast tortillas in dry skillet over medium-high heat until softened and speckled brown, 30 seconds per side.

QUICK PICKLED SHALLOTS AND RADISHES

MAKES ABOUT 1 CUP

  5 **radishes, trimmed and sliced thin**
  1 **shallot, sliced thin**
  ¼ **cup lime juice (2 limes)**
  1 **teaspoon sugar**
  ⅛ **teaspoon salt**

Combine all ingredients in bowl and serve.

MEXICAN CREMA

MAKES ABOUT ½ CUP
You can substitute plain yogurt for the sour cream in this recipe.

  ¼ **cup heavy cream**
  3 **tablespoons sour cream**
  ¼ **teaspoon finely grated lime zest**
      plus 1 teaspoon juice
  1 **teaspoon minced fresh cilantro**
  ½ **teaspoon extra-virgin olive oil**

Combine all ingredients in bowl and serve.

To balance the rich cheese and beans in our baked burritos, we add hearty, healthy Swiss chard to the mix.

Baked Burritos with Pinto Beans and Swiss Chard

SERVES 6

✔ **WHY THIS RECIPE WORKS:** To create an interesting burrito that balanced the usual rich beans and cheese with a fresh, hearty vegetable, we decided to add a pound of flavorful Swiss chard to our filling, simmering the leaves in vegetable broth until tender. The tough stems take much longer to soften than the leaves, so we left them out to save time. To give the filling a cohesive texture, we mashed some of the beans with more vegetable broth. To build a base of savory flavor, we sautéed onion until softened, then cooked tomato paste, garlic, cumin, oregano, and chipotle chile until fragrant before adding the chard and broth to the pan. White rice, cooked in flavorful broth and sprinkled with fresh cilantro, ensured our burritos were satisfying. For the cheese, we chose mild and easy-melting Monterey Jack cheese. We added some to the filling and sprinkled more on top of the rolled burritos, then broiled them until the cheese was melted and browned.

2¼ cups vegetable broth

¾ cup long-grain white rice, rinsed

6 garlic cloves, minced

Salt

¼ cup minced fresh cilantro

1 tablespoon vegetable oil

1 onion, chopped fine

3 tablespoons tomato paste

1 teaspoon minced chipotle chile in adobo sauce

1 tablespoon ground cumin

1 teaspoon dried oregano

1 pound Swiss chard, stemmed, leaves sliced into 1-inch-wide strips

1 (15-ounce) can pinto beans, rinsed

1 tablespoon lime juice

6 (10-inch) flour tortillas

10 ounces Monterey jack, shredded (2½ cups)

1. Bring 1¼ cups broth, rice, half of garlic, and ½ teaspoon salt to boil in small saucepan over medium-high heat. Cover, reduce heat to low, and cook until rice is tender and broth is absorbed, about 20 minutes. Remove rice from heat and let sit, covered, for 10 minutes. Add cilantro and fluff with fork to incorporate; cover to keep warm.

2. Meanwhile, heat oil in Dutch oven over medium heat until shimmering. Add onion and cook until just beginning to brown, about 5 minutes. Stir in tomato paste, chipotle, cumin, oregano, remaining garlic, and ½ teaspoon salt and cook until fragrant, about 1 minute. Add chard and ½ cup broth, cover, and simmer until chard is tender, about 15 minutes.

3. Using potato masher, coarsely mash half of beans with remaining ½ cup broth in bowl, then stir into pot. Cook, stirring constantly, until liquid is nearly evaporated, about 3 minutes. Off heat, stir in lime juice and remaining whole beans; cover to keep warm.

4. Adjust oven rack 6 inches from broiler element and heat broiler. Wrap tortillas in damp dish towel and microwave until warm and pliable, about 1 minute. Lay warm tortillas on counter. Mound warm rice, chard-bean mixture, and 1½ cups Monterey Jack across center of tortillas, close to bottom edge. Working with 1 tortilla at a time, fold sides of tortilla over filling, then fold up bottom of tortilla, pulling back on it firmly to tighten it around filling and continue to roll tightly into burrito.

5. Place burritos, seam side down, on aluminum foil–lined baking sheet, and sprinkle remaining 1 cup Monterey Jack over top. Broil until cheese is melted and starting to brown, 3 to 5 minutes. Serve.

Burritos with Tofu, Poblanos, and Tomatillos

SERVES 6

✓ WHY THIS RECIPE WORKS: With its creamy texture and exceptional ability to soak up flavor, tofu is the perfect choice for a burrito filling. We wanted to pair it with fresh, mildly spicy poblano chiles and plenty of flavorful spices and aromatics. First, we cooked white rice with broth and minced garlic to give it good savory flavor, then we tossed it with fresh cilantro. To ensure we'd have distinct bites of tofu in the filling, we drained the tofu on paper towels for 20 minutes, coarsely chopped it in the food processor, then browned it in a skillet. Next we bloomed a hefty amount of cumin and garlic along with some oregano to create a good base of flavor. To finish the filling, we added in tomatillos (also quickly chopped in the food processor), the poblanos, onions, and a jalapeño for a little more heat. We let the vegetables simmer until softened, then added our tofu back into the mix. The cilantro rice and some mellow Monterey Jack cheese nicely rounded out the fresh filling.

1¼ cups vegetable broth

¾ cup long-grain white rice, rinsed

3 garlic cloves, minced

Salt and pepper

¼ cup minced fresh cilantro

14 ounces firm tofu, quartered

1½ pounds tomatillos, husks and stems removed, rinsed well, dried, halved or quartered if large

3 tablespoons vegetable oil

5 garlic cloves, minced

1 tablespoon ground cumin

¼ teaspoon dried oregano

3 poblano chiles, stemmed, seeded, and cut into ½-inch pieces

2 onions, chopped fine

1 jalapeño chile, stemmed, seeded, and minced

6 (10-inch) flour tortillas

6 ounces Monterey Jack cheese, shredded (1½ cups)

1. Bring broth, rice, garlic, and ½ teaspoon salt to boil in small saucepan over medium-high heat. Cover, reduce heat to low, and cook until rice is tender and broth is absorbed, about 20 minutes. Remove rice from heat and let sit, covered, for 10 minutes. Add cilantro and fluff with fork to incorporate; cover to keep warm.

2. Meanwhile, pulse tofu in food processor until coarsely chopped into roughly ¼-inch pieces, 3 to 4 pulses. Spread chopped tofu over paper towel–lined baking sheet, let drain for 20 minutes, then gently pat dry with paper towels and season with salt and pepper. Pulse tomatillos in now-empty food processor until finely chopped, 8 to 10 pulses.

3. Heat 2 tablespoons oil in 12-inch nonstick skillet over medium-high heat until shimmering. Add tofu and cook until browned, 10 to 15 minutes; transfer to plate.

4. Add remaining 1 tablespoon oil, garlic, cumin, oregano, and ½ teaspoon salt to now-empty skillet and cook over medium heat until fragrant, about 30 seconds. Stir in chopped tomatillos, poblanos, onions, and jalapeño, cover, and cook until vegetables have released liquid, 5 to 7 minutes. Uncover, increase heat to medium-high, and simmer until pan is almost dry, 10 to 12 minutes. Return tofu to skillet and cook until flavors meld, about 2 minutes.

5. Wrap tortillas in damp dish towel and microwave until warm and pliable, about 1 minute. Arrange tortillas on counter. Mound warm rice, tofu filling, and Monterey Jack across center of tortillas, close to bottom edge. Working with 1 tortilla at a time, fold sides of tortilla over filling, then fold up bottom of tortilla, pulling back on it firmly to tighten it around filling and continue to roll tightly into burrito. Serve.

Rolling Burritos

1. Divide rice, filling, and cheese evenly among tortillas. Fold sides of tortilla in over filling.

2. Fold bottom of tortilla over sides and filling and roll tightly into burrito.

For a fresh take on simple cheese quesadillas, we add in crisp-tender sautéed zucchini and pickled jalapeños.

Zucchini Quesadillas
SERVES 2 **FAST**

✔ WHY THIS RECIPE WORKS: For a vegetarian quesadilla with a new spin, we introduced zucchini into the equation. We sautéed the zucchini with garlic and cumin to give it great flavor and the perfect crisp-tender texture. We kept the tortillas crisp by lightly toasting them in a dry skillet. Then we filled the quesadillas with the zucchini, Monterey Jack cheese for its gooey meltability, *queso fresco* for its salty tang, and pickled jalapeños for a little briny kick. We lightly coated the filled tortillas with oil and returned them to the skillet until they were well browned and the cheese was fully melted. Use a light hand when seasoning with kosher salt, as the cheese itself is rather salty. Let the quesadillas cool slightly before cutting and serving them; straight from the skillet, the cheese is molten and will ooze out. Serve with salsa, guacamole, and/or sour cream.

1 tablespoon vegetable oil, plus extra for brushing tortillas

1 zucchini, cut into ½-inch pieces

¼ teaspoon salt

⅛ teaspoon pepper

1 garlic clove, minced

½ teaspoon ground cumin

2 (8-inch) flour tortillas

2 ounces Monterey Jack cheese, shredded (½ cup)

1 ounce queso fresco, crumbled (¼ cup)

1 tablespoon minced jarred jalapeños

Kosher salt

1. Heat oil in 10-inch nonstick skillet over medium-high heat until shimmering. Add zucchini, salt, and pepper and cook, stirring occasionally, until zucchini is browned and tender, 5 to 7 minutes. Add garlic and cumin and cook until fragrant, about 30 seconds. Transfer to bowl. Wipe out skillet with paper towels.

2. Heat now-empty skillet over medium heat until hot, about 2 minutes. Place 1 tortilla in skillet and toast until soft and puffed slightly at edges, about 2 minutes. Flip tortilla and toast until puffed and slightly browned, 1 to 2 minutes longer. Transfer tortilla to cutting board. Repeat to toast second tortilla while assembling first quesadilla.

3. Sprinkle half of zucchini, half of Monterey Jack, half of queso fresco, and half of jalapeños over half of tortilla, leaving ½-inch border around edge. Fold other tortilla half over top and press to flatten. Brush surface generously with oil, sprinkle lightly with kosher salt, and set aside. Repeat to assemble second quesadilla.

4. Place both quesadillas in skillet, oiled sides down; cook over medium heat until crisp and well browned, 1 to 2 minutes. Brush tops with oil and sprinkle lightly with kosher salt. Flip quesadillas and cook until second sides are crisp and browned, 1 to 2 minutes longer. Transfer quesadillas to cutting board. Let cool at least 3 minutes, then slice each quesadilla in half and serve.

Cooking Quesadillas

Cook both quesadillas together in 10-inch nonstick skillet until crisp and well browned.

Types of Masa Flour

Masarepa, also called *harina precocida* and *masa al instante*, is a precooked corn flour that's prepared from starchier large-kernel white corn (as opposed to the small-kernel yellow corn familiar to most Americans). The germ is removed from the kernels during processing, and the kernels are then dried and ground to a fine flour. Both white and yellow masarepa can be found at many large supermarkets in the United States; the white variety, or *masarepa blanca,* is most often used in Colombia and Venezuela, so we chose to use it in our arepas recipe.

Masa harina is the traditional flour used to make tortillas. It is made from dried corn that is treated in a solution of lime and water, called slaked lime, to loosen the hulls from the kernels and soften the corn. The softened corn is ground into a dough, called masa, that is then dried and powdered to make masa harina. Masa harina can be found in well-stocked supermarkets and specialty Latin markets. Do not substitute cornmeal or regular corn flour for either masa harina or masarepa; they're produced from different types of corn and are processed differently.

Black Bean and Cheese Arepas

MAKES 8, SERVES 4 `FAST` `GF`

✔ **WHY THIS RECIPE WORKS:** Arepas are a type of corn cake popular in Venezuela and Colombia, though iterations exist in other Latin countries. The Venezuelan variety is served as sandwiches that are split open and stuffed with anything from meat and cheese to corn, beans, or even fish. The arepa itself is made using *masarepa* (a precooked corn flour) along with water and salt, but getting the consistency right proved to be a challenge. In the end, we found that using just a half-cup more water than masarepa produced a dough that was easy to shape, and a small amount of baking powder lightened its texture just enough. We shaped the dough into rounds, browned them in a skillet with some oil, and finished them in the oven. To stuff our arepas, we made a filling of mashed black beans mixed with Monterey Jack cheese. Cilantro added freshness, lime juice injected a bit of acidity, and chili powder brought a hint of heat. Masarepa is also called *harina precocida* and *masa al instante* and is available in the international aisle of well-stocked supermarkets and specialty Latin markets.

AREPAS

    2   cups (10 ounces) masarepa blanca
    1   teaspoon salt
    1   teaspoon baking powder
    2½ cups warm water
    ¼   cup vegetable oil

BLACK BEAN FILLING

    1   (15-ounce) can black beans, rinsed
    4   ounces Monterey Jack cheese, shredded (1 cup)
    2   tablespoons minced fresh cilantro
    2   scallions, sliced thin
    1   tablespoon lime juice
    ¼   teaspoon chili powder
        Salt and pepper

1. FOR THE AREPAS: Adjust oven rack to middle position and heat oven to 400 degrees. Whisk masarepa, salt, and baking powder together in large bowl. Gradually add water and stir until combined. Using generous ⅓ cup dough for each round, form eight 3-inch rounds, each about ½ inch thick.

2. Heat 2 tablespoons oil in 12-inch nonstick skillet over medium-high heat until shimmering. Add 4 arepas and cook until golden on both sides, about 4 minutes per side. Transfer arepas to wire rack set in rimmed baking sheet. Wipe out skillet with paper towels and repeat with remaining 2 tablespoons oil and remaining 4 arepas; transfer to baking sheet. (Fried arepas can be refrigerated for up to 3 days or frozen for up to 1 month. Increase baking time as needed in step 3; if frozen, do not thaw before baking.)

3. Bake arepas on wire rack until they sound hollow when tapped on bottom, about 10 minutes.

4. FOR THE FILLING: Meanwhile, using potato masher or fork, mash beans in bowl until most are broken. Stir in Monterey Jack, cilantro, scallions, lime juice, and chili powder and season with salt and pepper to taste.

5. Using fork, gently split hot, baked arepas open. Stuff each with generous 3 tablespoons filling. Serve.

VARIATION

Avocado, Tomato, and Bell Pepper Arepas `FAST` `VEGAN` `GF`

Omit black beans and cheese. Increase cilantro to ¼ cup, scallions to 4, lime juice to 3 tablespoons, and chili powder to ½ teaspoon. Add to filling 2 halved and pitted avocados, 1 chopped and 1 mashed; 2 tomatoes, cored and chopped into ½-inch pieces; and 1 yellow bell pepper, cut into ¼-inch pieces.

Pupusas with Tangy Cabbage Slaw
MAKES 10, SERVES 4 TO 6 `GF`

✔ **WHY THIS RECIPE WORKS:** *Pupusas* are the ultimate Salvadoran comfort food: A thick handmade corn tortilla is stuffed with cheese and griddled until golden brown. The stuffed corn tortilla is traditionally topped with *curtido*, a tart cabbage slaw. While traditionally eaten as a side dish, we think pupusas make a great lunch or a light dinner. The dough is similar to the one we use for thin corn tortillas, but with a bit more water so it's more malleable and easy to stuff. For the filling, we stuck to the classic combination of cheese, spices, and cilantro. Monterey Jack cheese worked best—just a few minutes in a hot skillet was all it took to melt, and its mild

Making Arepas

1. BROWN AREPAS: Heat oil in 12-inch nonstick skillet until shimmering. Cook arepas until golden on both sides, about 4 minutes per side.

2. BAKE AREPAS: Bake arepas on wire rack set inside baking sheet until they sound hollow when tapped on bottom, about 10 minutes.

3. SPLIT AREPAS: Using fork, gently split hot arepas open.

4. STUFF AREPAS: Stuff each arepa with generous 3 tablespoons filling.

Salvadorian *pupusas* are thick, griddled tortillas stuffed with cheese and topped with a bright, crunchy cabbage slaw.

flavor didn't overpower the flavor of the corn flour. Make the cabbage slaw before you begin making the pupusas; as the slaw sits, the vinegar, salt, and sugar soften the cabbage, and the flavor of the slaw improves. Masa harina is an instant corn masa flour. We've had good luck using Maseca, Goya Masarica, and Bob's Red Mill brands; if using Goya brand, do not confuse it with a cornmeal product called *masarepa,* which is similar in appearance.

TANGY CABBAGE SLAW

- 4 cups shredded green cabbage
- 1 carrot, peeled and shredded
- ¼ cup cider vinegar
- 2 tablespoons water
- 2 tablespoons minced fresh cilantro
- 1 jalapeño chile, stemmed, seeded, and sliced thin
- ½ teaspoon sugar
- ⅛ teaspoon minced fresh oregano
  Salt and pepper

Filling Pupusas

1. Wet hands slightly. Flatten heaping ¼ cup of dough (2½ ounces) into 4-inch-wide round. Place 2 tablespoons of cheese mixture in center of dough.

2. Bring sides of dough up around filling and pinch top to seal. Press on pinched side to flatten dough into 1-inch-thick disk.

3. Cut apart sides of small zipper-lock bag, leaving bottom seam intact. Place disk of dough on 1 side of bag and fold other side over top. Using plate, press dough gently into ¼-inch-thick pupusa.

PUPUSAS

- 6 ounces Monterey Jack cheese, shredded (1½ cups)
- 2 scallions, sliced thin
- 2 tablespoons minced fresh cilantro
- 1 tablespoon lime juice
- ¼ teaspoon chili powder
  Salt and pepper
- 2 cups (10 ounces) masa harina
- 2 cups warm water
- 1 teaspoon vegetable oil

1. FOR THE SLAW: Combine all ingredients in bowl and season with ½ teaspoon salt and pepper to taste. Cover and refrigerate until cabbage wilts slightly, about 1 hour.

2. FOR THE PUPUSAS: Combine Monterey Jack, scallions, cilantro, lime juice, and chili powder in bowl and season with salt and pepper to taste.

3. Using rubber spatula, stir masa, water, and ¼ teaspoon salt together in bowl to form soft dough. Using hands, knead dough in bowl until soft and slightly tacky but not sticky, about 1 minute. Cover dough with damp paper towel.

4. Cut apart sides of small zipper-lock bag but leave bottom seam intact. Pinch off heaping ¼ cup dough (2½ ounces) and roll into ball; keep remaining dough covered. Using slightly wet hands, flatten dough into 4-inch-wide round and place 2 tablespoons cheese mixture in center. Bring sides of dough up around filling and pinch top to seal. Press on pinched side to flatten dough into 1-inch-thick disk. Place on 1 side of plastic bag and fold other side over top. Using large plate, press dough gently into ¼-inch-thick pupusa; transfer to baking sheet and cover with damp paper towel. Repeat with remaining dough and cheese filling.

5. Heat oil in 12-inch nonstick skillet over medium-high heat until shimmering. Wipe out skillet with paper towel, leaving thin film of oil. Working in batches, cook pupusas in skillet until spotty brown on both sides, about 3 minutes per side; transfer to platter. Serve warm with slaw.

Ultimate Veggie Burgers

MAKES 12 BURGERS

✔ **WHY THIS RECIPE WORKS:** Store-bought frozen veggie burgers are convenient but notoriously inedible. We wanted to develop a homemade version that was more than worth the trouble, with complex savory flavor and a satisfying texture. We tried a variety of soy products, but none had a texture that we liked in a burger. When we turned to a more traditional base for veggie burgers we had better luck. Lentils had the best flavor, and bulgur and panko further bulked up our burgers, plus they absorbed the excess moisture the lentils retained even after thorough drying. Adding aromatic vegetables was a no-brainer; onions, celery, leek, and garlic provided great depth of flavor without being overwhelming. We knew that cremini mushrooms would give our burgers a meaty flavor, but we were surprised to find that adding ground cashews took them to the next level. Pulsing everything together in the food processor made for a more cohesive and even-textured mix, and mayonnaise provided the necessary fat and binding qualities. After forming the mixture into patties, we simply seared them in a skillet to give them a crunchy, browned exterior. Cremini mushrooms are also known as baby bella mushrooms. Serve with your favorite burger toppings.

¾ **cup brown lentils, picked over and rinsed**
   Salt and pepper
½ **cup vegetable oil, plus extra as needed**

With lentils, mushrooms, bulgur, and ground cashews, these veggie burgers have both complex flavor and great texture.

1 **pound cremini mushrooms, trimmed and sliced thin**
2 **onions, chopped fine**
1 **celery rib, minced**
1 **small leek, white and light green parts only, chopped fine and washed thoroughly (½ cup)**
2 **garlic cloves, minced**
¾ **cup medium-grind bulgur, rinsed**
1 **cup raw cashews**
⅓ **cup mayonnaise**
2 **cups panko bread crumbs**
12 **burger buns**

1. Bring 3 cups water, lentils, and 1 teaspoon salt to boil in medium saucepan over high heat. Reduce heat to medium-low and simmer, stirring occasionally, until lentils just begin to fall apart, about 25 minutes. Drain lentils well, transfer to paper towel–lined baking sheet, and gently pat dry.

2. Meanwhile, heat 2 tablespoons oil in 12-inch nonstick skillet over medium heat until shimmering. Add mushrooms and cook, stirring occasionally, until released liquid has evaporated and mushrooms are softened, about 8 minutes. Add onions, celery, leek, and garlic and cook until vegetables are softened and just beginning to brown, 10 to 15 minutes. Transfer to sheet with lentils and let mixture cool to room temperature, about 30 minutes.

3. Combine 2 cups water, bulgur, and ¼ teaspoon salt in large bowl and microwave, covered, until bulgur is softened, about 5 minutes. Drain well in fine-mesh strainer, using rubber spatula to press out excess moisture, and return to now-empty bowl; let cool slightly. Pulse cashews in food processor until finely ground, about 25 pulses, scraping down sides of bowl as needed.

4. Stir ground cashews, cooled lentil-vegetable mixture, and mayonnaise into bowl with bulgur until combined. Transfer half of mixture to now-empty food processor and pulse until coarsely ground, about 15 pulses; mixture should be cohesive but roughly textured. Transfer processed mixture to separate large bowl; repeat with remaining bulgur mixture. Stir in panko, 1 teaspoon salt, and pepper to taste until uniform. Divide mixture into 12 equal portions (about ½ cup each), then tightly pack each portion into ½-inch-thick patty.

5. Heat 2 tablespoons oil in 12-inch nonstick skillet over medium heat until shimmering. Add 4 burgers to skillet and cook until well browned on first side, about 4 minutes. Flip burgers, add additional oil if skillet looks dry, and cook until well browned on second side, about 4 minutes longer; transfer burgers to plate and tent loosely with aluminum foil. Repeat with remaining oil and burgers. Serve on burger buns.

TO MAKE AHEAD: Patties can be prepared through step 4, then transferred to 2 parchment paper–lined baking sheets, covered with plastic wrap, and frozen until firm, about 1 hour. Stack frozen patties between small sheets of parchment paper, wrap stacks tightly in plastic, and freeze in zipper-lock freezer bags for up to 1 month. Do not thaw before cooking. After browning frozen patties on both sides, bake in 350-degree oven until warmed through, about 10 minutes.

Grilled Portobello Burgers

SERVES 4

✓ **WHY THIS RECIPE WORKS:** To avoid mushroom burgers with soggy buns, we knew we had to find a way to rid the mushrooms of their excess moisture. We decided to try scoring them, a technique that had worked for us in the past with oven-roasted mushrooms. It worked like a charm on the grill. Before cooking, we lightly scored the mushrooms on the smooth, nongill side in a crosshatch pattern. This helped expedite the release of moisture, which dripped out and evaporated on the

grill, ensuring intense mushroom flavor and dry and toasty buns. The crosshatching also allowed the mushrooms to absorb more marinade—a flavorful mixture of olive oil, red wine vinegar, and garlic. Once they were charred and cooked through, we filled the caps with a savory mixture of feta, sun-dried tomatoes, and roasted red peppers before stacking them on grilled buns with basil mayo, baby arugula, and sweet grilled onions. If your mushrooms are larger or smaller than 4 to 5 inches, you may need to adjust the cooking time accordingly. If the mushrooms absorb all the marinade, simply brush the onions with olive oil before grilling them in step 4.

- 4 portobello mushroom caps (4 to 5 inches in diameter), gills removed
- ½ cup extra-virgin olive oil
- 3 tablespoons red wine vinegar
- 1 garlic clove, minced
- 1 teaspoon salt
- ½ teaspoon pepper
- 4 ounces feta cheese, crumbled (1 cup)
- ½ cup jarred roasted red peppers, patted dry and chopped
- ½ cup oil-packed sun-dried tomatoes, patted dry and chopped
- ½ cup mayonnaise
- ½ cup chopped fresh basil
- 4 (½-inch-thick) slices red onion
- 4 kaiser rolls, split and toasted
- 1 ounce (1 cup) baby arugula

1. Using tip of paring knife, cut ½-inch crosshatch pattern, 1/16 inch deep, on tops of mushroom caps. Combine oil, vinegar, garlic, salt, and pepper in 1-gallon zipper-lock bag. Add mushrooms, seal bag, turn to coat, and let sit for at least 30 minutes or up to 1 hour.

2. Combine feta, red peppers, and sun-dried tomatoes in bowl. Whisk mayonnaise and basil together in separate bowl. Push 1 toothpick horizontally through each onion slice to keep rings intact while grilling.

3A. FOR A CHARCOAL GRILL: Open bottom vent completely. Light large chimney starter filled with charcoal briquettes (6 quarts). When top coals are partially covered with ash, pour evenly over grill. Set cooking grate in place, cover, and open lid vent completely. Heat grill until hot, about 5 minutes.

3B. FOR A GAS GRILL: Turn all burners to high, cover, and heat grill until hot, about 15 minutes. Turn all burners to medium-high.

4. Clean and oil cooking grate. Remove mushrooms from marinade, reserving excess. Brush onions all over with reserved mushroom marinade. Place onions and mushrooms, gill side up, on grill. Cook (covered if using gas) until mushrooms have released their liquid and are charred on first side, 4 to 6 minutes. Flip mushrooms and onions and continue to cook (covered if using gas) until mushrooms are charred on second side, 3 to 5 minutes.

5. Transfer onions to platter; remove toothpicks. Transfer mushrooms to platter, gill side up, and divide feta mixture evenly among caps, packing down mixture. Return mushrooms to grill, feta side up, and cook, covered, until heated through, about 3 minutes.

6. Return mushrooms to platter and tent with aluminum foil. Spread basil mayonnaise on roll bottoms and top each with 1 mushroom and 1 onion slice. Divide arugula evenly among burgers, then cap with roll tops. Serve.

Scoring Portobello Mushrooms for Grilling

Using tip of sharp knife, lightly score top of each mushroom cap in crosshatch pattern 1/16 inch deep.

Mashed and whole black beans give these tasty and easy-to-make burgers the perfect texture.

Black Bean Burgers

SERVES 6   **FAST**

 **WHY THIS RECIPE WORKS:** Hearty, healthy black beans make the perfect base for a flavorful vegetarian burger, and using convenient canned beans means these burgers can be on the table in just 30 minutes. We found that mashing most of the beans but leaving about 1/2 cup of them whole made a bean burger that was not too crumbly, nor too dense and pasty. To ensure that the burgers held together once cooked, we added two eggs and also incorporated bread crumbs—both are binding ingredients often used in meatloaf and meatball recipes. The eggs also provided more protein and added richness. To flavor the beans, we liked a combination of shallot, cumin, and a little cayenne pepper. Finely chopped red bell pepper and minced cilantro added freshness and a little more texture. Avoid overmixing the bean mixture in step 1 or the burgers will have a mealy texture. Serve with your favorite burger toppings over salad greens or on a burger bun.

2 (15-ounce) cans black beans, rinsed
2 large eggs
5 tablespoons extra-virgin olive oil
1 teaspoon ground cumin
¼ teaspoon salt
⅛ teaspoon cayenne pepper
1 cup panko bread crumbs
1 red bell pepper, stemmed, seeded, and chopped fine
¼ cup minced fresh cilantro
1 shallot, minced

1. Place 2½ cups beans in large bowl and mash with potato masher until mostly smooth. In separate bowl, whisk together eggs, 1 tablespoon oil, cumin, salt, and cayenne. Stir egg mixture, remaining beans, panko, bell pepper, cilantro, and shallot into mashed beans until just combined. Divide mixture into 6 equal portions and lightly pack into 1-inch-thick patties.

2. Heat 2 tablespoons oil in 12-inch nonstick skillet over medium heat until shimmering. Carefully lay 3 patties in skillet and cook until well browned on both sides, 4 to 5 minutes per side.

3. Transfer burgers to plate and tent loosely with aluminum foil. Repeat with remaining 2 tablespoons oil and remaining patties. Serve.

VARIATION

Black Bean Burgers with Corn and Chipotle Chile FAST

Substitute 1 tablespoon minced canned chipotle chile in adobo sauce for cayenne. Reduce amount of red bell pepper to ¼ cup and add ¾ cup frozen corn, thawed and patted dry, to bean mixture.

Pinto Bean, Beet, and Bulgur Burgers

SERVES 8 VEGAN

✔ **WHY THIS RECIPE WORKS:** For these modern bean burgers, we combined pinto beans with sweet, earthy shredded beets and hearty, chewy bulgur. While the bulgur cooked, we pulsed the rest of the ingredients in a food processor to get just the right consistency. Along with the beets and beans, we added basil for freshness and walnuts for richness and texture. Garlic and mustard deepened the savory flavors. Using carrot baby food (which was already conveniently pureed) as a binder instead of eggs lent the patties a subtle sweetness—and, as an added bonus, it kept the recipe vegan. Panko bread crumbs further bound the mixture and helped the patties to sear up with a nice, crisp crust. Any brand of plain carrot baby food will work here. Use a coarse grater or the shredding disk of a food processor to shred the beets. If using the food processor, you may need to cut the beet into smaller pieces to fit inside the feed tube. We like to serve these burgers with Tahini Sauce (page 362), Cucumber-Yogurt Sauce (page 43), or Sriracha Mayo (page 43) over salad greens or on a burger bun.

　Salt and pepper
⅔　cup medium-grind bulgur, rinsed
　1　large beet (9 ounces), peeled and shredded
¾　cup walnuts
½　cup fresh basil leaves
　2　garlic cloves, minced
　1　(15-ounce) can pinto beans, rinsed
　1　(4-ounce) jar carrot baby food
　1　tablespoon whole-grain mustard
1½　cups panko bread crumbs
¼　cup vegetable oil

We combine pinto beans, hearty bulgur, and sweet, earthy beets for a modern take on a vegetarian burger.

1. Bring 1½ cups water and ½ teaspoon salt to boil in small saucepan. Off heat, stir in bulgur, cover, and let stand until tender, 15 to 20 minutes. Drain bulgur, spread onto rimmed baking sheet, and let cool slightly.

2. Meanwhile, pulse shredded beet, walnuts, basil, and garlic together in food processor until finely chopped, about 12 pulses, scraping down sides of bowl as needed. Add beans, carrot baby food, 2 tablespoons water, mustard, 1½ teaspoons salt, and ½ teaspoon pepper and pulse until well combined, about 8 pulses.

3. Transfer mixture to large bowl and stir in panko and cooled bulgur. Divide mixture into 8 equal portions and pack into 4-inch-wide patties.

4. Heat 2 tablespoons oil in 12-inch nonstick skillet over medium-high heat until shimmering. Gently lay 4 patties in skillet and cook until crisp and well browned on both sides, 4 to 5 minutes per side, turning gently halfway through cooking and reducing heat if burgers begin to scorch. Transfer burgers to plate and tent loosely with aluminum foil.

5. Wipe out skillet with paper towels and repeat with remaining 2 tablespoons oil and remaining patties. Serve.

CHAPTER 10

Eggs for Breakfast
and Dinner

■ FAST (Less than 45 minutes start to finish)   ■ VEGAN   ■ GLUTEN-FREE
Photos: Huevos Rancheros; Foolproof Soft-Cooked Eggs

Whether poached, hard- or soft-cooked, or fried, an egg is the perfect way to make a light vegetarian meal a little heartier. Here are our foolproof methods for cooking eggs every way.

Fried Eggs

MAKES 4 `FAST` `GF`

When checking the eggs for doneness, lift the lid just a crack to prevent loss of steam in case they need further cooking. When cooked, the thin layer of white surrounding the yolk will turn opaque, but the yolk should remain runny. To cook two eggs, use an 8-inch nonstick skillet and halve the amounts of oil and butter. You can use this method with extra-large or jumbo eggs without altering the timing. You will need a 12- or 14-inch nonstick skillet with a tight-fitting lid for this recipe.

  2 teaspoons vegetable oil
  4 large eggs
     Salt and pepper
  2 teaspoons unsalted butter,
     cut into 4 pieces and chilled

1. Heat oil in 12- or 14-inch nonstick skillet over low heat for 5 minutes. Meanwhile, crack 2 eggs into small bowl and season with salt and pepper. Repeat with remaining 2 eggs and second small bowl.

2. Increase heat to medium-high and heat until oil is shimmering. Add butter to skillet and quickly swirl to coat pan. Working quickly, pour 1 bowl of eggs in 1 side of pan and second bowl of eggs in other side. Cover and cook for 1 minute.

3. Remove skillet from heat and let stand, covered, 15 to 45 seconds for runny yolks (white around edge of yolk will be barely opaque), 45 to 60 seconds for soft but set yolks, and about 2 minutes for medium-set yolks. Slide eggs onto plates and serve immediately.

Poached Eggs

MAKES 4 `FAST` `GF`

You will need a 12-inch nonstick skillet with a tight-fitting lid for this recipe. See below for more information on poaching eggs.

     Salt and pepper
  2 tablespoons distilled white
     vinegar
  4 large eggs

1. Fill 12-inch nonstick skillet nearly to rim with water, add 1 teaspoon salt and vinegar, and bring to boil over high heat. Meanwhile, crack eggs into 2 teacups with handles (2 eggs per cup).

2. Lower lips of cups into water and tip eggs into skillet. Cover, remove from heat, and let sit until whites are set, about 4 minutes (yolks will be slightly runny; for firmer yolks, let sit an additional 30 to 60 seconds).

3. Using slotted spoon, carefully remove each egg, letting water drain back into skillet, and transfer to paper towel–lined plate. Season with salt and pepper to taste and serve immediately.

Fried Eggs

Foolproof Soft-Cooked Eggs

MAKES 4 `FAST` `GF`

Be sure to use large eggs that have no cracks and that are taken cold right from the refrigerator. Because precise timing is vital to the success of this recipe, we strongly recommend using a digital timer. If you have one, a steamer basket makes lowering the eggs into the boiling water easier. We recommend serving these eggs in eggcups and with buttered toast for dipping, or you may simply use the dull side of a butter knife to crack the egg along the equator, break the egg in half, and scoop out the insides with a teaspoon.

  4 large eggs, cold

1. Bring ½ inch water to boil in medium saucepan over medium-high heat. Using tongs, gently place eggs in boiling water (eggs will not be submerged). Cover saucepan and cook eggs for 6½ minutes.

2. Remove cover, transfer saucepan to sink, and place under cold running water for 30 seconds. Remove eggs from pan and serve.

COOKING TIMES FOR POACHED EGGS

If you want to cook more or fewer than four eggs, use the following times.

NUMBER OF EGGS	COOKING TIME
2 large	3½ minutes
4 large	4 minutes
8 large	5 minutes
12 large	6 minutes

Foolproof Hard-Cooked Eggs

MAKES 4 FAST GF

You can double or triple this recipe as long as you use a pot large enough to hold the eggs in a single layer, covered by an inch of water.

4 large eggs

Place eggs in medium saucepan, cover by 1 inch water, and bring to boil over high heat. Remove pan from heat, cover, and let sit 10 minutes. Meanwhile, fill medium bowl with 4 cups water and 1 tray of ice cubes. Transfer eggs to ice water bath with slotted spoon; let sit for 5 minutes. Peel eggs and serve.

Best Scrambled Eggs

SERVES 4 FAST GF

It's important to follow visual cues, as skillet thickness will have an effect on cooking times. If you don't have half-and-half, you can substitute 2 tablespoons plus 2 teaspoons whole milk and 4 teaspoons heavy cream. To dress up the eggs, add 2 tablespoons minced fresh parsley, chives, basil, or cilantro, or 1 tablespoon minced fresh dill or tarragon, after reducing the heat to low.

8 large eggs plus 2 large yolks
¼ cup half-and-half
Salt and pepper
1 tablespoon unsalted butter, chilled

1. Beat eggs and yolks, half-and-half, ¼ teaspoon salt, and ¼ teaspoon pepper together with fork in bowl until thoroughly combined and mixture is pure yellow; do not overbeat.

2. Melt butter in 10-inch nonstick skillet over medium-high heat, swirling to coat pan. Add egg mixture and, using heat-resistant rubber spatula, constantly and firmly scrape along bottom and sides of skillet until eggs begin to clump and spatula leaves trail on bottom of skillet, 1½ to 2½ minutes.

Best Scrambled Eggs

3. Reduce heat to low and gently but constantly fold eggs until clumped and slightly wet, 30 to 60 seconds. Immediately transfer eggs to warmed plates and season with salt to taste. Serve immediately.

FORMULA FOR SCRAMBLED EGGS

Half-and-half adds liquid that turns to steam when eggs are cooked, thus helping them cook into soft, fluffy mounds. You need 1 tablespoon of half-and-half for each serving of eggs. In addition to varying the half-and-half to match the number of eggs, you will need to vary the seasonings, pan size, and cooking time. Here's how to do that.

SERVINGS	EGGS	HALF-AND-HALF	SEASONINGS	BUTTER	SKILLET SIZE	COOKING TIME
1	2 large, plus 1 yolk	1 tablespoon	pinch salt pinch pepper	¼ tablespoon	8 inches	30–60 seconds over medium-high, 30–60 seconds over low
2	4 large, plus 1 yolk	2 tablespoons	⅛ teaspoon salt ⅛ teaspoon pepper	½ tablespoon	8 inches	45–75 seconds over medium-high, 30–60 seconds over low
3	6 large, plus 1 yolk	3 tablespoons	¼ teaspoon salt ⅛ teaspoon pepper	¾ tablespoon	10 inches	1–2 minutes over medium-high, 30–60 seconds over low
4	8 large, plus 2 yolks	¼ cup	¼ teaspoon salt ¼ teaspoon pepper	1 tablespoon	10 inches	1½–2½ minutes over medium-high, 30–60 seconds over low

Scrambled Eggs with Goat Cheese, Arugula, and Sun-Dried Tomatoes

SERVES 4 TO 6 `FAST` `GF`

✓ **WHY THIS RECIPE WORKS:** To keep our scrambled egg recipe light and fluffy while adding hearty ingredients such as cheese and vegetables, we had to eliminate as much of the added moisture as we could. We started by choosing ingredients that didn't add too much moisture: leafy arugula, sun-dried tomatoes, and tangy crumbled goat cheese. To further reduce any wetness, after we sautéed the onion and wilted the arugula, we wiped the pan dry before adding the eggs. Rinsing and patting the sun-dried tomatoes dry prevented them from making the eggs greasy. And rather than whisking milk into the eggs, we chose half-and-half, which has more fat and less moisture. We started by cooking the egg mixture until large curds formed, then we folded in the vegetables off the heat and sprinkled the eggs with the cheese.

To give scrambled eggs an elegant twist, we add peppery arugula, crumbled goat cheese, and sun-dried tomatoes.

12	**large eggs**
6	**tablespoons half-and-half**
	Salt and pepper
2	**teaspoons extra-virgin olive oil**
½	**onion, chopped fine**
⅛	**teaspoon red pepper flakes**
5	**ounces (5 cups) baby arugula**
1	**tablespoon unsalted butter**
¼	**cup oil-packed sun-dried tomatoes, rinsed, patted dry, and chopped fine**
3	**ounces goat cheese, crumbled (¾ cup)**

1. Beat eggs, half-and-half, ¾ teaspoon salt, and ¼ teaspoon pepper together with fork in bowl until thoroughly combined.

2. Heat oil in 12-inch nonstick skillet over medium heat until shimmering. Add onion and pepper flakes and cook until onion has softened, about 5 minutes. Add arugula and cook, stirring gently, until arugula begins to wilt, 30 to 60 seconds. Spread mixture in single layer on plate.

3. Wipe out now-empty skillet with paper towels, add butter, and melt over medium heat, swirling to coat pan. Add egg mixture. Using heat-resistant rubber spatula, stir eggs constantly, slowly pushing them from side to side, scraping along bottom and sides of skillet, and lifting and folding eggs as they form curds (do not overscramble or curds formed will be too small). Cook until large curds form but eggs are still very moist, 2 to 3 minutes.

4. Off heat, gently fold in arugula mixture and sun-dried tomatoes until evenly distributed; if eggs are still underdone, return skillet to medium heat for no longer than 30 seconds. Season with salt and pepper to taste. Divide eggs among individual plates and sprinkle with goat cheese. Serve.

VARIATION

Scrambled Eggs with Zucchini, Feta, and Mint `FAST` `GF`

Omit red pepper flakes, arugula, and sun-dried tomatoes. Add 1 large zucchini, cut into ¼-inch pieces, to skillet with onion in step 2, and cook until crisp-tender, about 4 minutes. In step 4, off heat, fold zucchini mixture and 1½ tablespoons minced fresh mint into eggs until evenly distributed. Substitute crumbled feta cheese for goat cheese.

Mexican-Style Scrambled Eggs (Migas)

SERVES 4 **FAST** **GF**

🗸 **WHY THIS RECIPE WORKS:** A breakfast staple throughout the Southwest, *migas* is an appealing version of fluffy scrambled eggs, with onion, chiles, cheese, and an unexpected ingredient: tortilla chips, which soften in the egg mixture to a pleasantly chewy texture. Nearly all the recipes we found for this simple dish use fried chips, but we found that these gave the eggs an off-flavor and made the dish taste overly greasy. We had much better luck using baked tortilla chips, which had a clean, corn flavor. To keep the eggs from getting soggy and to deepen the flavor of the dish, we sautéed the aromatics before adding the egg and tortilla chip mixture. For the cheese, we liked subtly spicy, melty pepper Jack. A little cilantro stirred in with the cheese added color and fresh flavor. For more spice, add in the ribs and seed from the jalapeño. In order for this recipe to be gluten-free, you must use gluten-free tortilla chips. To bake your own tortilla chips, spray 4 (6-inch) corn tortillas with vegetable oil spray, cut into wedges, and bake in 350-degree oven until crisp, 15 to 20 minutes. Serve with salsa.

- 8 large eggs
- 2 ounces baked tortilla chips, broken into ½-inch pieces (1 cup)
  Salt and pepper
- 2 tablespoons unsalted butter
- 1 red onion, chopped fine
- 1 red bell pepper, stemmed, seeded, and chopped fine
- 3 garlic cloves, minced
- 1 jalapeño chile, stemmed, seeded, and minced
- 3 ounces pepper Jack cheese, shredded (¾ cup)
- 2 tablespoons minced fresh cilantro

1. Mix eggs, tortilla chips, ¼ teaspoon salt, and pinch pepper together in bowl. Melt butter in 12-inch nonstick skillet over medium-high heat. Add onion and bell pepper and cook until softened, about 5 minutes. Stir in garlic and jalapeño and cook until fragrant, about 30 seconds.

2. Reduce heat to medium. Add egg mixture and cook, using heat-resistant rubber spatula to push mixture back and forth, until curds begin to form. Continue to cook, lifting and folding curds from side to side, until they clump in single mound but are still very moist, about 3 minutes. Off heat, gently fold in cheese and cilantro. Serve.

NOTES FROM THE TEST KITCHEN

Buying Eggs

There are numerous—and often confusing—options when buying eggs at the supermarket. And when eggs are the focal point of a dish, their quality makes a big difference. Here's what we've learned in the test kitchen about buying eggs.

COLOR

The shell's hue depends on the breed of the chicken. The run-of-the-mill leghorn chicken produces the typical white egg. Brown-feathered birds, such as Rhode Island Reds, produce ecru- to coffee-colored eggs. Despite marketing hype extolling the virtues of nonwhite eggs, our tests proved that shell color has no effect on flavor.

FARM-FRESH AND ORGANIC

In our taste tests, farm-fresh eggs were standouts. The large yolks were bright orange and sat very high above the comparatively small whites, and the flavor of these eggs was exceptionally rich and complex. The organic eggs followed in second place, with eggs from hens raised on a vegetarian diet in third, and the standard supermarket eggs last. Differences were easily detected in egg-based dishes like an omelet or a frittata, but not in cakes or cookies.

EGGS AND OMEGA-3S

Several companies are marketing eggs with a high level of omega-3 fatty acids, the healthful unsaturated fats also found in some fish. In our taste test, we found that more omega-3s translated into a richer egg flavor. Why? Commercially raised chickens usually peck on corn and soy, while chickens on an omega-3-enriched diet have supplements of greens, flaxseeds, and algae, which also add flavor, complexity, and color to their eggs. Read labels carefully and look for brands that guarantee at least 200 milligrams of omega-3s per egg.

HOW OLD ARE MY EGGS?

Egg cartons are marked with both a sell-by date and a pack date. The pack date is the day the eggs were packed, which is generally within a week of when they were laid but may be as much as 30 days later. The sell-by date is within 30 days of the pack date, which is the legal limit set by the U.S. Department of Agriculture (USDA). In short, a carton of eggs may be up to two months old by the end of the sell-by date. But according to the USDA, eggs are still fit for consumption for an additional three to five weeks past the sell-by date.

Tofu Scramble with Shallots and Herbs

SERVES 4 **FAST** **VEGAN** **GF**

✔ **WHY THIS RECIPE WORKS:** Recipes for tofu scrambles are numerous, but most result in nothing but bland and boring imitations of scrambled eggs. We wanted a recipe that offered a creamy, egglike texture and a subtle, satisfying flavor. Soft tofu proved to have a texture closest to eggs, yielding pieces that, when crumbled, were smooth and creamy. A small amount of curry powder was key, contributing depth of flavor and a nice touch of color, without overwhelming the dish with actual curry flavor. A sautéed shallot lent the tofu a mild aromatic flavor. We also found that the tofu could be crumbled into smaller or larger pieces to resemble egg curds of different sizes. Once we had perfected our scrambled tofu, we came up with a few hearty variations. Do not substitute firm tofu for the soft tofu in this recipe. Be sure to press the tofu dry thoroughly before cooking.

- 14 ounces soft tofu, pressed dry with paper towels
- 1½ teaspoons vegetable oil
- 1 shallot, minced
- ¼ teaspoon curry powder
- ¾ teaspoon salt
- ⅛ teaspoon pepper
- 2 tablespoons minced fresh basil, parsley, tarragon, or marjoram

Crumble tofu into ¼- to ½-inch pieces. Heat oil in 10-inch nonstick skillet over medium heat until shimmering. Add shallot and cook until softened, about 2 minutes. Stir in crumbled tofu, curry powder, salt, and pepper and cook until tofu is hot, about 2 minutes. Off heat, stir in basil and serve.

VARIATIONS

Tofu Scramble with Spinach and Feta **FAST** **GF**

Before adding tofu to skillet, add 4 cups baby spinach and cook until wilted, about 1 minute. Add ½ cup crumbled feta cheese to pan with tofu.

Tofu Scramble with Tomato, Scallions, and Parmesan **FAST** **GF**

Add 1 seeded and finely chopped tomato and 1 minced garlic clove to pan with shallot; cook until tomato is no longer wet, 3 to 5 minutes. Add ¼ cup grated Parmesan cheese and 2 tablespoons minced scallions to pan with tofu.

Tofu Scramble with Shiitakes, Red Bell Pepper, and Goat Cheese **FAST** **GF**

Before adding shallot to pan, cook 4 ounces stemmed and thinly sliced shiitake mushrooms, 1 finely chopped small red bell pepper, and pinch red pepper flakes, covered, until mushrooms have released their liquid, about 5 minutes. Uncover, add shallot, and continue to cook until mushrooms are dry and shallot is softened, about 2 minutes. Add ¼ cup crumbled goat cheese to pan with tofu.

Hearty Egg and Black Bean Burritos

SERVES 6 **FAST**

✔ **WHY THIS RECIPE WORKS:** Breakfast burritos can make a supersatisfying morning meal, but they typically rely on chorizo or breakfast sausage to provide bulk and flavor. We wanted to develop an equally hearty vegetarian version. Black beans were the perfect choice to bulk up our burritos alongside the fluffy, tender scrambled eggs. To freshen up the filling, we added sweet, bright bell peppers, fresh cilantro, and sliced scallions. Sharp cheddar cheese added richness and bold flavor, and a little cayenne pepper provided just the right amount of balancing heat. To make this an easy one-dish meal, we cooked the bell pepper and beans in the skillet before scrambling the eggs, then folded them into the eggs with the cheese and cilantro. You can substitute whole milk for the half-and-half in this recipe, but the eggs will be less rich and less tender. Serve with hot sauce or salsa, sour cream, and sliced avocado.

- 2 tablespoons vegetable oil
- 1 red bell pepper, stemmed, seeded, and chopped into ¼-inch pieces
- 1 (15-ounce) can black beans, rinsed
- 3 scallions, sliced thin
- ⅛ teaspoon cayenne pepper
- 12 large eggs
- ¼ cup half-and-half
  Salt and pepper
- 4 ounces sharp cheddar cheese, shredded (1 cup)
- 3 tablespoons minced fresh cilantro
- 6 (10-inch) flour tortillas

Our quick, hearty breakfast burritos are stuffed with black beans, scrambled eggs, red bell pepper, and cheddar cheese.

1. Heat 1 tablespoon oil in 12-inch nonstick skillet over medium-high heat until shimmering. Add bell pepper and cook until softened and beginning to brown, about 5 minutes. Stir in black beans, scallions, and cayenne, and cook until heated through, about 1 minute; transfer to bowl.

2. Beat eggs, half-and-half, ½ teaspoon salt, and ¼ teaspoon pepper with fork in bowl until thoroughly combined. Wipe out now-empty skillet with paper towels, add remaining 1 tablespoon oil, and return to medium heat. Add egg mixture and cook, using heat-resistant rubber spatula to push mixture back and forth, until curds begin to form. Continue to cook, lifting and folding curds from side to side, until they clump in single mound but are still very moist, about 3 minutes. Off heat, gently fold in bell pepper–bean mixture, cheddar, and cilantro. Season with salt and pepper to taste.

3. Stack tortillas between paper towels on plate and microwave until hot and pliable, 30 to 60 seconds. Divide egg mixture evenly across center of each tortilla, close to bottom edge. Fold sides then bottom of tortilla over filling, pulling back on it firmly to tighten it around filling, then continue to roll tightly into burritos. Serve.

Open-Faced Poached Egg Sandwiches

SERVES 4   **FAST**

✔ **WHY THIS RECIPE WORKS:** Classic poached egg dishes like eggs Benedict are decadently delicious but time-consuming to make. We wanted a fresher take that featured juicy tomatoes, greens, and cheese and relied on the soft egg yolk to provide richness. For the greens, we chose tender baby spinach, which needed just a couple of minutes to wilt in the skillet. Sautéed garlic and mild shallot gave it great flavor. Next, to get perfect, tender poached eggs, we stuck with our foolproof method: We traded in the usual saucepan for a shallow nonstick skillet, which gave us much easier access to the eggs. We cracked the eggs into teacups and tipped them simultaneously into the boiling water to ensure they cooked evenly. Adding vinegar to the cooking water helped to set the eggs quickly, and salting the water seasoned the eggs nicely. Then we simply spread toasted English muffins with creamy goat cheese brightened with lemon juice and topped them with fresh tomato slices, the spinach, and a perfectly poached egg. You will need a 12-inch nonstick skillet with a tight-fitting lid for this recipe.

4   ounces goat cheese, crumbled and softened (1 cup)
1   teaspoon lemon juice
    Salt and pepper
4   English muffins, split in half, toasted,
    and still warm
2   small tomatoes, cored and sliced thin (16 slices)
4   teaspoons extra-virgin olive oil
2   shallots, minced
1   garlic clove, minced
8   ounces (8 cups) baby spinach
2   tablespoons distilled white vinegar
8   large eggs

1. Adjust oven rack to middle position and heat oven to 300 degrees. Stir goat cheese, lemon juice, and ¼ teaspoon pepper together in bowl until smooth.

2. Spread goat cheese mixture evenly over warm English muffin halves and top with tomato slices. Arrange English muffins on baking sheet and keep warm in oven while preparing spinach and eggs.

3. Heat oil in 12-inch nonstick skillet over medium heat until shimmering. Add shallots and cook until softened, about 2 minutes. Stir in garlic and cook until fragrant, about 30 seconds. Stir in spinach and ¼ teaspoon salt and cook until spinach is wilted, about 2 minutes. Using tongs, squeeze out any excess moisture from spinach, then divide evenly among English muffins. Return English muffins to oven.

4. Wipe out now-empty skillet with paper towels, then fill nearly to rim with water. Add vinegar and 1 teaspoon salt and bring to boil over high heat. Meanwhile, crack eggs into 4 teacups with handles (2 eggs per cup). Lower lips of cups into water and tip eggs into skillet. Cover, remove from heat, and let sit until whites are set, about 5 minutes (yolks will be slightly runny; for firmer yolks, let sit an additional 30 to 60 seconds).

5. Using slotted spoon, carefully remove each egg, letting water drain back into skillet, and transfer to paper towel–lined plate to drain briefly. Arrange 1 poached egg on top of each English muffin, season with salt and pepper to taste, and serve immediately.

Poaching Eggs

1. Fill 12-inch nonstick skillet nearly to rim with water, add 1 teaspoon salt and 2 tablespoons vinegar, and bring to boil over high heat.

2. Crack eggs into 4 teacups (2 eggs per cup).

3. Lower lips of cups into water and tip eggs into skillet.

4. Cover, remove from heat, and let sit until whites are set. (Cooking time will vary based on number of eggs being cooked; see Cooking Times for Poached Eggs chart on page 378.)

A buttered, preheated baking sheet (set in a second sheet for insulation) makes it easy to make six eggs in a hole at once.

Eggs in a Hole
MAKES 6 `FAST`

✔ **WHY THIS RECIPE WORKS:** An egg fried in the cutout center of a piece of toast makes a fun and delicious breakfast. But without a griddle, you can't make more than two at a time, turning you into an unwilling short-order cook. We tried making them in batches, keeping the first ones warm in the oven, but those overcooked. So we decided to move the process entirely to the oven, toasting the bread on both sides there. A preheated buttered baking sheet ensured that the bread browned without sticking, and cracking the eggs onto the hot pan helped them set up right away. Stacking the baking sheet in a second sheet provided insulation and allowed the eggs to cook quickly but gently. If you don't have a biscuit cutter, you can cut the holes in the toast with a drinking glass.

  6 **slices hearty white sandwich bread**
  5 **tablespoons unsalted butter, softened**
  6 **large eggs**
      Salt and pepper

1. Adjust oven racks to lowest and highest positions, place rimmed baking sheet on lowest rack, and heat oven to 500 degrees. Spread 1 side of bread slices evenly with 2½ tablespoons butter. Using 2½-inch biscuit cutter, cut out and remove circle from center of each piece of buttered bread.

2. Remove hot sheet from oven, add remaining 2½ tablespoons butter, and let melt, tilting sheet to cover pan evenly. Place bread circles down center of sheet and bread slices on either side of circles, buttered side up. Return sheet to lowest oven rack and bake until bread is golden, 3 to 5 minutes, flipping bread and rotating sheet halfway through baking.

3. Remove sheet from oven and set inside second (room-temperature) rimmed baking sheet. Crack 1 egg into each bread hole. Season eggs with salt and pepper. Bake on highest oven rack until whites are barely set, 4 to 6 minutes, rotating sheet halfway through baking.

4. Transfer sheets to wire rack and let eggs sit until whites are completely set, about 2 minutes. Serve.

VARIATION

Spicy Eggs in a Hole `FAST`

Mix butter with 2 teaspoons hot sauce before spreading over bread. Sprinkle ½ cup shredded pepper Jack cheese over eggs before baking.

Classic Filled Omelet

SERVES 2 `FAST` `GF`

✔ **WHY THIS RECIPE WORKS:** Omelets seem simple, but cooking the eggs properly in a hot pan can be a delicate matter. Add cheese, which must melt before the omelet turns brown and rubbery, and you've got a truly temperamental dish on your hands. We wanted a foolproof cooking method for a creamy, supple omelet with perfectly melted cheese that didn't leak all over the pan. We found a good-quality nonstick skillet and an easy-melting cheese were essential. A heat-resistant rubber spatula kept the eggs from tearing as we shaped the omelet with the sides of the pan. To ensure the cheese melted before the eggs overcooked, we shredded it fine for quick melting and removed the pan from the heat after adding the cheese. The residual heat was enough to melt the cheese without overcooking the eggs. This technique gave us the omelet we had been looking for: moist and creamy, with plenty of perfectly melted cheese. You can substitute cheddar, Monterey Jack, or any semisoft, grateable cheese for the Gruyère.

Shaping a Filled Omelet

1. Pull cooked eggs from edges of skillet toward center, tilting skillet so any uncooked eggs run to skillet's edges.

2. Sprinkle cheese and filling across center of omelet. Off heat, fold lower third of omelet over filling, then press seam to secure.

3. Pull skillet sharply toward you so that unfolded edge of omelet slides up far side of skillet.

4. Fold far edge of omelet toward center and press to secure seam. Invert omelet onto plate.

6 **large eggs**
   Salt and pepper
1 **tablespoon unsalted butter, plus 1 tablespoon melted butter for brushing omelets**
6 **tablespoons finely shredded Gruyère cheese**
1 **recipe filling**

1. Add 3 eggs to small bowl, season with salt and pepper, and beat with fork until thoroughly combined. Repeat with remaining 3 eggs in separate bowl.

2. Melt 1½ teaspoons butter in 10-inch nonstick skillet over medium-high heat. Add 1 bowl of egg mixture and cook until edges begin to set, 2 to 3 seconds. Using heat-resistant rubber spatula, stir eggs in circular motion until slightly thickened, about 10 seconds. Use spatula to pull cooked edges of eggs in toward center, then tilt skillet to 1 side so that uncooked eggs run to edge of skillet. Repeat until omelet is just set but still moist on surface, 20 to 25 seconds. Sprinkle 3 tablespoons Gruyère and half of filling across center of omelet.

3. Off heat, use spatula to fold lower third (portion nearest you) of omelet over filling; press gently with spatula to secure seams, maintaining fold.

CLASSIC OMELET FILLINGS

MUSHROOM AND THYME FILLING `FAST` `GF`

- 1 tablespoon unsalted butter
- 1 small shallot, minced
- 2 ounces white mushrooms, trimmed and sliced ¼ inch thick
- 1 teaspoon minced fresh thyme
  Salt and pepper

Melt butter in 10-inch skillet over medium heat. Add shallot and cook until softened, about 2 minutes. Add mushrooms and cook until lightly browned, about 3 minutes. Off heat, stir in thyme and season with salt and pepper to taste. Transfer to bowl, cover, and set aside until needed.

RED BELL PEPPER, MUSHROOM, AND ONION FILLING `FAST` `GF`

Monterey Jack or pepper Jack cheese will taste good with this filling.

- 1 tablespoon unsalted butter
- ½ small onion, chopped fine
- 1 ounce white mushrooms, trimmed and sliced ¼ inch thick
- ¼ red bell pepper, cut into ½-inch pieces
- 1 teaspoon minced fresh parsley
  Salt and pepper

Melt butter in 10-inch skillet over medium heat. Add onion and cook until softened, about 2 minutes. Add mushrooms and cook until softened and beginning to brown, about 2 minutes. Add bell pepper and cook until softened, about 2 minutes. Off heat, stir in parsley and season with salt and pepper to taste. Transfer to bowl, cover, and set aside until needed.

4. Run spatula between outer edge of omelet and skillet to loosen. Pull skillet sharply toward you few times to slide unfolded edge of omelet up far side of skillet. Jerk skillet again so that unfolded edge folds over itself, or use spatula to fold edge over. Invert omelet onto warm plate. Tidy edges with spatula, brush with half of melted butter, and serve immediately.

5. Wipe out skillet and repeat with remaining 1½ teaspoons butter, remaining egg mixture, remaining 3 tablespoons Gruyère, remaining filling, and remaining melted butter.

Asparagus Omelet
SERVES 2 `FAST` `GF`

✔ **WHY THIS RECIPE WORKS:** For a substantial diner-style asparagus omelet that would be moist, tender, and sturdy, we focused on how to manipulate the eggs in the pan, and the temperature at which the omelet cooked. We opted for the easy approach of lifting the setting omelet with a rubber spatula to allow the uncooked eggs to pool underneath and cook. We cooked the omelet over medium-low heat until it was partway done, then we took it off the heat and sprinkled the filling and cheese over the top. After the omelet sat covered for about 5 minutes, the cheese was melted and the eggs were perfectly set but still tender. It is important to lift the edges of the omelet when cooking the eggs, rather than push them toward the center. You will need a 10-inch nonstick skillet with a tight-fitting lid for this recipe.

- 2 tablespoons unsalted butter
- ½ pound asparagus, trimmed and cut on bias into ¼-inch pieces
  Salt and pepper
- 1 shallot, halved and sliced thin
- 1 teaspoon lemon juice
- 5 large eggs
- 1½ ounces Gruyère cheese, grated (⅓ cup)

1. Heat 1 tablespoon butter in 10-inch nonstick skillet over medium-high heat. Stir in asparagus, pinch salt, and pinch pepper and cook for 2 minutes. Stir in shallot and continue to cook until asparagus is lightly browned and tender, 2 to 4 minutes. Stir in lemon juice, then transfer to bowl. Wipe out skillet with paper towels.

2. Whisk eggs together in bowl and season with salt and pepper. Heat remaining 1 tablespoon butter in now-empty skillet over medium-low heat, swirling to coat pan. Pour in eggs and cook, without stirring, until eggs begin to set, 45 seconds to 1 minute. Using heat-resistant rubber spatula, lift edge of cooked egg, then tilt pan to 1 side so that uncooked egg runs underneath. Repeat process, working around pan edge. Using spatula, gently scrape uncooked egg toward rim of skillet, until top is just slightly wet. Entire process should take 1½ to 2 minutes. Let pan sit on heat without moving for 30 seconds. Off heat, sprinkle asparagus mixture in even layer over omelet, then sprinkle Gruyère evenly over asparagus. Cover and let sit until eggs no longer appear wet, 4 to 5 minutes.

3. Return skillet to medium heat for 30 seconds. Using rubber spatula, loosen edges of omelet from skillet. Slide omelet halfway out of pan onto plate or cutting board. Tilt pan so top of omelet folds over itself. Cut omelet in half and serve immediately.

VARIATION

Asparagus Omelet with Roasted Red Peppers and Garlic FAST GF

Before adding lemon juice to asparagus mixture, add 1 teaspoon minced fresh thyme, 1 minced garlic clove, and pinch cayenne pepper and cook until fragrant, about 30 seconds. Add ⅓ cup roasted red peppers, rinsed, patted dry, and cut into ¼-inch pieces, to omelet with asparagus mixture. Substitute ½ cup grated fontina cheese for Gruyère.

To make an omelet substantial enough for lunch or dinner, we add in asparagus, roasted red peppers, and fontina cheese.

Making an Asparagus Omelet

1. SAUTÉ ASPARAGUS: Cook asparagus, pinch salt, and pinch pepper in hot, buttered skillet for 2 minutes. Stir in shallot and continue to cook until asparagus is lightly browned and tender, 2 to 4 minutes. Stir in lemon juice, then transfer to bowl.

2. COOK EGGS: Coat pan with more butter. Pour in eggs and cook until eggs begin to set, 45 seconds to 1 minute. Lift edge of cooked egg, then tilt pan to 1 side so that uncooked egg runs underneath. Repeat process, working around pan edge.

3. ADD FILLING: Off heat, sprinkle asparagus mixture in even layer over omelet, then sprinkle Gruyère evenly over asparagus. Cover and let sit until eggs no longer appear wet, 4 to 5 minutes. Return skillet to medium heat for 30 seconds.

4. TRANSFER TO PLATE: Using rubber spatula, loosen edges of omelet from skillet. Slide omelet halfway out of pan onto plate. Tilt pan so top of omelet folds over itself. Cut omelet in half and serve immediately.

Frittata with Parmesan and Herbs

SERVES 6 TO 8   **FAST**   **GF**

✓ **WHY THIS RECIPE WORKS:** Since few cookbooks agree on a method for making frittatas, we had to test a number of techniques to determine which would consistently yield the best frittata, an Italian version of the filled omelet. Whereas an omelet should be soft, delicate, and slightly runny, a frittata should be tender but firm. And whereas an omelet usually encases its filling, a frittata incorporates it evenly throughout. It should also be easy to make. Our testing found that starting the frittata on the stovetop and finishing it in the oven set it evenly so it didn't burn or dry out. Conventional skillets required so much oil to prevent sticking that frittatas cooked in them were likely to be greasy, so we used an ovensafe non-stick pan for a clean release. Because broilers vary in intensity, watch the frittata carefully as it cooks. You will need a 12-inch ovensafe nonstick skillet for this recipe.

12	large eggs
3	tablespoons half-and-half
¾	teaspoon salt
¼	teaspoon pepper
2	teaspoons extra-virgin olive oil
1	onion, chopped fine
1	garlic clove, minced
2	ounces Parmesan cheese, grated (1 cup)
¼	cup minced fresh parsley, basil, dill, tarragon, and/or mint

1. Adjust oven rack 5 inches from broiler element and heat broiler. Whisk eggs, half-and-half, ½ teaspoon salt, and pepper in medium bowl until well combined, about 30 seconds.

2. Heat oil in 12-inch ovensafe nonstick skillet over medium heat until shimmering. Add onion and remaining ¼ teaspoon salt and cook until onion is softened and lightly browned, 5 to 7 minutes. Add garlic and cook until fragrant, about 30 seconds. Stir Parmesan and herbs into eggs; add egg mixture to skillet and cook, using heat-resistant rubber spatula to

To keep this frittata simple and classic, we flavor it with just onion, garlic, Parmesan cheese, and fresh herbs.

stir and scrape bottom of skillet, until large curds form and spatula begins to leave wake but eggs are still very wet, about 2 minutes. Shake skillet to distribute eggs evenly; cook without stirring for 30 seconds to let bottom set.

3. Transfer skillet to oven and broil until frittata has risen and surface is puffed and spotty brown, 3 to 4 minutes; when cut into with paring knife, eggs should be slightly wet and runny. Remove skillet from oven and let sit for 5 minutes. Using spatula, loosen frittata from skillet and slide onto serving platter or cutting board. Cut into wedges and serve.

VARIATIONS

Frittata with Broccoli Rabe, Sun-Dried Tomatoes, and Fontina   **FAST**   **GF**

Substitute 8 ounces broccoli rabe, cut into 1-inch pieces, for onion, and increase cooking time to 6 to 8 minutes, until broccoli rabe is beginning to brown and soften. Add ⅛ teaspoon red pepper flakes to skillet with garlic. Substitute 3 ounces Italian fontina cheese, cut into ¼-inch cubes, for Parmesan. Stir ¼ cup rinsed, patted dry, and coarsely chopped oil-packed sun-dried tomatoes into eggs with fontina and herbs in step 2.

Removing Frittata from the Pan

Run spatula around skillet edge to loosen frittata, then carefully slide it out onto serving platter or cutting board.

Frittata with Asparagus and Goat Cheese FAST GF

Substitute 8 ounces thin asparagus, trimmed and cut on bias into ¼-inch pieces, for onion. Cook until asparagus is lightly browned and crisp-tender, about 3 minutes. Substitute 1 minced shallot for garlic and cook until shallot is softened, about 2 minutes. Substitute 1 cup crumbled goat cheese for Parmesan. Omit herbs.

Fried Eggs with Parmesan and Potato Roesti

SERVES 4 FAST GF

✔ WHY THIS RECIPE WORKS: When topped with a fried egg, Swedish roesti—a broad, golden-brown cake of simply seasoned grated potatoes fried in butter—makes a hearty breakfast or supper. Producing a golden-brown crust for our roesti recipe wasn't much of a problem, but the inside always came out gluey and half-cooked. To fix this, we eliminated moisture by wringing the raw grated potatoes in a dish towel. Covering the potatoes to start, then uncovering them to finish cooking, created surprisingly light potatoes. Our final breakthrough came when we removed excess starch by rinsing the raw potatoes in cold water, then tossed them with 1½ teaspoons of cornstarch to provide just enough starch to hold the cake together. For the best texture, shred the potatoes on the large shredding disk of a food processor. If using a coarse grater, cut the potatoes lengthwise so you are left with long shreds. Be sure to squeeze the potatoes as dry as possible. You will need a 12-inch nonstick skillet with a tight-fitting lid for this recipe. A well-seasoned cast-iron skillet with a tight-fitting lid can be used in place of the nonstick skillet.

2½ pounds Yukon Gold potatoes, peeled and shredded
1½ teaspoons cornstarch
Salt and pepper
5 tablespoons unsalted butter, plus 1 tablespoon cut into 4 pieces and chilled
8 large eggs
2 teaspoons vegetable oil
1 ounce Parmesan cheese, grated (½ cup)

1. Place potatoes in large bowl and fill with cold water. Using hands, swirl to remove excess starch, then drain, leaving potatoes in colander.

2. Wipe bowl dry. Place one-third of potatoes in center of dish towel. Gather towel ends together and twist tightly to

Storing Eggs

In the test kitchen, we've tasted two- and three-month-old eggs and found them perfectly palatable. However, at four months, the white was very loose and the yolk had off-flavors, though it was still edible. Our advice is to use your discretion; if eggs smell odd or are discolored, pitch them. Older eggs also lack the structure-lending properties of fresh eggs, so beware when baking.

IN THE REFRIGERATOR

Eggs often suffer more from improper storage than from age. If your refrigerator has an egg tray in the door, don't use it— eggs should be stored on a shelf, where the temperature is below 40 degrees (the average refrigerator door temperature in our kitchen is closer to 45 degrees). Eggs are best stored in their cardboard or plastic carton, which protects them from absorbing flavors from other foods. The carton also helps maintain humidity, which slows down the evaporation of the eggs' moisture.

IN THE FREEZER

Extra whites can be frozen for later use, but we have found their rising properties compromised. Frozen whites are best in recipes that call for small amounts (like an egg wash) or that don't depend on whipping (like an omelet). Yolks can't be frozen as is, but adding sugar syrup (microwave 2 parts sugar to 1 part water, stirring occasionally, until sugar is dissolved) to the yolks allows them to be frozen. Stir a scant ¼ teaspoon sugar syrup per yolk into the yolks before freezing. Defrosted yolks treated this way will behave just like fresh yolks in custards and other recipes.

squeeze out moisture. Transfer potatoes to now-empty bowl and repeat process with remaining potatoes in 2 batches.

3. Sprinkle cornstarch, ¾ teaspoon salt, and pinch pepper over potatoes. Using hands or fork, toss ingredients together until well blended.

4. Melt 2½ tablespoons butter in 12-inch nonstick skillet over medium heat. Add potato mixture and spread into even layer. Cover and cook for 6 minutes. Uncover and, using spatula, gently press potatoes down to form round cake. Cook, occasionally pressing on potatoes to shape into uniform round cake, until bottom is deep golden brown, 8 to 10 minutes longer.

5. Shake skillet to loosen roesti and slide onto large plate. Add 2½ tablespoons butter to skillet and swirl to coat pan. Invert roesti onto second plate and slide roesti, browned side

up, back into skillet. Cook, occasionally pressing down on roesti, until bottom is well browned, 8 to 10 minutes. Transfer roesti to cutting board and let cool slightly while making eggs. Wipe out now-empty skillet with paper towels.

6. Crack eggs into 2 small bowls (4 eggs per bowl) and season with salt and pepper. Heat oil in now-empty skillet over medium heat until shimmering. Add remaining 1 tablespoon chilled butter to skillet and quickly swirl to coat pan. Working quickly, pour 1 bowl of eggs in 1 side of pan and second bowl of eggs in other side. Cover and cook for 2 minutes.

7. Remove skillet from heat and let stand, covered, about 2 minutes for runny yolks (white around edge of yolk will be barely opaque), about 3 minutes for soft but set yolks, and about 4 minutes for medium-set yolks. Slide eggs onto roesti, sprinkle with Parmesan cheese, and season with salt to taste. Cut into wedges and serve.

Shakshuka

SERVES 4 `GF`

✔ **WHY THIS RECIPE WORKS:** Shakshuka is a Tunisian dish featuring eggs poached in a spiced tomato, onion, and pepper sauce. The name *shakshuka* is derived from a term meaning "all mixed up," and the key to great shakshuka is balancing the piquancy, acidity, richness, and sweetness of its ingredients. Choosing the right pepper to star in this dish made all the difference. We compared the results when using fresh red bell peppers, roasted red bell peppers, and piquillo peppers, which are sweet roasted chiles. The fresh red bell peppers tasted flat and lackluster. We liked the roasted red bell peppers just fine, but the piquillo peppers were our favorite, boasting spicy-sweet and vibrant flavors. These small red peppers from Spain, sold in jars or cans, have a subtle hint of smokiness from being roasted over a wood fire. We added yellow bell peppers to the mix for a clean, fresh flavor and a bright contrast to the deep red sauce. We finished our shakshuka with a sprinkling of bright cilantro and salty, creamy feta cheese. Jarred roasted red peppers can be substituted for the piquillo peppers. Serve with pita or crusty bread to mop up the sauce. You will need a 12-inch skillet with a tight-fitting lid for this recipe.

3 tablespoons vegetable oil
2 onions, chopped fine
2 yellow bell peppers, stemmed, seeded, and cut into ¼-inch pieces
4 garlic cloves, minced
2 teaspoons tomato paste

This Tunisian dish makes a convenient skillet supper—the eggs are poached right in the fragrant tomato-and-pepper sauce.

1 teaspoon ground cumin
1 teaspoon turmeric
Salt and pepper
⅛ teaspoon cayenne pepper
1½ cups jarred piquillo peppers, chopped coarse
1 (14.5-ounce) can diced tomatoes
¼ cup water
2 bay leaves
⅓ cup chopped fresh cilantro
8 large eggs
2 ounces feta cheese, crumbled (½ cup)

1. Heat oil in 12-inch skillet over medium-high heat until simmering. Add onions and bell peppers and cook until softened and beginning to brown, 8 to 10 minutes. Add garlic, tomato paste, cumin, turmeric, 1½ teaspoons salt, ¼ teaspoon pepper, and cayenne, and cook, stirring frequently, until tomato paste begins to darken, about 3 minutes.

2. Stir in piquillo peppers, tomatoes and their juice, water, and bay leaves and bring to simmer. Reduce heat to medium-low and cook, stirring occasionally, until sauce is slightly thickened, 10 to 15 minutes.

3. Off heat, discard bay leaves and stir in ¼ cup cilantro. Transfer 2 cups sauce to blender and process until smooth, about 60 seconds. Return puree to skillet and bring sauce to simmer over medium-low heat.

4. Off heat, make 4 shallow indentations (about 2 inches wide) in surface of sauce using back of spoon. Crack 2 eggs into each indentation and season eggs with salt and pepper. Cover and cook over medium-low heat until egg whites are just set and yolks are still runny, 5 to 10 minutes. Sprinkle with feta and remaining cilantro and serve.

Poaching Eggs in Sauce or Hash

1. Off heat, make 4 shallow indentations (about 2 inches wide) in surface of sauce (or hash) using back of spoon.

2. Crack 2 eggs into each indentation and season eggs with salt and pepper. Cover and cook over medium-low heat until egg whites are just set and yolks are still runny, 5 to 10 minutes.

Cajun-Style Eggs in Purgatory with Cheesy Grits

SERVES 4   `FAST` `GF`

WHY THIS RECIPE WORKS: A Cajun take on Eggs in Purgatory, this devilish dish gets its name from the spicy sauce used to poach the eggs. We tried a variety of hot sauces and chiles in order to find just the right balance of spice and heat for our sauce, and in the end we loved the moderate spice level and convenience of using canned Ro-tel tomatoes. A blend of tomatoes, green chiles, and spices, Ro-tel tomatoes are a staple in many Southern pantries. Not only did these spicy, tangy tomatoes add heat, they also formed the base of the sauce. To give the sauce more substance, we sautéed an onion and a green bell pepper and added some garlic and chili powder before stirring in the Ro-tel tomatoes, along with a can of plain tomato sauce for balance. Creamy, cheesy grits made the perfect foil for the eggs and sauce. In order for this recipe to be gluten-free, you must use gluten-free grits. You will need a 12-inch nonstick skillet with a tight-fitting lid for this recipe. Serve with hot sauce.

GRITS

3½	**cups water**
	Salt and pepper
1	**cup old-fashioned grits**
6	**ounces sharp cheddar cheese, shredded (1½ cups)**
3	**scallions, sliced thin**

EGGS

2	**tablespoons unsalted butter**
1	**onion, chopped fine**
1	**green bell pepper, stemmed, seeded, and cut into ⅓-inch pieces**
2	**garlic cloves, minced**
1	**teaspoon chili powder**
	Salt and pepper
1	**(10-ounce) can Ro-tel Diced Tomatoes & Green Chilies**
1	**(8-ounce) can tomato sauce**
8	**large eggs**

1. FOR THE GRITS: Bring water and ½ teaspoon salt to boil in medium saucepan. Add grits in very slow stream while whisking constantly in circular motion to prevent clumping. Cover, reduce heat to low, and cook, stirring often and scraping corners of pot, until grits are thick and creamy, 10 to 15 minutes. Stir in cheese and scallions and season with salt and pepper to taste; cover to keep warm.

2. FOR THE EGGS: Melt butter in 12-inch nonstick skillet over medium-high heat. Add onion and bell pepper and cook until softened, 5 to 7 minutes. Stir in garlic, chili powder, and ½ teaspoon salt, and cook until fragrant, about 30 seconds. Stir in Ro-tel tomatoes and tomato sauce and simmer until sauce is thickened, about 5 minutes.

3. Off heat, make 4 shallow indentations (about 2 inches wide) in surface of sauce using back of spoon. Crack 2 eggs into each indentation and season eggs with salt and pepper. Cover and cook over medium-low heat until egg whites are just set and yolks are still runny, 5 to 10 minutes. Portion grits into shallow bowls, top with eggs, and serve.

Huevos Rancheros

SERVES 4 `GF`

✔ **WHY THIS RECIPE WORKS:** The huevos rancheros found on American brunch menus tend to resemble heaping plates of nachos rather than the simple, satisfying Mexican meal of tortillas, eggs, and salsa. We wanted to use supermarket staples to produce the most authentic version possible. For the salsa, we enhanced canned diced tomatoes with green chiles, onion, chili powder, and garlic and roasted the mixture until it was spottily charred. Then we spread the salsa in a baking dish and topped it with cheese. To poach the eggs in the sauce, we made divots in the mixture, added the eggs, and baked the dish for about 15 minutes, until the eggs were just set. Then we topped the dish with avocado, scallions, and cilantro and served it with warm corn tortillas. Use a heavyweight rimmed baking sheet to roast the salsa; flimsy sheets will warp. Serve with Refried Pinto Beans (page 218) and hot sauce.

- 2 (28-ounce) cans diced tomatoes
- 1 tablespoon packed brown sugar
- 1 tablespoon lime juice
- 1 onion, chopped
- ½ cup canned chopped green chiles
- ¼ cup extra-virgin olive oil
- 3 tablespoons chili powder
- 4 garlic cloves, sliced thin
  Salt and pepper
- 4 ounces pepper Jack cheese, shredded (1 cup)
- 8 large eggs
- 1 avocado, halved, pitted, and diced
- 3 scallions, sliced thin
- ⅓ cup minced fresh cilantro
- 8 (6-inch) corn tortillas, warmed

1. Adjust oven rack to middle position and heat oven to 500 degrees. Drain tomatoes in fine-mesh strainer set over bowl, pressing with rubber spatula to extract 1¾ cups tomato juice; discard extra juice. Whisk in sugar and lime juice.

2. In separate bowl, combine drained tomatoes, onion, chiles, oil, chili powder, garlic, and ½ teaspoon salt. Spread tomato mixture evenly over parchment paper–lined rimmed baking sheet. Roast until charred in spots, 35 to 40 minutes, stirring halfway through baking. (Tomato juice mixture and roasted vegetables can be refrigerated separately for up to 24 hours; reheat vegetables in microwave for 45 seconds and bring juice to room temperature before continuing.)

3. Reduce oven temperature to 400 degrees. Combine roasted vegetables and tomato juice in 13 by 9-inch baking dish, season with salt and pepper to taste, and sprinkle evenly

with cheese. Using spoon, hollow out 8 holes in tomato mixture. Crack 1 egg into each hole and season eggs with salt and pepper.

4. Bake until whites are just beginning to set but still have some movement when dish is shaken, 13 to 16 minutes. Transfer dish to wire rack, tent with aluminum foil, and let sit for 5 minutes. Sprinkle with avocado, scallions, and cilantro. Serve with warm tortillas.

Sweet Potato Hash

SERVES 4 `FAST` `GF`

✔ **WHY THIS RECIPE WORKS:** To put a sweet twist on traditional potato hash, we looked to swap out regular spuds for sweet potatoes and boost the flavor with a backbone of chili powder. Unfortunately, our first attempts resulted in a very soft, mushy hash—sweet potatoes don't boast the same starchiness as russets, so they don't retain their shape as well once cooked. We got better results by mixing in some starchy russets with the sweet potatoes; the russets softened and crumbled, binding the hash together. To speed things up, we parcooked the potatoes in the microwave until tender, then moved them to the skillet to brown and crisp. We rounded out the flavors with onion, garlic, thyme, and a dash of hot sauce, plus heavy cream for richness. To make our hash a hearty meal, we poached eight eggs right in the hash. This hash was such a hit that we decided to develop a Red Flannel Hash variation, mottled with sweet, vibrant beets. If you

We put a new spin on classic breakfast hash by mixing the usual russets with earthy sweet potatoes.

notice that the potatoes aren't getting brown in step 3, turn up the heat (but don't let them burn). You will need a 12-inch nonstick skillet with a tight-fitting lid for this recipe.

- 12 **ounces russet potatoes, peeled and cut into ¼-inch pieces**
- 12 **ounces sweet potatoes, peeled and cut into ¼-inch pieces**
- 2 **tablespoons vegetable oil**
  Salt and pepper
- 1 **onion, chopped fine**
- 2 **garlic cloves, minced**
- ½ **teaspoon minced fresh thyme or ¼ teaspoon dried**
- ½ **teaspoon chili powder**
- ⅓ **cup heavy cream**
- ¼ **teaspoon hot sauce**
- 8 **large eggs**

1. Microwave russets, sweet potatoes, 1 tablespoon oil, ½ teaspoon salt, and ¼ teaspoon pepper in covered bowl until potatoes are translucent around edges, 5 to 8 minutes, stirring halfway through microwaving.

2. Meanwhile, heat remaining 1 tablespoon oil in 12-inch nonstick skillet over medium-high heat until shimmering. Add onion and cook until softened and lightly browned, 5 to 7 minutes.

3. Stir in garlic, thyme, and chili powder and cook until fragrant, about 30 seconds. Stir in hot potatoes, cream, and hot sauce. Using back of spatula, gently pack potatoes into pan and cook undisturbed for 2 minutes. Flip hash, 1 portion at a time, and lightly repack into pan. Repeat flipping process every few minutes until potatoes are nicely browned, 6 to 8 minutes.

4. Off heat, make 4 shallow indentations (about 2 inches wide) in surface of hash using back of spoon. Crack 2 eggs into each indentation and season eggs with salt and pepper. Cover and cook over medium-low heat until egg whites are just set and yolks are still runny, 5 to 10 minutes. Serve.

VARIATION

Sweet Potato Red Flannel Hash FAST GF

In order for this recipe to be gluten-free, you will need to use gluten-free Worcestershire sauce. Note that the beets will not brown like the potatoes; they will burn if the pan gets too dry.

Reduce russet potatoes and sweet potatoes to 8 ounces each. Microwave 8 ounces beets, peeled and cut into ¼-inch pieces, with potatoes. Add ¼ teaspoon vegetarian Worcestershire sauce to skillet with cream and hot sauce.

Brussels Sprouts Hash

SERVES 4 FAST GF

✓ **WHY THIS RECIPE WORKS:** For this hearty vegetable hash, we wanted to combine the potatoes with earthy Brussels sprouts and sweet carrots. But hashing together different vegetables presented a challenge: The potatoes and carrots took longer than the Brussels sprouts to soften. Starting the potatoes and carrots in the microwave with a little oil solved the problem, turning them tender in only 5 minutes. Meanwhile, we cooked the Brussels sprouts in the skillet to get good browning. We tried slicing or shredding the sprouts, but the small pieces tended to steam rather than brown. Cutting the sprouts into wedges provided nice flat surfaces that picked up flavorful browning. Next, we added in the microwaved carrots and potatoes along with onion, garlic, thyme, and a little water to help the Brussels sprouts cook through. Finally, we made divots in the flavorful hash and cracked eggs into them to poach gently over medium-low heat. Look for small Brussels sprouts no bigger than a golf ball, as they're likely to be sweeter and more tender than large sprouts. If you can find only large sprouts, halve them and cut each half into thirds.

1 pound red potatoes, unpeeled,
   cut into ½-inch chunks

2 carrots, peeled and cut into ½-inch chunks

3 tablespoons extra-virgin olive oil
   Salt and pepper

1 pound Brussels sprouts, trimmed and
   quartered lengthwise

1 onion, chopped fine

2 tablespoons water

1 tablespoon minced fresh thyme

1 garlic clove, minced

1 tablespoon unsalted butter

8 large eggs

2 scallions, sliced thin

1. Toss potatoes, carrots, 1 tablespoon oil, ½ teaspoon salt, and ¼ teaspoon pepper together in large bowl. Cover and microwave until vegetables are tender, 5 to 7 minutes, stirring halfway through cooking.

2. Meanwhile, heat 1 tablespoon oil in 12-inch nonstick skillet over medium-high heat until shimmering. Add Brussels sprouts and cook until browned, 6 to 8 minutes, stirring occasionally. Add microwaved vegetables, onion, water, thyme, garlic, remaining 1 tablespoon oil, ¾ teaspoon salt, and ¼ teaspoon pepper. Reduce heat to medium, cover, and cook until Brussels sprouts are just tender, 5 to 7 minutes longer, stirring halfway through cooking.

3. Off heat, stir in butter and season with salt and pepper to taste. Make 4 shallow indentations (about 2 inches wide) in surface of hash using back of spoon. Crack 2 eggs into each indentation and season eggs with salt and pepper. Cover and cook over medium-low heat until egg whites are just set and yolks are still runny, 5 to 10 minutes. Sprinkle with scallions and serve.

Spanish Tortilla with Roasted Red Peppers and Peas

SERVES 4 TO 6 GF

✔ **WHY THIS RECIPE WORKS:** This tapas bar favorite, boasting meltingly tender potatoes in a dense, creamy omelet, is immensely appealing. But the typical recipe calls for simmering the potatoes in up to 4 cups of extra-virgin olive oil. Using so much oil for a single and somewhat humble meal seemed excessive. We were able to cut the oil to a mere 6 tablespoons by substituting firmer, less starchy Yukon Gold potatoes for the standard russets. Traditional recipes call for flipping the tortilla with the help of a single plate, but when we tried this, the result was an egg-splattered floor. Sliding the omelet onto the plate—and then using a second plate to flip it—made a once-messy task foolproof. And while the tortilla was perfectly good plain, we liked it even better with roasted red peppers and peas, and a side of garlicky aïoli. Spanish tortillas are often served warm or at room temperature alongside olives and pickles as an appetizer. They may also be served with a salad as a light entrée. You will need a 10-inch nonstick skillet with a tight-fitting lid for this recipe.

6 tablespoons plus 1 teaspoon extra-virgin olive oil

1½ pounds Yukon Gold potatoes, peeled,
    quartered, and cut into ⅛-inch-thick slices

1 small onion, halved and sliced thin
   Salt and pepper

8 large eggs

½ cup jarred roasted red peppers, rinsed,
   patted dry, and cut into ½-inch pieces

½ cup frozen peas, thawed

1 recipe Garlic Aïoli (page 43)

Flipping a Spanish Tortilla

1. After browning first side, loosen tortilla with heat-resistant rubber spatula and slide it onto large plate.

2. Place second plate face down over tortilla. Invert tortilla onto second plate so that it is browned side up.

3. Slide tortilla back into pan, browned side up, then tuck edges into pan with rubber spatula.

1. Toss ¼ cup oil, potatoes, onion, ½ teaspoon salt, and ¼ teaspoon pepper together in large bowl. Heat 2 tablespoons oil in 10-inch nonstick skillet over medium-high heat until shimmering. Add potato mixture to pan and reduce heat to medium-low. Cover and cook, stirring every 5 minutes, until potatoes are tender, about 25 minutes.

2. Whisk eggs and ½ teaspoon salt together in now-empty bowl, then gently fold in cooked potato mixture, red peppers, and peas. Make sure to scrape all of potato mixture out of skillet.

3. Heat remaining 1 teaspoon oil in now-empty skillet over medium-high heat until just smoking. Add egg mixture and cook, shaking pan and folding mixture constantly for 15 seconds. Smooth top of egg mixture, reduce heat to medium, cover, and cook, gently shaking pan every 30 seconds, until bottom is golden brown and top is lightly set, about 2 minutes.

4. Off heat, run heat-resistant rubber spatula around edge of pan and shake pan gently to loosen tortilla; it should slide around freely in pan. Slide tortilla onto large plate, then invert onto second large plate and slide back into skillet browned side up. Tuck edges of tortilla into skillet with rubber spatula. Continue to cook over medium heat, gently shaking pan every 30 seconds, until second side is golden brown, about 2 minutes. Slide tortilla onto cutting board and let cool slightly. Serve warm or at room temperature with aïoli.

The key to a pasta frittata with a perfectly balanced texture is using thin, delicate angel hair for the pasta.

Pasta Frittata

SERVES 4 TO 6

✔ **WHY THIS RECIPE WORKS:** For a pasta frittata that would showcase the egg and pasta in equal measure, we opted for angel hair pasta. The superthin strands of angel hair formed a delicate network throughout the eggy interior. For convenience, we skipped the traditional pasta cooking method and instead cooked the angel hair in just 3 cups of water in the same 10-inch nonstick skillet we later used for cooking the frittata. Adding some oil to the pasta cooking water allowed us to create a crispy browned pasta crust; as the water evaporated, the bottom layer of pasta fried in the oil left in the skillet. We kept the eggs tender by whisking them with extra-virgin olive oil, and we added some Parmesan for rich flavor. Finally, we stirred in tender sautéed broccoli rabe to lend fresh flavor and heartiness. To ensure the proper texture, it's important to use angel hair pasta for this recipe. We like to serve the frittata warm or at room temperature, and with a side salad. You will need a 10-inch nonstick skillet with a tight-fitting lid for this recipe.

8 **large eggs**
1 **ounce Parmesan cheese, grated (½ cup)**
3 **tablespoons extra-virgin olive oil**
   Salt and pepper
3 **tablespoons vegetable oil**
2 **garlic cloves, sliced thin**
⅛ **teaspoon red pepper flakes**
8 **ounces broccoli rabe, trimmed and cut into ½-inch pieces**
3 **cups plus 1 tablespoon water**
1 **tablespoon white wine vinegar**
6 **ounces angel hair pasta, broken in half**

1. Whisk eggs, Parmesan, olive oil, ½ teaspoon salt, and ½ teaspoon pepper together in large bowl until egg is even yellow color.

2. Heat 2 teaspoons vegetable oil in 10-inch nonstick skillet over medium heat until shimmering. Add garlic and pepper flakes and cook until fragrant, about 1 minute. Stir in broccoli rabe, 1 tablespoon water, and ¼ teaspoon salt. Cover and

cook until broccoli rabe is bright green and crisp-tender, 2 to 3 minutes. Off heat, stir in vinegar, then transfer broccoli rabe mixture to bowl with egg mixture.

3. Wipe out now-empty skillet with paper towels, then add remaining 3 cups water, pasta, remaining 7 teaspoons vegetable oil, and ¾ teaspoon salt. Bring to boil over high heat and cook, stirring occasionally, until pasta is tender, water has evaporated, and pasta starts to sizzle in oil, 8 to 12 minutes. Reduce heat to medium and cook, swirling pan and scraping under edge of pasta with heat-resistant rubber spatula frequently (do not stir), until bottom turns golden and starts to crisp, 5 to 7 minutes.

4. Using spatula, push some pasta up sides of skillet to cover entire surface of pan. Pour egg mixture over pasta. Using tongs, lift up loose strands of pasta to allow egg to flow toward pan, being careful not to pull up crispy bottom crust. Cover skillet and continue to cook over medium heat until bottom crust turns golden brown and top of frittata is just set (egg below very top will still be raw), 5 to 8 minutes.

5. Slide frittata onto large plate, then invert onto second large plate and slide back into skillet browned side up. Tuck edges of frittata into skillet with rubber spatula. Continue to cook over medium heat until second side is golden brown, 2 to 4 minutes. Remove skillet from heat and let stand for 5 minutes. Using your hand or pan lid, invert frittata onto cutting board. Cut into wedges and serve.

NOTES FROM THE TEST KITCHEN

Substituting Eggs

Eggs vary in size, which will make a difference in recipes, especially those that call for several eggs. We use large eggs in all of our recipes, but you can substitute one size for another. For instance, four jumbo eggs are equivalent to five large eggs—each combination weighs a total of 10 ounces. See the chart below for help in making accurate calculations. For half of an egg, whisk the yolk and white together, measure, and then divide in half.

LARGE 2 oz		JUMBO 2.5 oz	EXTRA-LARGE 2.25 oz	MEDIUM 1.75 oz
1	=	1	1	1
2	=	1½	2	2
3	=	2½	2½	3½
4	=	3	3½	4½
5	=	4	4	6
6	=	5	5	7

Elegant, decadent, and easy to make ahead, this simple cheese quiche makes the perfect weekend brunch showstopper.

Simple Cheese Quiche

SERVES 6 TO 8

✓ **WHY THIS RECIPE WORKS:** Our ideal quiche has a tender, buttery pastry crust enveloping a velvety smooth custard that is neither too rich nor too lean. We tested numerous combinations of dairy and eggs to find the perfect combination: 5 eggs and 2 cups half-and-half. The baking temperature was equally important; 350 degrees was low enough to set the custard gently and hot enough to brown the top before the filling dried out and became rubbery. To keep the crust from becoming soggy, we parbaked it before adding the filling. To avoid spilling the custard, we set the parbaked crust in the oven before pouring the custard into the pastry shell. For perfectly baked quiche every time, we pulled it out of the oven when it was still slightly soft and allowed it to set up as it cooled. Be sure to add the custard to the pie shell while the crust is still warm so that the quiche will bake evenly. You can substitute other fresh herbs for the chives, like thyme, parsley, or marjoram. You can use the All-Butter Single-Crust Pie Dough (page 398) or store-bought pie dough in this recipe.

5 large eggs

2 cups half-and-half

¼ teaspoon salt

¼ teaspoon pepper

4 ounces cheddar cheese, shredded (1 cup)

1 tablespoon minced fresh chives

1 recipe single-crust pie dough, partially baked and still warm

1. Adjust oven rack to lower-middle position and heat oven to 350 degrees. Whisk eggs, half-and-half, salt, and pepper together in large bowl. Stir in cheddar and chives. Transfer filling to 4-cup liquid measuring cup.

2. Place warm pie shell on rimmed baking sheet and place in oven. Carefully pour egg mixture into warm shell until it reaches about ½ inch from top edge of crust (you may have extra egg mixture).

3. Bake quiche until top is lightly browned, center is set but soft, and knife inserted about 1 inch from edge comes out clean, 40 to 50 minutes. Let quiche cool for at least 1 hour or up to 3 hours. Serve slightly warm or at room temperature.

TO MAKE AHEAD: Let baked quiche cool completely, then cover with plastic wrap and refrigerate for up to 6 hours. (Crust of refrigerated quiche will be less crisp.) Quiche can be served slightly chilled, at room temperature, or warm; to serve warm, reheat in 350-degree oven for 10 to 15 minutes.

Quiche with Broccoli and Cheddar
Do not substitute frozen broccoli here.

Bring 4 cups chopped broccoli florets, ½ cup water, and ¼ teaspoon salt to boil in covered 12-inch skillet and cook until broccoli is bright green, about 3 minutes. Uncover and continue to cook until broccoli is tender and water has evaporated, about 3 minutes; transfer to paper towel–lined plate. Distribute broccoli over warm pie shell before adding egg mixture.

Quiche with Leek and Goat Cheese
Melt 2 tablespoons unsalted butter in 10-inch skillet over medium-high heat. Add 2 finely chopped leeks, white and light green parts only, and cook until softened, about 6 minutes; transfer to plate. Substitute 1 cup crumbled goat cheese for cheddar, and stir leeks into eggs with cheese and chives.

Quiche with Spinach and Feta
Removing the excess moisture from the spinach is crucial here.

Omit chives and substitute 1 cup crumbled feta cheese for cheddar. Stir 1 (10-ounce) package frozen chopped spinach, thawed and squeezed dry, into eggs with cheese.

Quiche with Asparagus and Gruyère
Do not substitute precooked or frozen asparagus here.

Substitute Gruyère cheese for cheddar, and stir 1 pound asparagus, trimmed and sliced on bias into ¼-inch-thick pieces, into eggs with cheese and chives.

Making Simple Cheese Quiche

1. PARBAKE CRUST: After making and chilling crust, line chilled crust with double layer of aluminum foil and fill with pie weights. Bake at 400 degrees until crust looks dry and is light in color, 25 to 30 minutes.

2. MAKE CUSTARD: In large bowl, whisk together eggs, half-and-half, salt, and pepper, then stir in cheese and chives.

3. FILL WARM PIE SHELL IN OVEN: Lower oven temperature to 350 degrees. Place pie shell on rimmed baking sheet and transfer to oven. Pour custard into large measuring cup, then fill pie shell, stopping ½ inch from top edge.

4. BAKE QUICHE: Bake until top of quiche is lightly browned, center is set but soft, and knife inserted about 1 inch from edge comes out clean, 40 to 50 minutes. Let quiche cool for at least 1 hour or up to 3 hours.

All-Butter Single-Crust Pie Dough

MAKES ONE 9-INCH PIE CRUST

✓ **WHY THIS RECIPE WORKS:** All-butter pie dough possesses great flavor, but it often fails to be flaky and is notoriously difficult to work with. We wanted an all-butter dough that was easier to mix, handle, and roll, with all the tenderness and flavor that "all-butter" promises. For easier handling, we tried simply using less butter, but this resulted in bland flavor and dry texture. Instead, we experimented with other forms of fat, including heavy cream, cream cheese, and sour cream. In the end, we found that sour cream not only added flavor to the crust, but it also helped keep the dough tender and flaky, because acid reduces gluten development. To distribute the sour cream evenly, mix it first with the water. Freezing the butter is crucial to the flaky texture of this crust—do not skip this step. If preparing the dough in a very warm kitchen, refrigerate all of the ingredients (including the flour) before making the dough.

3 tablespoons ice water, plus extra as needed

4 teaspoons sour cream

1¼ cups (6¼ ounces) all-purpose flour

1½ teaspoons sugar

½ teaspoon salt

8 tablespoons unsalted butter, cut into
   ¼-inch pieces and frozen for 10 to 15 minutes

1. Whisk ice water and sour cream together in bowl. Process flour, sugar, and salt in food processor until combined, about 3 seconds. Scatter frozen butter over top and pulse mixture until butter is size of large peas, about 10 pulses.

2. Pour half of sour cream mixture over flour mixture and pulse until incorporated, about 3 pulses. Repeat with remaining sour cream mixture. Pinch dough with your fingers; if dough feels dry and does not hold together, sprinkle 1 to 2 tablespoons more ice water over mixture and pulse until dough forms large clumps and no dry flour remains, 3 to 5 pulses.

3. Turn dough onto sheet of plastic wrap and flatten into 4-inch disk. Wrap tightly and refrigerate for 1 hour. Before rolling dough out, let it sit on counter to soften slightly, about 10 minutes. (Dough can be refrigerated for up to 2 days or frozen for up to 1 month. If frozen, let dough thaw completely on counter before rolling it out.)

4. Roll dough between 2 large sheets parchment paper to 12-inch circle. (If dough is soft and/or sticky, refrigerate until firm.) Remove parchment on top of dough round and flip into 9-inch pie plate; peel off second layer parchment. Lift dough and gently press it into pie plate, letting excess hang over plate's edge. Cover loosely with plastic and refrigerate until firm, about 30 minutes.

5. Trim all but ½ inch of dough overhanging edge of pie plate. Tuck dough underneath itself to form tidy, even edge that sits on lip of pie plate. Crimp dough evenly around edge of pie using fingers. Wrap dough-lined pie plate loosely in plastic and refrigerate until firm, about 15 minutes.

6. Adjust oven rack to middle position and heat oven to 400 degrees. Line chilled pie crust with double layer of aluminum foil, covering edges to prevent burning, and fill with pie weights or pennies.

7A. FOR A PARTIALLY BAKED CRUST: Bake until pie dough looks dry and is pale in color, 25 to 30 minutes. Transfer pie plate to wire rack and remove weights and foil. Following particular pie recipe, use crust while it is still warm or let it cool completely.

7B. FOR A FULLY BAKED CRUST: Bake until pie dough looks dry and is pale in color, 25 to 30 minutes. Remove weights and foil and continue to bake crust until deep golden brown, 5 to 10 minutes. Transfer pie plate to wire rack. Following particular pie recipe, use crust while it is still warm or let it cool completely.

Shaping a Single-Crust Pie Shell

1. Gently press dough into pie plate, letting excess hang over plate's edge. Trim all but ½ inch of excess dough. Tuck dough underneath itself to form tidy, even edge that sits on lip of pie plate.

2. Use index finger of one hand and thumb and index finger of other hand to create fluted ridges perpendicular to edge of pie plate.

A Parmesan and Gruyère béchamel seasoned with cayenne, paprika, and nutmeg gives our airy soufflé nuanced flavor.

Cheese Soufflé

SERVES 4 TO 6

✓ **WHY THIS RECIPE WORKS:** We wanted a cheese soufflé with bold cheese flavor, good stature, and a light but not-too-airy texture, without the fussiness of most recipes. To add cheese flavor without weight, we added airy, potent Parmesan cheese to the Gruyère. To get the texture just right and keep things simple, we beat the egg whites to stiff peaks, then—rather than carefully folding them into the béchamel—added the sauce right to the mixer and beat everything until uniform. For well-rounded flavor, we seasoned the béchamel with a little paprika, cayenne, white pepper, and nutmeg. Serve this soufflé with a green salad for a light dinner. Comté, sharp cheddar, or gouda cheese can be substituted for the Gruyère. To prevent the soufflé from overflowing the soufflé dish, leave at least 1 inch of space between the top of the batter and the rim of the dish; discard any excess batter. The most foolproof way to test for doneness is with an instant-read thermometer. Alternatively, use two large spoons to pry open the soufflé; the center should appear thick and creamy but not soupy.

Mixing and Baking a Cheese Soufflé

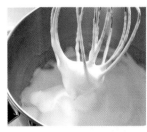

1. Whip egg whites and cream of tartar on medium-low speed until foamy, about 1 minute. Increase speed to medium-high and whip until stiff peaks form, 3 to 4 minutes.

2. Add cheese mixture and continue to whip until fully combined, about 15 seconds.

3. Pour mixture into prepared dish and sprinkle with remaining 1 tablespoon Parmesan.

4. Bake until risen above rim, top is deep golden brown, and interior registers 170 degrees, 30 to 35 minutes.

1	ounce Parmesan cheese, grated (½ cup)
¼	cup (1¼ ounces) all-purpose flour
¼	teaspoon paprika
¼	teaspoon salt
⅛	teaspoon cayenne pepper
⅛	teaspoon white pepper
	Pinch ground nutmeg
4	tablespoons unsalted butter
1⅓	cups whole milk
6	ounces Gruyère cheese, shredded (1½ cups)
6	large eggs, separated
2	teaspoons minced fresh parsley
¼	teaspoon cream of tartar

1. Adjust oven rack to middle position and heat oven to 350 degrees. Spray 8-inch round (2-quart) soufflé dish with vegetable oil spray, then sprinkle with 2 tablespoons Parmesan.

2. Combine flour, paprika, salt, cayenne, white pepper, and nutmeg in bowl. Melt butter in small saucepan over medium heat. Stir in flour mixture and cook for 1 minute. Slowly whisk in milk and bring to simmer. Cook, whisking constantly, until mixture is thickened and smooth, about 1 minute. Remove pan from heat and whisk in Gruyère and 5 tablespoons Parmesan until melted and smooth. Let cool for 10 minutes, then whisk in egg yolks and 1½ teaspoons parsley.

3. Using stand mixer fitted with whisk, whip egg whites and cream of tartar on medium-low speed until foamy, about 1 minute. Increase speed to medium-high and whip until stiff peaks form, 3 to 4 minutes. Add cheese mixture and continue to whip until fully combined, about 15 seconds.

4. Pour mixture into prepared dish and sprinkle with remaining 1 tablespoon Parmesan. Bake until soufflé has risen above rim, top is deep golden brown, and interior registers 170 degrees, 30 to 35 minutes. Sprinkle with remaining ½ teaspoon parsley and serve immediately.

VARIATION

Cheese Soufflé with Fines Herbes

Whisk 1 tablespoon minced fresh chives and 1½ teaspoons minced fresh tarragon into soufflé base with egg yolks and parsley in step 2.

Savory Breakfast Pizza

SERVES 4 **FAST**

✔ **WHY THIS RECIPE WORKS:** Topped with sunny-side-up eggs, breakfast pizza works equally well as an elegant brunch or as a fun weeknight dinner. The trick to cooking eggs on top of a pizza was to parbake the crust to get it crisp and flat. We shaped the dough on an oiled rimmed baking sheet and pressed the dough flat if it puffed while baking. Next we considered the toppings. We wanted to pair the eggs with a cheesy cream sauce and savory cremini mushrooms. For the sauce, we mixed ricotta with heavy cream and seasoned it with garlic, scallion, oregano, and cayenne. Once the crust was baked, we spread it with the sauce and toppings, then cracked the eggs over the top. After just 10 minutes more in the oven, the eggs were perfectly set. Cremini mushrooms are also known as baby bella mushrooms. You can use our recipe for Classic Pizza Dough (page 331) or store-bought pizza dough in this recipe. Let the dough sit out at room temperature while preparing the remaining ingredients, otherwise it will be difficult to stretch.

½ cup whole-milk ricotta cheese
3 tablespoons extra-virgin olive oil
2 tablespoons heavy cream
2 garlic cloves, minced
1 scallion, sliced thin
1 teaspoon minced fresh oregano
Salt and pepper
Pinch cayenne pepper
1 pound pizza dough
4 ounces mozzarella cheese, shredded (1 cup)
½ ounce Parmesan cheese, finely grated (¼ cup)
2 ounces cremini mushrooms, trimmed and sliced thin
4 large eggs

1. Whisk ricotta, 2 tablespoons oil, cream, garlic, scallion, oregano, ¼ teaspoon salt, ⅛ teaspoon pepper, and cayenne together in bowl; refrigerate until ready to use.

2. Adjust oven rack to lower-middle position and heat oven to 500 degrees. Grease rimmed baking sheet with remaining 1 tablespoon oil. Press and roll dough into 13 by 11-inch rectangle on lightly floured counter. Transfer dough to prepared baking sheet and reshape as needed. Bake until dough just begins to brown in spots, about 8 minutes; use spatula to gently press on center if dough puffs during baking.

3. Using back of spoon, spread ricotta sauce in thin layer evenly over dough, leaving ¼-inch border. Sprinkle mozzarella, Parmesan, and mushrooms evenly over sauce. Gently crack eggs onto pizza, being careful not to break yolks or let them run over edge of crust, and season eggs with salt and pepper.

4. Return pizza to oven and bake until crust is golden, egg whites are just set, and yolks are still runny when pan is lightly shaken, 9 to 11 minutes. Transfer pizza to cutting board. Let cool for 5 minutes, slice, and serve.

Preparing Breakfast Pizza

1. Gently tamp center of pizza dough down lightly during baking to ensure level surface for eggs, leaving rim of crust to prevent eggs from running over sides.

2. Gently crack eggs on top of assembled pizza, without letting them run over edge, and season eggs with salt and pepper.

Savory Breakfast Pizza with Arugula Salad `FAST`

Whisk 2 teaspoons extra-virgin olive oil, ½ tablespoon red wine vinegar, ¼ teaspoon Dijon mustard, pinch salt, and pinch pepper together in medium bowl. Add 2 cups baby arugula and toss to combine. Sprinkle arugula evenly over pizza when it is removed from oven, and let pizza cool until arugula is slightly wilted, about 5 minutes.

Egg Gratin with Swiss Chard and Cherry Tomatoes

SERVES 4 TO 6 `GF`

✔ **WHY THIS RECIPE WORKS:** Our ideal egg gratin should have a luxurious custard base with a healthy dose of perfectly cooked fresh vegetables. With a little trial and error, we found just the right ratio of eggs to liquid for a smooth, velvety custard, but the addition of juicy vegetables threatened the stability and consistency of our base. In order to add the fillings without affecting our perfect custard, we whisked in a little cornstarch. This kept the custard glossy and rich from one edge to the other, even when packed with plump, sweet, pan-roasted cherry tomatoes, buttery, nutty Manchego cheese, and earthy, bitter Swiss chard. Finishing the baked custard under the broiler gave it an appealing golden-brown, cheesy top. We loved the chewy contrast between the crust and the silky, tender custard, but we wanted more of it. By greasing the gratin dish with butter and dusting it with extra Manchego cheese, we were able to form a toasty cheese "crust" on the bottom and sides of our decadent vegetable gratin as well.

3	tablespoons unsalted butter, plus extra for dish
2½	ounces Manchego cheese, grated (1¼ cups)
8	ounces cherry tomatoes
	Salt and pepper
2	garlic cloves, minced
8	ounces Swiss chard, stemmed and cut into ½-inch pieces
2	tablespoons cornstarch
1¼	cups half-and-half
4	large eggs

1. Adjust 1 oven rack to middle position and second rack 6 inches from broiler element. Heat oven to 350 degrees. Grease bottom and sides of broiler-safe 2-quart gratin dish with butter and sprinkle ¼ cup Manchego evenly over bottom and sides of dish. Melt 1 tablespoon butter in 10-inch nonstick skillet over medium-low heat. Add tomatoes, ½ teaspoon salt,

Cornstarch keeps the custard for our egg gratin from breaking, even when packed with tomatoes and Swiss chard.

and ¼ teaspoon pepper and cook until tomatoes begin to break down and release their liquid, 3 to 5 minutes; transfer tomatoes to prepared dish.

2. Wipe out now-empty skillet with paper towels and melt remaining 2 tablespoons butter over medium-low heat. Add garlic and cook, stirring occasionally, until lightly golden, about 2 minutes. Stir in chard and increase heat to medium-high. Cover and cook until chard is wilted but still bright green, about 2 minutes. Uncover and cook, stirring frequently, until liquid evaporates, about 1 minute. Transfer chard to gratin dish and spread evenly over tomatoes.

3. Whisk cornstarch and ½ teaspoon salt together in medium bowl. Whisk in half-and-half, eggs, and ¾ cup Manchego until thoroughly combined. Pour egg mixture over tomatoes and greens. Sprinkle with remaining ¼ cup Manchego. Bake gratin on middle rack until toothpick inserted in center comes out clean, 30 to 40 minutes, rotating dish halfway through baking. Remove gratin from oven.

4. Heat broiler. Broil gratin on top rack until cheese is golden brown, about 2 minutes. Let gratin cool until custard has set up, about 5 minutes. Serve.

CHAPTER 11

Small Bites and Savory Snacks

■ FAST (Less than 45 minutes start to finish)   ■ VEGAN   ■ GLUTEN-FREE
Photos: Sweet Potato Hummus; Marinated Feta and Green Olives

This fresh, chunky Mexican-style salsa can be made with any tomatoes, even ordinary supermarket ones.

Fresh Tomato Salsa

MAKES ABOUT 3 CUPS **FAST** **VEGAN** **GF**

☑ WHY THIS RECIPE WORKS: We wanted a fresh, chunky salsa that emphasized the tomatoes. To solve the problem of watery salsa, we diced the tomatoes, then let them drain in a colander. This put all tomatoes, regardless of ripeness or juiciness, on a level playing field. Next, we chose red onion over yellow or white for its pretty color and milder flavor, and jalapeño chile for its slight vegetal flavor and moderate heat. Lime juice lent some acidity and tasted more authentic (and better) than vinegar or lemon juice. We found the best, and simplest, way to combine the ingredients was to layer each chopped ingredient on top of the tomatoes while they drained. Once the tomatoes were ready, all that was needed were a few stirs before finishing the salsa with the lime juice, salt, and sugar. The amount of sugar and lime juice you will need depends on the ripeness of the tomatoes. For a spicier salsa, add in the jalapeño seeds. The salsa can be made 2 to 3 hours in advance; add the lime juice, salt, and sugar just before serving.

Chopping a Tomato

1. Using paring knife, cut out cone-shaped tomato core along with any hard flesh.

2. Using chef's knife, cut tomato into ½-inch-thick slices.

3. Stack several tomato slices, then cut both lengthwise and widthwise into pieces as directed in recipe.

1½ pounds tomatoes, cored and cut into
    ½-inch pieces
½ cup finely chopped red onion
¼ cup chopped fresh cilantro
1 large jalapeño chile, stemmed,
    seeded, and minced
1 small garlic clove, minced
2 teaspoons lime juice, plus extra to taste
½ teaspoon salt
    Pinch pepper
    Sugar

1. Place tomatoes in colander set over large bowl and let drain 30 minutes. As tomatoes drain, layer onion, cilantro, jalapeño, and garlic on top.

2. Shake colander to drain excess tomato juice. Discard juice, wipe out bowl, and transfer tomato mixture to bowl. Stir in lime juice, salt, and pepper. Season with sugar and extra lime juice to taste before serving.

This vibrant green salsa features the bright, citrusy flavor of fresh tomatillos blended with jalapeño, cilantro, and lime juice.

Tomatillo Salsa

MAKES ABOUT 2 CUPS **FAST** **VEGAN** **GF**

✔ **WHY THIS RECIPE WORKS:** To make a well-balanced tomatillo salsa that highlighted the green, citrusy notes of the fruit, we started by roasting half of the tomatillos to soften their firm texture and tame their acidity. As an added bonus, we also liked the subtle smokiness their charred skins gave the salsa. Once the tomatillos were spotty brown, we let them cool completely. A few quick pulses in a food processor (along with more fresh tomatillos, onion, garlic, jalapeño, cilantro, and lime juice), and the salsa was ready to serve. The outer husk of a fresh tomatillo should be dry, and the tomatillo itself should be bright green, with a fresh, fruity smell. The amount of sugar you will need depends on the ripeness of the tomatillos. For a spicier salsa, add in the jalapeño seeds.

1 **pound tomatillos, husks and stems removed, tomatillos rinsed well and dried**
1 **teaspoon vegetable oil**
1 **small onion, chopped**

Tomatillos

Called *tomates verdes* (green tomatoes) in much of Mexico, small green tomatillos have a tangier, more citrusy flavor than true green tomatoes. When choosing tomatillos, look for pale-green orbs with firm flesh that fills and splits open the fruit's outer papery husk, which must be removed before cooking. Avoid tomatillos that are too yellow and soft, as these specimens are past their prime and will taste sour and muted. Canned tomatillos are a reasonable substitute for fresh, though they won't contribute the same depth of flavor.

1 **jalapeño chile, stemmed and seeded**
½ **cup fresh cilantro leaves**
2 **tablespoons lime juice**
1 **garlic clove, minced**
   Salt
2 **teaspoons extra-virgin olive oil**
   Sugar

1. Adjust oven rack 6 inches from broiler element and heat broiler. Line rimmed baking sheet with aluminum foil. Toss half of tomatillos with vegetable oil and transfer to prepared sheet. Broil until tomatillos are spotty brown and skins begin to burst, 7 to 10 minutes. Transfer tomatillos to food processor and let cool completely.

2. Halve remaining tomatillos and add to food processor with broiled tomatillos. Add onion, jalapeño, cilantro, lime juice, garlic, and ¼ teaspoon salt. Pulse until slightly chunky, 16 to 18 pulses. Transfer to bowl and let sit at room temperature for 15 minutes. Stir in olive oil and season with salt and sugar to taste. Serve.

Husking Tomatillos

1. Pull papery husks and stems off of tomatillos; discard.

2. Rinse tomatillos in colander to rid them of sticky residue from husks. Dry tomatillos thoroughly.

The key to perfectly chunky guacamole is to dice two avocados and mash one, then gently stir them together.

Chunky Guacamole

MAKES 2½ TO 3 CUPS `FAST` `VEGAN` `GF`

✔ **WHY THIS RECIPE WORKS:** Most guacamole recipes sacrifice the extraordinary character of the avocados by reducing them to a listless puree and adding too many other flavors. We wanted to highlight the avocados' buttery texture and nutty flavor. Neither pureeing nor mashing all the avocados gave us guacamole with the right texture. Instead, mashing one of the avocados lightly with a fork, then gently mixing in the remaining diced avocado along with the other ingredients, gave us an appealingly chunky yet cohesive dip. For the flavorings, we added judicious amounts of onion, garlic, cumin, and jalapeño. Lime juice was a necessity, not only for flavor but also to help preserve the guacamole's green color. To minimize the risk of discoloration, prepare the minced ingredients first so they are ready to mix with the avocados as soon as they are cut. Ripe avocados are essential here. To test for ripeness, flick the small stem off the end of the avocado. If it comes off easily and you can see green underneath it, the avocado is ripe. For a spicier guacamole, add in the jalapeño seeds.

3 avocados, halved, pitted, and cut into
  ½-inch pieces
  Salt
¼ cup minced fresh cilantro
2 tablespoons finely chopped onion
1 small jalapeño chile, stemmed,
  seeded, and minced
1 garlic clove, minced
2 tablespoons lime juice
½ teaspoon ground cumin (optional)

Using fork, mash 1 avocado and ¼ teaspoon salt into relatively smooth puree in medium bowl. Gently fold in remaining 2 diced avocados, cilantro, onion, jalapeño, garlic, lime juice, and cumin, if using. Season with salt to taste and serve. (Guacamole can be refrigerated, with plastic wrap pressed directly onto its surface to prevent browning, for up to 1 day; bring to room temperature before serving.)

Classic Hummus

MAKES ABOUT 2 CUPS `FAST` `VEGAN` `GF`

✔ **WHY THIS RECIPE WORKS:** We wanted hummus with a light, silky-smooth texture and a balanced flavor profile. Since we didn't want to spend hours making it, we started with convenient canned chickpeas. In theory, the best way to guarantee a creamy texture is to remove the chickpeas' tough skins, but we couldn't find an approach that wasn't tedious or futile. Instead, we turned to the food processor. When we pureed the chickpeas alone, the hummus was still grainy, but when we used it to make an emulsion (much like mayonnaise), we got just the light, creamy texture we were after. We started by grinding just the chickpeas, then slowly added in a small amount of water and lemon juice. Then we whisked the olive oil and a generous amount of tahini together and drizzled the mixture into the chickpeas while processing; this created a lush, light, and flavorful puree. Earthy cumin, garlic, and a pinch of cayenne kept the flavors balanced, then we finished with a sprinkling of fresh herbs.

¼ cup water
3 tablespoons lemon juice
6 tablespoons tahini
2 tablespoons extra-virgin olive oil,
  plus extra for drizzling
1 (15-ounce) can chickpeas, rinsed
1 small garlic clove, minced
½ teaspoon salt

¼ teaspoon ground cumin
Pinch cayenne pepper
1 tablespoon minced fresh cilantro or parsley

1. Combine water and lemon juice in small bowl. In separate bowl, whisk tahini and oil together. Set aside 2 tablespoons of chickpeas for garnish.

2. Process remaining chickpeas, garlic, salt, cumin, and cayenne in food processor until almost fully ground, about 15 seconds. Scrape down bowl with rubber spatula. With machine running, add lemon juice mixture in steady stream. Scrape down bowl and continue to process for 1 minute. With machine running, add tahini mixture in steady stream and process until hummus is smooth and creamy, about 15 seconds, scraping down bowl as needed.

3. Transfer hummus to serving bowl, cover with plastic wrap, and let sit at room temperature until flavors meld, about 30 minutes. Sprinkle with reserved chickpeas and cilantro, drizzle with oil, and serve. (Hummus can be refrigerated for up to 5 days; refrigerate garnishes separately. Before serving, stir in 1 tablespoon warm water to loosen hummus texture if necessary.)

VARIATIONS
Artichoke-Lemon Hummus FAST VEGAN GF
Rinse 1 cup drained canned artichoke hearts and pat dry with paper towels. Chop ¼ cup artichoke hearts and set aside for garnish. Increase lemon juice to 4 tablespoons (2 lemons) and omit cumin. Process entire can of chickpeas (do not reserve 2 tablespoons) along with remaining ¾ cup artichokes and ¼ teaspoon grated lemon zest. Omit cilantro. Garnish hummus with reserved artichokes, 2 teaspoons minced fresh parsley or mint, and olive oil.

Hummus with Smoked Paprika FAST VEGAN GF
Process entire can of chickpeas (do not reserve 2 tablespoons), and substitute 1 teaspoon smoked paprika for cumin. Omit cilantro. Garnish hummus with 2 tablespoons toasted pine nuts, 1 tablespoon thinly sliced scallion greens, and olive oil.

Roasted Garlic Hummus VEGAN GF
Remove outer papery skins from 2 heads garlic; cut top quarters off heads and discard. Wrap garlic in aluminum foil and roast in 350-degree oven until browned and very tender, about 1 hour. Meanwhile, heat 2 tablespoons extra-virgin olive oil and 2 thinly sliced garlic cloves in 8-inch skillet over medium-low heat. Cook, stirring occasionally, until garlic is golden brown, about 15 minutes. Using slotted spoon, transfer garlic slices to paper towel–lined plate and set aside; reserve oil. Once roasted garlic is cool, squeeze cloves from their skins

(you should have about ¼ cup). Substitute garlic cooking oil for olive oil in step 1 and omit cumin. Process entire can of chickpeas (do not reserve 2 tablespoons) along with roasted garlic puree. Omit cilantro. Garnish hummus with toasted garlic slices, 2 teaspoons minced fresh parsley, and olive oil.

Roasted Red Pepper Hummus FAST VEGAN GF
Omit water and cumin. Process entire can of chickpeas (do not reserve 2 tablespoons) along with ¼ cup jarred roasted red peppers that have been rinsed and thoroughly patted dry with paper towels. Omit cilantro. Garnish hummus with 2 tablespoons toasted sliced almonds, 2 teaspoons minced fresh parsley, and olive oil.

Sweet Potato Hummus
MAKES ABOUT 3½ CUPS VEGAN GF

✓ **WHY THIS RECIPE WORKS:** To put a twist on classic hummus, we married it with earthy, vibrant sweet potato. We found the trick to this rendition was finding the right balance of ingredients and bringing out the best in the sweet potato's subtle flavor. We started with our recipe for Classic Hummus and added varying amounts of tender sweet potato pulp. One large sweet potato (about 1 pound) gave us just the right balance. We found that microwaving the sweet potato resulted in flavor that was nearly as intense as when we roasted it, and this method was far faster and easier, which we though was important for such a simple dish. Tasters preferred less tahini here than in the plain hummus, so we reduced it to ¼ cup. To play up the sweet potato's flavor, we used complementary warm spices: sweet paprika, coriander, cinnamon, and cumin. A dash of cayenne pepper and a single clove of garlic cut the sweetness and accented the spices well.

1 large sweet potato (about 1 pound), unpeeled
¾ cup water
¼ cup lemon juice (2 lemons)
¼ cup tahini
2 tablespoons extra-virgin olive oil, plus extra for drizzling
1 (15-ounce) can chickpeas, rinsed
1 small garlic clove, minced
1 teaspoon paprika
1 teaspoon salt
½ teaspoon ground coriander
¼ teaspoon ground cumin
⅛ teaspoon ground cinnamon
⅛ teaspoon cayenne pepper

1. Prick sweet potato several times with fork, place on plate, and microwave until very soft, about 12 minutes, flipping halfway through microwaving. Slice potato in half lengthwise, let cool, then scrape sweet potato flesh from skin; discard skin.

2. Combine water and lemon juice in small bowl. In separate bowl, whisk tahini and oil together.

3. Process sweet potato, chickpeas, garlic, paprika, salt, coriander, cumin, cinnamon, and cayenne in food processor until almost fully ground, about 15 seconds. Scrape down bowl with rubber spatula. With machine running, add lemon juice mixture in steady stream. Scrape down bowl and continue to process for 1 minute. With machine running, add tahini mixture in steady stream and process until hummus is smooth and creamy, about 15 seconds, scraping down bowl as needed.

4. Transfer hummus to serving bowl. Cover with plastic wrap and let sit at room temperature until flavors meld, about 30 minutes. Drizzle with olive oil and serve. (Hummus can be refrigerated for up to 5 days; before serving, stir in 1 tablespoon warm water to loosen hummus texture if necessary.)

VARIATION

Parsnip Hummus `VEGAN` `GF`
Look for tender, thin parsnips; large parsnips can taste bitter. Substitute 1 pound parsnips, peeled and cut into 1-inch lengths, for sweet potato; microwave parsnips in covered bowl until tender, about 10 minutes. Omit paprika.

Baba Ghanoush
MAKES ABOUT 2 CUPS `VEGAN` `GF`

✔ **WHY THIS RECIPE WORKS:** For baba ghanoush boasting great eggplant flavor, we kept the flavorings simple: just tahini, lemon juice, garlic, and parsley. We found that it was critical to start with fresh eggplant and cook it until the flesh was almost sloshy; undercooked eggplant, while misleadingly soft to the touch, tasted spongy and raw in the finished dish. We found that it took anywhere from 40 minutes to an hour to cook the eggplant fully, depending on how much moisture the eggplant had. To avoid a watery texture, we drained the cooked eggplant before processing it. Pricking the eggplant all over with a fork before roasting also helped it to release moisture. Look for eggplants with shiny, taut, and unbruised skins and an even shape (eggplants with a bulbous shape won't cook evenly). We prefer to serve baba ghanoush only lightly chilled;

We found that grilling the eggplant until it's completely soft is essential for baba ghanoush with a complex, smoky flavor.

if cold, let it stand at room temperature for about 20 minutes before serving. Serve with Olive Oil–Sea Salt Pita Chips (page 424), pita wedges, tomato wedges, or cucumber slices.

> 2 **pounds eggplant, pricked all over with fork**
> 2 **tablespoons tahini**
> 2 **tablespoons extra-virgin olive oil,**
> **plus extra for drizzling**
> 4 **teaspoons lemon juice**
> 1 **small garlic clove, minced**
> **Salt and pepper**
> 2 **teaspoons chopped fresh parsley**

1. Adjust oven rack to middle position and heat oven to 500 degrees. Place eggplants on aluminum foil–lined rimmed baking sheet and roast, turning eggplants every 15 minutes, until uniformly soft when pressed with tongs, 40 to 60 minutes. Let eggplants cool for 5 minutes on baking sheet.

2. Set colander over bowl. Trim top and bottom off each eggplant. Slit eggplants lengthwise and use spoon to scoop hot pulp from skins. Place pulp in colander (you should have about 2 cups packed pulp); discard skins. Let pulp drain for 3 minutes.

3. Transfer pulp to food processor. Add tahini, oil, lemon juice, garlic, ¾ teaspoon salt, and ¼ teaspoon pepper. Process mixture into coarse puree, about 8 pulses. Season with salt and pepper to taste. Transfer to serving bowl, cover with plastic wrap flush with surface of dip, and refrigerate until chilled, about 1 hour. (Dip can be refrigerated for up to 1 day; let sit at room temperature for 30 minutes and season with extra lemon juice and salt to taste before serving.) Drizzle with extra oil, sprinkle with parsley, and serve.

Making Baba Ghanoush

1. ROAST EGGPLANT:
Roast and turn eggplants in 500-degree oven, until skins darken and wrinkle and eggplants are uniformly soft when pressed with tongs, 40 to 60 minutes. Let cool.

2. DRAIN EXCESS LIQUID:
Trim top and bottom off each eggplant. Slit eggplants lengthwise and use spoon to scoop hot pulp from skins. Let pulp drain in colander for 3 minutes.

3. PULSE DIP: Transfer pulp to food processor. Add tahini, oil, lemon juice, garlic, salt, and pepper. Pulse until mixture has coarse texture, about 8 pulses. Season with salt and pepper to taste.

4. CHILL: Transfer to serving bowl, cover with plastic wrap flush with surface of dip, and refrigerate until chilled, 45 minutes to 1 hour.

Toasted walnuts and wheat crackers add both nutty flavor and texture to this easy roasted red pepper dip.

Muhammara

MAKES ABOUT 2 CUPS **FAST**

☑ **WHY THIS RECIPE WORKS:** Our quick version of this traditional Middle Eastern red pepper dip is simple to make and bursting with authentic flavors. We started with roasted red peppers and whirred them in the food processor to process them to a smooth consistency. We flavored the dip with cumin, cayenne, and lemon juice and added honey and molasses for sweetness and a velvety texture. Toasted walnuts and crumbled wheat crackers ground with the peppers lent complexity and richness, amplifying the sweet, smoky, and savory flavors that are unique to this dip. We've had good luck using Carr's Whole Wheat Crackers in this recipe. Serve this dip with Olive Oil–Sea Salt Pita Chips (page 424), pita wedges, or thinly sliced baguette.

1½ **cups jarred roasted red peppers,**
rinsed and patted dry
1 **cup walnuts, toasted**
¼ **cup plain wheat crackers, crumbled**

3 tablespoons lemon juice

2 tablespoons extra-virgin olive oil

1 tablespoon molasses

1 teaspoon honey

¾ teaspoon salt

½ teaspoon ground cumin

⅛ teaspoon cayenne pepper

1 tablespoon minced fresh parsley (optional)

Pulse all ingredients except parsley in food processor until smooth, about 10 pulses. Transfer to serving bowl, cover, and refrigerate for 15 minutes. (Dip can be refrigerated for up to 1 day; let sit at room temperature for 30 minutes and season with extra lemon juice, salt, and cayenne to taste before serving.) Sprinkle with parsley, if using, and serve.

Butter Bean and Pea Dip with Mint

MAKES ABOUT 2 CUPS `GF`

✓ **WHY THIS RECIPE WORKS:** Bean dips tend to be dense and gluey with lots of spices and flavorings—rarely do they actually highlight the beans. We wanted a lighter, fresher dip that would play up the beans' earthy-sweet flavors and their smooth, creamy texture. We chose butter beans for their velvety texture and mild flavor. Using canned beans kept the dip easy. To make our bean dip creamy and complex-tasting, we paired the starchy beans with delicate baby peas. By adding in the lighter peas, we avoided the pastiness of dips that used only beans. To further freshen the dip, we added creamy Greek-style yogurt, a healthy dose of lemon juice, and a full ¼ cup of mint. We prefer this dip when made with whole Greek yogurt, but 2 percent or 0 percent Greek yogurt can be substituted. Serve with chips, crackers, or vegetables.

1 small garlic clove, minced

¼ teaspoon grated lemon zest plus 2 tablespoons juice

1 cup frozen baby peas, thawed and patted dry

1 (15-ounce) can butter beans, 2 tablespoons liquid reserved, beans rinsed

¼ cup fresh mint leaves

1 scallion, white and light green parts cut into ½-inch pieces, dark green part sliced thin on bias
   Salt

¼ teaspoon ground coriander
   Pinch cayenne pepper

¼ cup plain Greek yogurt
   Extra-virgin olive oil

We process navy beans and artichokes with Greek yogurt and mint for an easy light and creamy dip.

1. Combine garlic and lemon zest and juice in bowl and let stand for 15 minutes. Set aside 2 tablespoons peas for garnish.

2. Pulse butter beans, reserved liquid, remaining peas, mint, white and light green scallion pieces, ¾ teaspoon salt, coriander, cayenne, and garlic–lemon juice mixture in food processor until fully ground, 5 to 10 pulses. Scrape down bowl with rubber spatula. Continue to process until uniform paste forms, about 1 minute, scraping down bowl twice.

3. Add yogurt and continue to process until smooth, about 15 seconds, scraping down bowl as needed. Transfer to serving bowl, cover, and let stand at room temperature for 30 minutes. (Dip can be refrigerated for up to 1 day; let sit at room temperature for 30 minutes before serving.) Season with salt to taste. Sprinkle with reserved peas and dark green scallion parts, drizzle with oil, and serve.

VARIATION

Navy Bean and Artichoke Dip with Parsley `GF`

Increase lemon zest to 1 teaspoon. Substitute frozen artichoke hearts, thawed and patted dry, for peas (reserving 2 chopped tablespoons for garnish), navy beans for butter beans, parsley for mint, and ground fennel seeds for coriander.

Lemon-Dill Yogurt Cheese

MAKES ABOUT 1 CUP GF

✓ **WHY THIS RECIPE WORKS:** Strained yogurt is simply plain yogurt that has been slowly strained to remove its whey, giving it a thicker, creamier consistency and a richer flavor. Mixed with a few simple flavorings, it makes a lighter, fresher alternative to heavier mayonnaise- or cream cheese–based dips, and it couldn't be easier to make—all it takes is a little hands-off time. To end up with about 1 cup of strained yogurt, we started with 2 cups of traditional yogurt. A strainer lined with several coffee filters or a double layer of cheesecloth was ideal for slowly draining away the whey. After about 10 hours, a full cup of whey had drained off, leaving us with a thick, luscious strained yogurt with a consistency close to cream cheese. For the flavorings, we chose a bright combination of lemon zest and fresh dill, plus a little salt and pepper. Both regular and low-fat yogurt will work well here; do not use nonfat yogurt. Avoid yogurts containing modified food starch, gelatin, or gums since they prevent the yogurt from draining. After straining, the plain yogurt also makes a good substitute for Greek yogurt or cream cheese.

- 2 **cups plain yogurt**
- 1 **tablespoon minced fresh dill**
- 2 **teaspoons grated lemon zest**
- ⅛ **teaspoon salt**
- **Pinch pepper**

1. Line fine-mesh strainer with 3 basket-style coffee filters or double layer of cheesecloth. Set strainer over large measuring cup or bowl (there should be enough room for about 1 cup of liquid to drain without touching strainer).

2. Spoon yogurt into strainer, cover tightly with plastic wrap, and refrigerate until yogurt has released about 1 cup liquid and has creamy, cream cheese–like texture, at least 10 hours or up to 2 days.

3. Transfer drained yogurt to clean container; discard liquid. Stir in dill, lemon zest, salt, and pepper. Cover and refrigerate until flavors have blended, about 1 hour. Season with salt and pepper to taste before serving. (Yogurt can be refrigerated for up to 2 days; season with extra salt and pepper to taste before serving.)

VARIATION

Honey-Walnut Yogurt Cheese GF

Omit dill, lemon zest, and pepper. Stir 3 tablespoons toasted, chopped walnuts and 1 tablespoon honey into drained cheese with salt in step 3.

Straining Yogurt Cheese

Line fine-mesh strainer with 3 coffee filters or double layer of cheesecloth and set it over large measuring cup or bowl. Spoon yogurt into strainer, cover tightly with plastic wrap, and refrigerate at least 10 hours.

Tzatziki

MAKES ABOUT 2 CUPS GF

✓ **WHY THIS RECIPE WORKS:** *Tzatziki* is a traditional Greek sauce made from strained yogurt and cucumber. It is endlessly versatile; it is as delicious eaten as a dip with raw vegetables or pita bread as it is dolloped on a veggie burger or spread on a sandwich. To make our own classic version, we started by shredding a cucumber on a coarse grater, salting it, and letting it drain to keep its excess liquid from watering down the dip. Then we simply stirred the cucumber into rich, creamy Greek yogurt flavored with fresh mint and a little garlic. The hardest part was waiting until the dip was chilled to dig in. Using Greek yogurt here is key; do not substitute regular plain yogurt or the sauce will be very watery. Serve with raw vegetables, pita wedges, or Olive Oil–Sea Salt Pita Chips (page 424).

- 1 **(12-ounce) cucumber, peeled, halved lengthwise, seeded, and shredded**
- **Salt and pepper**
- 1 **cup whole Greek yogurt**
- 2 **tablespoons extra-virgin olive oil**
- 2 **tablespoons minced fresh mint and/or dill**
- 1 **small garlic clove, minced**

1. Toss cucumber and ½ teaspoon salt together and let drain in colander for 15 minutes.

2. Whisk yogurt, oil, mint, and garlic together in bowl, then stir in drained cucumber. Cover and refrigerate until chilled, at least 1 hour or up to 2 days. Season with salt and pepper to taste before serving.

VARIATION

Beet Tzatziki GF

Reduce amount of cucumber to 6 ounces and add 6 ounces raw beets, peeled and grated, to cucumber and salt in step 1.

Turkish Nut Sauce

MAKES ABOUT 1 CUP **FAST** **VEGAN**

✔ **WHY THIS RECIPE WORKS:** *Tarator* is a rich, smooth sauce made from nuts, bread, water, olive oil, garlic, and lemon; it is served throughout Turkey as a dip with pita bread and vegetables. This dip relies on the combination of ground nuts, bread, and oil, rather than eggs or dairy, for its velvety texture. The best part about it is that it is incredibly easy to make—all the ingredients are simply processed in a blender or food processor until smooth. Our first step was to decide which type of nut to use. Traditionally, tarator is made with hazelnuts, but our research turned up versions that called for almonds, walnuts, and pine nuts. We made batches with all four nuts and found that they all worked equally well in the recipe. Next, we compared toasted and untoasted nuts in a side-by-side tasting. We concluded that toasting the nuts really was essential; it brought out the complexity of the nuts and deepened the sauce's overall flavor. If using almonds or hazelnuts, make sure they are skinless. A generous dose of lemon juice and a little garlic helped balance the richness of the nuts, while a touch of cayenne pepper added welcome heat. Serve with Olive Oil–Sea Salt Pita Chips (page 424), wedges of warm pita bread, or raw vegetables.

1   **slice hearty white sandwich bread, crusts removed, torn into 1-inch pieces**
¾   **cup water, plus extra as needed**
1   **cup blanched almonds, blanched hazelnuts, pine nuts, or walnuts, toasted**
¼   **cup extra-virgin olive oil**
2   **tablespoons lemon juice, plus extra as needed**
1   **small garlic clove, minced**
    Salt and pepper
    Pinch cayenne pepper

1. Mash bread and water together in bowl with fork into paste. Process bread mixture, nuts, oil, lemon juice, garlic, ½ teaspoon salt, ⅛ teaspoon pepper, and cayenne in blender until smooth, about 2 minutes. Add additional water as needed until sauce is barely thicker than consistency of heavy cream.

2. Season with salt, pepper, and additional lemon juice to taste. Serve at room temperature. (Sauce can be refrigerated for up to 2 days; bring to room temperature before serving.)

A combination of white mushrooms and potent dried porcini gives our mushroom paté deep savory flavor.

Easy Mushroom Pâté

MAKES 2 CUPS, SERVES 8 **GF**

✔ **WHY THIS RECIPE WORKS:** To achieve a spread full of heady, earthy mushroom flavor without foraging the forests for wild specimens, we supplemented everyday white button mushrooms with dried porcini, which are intensely flavored but widely available year-round. Rather than aiming for a smooth texture, we found we got the best results when we pulsed the mushrooms in the food processor until still slightly chunky. Rehydrating the dried porcini before chopping them in the food processor was essential to keep the texture of the dish from ending up grainy, and we reserved some of the potent soaking liquid to give the pâté even more mushroom flavor. Cream cheese and a couple of tablespoons of heavy cream provided a rich, creamy base. Sautéed shallots, thyme, and garlic contributed deep flavor, while lemon juice and parsley offset the earthy flavors with some brightness. Serve with crackers, a thinly sliced baguette, or Crostini (page 424).

1 ounce dried porcini mushrooms, rinsed

1 pound white mushrooms, trimmed and halved

3 tablespoons unsalted butter

2 large shallots, minced

Salt and pepper

3 garlic cloves, minced

1½ teaspoons minced fresh thyme

2 ounces cream cheese

2 tablespoons heavy cream

1 tablespoon minced fresh parsley

1½ teaspoons lemon juice

1. Microwave 1 cup water and porcini mushrooms in covered bowl until steaming, about 1 minute. Let sit until softened, about 5 minutes. Drain porcini through fine-mesh strainer lined with coffee filter set over bowl. Reserve ⅓ cup liquid. Pulse porcini and white mushrooms in food processor until finely chopped and all pieces are pea-size or smaller, about 10 pulses, scraping down bowl as needed.

2. Melt butter in 12-inch skillet over medium heat. Add shallots and ¾ teaspoon salt and cook until shallots are softened, 3 to 5 minutes. Stir in garlic and thyme and cook until fragrant, 30 seconds. Stir in processed mushrooms and cook, stirring occasionally, until liquid released from mushrooms evaporates and mushrooms begin to brown, 10 to 12 minutes.

3. Stir in reserved porcini liquid and cook until nearly evaporated, about 1 minute. Off heat, stir in cream cheese, cream, parsley, and lemon juice, and season with salt and pepper to taste. Transfer to serving bowl and smooth top. Press plastic wrap flush to surface of pâté and refrigerate until firm, at least 2 hours or up to 3 days. Before serving, bring pâté to room temperature to soften.

Baked Goat Cheese with Olive Oil and Herbs

SERVES 8 FAST GF

✓ **WHY THIS RECIPE WORKS:** With its exceptionally creamy texture and mild, slightly grassy flavor, goat cheese is the perfect base for a simple but elegant appetizer. To start, we cut a log of goat cheese into attractive rounds and shingled them into a casserole dish. Chilling the cheese before slicing made it easier to get neat slices. Then we mixed olive oil with honey, bright citrus zest, floral herbes de Provence, salt and pepper, and some red pepper flakes for just a hint of heat. We drizzled this flavorful mixture over the cheese rounds, then baked them until they were brown and bubbling. Serve warm with crackers or a thinly sliced baguette.

Our Favorite Pepper Mill

A pepper mill has one purpose: to swiftly crank out fresh ground pepper, without any strain or guesswork in grind selection. Yet many models fail to measure up. To find our favorite, we chose nine contenders and got grinding.

To evaluate grind speed and ease of operation, we timed how long it took for each model to produce 2 tablespoons of finely ground pepper. Speeds ranged from 90 seconds to a whopping 14 minutes. Surprisingly, the bigger mills were not always the fastest. Mills with smooth, padded handles or rounded tops that fit users' hands aided, rather than hampered, grinding. And though they sound enticing, battery-driven mills turned out to be nonstarters. One, which cost an astounding $99.95, had us prying apart a complicated mechanism at the base to insert six AAA batteries. Another took a painful 14 minutes to grind 2 tablespoons of pepper.

Next we evaluated grind size and quality. We often want a specific-size grind of pepper depending on the dish, and changing the grind on many of the mills caused trouble. Our favorite mills had clear markings that shifted neatly into place. And getting a mix of fine powder and coarse chunks doesn't help in recipes when you want one or the other. Only two out of the 10 models in our lineup consistently produced just the right grind size in every setting; the rest spat out a mix of dust and cracked peppercorns.

At the end of testing, we finally had a winner: the **Cole & Mason Derwent Gourmet Precision Pepper Mill**, $40. The carbon steel grind mechanism in our winning model features seven large grooves on the nut (most have only five) that taper into finer grooves at the base. These allow it to swiftly channel peppercorns toward the deep, sharp serrations on its ring, for fast, efficient grinding. Its spring provides just the right tension to bring the nut and the ring the appropriate distance together (or apart) to create a uniform grind in each of its six fixed, clearly marked grind sizes. We also appreciated its clear acrylic body, which allows you to track when you need a refill.

1 (12-ounce) log goat cheese, well chilled

⅓ cup extra-virgin olive oil

2 teaspoons honey

½ teaspoon grated orange or lemon zest

½ teaspoon herbes de Provence

¼ teaspoon salt

⅛ teaspoon pepper

⅛ teaspoon red pepper flakes

All About Pepper

Freshly ground pepper has distinctive flavor and heat. Once the shell of the peppercorn is cracked, its aroma immediately starts to fade, and most of its scent and flavor disappears within a half-hour. We don't recommend buying ground pepper. Replacing your pepper shaker with a good pepper mill is one of the simplest ways to enhance your cooking.

BLACK PEPPER

This is the classic choice when cooking. Until recently, supermarket brands never specified origin or variety of peppercorns. But specialty retailers offering exotically named varieties like Sarawak, Lampong, and Tellicherry have raised awareness. When we tested eight varieties, we could detect differences—some are floral, others more spicy—but it was hard to make value judgments. Personal preferences really come into play.

WHITE PEPPER

White pepper is simply black pepper harvested at a riper stage. The hulls are then removed, and with them goes the heat that is characteristic of black pepper. What's left is more floral and aromatic than spicy. White pepper is useful in dishes where black specks might be unwelcome (such as a white sauce), or where its floral flavor works well with other ingredients. We especially like white pepper in Thai dishes with citrus, lemon grass, and chiles.

GREEN PEPPER

Green peppercorns are peppercorns picked before they ripen. They are available both in dried form and preserved in brine or vinegar. Dried green pepper adds a fresh, clean flavor to dishes, while the preserved form adds a little heat and tang.

PINK PEPPER

This rose-hued pepper isn't a peppercorn at all. It's actually a berry from a tropical evergreen. It has a savory heat, but its "light, fruity flavor," as well as its pretty color, make it an excellent addition to soft cheeses, salads, and popcorn. It's often sold as part of a mixed peppercorn medley.

Adjust oven rack to middle position and heat oven to 400 degrees. Using cheese wire or dental floss, slice goat cheese into ⅓-inch-thick rounds. Shingle cheese into small casserole dish. Combine all remaining ingredients in bowl, then drizzle over cheese. Bake cheese until oil is bubbling and cheese begins to brown around edges, 10 to 15 minutes. Serve warm.

Slicing Goat Cheese

Using cheese wire or dental floss, slice goat cheese into ⅓-inch-thick rounds.

Goat Cheese with Pink Peppercorns and Herbs

SERVES 6 TO 8 **FAST** **GF**

✔ **WHY THIS RECIPE WORKS:** Goat cheese is often sold rolled in herbs, and although the coated log is always more appealing than the naked log, it seldom lives up to expectations. These herb coatings usually taste dusty or stale, and they tend to overpower the flavor of the cheese itself. To liven up a plain log, we decided to make our own coating, starting with a base of bright, eye-catching pink peppercorns. Pink peppercorns have some of the familiar pungency of black peppercorns but boast a much more delicate flavor that's a bit fruity and floral. Minced thyme and crushed fennel seeds rounded out the flavor of the coating, and extra-virgin olive oil, drizzled over the top before serving, gave our attractive appetizer a little extra panache. Serve with baguette slices or crackers.

1 teaspoon fennel seeds
4 teaspoons whole pink peppercorns
4 teaspoons minced fresh thyme
1 (10-ounce) log goat cheese, well chilled
¼ cup extra-virgin olive oil

1. Toast fennel seeds in 8-inch skillet over medium heat, shaking pan, until first wisps of smoke appear, about 2 minutes. Let cool, then place in zipper-lock bag and crush coarsely with meat pounder. Place peppercorns in zipper-lock bag with fennel seeds and crush coarsely with meat pounder.

Colorful pink peppercorns and fennel seeds transform a log of goat cheese into an impressive appetizer.

2. Combine crushed fennel and peppercorns with thyme in shallow dish. Roll goat cheese log in mixture to coat thoroughly, pressing gently to adhere. Transfer cheese to serving plate and sprinkle with any remaining herb mixture. (Cheese can be refrigerated for up to 8 hours.) Drizzle with oil before serving.

Preparing a Goat Cheese Log

1. Place toasted fennel seeds in zipper-lock bag and crush coarsely with meat pounder. Then add peppercorns to bag and crush again.

2. Combine fennel seeds, peppercorns, and minced thyme in shallow dish, then roll goat cheese in mixture, pressing gently to adhere.

Cheddar-Beer Spread

SERVES 8 TO 10 `GF`

☑ **WHY THIS RECIPE WORKS:** For this addictive cheese spread, we made extra-sharp cheddar smooth and creamy by processing it in the food processor and flavoring it with lots of bold ingredients plus mild, hoppy beer. We discovered that simmering the beer before adding it to the spread eliminated the harsh bite of raw alcohol. And while it may seem strange to rinse minced onion, this step washed away some of the pungent flavor compounds, called thiosulfinates, that are created when the onion is cut, keeping the onion from overpowering the spread. We rounded out the dip with sweet ketchup, Dijon mustard, Worcestershire sauce, hot sauce, and a little garlic and refrigerated it until firm. We have found that a lager-style beer and a sharp or extra-sharp cheddar cheese make this spread most flavorful. Serve with raw vegetables, crackers, a thinly sliced baguette, or Crostini (page 424). In order for this spread to be gluten-free, you must use gluten-free beer and gluten-free Worcestershire sauce.

½ cup mild beer
1 pound sharp or extra-sharp cheddar cheese, shredded (4 cups)
¼ cup minced onion, rinsed and patted dry
2 tablespoons ketchup
1 tablespoon Dijon mustard
1 tablespoon vegetarian Worcestershire sauce
1½ teaspoons hot sauce
1 garlic clove, minced

1. Bring beer to boil in small saucepan over high heat, then reduce heat to low and simmer for 1 minute. Transfer to bowl and let cool to room temperature.

2. Process cheddar, onion, ketchup, mustard, Worcestershire, hot sauce, and garlic in food processor until very smooth, about 1½ minutes. With machine running, slowly add beer in steady stream and process until mixture is smooth, about 1 minute. Transfer to serving bowl, cover tightly with plastic wrap, and refrigerate until firm, about 2 hours. (Spread can be refrigerated for up to 1 week; bring to room temperature before serving.)

ALL ABOUT **CHEESES**

There is a vast variety of American and European cheeses, both in high-end cheese shops and at the supermarket. The selection listed here includes some of the more popular and widely available cheeses, with descriptions of their flavor and texture to help you put together a balanced cheese platter. Always consider pairing different flavors (strong to mild), textures (soft, semisoft, semifirm, and firm), and types of cheeses (such as goat's milk and cow's milk) to make the platter interesting. For accompaniments, choose mild-flavored bread and crackers that don't overshadow the cheese. Fresh and dried fruit, chutneys and jams, and olives are all good additions. As for portion size, figure on 2 to 3 ounces of cheese per person.

Cheese is best served at room temperature, as the flavors and aromas are muted by the cold. Remove cheeses from the refrigerator 1 to 2 hours before serving and keep them wrapped until serving time to prevent them from drying out. For long-term storage in the refrigerator, we find that cheeses are best wrapped in parchment paper and then in aluminum foil. The paper allows the cheese to breathe, while the foil keeps out off-flavors and prevents the cheese from drying out.

Asiago
This cow's-milk cheese is sold at various ages. Fresh Asiago is firm like cheddar or Havarti, and the flavor is fairly mild. Aged Asiago is drier, almost like Parmesan, and has a much sharper, saltier flavor.

Brie
A popular soft cow's-milk cheese from France, Brie is creamy with a slight mushroom flavor, subtle nuttiness, and an edible rind. It is a classic choice for a cheese tray. With the rind removed, it's a good melting cheese.

Camembert
Camembert is a soft cow's-milk cheese from France with an edible rind. Similar to Brie in texture, Camembert is more pungent, with a stronger flavor.

Cheddar
This cow's-milk cheese is made predominantly in Great Britain and the United States. The American versions are usually softer in texture, with a tangy sharpness, whereas British cheddars are drier—even crumbly—with a nutty sharpness. Older farmhouse cheddar is best eaten by itself. Young cheddar is the quintessential melting cheese. Cheddar can also be found smoked. It is made in both white and orange forms.

Colby
Colby is a semisoft cow's-milk cheese from the United States that is very mild in flavor. One of only a few cheeses that have true American roots, Colby is a wonderful melting cheese.

Emmentaler
This semifirm cow's-milk cheese from Switzerland and France is a classic Swiss-style cheese. It has a fruity flavor with a sweet, buttery nuttiness.

Feta
A fresh cheese made from cow's, goat's, or sheep's milk (or a combination thereof), feta is a staple in many Mediterranean countries. It can be made in a variety of styles, from dry and crumbly to soft and creamy; flavors range from mild to tangy and salty. It is often eaten with fresh vegetables or crumbled over salads.

Fontina
Known more formally as Fontina Val d'Aosta, true fontina is a semisoft cow's-milk cheese from Italy and has an earthy and delicately herbaceous flavor. The domestic variety (with its bright red coating) is buttery and melts well but lacks the complex flavor of the Italian original.

Goat Cheese
Produced in many countries in numerous forms, goat cheeses range from creamy fresh cheeses with a mild tanginess to aged cheeses that are firm, dry, and pungent. French goat cheeses (called *chèvres*) are typically more complex in flavor than most of their American counterparts.

Gorgonzola

Gorgonzola can be aged and quite crumbly, or fairly young and creamy. Aged Gorgonzola has a much more potent blue cheese flavor, similar to Roquefort. In general, we like young Gorgonzola; its flavor is less overwhelming. Look for Gorgonzola dolce (sweet Gorgonzola).

Gouda

Gouda is a semifirm-to-firm cow's-milk cheese from Denmark. Semisoft gouda is mild and slightly sweet, whereas aged gouda is dry and crumbly, with a deep caramel flavor and a sharp zing.

Gruyère

Gruyère is a semifirm cow's-milk cheese from France and Switzerland. It is strong, fruity, and earthy in flavor, with a hint of honey-flavored sweetness.

Havarti

This semisoft cow's-milk cheese from Denmark is often flavored with herbs or caraway seeds to augment its mild flavor.

Jarlsberg

Jarlsberg is a Swiss-style cow's-milk cheese from Norway that has a waxy texture and a straightforward Swiss cheese flavor, with a hint of fruitiness.

Manchego

Manchego is a semifirm-to-firm sheep's-milk cheese from Spain that is nutty, salty, and acidic. Serve it with crackers and fresh fruit.

Mozzarella

This popular cow's- or water buffalo's–milk cheese from Italy is available fresh or semisoft (the semisoft is also available smoked). The semisoft version, sold in blocks, is mild in flavor and usually shredded and melted on top of pizza or in other dishes. Fresh mozzarella is sold in oval-shaped balls of various sizes and is usually served on its own. Fresh mozzarella has a rich milk flavor and a good balance of brininess and sweetness.

Parmesan

Parmesan is a hard, grainy cheese made from cow's milk. We recommend authentic Italian Parmigiano-Reggiano, which has an unmistakable sweet, fruity, and nutty flavor. Commonly used for grating over pasta, Parmesan is excellent served on its own with fresh fruit.

Pecorino Romano

Pecorino Romano is a bone-white cheese with an intense peppery flavor and a strong sheepy quality. Like Parmesan, Pecorino Romano is designed for grating, but it has a much saltier and more pungent flavor. It is traditionally made entirely from sheep's milk.

Provolone

Provolone, a cow's-milk cheese from Italy, is made in two styles. The semifirm mild version is widely available and is usually sold sliced. There is also a firm, aged style that is salty, nutty, and spicy, with a light caramel sweetness. The latter makes a nice addition to any cheese platter.

Ricotta Salata

Fresh ricotta cheese is salted and pressed to make this firm but crumbly cheese with a texture that is similar to feta but with a flavor that is milder and far less salty. Ricotta salata is pleasingly piquant.

Roquefort

Roquefort is a blue-veined sheep's-milk cheese from France. Aged in specially designated caves, it's probably the oldest cheese known. Roquefort's flavor is bold but not overpowering, and salty with a slight mineral tinge.

Flavored with sweet pimento peppers, this creamy cheddar cheese spread is a perennial Southern favorite.

jarred pimentos, an equal amount of roasted red peppers may be substituted. In order for this spread to be gluten-free, you must use gluten-free Worcestershire sauce.

½ cup jarred pimentos, drained and patted dry
6 tablespoons mayonnaise
2 garlic cloves, minced
1½ teaspoons vegetarian Worcestershire sauce
1 teaspoon hot sauce, plus extra to taste
1 pound extra-sharp cheddar cheese, shredded (4 cups)
Salt and pepper

Process pimentos, mayonnaise, garlic, Worcestershire, and hot sauce together in food processor until smooth, about 20 seconds. Add cheese and pulse until uniformly blended, with fine bits of cheese throughout, about 20 pulses. Season with salt, pepper, and extra hot sauce to taste, and serve. (Spread can be refrigerated for up to 2 weeks; bring to room temperature before serving.)

Pimento Cheese Spread

SERVES 8 **FAST** **GF**

✔ **WHY THIS RECIPE WORKS:** This deconstructed cheese ball is a popular Southern spread that can be slathered on anything from crackers and sandwiches to crudités. Drained jarred pimentos give the cheesy spread its name and trade-mark color. You can buy it premade at the grocery store, but homemade spreads are infinitely better and take just about 10 minutes. Most recipes use a combination of extra-sharp cheddar cheese and a milder cheddar or Monterey Jack, but we found that batches made with all extra-sharp cheese tasted more complex and satisfying. To give our spread a well-rounded flavor and a little kick, we also added some Worcestershire sauce, minced garlic, and a dash or two of hot sauce. Finally, we mixed in just enough mayonnaise to bind everything together. Both white and orange extra-sharp cheddar work well here. Don't substitute store-bought preshredded cheese; it doesn't blend well and produces a dry spread. If you can't find

Spicy Whipped Feta

MAKES 2 CUPS, SERVES 8 **FAST** **GF**

✔ **WHY THIS RECIPE WORKS:** The return on investment is huge with this Greek meze classic; you simply process tangy, salty feta to a smooth consistency with a few simple flavors to get a rich yet light, cheesy dip. We found rinsing the feta was the key to preventing an overly salty dip. To allow the flavor of the feta to take center stage, we kept the other flavorings simple. A hefty dose of cayenne pepper gave the dip a subtle background heat that didn't compete with the feta. Olive oil imparted fruity notes and some richness, and bright lemon juice balanced the saltiness of the cheese. While a pound of feta may seem like a lot, its volume will condense dramatically when processed. This dip is fairly spicy; to make it less spicy, reduce the amount of cayenne to ¼ teaspoon. Our favorite brand of feta cheese is Mt. Vikos Traditional Feta. Serve with Olive Oil–Sea Salt Pita Chips (page 424) or pita wedges.

1 pound feta cheese, crumbled (4 cups)
⅓ cup extra-virgin olive oil, plus extra for drizzling
1 tablespoon lemon juice
½ teaspoon cayenne pepper
½ teaspoon pepper

Rinse feta under cold running water and pat dry with paper towels. Process feta, oil, lemon juice, cayenne, and pepper in food processor until smooth, about 20 seconds. Transfer mixture to serving bowl, drizzle with additional oil to taste, and serve. (Feta can be refrigerated for up to 2 days; bring to room temperature before serving.)

Marinated Feta and Green Olives

SERVES 6 TO 8 `GF`

✔ **WHY THIS RECIPE WORKS:** We wanted a brightly flavored, chunky mix of marinated feta and olives that could take center stage on an elegant cheese board. Thinly sliced garlic, orange zest, oregano, cumin seeds, and a sprinkling of red pepper flakes gave the marinade complexity and brightness. Toasting the cumin seeds and briefly warming the marinade deepened the flavors, and the warm marinade easily infused the cubed feta and chopped olives. Letting the feta and olives sit in the marinade for 90 minutes before serving allowed the flavors to meld. For more richness, we added a little extra oil just before serving. Don't use marinated olives here; look for plain, brined olives, which can be found in the deli section at most supermarkets. Be sure to buy a block of feta, not crumbled feta, for this recipe. Our favorite brand of feta cheese is Mt. Vikos Traditional Feta. Serve with Crostini (page 424), Olive Oil–Sea Salt Pita Chips (page 424), or pita wedges.

1	teaspoon cumin seeds
1¼	cups extra-virgin olive oil
1	tablespoon minced fresh oregano
2	garlic cloves, sliced thin
1½	teaspoons grated orange zest
¼	teaspoon red pepper flakes
12	ounces feta cheese, cut into ½-inch cubes (2 cups)
1½	cups pitted green olives, chopped coarse

1. Toast cumin seeds in small saucepan over medium heat, shaking pan, until first wisps of smoke appear, about 2 minutes. Stir in 1 cup oil, oregano, garlic, orange zest, and pepper flakes. Reduce heat to low and cook until garlic is softened, about 10 minutes.

2. Place feta and olives in medium bowl, pour warm marinade over top, and toss gently to combine. Cover and let sit until mixture reaches room temperature, about 1½ hours. Stir in remaining ¼ cup oil before serving. (Marinated olives and feta can be refrigerated for up to 1 week; bring to room temperature before serving.)

Marinated Baby Mozzarella

SERVES 8 TO 10 `GF`

✔ **WHY THIS RECIPE WORKS:** We wanted to create a simple marinade with herbs and bright citrus notes that would play up the delicate flavor of fresh baby mozzarella. We chose a classic combination of shallot, garlic, oregano, lemon zest, and red pepper flakes. To bloom the flavors of the marinade and help them to be readily absorbed by the cheese, it was important to heat the marinade gently on the stovetop. Adding more uncooked olive oil to the marinade after it had cooled freshened its flavor. To keep the warm marinade from melting the mozzarella, we set it in the refrigerator while it marinated. Make sure to bring the mixture to room temperature before serving or the oil will look cloudy and congealed. Small mozzarella balls measuring 1 inch or less (sometimes called "pearls") work best here; if the mozzarella balls are larger, cut them into 1-inch pieces before marinating. A rasp-style grater makes quick work of turning the garlic into a paste. Serve with toothpicks and a thinly sliced baguette or crackers.

1	pound fresh baby mozzarella cheese balls (bocconcini)
½	cup extra-virgin olive oil
1	shallot, sliced thin
1	small garlic clove, minced to paste
½	teaspoon minced fresh oregano or thyme
½	teaspoon salt
¼	teaspoon grated lemon zest
⅛	teaspoon red pepper flakes

Rinse mozzarella thoroughly in colander, then drain well and pat dry with paper towels; transfer to medium bowl. Heat 6 tablespoons oil, shallot, garlic, oregano, salt, lemon zest, and pepper flakes in small saucepan over low heat until shallot is softened, about 10 minutes. Pour oil mixture over mozzarella and toss to combine. Cover and refrigerate until flavors have melded, at least 4 hours or up to 2 days. Bring to room temperature and stir in remaining 2 tablespoons oil before serving.

Mincing Garlic to a Paste

Finely mince garlic, then sprinkle with salt. Scrape blade of knife back and forth over garlic until it forms sticky paste.

Thanks to its high melting point, creamy, salty halloumi cheese is ideal for pan-frying to a crisp golden brown.

Pan-Fried Halloumi

SERVES 4 FAST

✔ **WHY THIS RECIPE WORKS:** Halloumi is a firm, brined cheese popular in Greece, Cyprus, and Turkey. It is made from goat's or sheep's milk (or a combination of both) and has a solid consistency and a high melting point, making it perfect for pan searing. To get a crisp, browned crust that would offer a satisfying contrast to the chewy cheese, we tried pan frying the halloumi both plain and dusted with flour, bread crumbs, and cornmeal. A combination of stone-ground cornmeal and a little all-purpose flour provided just the right golden-brown, textured coating. The salty, creamy, chewy cheese was so good, all it needed was a squeeze of bright lemon juice. However, to make a slightly more dressed-up version, we made a quick butter sauce with thinly sliced garlic, fresh parsley, and red pepper flakes to drizzle over the top. The pan-fried halloumi also tastes great with a drizzle of honey.

2 tablespoons cornmeal
1 tablespoon all-purpose flour
1 (8-ounce) block halloumi cheese
2 tablespoons extra-virgin olive oil
  Lemon wedges

1. Combine cornmeal and flour in shallow dish. Slice block of cheese crosswise into ½-inch-thick slabs. Working with 1 slab at a time, coat both wide sides in cornmeal mixture, pressing to help coating adhere; transfer to plate.

2. Heat oil in 12-inch nonstick skillet over medium heat until shimmering. Arrange halloumi in even layer in skillet and cook until golden brown on both sides, 2 to 4 minutes per side. Transfer to platter and serve with lemon wedges.

VARIATION

Pan-Fried Halloumi with Garlic-Parsley Sauce FAST

After frying halloumi, discard oil left in skillet and wipe out skillet with paper towels. Add 2 tablespoons unsalted butter to now-empty skillet and melt over medium heat. Add 1 thinly sliced garlic clove, 2 tablespoons chopped fresh parsley, and ¼ teaspoon red pepper flakes and cook until garlic is golden brown and fragrant, about 1 minute. Drizzle butter mixture over pan-fried halloumi and serve with lemon wedges.

Frico (Baked Cheese Crisps)

MAKES 8 LARGE WAFERS FAST GF

✔ **WHY THIS RECIPE WORKS:** This one-ingredient wonder is probably the simplest and most addictive snack you'll ever eat. A thin, golden, flavorful cheese crisp, classically made from Montasio cheese, frico is nothing more than shredded cheese sprinkled into a pan, melted, and then browned to form a crisp wafer. When made well, frico is perfectly light and airy, with a heavenly and intense cheese flavor. A 10-inch nonstick skillet worked best to ensure a smooth and effortless release without the need for oil or butter. Removing the pan from the heat after browning the first side allowed the crisp to begin to set without burning and made our job of flipping the crisp to brown the second side much easier. Using the right level of heat was also essential. If the pan was too hot, the cheese cooked too fast and turned bitter. But when cooked slowly over low heat, the cheese dried out and never browned. We found it necessary to adjust the heat between medium-high and medium between flips. Montasio cheese may be hard to find in the United States, but it's worth tracking down. If you can't find it, aged Asiago is a good substitute.

1 pound Montasio or aged Asiago cheese, shredded (4 cups)

1. Sprinkle ½ cup cheese over bottom of 10-inch nonstick skillet. Cook over medium-high heat, shaking pan occasionally to ensure even distribution of cheese over bottom of pan, until edges are lacy and toasted, about 4 minutes. As cheese begins to melt, use spatula to tidy lacy outer edges of cheese and prevent them from burning.

2. Remove pan from heat and allow cheese to set, about 30 seconds. Using fork and spatula, carefully flip cheese wafer over and return pan to medium-high heat. Cook until second side is golden brown, about 2 minutes. Slide cheese wafer out of pan onto plate. Repeat with remaining cheese. Serve.

Flipping Frico

Once first side is browned, remove pan from heat and let cool briefly. Then use fork and spatula to carefully flip cheese wafer over and return pan to medium-high heat to cook second side.

To keep our cheddar cheese coins tender, we add a little cornstarch to the flour and mix the dough together quickly.

Cheddar Cheese Coins

MAKES ABOUT 5 DOZEN COINS

✔ **WHY THIS RECIPE WORKS:** Cheddar cheese coins should be cheesy, buttery crackers with just a little spice, but more often they're greasy, bland, and tough. We wanted to come up with a simple, foolproof version. Cheese coins are made from flour, sharp cheddar cheese, butter, and seasonings. We kept our seasonings simple—just salt, cayenne, and paprika. We used the food processor to combine the dry ingredients and the shredded cheese, which helped to keep the coins tender by limiting the handling of the dough. Adding a little cornstarch with the flour further ensured the coins baked up tender. We processed the dry ingredients with chilled butter until the mixture resembled wet sand, then added water and

processed until the dough came together. Next, we rolled the dough into logs, refrigerated them until firm, then sliced them into thin coins. We baked the cheesy coins in a moderate oven until they were just lightly golden and perfectly crisp.

8 ounces extra-sharp cheddar cheese, shredded (2 cups)
1½ cups (7½ ounces) all-purpose flour
1 tablespoon cornstarch
½ teaspoon salt
¼ teaspoon cayenne pepper
¼ teaspoon paprika
8 tablespoons unsalted butter, cut into 8 pieces and chilled
3 tablespoons water

1. Process cheddar, flour, cornstarch, salt, cayenne, and paprika in food processor until combined, about 30 seconds. Scatter butter pieces over top and process until mixture resembles wet sand, about 20 seconds. Add water and process until dough forms ball, about 10 seconds. Transfer dough to counter and divide in half. Roll each half into 10-inch log, wrap in plastic wrap, and refrigerate until firm, at least 1 hour or up to 3 days. (Dough can be frozen for up to 1 month; thaw completely before slicing and baking.)

2. Adjust oven racks to upper-middle and lower-middle positions and heat oven to 350 degrees. Line 2 rimmed baking sheets with parchment paper. Unwrap logs and slice into ¼-inch-thick coins, giving dough quarter turn after each slice to keep log round. Place coins on prepared sheets, spaced ½ inch apart.

3. Bake until light golden around edges, 22 to 28 minutes, switching and rotating sheets halfway through baking. Let coins cool completely on sheets before serving. (Coins can be stored at room temperature for up to 3 days.)

VARIATIONS
Parmesan and Rosemary Cheese Coins
Substitute 8 ounces finely grated Parmesan for cheddar, black pepper for cayenne, and 1 teaspoon minced fresh rosemary for paprika.

Gruyère, Mustard, and Caraway Cheese Coins
Substitute Gruyère for cheddar. Add 1 teaspoon caraway seeds to food processor with spices. Substitute 4 tablespoons whole-grain mustard for water.

Blue Cheese and Celery Seed Cheese Coins
Substitute 1 cup crumbled blue cheese for 1 cup cheddar. Increase paprika to 2 teaspoons and cayenne to ½ teaspoon. Add 1 teaspoon celery seeds to food processor with spices. Omit water.

Shaping Cheese Coins

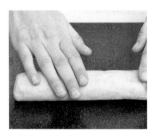 

1. Using hands, roll each piece of dough into 10-inch log on clean counter, then wrap in plastic wrap and chill for at least 1 hour.

2. Slice chilled dough into ¼-inch-thick coins. Give dough log quarter turn after each slice to help keep log round.

Lavash Crackers
MAKES ABOUT 1 POUND, SERVES 6 TO 8

✓ **WHY THIS RECIPE WORKS:** Lavash crackers are a little bit nutty and a little bit sweet, and they have a crisp and airy texture perfect for topping with a bit of goat cheese or eaten as is. To get just the right flavor and texture, we used a combination of three flours: fine semolina flour, nutty whole-wheat flour, and all-purpose flour. To make the dough, we mixed the flours (and a little salt) in a stand mixer, then gradually added water and oil until the dough was smooth and elastic. Letting the dough rest for an hour made it much easier to roll out. Once the dough had rested, we rolled it out over oiled baking sheets, pricked it all over with a fork to prevent air bubbles, brushed it with a beaten egg, and sprinkled it with sesame seeds, salt, and pepper. Finally, we baked the crackers until deeply golden brown and let them cool before breaking the large sheets into crispy, crunchy crackers.

1½   cups (8⅝ ounces) semolina flour
¾   cup (4⅛ ounces) whole-wheat flour
¾   cup (3¾ ounces) all-purpose flour
¾   teaspoon salt
1   cup warm water
⅓   cup extra-virgin olive oil,
      plus extra for brushing
1   large egg, lightly beaten
2   tablespoons sesame seeds
2   teaspoons kosher salt
1   teaspoon coarsely ground pepper

1. Using stand mixer fitted with dough hook, mix flours and salt on low speed. Gradually add water and oil and knead until dough is smooth and elastic, 7 to 9 minutes. Turn dough out onto lightly floured counter and knead by hand to form smooth, round ball. Divide dough into 4 equal pieces, brush with oil, and cover with plastic wrap. Let rest at room temperature for 1 hour.

2. Adjust oven racks to upper-middle and lower-middle positions and heat oven to 425 degrees. Lightly coat two 18 by 13-inch rimless (or inverted) baking sheets with vegetable oil spray.

3. Working with 1 piece of dough at a time (keep remaining dough covered with plastic), press dough into small rectangle, then transfer to one of prepared sheets. Using rolling pin and hands, roll and stretch dough evenly to edges of sheet. Using

Shaping Lavash Crackers

1. Using rolling pin and hands, roll and stretch 1 piece of dough evenly to edges of sheet.

2. Using fork, poke holes in dough at 2-inch intervals.

3. Brush dough with beaten egg and sprinkle with sesame seeds, kosher salt, and pepper, pressing gently to help seasonings adhere.

4. Once lavash is baked and cooled, break crackers into large pieces using hands.

fork, poke holes in dough at 2-inch intervals. Repeat with second piece of dough on second prepared sheet. Brush doughs with beaten egg, then sprinkle evenly with sesame seeds, kosher salt, and pepper, pressing gently to help seasonings adhere.

4. Bake crackers until deeply golden brown, 15 to 18 minutes, switching and rotating sheets halfway through baking. Transfer crackers to wire rack and let cool completely. Let baking sheets cool completely before rolling out and baking remaining dough. Break cooled lavash into large crackers and serve. (Lavash can be stored at room temperature for up to 2 weeks.)

All About Salt

Salt is one of the most essential ingredients in cooking. We season nearly everything we cook, we use it to bring out the flavors of vegetables and to brine beans, and we salt the cooking water for pasta, rice, and grains. Whether mined from underground or obtained by evaporating seawater, salt in its most basic form is the same: sodium chloride. What distinguishes one salt from another is texture, shape, and mineral content. These qualities can affect how a salt tastes.

TABLE SALT

Table salt consists of tiny, uniformly shaped crystals created during rapid vacuum evaporation. It usually includes anticaking agents that help it pour smoothly. Table salt can be used in any application. It dissolves easily, making it our go-to for most recipes, both sweet and savory. Avoid iodized salt, which can impart a chemical flavor.

KOSHER SALT

Kosher salt is raked during the evaporation process to yield large, flaky crystals that were originally used for koshering meat. Unlike table salt, kosher salt doesn't contain any additives. Its large grains distribute easily and cling well to surfaces, making it great for seasoning. The two major brands of kosher salt—Morton and Diamond Crystal—work equally well.

SEA SALT

Sea salt is the product of seawater evaporation—a time-consuming, expensive process that yields irregularly shaped, mineral-rich flakes that vary in color but only slightly in flavor. Don't bother cooking with pricey sea salt; mixed into food, it doesn't taste any different than table salt. Instead, use it as a "finishing salt," where its delicate crunch stands out. When buying sea salt, texture—not exotic provenance—is the main consideration. Look for brands boasting large, flaky crystals.

SUBSTITUTING SALT

Given its coarser crystal structure, kosher salt packs a lot less into each teaspoon when compared with table salt. In fact, even the volume measurements between the two major brands of kosher salt—Morton and Diamond Crystal—vary significantly. If you want to substitute one for another, here's how they measure up:

1 teaspoon table salt = 1½ teaspoons Morton kosher salt = 2 teaspoons Diamond Crystal kosher salt

Crostini

MAKES 25 TO 30 TOASTS   `FAST` `VEGAN`

✅ **WHY THIS RECIPE WORKS:** Crostini—Italian for "little toasts"—are simply small slices of toasted or grilled bread, usually made with baguette or ciabatta, that make a perfect base for dips, spreads, cheeses, vegetables, or pâtés. We found that thin slices of baguette were the best choice for our crostini recipe. Baking the toasts for 10 minutes in a 400-degree oven turned them crisp enough to hold even hefty toppings, and rubbing the hot toasts with a raw garlic clove added just the right subtle garlicky flavor. Finally, brushing them with olive oil added richness and moisture. Arrange these little toasts next to a cheese platter or dip, or serve them alongside a soup, stew, or salad. Crostini taste best straight from the oven.

1 large (12- to 15-inch) baguette, cut into ½-inch-thick slices on bias
1 garlic clove, peeled and sliced in half
2 tablespoons extra-virgin olive oil
   Salt and pepper

Adjust oven rack to middle position and heat oven to 400 degrees. Arrange bread in single layer on baking sheet. Bake bread until dry and crisp, about 10 minutes, flipping slices over halfway through baking. Rub garlic clove over 1 side of each piece of toasted bread, then brush with oil. Season with salt and pepper to taste and serve.

Olive Oil–Sea Salt Pita Chips

SERVES 8   `FAST` `VEGAN`

✅ **WHY THIS RECIPE WORKS:** Homemade pita chips are surprisingly easy to make and taste much better than store-bought, plus making your own means you customize the flavors. First we separated the two layers of each pita to get thinner, crispier chips. Next, we brushed each round with plenty of oil (we chose extra-virgin olive oil for its robust flavor) and sprinkled it with coarse salt. To quickly cut the rounds into wedges, we stacked them up, then sliced the stacked rounds into eight wedges all at once. This method also meant that we needed to oil and season the rounds only on one side, because the unseasoned sides of the stacked pita rounds absorbed the seasoned oil from the adjacent rounds. Finally, we arranged the wedges on two rimmed baking sheets in a single layer to ensure they would bake evenly. We tried

Homemade pita chips are surprisingly easy—all they need is a brush of oil, a sprinkle of salt, and 15 minutes in the oven.

flipping the chips halfway through baking, but we found that it wasn't worth the hassle—even without flipping, the bottom side of the chips browned nicely from contact with the baking sheet. Both white and whole-wheat pita breads will work well here. We prefer the larger crystal size of kosher salt here; if using table salt, reduce the amount of salt by half.

4 (8-inch) pita breads
½ cup extra-virgin olive oil
1 teaspoon sea salt or kosher salt

1. Adjust oven racks to upper-middle and lower-middle positions and heat oven to 350 degrees. Using kitchen shears, cut around perimeter of each pita and separate into 2 thin rounds.

2. Working with 1 round at a time, brush rough side generously with oil and sprinkle with salt. Stack rounds on top of one another, rough side up, as you go. Using chef's knife, cut pita stack into 8 wedges. Spread wedges, rough side up and in single layer, on 2 rimmed baking sheets. Bake until wedges are golden brown and crisp, about 15 minutes, rotating and switching sheets halfway through baking. Let cool before serving. (Pita chips can be stored at room temperature for up to 3 days).

VARIATIONS
Rosemary-Parmesan Pita Chips `FAST`
Reduce salt to ½ teaspoon and toss with ½ cup grated Parmesan and 2 tablespoons minced fresh rosemary before sprinkling over pitas.

Chili-Spiced Pita Chips `FAST` `VEGAN`
Mix 1 tablespoon chili powder, ½ teaspoon garlic powder, and pinch cayenne pepper with salt before sprinkling over pitas.

Buttermilk-Ranch Pita Chips `FAST`
Mix 1 tablespoon buttermilk powder, 2 teaspoons dried dill, ¼ teaspoon garlic powder, and ¼ teaspoon onion powder with salt before sprinkling over pitas.

Cinnamon-Sugar Pita Chips `FAST`
Substitute 8 tablespoons melted unsalted butter for oil. Reduce salt to ¼ teaspoon. Mix 3 tablespoons sugar and 1 tablespoon cinnamon with salt before sprinkling over pitas.

Cutting Pitas into Chips

1. Using kitchen shears, cut around perimeter of each pita to yield 2 thin rounds.

2. After brushing rough side of each pita round with oil and seasoning with salt, stack rounds on top of one another, rough side up. Using chef's knife, cut stack into 8 wedges.

3. Arrange wedges, rough side up and in single layer, on 2 rimmed baking sheets, fitting them together tightly without overlapping.

To get truly crisp kale chips, we bake the kale low-and-slow on a wire rack so the leaves fully dehydrate.

Kale Chips
SERVES 4 `VEGAN` `GF`

✔ **WHY THIS RECIPE WORKS:** Kale chips should boast a crisp texture and great earthy flavor, but often they just don't stay crispy. We found there were three key steps to getting kale chips with the perfect crisp texture. First, we lengthened the cooking time and lowered the oven temperature to mimic the effects of a dehydrator. Next, we baked the leaves on a wire rack to allow the oven air to circulate above and beneath the kale leaves. Finally, we made sure that we started with completely dry leaves—we spun them dry using a salad spinner, then blotted them between two dish towels to make sure no water was left clinging. Tossed with olive oil and seasoned lightly with crunchy kosher salt, these ultracrisp kale chips were a supersatisfying snack. We prefer to use Lacinato (Tuscan) kale in this recipe, but curly-leaf kale can be substituted; chips made with curly leaf kale will taste a bit chewy at the edges and won't hold as well. We prefer the larger crystal size of kosher salt here; if using table salt, reduce the amount of salt by half.

All About Olives

BRINE-CURED VERSUS SALT-CURED

Jarred olives come in three basic types at the supermarket: brine-cured green, brine-cured black, and salt-cured black (often labeled "oil-cured"). Brine-cured olives are soaked in a salt solution for periods of up to a year to remove bitterness and develop flavor. Salt-cured olives are packed in salt until nearly all their liquid has been extracted, then covered in oil to be replumped. Both processes traditionally take weeks or even months. Generally we find that brine-cured black and green olives can be used interchangeably in any recipe based on personal preference. Among our test cooks, only a few olive aficionados favored the concentrated, bitter taste of salt-cured olives—we don't recommend cooking with them unless a recipe specifically calls for them. And as for canned olives? We avoid them entirely, finding them almost tasteless, with a firm yet oddly slippery texture.

GREEN OLIVES

Often labeled "Spanish" olives, green olives are picked before they fully ripen, and their mild flavor adds a bright, acidic dimension to food. Manzanillas, produced in Spain and California, are the pimento-stuffed olives best known for garnishing martinis. Add these olives at the end of cooking to avoid bitterness.

BLACK OLIVES

Picked when mature, black olives lend a more robust, fruity taste. The most common types are kalamata olives, which have an earthy flavor and creamy flesh, and niçoise olives, which boast an assertive, somewhat bitter flavor. We prefer the fresher kalamatas from the refrigerator section of the supermarket; the jarred shelf-stable ones are bland and mushy in comparison. If you can't find kalamatas in the refrigerator section of your market, look for them at the salad bar.

PITTED VERSUS UNPITTED

Pitted olives are certainly convenient, but they lack the complex, fruity flavors of unpitted olives and often have a mushier texture. After being brined for up to a year, the pitted olives are returned to the brine for packing, which can penetrate the inside of the olive and turn it mushy and pasty, as well as increase the absorption of salt. That saltier taste can mask subtler flavors. If you have the time, we recommend that you buy unpitted olives and pit them yourself.

12 ounces Lacinato kale, stemmed and torn into 3-inch pieces
1 tablespoon extra-virgin olive oil
½ teaspoon kosher salt

1. Adjust oven racks to upper-middle and lower-middle positions and heat oven to 200 degrees. Set wire racks in 2 rimmed baking sheets. Dry kale thoroughly between dish towels, transfer to large bowl, and toss with oil and salt.

2. Arrange kale on prepared racks, making sure leaves overlap as little as possible. Bake kale until very crisp, 45 to 60 minutes, switching and rotating sheets halfway through baking. Let chips cool for several minutes before serving. (Kale chips can be stored in paper towel–lined airtight container for up to 1 day.)

Making Kale Chips

1. TEAR LEAVES: Stem kale, then tear leaves into rough 3-inch pieces.

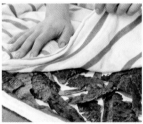

2. DRY WELL: Wash and dry kale using salad spinner, then dry it thoroughly between dish towels. Transfer to large bowl and toss with oil and salt.

3. ARRANGE ON WIRE RACK: Arrange kale on prepared racks, making sure leaves don't overlap too much.

4. BAKE UNTIL CRISP: Bake kale on upper-middle and lower-middle positions in 200-degree oven until very crisp, 45 to 60 minutes, switching and rotating sheets halfway through baking.

Boozy Marinated Black and Green Olives

MAKES ABOUT 3 CUPS, SERVES 8 TO 10 `VEGAN` `GF`

✓ **WHY THIS RECIPE WORKS:** The most important step when making marinated olives is to start with good olives and good olive oil—but why bother if the rest of the flavors are boring or bland? We wanted marinated olives that were easy to put together and worth the wait. We started with olives with pits (pitted olives tend to have less flavor), packed in brine not oil. To give the dish more variety, we liked a combination of green and black olives. We started with the usual aromatics—garlic, thyme, and red pepper flakes—and added sliced shallots, a little cayenne for complex heat, and grated orange zest for a bright citrus note. But the ingredient that really put our olives over the top turned out to be sambuca; this sweet, anise-flavored Italian liqueur gave the marinade depth and an interesting flavor. You can substitute ouzo, a Greek liqueur with a similar taste, for the sambuca.

- 1½ **cups large brine-cured green olives with pits**
- 1½ **cups large brine-cured black olives with pits**
- ¼ **cup extra-virgin olive oil**
- 3 **shallots, sliced thin**
- 3 **garlic cloves, crushed and peeled**
- 2 **tablespoons sambuca**
- 1 **teaspoon minced fresh thyme**
- ¾ **teaspoon salt**
- ¼ **teaspoon grated orange zest**
- ¼ **teaspoon red pepper flakes**
  Pinch cayenne pepper

Rinse olives thoroughly, then drain and pat dry with paper towels. Toss olives with remaining ingredients in bowl, cover, and refrigerate for at least 12 hours or up to 5 days. Let sit at room temperature for 30 minutes before serving.

Pitting Olives

To pit olives, place olive on counter and hold flat edge of knife over olive. Press blade firmly with hand to loosen olive meat from pit, then remove pit with fingers.

Simmering marinated artichokes in the aromatic packing oil before storing them infuses them with bright flavor.

Marinated Artichokes

MAKES FOUR 1-PINT JARS `VEGAN` `GF`

✓ **WHY THIS RECIPE WORKS:** Marinated artichokes have so many uses that they should be considered a pantry staple; they're perfect for everything from throwing on pizzas to tossing into a salad or pasta, to eating on an antipasto platter. But store-bought versions tend to be mushy and bland—and expensive. We set out to make our own recipe for easy, inexpensive, and boldly flavorful marinated artichokes. To get the best tender-yet-meaty texture and sweet, nutty artichoke flavor, we started with fresh baby artichokes. We simmered them gently in olive oil with strips of lemon zest, garlic, red pepper flakes, and thyme, then let them sit off the heat until they were perfectly fork-tender and infused with the aromatic flavors. Then we stirred in fresh lemon juice and more zest, minced garlic, and mint before transferring the artichokes to jars and topping them with the aromatic-infused oil for storage.

3 lemons

5 cups extra-virgin olive oil

6 pounds baby artichokes (2 to 4 ounces each)

16 garlic cloves, peeled (12 smashed, 4 minced)

½ teaspoon red pepper flakes

4 sprigs fresh thyme

Salt and pepper

½ cup minced fresh mint

1. Using vegetable peeler, remove 6 (2-inch) strips zest from 1 lemon. Grate and reserve 1 teaspoon zest from second lemon. Halve and juice lemons to yield ½ cup juice, reserving spent lemon halves.

2. Combine oil and lemon zest strips in large saucepan. Working with 1 artichoke at a time, cut top quarter off each artichoke, snap off outer leaves, and trim away dark skin. Peel and trim stem, then cut artichoke in half lengthwise (quarter artichoke if large). Rub each artichoke half with spent lemon half and place in saucepan.

3. Add smashed garlic, pepper flakes, thyme sprigs, 2 teaspoons salt, and ½ teaspoon pepper to saucepan and bring to rapid simmer over high heat. Reduce heat to medium-low and simmer, stirring occasionally to submerge all artichokes, until artichokes can be pierced with fork but are still firm, about 5 minutes. Remove from heat, cover, and let sit until artichokes are fork-tender and fully cooked, about 20 minutes.

4. Gently fold in reserved grated lemon zest, reserved lemon juice, remaining minced garlic, and mint. Season with salt to taste. Using slotted spoon, transfer artichokes to four 1-pint jars with tight-fitting lids. Strain oil through fine-mesh strainer

set over 8-cup liquid measuring cup. Discard thyme sprigs, then spoon strained solids evenly into jars. Cover artichokes with strained oil, let cool to room temperature, and serve. (Artichokes, and any leftover strained oil, can be refrigerated for up to 4 days.)

Giardiniera

MAKES FOUR 1-PINT JARS `VEGAN` `GF`

✔ WHY THIS RECIPE WORKS: In Italy, *giardiniera* refers to pickled vegetables that are typically eaten as an antipasto. But here in the United States, it's most recognized as a combination of pickled cauliflower, carrots, celery, and sweet and hot peppers that is served alongside sandwiches or other lunch fare. Although humble-looking, giardiniera can be surprisingly good: crunchy, with a vinegary bite, and almost dangerously hot. But grocery store versions tend to fall flat, with too-salty brines and washed-out flavors. To make our own quick-pickled version (no sterilization required), we prepped the vegetables, transferred them to jars, and topped them with a hot, flavorful brine. Once the jars were cool, we simply refrigerated them until the vegetables had absorbed the bright, briny flavors, which took about a week. For the brine, we stuck with traditional pickling flavors: garlic, dill, sugar, salt, and mild white wine vinegar. Different types and brands of salt measure differently and can alter the flavor of this recipe. If using Morton Kosher Salt, reduce the amount of salt to 3 tablespoons. If using table salt, reduce the amount of salt to 2 tablespoons.

Making Marinated Artichokes

1. PREP ARTICHOKES: Cut top quarter off each artichoke, snap off outer leaves, and trim away dark skin. Peel and trim stem, then cut artichoke in half lengthwise. Rub each artichoke half with lemon half and place in saucepan with oil and lemon zest.

2. SIMMER IN OIL: Add smashed garlic, pepper flakes, thyme sprigs, salt, and pepper to saucepan. Bring oil to rapid simmer over high heat, then reduce heat to medium-low and cook, stirring occasionally, about 5 minutes.

3. LET SIT UNTIL TENDER: When artichokes can be pierced with fork but are still firm, remove pot from heat, cover, and let sit until artichokes are fork-tender and fully cooked, about 20 minutes.

4. ADD AROMATICS: Fold in grated lemon zest, lemon juice, minced garlic, and mint and season with salt to taste. Transfer artichokes to jars with tight-fitting lids. Cover with infused oil and let cool to room temperature.

½ head cauliflower (1 pound), cored and
   cut into ½-inch florets
3 carrots, peeled and sliced ¼ inch thick on bias
3 celery ribs, cut crosswise into ½-inch pieces
1 red bell pepper, stemmed, seeded,
   and cut into ½-inch-wide strips
2 serrano chiles, stemmed and sliced thin
4 garlic cloves, sliced thin
1 cup chopped fresh dill
2¾ cups white wine vinegar
2¼ cups water
¼ cup sugar
¼ cup Diamond Crystal kosher salt

1. Combine cauliflower, carrots, celery, bell pepper, serranos, and garlic in large bowl, then transfer to four 1-pint jars with tight-fitting lids.

2. Bundle dill in cheesecloth and tie with kitchen twine to secure. Bring dill sachet, vinegar, water, sugar, and salt to boil in large saucepan over medium-high heat. Remove from heat and let steep for 10 minutes. Discard dill sachet.

3. Return brine to brief boil, then pour evenly over vegetables. Let cool to room temperature, then cover and refrigerate until vegetables taste pickled, at least 7 days or up to 1 month.

To make a creamy, tangy filling for deviled eggs, we mix the yolks with mayo, sour cream, mustard, and vinegar.

Deviled Eggs

MAKES 1 DOZEN **FAST** **GF**

 **WHY THIS RECIPE WORKS:** The first step to getting a great deviled egg is getting a perfect hard-cooked egg. After countless tests, we found the best method was to cover the eggs with an inch of water, bring the water to a boil, then remove it from the heat to avoid overcooking. After a few minutes' rest off the heat, we drained the eggs and rapidly cooled them in an ice water bath. The gentle residual heat perfectly cooked the eggs—not a chance of a green tinge or chalky yolk. For a filling with the creamiest texture, we forced the yolks through a fine-mesh strainer before mixing them with the other ingredients. We added both mayonnaise and a little sour cream for flavor and silkiness. Spicy brown mustard provided punch, and white vinegar gave our deviled eggs a bit of tang. You can use reduced-fat mayonnaise and sour cream in this recipe. To fill the eggs, a spoon works just fine, but we like to pipe the filling using either a zipper-lock bag with a corner snipped off or—for the most elegant presentation—a pastry bag fitted with a fluted (star) tip.

6 large eggs
2 tablespoons mayonnaise
1 tablespoon sour cream
½ teaspoon distilled white vinegar
½ teaspoon spicy brown mustard
¼ teaspoon sugar
⅛ teaspoon salt
⅛ teaspoon pepper

1. Combine 4 cups water and 4 cups ice cubes in large bowl; set aside. Place eggs in large saucepan, cover with 1 inch of water, and bring to boil over high heat. Remove pan from heat, cover, and let stand 10 minutes. Pour off water from saucepan and gently shake pan back and forth to crack egg shells. Transfer eggs to ice water and let cool 5 minutes.

2. Peel eggs and halve lengthwise. Transfer yolks to fine-mesh strainer set over bowl. Using spatula, press yolks through strainer into bowl. Stir in remaining ingredients until smooth.

3. Arrange whites on serving platter. Divide yolk mixture among whites. Serve. (Egg white halves and filling can be refrigerated separately for 2 days. Wrap egg whites in double layer of plastic wrap. Transfer filling mixture to zipper-lock bag, squeeze out air, and seal.)

VARIATIONS

Herbed Deviled Eggs `FAST` `GF`

Fresh herbs are a must here; do not substitute dried herbs.

Substitute white wine vinegar for distilled white vinegar, and Dijon mustard for spicy brown mustard. Stir 2 teaspoons each minced fresh tarragon, parsley, and chives into filling in step 2.

Spanish-Style Deviled Eggs `FAST` `GF`

Either smoked or sweet paprika will work well here.

Substitute sherry vinegar for distilled white vinegar. Stir ¼ cup finely chopped pimento-stuffed green olives, ¼ cup shredded cheddar cheese, and 1 teaspoon paprika into filling in step 2.

Dill-Pickled Deviled Eggs `FAST` `GF`

Fresh dill is a must here; do not substitute dried dill.

Substitute dill pickle juice for distilled white vinegar, and yellow mustard for spicy brown mustard. Stir 1 tablespoon finely chopped dill pickles and 1 tablespoon minced fresh dill into filling in step 2.

Blue Cheese Deviled Eggs `FAST` `GF`

A relatively mild blue cheese, such Stella Blue, works best here.

Substitute cider vinegar for distilled white vinegar, and Dijon mustard for spicy brown mustard. Increase pepper to ¼ teaspoon and stir ¼ cup crumbled blue cheese into filling in step 2.

Filling Deviled Eggs without a Pastry Bag

1. Set zipper-lock bag inside measuring cup and fold bag over rim of cup. Transfer filling to bag, then, using scissors, snip about ½ inch off corner of bag.

2. Twist top of bag and squeeze to force filling to snipped corner. Squeeze filling through hole to fill egg whites.

Stuffed Jalapeños

SERVES 8 `FAST`

✔ **WHY THIS RECIPE WORKS:** Stuffed jalapeños are classic bar food: spicy jalapeños stuffed with cream cheese or cheddar, then battered and deep-fried to a golden brown. But between the stuffing and deep frying, this recipe is a pain, and all too often the first bite leaves you holding an empty batter shell while you struggle to eat the entire jalapeño. To make these appetizers easier to prepare (and eat), we opted to swap the deep-fried batter for a crunchy bread-crumb topping and bake them open-faced. For the creamy filling, we liked a blend of cheeses for optimal flavor and texture; cheddar provided bold flavor, and cream cheese added just enough silkiness to the mix. Scallions and chili powder added complexity and a little heat, and a bit of lime juice added brightness. To ensure the topping stayed crisp, we chose extra-crunchy panko bread crumbs and toasted them in a skillet before sprinkling them over the filling. Then we baked the stuffed jalapeños just until they were hot throughout. To make the peppers spicier, reserve and add the jalapeño seeds to the filling.

½ cup panko bread crumbs
1 tablespoon vegetable oil
12 medium jalapeño chiles, preferably with stems
6 ounces cheddar cheese, shredded (1½ cups)
4 ounces cream cheese, softened
2 scallions, chopped fine
2 teaspoons lime juice
1 teaspoon chili powder
½ teaspoon salt
  Vegetable oil spray

1. Adjust oven rack to middle position and heat oven to 350 degrees. Line rimmed baking sheet with aluminum foil. Toss panko with oil and toast in 12-inch nonstick skillet over medium-high heat, stirring often, until well browned, 5 to 10 minutes.

2. Cut each jalapeño in half lengthwise through stem, then remove ribs and seeds. Combine cheddar, cream cheese, scallions, lime juice, chili powder, and salt in bowl. Spoon cheese mixture evenly into jalapeños and transfer to prepared sheet. Top with toasted panko and spray lightly with vegetable oil spray. Bake until hot, 15 to 20 minutes. Serve.

Quick Toasted Almonds

MAKES 2 CUPS `FAST` `VEGAN` `GF`

✔ **WHY THIS RECIPE WORKS:** We wondered if making our own quick toasted almonds would be better than buying canned almonds, which are often stale-tasting or too salty. We found that toasting raw almonds for just 8 minutes in hot oil gave them a round, complex toasted flavor that was fresher than store-bought versions. Best of all, we could season them with a variety of herbs and spices much more interesting than the ubiquitous store-bought smoked variety. Bottom line: You simply can't buy almonds this good.

- 1 tablespoon extra-virgin olive oil
- 2 cups skin-on raw whole almonds
- 1 teaspoon salt
- ¼ teaspoon pepper

Heat oil in 12-inch nonstick skillet over medium-high heat until just shimmering. Add almonds, salt, and pepper and reduce heat to medium-low. Cook, stirring often, until fragrant and color deepens slightly, about 8 minutes. Transfer almonds to paper towel–lined plate and let cool before serving. (Almonds can be stored at room temperature for up to 5 days.)

VARIATIONS

Rosemary Almonds `FAST` `VEGAN` `GF`

Add ½ teaspoon dried rosemary to skillet with almonds.

Warm Spiced Almonds `FAST` `GF`

Substitute unsalted butter for olive oil. Add 2 tablespoons sugar, ½ teaspoon ground cinnamon, ⅛ teaspoon ground cloves, and ⅛ teaspoon ground allspice to skillet with almonds.

Spanish-Style Almonds `FAST` `VEGAN` `GF`

Add ¾ teaspoon smoked paprika to skillet with almonds.

Chinese Five-Spice Almonds `FAST` `VEGAN` `GF`

Add 1 teaspoon five-spice powder to skillet with almonds.

Orange-Fennel Almonds `FAST` `VEGAN` `GF`

Add 1 teaspoon grated orange zest and ½ teaspoon ground fennel seeds to skillet with almonds.

NOTES FROM THE TEST KITCHEN

All About Nuts

With their meaty texture, great flavor, and abundant healthy fats and protein, nuts are an essential ingredient in vegetarian cooking. We often use them to lend richness, flavor, and crunch to recipes, and, of course, they make a great snack all on their own. Here's what you need to know.

STORING NUTS

All nuts are high in oil and will become rancid rather quickly. In the test kitchen, we store all nuts in the freezer in freezer-safe zipper-lock bags. Frozen nuts will keep for months, and there's no need to defrost before toasting or chopping.

TOASTING NUTS

Toasting nuts brings out their flavors and gives them a satisfying crunchy texture. To toast a small amount (under 1 cup), put the nuts (or seeds) in a dry small skillet over medium heat. Shake the skillet occasionally to prevent scorching and toast until they are lightly browned and fragrant, 3 to 8 minutes. Watch them closely since they can go from golden to burnt very quickly. To toast more than 1 cup of nuts, spread the nuts in a single layer on a rimmed baking sheet and toast in a 350-degree oven. To promote even toasting, shake the baking sheet every few minutes, and toast until the nuts are lightly browned and fragrant, 5 to 10 minutes.

SKINNING NUTS

The skins from some nuts, such as walnuts and hazelnuts, can impart a bitter flavor and undesirable texture in some dishes. To remove the skins, simply rub the hot toasted nuts inside a clean dish towel.

ALMOND PRIMER

Most nuts can be found either raw, toasted, or roasted, but almonds are sold in a dizzying array of varieties: raw, roasted, blanched, slivered, sliced, and smoked. So which almonds do we prefer? When it comes to decorating cookies, we like the clean presentation of whole skinless blanched almonds. For other baked goods, leafy salads, and simple side dishes, we find that thinly sliced raw almonds (with or without their skins) deliver a nice, light flavor and texture. In stir-fries and pilafs, we love the substantial crunch of thick-cut slivered almonds. Roasted almonds are best for eating out of hand. As for smoked almonds, we find their bold flavor and crunch are best in snacks like spiced nuts or party mixes. Like all nuts, almonds are highly perishable (the oils in the nuts go rancid quickly) and are best stored in the freezer to prevent spoilage.

Almond Granola with Dried Fruit

MAKES ABOUT 9 CUPS VEGAN GF

✔ **WHY THIS RECIPE WORKS:** Store-bought granola suffers from many shortcomings. It's often loose and gravelly, overly sweet, and infuriatingly expensive. We wanted to make our own granola at home, with big clusters and a crisp texture. We found that the secret to getting the perfect texture was to firmly pack the granola mixture into a rimmed baking sheet before baking. Once it was baked, we could break it into crunchy clumps of any size. Chopping the almonds by hand was best for superior texture and crunch—the food processor did a lousy job of chopping the nuts evenly. To complement the nuts, we also liked plenty of chewy, wholesome dried fruit. For sweetness and to bind the granola together, we added modest amounts of light brown sugar and maple syrup. A little salt and vanilla were the only other flavorings we needed. You can substitute an equal quantity of slivered or sliced almonds. Do not use quick oats in this recipe. In order for this recipe to be gluten-free, you must use gluten-free oats.

- ⅓ cup maple syrup
- ⅓ cup packed (2⅓ ounces) light brown sugar
- 4 teaspoons vanilla extract
- ½ teaspoon salt
- ½ cup vegetable oil
- 5 cups old-fashioned rolled oats
- 2 cups raw almonds, chopped coarse
- 2 cups raisins or other dried fruit, chopped

1. Adjust oven rack to upper-middle position and heat oven to 325 degrees. Whisk maple syrup, sugar, vanilla, and salt together in large bowl. Whisk in oil. Fold in oats and almonds until thoroughly coated.

2. Transfer oat mixture to parchment paper–lined rimmed baking sheet and spread across sheet into thin, even layer (about ⅜ inch thick). Using stiff metal spatula, compress oat mixture until very compact. Bake until lightly browned, 40 to 45 minutes, rotating pan halfway through baking.

3. Remove granola from oven and let cool on baking sheet to room temperature, about 1 hour. Break cooled granola into pieces of desired size. Stir in raisins and serve. (Granola can be stored at room temperature for up to 2 weeks.)

VARIATIONS

Spiced Walnut Granola with Dried Apple VEGAN GF

Add 2 teaspoons ground cinnamon, 1½ teaspoons ground ginger, ¾ teaspoon ground allspice, ½ teaspoon freshly grated nutmeg, and ½ teaspoon pepper to maple syrup mixture in step 1. Substitute coarsely chopped walnuts for almonds, and chopped dried apples for raisins.

Pecan-Orange Granola with Dried Cranberries VEGAN GF

Add 2 tablespoons finely grated orange zest and 2½ teaspoons ground cinnamon to maple syrup mixture in step 1. Substitute coarsely chopped pecans for almonds, and dried cranberries for raisins.

Tropical Granola with Dried Mango VEGAN GF

Reduce vanilla extract to 2 teaspoons and add 1½ teaspoons ground ginger and ¾ teaspoon freshly grated nutmeg to maple syrup mixture in step 1. Substitute coarsely chopped macadamias for almonds, 1½ cups unsweetened shredded coconut for 1 cup oats, and chopped dried mango for raisins.

Crispy Spiced Chickpeas

SERVES 6 FAST VEGAN GF

✔ **WHY THIS RECIPE WORKS:** Chickpeas aren't just for salads and curries anymore. Tossed in oil and roasted, these beans become ultracrisp and deeply nutty in flavor—the perfect cocktail snack. Most recipes call for roasting chickpeas in the oven, but we found they never became crisp enough. Switching to the stovetop and frying the chickpeas in olive oil gave us the big crunch factor we were seeking. A quick toss in a sweet and savory mixture of sugar and smoked paprika made our chickpeas incredibly addictive. Make sure to dry the chickpeas thoroughly with paper towels before placing them in the oil. In order to get crisp chickpeas, it is important to keep the heat high enough to ensure the oil is simmering the entire time. After about 12 minutes, test for doneness by removing a few chickpeas and placing them on a paper towel to cool slightly before tasting. If they are not quite crisp yet, continue to cook 2 to 3 minutes longer, checking occasionally for doneness.

- 1 teaspoon smoked paprika
- 1 teaspoon sugar
- ½ teaspoon salt
- ¼ teaspoon pepper
- 1 cup extra-virgin olive oil
- 2 (15-ounce) cans chickpeas, rinsed and patted dry

Shallow-fried in olive oil then tossed with smoked paprika, these chickpeas are light, crisp, and deeply flavorful.

Combine paprika, sugar, salt, and pepper in large bowl. Heat oil in Dutch oven over high heat until just smoking. Add chickpeas to oil and cook, stirring occasionally, until deep golden brown and crisp, 12 to 15 minutes. Using slotted spoon, transfer chickpeas to paper towel–lined baking sheet to drain briefly, then toss with spices. Serve. (Chickpeas can be stored at room temperature for up to 24 hours.)

Frying Chickpeas

1. Rinse chickpeas, then thoroughly pat dry with paper towels.

2. Fry chickpeas in hot oil until deep golden brown and very crisp, 12 to 15 minutes.

Perfect Popcorn
MAKES 4 QUARTS, SERVES 6 TO 8 `FAST` `GF`

✔ **WHY THIS RECIPE WORKS:** Most of us reach for those preseasoned, microwavable bags when we're in the mood for popcorn, but between the artificial flavors and the near certainty of burning, they usually disappoint. Our goal was to come up with a recipe for perfect popcorn that was easy enough to supplant the microwave. We found that the key to this recipe was making the popcorn in a big, heavy-bottomed Dutch oven. The Dutch oven did the best job of heating the oil evenly, which ensured that the kernels heated and popped at the same rate, giving us few unpopped kernels and less risk of burning. Once we had the technique down, we came up with lots of flavorful variations to dress up the light, fluffy popcorn. You'll want a good-size Dutch oven to make popcorn—at least 5 or 6 quarts. Be sure to shake the pan vigorously when cooking to prevent the popcorn from scorching.

3   **tablespoons unsalted butter**
2   **tablespoons vegetable oil**
½   **cup popcorn kernels**
    Salt

Microwave butter in bowl on 50 percent power until just melted, 1 to 3 minutes. Combine oil and popcorn in large Dutch oven. Cover and place over medium-high heat, shaking occasionally, until first few kernels begin to pop. Continue to cook, shaking pot vigorously, until popping has mostly stopped. Transfer to large bowl, toss with melted butter, and season with salt to taste. Serve.

VARIATIONS
Garlic and Herb Popcorn `FAST` `GF`
Add 2 minced garlic cloves and 1 tablespoon minced fresh or 1 teaspoon dried rosemary, thyme, or dill to butter before melting.

Parmesan-Pepper Popcorn `FAST` `GF`
Add ½ teaspoon pepper to butter before melting. Add ½ cup grated Parmesan to popcorn when tossing with butter.

Cajun-Spiced Popcorn `FAST` `GF`
Add 1 teaspoon red pepper flakes, 1 teaspoon minced fresh thyme (or ½ teaspoon dried), ¾ teaspoon hot sauce, ½ teaspoon garlic powder, ½ teaspoon paprika, and ¼ teaspoon onion powder to butter before melting.

Hot and Sweet Popcorn `FAST` `GF`
Add 2 tablespoons sugar, 1 teaspoon ground cinnamon, and ½ teaspoon chili powder to butter before melting.

Conversions and Equivalents

Some say cooking is a science and an art. We would say that geography has a hand in it, too. Flour milled in the United Kingdom and elsewhere will feel and taste different from flour milled in the United States. So we cannot promise that the loaf of bread you bake in Canada or England will taste the same as a loaf baked in the States, but we can offer guidelines for converting weights and measures. We also recommend that you rely on your instincts when making our recipes. Refer to the visual cues provided. If the bread dough hasn't "come together in a ball," as described, you may need to add more flour—even if the recipe doesn't tell you to. You be the judge.

The recipes in this book were developed using standard U.S. measures following U.S. government guidelines. The charts below offer equivalents for U.S., metric, and imperial (U.K.) measures. All conversions are approximate and have been rounded up or down to the nearest whole number.

EXAMPLE:

| 1 teaspoon | = | 4.9292 milliliters, rounded up to 5 milliliters |
| 1 ounce | = | 28.3495 grams, rounded down to 28 grams |

VOLUME CONVERSIONS

U.S.	METRIC
1 teaspoon	5 milliliters
2 teaspoons	10 milliliters
1 tablespoon	15 milliliters
2 tablespoons	30 milliliters
¼ cup	59 milliliters
⅓ cup	79 milliliters
½ cup	118 milliliters
¾ cup	177 milliliters
1 cup	237 milliliters
1¼ cups	296 milliliters
1½ cups	355 milliliters
2 cups (1 pint)	473 milliliters
2½ cups	591 milliliters
3 cups	710 milliliters
4 cups (1 quart)	0.946 liter
1.06 quarts	1 liter
4 quarts (1 gallon)	3.8 liters

WEIGHT CONVERSIONS

OUNCES	GRAMS
½	14
¾	21
1	28
1½	43
2	57
2½	71
3	85
3½	99
4	113
4½	128
5	142
6	170
7	198
8	227
9	255
10	283
12	340
16 (1 pound)	454

CONVERSIONS FOR COMMON BAKING INGREDIENTS

Baking is an exacting science. Because measuring by weight is far more accurate than measuring by volume, and thus more likely to achieve reliable results, in our recipes we provide ounce measures in addition to cup measures for many ingredients. Refer to the chart below to convert these measures into grams.

INGREDIENT	OUNCES	GRAMS
1 cup all-purpose flour*	5	142
1 cup cake flour	4	113
1 cup whole-wheat flour	5½	156
1 cup granulated (white) sugar	7	198
1 cup packed brown sugar (light or dark)	7	198
1 cup confectioners' sugar	4	113
1 cup cocoa powder	3	85
4 tablespoons butter† (½ stick, or ¼ cup)	2	57
8 tablespoons butter† (1 stick, or ½ cup)	4	113

* U.S. all-purpose flour, the most frequently used flour in this book, does not contain leaveners, as some European flours do. These leavened flours are called self-rising or self-raising. If you are using self-rising flour, take this into consideration before adding leavening to a recipe.

† In the United States, butter is sold both salted and unsalted. We generally recommend unsalted butter. If you are using salted butter, take this into consideration before adding salt to a recipe.

CONVERTING OVEN TEMPERATURES

FAHRENHEIT	CELSIUS	GAS MARK (IMPERIAL)
225	105	¼
250	120	½
275	135	1
300	150	2
325	165	3
350	180	4
375	190	5
400	200	6
425	220	7
450	230	8
475	245	9

CONVERTING FAHRENHEIT TO CELSIUS

We include doneness temperatures in a few of the recipes in this book. We recommend an instant-read thermometer for the job. Refer to the above table to convert Fahrenheit degrees to Celsius. Or, for temperatures not represented in the chart, use this simple formula:

Subtract 32 degrees from the Fahrenheit reading, then divide the result by 1.8 to find the Celsius reading.

EXAMPLE:

"Bake until soufflé has risen above rim, top is deep golden brown, and interior registers 170 degrees, 30 to 35 minutes." To convert:

$$170°F - 32 = 138°$$
$$138° \div 1.8 = 76.67°C, \text{ rounded up to } 77°C$$

Index

Note: Page references in *italics* indicate recipe photographs.

■ FAST (Less than 45 minutes start to finish)   ■ VEGAN   ■ GLUTEN-FREE

A

Algerian-Style Fennel, Orange, and Olive Salad, ■ ■ ■ 267

All-Butter Press-In Tart Dough, 340

All-Butter Single-Crust Pie Dough, 398

Almond(s)

and Carrots, Bulgur Salad with, ■ 183

Chinese Five-Spice, ■ ■ ■ 431

and Cranberries, Baked Wild Rice with, ■ ■ 162

and Cranberries, Broccoli Salad with, ■ ■ 259

Frisée, and Goat Cheese, Pan-Roasted Pear Salad with, ■ 254

Granola with Dried Fruit, ■ ■ 432

Green Olive and Orange Pesto, ■ ■ 139

Hot Quinoa Cereal, ■ ■ 201

Jeweled Rice, ■ ■ 161, *161*

and Lemon, Braised Beets with, ■ ■ 282–83, *283*

Orange-Fennel, ■ ■ ■ 431

Oranges, and Olives, Rice Salad with, ■ ■ 174

primer on, 431

Rosemary, ■ ■ ■ 431

Smoked, Radicchio, and Dates, Citrus Salad with, ■ ■ ■ 246

and Smoked Paprika, Sautéed Green Beans with, ■ ■ 300

Spanish-Style, ■ ■ ■ 431

Toasted, and Sage, Pureed Butternut Squash with, ■ ■ 313

Toasted, Quick, ■ ■ ■ 431

and Tomato Pesto, ■ ■ 138

Warm Spiced, ■ ■ 431

White Gazpacho, ■ 84–85

Almost Hands-Free Risotto

with Fennel and Saffron, ■ 172

with Herbs, ■ 172

with Parmesan, ■ 156, 171–72

with Porcini, ■ 172

Amaranth, 180, 184

Apple(s)

Blue Cheese, and Pecans, Warm Spinach Salad with, ■ ■ 255

Apple(s) *(cont.)*

and Butternut Squash Soup, Curried, ■ 82

Caraway, and Horseradish, Celery Root Salad with, ■ ■ 262

Celeriac, and Fennel Chowder, 90–91, *91*

Cheddar, and Hazelnuts, Brussels Sprout Salad with, ■ ■ 260

Cider-Braised Belgian Endives with, ■ ■ 299

-Cinnamon Overnight Steel-Cut Oatmeal, ■ 201

Dried, Spiced Walnut Granola with, ■ ■ 432

and Fennel, Sweet and Sour Cabbage Salad with, ■ ■ 260–61

and Fennel Chopped Salad, ■ ■ 264

and Parsley, Celery Root Salad with, ■ ■ 262

Sweet and Red Potato Salad, ■ ■ ■ 271, *271*

Walnuts, Dried Cherries, and Herbed Baked Goat Cheese, Salad with, 247–48

Apricots

Aged Gouda, and Pistachios, Quinoa Pilaf with, ■ 196

Swiss Chard, and Pistachios, Socca with, ■ ■ *328*, 328–29

Arepas

Avocado, Tomato, and Bell Pepper, ■ ■ ■ 370

Black Bean and Cheese, ■ ■ 369–70

Artichoke(s)

about, 12

Hearts and Parmesan, Bruschetta with, ■ 352

-Lemon Hummus, ■ ■ ■ 407

Marinated, ■ ■ *427*, 427–28

and Navy Bean Dip with Parsley, ■ ■ *410*, 410

Pepper, and Chickpea Tagine, 104

preparing, 17

preparing for roasting, 280

Roasted, with Lemon Vinaigrette, ■ ■ 281

Roasted, ■ ■ *280*, 280–81

selecting, 281

Shallot, and Goat Cheese Tarts, 337

Vegetable Paella in a Paella Pan, ■ ■ 171

Vegetable Paella, ■ ■ *170*, 170–71

Arugula

about, 252

Caramelized Onions, and Ricotta, Pizza with, 330–31

Edamame Salad, ■ ■ 213, *213*

Goat Cheese, and Sun-Dried Tomatoes, Scrambled Eggs with, ■ ■ 380, *380*

Golden Raisins, and Walnuts, Citrus Salad with, ■ ■ 246

Lemon, and Parmesan, Farro Risotto with, ■ 190

Oat Berry, and Chickpea Salad, ■ 192, *192*

Parsley, and Ricotta Pesto, ■ ■ 139

Pesto, Grape Tomatoes, and Goat Cheese, Bruschetta with, ■ 352

Salad, Savory Breakfast Pizza with, ■ 401

Salad with Grapes, Fennel, Gorgonzola, and Pecans, ■ ■ 244

Salad with Oranges, Feta, and Sugared Pistachios, ■ ■ 244

and Sun-Dried Tomato Vinaigrette, Pasta Salad with, 142–43

Super Greens Soup with Lemon-Tarragon Cream, ■ 83, 83–84

Asiago, 416

and Dates, Grilled Cheese Sandwiches with, ■ 354

and Herbs, Vegetable Torta with, *320*, 344–45

Asian Braised Tofu with Winter Squash and Coconut Milk, ■ ■ 231–32

Asian ingredients, 54–55

Asian noodles, types of, 147

Asian-Style Swiss Chard, ■ ■ ■ 294

Asparagus

about, 12

Broiled, with Balsamic Glaze, ■ ■ ■ 282

Broiled, with Soy-Ginger Vinaigrette, ■ ■ ■ 282

Broiled, ■ ■ ■ 282

Brown Rice Salad, ■ *175*, 175–76

cutting on the bias, 243

and Fresh Basil Dressing, Tortellini Salad with, 144

and Goat Cheese, Frittata with, ■ ■ 389

grilling, 297

AMERICA'S TEST KITCHEN
17 Station Street, Brookline, MA 02445

Library of Congress Cataloging-in-Publication Data
The complete vegetarian cookbook : a fresh guide to eating well with 700 foolproof recipes / by the editors at America's test kitchen.
    pages cm
 Includes index.
 ISBN 978-1-936493-96-8
1. Vegetarian cooking. I. America's test kitchen (Television program)
 TX837.C5943 2015
 641.5'636--dc23

                    2014042807
Manufactured in the United States of America
10 9 8 7 6 5 4 3 2 1

DISTRIBUTED BY
America's Test Kitchen
17 Station Street, Brookline, MA 02445

PICTURED OPPOSITE TITLE PAGE: Thai-Style Tofu and Basil Lettuce Cups (page 232)
PICTURED OPPOSITE TABLE OF CONTENTS PAGE: Roasted Winter Squash Halves with Browned Butter and Sage (page 314)
PICTURED ON FRONT COVER: Tomato Tart (page 338)
PICTURED ON BACK COVER: Millet Cakes with Spinach and Carrots (page 44); Stuffed Eggplant with Bulgur (page 46); Salad with Crispy Spiced Chickpeas (page 246); Chilled Marinated Tofu (page 222)

EDITORIAL DIRECTOR: Jack Bishop
EDITORIAL DIRECTOR, BOOKS: Elizabeth Carduff
EXECUTIVE FOOD EDITOR: Julia Collin Davison
SENIOR EDITOR: Suzannah McFerran
ASSOCIATE EDITORS: Alyssa King and Stephanie Pixley
EDITORIAL ASSISTANT: Kate Ander
TEST COOKS: Sara Mayer and Anne Wolf
ADDITIONAL RECIPE DEVELOPMENT: Matthew Card and Raquel Pelzel
DESIGN DIRECTOR: Amy Klee
ART DIRECTOR: Greg Galvan
DESIGNER: Allison Boales
PHOTOGRAPHY DIRECTOR: Julie Cote
ASSOCIATE ART DIRECTOR, PHOTOGRAPHY: Steve Klise
STAFF PHOTOGRAPHER: Daniel J. van Ackere
ADDITIONAL PHOTOGRAPHY: Keller + Keller and Carl Tremblay
FOOD STYLING: Catrine Kelty and Marie Piraino
PHOTOSHOOT KITCHEN TEAM:
  ASSOCIATE EDITOR: Chris O'Connor
  TEST COOK: Daniel Cellucci
  ASSISTANT TEST COOK: Matthew Fairman
PRODUCTION DIRECTOR: Guy Rochford
SENIOR PRODUCTION MANAGER: Jessica Quirk
PRODUCTION MANAGEMENT SPECIALIST: Christine Walsh
PRODUCTION AND IMAGING SPECIALISTS: Heather Dube, Dennis Noble, Lauren Robbins, and Jessica Voas
PROJECT MANAGER: Britt Dresser
COPYEDITOR: Jeff Schier
PROOFREADER: Annie Imbornoni
INDEXER: Elizabeth Parson